T H E

Bach
Flower Remedies

D0813732

THE Bach flower Remedies

INCLUDING

HEAL THYSELF
by Edward Bach, M.D.

THE TWELVE HEALERS
by Edward Bach, M.D.

THE BACH REMEDIES REPERTORY
by F. J. Wheeler, M.D.

Updated, revised and enlarged by The Dr. Edward Bach Centre

KEATS PUBLISHING, INC. NEW CANAAN, CONNECTICUT

The Bach Flower Remedies is intended solely for informational and educational purposes, and not as medical advice. Please consult a medical or health professional if you have questions about your health.

THE BACH FLOWER REMEDIES

Copyright © 1997 by The Dr. Edward Bach Centre
All Rights Reserved

Published by arrangement with The C. W. Daniel Company Ltd.,
Saffron Walden, Essex, England

Library of Congress Cataloging-in-Publication Data

Bach, Edward, 1886–1936.
    The Bach flower remedies. Including Heal thyself / by Edward Bach : The twelve healers / by Edward Bach : The Bach remedies repertory / by F.J. Wheeler. Updated, rev. and enlarged / by the Dr. Edward Bach Centre.
    x. cm.
    Includes index.
    ISBN 0-87983-869-8
    1. Flowers—Therapeutic use. 2. Homeopathy—Materia medica and therapeutics. I. Bach, Edward, 1886–1936. Twelve healers. II. Wheeler, F. J. Bach remedies repertory. III. Dr. Edward Bach Centre.
RX615.F55B326   1997
615'.321—dc21   97-29689
                                                                                        CIP

Printed in the United States of America

Keats Publishing, Inc.
27 Pine Street (Box 876)
New Canaan, Connecticut 06840-0876

Keats Publishing website address: www.keats.com

This book is dedicated

to

all who suffer

or

who are in distress

Contents

Heal Thyself
EDWARD BACH, M.D.

The Twelve Healers and Other Remedies
EDWARD BACH, M.D.

The Bach Remedies Repertory
F.J. Wheeler, M.D.

Updated, revised and enlarged 1996 by
The Dr. Edward Bach Centre

Publisher's Introduction

EDWARD BACH (1886–1936) believed the ills of the heart and the spirit must be the focus of a healer's attention. The bodily ills are symptoms. He felt that it is ". . . our fears, our cares, our anxieties and such like that open the path to the invasion of illness."

Historically, herbal medicine has offered means of cheering, consoling, quieting, uplifting, settling the mind and the emotions. Culpepper or Gerard might also have known what plant to prescribe for melancholy or mental indecisiveness. But Bach went further in making a medical connection between feelings and actual physical illness. He also developed a specialized branch of herbal medicine which employed only the flowers—the highly potent and vital seed-bearing organ—and only nonpoisonous ones (unlike the aconite or digitalis of herbal medicine).

Bach used his flower remedies to relieve mental distress until problems could be dealt with in the inner man; and also, in part, to actually heal such attitudes as remorse or lack of confidence. This was, however, only part of the cure, which also involved positive interaction and encouraging guidance from the doctor. A good doctor would be able to recognize disease—on the basis of certain moods and attitudes—before it became manifest as a physical breakdown. He could then, truly, practice preventive medicine.

No scientific explanation of how or why these remedies worked was offered by Edward Bach. Indeed, he was wary of the "'trends" that science is prone to, and encouraged others to keep his remedies "free from science, free from theories." If certain observable principles were operative in nature, there was no need to complicate the issue. Wild animals did not need an explanation of why certain plants helped them when they were ill. What Bach did offer was hundreds of successful case histories.

The remedies themselves are simple in their preparation. The materials required are pure water, sunlight, fresh blossoms and a clean glass bowl. Their action is always gentle and strengthening.

April, 1979   *New Canaan, Connecticut*

The Bach Remedies

A Talk with John Diamond, M.D.

The following interview appeared originally in The Health Quarterly *magazine. We feel it is a clear and valuable explanation of how one doctor, among a great many in this country, has come to understand and use the Bach Flower Remedies in his own practice.*

Interviewer: It is difficult to categorize Dr. Bach into a particular discipline, isn't it?

Dr. Diamond: Dr. Bach came to develop the flower remedies through his work in homeopathy. He had perfected the more modern homeopathic remedies of bacteriological origin. The flower remedies are closer to homeopathy than anything else.

I: Two salient characteristics of homeopathy are extreme dilution and the Law of Similars—like cures like. Do these also characterize the flower remedies?

D: First of all, homeopathy requires more than dilution. It requires potentiating a dilution by means of working in a specific rhythmic method. The preparation of flower remedies does not require this, nor do they work according to the Law of Similars, necessarily. However, they are dilute, harmless, natural and gentle.

Dr. Bach also departs from homeopathy in believing that by correcting harmful mental attitudes you can stop the disease from becoming physical or, more probably, you can treat the disease when it is at an energy level rather than grossly pathological. Even when it is grossly pathological you can *assist*, because you can greatly alleviate the mental component which may be causative or reactive to the physical problem. (By the way, I think that his little book, *Heal Thyself*, is one of the best statements of proper medicine that anyone can make.)

The flower remedies have a great role to play in the more psycho-somatic type of illness. In extremely pathological cases other remedies are needed as well.

Let's take a look at a specific flower to see what kind of application it has. The symptoms that call for Agrimony as a treatment are: hiding worries from others under a cloak of cheerfulness and good humor; restlessness; putting on a fair front but underneath tense and worried.

I: In diagnosing symptoms like these—a subjective matter—what would happen if the doctor misjudged an attitude and gave the wrong flower remedy?

D: These remedies can do no harm. But there are certain ways they should be used. There are certain flowers that the practitioner should start off with, for instance. Also, the need for a particular remedy changes.

Suppose that a man came in saying, "Nothing is wrong with me . . . I'm fine." And you can see that underneath he is tense and worried. You could very well give him Agrimony. The next visit he might say, "You know, you're right. I now realize that there are things that are bothering me. I keep dwelling back on an old, unpleasant situation. And I can't seem to bury it." The appropriate remedy for this is honeysuckle, which is for overly retrospective people. The next week he comes in with another, entirely different problem.

Another interesting possibility with the flower remedies is the opportunity to do something for the relatives of the patient. In the case of an accident or acute illness, I might be giving the patient the rescue remedy [a composite remedy in addition to the 38 flower remedies]. At the same time red chestnut would be helpful for the anxious and concerned relatives. The Bach flower remedies comprise the only system which offers this kind of help.

Some of the remedies are deeper than others; some treat more superficial characteristics. Each one has a positive and negative aspect. During treatment we tend to look more at the negative aspect because this is what we are trying to overcome; we are trying to encourage the other side. The negative aspect of Wild Oat, for instance, is uncertainty about what to do and an inability to put down roots and grow. This often applies to talented people who can't decide on what their course in life should be. You are then trying to encourage the Wild Oat to settle down and grow—this is the positive aspect.

The usual diagnostic formula is to sit down and talk with the patient and to go through, in your mind, the particular remedies to see what applies. This is often a dynamic and on-going process. As one mental attitude or layer settles, another layer is revealed.

I: Do you also check the person out physically?

D: Oh yes. You use all of your other techniques and add this last one to them. The flower remedies are very good in cases of chronic illness, but can also be used in acute cases. They usually work best over a period of time, although you can get very dramatic results too (particularly in psychotic patients).

I: Are the flower remedies lasting in their effects, or do you have to keep taking them?

D: Well, again, you have to understand the dynamic quality of a personality and what you call problems. You might deal with the initial problem, to some extent, and then find that there are others underneath which require different remedies. It is like psychotherapy in the sense that you can start where you like, finish when you like. In a case when a person does not want to become too involved in the therapy, we might give him the remedy for his immediate problem and tell him to take it for an indefinite amount of time to help him over that initial period. It is preferable to give the person the remedy and then to continue seeing him regularly. By the next week he may not be so bothered by the original problem, but another difficulty may have turned up. As each layer is dealt with, new layers emerge. It can go on and on. What was negative becomes positive, and growth takes place.

I: I am wondering if people go back to being bothered by the same problems, after they stop taking the remedies?

D: People do tend to repeat patterns, but they also grow and change. It also depends on what else the doctor does beside giving the remedy. He must work with the patient, helping him to learn to deal positively with situations. *There is no such thing as "take a pill and you are cured."* Curing is a lifelong process that ends when you die. [Italics are the editor's.]

Now, what I have described is the predominant way of working with the Bach flower remedies. People have added other elements, such as a psychic component, which I feel is unnecessary and wrong. It is just a matter of sitting down and listening to a patient and sorting out the remedy for the attitude at that time. To understand the remedies, the thing to keep in mind is simply that if the mental attitudes are treated, the physical problems—if they are in the early stages—will be reversed. Or at least the "psycho" component of the psychosomatic problem can be relieved. If the problem has become fully developed into the physical stage, then the somatopsychic element can be relieved, the feedback from the body to the mind (the mental distress that ill health causes of itself).

You can see that the flower remedies have particular value in terms of prevention. If you have anxieties and fears that could eventually lead to an ulcer, we can treat these quite easily. This is *primary* prevention. It does not require the remedial measures that medicine takes when a problem has begun but has not yet overcome the person (and which is usually called prevention); nor does it involve intense psychotherapy. It is true that these remedies are more for healthy people rather than very sick people. They are not remedies for advanced cases of cancer and the like. These remedies are most helpful in preventing a physical illness that is about to attack. The thoughts or attitudes which create illness may be present for twenty or thirty years before they show up as physical disease. In that time they can be treated. One should not wait until the disease has become physical, and then try to change attitudes overnight.

I: But precisely how do these emotions affect the physical body? Take the strong emotion of "hate" as an example.

D: Hate and envy seem to rob the body and all the organs of energy, the kind of energy that is associated with acupuncture. The gland that seems to be particularly affected by hate and envy is the thymus. As long as the patient has an underactive thymus gland, none of the immune systems will work properly. Twenty years ago it was known that cancer, as a disease, comes about when the body ceases to be able to recognize abnormal cells, which is part of the function of the thymus. (I am stressing this aspect to illustrate one way that hate might, after a period of ten or twenty years, settle into the physical.) How does that relate, exactly to a specific biochemical sequence? . . . it is just a matter of time, and the answer is immaterial.

Bach had the further insight that illness, disharmony, imbalance are often a result of a gap between the inner state and the "face" that a person daily puts on to those around him. The closer the two faces (inner and outer) are together, the better. A primary characteristic of degenerative disease is the difference between the way a person appears and the way he really feels. The pretense. This is very often part of a disease. It takes a long time for what we really are to intrude on our outer face. In all those years the gap is continually eating away at our health. Every time a person thinks a negative or depressing thought, it is also chipping away at health—the thymus stops working for that moment. This is why I am against most psychotherapy: it focuses on the negative, and the thymus is continually being pounded. A healthy thymus is associated with love, joy, youth and enthusiasm.

One of the basic requirements, I might add, for treating any illness is that the person must *want* to get well, and must be willing to take some responsibility for that. The element of will is definitely involved. Often, by the time the patient has a severe illness, he has made up his mind that he doesn't want to get well. Furthermore, by the time a person is ill, and goes to a conventional doctor, structural changes have taken place and it is rare that the condition can be returned completely to normal again. The whole object is to treat before it gets to that point. Primary prevention! If you have the right attitudes you should never get sick—just slow down and die, as wild animals do.

(At this point the interviewer became the "patient." Imagining hate, during the simple kinesiological testing of muscle strength, the muscle under consideration tested weak. Imagining love, the muscle tested strong!)

I: Can you explain the work that you are doing now in using flower remedies as part of your other therapies?

D: My own new work with the flower remedies is related to the energy involved in acupuncture. It is intimately connected with the central nervous system. We are now working out three interrelating elements: the acupuncture meridian, its corresponding flower remedy and a psychological attitude. So, if we are presented with an attitude, we double check it against the meridian to see if that energy circuit is indeed impaired, and then we can tell the patient what attitude is operating at that moment and help to guide him into transmuting that attitude— flooding himself with its opposite. This can be done instantly, and the effects of a change in attitude can be demonstrated instantly. (The art of healing that is involved here is learning how to mobilize a patient's will.) The relief can be instantaneous with the transmutation. Then we follow up by giving the appropriate flower remedy to cement or reinforce the change. But the important thing is that the patient really treat himself.

Eventually, we would like to see people reach the point where they realize how these principles work so they can take over the responsibility and control of their own bodies . . . through understanding the effects of emotional states, and cementing their mental efforts with helpful substances, such as the flower remedies.

In conclusion, then, the new combination of elements that we use together are: 1) a physical diagnosis of a mental problem, 2) transmutation of feelings, 3) cementing with flower remedies, 4) and all the other available therapies such as homeopathic medicine, diet and nutrition, helping postural problems, fasting, and so on.

Heal Thyself

AN EXPLANATION OF THE REAL CAUSE AND CURE OF DISEASE

EDWARD BACH

M.D., B.S., D.P.H.

Chapter 1

IT IS NOT THE OBJECT of this book to suggest that the art of healing is unnecessary; far be it from any such intention; but it is humbly hoped that it will be a guide to those who suffer, to seek within themselves the real origin of their maladies so that they may assist themselves in their own healing. Moreover, it is hoped that it may stimulate those, both in the medical profession and in religious orders, who have the welfare of humanity at heart, to redouble their efforts in seeking the relief of human suffering, and so hasten that day when the victory over disease will be complete.

The main reason for the failure of modern medical science is that it is dealing with results and not causes. For many centuries the real nature of disease has been masked by materialism, and thus disease itself has been given every opportunity of extending its ravages, since it has not been attacked at its origin. The situation is like to an enemy strongly fortified in the hills, continually waging guerrilla warfare in the country around, while the people, ignoring the fortified garrison, content themselves with repairing the damaged houses and burying the dead, which are the results of the raids of the marauders. So, generally, speaking, is the situation in medicine to-day; nothing more than the patching up of those attacked and the burying of those who are slain, without a thought being given to the real stronghold.

Disease will never be cured or eradicated by present materialistic methods, for the simple reason that disease in its origin is not material. What we know as disease is an ultimate result produced in the body, the end product of deep and long-acting forces, and even if material treatment alone is apparently successful this is nothing more than a temporary relief unless the real cause has been removed. The modern trend of medical science, by misinterpreting the true nature of disease and concentrating it in materialistic terms in the physical body, has enormously increased its power, firstly, by distracting the thoughts of people from its true origin and hence from the effective method of attack, and secondly, by localising it in the body, thus obscuring true hope of recovery and raising a mighty disease complex of fear, which never should have existed.

Disease is in essence the result of conflict between Soul and Mind, and will never be eradicated except by spiritual and mental effort. Such efforts, if properly made with understanding, as we shall see later, can cure and prevent disease by removing those basic factors which are its primary cause. No effort directed to the body alone can do more than superficially repair damage, and in this there is no cure, since the cause is still operative and may at any moment again demonstrate its presence in another form. In fact, in many cases apparent recovery is harmful, since it hides from the patient the true cause of his trouble, and in the satisfaction of apparently renewed health the real factor, being unnoticed, may gain in strength. Contrast these cases with that of the patient who knows, or who is by some wise physician instructed in the nature of the adverse spiritual or mental forces at work, the result of which has precipitated what we call disease in the physical body. If that patient directly attempts to neutralise those forces, health improves as soon as this is successfully begun, and when it is completed the disease will disappear. This is true healing by attacking the stronghold, the very base of the cause of suffering.

One of the exceptions to materialistic methods in modern science is that of the great Hahnemann, the founder of Homeopathy, who with his realisation of the beneficent love of the Creator and of the Divinity which resides within man, by studying the mental attitude of his patients toward life, environment and their respective diseases, sought to find in the herbs of the field and in the realms of nature the remedy which would not only heal their bodies but would at the same time uplift their mental outlook. May his science be extended and developed by those true physicians who have the love of humanity at heart.

Five hundred years before Christ some physicians of ancient India, working under the influence of the Lord Buddha, advanced the art of healing to so perfect a state that they were able to abolish surgery, although the surgery of their time was as efficient, or more so, than that of the present day. Such men as Hippocrates with his mighty ideals of healing, Paracelsus with his certainty of the divinity of man, and Hahnemann who realised that disease originated in a plane above the physical—all these knew much of the real nature and remedy of suffering. What untold misery would have been spared during the last twenty or twenty-five centuries had the teaching of these great masters of their art been followed, but, as in other things, materialism has appealed too strongly to the Western world, and for so long a time, that the voices of the practical obstructors have risen above the advice of those who knew the truth.

Let it be briefly stated that disease, though apparently so cruel, is in itself beneficent and for our good and, if rightly interpreted, it will guide us to our essential faults. If properly treated it will be the cause of the removal of those faults and leave us better and greater than before. Suffering is a corrective to point out a lesson which by other means we have failed to grasp, and never can it be eradicated until that lesson is learnt. Let is also be known that in those who understand and are able to read the significance of premonitory symptoms disease may be prevented before its onset or aborted in its earlier stages if the proper corrective spiritual and mental efforts be undertaken. Nor need any case despair, however severe, for the fact that the individual is still granted physical life indicates that the Soul who rules is not without hope.

Chapter 2

To understand the nature of disease certain fundamental truths have to be acknowledged.

The first of these is that man has a Soul which is his real self; a Divine, Mighty Being, a Son of the Creator of all things, of which the body, although the earthly temple of that Soul, is but the minutest reflection: that our Soul, our Divinity Who resides in and around us, lays down for us our lives as He wishes them to be ordered and, so far as we will allow, ever guides, protects and encourages us, watchful and beneficent to lead us always for our utmost advantage: that He, our Higher Self, being a spark of the Almighty, is thereby invincible and immortal.

The second principle is that we, as we know ourselves in this world, are personalities down here for the purpose of gaining all the knowledge and experience which can be obtained through earthly existence, of developing virtues which we lack and of wiping out all that is wrong within us, thus advancing towards the perfection of our natures. The Soul knows what environment and what circumstances will best enable us to do this, and hence He places us in that branch of life most suited for that object.

Thirdly, we must realise that the short passage on this earth, which we know as life, is but a moment in the course of our evolution, as one day at school is to a life, and although we can for the present only see and comprehend that one day, our intuition tell us that birth was infinitely far from our beginning and death infinitely far from our ending. Our Souls, which are really we, are immortal, and the bodies of which we are conscious are temporary, merely as horses we ride to go a journey, or instruments we use to do a piece of work.

Then follows a fourth great principle, that so long as our Souls and personalities are in harmony all is joy and peace, happiness and health. It is when our personalities are led astray from the path laid down by the Soul, either by our own worldly desires or by the persuasion of others, that a conflict arises. This conflict is the root cause of disease and unhappiness. No matter what our work in the world—bootblack or monarch, landlord or peasant, rich or poor—so long as we do that particular work according to the dictates of the Soul, all is well; and we can further rest assured that in whatever station of life we are placed, princely or lowly, it contains the lessons and experiences necessary at the moment of our evolution, and gives us the best advantage for the development of ourselves.

The next great principle is the understanding of the Unity of all things: that the Creator of all things is Love, and that everything of which we are conscious is in all its infinite number of forms a manifestation of that Love, whether it be a planet or a pebble, a star or a dewdrop, man or the lowliest form of life. It may be possible to get a glimpse of this conception by thinking of our Creator as a great blazing sun of beneficence and love and from the centre an infinite number of beams radiate in every direction, and that we and all of which we are conscious are particles at the end of those beams, sent out to gain experience and knowledge, but ultimately to return to the great centre. And though to us each ray may appear separate and distinct, it is in reality part of the great central Sun. Separation is impossible, for as soon as a beam of light is cut off from its source it ceases to exist. Thus we may comprehend a little of the impossibility of separateness as, although each ray may have its individuality, it is nevertheless part of the great central creative power. Thus any action against ourselves or against another affects the whole, because by causing imperfection in a part it reflects on the whole, every particle of which must ultimately become perfect.

So we see there are two great possible fundamental errors: dissociation between our Souls and our personalities, and cruelty or wrong to others, for this is a sin against Unity. Either of these brings conflict, which leads to disease. An understanding of where we are making an error (which is so often not realised by us) and an earnest endeavour to correct the fault will lead not only to a life of joy and peace, but also to health.

Disease is in itself beneficent, and has for its object the bringing back of the personality to the Divine will of the Soul; and thus we can see that it is both preventable and avoidable, since if we could only realise for ourselves the mistakes we are making and correct these by spiritual and mental means there could be no need for the severe lessons of suffering. Every opportunity is given us by the Divine Power to mend our ways before, as a last resort, pain and suffering have to be applied. It may not be the errors of this life, this day at school, which we are combating; and although we in our physical minds may not be conscious of the reason of our suffering, which may to us appear cruel and without reason, yet our Souls (which are ourselves) know the full purpose and are guiding us to our best advantage. Nevertheless, understanding and correction of our errors would shorten our illness and bring us back to health. Knowledge of the Soul's purpose and acquiescence in that knowledge means the relief of earthly suffering and distress, and leaves us free to develop our evolution in joy and happiness.

There are two great errors: first, to fail to honour and obey the dictates of our Soul, and second, to act against Unity. On account of the former, be ever reluctant to judge others, because what is right for one is wrong for another. The merchant, whose work it is to build up a big trade not only to his own advantage but also to that of all those whom he may employ, thereby gaining knowledge of efficiency and control and developing the virtues associated with each, must of necessity use different qualities and different virtues from those of a nurse, sacrificing her life in the care of the sick; and yet both, if obeying the dictates of their Souls, are rightly learning those qualities necessary for their evolution. It is obeying the commands of our Soul, our Higher Self, which we learn through conscience, instinct and intuition, that matters.

Thus we see that, by its very principles and in its very essence, disease is both preventable and curable, and it is the work of spiritual healers and physicians to give, in addition to material remedies, the knowledge to the suffering of the error of their lives, and of the manner in which these errors can be eradicated, and so to lead the sick back to health and joy.

Chapter 3

❦

WHAT WE KNOW AS DISEASE is the terminal stage of a much deeper disorder, and to ensure complete success in treatment it is obvious that dealing with the final result alone will not be wholly effective unless the basic cause is also removed. There is one primary error which man can make, and that is action against Unity; this originates in self-love. So also we may say that there is but one primary affliction—discomfort, or disease. And as action against Unity may be divided into various types, so also may disease—the result of these actions—be separated into main groups corresponding to their causes. The very nature of an illness will be a useful guide to assist in discovering the type of action which is being taken against the Divine Law of Love and Unity.

If we have in our nature sufficient love of all things, then we can do no harm; because that love would stay our hand at any action, our mind at any thought which might hurt another. But we have not yet reached that state of perfection; if we had, there would be no need for our existence here. But all of us are seeking and advancing towards that state, and those of us who suffer in mind or body are by this very suffering being led toward that ideal condition; and if we will but read it aright, we may not only hasten our steps towards that goal, but also save ourselves illness and distress. From the moment the lesson is understood and the error eliminated there is no longer need for the correction, because we must remember that suffering is in itself beneficent, in that it points out to us when we are taking wrong paths and hastens our evolution to its glorious perfection.

The real primary diseases of man are such defects as pride, cruelty, hate, self-love, ignorance, instability and greed; and each of these, if considered, will be found to be adverse to Unity. Such defects as these are the real diseases (using the word in the modern sense), and it is a continuation and persistence in such defects after we have reached that stage of development when we know them to be wrong, which precipitates in the body the injurious results which we know as illness.

Pride is due, firstly, to lack of recognition of the smallness of the personality and its utter dependence on the Soul, and all the successes it may have are not of itself but are blessings bestowed by the Divinity within; secondly, the loss of the sense of proportion, of the minuteness of one amidst the scheme of Creation. As Pride invariably refuses to bend with humility and resignation to the Will of the Great Creator, it commits actions contrary to that Will.

Cruelty is a denial of the unity of all and a failure to understand that any action adverse to another is in opposition to the whole, and hence an action against Unity. No man would practise its injurious effects against those near and dear to him, and by the law of Unity we have to grow until we understand that everyone, as being part of a whole, must become near and dear to us, until even those who persecute us call up only feelings of love and sympathy.

Hate is the opposite of Love, the reverse of the Law of Creation. It is contrary to the whole Divine scheme and is a denial of the Creator; it leads only to such actions and thoughts which are adverse to Unity and the opposite of those which would be dictated by Love.

Self-love again is a denial of Unity and the duty we owe to our brother men by putting the interests of ourselves before the good of humanity and the care and protection of those immediately around us.

Ignorance is the failure to learn, the refusal to see Truth when the opportunity is offered, and leads to many wrong acts such as can only exist in darkness and are not possible when the light of Truth and Knowledge is around us.

Instability, indecision and weakness of purpose result when the personality refuses to be ruled by the Higher Self, and lead us to betray others through our weakness. Such a condition would not be possible had we within us the knowledge of the Unconquerable Invincible Divinity which is in reality ourselves.

Greed leads to a desire for power. It is a denial of the freedom and individuality of every soul. Instead of recognising that every one of us is down here to develop freely upon his own lines according to the dictates of the soul alone, to increase his individuality, and to work free and unhampered, the personality with greed desires to dictate, mould and command, usurping the power of the Creator.

Such are examples of real disease, the origin and basis of all our suffering and distress. Each of such defects, if persisted in against the voice of the Higher Self, will produce a conflict which must of necessity be reflected in the physical body, producing its own specific type of malady.

We can now see how any type of illness from which we may suffer will guide us to the discovery of the fault which lies behind our affliction. For example, Pride, which is arrogance and rigidity of mind, will give rise to those diseases which produce rigidity and stiffness of the body. Pain is the result of cruelty, whereby the patient learns through personal suffering not to inflict it upon others, either from a physical or from a mental standpoint. The penalties of Hate are loneliness, violent uncontrollable temper, mental nerve storms and conditions of hysteria. The diseases of introspection—neurosis, neurasthenia and similar conditions—which rob life of so much enjoyment, are caused by excessive Self-love. Ignorance and lack of wisdom bring their own difficulties in everyday life, and in addition, should there be a persistence in refusing to see truth when the opportunity has been given, short-sightedness and impairment of vision and hearing are the natural consequences. Instability of mind must lead to the same quality in the body with those various disorders which affect movement and co-ordination. The result of greed and domination of others is such diseases as will render the sufferer a slave to his own body, with desires and ambitions curbed by the malady.

Moreover, the very part of the body affected is no accident, but is in accordance with the law of cause and effect, and again will be a guide to help us. For example, the heart, the fountain of life and hence of love, is attacked when especially the love side of the nature towards humanity is not developed or is wrongly used; a hand affected denotes failure or wrong in action; the brain being the centre of control, if afflicted, indicates lack of control in the personality. Such must follow as the law lays down. We are all ready to admit the many results which may follow a fit of violent temper, the shock of sudden bad news; if trivial affairs can thus affect the body, how much more serious and deep-rooted must be a prolonged conflict between soul and body. Can we wonder that the result gives rise to such grievous complaints as the diseases amongst us to-day?

But yet there is no cause for depression. The prevention and cure of disease can be found by discovering the wrong within ourselves and eradicating this fault by the earnest development of the virtue which will destroy it; not by fighting the wrong, but by bringing in such a flood of its opposing virtue that it will be swept from our natures.

Chapter 4

※☾※

SO WE FIND THAT THERE is nothing of the nature of accident as regards disease, either in its type or in that part of the body which is affected; like all other results of energy, it follows the law of cause and effect. Certain maladies may be caused by direct physical means, such as those associated with some poisons, accidents and injuries, and gross excesses; but disease in general is due to some basic error in our constitution, as in the examples already given.

And thus for a complete cure not only must physical means be used, choosing always the best methods which are known to the art of healing, but we ourselves must also endeavour to the utmost of our ability to remove any fault in our nature; because final and complete healing ultimately comes from within, from the Soul itself, which by His beneficence radiates harmony throughout the personality, when allowed to do so.

As there is one great root cause of all disease, namely self-love, so there is one great certain method of relief of all suffering, the conversion of self-love into devotion to others. If we but sufficiently develop the quality of losing ourselves in the love and care of those around us, enjoying the glorious adventure of gaining knowledge and helping others, our personal griefs and sufferings rapidly come to an end. It is the great ultimate aim: the losing of our own interests in the service of humanity. It matters not the station in life in which our Divinity has placed us. Whether engaged in trade or profession, rich or poor, monarch or beggar, for one and all it is possible to carry on the work of their respective vocations and yet be veritable blessings to those around by communicating to them the Divine Love of Brotherhood.

But the vast majority of us have some way to travel before we can reach this state of perfection, although it is surprising how rapidly any individual may advance along these lines if the effort is seriously made, providing he trusts not in his poor personality alone but has implicit faith, that by the example and teaching of the great masters of the world he may be enabled to unite himself with his own Soul, the Divinity within, when all things become possible. In most of us there is one, or more, adverse defect which is particularly hindering our advancement, and it is such defect, or defects, which we must especially seek out within ourselves, and whilst striving to develop and extend the love side of our nature towards the world, endeavour at the same time to wash away any such defect in particular by the flooding of our nature with the opposing virtue. At first this may be a little difficult, but only just at first, for it is remarkable how rapidly a truly encouraged virtue will increase, linked with the knowledge that with the aid of the Divinity within us, if we but persevere, failure is impossible.

In the development of Universal Love within ourselves we must learn to realise more and more that every human being, however lowly, is a son of the Creator, and that one day and in due time he will advance to perfection just as we all hope to do. However base a man or creature may appear, we must remember that there is the Divine Spark within, which will slowly but surely grow until the glory of the Creator irradiates that being.

Moreover, the question of right or wrong, of good and evil, is purely relative. That which is right in the natural evolution of the aboriginal would be wrong for the more enlightened of our civilisation, and that which might even be a virtue in such as ourselves might be out of place, and hence wrong, in one who has reached the stage of discipleship. What we call wrong or evil is in reality good out of place, and hence is purely relative. Let us remember also that our standard of idealism again is relative; to the animals we must appear as veritable gods, whereas we in ourselves are very far below the standards of the great Brotherhood of Saints and Martyrs who have given their all to be examples to us. Hence we must have compassion and sympathy for the lowliest, for whilst we may consider ourselves as having advanced far above their level, we are in ourselves minute indeed, and have yet a long journey before us to reach the standard of our older brothers, whose light shines throughout the world in every age.

If Pride assails us, let us try to realise that our personalities are in themselves as nothing, unable to do any good work or acceptable service, or to resist the powers of darkness, unless assisted by that Light which is from above, the Light of our Soul; endeavour to comprehend a glimpse of the omnipotence and unthinkable mightiness of our Creator, Who makes in all perfection a world in one drop of water and systems upon systems of universes, and try to realise the relative humility we owe and our utter dependence upon Him. We learn to pay homage and give respect to our human superiors; how infinitely more should we acknowledge our own frailty with utmost humility before the Great Architect of the Universe!

If Cruelty, or Hate, bar our way to progress, let us remember that Love is the foundation of Creation, that in every living soul there is some good, and that in the best of us there is some bad. By seeking the good in others, even in those who at first offend us, we shall learn to develop, if nothing more, some sympathy and a hope that they will see better ways; then it follows that the desire will arise to help them to that uplift. The ultimate conquest of all will be through love and gentleness, and when we have sufficiently developed those two qualities nothing will be able to assail us, since we shall ever have compassion and not offer resistance; for, again, by the same law of cause and effect it is resistance which damages. Our object in life is to follow the dictates of our Higher Self, undeterred by the influence of others, and this can only be achieved if we gently go our own way, but at the same time never interfere with the personality of another or cause the least harm by any method of cruelty or hate. We must strive to learn love of others, beginning perhaps with one individual or even an animal, and let this love develop and extend over a wider and wider range, until its opposing defects will automatically disappear. Love begets Love, as Hate does Hate.

The cure of self-love is effected by the turning outwards to others of the care and attention which we are devoting to ourselves, becoming so engrossed in their welfare that we forget ourselves in that endeavour. As one great order of Brotherhood expresses it, "to seek the solace of our own distress by extending relief and consolation to our fellow-creatures in the hour of their affliction," and there is no surer way of curing self-love and the disorders which follow it than by such a method.

Instability can be eradicated by the development of self-determination, by making up the mind and doing things with definiteness instead of wavering and hovering. Even if at first we may sometimes make errors, it were better to act than to let opportunities pass for the want of decision. Determination will soon grow; fear of plunging into life will disappear, and the experiences gained will guide our mind to better judgment.

To eradicate Ignorance, again let us not be afraid of experience, but with mind awake and with eyes and ears wide open take in every particle of knowledge which may be obtained. At the same time we must keep flexible in thought, lest preconceived ideas and former convictions rob us of the opportunity of gaining fresh and wider knowledge. We should be ever ready to expand the mind and to disregard any idea, however firmly rooted, if under wider experience a greater truth shows itself.

Like Pride, Greed is a great obstacle to advancement, and both of these must be ruthlessly washed away. The results of Greed are serious indeed, because it leads us to interfere with the soul-development of our fellow-men. We must realise that every being is here to develop his own evolution according to the dictates of his Soul, and his Soul alone, and that none of us must do anything but encourage our brother in that development. We must help him to hope and, if in our power, increase his knowledge and worldly opportunities to gain his advancement. Just as we would wish others to help us up the steep and difficult mountain path of life, so let us be ever ready to lend a helping hand and give the experience of our wider knowledge to a weaker or younger brother. Such should be the attitude of parent to child, master to man or comrade to comrade, giving care, love, and protection as far as may be needed and beneficial, yet never for one moment interfering with the natural evolution of the personality, as this must be dictated by the Soul.

Many of us in our childhood and early life are much nearer to our own Soul than we are in later years, and have then clearer ideas of our work in life, the endeavours we are expected to make and the character we are required to develop. The reason for this is that the materialism and circumstances of our age, and the personalities with whom we associate, lead us away from the voice of our Higher Self and bind us firmly to the commonplace with its lack of ideals, all too evident in this civilisation. Let the parent, the master and the comrade ever strive to encourage the growth of the Higher Self within those over whom they have the wonderful privilege and opportunity to exert their influence, but let them ever allow freedom to others, as they hope to have freedom given to them.

So in a similar way may we seek out any faults in our constitution and wash them out by developing the opposing virtue, thus removing from our nature the cause of the conflict between Soul and personality, which is the primary basic cause of disease. Such action alone, if the patient has faith and strength, will bring relief, health and joy, and in those not so strong will materially assist the work of the earthly physician in bringing about the same result.

We must earnestly learn to develop individuality according to the dictates of our own Soul, to fear no man and to see that no one interferes with, or dissuades us from, the development of our evolution, the fulfilment of our duty and the rendering of help to our fellow-men, remembering that the further we advance, the greater blessing we become to those around. Especially must we be on guard in the giving of help to other people, no matter whom they be, to be certain that the desire to help comes from the dictates of the Inner Self and is not a false sense of duty imposed by the suggestion or persuasion of a more dominant personality. One tragedy resulting from modern convention is of such a type, and it is impossible to calculate the thousands of hindered lives, the myriads of missed opportunities, the sorrow and the suffering so caused, the countless number of children who from a sense of duty have perhaps for years waited upon an invalid when the only malady the parent has known has been the greed of attention. Think of the armies of men and women who have been prevented from doing perhaps some great and useful work for humanity because their personality has been captured by some one individual from whom they have not had the courage to win freedom; the children who in their early days know and desire their ordained calling, and yet from difficulties of circumstance, dissuasion by others and weakness of purpose glide into some other branch of life, where they are neither happy nor able to develop their evolution as they might otherwise have done. It is the dictates of our conscience alone which can tell us whether our duty lies with one or many, how and whom we should serve; but whichever it may be, we should obey that command to the utmost of our ability.

Finally, let us not fear to plunge into life; we are here to gain experience and knowledge, and we shall learn but little unless we face realities and seek to our utmost. Such experience can be gained in every quarter, and the truths of nature and of humanity can be won just as effectively, perhaps even more so, in a country cottage as amongst the noise and hustle of a city.

Chapter 5

❦

As lack of individuality (that is, the allowing of interference with the personality, such interference preventing it from complying with the demands of the Higher Self) is of such great importance in the production of disease, and as it often begins early in life, let us now consider the true relation between parent and child, teacher and pupil.

Fundamentally, the office of parenthood is to be the privileged means (and, indeed, it should be considered as divinely privileged) of enabling a soul to contact this world for the sake of evolution. If properly understood, there is probably no greater opportunity offered to mankind than this, to be the agent of the physical birth of a soul and to have the care of the young personality during the first few years of its existence on earth. The whole attitude of parents should be to give the little newcomer all the spiritual, mental and physical guidance to the utmost of their ability, ever remembering that the wee one is an individual soul come down to gain his own experience and knowledge in his own way according to the dictates of his Higher Self, and every possible freedom should be given for unhampered development.

The office of parenthood is one of divine service, and should be respected as much as, or perhaps even more than, any other duty we may be called upon to undertake. As it is one of sacrifice, it must ever be borne in mind that nothing whatever should be required in return from the child, the whole object being to give, and give alone, gentle love, protection and guidance until the soul takes charge of the young personality. Independence, individuality and freedom should be taught from the beginning, and the child should be encouraged as early as possible in life to think and act for himself. All parental control should be relinquished step by step as the ability for self-management is developed, and later on no restraint or false idea of duty to parenthood should hamper the dictates of the child's soul.

Parenthood is an office in life which passes from one to another, and is in essence a temporary giving of guidance and protection for a brief period, after which time it should then cease its efforts and leave the object of its attention free to advance alone. Be it remembered that the child for whom we may become a temporary guardian may be a much older and greater soul than ourselves, and spiritually our superior, so that control and protection should be confined to the needs of the young personality.

Parenthood is a sacred duty, temporary in its character and passing from generation to generation. It carries with it nothing but service and calls for no obligation in return from the young, since they must be left free to develop in their own way and become as fitted as possible to fulfil the same office in but a few years' time. Thus the child should have no restrictions, no obligations and no parental hindrances, knowing that parenthood had previously been bestowed on his father and mother and that it may be his duty to perform the same office for another.

Parents should be particularly on guard against any desire to mould the young personality according to their own ideas or wishes, and should refrain from any undue control or demand of favours in return for their natural duty and divine privilege of being the means of helping a soul to contact the world. Any desire for control, or wish to shape the young life for personal motives, is a terrible form of greed and should never be countenanced, for if in the young father or mother this takes root it will in later years lead them to be veritable vampires. If there is the least desire to dominate, it should be checked at the onset. We must refuse to be under the slavery of greed, which compels in us the wish to possess others. We must encourage in ourselves the art of giving, and develop this until it has washed out by its sacrifice every trace of adverse action.

The teacher should ever bear in mind that it is his office merely to be the agent of giving to the young guidance and an opportunity of learning the things of the world and of life, so that each child may absorb knowledge in his own way, and, if allowed freedom, instinctively choose that which is necessary for the success of his life. Again, therefore, nothing more than the gentlest care and guidance should be given to enable the student to gain the knowledge he requires.

Children should remember that the office of parenthood, as emblematical of creative power, is divine in its mission, but that it calls for no restriction of development and no obligations which might hamper the life and work dictated to them by their own Soul. It is impossible to estimate in this present civilisation the untold suffering, the cramping of natures and the developing of dominant characters which the lack of a realisation of this fact produces. In almost every home parents and children build themselves prisons from entirely false motives and a wrong conception of the relationship of parent and child. These prisons bar the freedom, cramp the life, prevent the natural development and bring unhappiness to all concerned, and the mental, nervous and even physical disorders which afflict such people form a very large proportion indeed of the sickness of our present time.

It cannot be too firmly realised that every soul in incarnation is down here for the specific purpose of gaining experience and understanding, and of perfecting his personality towards those ideals laid down by the soul. No matter what our relationship be to each other, whether husband and wife, parent and child, brother and sister, or master and man, we sin against our Creator and against our fellowmen if we hinder from motives of personal desire the evolution of another soul. Our sole duty is to obey the dictates of our own conscience, and this will never for one moment brook the domination of another personality. Let everyone remember that his Soul had laid down for him a particular work, and that unless he does this work, though perhaps not consciously, he will inevitably raise a conflict between his Soul and personality which of necessity reacts in the form of physical disorders.

True, it may be the calling of any one individual to devote his life to one other alone, but before doing so let him be absolutely certain that this is the command of his Soul, and that it is not the suggestion of some other dominant personality over-persuading him, or false ideas of duty misdirecting him. Let him also remember that we come down into this world to win battles, to gain strength against those who would control us, and to advance to that stage when we pass through life doing our duty quietly and calmly, undeterred and uninfluenced by any living being, calmly guided always by the voice of our Higher Self. For very many their greatest battle will be in their own home, where before gaining their liberty to win victories in the world they will have to free themselves from the adverse domination and control of some very near relative.

Any individual, whether adult or child, part of whose work it is in this life to free himself from the dominant control of another, should remember the following: firstly, that his would-be oppressor should be regarded in the same way as we look upon an opponent in sport, as a personality with whom we are playing the game of Life, without the least trace of bitterness, and that if it were not for such opponents we should be lacking the opportunity of developing our own courage and individuality; secondly, that the real victories of life come through love and gentleness, and that in such a contest no force whatever must be used: that by steadily growing in his own nature, bearing sympathy, kindness and, if possible, affection—or, even better, love—towards the opponent, he may so develop that in time he may very gently and quietly follow the call of conscience without allowing the least interference.

Those who are dominant require much help and guidance to enable them to realise the great universal truth of the Unity and to understand the joy of Brotherhood. To miss such things is to miss the real happiness of Life, and we must help such folk as far as lies within our power. Weakness on our part, which allows them to extend their influence, will in no way assist them; a gentle refusal to be under their control and an endeavour to bring to them the realisation of the joy of giving will help them along the upward path.

The gaining of our freedom, the winning of our individuality and independence, will in most cases call for much courage and faith. But in the darkest hours, and when success seems well-nigh impossible, let us ever remember that God's children should never be afraid, that our Souls only give us such tasks as we are capable of accomplishing, and that with our own courage and faith in the Divinity within us victory must come to all who continue to strive.

Chapter 6

AND NOW, DEAR BROTHERS AND sisters, when we realise that Love and Unity are the great foundations of our Creation, that we ourselves are children of the Divine Love, and that the eternal conquest of all wrong and suffering will be accomplished by means of gentleness and love, when we realise all this, where in this beauteous picture are we to place such practices as vivisection and animal gland grafting? Are we still so primitive, so pagan, that we yet believe that by the sacrifice of animals we are enabled to escape the results of our own faults and failings? Nearly 2,500 years ago the Lord Buddha showed to the world the wrongness of sacrificing the lower creatures. Humanity already owes a mighty debt to the animals which it has tortured and destroyed, and far from any good resulting to man from such inhuman practices, nothing but harm and damage can be wrought to both the human and animal kingdoms. How far have we of the West wandered from those beautiful ideals of our Mother India of old times, when so great was the love for the creatures of the earth that men were trained and skilled to attend the maladies and injuries of not only the animals, but also the birds. Moreover, there were vast sanctuaries for all types of life, and so averse were the people to hurting a lower creature that any man who hunted was refused the attendance of a physician in time of sickness until he had vowed to relinquish such a practice.

Let us not speak against the men who practice vivisection, for numbers of these are working with truly humanitarian principles, hoping and striving to find some relief for human suffering; their motive is good enough, but their wisdom is poor, and they have little understanding of the reason of life. Motive alone, however right, is not enough; it must be combined with wisdom and knowledge.

Of the horror of the black magic associated with gland grafting let us not even write, but implore every human being to shun it as ten thousand times worse than any plague, for it is a sin against God, man and animal.

With just such one or two exceptions there is no point in dwelling on the failure of modern medical science; destruction is useless unless we rebuild a better edifice, and as in medicine the foundation of the newer building is already laid, let us concentrate on adding one or two stones to that temple. Neither is adverse criticism of the profession to-day of value; it is the system which is mainly wrong, not the men; for it is a system whereby the physician, from economic reasons alone, has not the time for administering quiet, peaceful treatment or the opportunity for the necessary meditation and thought which should be the heritage of those who devote their lives to attendance on the sick. As Paracelsus said, the wise physician attends five, not fifteen, patients in a day—an ideal impracticable in this age for the average practitioner.

The dawn of a new and better art of healing is upon us. A hundred years ago the Homeopathy of Hahnemann was as the first streak of the morning light after a long night of darkness, and it may play a big part in the medicine of the future. Moreover, the attention which is being given at the present time to improving conditions of life and providing purer and cleaner diet is an advance towards the prevention of sickness; and those movements which are directed to bring to the notice of the people both the connection between spiritual failings and disease and the healing which may be obtained through perfection of the mind, are pointing the way towards the coming of that bright sunshine in whose radiant light the darkness of disease will disappear.

Let us remember that disease is a common enemy, and that every one of us who conquers a fragment of it is thereby helping not only himself but the whole of humanity. A certain, but definite, amount of energy will have to be expended before its overthrow is complete; let us one and all strive for this result, and those are greater and stronger than the others may not only do their share, but materially assist their weaker brothers.

Obviously the first way to prevent the spread and increase of disease is for us to cease committing those actions which extend its power; the second, to wipe out from our natures our own defects, which would allow further invasion. The achievement of this is victory indeed; then, having freed ourselves, we are free to help others. And it is not so difficult as it may at first appear; we are but expected to do our best, and we know that this is possible for all of us if we will but listen to the dictates of our own Soul. Life does not demand of us unthinkable sacrifice; it asks us to travel its journey with joy in our heart and to be a blessing to those around, so that if we leave the world just that trifle better for our visit, then have we done our work.

The teachings of religions, if properly read, plead with us "to forsake all and follow Me", the interpretation of which is to give ourselves entirely up to the demands of our Higher Self, but not, as some imagine, to discard home and comfort, love and luxury; very far from this is the truth. A prince of the realm, with all the glories of the palace, may be a Godsend and a blessing indeed to his people, to his country—nay, even to the world; how much might have been lost had that prince imagined it his duty to enter a monastery. The offices of life in every branch, from the lowliest to the most exalted, have to be filled, and the Divine Guide of our destinies knows into which office to place us for our best advantage; all we are expected to do is to fulfil that duty cheerfully and well. There are saints at the factory bench and in the stokehold of a ship as well as among the dignitaries of religious orders. Not one of us upon this earth is being asked to do more than is within his power to perform, and if we strive to obtain the best within us, ever guided by our Higher Self, health and happiness is a possibility for each one.

For the greater part of the last two hundred years Western civilisation has passed through an age of intense materialism, and the realisation of the spiritual side of our natures and existence has been greatly lost in the attitude of mind which has placed worldly possessions, ambitions, desires and pleasures above the real things of life. The true reason of man's existence on earth has been overshadowed by his anxiety to obtain from his incarnation nothing but worldly gain. It has been a period when life has been very difficult because of the lack of the real comfort, encouragement and uplift which is brought by a realisation of greater things than those of the world. During the last centuries religions have to many people appeared rather as legends having no bearing on their lives instead of being the very essence of their existence. The true nature of our Higher Self, the knowledge of previous and later life, apart from this present one, has meant but very little to us instead of being the guide and stimulus of our every action. We have rather shunned the great things and attempted to make life as comfortable as possible by putting the super-physical out of our minds and depending upon earthly pleasures to compensate us for our trials. Thus have position, rank, wealth and worldly possessions become the goal of these centuries; and as all such things are transient and can only be obtained and held with much anxiety and concentration on material things, so has the real internal peace and happiness of the past generations been infinitely below that which is the due of mankind.

The real peace of the Soul and mind is with us when we are making spiritual advance, and it cannot be obtained by the accumulation of wealth alone, no matter how great. But the times are changing, and the indications are many that this civilisation has begun to pass from the age of pure materialism to a desire for the realities and truths of the universe. The general and rapidly increasing interest exhibited to-day for knowledge of super-physical truths, the growing number of those who are desiring information on existence before and after this life, the founding of methods to conquer disease by faith and spiritual means, the quest after the ancient teachings and wisdom of the East— all these are signs that people of the present time have glimpsed the reality of things. Thus, when we come to the problem of healing we can understand that this also will have to keep pace with the times and change its methods from those of gross materialism to those of a science founded upon the realities of Truth and governed by the same Divine laws which rule our very natures. Healing will pass from the domain of physical methods of treating the physical body to that of spiritual and mental healing, which, by bringing about harmony between the Soul and mind, will eradicate the very basic cause of disease, and then allow such physical means to be used as may be necessary to complete the cure of the body.

It seems quite possible that, unless the medical profession realises these facts and advances with the spiritual growth of the people, the art of healing may pass into the hands of religious orders or into those of the trueborn healers of men who exist in every generation, but who yet have lived more or less unobserved, prevented from following their natural calling by the attitude of the orthodox. So that the physician of the future will have two great aims. The first will be to assist the patient to a knowledge of himself and to point out to him the fundamental mistakes he may be making, the deficiencies in his character which he should remedy, and the defects in his nature which must be eradicated and replaced by the corresponding virtues. Such a physician will have to be a great student of the laws governing humanity and of human nature itself, so that he may recognise in all who come to him those elements which are causing a conflict between the Soul and the personality. He must be able to advise the sufferer how best to bring about the harmony required, what actions against Unity he must cease to perform and the necessary virtues he must develop to wipe out his defects. Each case will need a careful study, and it will only be those who have devoted much of their life to the knowledge of mankind and in whose heart burns the desire to help, who will be able to undertake successfully this glorious and divine work for humanity, to open the eyes of a sufferer and enlighten him on the reason of his being, and to inspire hope, comfort and faith which will enable him to conquer his malady.

The second duty of the physician will be to administer such remedies as will help the physical body to gain strength and assist the mind to become calm, widen its outlook and strive towards perfection, thus bringing peace and harmony to the whole personality. Such remedies there are in nature, placed there by the mercy of the Divine Creator for the healing and comfort of mankind. A few of these are known, and more are being sought at the present time by physicians in different parts of the world, especially in our Mother India, and there is no doubt that when such researches have become more developed we shall regain much of the knowledge which was known more than two thousand years ago, and the healer of the future will have at his disposal the wonderful and natural remedies which were divinely placed for man to relieve his sickness.

Thus the abolition of disease will depend upon humanity realising the truth of the unalterable laws of our Universe and adapting itself with humility and obedience to those laws, thus bringing peace between its Soul and itself, and gaining the real joy and happiness of life. And the part of the physician will be to assist any sufferer to a knowledge of such truth, to point out to him the means by which he can gain harmony, to inspire him with faith in his Divinity which can overcome all, and to administer such physical remedies as will help in the harmonising of the personality and the healing of the body.

Chapter 7

AND NOW WE COME TO the all-important problem, how can we help ourselves? How can we keep our mind and body in that state of harmony which will make it difficult or impossible for disease to attack us, for it is certain that the personality without conflict is immune from illness.

First let us consider the mind. We have already discussed at some length the necessity of seeking within ourselves those defects we possess which cause us to work against Unity and out of harmony with the dictates of the Soul, and of eliminating these faults by developing the opposing virtues. This can be done on the lines already indicated, and an honest self-examination will disclose to us the nature of our errors. Our spiritual advisers, true physicians and intimate friends should all be able to assist us to obtain a faithful picture of ourselves, but the perfect method of learning this is by calm thought and meditation, and by bringing ourselves to such an atmosphere of peace that our Souls are able to speak to us through our conscience and intuition, and to guide us according to their wishes. If we can only set aside a short time every day, quite alone and in as quiet a place as possible, free from interruption, and merely sit or lie quietly, either keeping the mind a blank or calmly thinking of one's work in life, it will be found after a time that we get great help at such moments and, as it were, flashes of knowledge and guidance are given to us. We find that the questions of the difficult problems of life are unmistakably answered and we become able to choose with confidence the right course. Throughout such times we should keep an earnest desire in the heart to serve humanity and work according to the dictates of our Soul.

Be it remembered that when the fault is found the remedy lies not in a battle against this and not in a use of will power and energy to suppress a wrong, but in a steady development of the opposite virtue, thus automatically washing from our natures all trace of the offender. This is the true and natural method of advancement and of the conquest of wrong, vastly easier and more effective than fighting a particular defect. To struggle against a fault increases its power, keeps our attention riveted on its presence, and brings us a battle indeed, and the most success we can then expect is conquest by suppression, which is far from satisfactory, as the enemy is still with us and may in a weak moment show itself afresh. To forget the failing and consciously to strive to develop the virtue which would make the former impossible, this is true victory.

For example, should there be cruelty in our nature, we can continually say, "I will not be cruel," and so prevent ourselves from erring in that direction; but the success of this depends on the strength of the mind, and should it weaken we might for the moment forget our good resolve. But should we, on the other hand, develop real sympathy towards our fellow-men, this quality will once and for all make cruelty impossible, for we should shun the very act with horror because of our fellow-feeling. About this there is no suppression, no hidden enemy to come forward at moments when we are off our guard, because our sympathy will have completely eradicated from our nature the possibility of any act which could hurt another.

As we have previously seen, the nature of our physical maladies will materially help in pointing out to us the mental disharmony which is the basic cause of their origin; and another great factor of success is that we must have a zest for life and look upon existence not merely as a duty to be borne with as much patience as possible, developing a real joy in the adventure of our journey through this world.

Perhaps one of the greatest tragedies of materialism is the development of boredom and the loss of real inner happiness; it teaches people to seek contentment and compensation for troubles in earthly enjoyments and pleasures, and these can never bring anything but temporary oblivion of our difficulties. Once we begin to seek compensation for our trials at the hands of the paid jester we start a vicious circle. Amusement, entertainment and frivolity are good for us all, but not when we persistently depend upon these to alleviate our troubles. Worldly amusements of every kind have to be steadily increased in their intensity to keep their hold, and the thrill of yesterday becomes the bore of to-morrow. So we go on seeking other and greater excitements until we become satiated and can no longer obtain relief in that direction. In some form or another reliance on worldly entertainment makes Fausts of us all, and though perhaps we may not fully realise it in our conscious self, life becomes for us little more than a patient duty and all its true zest and joy, such as should be the heritage of every child and be maintained until our latest hours, departs from us. The extreme stage is reached to-day in the scientific efforts being evolved to obtain rejuvenation, prolongation of natural life and increase of sensual pleasures by means of devilish practices.

The state of boredom is responsible for the admittance into ourselves of much more disease than would be generally realised, and as it tends to-day to occur early in life, so the maladies associated with it tend to appear at a younger age. Such a condition cannot occur if we acknowledge the truth of our Divinity, our mission in the world, and thereby possess the joy of gaining experience and helping others. The antidote for boredom is to take an active and lively interest in all around us, to study life throughout the whole day, to learn and learn and learn from our fellow-men, and from the occurrences in life, the Truth that lies behind all things, to lose ourselves in the art of gaining knowledge and experience, and to watch for opportunities when we may use such to the advantage of a fellow-traveller. Thus every moment of our work and play will bring with it a zeal for learning, a desire to experience real things, real adventures and deeds worthwhile, and as we develop this faculty we shall find that we are regaining the power of obtaining joy from the smallest incidents, and occurrences we have previously regarded as commonplace and of dull monotony will become the opportunity for research and adventure. It is in the simple things of life—the simple things because they are nearer the great Truth—that real pleasure is to be found.

Resignation, which makes one become merely an unobservant passenger on the journey of life, opens the door to untold adverse influences which would never have an opportunity of gaining admittance as long as our daily existence brought with it the spirit and joy of adventure. Whatever may be our station, whether a worker in the city with its teeming myriads or a lonely shepherd in the hills, let us strive to turn monotony into interest, dull duty into a joyous opportunity for experience, and daily life into an intense study of humanity and the great fundamental laws of the Universe. In every place there is ample opportunity to observe the laws of Creation, either in the mountains or valleys or amongst our brother men. First let us turn life into an adventure of absorbing interest, when boredom will be no longer possible, and from the knowledge thus gained seek to harmonise our mind with our Soul and with the great Unity of God's Creation.

Another fundamental help to us is to put away all fear. Fear in reality holds no place in the natural human kingdom, since the Divinity within us, which is ourself, is unconquerable and immortal, and if we could but realise it we, as Children of God, have nothing of which to be afraid. In materialistic ages fear naturally increases in earthly possessions (whether they be of the body itself or external riches), for if such things be our world, since they are so transient, so difficult to obtain and so impossible to hold save for a brief spell, they arouse in us the utmost anxiety lest we miss an opportunity of grasping them while we may, and we must of necessity live in a constant state of fear, conscious or subconscious, because in our inner self we know that such possessions may at any moment be snatched from us and that at the most we can only hold them for a brief life.

In this age the fear of disease has developed until it has become a great power for harm, because it opens the door to those things we dread and makes it easier for their admission. Such fear is really self-interest, for when we are earnestly absorbed in the welfare of others there is no time to be apprehensive of personal maladies. Fear at the present time is playing a great part in intensifying disease, and modern science has increased the reign of terror by spreading abroad to the general public its discoveries, which as yet are but half-truths. The knowledge of bacteria and the various germs associated with disease has played havoc in the minds of tens of thousands of people, and by the dread aroused in them has in itself rendered them more susceptible of attack. While lower forms of life, such as bacteria, may play a part in or be associated with physical disease, they constitute by no means the whole truth of the problem, as can be demonstrated scientifically or by everyday occurrences. There is a factor which science is unable to explain on physical grounds, and that is why some people become affected by disease whilst others escape, although both classes may be open to the same possibility of infection. Materialism forgets that there is a factor above the physical plane which in the ordinary course of life protects or renders susceptible any particular individual with regard to disease, of whatever nature it may be. Fear, by its depressing effect on our mentality, thus causing disharmony in our physical and magnetic bodies, paves the way for invasion, and if bacteria and such physical means were the sure and only cause of disease, then indeed there might be but little encouragement not to be afraid. But when we realise that in the worst epidemics only a proportion of those exposed to infection are attacked and that, as we have already seen, the real cause of disease lies in our own personality and is within our control, then have we reason to go about without dread and fearless, knowing that the remedy lies with ourselves. We can put all fear of physical means alone as a cause of disease out of our minds, knowing that such anxiety merely renders us susceptible, and that if we are endeavouring to bring harmony into our personality we need anticipate illness no more than we dread being struck by lightning or hit by a fragment of a falling meteor.

Now let us consider the physical body. It must never be forgotten that this is but the earthly habitation of the Soul, in which we dwell only for a short time in order that we may be able to contact the world for the purpose of gaining experience and knowledge. Without too much identifying ourselves with our bodies, we should treat them with respect and care, so that they may be healthy and last the longer to do our work. Never for one moment should we become engrossed or over-anxious about them, but learn to be as little conscious of their existence as possible, using them as a vehicle of our Soul and mind and as servants to do our will. External and internal cleanliness are of great importance. For the former we of the West use our water too hot; this opens the skin and allows the admission of dirt. Moreover, the excessive use of soap renders the surface sticky. Cool or tepid water, either running as a shower bath or changed more than once is nearer the natural method and keeps the body healthier; only such an amount of soap as is necessary to remove obvious dirt should be used, and this should afterwards be well washed off in fresh water.

Internal cleanliness depends on diet, and we should choose everything that is clean and wholesome and as fresh as possible, chiefly natural fruits, vegetables and nuts. Animal flesh should certainly be avoided; first, because it gives rise to much physical poison in the body; secondly, because it stimulates an abnormal and excessive appetite; and thirdly, because it necessitates cruelty to the animal world. Plenty of fluid should be taken to cleanse the body, such as water and natural wines and products made direct from Nature's storehouse, avoiding the more artificial beverages of distillation.

Sleep should not be excessive, as many of us have more control over ourselves whilst awake than when asleep. The old saying, "Time to turn over, time to turn out," is an excellent guide as to when to rise.

Clothing should be as light in weight as is compatible with warmth; it should allow air to reach the body, and sunshine and fresh air should be permitted to contact the skin on all possible occasions. Water and sun bathing are great donors of health and vitality.

In all things cheerfulness should be encouraged, and we should refuse to be oppressed by doubt and depression, but remember that such are not of ourselves, for our Souls know only joy and happiness.

Chapter 8

THUS WE SEE THAT OUR conquest of disease will mainly depend on the following: firstly, the realisation of the Divinity within our nature and our consequent power to overcome all that is wrong: secondly, the knowledge that the basic cause of disease is due to disharmony between the personality and the Soul; thirdly, our willingness and ability to discover the fault which is causing such a conflict; and fourthly, the removal of any such fault by developing the opposing virtue.

The duty of the healing art will be to assist us to the necessary knowledge and means by which we may overcome our maladies, and in addition to this to administer such remedies as will strengthen our mental and physical bodies and give us greater opportunities of victory. Then shall we indeed be capable of attacking disease at its very base with real hope of success. The medical school of the future will not particularly interest itself in the ultimate results and products of disease, nor will it pay so much attention to actual physical lessons, or administer drugs and chemicals merely for the sake of palliating our symptoms, but knowing the true cause of sickness and aware that the obvious physical results are merely secondary, it will concentrate its efforts upon bringing about that harmony between body, mind and soul which results in the relief and cure of disease. And in such cases as are undertaken early enough the correction of the mind will avert the imminent illness.

Among the types of remedies that will be used will be those obtained from the most beautiful plants and herbs to be found in the pharmacy of Nature, such as have been divinely enriched with healing powers for the mind and body of man.

For our own part we must practise peace, harmony, individuality and firmness of purpose and increasingly develop the knowledge that in essence we are of Divine origin, children of the Creator, and thus have within us, if we will but develop it, as in time we ultimately surely must, the power to attain perfection. And this reality must increase within us until it becomes the most outstanding feature of our existence. We must steadfastly practise peace, imagining our minds as a lake ever to be kept calm, without waves, or even ripples, to disturb its tranquillity, and gradually develop this state of peace until no event of life, no circumstance, no other personality is able under any condition to ruffle the surface of that lake or raise within us any feelings of irritability, depression or doubt. It will materially help to set apart a short time each day to think quietly of the beauty of peace and the benefits of calmness, and to realise that it is neither by worrying nor hurrying that we accomplish most, but by calm, quiet thought and action become more efficient in all we undertake. To harmonise our conduct in this life in accordance with the wishes of our own Soul, and to remain in such a state of peace that the trials and disturbances of the world leave us unruffled, is a great attainment indeed and brings to us that Peace which passeth understanding; and though at first it may seem to be beyond our dreams, it is in reality, with patience and perseverance, within the reach of us all.

We are not all asked to be saints or martyrs or men of renown; to most of us less conspicuous offices are allotted. But we are all expected to understand the joy and adventures of life and to fulfil with cheerfulness the particular piece of work which has been ordained for us by our Divinity.

For those who are sick, peace of mind and harmony with the Soul is the greatest aid to recovery. The medicine and nursing of the future will pay much more attention to the development of this within the patient than we do today when, unable to judge the progress of a case except by materialistic scientific means, we think more of the frequent taking of temperature and a number of attentions which interrupt, rather than promote, that quiet rest and relaxation of body and mind which are so essential to recovery. There is no doubt that at the very onset of it, at any rate, minor ailments, if we could but get a few hours' complete relaxation and in harmony with our Higher Self the illness would be aborted. At such moments we need to bring down into ourselves but a fraction of that calm, as symbolised by the entry of Christ into the boat during the storm on the lake of Galilee, when He ordered "Peace, be still."

Our outlook on life depends on the nearness of the personality to the Soul. The closer the union the greater the harmony and peace, and the more clearly will shine the light of Truth and the radiant happiness which is of the higher realms; these will hold us steady and undismayed by the difficulties and terrors of the world, since they have their foundations on the Eternal Truth of Good. The knowledge of Truth also gives to us the certainty that, however tragic some of the events of the world may appear to be, they form but a temporary stage in the evolution of man; and that even disease is in itself beneficent and works under the operation of certain laws designed to produce ultimate good by exerting a continual pressure towards perfection. Those who have this knowledge are unable to be touched or depressed or dismayed by those events which are such a burden to others, and all uncertainty, fear and despair go for ever. If we can but keep in constant communion with our own Soul, our Heavenly Father, then indeed is the world a place of joy, nor can any adverse influence be exerted upon us.

We are not permitted to see the magnitude of our own Divinity, or to realise the mightiness of our Destiny and the glorious future which lies before us; for, if we were, life would be no trial and would involve no effort, no test of merit. Our virtue lies in being oblivious for the most part to those great things, and yet having faith and courage to live well and master the difficulties of this earth. We can, however, by communion with our Higher Self, keep that harmony which enables us to overcome all worldly opposition and make our journey along the straight path to fulfil our destiny, undeterred by the influences which would lead us astray.

Next must we develop individuality and free ourselves from all worldly influences, so that obeying only the dictates of our own Soul and unmoved by circumstances or other people we become our own masters, steering our bark over the rough seas of life without ever quitting the helm of rectitude, or at any time leaving the steering of our vessel to the hands of another. We must gain our freedom absolutely and completely, so that all we do, our every action—nay, even our every thought—derives its origin in ourselves, thus enabling us to live and give freely of our own accord, and of our own accord alone.

Our greatest difficulty in this direction may lie with those nearest to us in this age when the fear of convention and false standards of duty are so appallingly developed. But we must increase our courage, which with so many of us is sufficient to face the apparently big things of life, but which yet fails at the more intimate trials. We must be able with impersonality to determine right and wrong and to act fearlessly in the presence of relative or friend. What a vast number of us are heroes in the outer world, but cowards at home! Though subtle indeed may be the means used to prevent us from fulfilling our Destiny, the pretence of love and affection, or a false sense of duty, methods to enslave us and keep us prisoners to the wishes and desires of others, yet must all such be ruthlessly put aside. The voice of our own Soul, and that voice alone, must be heeded as regards our duty if we are not to be hampered by those around us. Individuality must be developed to the utmost, and we must learn to walk through life relying on none but our own Soul for guidance and help, to take our freedom with both hands and plunge into the world to gain every particle of knowledge and experience which may be possible.

At the same time we must be on our guard to allow to everyone their freedom also, to expect nothing from others, but, on the contrary, to be ever ready to lend a helping hand to lift them upwards in times of their need and difficulty. Thus every personality we meet in life, whether mother, husband, child, stranger or friend, becomes a fellow-traveller, and any one of them may be greater or smaller than ourselves as regards spiritual development; but all of us are members of a common brotherhood and part of a great community making the same journey and with the same glorious end in view.

We must be steadfast in the determination to win, resolute in the will to gain the mountain summit; let us not give a moment's regret to the slips by the way. No great ascent was ever made without faults and falls, and they must be regarded as experiences which will help us to stumble less in the future. No thoughts of past errors must ever depress us; they are over and finished, and the knowledge thus gained will help to avoid a repetition of them. Steadily must we press forwards and onwards, never regretting and never looking back, for the past of even one hour ago is behind us, and the glorious future with its blazing light ever before us. All fear must be cast out; it should never exist in the human mind, and is only possible when we lose sight of our Divinity. It is foreign to us because as Sons of the Creator, Sparks of the Divine Life, we are invincible, indestructible and unconquerable. Disease is apparently cruel because it is the penalty of wrong thought and wrong action, which must result in cruelty to others. Thus the necessity of developing the love and brotherhood side of our natures to the utmost, since this will make cruelty in the future an impossibility.

The development of Love brings us to the realisation of Unity, of the truth that one and all of us are of the One Great Creation.

The cause of all our troubles is self and separateness, and it vanishes as soon as Love and the knowledge of the great Unity become part of our natures. The Universe is God rendered objective; at its birth it is God reborn; at its close it is God more highly evolved. So with man; his body is himself externalised, an objective manifestation of his internal nature; he is the expression of himself, the materialisation of the qualities of his consciousness.

In our Western civilisation we have the glorious example, the great standard of perfection and the teachings of the Christ to guide us. He acts for us as Mediator between our personality and our Soul. His mission on earth was to teach us how to obtain harmony and communion with our Higher Self, with Our Father which is in Heaven, and thereby to obtain perfection in accordance with the Will of the Great Creator of all.

Thus also taught the Lord Buddha and other great Masters who have come down from time to time upon the earth to point out to men the way to attain perfection. There is no halfway path for humanity. The Truth must be acknowledged, and man must unite himself with the infinite scheme of Love of his Creator.

And so come out, my brothers and sisters, into the glorious sunshine of the knowledge of your Divinity, and earnestly and steadfastly set to work to join in the Grand Design of being happy and communicating happiness, uniting with that great band of Brotherhood whose whole existence is to obey the wish of their God, and whose great joy is in the service of their younger brother men.

The Twelve Healers

AND OTHER REMEDIES

EDWARD BACH

M.D., B.S., M.R.C.S, L.R.C.P., D.P.H.

The Twelve Healers

INTRODUCTION

THIS SYSTEM OF TREATMENT IS the most perfect that has been given to mankind within living memory. It has the power to cure disease; and, in its simplicity, it may be used in the household.

It is its simplicity, combined with its all-healing effects, that is so wonderful.

No science, no knowledge is necessary, apart from the simple methods described herein; and they who will obtain the greatest benefit from this God-sent Gift will be those who keep it pure as it is; free from science, free from theories, for everything in Nature is simple.

This system of healing, which has been Divinely revealed unto us, shows that it is our fears, our cares, our anxieties and such like that open the path to the invasion of illness. Thus by treating our fears, our cares, our worries and so on, we not only free ourselves from our illness, but the Herbs given unto us by the Grace of the Creator of all, in addition take away out fears and worries, and leave us happier and better in ourselves.

As the Herbs heal our fears, our anxieties, our worries, our faults and our failings, it is these we must seek, and then the disease, no matter what it is, will leave us.

There is little more to say, for the understanding mind will know all this, and may there be sufficient of those with understanding minds, unhampered by the trend of science, to use these Gifts of God for the relief and the blessing of those around them.

Thus, behind all disease lie our fears, our anxieties, our greed, our likes and dislikes. Let us seek these out and heal them, and with the healing of them will go the disease from which we suffer.

From time immemorial it has been known that Providential Means have placed in Nature the prevention and cure of disease, by means of divinely enriched herbs and plants and trees. The remedies of Nature given in this book have proved that they are blest above others in their work of mercy; and that they have been given the power to heal all types of illness and suffering.

In treating cases with these remedies no notice is taken of the nature of the disease. The individual is treated, and as he becomes well the disease goes, having been cast off by the increase of health.

All know that the same disease may have different effects on different people; it is the effects that need treatment, because they guide to the real cause.

The mind, being the most delicate and sensitive part of the body, shows the onset and the course of disease much more definitely than the body, so that the outlook of mind is chosen as the guide as to which remedy or remedies are necessary.

In illness there is a change of mood from that in ordinary life, and those who are observant can notice this change often before, and sometimes long before, the disease appears, and by treatment can prevent the malady from ever appearing. When illness has been present for some time, again the mood of the sufferer will guide to the correct remedy.

Take no notice of the disease, think only of the outlook on life of the one in distress.

Thirty-eight different states are simply described: and there should be no difficulty either for oneself, or for another, to find that state or a mixture of states which are present, and so to be able to give the required remedies to effect a cure.

The title, *The Twelve Healers*, has been retained for this book, as it is familiar to many readers.

The relief of suffering was so certain and beneficial, even when there were only twelve remedies, that it was deemed necessary to bring these before the attention of the public at the time, without waiting for the discovery of the remaining twenty-six, which complete the series. The original twelve are indicated by asterisks.

The 38 Remedies

ARE PLACED UNDER THE FOLLOWING 7 HEADINGS

1.

FOR FEAR

2.

FOR UNCERTAINTY

3.

FOR INSUFFICIENT INTEREST IN PRESENT CIRCUMSTANCES

4.

FOR LONELINESS

5.

FOR THOSE OVER-SENSITIVE TO INFLUENCES AND IDEAS

6.

FOR DESPONDENCY OR DESPAIR

7.

FOR OVER-CARE FOR WELFARE OF OTHERS

For Those Who Have Fear

*ROCK ROSE

The rescue remedy. The remedy of emergency for cases where there even appears no hope. In accident or sudden illness, or when the patient is very frightened or terrified, or if the condition is serious enough to cause great fear to those around. If the patient is not conscious the lips may be moistened with the remedy. Other remedies in addition may also be required, as, for example, if there is unconsciousness, which is a deep, sleepy state, Clematis; if there is torture, Agrimony, and so on.

*MIMULUS

Fear of worldly things, illness, pain, accidents, poverty, of dark, of being alone, of misfortune. The fears of everyday life. These people quietly and secretly bear their dread, they do not freely speak of it to others.

CHERRY PLUM

Fear of the mind being over-strained, of reason giving way, of doing fearful and dreaded things, not wished and known wrong, yet there comes the thought and impulse to do them.

ASPEN

Vague unknown fears, for which there can be given no explanation, no reason.

Yet the patient may be terrified of something terrible going to happen, he knows not what.

These vague unexplainable fears may haunt by night or day.

Sufferers are often afraid to tell their trouble to others.

RED CHESTNUT

For those who find it difficult not to be anxious for other people.

Often they have ceased to worry about themselves, but for those of whom they are fond they may suffer much, frequently anticipating that some unfortunate thing may happen to them.

For Those Who Suffer Uncertainty

*Cerato

Those who have not sufficient confidence in themselves to make their own decisions.

They constantly seek advice from others, and are often misguided.

*Scleranthus

Those who suffer much from being unable to decide between two things, first one seeming right then the other.

They are usually quiet people, and bear their difficulty alone, as they are not inclined to discuss it with others.

*Gentian

Those who are easily discouraged. They may be progressing well in illness or in the affairs of their daily life, but any small delay or hindrance to progress causes doubt and soon disheartens them.

Gorse

Very great hopelessness, they have given up belief that more can be done for them.

Under persuasion or to please others they may try different treatments, at the same time assuring those around that there is so little hope of relief.

Hornbeam

For those who feel that they have not sufficient strength, mentally or physically, to carry the burden of life placed upon them; the affairs of every day seem too much for them to accomplish, though they generally succeed in fulfilling their task.

For those who believe that some part, of mind or body, needs to be strengthened before they can easily fulfil their work.

Wild Oat

Those who have ambitions to do something of prominence in life, who wish to have much experience, and to enjoy all that which is possible for them, to take life to the full.

Their difficulty is to determine what occupation to follow; as although their ambitions are strong, they have no calling which appeals to them above all others.

This may cause delay and dissatisfaction.

Not Sufficient Interest in Present Circumstances

*CLEMATIS

Those who are dreamy, drowsy, not fully awake, no great interest in life. Quiet people, not really happy in their present circumstances, living more in the future than in the present; living in hopes of happier times, when their ideals may come true. In illness some make little or no effort to get well, and in certain cases may even look forward to death, in the hope of better times; or maybe, meeting again some beloved one whom they have lost.

HONEYSUCKLE

Those who live much in the past, perhaps a time of great happiness, or memories of a lost friend, or ambitions which have not come true. They do not expect further happiness such as they have had.

WILD ROSE

Those who without apparently sufficient reason become resigned to all that happens, and just glide through life, take it as it is, without any effort to improve things and find some joy. They have surrendered to the struggle of life without complaint.

OLIVE

Those who have suffered much mentally or physically and are so exhausted and weary that they feel they have no more strength to make any effort. Daily life is hard work for them, without pleasure.

WHITE CHESTNUT

For those who cannot prevent thoughts, ideas, arguments which they do not desire from entering their minds. Usually at such times when the interest of the moment is not strong enough to keep the mind full.

Thoughts which worry and will remain, or if for a time thrown out, will return. They seem to circle round and round and cause mental torture.

The presence of such unpleasant thoughts drives out peace and interferes with being able to think only of the work or pleasure of the day.

MUSTARD

Those who are liable to times of gloom, or even despair, as though a cold dark cloud overshadowed them and hid the light and the joy of life. It may not be possible to give any reason or explanation for such attacks.

Under these conditions it is almost impossible to appear happy or cheerful.

CHESTNUT BUD

For those who do not take full advantage of observation and experience, and who take a longer time than others to learn the lessons of daily life.

Whereas one experience would be enough for some, such people find it necessary to have more, sometimes several, before the lesson is learnt.

Therefore, to their regret, they find themselves having to make the same error on different occasions when once would have been enough, or observation of others could have spared them even that one fault.

Loneliness

*Water Violet

For those who in health or illness like to be alone. Very quiet people, who move about without noise, speak little, and then gently. Very independent, capable and self-reliant. Almost free of the opinions of others. They are aloof, leave people alone and go their own way. Often clever and talented. Their peace and calmness is a blessing to those around them.

*Impatiens

Those who are quick in thought and action and who wish all things to be done without hesitation or delay. When ill they are anxious for a hasty recovery.

They find it very difficult to be patient with people who are slow, as they consider it wrong and a waste of time, and they will endeavour to make such people quicker in all ways.

They often prefer to work and think alone, so that they can do everything at their own speed.

Heather

Those who are always seeking the companionship of anyone who may be available, as they find it necessary to discuss their own affairs with others, no matter whom it may be. They are very unhappy if they have to be alone for any length of time.

Over-sensitive To Influences and Ideas

*AGRIMONY

The jovial, cheerful, humorous people who love peace and are distressed by argument or quarrel, to avoid which they will agree to give up much.

Though generally they have troubles and are tormented and restless and worried in mind or in body, they hide their cares behind their humour and jesting and are considered very good friends to know. They often taken alcohol or drugs in excess, to stimulate themselves and help themselves bear their trials with cheerfulness.

*CENTAURY

Kind, quiet, gentle people who are over-anxious to serve others. They overtax their strength in their endeavours.

Their wish so grows upon them that they become more servants than willing helpers. Their good nature leads them to do more than their own share of work, and in so doing they may neglect their own particular mission in life.

WALNUT

For those who have definite ideals and ambitions in life and are fulfilling them, but on rare occasions are tempted to be led away from their own ideas, aims and work by the enthusiasm, convictions or strong opinions of others.

The remedy gives constancy and protection from outside influences.

HOLLY

For those who are sometimes attacked by thoughts of such kind as jealousy, envy, revenge, suspicion.

For the different forms of vexation.

Within themselves they may suffer much, often when there is no real cause for their unhappiness.

For Despondency or Despair

LARCH

For those who do not consider themselves as good or capable as those around them, who expect failure, who feel that they will never be a success, and so do not venture or make a strong enough attempt to succeed.

PINE

For those who blame themselves. Even when successful they think they could have done better, and are never content with their efforts or the results. They are hard-working and suffer much from the faults they attach to themselves.

Sometimes if there is any mistake it is due to another, but they will claim responsibility even for that.

ELM

Those who are doing good work, are following the calling of their life and who hope to do something of importance, and this often for the benefit of humanity.

At times there may be periods of depression when they feel that the task they have undertaken is too difficult, and not within the power of a human being.

SWEET CHESTNUT

For those moments which happen to some people when the anguish is so great as to seem to be unbearable.

When the mind or body feels as if it had borne to the uttermost limit of its endurance, and that now it must give way.

When it seems there is nothing but destruction and annihilation left to face.

STAR OF BETHLEHEM

For those in great distress under conditions which for a time produce great unhappiness.

The shock of serious news, the loss of someone dear, the fright following an accident, and such like.

For those who for a time refuse to be consoled, this remedy brings comfort.

WILLOW

For those who have suffered adversity or misfortune and find these difficult to accept, without complaint or resentment, as they judge life much by the success which it brings.

They feel that they have not deserved so great a trial, that it was unjust, and they become embittered.

They often take less interest and are less active in those things of life which they had previously enjoyed.

OAK

For those who are struggling and fighting strongly to get well, or in connection with the affairs of their daily life. They will go on trying one thing after another, though their case may seem hopeless.

They will fight on. They are discontented with themselves if illness interferes with their duties or helping others.

They are brave people, fighting against great difficulties, without loss of hope or effort.

CRAB APPLE

This is the remedy of cleansing.

For those who feel as if they had something not quite clean about themselves.

Often it is something of apparently little importance: in others there may be more serious disease which is almost disregarded compared to the one thing on which they concentrate.

In both types they are anxious to be free from the one particular thing which is greatest in their minds and which seems so essential to them that it should be cured.

They become despondent if treatment fails.

Being a cleanser, this remedy purifies wounds if the patient has reason to believe that some poison has entered which must be drawn out.

Over-Care For Welfare of Others

*Chicory

Those who are very mindful of the needs of others; they tend to be over-full of care for children, relatives, friends, always finding something that should be put right. They are continually correcting what they consider wrong, and enjoy doing so. They desire that those for whom they care should be near them.

*Vervain

Those with fixed principles and ideas, which they are confident are right, and which they very rarely change.

They have a great wish to convert all around them to their own views of life.

They are strong of will and have much courage when they are convinced of those things that they wish to teach.

In illness they struggle on long after many would have given up their duties.

Vine

Very capable people, certain of their own ability, confident of success.

Being so assured, they think that it would be for the benefit of others if they could be persuaded to do things as they themselves do, or as they are certain is right. Even in illness they will direct their attendants.

They may be of great value in emergency.

Beech

For those who feel the need to see more good and beauty in all that surrounds them. And, although much appears to be wrong, to have the ability to see the good growing within. So as to be able to be more tolerant, lenient and understanding of the different way each individual and all things are working to their own final perfection.

ROCK WATER

Those who are very strict in their way of living; they deny themselves many of the joys and pleasures of life because they consider it might interfere with their work.

They are hard masters to themselves. They wish to be well and strong and active, and will do anything which they believe will keep them so. They hope to be examples which will appeal to others who may then follow their ideas and be better as a result.

Methods of Dosage

꧁꧂

As all these remedies are pure and harmless, there is no fear of giving too much or too often, though only the smallest quantities are necessary to act as a dose. Nor can any remedy do harm should it prove not to be the one actually needed for the case.

To prepare take about two drops from the stock bottle into a *small bottle nearly filled with water; if this is required to keep for some time a little brandy may be added as a preservative.

This bottle is used for giving doses, and but a few drops of this, taken in a little water, milk, or any way convenient, is all that is necessary.

In urgent cases the doses may be given every few minutes, until there is improvement; in severe cases about half-hourly; and in long-standing cases every two or three hours, or more often or less as the patient feels the need.

In those unconscious, moisten the lips frequently.

Whenever there is pain, stiffness, inflammation, or any local trouble, in addition a lotion should be applied. Take a few drops from the medicine bottle in a bowl of water and in this soak a piece of cloth and cover the affected part; this can be kept moist from time to time, as necessary.

Sponging or bathing in water with a few drops of the remedies added may at times be useful.

*Agrimony	*Agrimonia eupatoria*
Aspen	*Populus tremula*
Beech	*Fagus sylvatica*
*Centaury	*Centaurium umbellatum*
*Cerato	*Ceratostigma willmottiana*

*Up to 30 ml (1 oz.) size. Full instructions issued with remedies.

Cherry Plum	*Prunus cerasifera*
Chestnut Bud	*Æsculus hippocastanum*
*Chicory	*Cichorium intybus*
*Clematis	*Clematis vitalba*
Crab Apple	*Malus pumila*
Elm	*Ulmus procera*
*Gentian	*Gentiana amarella*
Gorse	*Ulex eruopæus*
Heather	*Calluna vulgaris*
Holly	*Ilex aquifolium*
Honeysuckle	*Lonicera caprifolium*
Hornbeam	*Carpinus betulus*
*Impatiens	*Impatiens glandulifera*
Larch	*Larix decidua*
*Mimulus	*Mimulus guttatus*
Mustard	*Sinapis arvensis*
Oak	*Quercus robur*
Olive	*Olea europæa*
Pine	*Pinus sylvestris*
Red Chestnut	*Æsculus carnea*
*Rock Rose	*Helianthemum nummularium*
Rock Water	
*Scleranthus	*Scleranthus annuus*
Star of Bethlehem	*Ornithogalum umbetlatum*
Sweet Chestnut	*Castanea sativa*
*Vervain	*Verbena officinalis*
Vine	*Vitis vinifera*
Walnut	*Juglans regia*
*Water Violet	*Hottonia palustris*
White Chestnut	*Æsculus hippocastanum*
Wild Oat	*Bromus ramosus†*
Wild Rose	*Rosa canina*
Willow	*Salix vitellina*

† There is no English name for Bromus ramosus.
Bromus is an ancient word meaning Oat.
(The alteration in the Latin names of certain of the plants in this edition of *The Twelve Healers* is due to changes of nomenclature governed by The International Rules of Botanical Nomenclature.)

And may we ever have joy and gratitude in our hearts that the great Creator of all things, in His Love for us, has placed the herbs in the fields for His healing.

A SUPPLEMENTARY GUIDE TO THE USE OF

HERBAL REMEDIES DISCOVERED BY EDWARD BACH

M.D., B.S., M.R.C.S., L.R.C.P., D.P.H.

M. J. WHEELER

M.D., M.R.C.S., L.R.C.P.

Updated, revised and enlarged 1996
by The Dr. Edward Bach Centre

$\mathscr{P}$reface

BETWEEN THE YEARS 1930 AND 1936 Edward Bach, M.D., B.S., M.R.C.S., L.R.C.P., D.P.H., found, perfected and put into use a system of medicine as simple as it had proved effective. After a successful career in London, he abandoned a lucrative practice to seek and find herbs which would heal the sick, but from which no ill-effects could be derived.

Dr. Bach taught that the basis of disease was to be found in disharmony between the spiritual and mental aspects of a human being. This disharmony, to be found wherever conflicting moods produced unhappiness, mental torture, fear, or lassitude and resignation, lowered the body's vitality and allowed disease to be present. For this reason the remedies he prepared were for the treatment of the mood and temperament of the patient, not for his physical illness; so that each patient becoming more himself could increase his or her own vitality and so draw from an inward strength and an inward peace the means to restore health.

Each patient must lead his own life and learn to lead it in freedom. Each is a different type, a different individual, and each must be treated for his personal mood and the need of the moment, not for his physical disease.

Bach wrote in his book, *The Twelve Healers and Other Remedies*: "In treating cases with these remedies, no notice is taken of the nature of the disease. The individual is treated and as he becomes well the disease goes, having been cast off by the increase in health.

"All know that the same disease may have different effects on different people; it is the effects that need treatment, because they guide to the real cause.

"The mind being the most delicate and sensitive part of the body, shows the onset and the course of disease much more definitely than the body, so that the outlook of mind is chosen as the guide as to which remedy or remedies are necessary."

Dr. Bach stressed that his remedies could be used in conjunction with any other form of treatment, and would not clash or interfere. Equally, they could achieve great results used alone.

In the following pages my father, Dr. F. J. Wheeler, who knew and worked with Dr. Bach from 1929 until his death in 1936, and who has himself achieved many remarkable results with the 38 remedies which Dr. Bach produced, has set out a repertory for the guidance and help of those who use these remedies.

These indications for the use of the remedies should be studied together with *The Twelve Healers*, to which they are intended to be a supplement. There can be no hard-and-fast rules in treating patients with these remedies, as each patient must be regarded as an individual to be helped in the light of his personal and particular circumstances and moods. But the basic states of minds and the remedies remain constant, and while always bearing in mind the need to retain flexibility and a mind ready to receive fresh inspiration while using these methods of treatment, this repertory should prove of assistance to those seeking to develop their own ability to choose and administer the right remedy either for themselves or for others.

It is in the sincere hope of making yet a further contribution to the understanding of the true art of healing that this book was prepared.

London, 1952.   FRANCES M. WHEELER.

Introduction to the Revised Edition

SINCE THIS BOOK WAS FIRST published, it has become a very helpful complement to the more descriptive books on the subject.

The Repertory provides an alphabetical listing of emotions and symptoms, alongside which are suggested remedies relating to the given state of mind. There are many thousands of words to describe the way we feel, and it would be impossible to list every one in a book of this nature. In revising and up-dating *The Bach Remedies Repertory*, it has been our aim to include as many words and cover as many variations as possible, thereby creating a comprehensive index of the most commonly—and in some cases, not so commonly—used terms.

In order to select the most appropriate remedy or remedies, it is important to consider the problem in relation to its cause and how it is experienced on a personal level because the characteristics expressed and experienced by the individual concerned are the guiding factors. For example, listed under DEPRESSION, there are several sub-categories describing a number of different reasons for a depressed state of mind, and the suggested choice of remedy is indicated alongside the most appropriate descriptive term.

Similarly, listed under SENSITIVITY, there are several sub-divisions: *to noise, to controversy, to criticism* and so on, and there are, in turn, a choice of remedies listed within each category. For example, *Sensitivity to noise* suggests Clematis, Mimulus, Water Violet and Impatiens. You would not need all four remedies, but should consider each one separately on its own merits, consulting the descriptive books such as *The Twelve Healers and Other Remedies, The Bach Flower Remedies Step by Step, The Handbook* or *The Dictionary* for clarification. **Clematis** people are sensitive to noise because they tend to day-dream and therefore find noise disturbs their thoughts. **Mimulus** people tend to be nervous and are therefore frightened by noise. **Water Violet** people enjoy peace and quiet and therefore find noise an intrusion into their privacy. **Impatiens** people think and work quickly, and therefore become irritated by noise because it hinders their progress.

It should be remembered that people interpret words in different ways so there will always be a subjective element to any descriptive term used. The Repertory is intended to be used for clarification when in doubt, to provide a few objective ideas, or simply to jog the memory. Always remember to consider the individual characteristics of the suggestions given because it is only by reading the full description of each remedy before finally deciding upon your choice, that satisfactory results can be obtained.

JUDY HOWARD
The Dr. Edward Bach Centre

Sotwell, 1995

Moods	Remedies

ABANDONED
  fear of being — Mimulus
  without hope — Sweet Chestnut
  see also Rejection and Loneliness

ABASHED
  with guilt or self-reproach — Pine

ABHORRENCE
  regarding with hatred — Holly
  disgust — Crab Apple

ABILITY
  lack of confidence in own — Larch
  lack of confidence, momentarily, — Elm
    due to pressure/responsibility
  lack of belief/trust in self — Larch, Cerato
  creative (positive) — Clematis
  aggressively certain of one's — Vervain, Vine, Beech,
    own — Impatiens

ABNORMALITY
  obsessed with personal defect — Crab Apple
  fear of mental — Cherry Plum
  thoughts of unfairness— — Willow
    "why me?"

ABRASIVE
  and critical — Beech, Chicory
  and short tempered — Impatiens, Holly
  and angry, hateful, jealous, — Holly
    envious
  with resentment, self-pity — Willow, Chicory
  and defiant — Vine

ABRUPT — Impatiens, Beech, Vine

Moods	Remedies

ABSENTEEISM
  to avoid responsibilities — Elm
  to avoid confrontation — Agrimony
  due to lack of interest/escapism — Clematis, Wild Rose, Hornbeam, Mustard
  due to fear — Larch, Mimulus, Rock Rose, Rescue Remedy

ABSENT MINDED
  due to drifting thoughts — Clematis
  due to tiredness — Olive

ABSORPTION
  with distant thoughts/daydreaming — Clematis
  with memories — Honeysuckle
  with enthusiasm or matters of principle — Vervain
  with self — Heather, Chicory
  with details — Crab Apple
  with worries — White Chestnut
  with vengeance/jealous/hatred — Holly

ABSTINENCE
  self-righteous/extreme self control — Rock Water
  adjustment to, after e.g. alcoholism — Walnut, Agrimony

ABSTRACT
  ideas and fantasies — Clematis
  lacking in ambition — Wild Rose

ABSURDITY
  intolerance with/accusation of — Beech
  frustration with — Vervain

MOODS	REMEDIES

ABUSE
sense of injustice of   Vervain
shock of   Star of Bethlehem
fear of   Mimulus, Rock Rose
sense of contamination by   Crab Apple

ABUSIVE
due to uncontrolled rage   Cherry Plum
due to aggressive dominance   Vine
due to selfish possessiveness   Chicory
due to vexation   Holly
due to critical intolerance   Beech
due to slowness   Impatiens
due to frustration   Vervain

ACCEPTANCE
resigned to the inevitable   Wild Rose
meek   Centaury

ACCIDENT PRONE
due to lack of concentration   Clematis
due to impatience/nervous   Impatiens
   tension
due to fearful nervousness   Aspen, Mimulus
due to over-enthusiasm   Vervain

ACCOMPLISHMENT
doubt of one's ability   Larch
eager to achieve   Vervain, Impatiens

ACCUSING
due to suspicion   Holly
due to desire for perfection   Rock Water, Vervain
as a "put-down"   Beech
due to irrational fears   Cherry Plum

ACHIEVE
ambitious desire to   Vervain, Vine
doubt of one's ability to   Larch

Moods	Remedies
ACID-TONGUED	
due to spitefulness/hatred	Holly
irritated annoyance/intolerance	Beech
and bitter/selfish	Willow, Chicory
critical, bitingly accusative	Chicory, Beech, Vine
ACQUIESCENCE	
generally	Centaury, Wild Rose
due to fear	Mimulus, Larch
ACQUISITIONS	
desire to cling to, selfishly	Chicory
clings to due to sentimental attachment	Honeysuckle
to aid release of emotional attachment to	Walnut
ACRIMONIOUS	Chicory, Willow, Holly, Vine, Beech
ACTING	
as a pretense	Agrimony
to gain attention/favour	Chicory
ACTIVE	
excessively, due to enthusiasm	Vervain
excessively, due to impatience/hastiness	Impatiens
overly, as hard task master to self	Rock Water
ADAMANT	Vervain, Vine
ADAPT	
helps to	Walnut
ADAPTABLE	Wild Rose, Clematis

MOODS	REMEDIES

ADDICTION
life controlled by — Centaury
used as means of escape — Agrimony, Clematis
to break habit of — Walnut, Chestnut Bud
see also Withdrawal

ADDLED — Scleranthus, Cerato

ADHERENCE
to principles — Vervain, Rock Water

ADMIRATION
for others/desire to copy or follow — Cerato
none for self — Pine, Crab Apple
with envy/jealousy — Holly

ADORATION
for others, with desire to possess — Chicory
of self — Heather, Chicory, Rock Water
none for self — Pine, Crab Apple

ADRENALINE (emotional)
feeling of having excess — Impatiens, Vervain, Aspen, Rock Rose, Rescue Remedy

ADRIFT — Wild Rose, Clematis

ADULATION
of self — Heather, Chicory, Rock Water

ADVENTURE
desire for — Clematis
great spirit of — Vervain
no desire for — Wild Rose, Mustard, Olive

Moods	Remedies
ADVERSITY	
struggles on in spite of	Oak
unaffected by	Oak, Vine, Vervain, Wild Rose
depressed by	Gentian, Gorse
ADVICE	
seeking	Cerato
influenced by and follows	Centaury, Cerato, Walnut
withholds until requested to give	Water Violet
eager to give	Chicory, Vervain
hurt if not taken	Chicory
AFFECTIONATE	Centaury, Chicory, Red Chestnut, Pine
AFRAID	
due to known cause	Mimulus
desperate/panic stricken	Rock Rose, Cherry Plum
irrationally	Cherry Plum, Aspen
due to unknown cause	Aspen
for welfare of others	Red Chestnut
of failure	Larch
see also Fear	
AFTER-SHOCK	Star of Bethlehem, Rescue Remedy
AGEING	
desire to reverse	Honeysuckle, Heather, Rock Water
dislike of look of self	Crab Apple
fear of	Mimulus, Rock Rose
AGGRAVATING	
due to intensity	Vervain
due to impatience	Impatiens
due to indecision	Scleranthus, Cerato
due to persistence	Vervain, Heather

Moods	Remedies

AGGRAVATED
 by the slowness of others — Impatiens
 by the stupidity of others — Beech
 by the weakness of others — Vine
 by injustice/unfairness — Vervain

AGGRESSION
 enthusiastic/passionate — Vervain
 spiteful — Holly
 demanding/dominant — Vine

AGGRIEVED
 and resentful — Willow
 and hurt — Chicory
 and angered by injustice — Vervain
 but does not protest — Centaury, Agrimony

AGITATED — Impatiens, Agrimony, White Chestnut

 with detail — Crab Apple
 with injustice — Vervain

AGONY (emotional)
 concealed, inner torture — Agrimony
 of grief — Star of Bethlehem, Sweet Chestnut

 of mental arguments — White Chestnut

AGREES
 readily, against better judgment — Cerato, Centaury
 to keep peace — Agrimony, Centaury, Wild Rose

AILMENTS
 obsessed with — Crab Apple, Heather
 enjoys talking in detail about — Heather
 feels unclean due to — Crab Apple
 afraid of — Mimulus
 exhausted/drained by — Olive
 see also Illness

Moods	Remedies
AIMLESS	Wild Rose, Wild Oat
AIR-HEAD	Clematis
AIR TRAVEL	
fear of	Mimulus, Rock Rose, Rescue Remedy
worried about	White Chestnut, Aspen
exhausted by	Olive
bemused and distracted by	Clematis
adjustment following	Walnut
jet lag	Walnut, Clematis, Olive
AIR-SICK	Rescue Remedy, Scleranthus, Walnut
ALCOHOL	
addiction to	Centaury, Agrimony, Cerato
breaking habit of addiction to	Walnut, Chestnut Bud
sickened by	Crab Apple
repeated hangovers	Chestnut Bud
used as a "crutch", to provide courage	Agrimony, Larch, Mimulus
ALIENATION	
due to aloof distancing	Water Violet
due to over-talkativeness	Heather
due to irritation	Impatiens
due to suffocating possessiveness	Chicory
due to influence/persuasive control of others	Walnut
ALONE	
preference for being	Water Violet
fear of being	Mimulus, Agrimony
dislike of being	Chicory, Heather
to work at own pace	Impatiens

MOODS	REMEDIES
ALOOFNESS	Water Violet
ALTRUISTIC	Oak, Centaury, Red Chestnut, Vervain

AMBITION
lack of	Wild Rose, Gorse
strong sense of	Vervain, Vine
definite but side-tracked	Walnut
ill-defined	Wild Oat
to possess/control others	Chicory, Vine
delayed/disappointed about, due to set-back	Gentian

AMBIVALENCE	Scleranthus, Cerato

AMUSEMENT
no sense of	Mustard, Gorse, Willow
malicious/spiteful sense of	Holly, Chicory
pretence—put on "brave/cheerful face"	Agrimony

ANALYTICAL	Rock Water, Beech, Vervain, Vine

ANGER
due to hatred/envy	Holly
due to injustice	Vervain
uncontrolled	Cherry Plum
with self for weakness	Centaury
with self for hesitancy/indecision	Scleranthus
with self for failure	Rock Water
with slowness	Impatiens
with stupidity of others	Beech

ANGST	Aspen

see also Anxiety

Moods	Remedies
ANGUISH	Sweet Chestnut, Agrimony
ANNOYANCE	
with others/trivial matters	Impatiens, Beech
due to physical restrictions of illness	Oak
due to frustration	Vervain, Oak
ANSWER BACK	
for attention	Chicory
resentfully	Willow
spitefully	Holly
with valid argument	Vervain
in defiance	Vine, Vervain, Chicory
ANTICIPATION	
vague fears/foreboding	Aspen
of trouble for others	Red Chestnut
of failure	Larch, Mimulus
ANTI-CLIMAX	Gentian
ANTI-SOCIAL	
appears to be	Water Violet
due to sulkiness	Willow
due to shyness/timidity	Mimulus
due to lack of confidence	Larch
due to self-opinionated/ pretentiousness	Vine
ANXIETY	
hidden/concealed restlessness	Agrimony
known cause	Mimulus
for welfare of others	Red Chestnut
unknown cause/vague anticipation	Aspen
with worrying thoughts	White Chestnut

Moods	Remedies

ANXIOUSNESS
with vague anticipation — Aspen
for welfare of others — Red Chestnut
concealed, restless — Agrimony

APATHY
generally — Wild Rose, Hornbeam, Clematis
due to depression — Gorse, Mustard
due to lack of energy/exhaustion — Olive

APOLOGETIC — Pine

APPREHENSIVE
through fear — Aspen, Mimulus, Rock Rose
for others — Red Chestnut
and doubtful/despondent — Gentian
about possible failure — Larch

APPROVAL
seeks, for reassurance — Cerato

ARDENT — Vervain

ARGUMENTATIVE — Beech, Vervain, Willow, Chicory, Holly, Impatiens

ARGUMENTS
mental — White Chestnut
enjoys — Vervain, Chicory, Willow, Beech
avoids — Agrimony, Centaury, Water Violet, Clematis, Wild Rose

ARROGANCE — Beech, Vine

ATTENTION
seeks — Chicory, Heather, Willow
dislikes — Water Violet

Moods	Remedies
AUTHORITARIAN	Vine
AUTOCRATIC	Vine
AVOIDANCE	
of arguments	Agrimony, Centaury, Water Violet, Clematis, Wild Rose
of people	Water Violet, Mimulus, Beech, Impatiens
of confronting reality	Agrimony, Clematis, Honeysuckle, Chestnut Bud
AWKWARDNESS	
concealed sense of	Agrimony
due to shyness	Mimulus
due to dislike of self	Crab Apple
due to lack of confidence	Larch
due to hesitancy/indecision	Scleranthus
due to apprehension	Aspen
due to subservience; sense of awe	Centaury
in children of feeble/puny build or character	Mimulus, Larch
BABY BLUES	
for no apparent reason	Mustard
with irrational fears/behavior	Cherry Plum
BACK-CHAT	Beech, Willow, Chicory
BAD NEWS	Star of Bethlehem
BELONGING	
no sense of, due to uncertainty	Cerato, Scleranthus, Larch
no sense of, due to loneliness	Heather, Sweet Chestnut, Mimulus
no sense of, and feels bitter/pities self	Willow, Chicory
no sense of, feels unwanted/ostracised	Willow, Chicory, Mimulus, Crab Apple, Gorse, Sweet Chestnut

Moods	Remedies
BEREAVEMENT	
initial shock/numbness	Star of Bethlehem
dejection, emptiness	Sweet Chestnut
longing for one's own death	Clematis
thoughts filled with past memories	Honeysuckle
for protection and adjustment	Walnut
with sense of guilt/self reproach	Pine
with resentment/self-pity	Willow
BEWILDERED	Clematis
BIG-HEADEDNESS	Vine, Beech
BIGOTRY	Vervain, Vine, Beech, Rock Water
BITCHINESS	Holly, Chicory, Beech
BITTERNESS	Willow, Chicory, Holly
BLABBER	
nervous chatter	Impatiens, Agrimony, Mimulus
for attentive company	Heather, Chicory
obsessive preaching	Vervain
BLAME	
others	Willow, Chicory, Beech, Vine
self	Pine, Crab Apple, Red Chestnut, Centaury, Agrimony
BLASE	Wild Rose, Clematis
see also Boredom	
BLEMISH	
obsessed with	Crab Apple
BLITHE	Agrimony

Moods	Remedies

BLOCKAGE
of ability to give love — Chicory, Holly
of progression in life due to frustrated ambition — Walnut, Wild Oat, Gorse, Sweet Chestnut, Willow
due to failure to learn — Chestnut Bud

BLOOD
fear for — Mimulus, Rock Rose
faints at sight of — Rescue Remedy
revolted by — Crab Apple

BLOODY-MINDED — Beech, Willow, Vine, Chicory, Vervain, Rock Water

BLUNT
due to intolerance — Beech, Vine
straightforwardness — Water Violet, Rock Water, Oak, Vervain

BLUSHES EASILY — Mimulus, Larch, Pine
see also Self-Consciousness

BODY IMAGE
poor sense of, due to self-dislike — Crab Apple
poor sense of, due to uncertainty — Cerato
poor sense of and tries to hide with joviality — Agrimony
excessively high regard for imposing strict regime for living — Rock Water

BOISTEROUS
due to excitement — Impatiens, Vervain
at means of seeking attention/ showing off — Chicory
and disobedient — Vine
purposely, as means of hiding inadequacies — Agrimony

MOODS	REMEDIES
BORE	
talkative	Heather
depressing	Gorse, Willow
BOREDOM	
generally	Clematis, Wild Oat
through impatient expectation	Impatiens
BOSSY	Chicory, Vine, Impatiens, Beech, Vervain
BRAIN-STORM	Cherry Plum
BRAINWASHING	
instrumental in	Vervain, Vine, Chicory, Rock Water
succumb to/influenced by	Walnut, Cerato, Clematis, Wild Rose, Centaury, Agrimony
BRAVE	
by nature	Oak, Vine, Vervain
finds it hard to be, through fear	Mimulus, Aspen, Rock Rose, Agrimony, Centaury
finds it hard to be, through lack of confidence/uncertainty	Larch, Scleranthus, Cerato, Centaury
BREAK-DOWN, mental	
due to over-work/burn-out	Oak, Vervain, Elm, Rock Water
due to mental torment/ restlessness	Agrimony, White Chestnut, Cherry Plum, Impatiens, Scleranthus
BROODY	
about future	Clematis, Gentian
about misfortune	Willow, White Chestnut, Sweet Chestnut
about making decisions	Scleranthus

Moods	Remedies
BUBBLY	Agrimony, Heather, Impatiens, Vervain
BURDEN	
believes one is a burden to others	Pine, Mustard
manipulates attention by claiming one is	Chicory
BURDENED	
with work	Oak, Vervain, Centaury, Rock Water
with responsibility	Elm
with mental torment	White Chestnut, Agrimony
with mental pressure	Elm, White Chestnut, Vervain
BURN-OUT	Olive, Walnut, Oak, Rock Water, Vervain
see also Break-down	
CAPABLE	
and reliable	Oak, Water Violet, Vine
but doubtful when under pressure	Elm
but has no confidence	Larch
but easily influenced	Walnut
but fusses	Chicory, Vervain
CAPITULATION	Gorse, Wild Rose, Centaury, Agrimony, Sweet Chestnut
CARELESS	
due to impatience	Impatiens
due to boredom	Clematis
due to tiredness	Olive

Moods	Remedies
CAUTIOUS	
by nature	Oak, Water Violet
due to suspicion	Holly
due to fear	Mimulus, Aspen
due to uncertainty	Scleranthus, Cerato
due to doubt	Cerato, Gentian
CHANGEABLE	Cerato, Scleranthus
CHATTER-BOX	Heather, Agrimony, Cerato, Chicory, Impatiens, Vervain
CHEERFULNESS, false	Agrimony
CLEANSER	Crab Apple
CLOWN	Agrimony
COMMUNICATOR, good	Vervain, Oak, Water Violet
COMPANY	
desires	Agrimony, Chicory, Heather, Cerato, Vervain
aversion to	Impatiens, Mimulus, Water Violet, Larch
COMPETITIVE	Vervain, Vine, Rock Water
COMPLACENCY	Wild Rose, Clematis
COMPLAIN	
about others	Beech, Chicory, Holly, Willow, Impatiens
on principle	Vervain
when ill	Willow, Gorse
never	Centaury, Agrimony, Oak
COMPOSURE	Water Violet, Rock Water, Oak

Moods	Remedies
COMPULSIVE	
habits	Crab Apple
talker	Heather, Chicory, Vervain
eating	Crab Apple, Agrimony
lying, for attention	Heather, Chicory
CONCEALMENT of emotions	Agrimony, Water Violet, Oak
CONCEIT	Beech, Rock Water, Vine, Vervain
CONCENTRATION	
lack of	Clematis, White Chestnut
lack of, through indecision	Scleranthus
lack of, through self-distrust	Cerato
over	Vervain, Rock Water
CONCERNED	
about details	Crab Apple
about others	Chicory, Red Chestnut, Oak, Vervain
about self	Heather, Rock Water, Chicory, Willow
CONDESCENDING	Vine, Water Violet, Rock Water
CONFIDENCE	
lack of	Larch, Cerato, Scleranthus, Elm
CONFIRMATION	
seeks	Cerato
CONFRONTATION	
avoids	Agrimony, Centaury, Clematis, Mimulus
enjoys	Vervain, Vine
CONFUSION	Scleranthus, Cerato, Wild Oat

Moods	Remedies

CONGESTION, mental
    through worry   White Chestnut
    through anxiousness for others   Red Chestnut
    through selfish absorption   Chicory, Heather
    through matters of principle   Vervain
    through concern over trivialities   Crab Apple

CONSOLATION
    enjoys and seeks   Willow, Chicory
    aversion to   Water Violet

CONSPIRACY
    suspicious of   Holly
    irrational fear of   Cherry Plum

CONSTANCY   Walnut

CONTAMINATION   Crab Apple

CONTEMPT
    for others   Beech, Vine, Holly, Impatiens
    for self   Crab Apple, Pine

CONTROL
    lack of mental   Cherry Plum
    desire to control others   Chicory, Vine

CONVALESCENCE
    fatigue during   Hornbeam, Olive
    undefined depression during   Mustard
    to assist in adjustment   Walnut

CONVERSATION
    enjoys   Heather, Vervain, Agrimony,
                                  Chicory
    finds difficult   Mimulus, Larch
    finds difficult with mundane/   Water Violet, Impatiens
      trivial chatter

Moods	Remedies
CONVENTIONS	
fond of	Wild Rose, Rock Water
to break old	Walnut
CONVERT	
desire to	Vervain, Beech, Rock Water
CONVICTION, strong sense of	Vervain, Vine, Rock Water, Chicory
COPE	
copes well, even under pressure	Oak
copes well until under pressure	Elm
COPIES others	Cerato
CORRECT	
wishes to	Chicory, Vervain, Beech
COURAGE	
possesses generally, by nature of convictions	Oak, Vervain
lack of, due to fear	Mimulus, Aspen, Rock Rose
lack of, due to fear of failure	Larch
COVETOUS	Chicory, Holly
COY	Mimulus
CRAZED	Cherry Plum, Vervain
CRIES EASILY	
generally	Chicory, Willow
due to mood changes	Scleranthus
because highly sensitive	Walnut, Mimulus, Centaury
due to indefinable depression/ melancholy	Mustard
due to emotional crisis	Rescue Remedy
see also Tearfulness, Sensitivity and Weepiness	

MOODS	REMEDIES
CRITICAL	
of others	Beech, Chicory, Vervain
of self	Pine, Rock Water, Crab Apple
CROSS-ROADS of life,	
uncertainty at	Wild Oat
CRUSADER	Vervain
CURIOSITY	
lack of	Wild Rose, Gorse
CYNICISM	Beech, Vine, Holly, Willow, Gorse
DAY-DREAMING	Clematis, Honeysuckle
DAZED	Clematis, Star of Bethlehem
DEATH	
fear of	Mimulus, Rock Rose
desires, with irrational desperation	Cherry Plum
desires, as means of escape	Agrimony, Clematis
morbid obsession with	Clematis, Mustard, Sweet Chestnut
DEBATE	
enjoys	Vervain
DECISION	
unable to make	Scleranthus, Cerato, Wild Oat
good at making	Vervain, Vine, Water Violet
DEFENSIVE	Willow, Holly, Vervain
DEFERENCE	Centaury, Cerato, Agrimony
DEFIANCE	Vine, Beech, Chicory

Moods	Remedies
DEFINITE	
sense of purpose	Walnut, Vervain, Rock Water, Vine
DEJECTION	Sweet Chestnut
DELEGATE	
does so with orders	Vine
finds it hard to; does job oneself	Vervain, Impatiens
too timid to	Mimulus, Centaury
no desire to	Oak, Chicory
happy to be relieved from duty	Wild Rose
feels a failure if has to	Elm, Rock Water
DELIRIUM	Cherry Plum
DELUSIONS	
generally, due to imagination	Aspen, Cherry Plum, Clematis
of grandeur	Cherry Plum, Vervain, Rock Water, Chicory
DEMANDING	Vine, Chicory, Heather
DEMENTED	
with irrational fears/out of control	Cherry Plum
with despair	Sweet Chestnut
with hidden fear/torment	Agrimony
with fear over others	Red Chestnut
with irritation	Impatiens
with confusion/indecision	Scleranthus
DEMONSTRATIVE	
generally	Vervain, Vine, Chicory, Holly, Impatiens
not inclined to be	Agrimony, Centaury, Water Violet

Moods	Remedies
DEMURE	Centaury, Water Violet, Mimulus
DEPENDABLE	Oak

DEPENDENT
on people to fuss over	Chicory
on people for advice	Cerato
on people to talk to	Heather
on people for support/strength	Centaury

DEPLETED of energy	Olive, Hornbeam, Sweet Chestnut

DEPRESSION
for known reason; due to set-back	Gentian
cause unknown	Mustard
pessimistic	Gorse, Gentian
hopeless	Gorse
utter dejection	Sweet Chestnt
descends suddenly, like dark cloud	Mustard
introspective	Willow

NB: *It is important to treat the cause of depression e.g. guilt, responsibility etc., as appropriate, in addition to the depression itself.*

DESIRE
lack of	Wild Rose, Olive, Hornbeam
excessive	Impatiens, Vervain, Chicory
denial/suppression of	Agrimony, Water Violet, Rock Water
repulsed by (sexual)	Crab Apple

DESIRABILITY
no sense of due to poor image of self	Crab Apple
needs reassurance about	Cerato

Moods	Remedies
DESPAIR	
materialistic	Gorse, Gentian
due to terror	Rock Rose
pessimistic hopelessness	Gorse
helpless, heartbroken, utter	Sweet Chestnut
cause unknown	Mustard
through self-blame/guilt	Pine
due to shock	Star of Bethlehem
of living	Cherry Plum
DESPERATION	Cherry Plum, Sweet Chestnut
DESPISE	
others	Holly, Beech
others for slowness	Impatiens
others for weakness	Vine
oneself	Crab Apple, Pine
DESPONDENCY	
through lack of confidence	Larch
from self-reproach/guilt	Pine
through feeling of inadequacy	Elm
from shock, bad news	Star of Bethlehem
through limitation of illness	Oak
from feeling of uncleanliness/ unworthiness	Crab Apple
due to embitterment	Willow
cause unknown	Mustard
through frustration	Vervain
through over-work	Vervain, Oak, Elm
through tiredness	Hornbeam, Olive
through slowness, e.g. of progress	Impatiens
complete anguish	Sweet Chestnut
DESTITUTE	Sweet Chestnut
DESTRUCTIVE	Crab Apple, Holly, Willow, Chicory

Moods	Remedies
DETACHED	Water Violet, Clematis, Impatiens
DETERMINATION	Vervain, Vine, Oak, Rock Water, Impatiens
DEVASTATED	Star of Bethlehem, Sweet Chestnut
DEVIOUS	Holly
DEVOID	Sweet Chestnut, Olive
DEVOUT	Rock Water
DIFFIDENT	Larch, Mimulus, Cerato, Centaury
DIGNITY	Water Violet
DILEMMA	Scleranthus, Wild Oat
DILIGENCE	Vervain, Oak
DIPLOMACY lack of	Beech, Impatiens, Vine, Holly, Vervain

DIRECTS
  others in illness etc.
  affairs of others
	Vine
	Chicory, Vine, Vervain

DIRT dislike of	Crab Apple
DISAGREE	Vervain, Beech, Rock Water, Vine
DISAPPOINTED	Gentian

MOODS	REMEDIES
DISAPPROVING	Rock Water, Chicory, Beech
DISCIPLINARIAN	Vine
DISCIPLINE, self	Rock Water
DISCONTENTMENT	
with life's ambitions	Wild Oat
with self	Rock Water, Pine, Oak
with others	Willow, Chicory, Beech, Impatiens
DISCOURAGEMENT	Gentian, Elm
DISCUSSION	
enjoys	Vervain
avoids, due to shyness	Mimulus
avoids, due to refusal to confront	Agrimony, Clematis
avoids, due to uncertainty of opinion	Cerato, Scleranthus
DISDAINFUL	
generally	Holly, Beech, Vine
may appear to be	Water Violet, Rock Water, Vervain
of oneself	Larch, Crab Apple, Centaury, Pine
DISGRUNTLED	Willow, Chicory
DISHEARTENED	Gentian
DISINCLINATION	
generally	Wild Rose
due to boredom	Clematis
due to tiredness	Olive, Hornbeam
due to depression	Mustard, Gorse, Willow, Sweet Chestnut

MOODS	REMEDIES
DISLIKE of self	Crab Apple, Pine
DISPASSIONATE	Wild Rose

DISSATISFACTION

due to unfulfilled ambitions	Wild Oat
due to frustration/restriction	Walnut, Vervain, Impatiens
due to limitations during illness	Oak
from resentment	Willow
from envy, jealousy	Holly
with self	Rock Water, Pine
with others	Beech, Chicory, Vine

DISTANT	Clematis

DISTRACTED

with thoughts of future	Clematis
with thoughts of past	Honeysuckle
with thoughts of nothing	Clematis
with worries	White Chestnut
by flitting thoughts	Impatiens, Scleranthus

DISTRAUGHT

with fear and concern for others	Red Chestnut
with events of life	Sweet Chestnut
with irrational fears	Cherry Plum
due to shock/bad news	Star of Bethlehem

DISTRUSTFUL	Holly

DITHER

due to uncertainty/indecision	Scleranthus, Cerato
due to fear	Mimulus, Rock Rose

DOGMA

rigidly follows	Rock Water
submits to	Centaury, Wild Rose, Cerato, Mimulus, Larch
rebels against	Vine

Moods	Remedies
DOGMATIC	Vine, Rock Water, Vervain
DOMINATION	Vine, Chicory, Heather, Vervain
DOMINATED	Centaury, Cerato, Mimulus, Agrimony
DOMINEERING	Vine, Chicory
DOUBT	Gentian, Cerato
DOWNCAST	Gentian, Willow, Mustard
DREAD	
apprehensive/terrifying	Aspen, Rock Rose
of known event e.g. performing, attending interviews, entertaining	Larch, Mimulus
hidden	Aspen, Agrimony
DREAMS	
night terrors	Aspen, Rock Rose, Rescue Remedy
nightmares	Rock Rose, Star of Bethlehem, Rescue Remedy
recurring	Honeysuckle, Chestnut Bud, Pine, Rescue Remedy
day-dreams	Clematis
vividly imaginative	Clematis, Vervain, Cherry Plum
DRIFTING in life	
due to lack of ambition	Wild Rose
with dissatisfaction due to lack of direction	Wild Oat
DROWSINESS	
dreamy, sleepy	Clematis
due to exhaustion	Olive
due to lethargy/mental weariness	Hornbeam
due to apathy	Wild Rose

Moods	Remedies
DUTIFUL	Centaury
DUTY, great sense of	Rock Water, Oak, Vervain
EAGERNESS	Impatiens, Vervain, Aspen
EATING	
greedily	Impatiens, Vervain
dislike of	Crab Apple
prefers to do so in private	Water Violet
afraid of	Mimulus, Aspen, Rock Rose
EFFICIENT	Oak, Rock Water, Water Violet, Vervain, Vine
EFFORT	
lack of due to dreaminess	Clematis
lack of due to exhaustion	Olive, Hornbeam
lack of due to apathetic resignation	Wild Rose
over-	Impatiens, Vervain, Rock Water
EGOTISTIC	Beech, Vine, Vervain
EMBARRASSMENT	Mimulus, Larch, Crab Apple
EMBITTERMENT	Willow
EMERGENCIES	Rescue Remedy
EMOTION	
hides	Agrimony, Water Violet, Oak
flat/apparent absence of	Wild Rose
EMPATHIC	Vervain
ENDURANCE	Oak, Centaury, Vervain, Rock Water

Moods	Remedies

EMPTY
   due to exhaustion — Olive
   due to lack of interest — Clematis, Honeysuckle
   due to sorrow — Star of Bethlehem
   due to utter dejection — Sweet Chestnut

ENERGY
   lack of — Olive, Hornbeam, Wild Rose
   excess of — Impatiens, Vervain, Aspen

ENMITY — Holly

ENRAGED
   generally — Holly, Cherry Plum
   about injustice — Vervain

ENTHUSIASTIC — Vervain

ENVY — Holly

EQUITY, great belief in — Vervain

ESCAPISM, mental — Clematis, Honeysuckle, Agrimony

EXACTITUDE — Rock Water, Vervain, Beech

EXAMINATIONS
   nervousness prior to — Mimulus, Rescue Remedy, Aspen, Larch
   lethargy prior to — Hornbeam
   exhaustion due to — Olive
   despondent over — Gentian
   indifference/lack of concentration — Wild Rose, Clematis

EXAMPLE
   would like to be, for others to follow — Rock Water

MOODS	REMEDIES
EXAGGERATES	
due to enthusiasm	Vervain
due to imagination	Clematis, Cherry Plum
for sympathy and attention	Chicory, Heather
symptoms	Heather
EXASPERATION	Vervain, Beech, Impatiens, Sweet Chestnut
EXCESSIVE	Agrimony, Vervain, Impatiens, Cherry Plum, Crab Apple
EXCITABLE	Impatiens, Vervain, Heather, Agrimony
EXCITEMENT	
seeks, desires, anxious for	Clematis, Agrimony, Heather
lacks emotional	Wild Rose, Hornbeam, Gorse, Mustard
unexplained feeling of	Aspen, Impatiens, Vervain
EXHAUSTION	
through overwork, due to weak will	Centaury
physical and mental	Olive
mental weariness/procrastination	Hornbeam
through strain and effort	Vervain
through lack of vitality	Clematis, Wild Rose
struggles on in spite of	Oak
with extreme helplessness/ despair	Sweet Chestnut
EXPECTANT	Aspen, Impatiens
EXPERIENCE	
does not learn from	Chestnut Bud

Moods	Remedies
EXPRESSION	
lacks	Wild Rose
avoids	Agrimony, Water Violet
glum	Mustard, Gorse, Willow
EXTROVERT	
by nature	Vervain, Vine, Impatiens, Heather
as a mask	Agrimony
EYE-CONTACT	
Avoids nervously	Mimulus, Aspen
avoids due to embarrassment	Mimulus, Larch, Pine, Crab Apple
avoids due to shyness/timidity	Mimulus, Centaury
avoids to hide feelings	Agrimony
powerful, intense	Vervain, Vine, Chicory, Heather, Impatiens
intense, but agitated due to nervous energy	Impatiens
stares dreamily/looks through subject	Clematis
close to face, direct	Heather
FABRICATION	
to get attention	Heather, Chicory, Willow
due to over-active imagination	Clematis, Cherry Plum
malicious	Holly
FACADE	Agrimony
FAILURE	
expects/fears	Larch, Mimulus
temporary feeling of	Elm
to reach high standards	Rock Water
to others	Pine
FAINTNESS	Clematis

Moods	Remedies
FAIRNESS	
great belief in	Vervain
FAITH	
lost	Gertian, Gorse, Sweet Chestnut
lacks in oneself	Cerato, Elm, Larch
FAMILY	
over-concerned with	Chicory, Red Chestnut
FANATICAL	Vervain
FANTASIES	Clematis, Cherry Plum
FAULT-FINDING	
with others	Beech, Chicory, Holly, Impatiens, Willow, Vervain
with self	Pine, Rock Water, Crab Apple
FEAR	
known cause (illness, poverty, pain etc.)	Mimulus
unknown cause	Aspen
of darkness	Aspen, Mimulus
of death	Aspen, Mimulus, Rock Rose
of fear	Aspen
extreme	Rock Rose
of insanity	Cherry Plum
of failure	Larch
of future	Aspen, Mimulus, Agrimony
for oneself when ill/for one's health	Heather, Mimulus
of losing friends	Chicory, Heather, Mimulus
of mind giving way/loss of control	Cherry Plum
of God	Aspen, Mimulus
secret	Aspen, Mimulus, Agrimony, Scleranthus
vague, unreasoning	Aspen
for oneself if ill	Heather, Mimulus
absence of, for self	Red Chestnut

Moods	Remedies
FEARFUL, by nature	Mimulus
FEARLESS	Oak
FERVENCY	Vervain
FICKLE	Scleranthus, Cerato
FIERY	Holly, Vervain, Impatiens, Cherry Plum
FIGHTING SPIRIT	Vervain, Oak
FIXATION	
with project	Vervain
with injustice	Vervain
with self	Heather, Crab Apple
with detail	Crab Apple
with cleanliness	Crab Apple
FIXED IDEAS & OPINIONS	Beech, Rock Water, Vervain, Vine
FLIPPANT	Impatiens, Holly
FLOATING, sensation of	Clematis
FOLLOWS others	
due to uncertainty	Cerato
because eager to please	Centaury
due to lack of self-confidence	Larch
FOOLISH	Cerato
FORCEFUL	Vine

Moods	Remedies
FREEDOM	
yearning desire for (from torment)	Sweet Chestnut, Clematis, Agrimony, Cherry Plum
desires, from responsibility	Elm
desires, from duty	Centaury
feels claustrophobic without	Water Violet, Impatiens
FORGETFUL	
due to mental turmoil	White Chestnut, Agrimony
due to lack of concentration	Clematis
due to apathy	Wild Rose
FORGIVE	
unable to, due to bitterness	Willow
unable to, due to injustice	Vervain
readily does so, as blames self	Pine, Centaury
FORTITUDE	Oak
FRANTIC	
with worry	White Chestnut
with worry/anxiety over others	Red Chestnut
with irrational fears	Cherry Plum, Aspen
in crisis situation	Rescue Remedy
FRETFUL	Chicory, Agrimony, White Chestnut, Red Chestnut
FRIGHT	Star of Bethlehem, Rock Rose
FRUSTRATION	
generally	Vervain, Walnut
with slowness	Impatiens
uncontrollable	Cherry Plum
FULFILMENT	
lack of, thus seeks	Wild Oat

MOODS	REMEDIES
FUSSINESS	
over other people's affairs/meddling	Chicory
over others, due to fear/anxiety	Red Chestnut
about detail, trivialities and cleanliness	Crab Apple
about making judgement	Cerato
about principles	Vervain
about correctness	Rock Water, Vervain
FUTURE	
fear of	Aspen, Mimulus, Agrimony
looks forward to	Clematis
has no interest in	Honeysuckle
worries about	White Chestnut, Agrimony
GABBLE	Heather, Impatiens, Agrimony, Vervain
GAIETY, false	Agrimony
GARRULOUS	Heather, Impatiens, Agrimony, Vervain
GAWKISH	Mimulus, Clematis
GENIAL, joyous	Agrimony
GIGGLE	
to hide feelings	Agrimoy
nervously	Mimulus, Agrimony, Larch
with nervous impatience	Impatiens
GLOOM	Gorse, Mustard, Willow
GOD	
fear of	Mimulus, Aspen
fear of due to guilt	Pine
self-righteous fear of	Rock Water, Crab Apple

MOODS	REMEDIES
GOD (continued)	
disbelief in	Gorse
anger/hatred of	Holly
bitterness/resentment of	Willow
loss of faith in	Sweet Chestnut
GREEDY	
for others' possessions	Chicory
for sympathy	Chicory, Heather, Willow
for information/advise	Cerato
for power/control	Vine, Chicory, Vervain
for perfection	Rock Water, Vervain
for love	Chicory
for company	Heather
GREGARIOUS	Agrimony, Heather
GRIEF	
sudden, shock	Star of Bethlehem, Rescue Remedy
grieves silently	Water Violet
chronic grieving despair	Sweet Chestnut
heartache	Sweet Chestnut, Star of Bethlehem
with longing for the past	Honeysuckle
with guilt/self blame	Pine
with self condemnation/disgust	Crab Apple
GRIEVANCE	
voices	Vervain, Holly, Vine
does not complain	Centaury, Agrimony, Mimulus, Larch
allows to fester inwardly	Willow, Chicory, White Chestnut, Holly, Agrimony
GRUDGE, bearing	Willow, Chicory
GRUMBLE	Willow

Moods	Remedies
GUIDANCE	
seeks	Cerato
gives	Vervain, Vine, Chicory
gives through criticism	Beech
gives by example	Rock Water
gives quietly when asked	Water Violet
GUILT	Pine
GULLIBLE	Cerato, Clematis
HABITS	
irritated by	Beech
to break	Walnut, Chestnut Bud
HALLUCINATE	Cherry Plum, Rock Rose, Clematis, Vervain, Agrimony
HAND-WASHING	
obsessive, due to sense of uncleanliness	Crab Apple
see also Dirt	
HAPPY-GO-LUCKY	Agrimony, Oak
HAPPINESS	
longs for	Clematis, Star of Bethlehem, Sweet Chestnut
HAPPEN	
fears something is about to	Aspen
can't wait for things to	Impatiens, Clematis
HARD TASK-MASTERS	
to themselves	Rock Water
to others	Beech, Chicory, Vine, Impatiens

MOODS	REMEDIES
HARASSED	
sense of being/irritated by	Impatiens, Vervain, Cherry Plum
sense of being, due to responsibility	Elm, White Chestnut
and bad-tempered	Impatiens, Vervain, Cherry Plum, Holly, Willow, Beech
ever willing but over-burdened	Centaury, White Chestnut
HASTY	Impatiens
HATE	
generally	Holly
festering resentment	Willow
can see no redeeming features in others	Beech
HAUGHTY	
appears to be, through pride/dignity	Water Violet
if self-opinionated/know-all/autocratic	Vine
through vanity/self obsessed	Heather
through self-righteousness	Rock Water
HAUNTING THOUGHTS	
suffers	Aspen, White Chestnut, Honeysuckle
protection from	Walnut
HEADSTRONG	Vervain, Vine
HELP	
in emergencies/distress	Rescue Remedy
seeks help in decision making	Cerato

Moods	Remedies
HELPFUL	
but maintains discreet distance	Water Violet
calmly, without question	Oak
but fusses	Chicory, Vervain
dutifully, eager to please	Centaury, Pine
HELPLESSNESS	Sweet Chestnut
HESITANCY	
through uncertainty	Scleranthus, Cerato
through fear	Mimulus
through lack of confidence	Larch
none, being self-assured	Impatiens, Vine, Water Violet, Vervain, Chicory
HIGHLY STRUNG	Vervain, Rock Water, Impatiens
through anticipation/living on a knife-edge	Aspen
HOME-SICKNESS	Honeysuckle
HOPELESSNESS	
pessimistic	Gorse
extreme	Sweet Chestnut
HORRIFIED	Rock Rose, Star of Bethlehem
HOSTILITY	
due to hatred/suspicion/envy/ jealousy	Holly
due to intolerance	Beech
due to irritation with slowness	Impatiens
HOUSE-PROUD	Crab Apple, Chicory, Rock Water

MOODS	REMEDIES

HUMOUR
    hides emotions behind, like clown   Agrimony
    lacks sense of   Willow, Mustard, Gorse

HYGIENE
    obsessed with   Crab Apple

HYPERACTIVE   Vervain, Impatiens, Cherry Plum

HYPNOTISED   Clematis

HYPOCHONDRIA   Heather, Crab Apple

HYPOCRISY   Scleranthus, Cerato, Centaury,
    Agrimony

HYSTERIA   Cherry Plum, Rescue Remedy

IDEALISTIC
    of future/fantasies   Clematis
    impractically   Clematis
    over-enthusiastic perfectionism   Vervain
    for self   Rock Water
    high ideals   Vervain, Beech, Impatiens,
    Rock Water

    unable to realise ambitions   Wild Oat

IDENTITY
    lack of   Cerato, Agrimony, Centaury

ILLNESS
    simulated   Chicory, Heather, Willow
    frustrated by   Oak
    feels unclean during   Crab Apple
    fear of   Mimulus
    depleted energy due to/help in   Olive
        convalescence
    see also Ailments

Moods	Remedies
IMAGE	
lacks definition	Cerato, Centaury
dislikes one's own	Crab Apple, Pine
high opinion of one's own	Rock Water, Heather, Chicory, Vine
IMAGINATION	
creative	Clematis
over-zealous	Cherry Plum, Rock Rose
lacks	Wild Rose, Gorse
vivid	Clematis, Cherry Plum
influenced by	Walnut
IMITATES	
through lack of self-identity/ certainty	Cerato
because easily led	Centaury, Walnut
IMMEDIACY	
demands	Impatiens, Vine
IMPARTIALITY	Wild Rose, Scleranthus, Cerato, Clematis
IMPATIENT	Impatiens
IMPETUOUS	Impatiens, Vervain, Cherry Plum
IMPRESSION	
tries to make	Willow, Chicory
tries to make, for sympathy	Willow, Chicory
tries to make, in order to convert	Vervain
tries to make, as example	Rock Water
IMPUDENT	Willow, Chicory, Beech

Moods	Remedies
IMPULSIVE	
quick and eager/hasty/ impetuous	Impatiens
irrational/uncontrolled/ fear of	Cherry Plum
over-enthusiastic/hasty	Vervain
acts out imaginary fantasy	Clematis
becoming a salve to impulses	Centaury, Walnut
IMPURITY	
dislikes/feels contaminated by	Crab Apple
INADEQUACY	
through lack of confidence	Larch, Elm
through self-distrust	Cerato, Scleranthus
through guilt	Pine
through fear/shyness/timidity	Mimulus
INATTENTIVE	Clematis, Honeysuckle, White Chestnut
INCENSED	Vervain
INDECISION	Scleranthus
about life's direction	Wild Oat
about one's judgement/instincts	Cerato
INDEPENDENCE	Water Violet, Oak, Impatiens, Vine
INDIFFERENCE	
to life	Clematis, Wild Rose, Mustard
towards needs of others	Beech, Vine, Chicory, Holly, Impatiens
INDIGNANT	Chicory, Vervain, Beech

Moods	Remedies

INDULGENCE
    in food, then feels disgusted   Crab Apple
    in projects, enthusiastically   Vervain
    hurriedly   Impatiens
    refrains from, through politeness   Water Violet
    refrains from, through self-restraint   Rock Water
    needs protection from   Walnut

INERTIA   Hornbeam, Wild Rose
    through exhaustion   Olive
    through depression   Mustard, Gorse

INFURIATED   Holly, Vervain, Vine, Cherry
    Plum, Beech

INFLUENCED
    from path in life   Walnut, Cerato, Wild Oat
    easily, by dominance of others   Centaury
    by decision of others   Cerato, Gorse, Centaury,
    Agrimony
    by delay and hindrance   Gentian
    for the sake of peace   Agrimony
    through jealousy/envy   Holly

INQUISITIVE   Vervain, Impatiens, Chicory,
    Clematis

INSANITY
    fears   Cherry Plum
    sense of   Clematis
    sense of, due to frustration   Vervain, Impatiens

INSECURITY
    generally   Cerato, Larch
    through fear   Mimulus, Red Chestnut
    and clings to others   Heather, Chicory
    needs to be loved/protected   Chicory

Moods	Remedies
INSENSITIVE	Vine, Beech, Chicory
INSTANT	
desires instant action	Impatiens, Vervain
INSTINCTS	
follows	Vervain
distrusts	Cerato, Scleranthus
INTENSE	Vervain
INTEREST	
lack of, due to distant thoughts	Clematis, Honeysuckle
lack of, due to fatigue	Olive, Hornbeam
lack of, due to apathy/resignation	Wild Rose
lack of, due to worry	White Chestnut
lack of, due to desperation	Gorse, Mustard
lack of, due to self-absorption	Heather
lack of, through embitterment	Willow
too much, generally, especially matters of principle	Vervain
too much, in affairs of others	Chicory
INTERFERENCE	
in affairs of others	Chicory
by fussing and criticising	Chicory
by talking of self	Heather
by dominating	Vine
by persuasion	Vervain
by asking questions	Cerato
by revenge	Holly
by thoughts/mental arguments	White Chestnut
by setting rigid example	Rock Water
no desire for	Water Violet
protection from	Walnut

Moods	Remedies
INTERVIEW	
nervousness about	Rescue Remedy, Mimulus, Larch
negative about	Gentian, Gorse
fearful/worried about	Mimulus, White Chestnut
INTIMIDATED	Centaury, Mimulus, Walnut, Agrimony
INTIMIDATING	Vine
INTOLERANCE	Beech
of slowness	Impatiens
of inaccuracy	Vervain, Rock Water
INTROSPECTION	Willow, Heather
through guilt	Pine
INTROVERTED	Centaury, Mimulus
due to dreaminess	Clematis
due to sulkiness/self-pity	Willow
appears to be, due to dignified aloofness	Water Violet
through worry	White Chestnut
through indecision	Scleranthus
for selfish reasons	Chicory
INTUITION, distrusts	Cerato
INVOKES ILLNESS	
to obtain sympathy	Chicory, Heather
to manipulate others	Chicory
through resentment/self-pity	Willow
to escape from reality	Clematis
to escape fear	Mimulus
due to lack of confidence	Larch

MOODS	REMEDIES
IRRATIONAL	
thoughts generally	Cherry Plum
fears of harmful act	Cherry Plum
anxiety	Aspen
IRRITABILITY	
generally	Impatiens
with mannerisms and habits of others	Beech
due to selfishness	Chicory
due to ill temper	Holly, Willow
due to frustration with insensitivity/injustices	Vervain
ISOLATION	
enjoys	Water Violet, Impatiens
cannot bear	Heather
JADED	Olive, Hornsbeam
JEALOUSY	Holly
JOKES	
to make light of problems	Agrimony
JOVIALITY, false	Agrimony
JUDGEMENTS	
distrusts one's own	Cerato
suspicious/distrustful of others'	Holly
afraid of	Mimulus, Rock Rose
makes hasty	Impatiens
overly critical	Vervain, Beech
JUMPY	Mimulus, Impatiens, Aspen, Agrimony
JUSTICE	
great belief in	Vervain

Moods	Remedies
KARMA	
submission to	Clematis
unquestioned acceptance of	Wild Rose
afraid of consequences of	Mimulus, Aspen, Rock Rose
over influenced by/feels controlled	Walnut, Crab Apple, Centaury
KEEN	Vervain
KEEPSAKES	
sentimental about	Honeysuckle
no attachment to	Clematis
irritated by	Impatiens, Beech, Vine
comforted by	Centaury, Mimulus, Larch, Cerato, Honeysuckle, Chicory
KILL	
irrational desire to	Cherry Plum
hateful desire to	Holly
over-concerned about accidental killing of insects	Red Chestnut, Pine, Centaury
over-concerned about slaughter of animals	Red Chestnut, Vervain, Centaury, Pine
KNOW-ALL	Vine, Beech
KNOWS BEST	Chicory, Vervain, Rock Water, Water Violet
LABORIOUS, work seems	Hornbeam, Wild Rose
LASSITUDE	
generally	Hornbeam, Wild Rose, Olive, Clematis
due to self-pity/resentment	Willow
due to depression	Gorse, Mustard, Sweet Chestnut

Moods	Remedies
LAUGHTER	
to hide feelings	Agrimony
nervous	Agrimony, Impatiens, Mimulus
uncontrollable	Cherry Plum
LAX	Wild Rose, Clematis, Hornbeam, Scleranthus, Cerato, Larch
LAZINESS	Wild Rose, Hornbeam, Clematis
LEADERSHIP	Vine, Vervain, Water Violet
LEARN	
unable to, from experience/ mistakes	Chestnut Bud
LECTURE	
desire to, due to enthusiasm	Vervain
does so, to dominate/control	Vine
does so, to get own way	Chicory
does so, to expose stupidity	Beech
LETHARGY	
generally	Hornbeam, Wild Rose
despises	Rock Water
LIBERATION	
desire for	Sweet Chestnut, Clematis, Cherry Plum
desire for, from duty	Centaury
desire for, from mental torment	White Chestnut, Agrimony

MOODS	REMEDIES
LIFE	
despaired of	Sweet Chestnut, Rescue Remedy
seems a drudgery	Centaury, Hornbeam, Olive, Gorse
loss of interest in	Clematis, Gorse
no pleasure in	Olive, Mustard
irrational desire to end	Cherry Plum
LIVELY	Impatiens, Vervain, Agrimony
LIVID	Holly, Vervain, Cherry Plum, Vine
LOATHSOME	
of others	Holly
of self	Crab Apple
LONELINESS	
enjoys	Water Violet
prefers, for work	Impatiens
dislikes	Agrimony, Heather, Chicory, Mimulus, Vervain
seeks, as an escape	Clematis
heartbreaking	Star of Bethlehem, Sweet Chestnut
LONGS FOR	
peace of mind	White Chestnut, Agrimony
home	Honeysuckle
loved ones	Honeysuckle, Chicory, Red Chestnut
freedom from mental torture	Agrimony, White Chestnut, Scleranthus, Sweet Chestnut, Cherry Plum
future, for better times	Clematis
something to look forward to	Clematis
release from envy, jealousy	Holly

MOODS	REMEDIES

LOSS
  sense of, e.g. through grief   Star of Bethlehem
  see also Bereavement and Grief

LOVE
  lack of, for others   Holly
  lack of, for self   Crab Apple, Pine
  desires more of/constant   Chicory
  desires as reassurance   Cerato

LOVE-STRUCK
  and dreamy   Clematis
  but jealous   Holly
  but possessive/clinging   Chicory

LOW
  in spirits   Mustard, Olive, Sweet Chestnut, Gentian, Gorse, Willow

  see also Depression and Downcast

LUNACY   Cherry Plum, Agrimony, Impatiens

LUST   Chicory, Vervain, Heather, Cherry Plum

MACABRE thoughts   Mustard, Cherry Plum, White Chestnut

MADNESS   Cherry Plum

MADDENING
  finds subject matter   Vervain
  finds people   Vervain, Beech, Vine
  finds slowness   Impatiens

MALICIOUS
  tendencies   Holly
  thoughts, mental arguments   White Chestnut, Holly, Willow

Moods	Remedies
MALINGER	
due to responsibility	Elm
due to exhaustion	Olive
due to laziness	Wild Rose
MANIC	
thoughts	Cherry Plum, White Chestnut
with depression	Mustard, Scleranthus
Suicidal	Cherry Plum
MANIPULATIVE	Chicory
MANIPULATED	Centaury, Agrimony
MANNERISMS	
irritated by	Beech
irritated by slowness of	Impatiens
uses plentifully to illustrate point	Vervain
MARTYR	
to a cause	Vervain
for affection/attention	Chicory, Heather
to resentment	Willow
to own ideals	Rock Water
as an example to others	Rock Water
MASK	
jovial, to hide fears, worries etc.	Agrimony
MASOCHISM, mental	Rock Water, Crab Apple, Pine, Cherry Plum, White Chestnut
MASQUERADE	Agrimony
MASTERFUL	Vervain, Vine
MAZE	
as though lost in	Wild Oat, Scleranthus, Clematis

Moods	Remedies
MEDDLE	
to control/manipulate	Chicory
to hasten	Impatiens
to convince	Vervain
MEDITATIVE	Clematis
MEEK	Centaury, Mimulus, Larch
MEGALOMANIA	Cherry Plum, Vervain, Rock Water, Chicory
MELANCHOLIA	Gorse, Sweet Chestnut
with no known reason	Mustard
MEMORY	
bad, due to lack of concentration	Clematis, Honeysuckle
bad, due to mind full of other things	Vervain, White Chestnut
MENTAL ARGUMENTS	White Chestnut
MERCILESS	Vine, Holly
MERRIMENT	
which hides true feelings	Agrimony
METABOLISM (of mental energy)	
lethargic	Hornbeam, Wild Rose
hyperactive	Impatiens, Vervain
hyperactive, due to fear/ anxiety	Rock Rose, Aspen
slow, dreamy	Clematis
slow, through depression	Mustard, Gorse, Sweet Chestnut
METAMORPHOSIS	
helps during	Walnut

Moods	Remedies
METHODICAL	Oak, Rock Water, Vervain, Wild Rose
METICULOUS	
generally, by nature	Rock Water, Vervain, Beech
over concentration to detail	Crab Apple
MIMIC	
due to uncertainty about self	Cerato
sarcastically/spitefully/to gain advantage	Holly, Willow, Chicory
MISANTHROPY	Holly, Beech
MISBEHAVIOUR	
to gain attention	Chicory, Heather, Willow
due to strength of own will	Vine
due to desire for own way	Vine, Chicory
due to fear	Mimulus, Rock Rose
due to being misled by stronger personality	Centaury, Walnut
in trying to impress	Agrimony, Chicory
due to being misled by stronger personalities	Centaury, Cerato, Walnut
MISERY	
generally, in outlook	Willow
with self pity	Willow, Chicory
with pessimism/doubt	Gentian, Gorse
with cloud of depression	Mustard
with bleak despair	Sweet Chestnut
hidden	Agrimony, Water Violet, Oak, Centaury
MISGUIDED BY OTHERS	Centaury, Cerato
on occasions	Walnut

MOODS	REMEDIES
MISTAKES	
does not learn by	Chestnut Bud
blames self for mistakes of others	Pine
MISTRUSTFUL	
of others	Holly
of self	Cerato
of self to do harm/act irrationally	Cherry Plum
MOAN	Willow, Chicory, Gorse
MOCK	Holly, Vine, Beech
MODEST	Centaury, Larch, Mimulus
MONOTONE	Mustard, Gorse, Wild Rose
MOODY	
depression comes and goes	Mustard
mood swings	Scleranthus
self-pitying, selfish	Willow, Chicory
MOPE	Willow, Chicory, Mustard, Gorse
MORALITY	
for self perfectionism	Rock Water
in support of others	Vervain
MORBID THOUGHTS	Mustard, Cherry Plum, White Chestnut
MOTHERLY	Chicory
possessively/selfishly/fussily	Chicory
selflessly anxious	Red Chestnut
gentle and selflessly protective	Centaury

Moods	Remedies

MOTIVATION
high degree of — Vervain, Vine, Impatiens
lack of, through listlessness — Wild Rose, Hornbeam, Olive

MOULDING OF CHARACTER
those who try to convert others — Vervain, Chicory, Rock Water
those who are affected by others — Cerato, Walnut, Centaury, Agrimony

MOURNING
in grief — Star of Bethlehem
with memories/regrets — Honesycukle
with bleak despair — Sweet Chestnut
with self-reproach/regrets — Pine
and desiring own demise — Clematis

NAG — Chicory, Beech, Vine

NARROW-MINDED — Rock Water, Beech

NAUSEOUS
feeling of, generally — Crab Apple
with fear — Mimulus, Rock Rose
due to travel — Scleranthus

NERVOUS BREAKDOWN — Cherry Plum, Oak, Scleranthus, Vervain, Agrimony, White Chestnut

NERVOUSNESS
generally, fearful/timid/shy — Mimulus
with vague anticipation — Aspen
with impatient eagerness — Impatiens

NERVY — Agrimony, Chicory, Impatiens, Mimulus, Vervain

NEUROSIS — Cherry Plum, Rock Rose

Moods	Remedies

NOISE
aversion to/peace disturbed by — Water Violet, Clematis, Mimulus, Walnut
intolerant of/annoyed with — Beech, Impatiens, Willow

NOSEY — Chicory, Heather, Vervain, Cerato

NOSTALGIA — Honeysuckle

NUISANCE
apologises for being — Pine
annoyed with/irritated by — Beech, Impatiens

NUMBNESS — Clematis, Star of Bethlehem

OBEDIENCE
demands — Vine
demands of self — Rock Water

OBEDIENT — Centaury, Cerato, Agrimony
through fear — Mimulus

OBESITY
disgusted by — Crab Apple
due to over indulgence, acting as crutch — Walnut, Centaury, Wild Rose, Gorse
see also Eating

OBLIGATION
feels under, due to sense of duty — Centaury, Pine
feels under, due to sense of principle — Vervain, Oak

OBLIVION
desires — Clematis, Sweet Chestnut

Moods	Remedies
OBSERVATION	
astute	Impatiens, Vervain, Rock Water
lack of	Clematis, Chestnut Bud, Honeysuckle, White Chestnut, Wild Rose
OBSESSIVE	
fear	Cherry Plum, Rock Rose
religiously	Rock Water, Vervain
with self-righteousness	Rock Water, Chicory
over details	Crab Apple
OBSTINATE	Vervain, Vine, Beech
OBSTRUCTIVE	Beech, Vervain, Vine, Willow, Holly
OFFENSE	
takes easily with introspection	Chicory, Willow
takes easily due to uncertainty	Cerato, Larch
takes easily due to injustice	Vervain
OLD TIES, TO BREAK	Walnut
OMNIPOTENT	Vine
OPINIONATED	Vine, Vervain, Beech, Chicory, Impatiens
OPPORTUNITY	
loses through doubt	Cerato, Gentian
loses through lack of confidence	Larch
loses through indecision	Scleranthus
loses through lack of faith in intuition	Cerato
loses through uncertainty of vocational path	Wild Oat

Moods	Remedies

OPTIONS
   undecided when confronted with — Scleranthus
   confused about ambitions — Wild Oat
   doubtful of own mind — Cerato, Scleranthus

OSTENTATION — Beech, Chicory, Heather, Vine

OSTRASISED
   due to selfishness/possessiveness — Chicory
   due to unrelenting talkativeness — Heather
   due to angry attitude — Holly, Willow
   due to critical attitude — Beech, Chicory

OUTBURST
   uncontrolled — Cherry Plum
   angered by injustice — Vervain
   of hateful/spiteful abuse — Holly

OUTRAGE
   deep sense of — Vervain

OVERACT
   for sympathy or attention — Chicory, Willow

OVER-ANXIOUS
   to please — Centaury
   to care for others — Chicory
   to influence others — Vervain
   for others' opinions — Cerato
   over details — Crab Apple
   for self — Heather, Rock Water, Willow
   for safety of others — Red Chestnut
   to set good example — Rock Water

OVER-INDULGENCE
   generally — Vervain, Heather, Chicory
   and feels disgusted — Crab Apple
   uncontrolled — Cherry Plum
   help in breaking habit of — Walnut, Chestnut Bud

Moods	Remedies

OVERRULES   Vine

OVER-SENSITIVITY
  hides   Agrimony
  through weakness   Centaury
  to strong influences   Walnut
  to fancied insults/suspicion   Holly, Vervain

OVERWHELMED
  by responsibility/pressure   Elm
  by demands of others   Centaury, Mimulus
  harrassed/irritated with constant   Impatiens
    demands

OVERWORK
  tendency to   Oak, Vervain, Centaury
  exhausted by   Olive

OVERWROUGHT
  with fear for others   Red Chestnut
  with despair   Sweet Chestnut
  with anxiety about how to cope Elm
  with anxiety and foreboding   Aspen
  with worry   White Chestnut

PACIFIST   Agrimony, Centaury, Vervain,
    Clematis, Wild Rose,
    Oak

PANGS OF GUILT   Pine

PANIC
  generally   Rock Rose, Rescue Remedy
  with irrational thoughts   Cherry Plum

PARANOIA
  with suspicion   Holly
  with irrational fears   Cherry Plum

Moods	Remedies

PARTICULAR
over detail — Crab Apple, Rock Water
about self-perfection — Rock Water
about cleanliness — Crab Apple
about upholding principles — Vervain

PASSIONATE
with enthusiasm — Vervain, Impatiens
without control — Cherry Plum

PASSIVE — Centaury, Mimulus, Wild Rose, Clematis

PAST
nostalgic memories of — Honeysuckle
no interest in — Clematis
regrets — Honeysuckle, Pine, Crab Apple

to let go of — Walnut

PATH IN LIFE
to help determine — Wild Oat
to help remain upon — Walnut

PATRONISING/condescending — Vine, Beech, Rock Water

PEACE OF MIND
disturbed by thoughts/worry — White Chestnut, Agrimony
disturbed by guilt — Pine
disturbed by mental arguments — White Chestnut, Vervain
disturbed by fear — Mimulus, Aspen, Rock Rose
disturbed by fear for others — Red Chestnut
disturbed by grief — Star of Bethlehem, Honeysuckle

disturbed by resentment — Willow
disturbed by indecision — Scleranthus
disturbed by obsession — Crab Apple

Moods	Remedies
PEACE AND QUIET	
enjoys, must have	Water Violet
avoids	Agrimony, Heather
PEEVED	Impatiens, Beech, Vervain
PENSIVE	Clematis
PERFECTIONISM	Beech, Rock Water, Vervain, Vine
PERSECUTION	
suspicious of	Holly, Cherry Plum
afraid of	Cherry Plum, Mimulus, Aspen
PERSISTENT	Vervain, Oak, Rock Water
PERSUASIVE	
enthusiastically	Vervain
quietly	Water Violet
PERSUADED BY OTHERS	
against inclination	Gorse, Wild Rose, Walnut
through self-distrust	Cerato
through weakness	Centaury
through kindness	Agrimony
through jealousy, envy	Holly
to please others	Centaury
PESSIMISM	Gorse, Gentian
PETRIFIED	Rock Rose
PETTY	Crab Apple, Chicory, Beech
PETULANT	Impatiens, Willow

MOODS	REMEDIES

PHILOSOPHICAL
generally, by nature — Oak, Water Violet, Clematis, Wild Rose

with strong opinions — Vervain

PHOBIAS
known, generally — Mimulus, Rock Rose, White Chestnut

about dirt/contamination/looks — Crab Apple
unknown/vague — Aspen
irrational — Cherry Plum

PIOUS — Rock Water, Beech

PINE — Honeysuckle, Clematis

PITY
self — Willow, Chicory
for others — Centaury, Pine, Red Chestnut, Vervain, Agrimony

PLACID — Oak, Water Violet, Wild Rose, Clematis, Centaury, Mimulus

PLAY-ACT — Chicory, Willow, Vervain, Vine, Clematis

PLEASURE
none, in life — Mustard, Sweet Chestnut
takes, in company of others — Heather
takes, in converting others — Vervain, Rock Water, Beech
seeks — Agrimony
takes, in being an exhibitionist — Vervain, Vine

PLODDERS — Oak

MOODS	REMEDIES

POISE
   lack of   Scleranthus
   possesses   Water Violet

POLLUTION
   sense of being contaminated by   Crab Apple
   fear of   Mimulus
   agitated by, for fear of harm to   Red Chestnut
      others
   agitated by, on principle   Vervain

PONDER
   on problem-solving   Vervain
   on worries/mental arguments   White Chestnut
   on future   Clematis
   on past   Honeysuckle
   on self   Heather, Chicory, Willow
   fearfully, about what *might*   Aspen
      happen

POSSESSIVENESS   Chicory, Heather

POUT
   with resentment   Willow
   with self-pity   Chicory, Willow

POWER
   desire for   Vine
   desire for, to manipulate   Chicory
   frustrated by lack of   Vine, Vervain

PRAGMATIC   Vine, Vervain, Oak, Chicory

PRAISE
   desires   Chicory
   seeks, for reassurance   Cerato
   wallows in   Vine, Chicory

MOODS	REMEDIES

PREACH
  tendency to   Vervain, Rock Water, Beech

PRECISE   Vervain, Rock Water, Beech

PRE-OCCUPATION
  with thoughts/worries   White Chestnut
  with future/fantasy   Clematis
  with past   Honeysuckle
  with injustice   Vervain
  with self   Heather, Rock Water, Crab
                            Apple, Chicory, Willow
  with cleanliness   Crab Apple
  with detail/trivialities   Crab Apple
  with jealousy   Holly, Willow
  with grievances   Holly, Willow, Vervain

PRESENTIMENT   Aspen

PRESSURE
  of responsibility, overwhelmed by Elm
  of work, thrives on   Vervain
  to serve/assist others   Centaury
  unaffected by/takes in stride Oak
  to conform, influenced by   Cerato, Walnut, Centaury

PRESUMPTUOUS   Vine, Chicory, Beech

PRETENCE
  of courage/happiness   Agrimony

PRETENTIOUS   Beech, Chicory, Vine

PRIDE   Water Violet, Rock Water,
                          Chicory, Crab Apple

PRINCIPLES
  feels strongly about   Vervain

MOODS	REMEDIES
PRIVACY	
enjoys, needs	Water Violet
PROCRASTINATION	
through lethargy	Hornbeam
through uncertainty	Scleranthus, Larch
through fear	Mimulus
PROTECTIVE	Centaury, Chicory, Red Chestnut, Vervain, Oak
PROTECTION	
from disturbing outside influences	Walnut
PROUD	Water Violet, Rock Water, Chicory, Crab Apple
PURIST	Rock Water, Vervain, Beech
QUALM	Aspen, Cerato, Pine, Gentian, Rock Water
QUARRELSOME	Willow, Vervain, Holly, Chicory, Beech, Impatiens
QUARRELS	
avoids	Agrimony, Centaury, Clematis, Wild Rose
QUESTIONS	
repeated, for confirmation	Cerato
out of keen interest	Vervain
out of suspicion	Holly, Willow
out of arrogance	Vine, Beech
QUICK	Impatiens, Vervain

MOODS	REMEDIES
QUIET	
generally, by nature	Aspen, Centaury, Scleranthus, Water Violet, Centaury
and dreamy	Clematis
and shy	Mimulus
QUIZZICAL	Cerato, Vervain
RACE AHEAD	
generally disposed to	Impatiens
thoughts tend to	Impatiens, Vervain, White Chestnut, Aspen
RAGE	
uncontrolled/irrational	Cherry Plum
due to authoritarianism	Vine
due to hatred/revenge/envy	Holly
due to injustice/sense of principle	Vervain
due to irritability/impatience	Impatiens
RAPE	
after effects of: shock	Star of Bethlehem, Rescue Remedy
disgust/sense of contamination/ uncleanliness	Crab Apple
guilt	Pine
nightmares/horror	Rock Rose
ghastly memory	Honeysuckle, Rock Rose, Star of Bethlehem
plagued by repetitive thoughts	White Chestnut
RASH	
acts rashly	Impatiens, Vervain
emotionally irritated by physical rash	Impatiens
emotionally feels unclean due to rash	Crab Apple

Moods	Remedies

REACTIVE
    in response to injustice or insult — Vervain
    as result of resentment/self pity — Willow, Chicory
    as result of humiliation — Vervain, Chicory
    as result of humiliation, but absorbed — Water Violet
    spitefully or as result of hatred/jealousy — Holly
    in authoritarian manner — Vine
    in form of rage/uncontrolled temper — Cherry Plum

REALITY
    no sense of/ungrounded — Clematis
    firm sense of — Oak, Vervain, Vine

REALIZATION (sudden) — Star of Bethlehem

REASSURANCE
    needs/seeks due to uncertainty — Cerato
    needs, to encourage — Mimulus, Larch

REBELLIOUSNESS — Beech, Impatiens, Vervain, Vine

REBIRTHING
    adjustment to/after — Walnut
    shock, as result of — Star of Bethlehem
    guilt, uncovered by — Pine
    grief/sadness, uncovered by — Star of Bethlehem
    inability to forgive, uncovered by — Willow
    self condemnation/disgust, as result of — Crab Apple

RECEPTIVE
    to other people's needs — Centaury, Walnut, Red Chestnut, Chicory
    to fantasies/creativity — Clematis

MOODS	REMEDIES
RECLUSE, by preference	Water Violet
due to fear	Aspen, Mimulus, Rock Rose, Cherry Plum
due to fear of contamination from outside	Crab Apple
as mark of self-martyrdom/self-perfectionism	Rock Water
due to resentment	Willow
RECOIL	
through shock	Star of Bethlehem
through disgust	Crab Apple
through horror	Rock Rose
through fear	Aspen, Mimulus, Rock Rose
through abusive verbal attack	Walnut, Mimulus, Centaury, Agrimony
RECOVERY	
adjustment during	Walnut
depletion of energy during	Hornbeam, Olive
depressed/weepy during	Mustard, Willow, Gorse (if due to poor prognosis)
diseased feeling during	Crab Apple
shock to the system during	Star of Bethlehem, Rescue Remedy
set-back during	Gentian
despair of serious set-back	Sweet Chestnut
RECTITUDE	Rock Water, Vervain
REFORMER	Rock Water, Vervain
REFRACTORY	Beech, Vine, Vervain, Impatiens
REFUSAL to conform	
due to own strength of character	Beech, Vervain, Vine, Chicory
due to unconventionalist ideas	Clematis

MOODS	REMEDIES

REFUSAL TO BE CONSOLED
   after shocking news — Star of Bethlehem
   wishes to be left alone to grieve/ — Water Violet, Honeysuckle
     reflect in peace and silence
   as shows signs of weakness — Vine, Rock Water
   yet manipulates consolation and — Chicory, Willow
     sympathy through self-pity
   has innate courage to face — Oak
     adversity

REGARD FOR SELF
   poor, due to self-detestation — Crab Apple
   poor, due to guilt/self-reproach — Pine
   high, but wants to be better — Rock Water

REGRESSION
   with thoughts of past — Honeysuckle
   shocked/saddened by — Star of Bethlehem
   frightened by — Mimulus, Rock Rose
   adjustment to — Walnut
   depressed by/denting ambition — Gentian

REGRETS — Honeysuckle, Pine

REJECTION
   with grief/sense of loss or shock — Star of Bethlehem
   with self-blame — Pine, Crab Apple
   with resentment/bitterness — Willow
   with hatred/jealousy — Holly
   with no confidence — Larch
   with sense of vulnerability — Cerato, Mimulus, Larch
   with over-concern/fearful anxiety — Red Chestnut
     over others
   with over-concern/possessiveness — Chicory, Heather

RELAPSE
   into old unproductive habits — Chestnut Bud
   depressed by — Gentian

Moods	Remedies

RELAXATION
  difficult, due to tension   Vervain, Rock Water, Vine
  easy, due to drowsiness   Olive, Clematis
  easy, due to apathy/lethargy   Wild Rose, Hornbeam
  difficult due to worrying   White Chestnut
    thoughts
  difficult due to fear/anxiety   Mimulus, Aspen, Rock Rose,
                                       Cherry Plum
  difficult due to fear for others   Red Chestnut
  difficult due to impatience/   Impatiens, Vervain
    cannot slow down
  see also Restlessness

RELEASE
  longs for, from servile work   Centaury
  longs for, as escape from present Clematis
    circumstances
  longs for, from life   Clematis
  longs for, from anguish   Sweet Chestnut
  longs for, from guilt   Pine
  longs for, from torment   Agrimony, White Chestnut
  longs for, from contamination of   Crab Apple
    disease

RELENTLESS   Oak, Vervain

REMINDED
  and saddened by memories   Honeysuckle
  needs to be, due to   Clematis
    forgetfulness
  needs to be, due to full mind   White Chestnut, Vervain
  needs to be, repeatedly   Chestnut Bud, Clematis
  irritated at being reminded of   Vervain, Vine, Impatiens
    short-comings

MOODS	REMEDIES
REMINDERS	
nostalgic	Honeysuckle
sentimental	Walnut, Honeysuckle
which provoke guilt	Pine
which provoke sadness/grief	Star of Bethlehem, Honeysuckle
which provokes self disgust	Crab Apple
about injustice	Vervain
which revive grudges	Willow
which cause set-back	Gentian
REMINISCENCE	Honeysuckle
REMORSE	Pine
REMOTENESS	
due to mental escapism/day-dreaming	Clematis
due to absorption with past	Honeysuckle
due to grief/shock	Star of Bethlehem
due to utter dejection/emptiness	Sweet Chestnut
through desire for private solitude	Water Violet
suffered by sensitive people	Larch, Mimulus, Centaury, Crab Apple
RENUNCIATION	Rock Water
REPEAT	
same mistakes	Chestnut Bud
oneself verbally	Heather, Vervain, Impatiens
REPELLED	Crab Apple
REPENTING	Pine

Moods	Remedies
REPRESSED EMOTIONS	
generally	Agrimony, Centaury, Water Violet
of guilt	Pine
of indecision	Scleranthus
of resentment/bitterness	Willow
festering thoughts/mental arguments	White Chestnut
REPUGNANCE	Crab Apple
REPULSION	
generally	Crab Apple
through horror	Star of Bethlehem, Rock Rose
RESENTMENT	Willow
vengeful	Holly
due to injustice	Vervain
when unappreciated	Chicory, Willow
due to jealousy/envy	Holly
RESERVED	
shy	Mimulus
subservient/weak	Centaury
by choice due to private nature	Water Violet
RESIGNATION	Wild Rose, Gorse
RESILIENCE	Oak, Vervain, Rock Water
RESPECT	
demands	Vine
yearns for, selfishly	Chicory
appreciates	Vervain
deserving of	Water Violet

Moods	Remedies
RESPONSIBILITY	
capable and thrives on	Vervain
copes unflustered with	Oak
feels overwhelmed by	Elm
despondency due to	Elm, Gentian
lost confidence due to	Elm, Larch
carries it with quiet dignified pride	Water Violet
RESTLESSNESS	
through mental torture/worries	Agrimony, White Chestnut
through indecision	Scleranthus
through impatience	Impatiens
through over-enthusiasm	Vervain
through apprehensive anxiety/ fears	Aspen, Mimulus, Red Chestnut
see also Relaxation	
RESTRAINT	
self-inflicted	Rock Water
RETICENCE	
due to indecision	Scleranthus, Cerato
due to doubt	Cerato, Gentian
due to fear/apprehension	Mimulus, Aspen
due to lack of confidence	Larch, Cerato
due to suspicion	Holly
RETIREMENT	
adjustment to/feels unsettled by	Walnut
finds it hard to "switch off" from active work	Vervain
causing recoil due to unaccustomed inactivity	Vervain, Willow, Clematis, Honeysuckle
causing uncertainty about future/ feels lost	Wild Oat

Moods	Remedies
RETROSPECTION	Honeysuckle, Pine, Gorse, Willow
REVENGE	Holly
REVOLT	
at uncleanliness	Crab Apple
at injustice unfairness	Vervain, Willow
at restrictions/slowness	Impatiens, Vervain, Vine
RIDICULE	
affected by	Mimulus, Centuary, Cerato, Scleranthus, Larch
despondency due to	Gentian
protection from influence of	Walnut
spitefully inflicting	Holly
arrogantly inflicting	Beech, Vine
RIGHT	
arrogantly believes one is always	Vine
believes one's principles are	Vervain, Beech, Rock Water
uncertain that one is	Cerato
RIGHTEOUS	Rock Water, Beech, Vervain
RIGIDITY, mental	Rock Water, Beech, Vine, Vervain
ROCK-SOLID	
and dependable	Oak
and convincingly determined	Vine
ROMANTIC	Clematis
RULE	
desire to	Vine

Moods	Remedies
RULED	
through lack of inner strength	Centaury, Agrimony
due to susceptibility to influence	Cerato, Walnut
rebels against attempts to be	Vine, Vervain, Beech
RUNS AWAY FROM	
responsibility	Elm
problems	Agrimony, Clematis
RUSHED	
sense of being	Impatiens
hyperactivity	Vervain, Impatiens
RUT	
sense of being in	Wild Rose, Clematis, Gorse
RUTHLESSNESS	Vine
SACRIFICE	
self	Rock Water, Pine, Crab Apple, Red Chestnut
self, as martyr	Rock Water, Chicory
SADNESS	Star of Bethlehem, Pine, Sweet Chestnut, Mustard, Willow
SADISTIC	
spiteful/hateful	Holly
and vindictive, with desire to control	Vine
SAFETY	
fear for others	Red Chestnut
fear for one's own	Mimulus, Rescue Remedy
SANCTIMONIOUS	Rock Water, Beech, Vervain, Vine

Moods	Remedies
SANITY	
fear for one's own	Cherry Plum
SARCASTIC	Holly, Willow, Vine, Beech, Chicory
SARDONIC	Willow, Holly, Beech, Vine
SATISFACTION	
lack of, with ambitions	Wild Oat
lack of, with life	Wild Rose, Hornbeam, Gorse, Sweet Chestnut
lack of, with self	Rock Water, Cerato, Crab Apple
SCARED	
generally	Rock Rose, Mimulus, Aspen
for others	Red Chestnut
without knowing why	Aspen
for sanity	Cherry Plum
SCATHING	Holly, Beech
SCATTER-BRAINED	Clematis, Scleranthus, Cherry Plum
SCEPTICAL	Beech, Vine, Gorse, Holly
SCRUFFINESS	
cannot tolerate	Rock Water, Crab Apple
prefers	Wild Rose, Hornbeam, Gorse

Moods	Remedies

SECRETIVE
  out of suspicion for others' motives — Holly
  for power/self importance — Vine
  enjoys being/clings selfishly to secrets/uses as way of manipulating attention — Chicory
  due to desire for privacy — Water Violet
  due to fear — Mimulus, Aspen, Rock Rose
  due to denial — Agrimony
  due to indecision — Scleranthus
  due to shame — Crab Apple, Pine
  with torturous thoughts — White Chestnut, Agrimony

SECURITY (emotional)
  seeks — Cerato, Mimulus, Heather, Chicory

SEDATE
  due to listlessness — Wild Rose, Hornbeam
  due to drowsiness — Clematis, Olive, Hornbeam
  composed/clean living/private person — Water Violet

SELF-ABSORPTION — Heather, Willow, Chicory, Rock Water, Beech, Crab Apple

SELF-ABUSE — Crab Apple

SELF-BLAME — Pine

SELF-CENTERED — Chicory, Heather, Willow

Moods	Remedies
SELF-CONFIDENCE	
lack of	Larch
lack of, through fear	Mimulus
lack of, momentarily, when under pressure	Elm
lack of, through self distrust	Cerato
lack of, through indecision	Scleranthus
lack of, through feeling of hopelessness	Gorse
SELF-CONSCIOUSNESS	Mimulus, Larch, Cherry Plum
SELF-CONTROL	
possesses, by nature	Water Violet, Oak
lack of	Cherry Plum, Holly
may lose, when seriously provoked	Vervain
SELF-DENIAL	
inclined to, by nature	Centaury, Rock Water, Red Chestnut, Pine
in a selfish manner—"don't worry about me"	Chicory
SELF-DETERMINATION	Vervain, Oak, Rock Water, Vine
SELF-DISLIKE	Crab Apple
SELF-DISTRUST	Cerato
SELF-ESTEEM	
lack of	Larch, Cerato, Pine, Crab Apple, Elm
SELF-IMPORTANT	Chicory, Heather, Vine
SELF-INDULGENT	Chicory, Heather
then feels disgusted	Crab Apple
then feels guilty	Pine

Moods	Remedies
SELF-INTEREST	Chicory, Heather, Rock Water, Beech, Willow
SELF-MARTYRDOM	Centaury, Rock Water, Chicory, Willow
SELF-OPINIONATED	Vine, Vervain, Beech, Chicory
SELF-PITY	Willow, Chicory
SELF-RELIANT	Impatiens, Vine, Water Violet, Oak, Vervain
SELF-REPROACH	Pine
SELF-RESPECT	
lack of	Pine, Crab Apple, Cerato
SELF-RIGHTEOUS	Rock Water, Beech, Vervain
SELF-SACRIFICIAL	
by nature	Rock Water
to gain sympathy	Chicory, Willow
SELF-SUFFICIENT	Water Violet, Oak, Vine
SENSITIVITY	
to noise	Clematis, Mimulus, Water Violet, Impatiens
to controversy/conflict/strife	Agrimony, Mimulus, Centaury
sensitive by nature	Walnut, Centaury, Agrimony, Clematis
to criticism	Willow, Chicory, Vervain
see also Cries easily, Fearfulness and Weepiness	
SENTIMENTAL	Honeysuckle, Walnut, Chicory, Red Chestnut, Centaury, Pine

MOODS	REMEDIES
SERENITY	Water Violet
SERVICE	
enjoys giving	Oak, Centaury, Chicory, Red Chestnut, Agrimony
begrudges giving	Willow
SERVILE	Centaury, Agrimony, Pine
SET-BACKS	
discouraged by	Gentian
perseveres in site of	Oak
gives in to	Gorse
frightened by	Mimulus
SEVERE	Vine, Rock Water
SEX	
dislike of	Crab Apple
afraid of	Mimulus, Larch
feels interfered by	Water Violet
over-excited about	Vervain, Impatiens
dominant	Vine
disinterested in	Clematis, Olive, Hornbeam, Wild Rose
SHAME	Crab Apple, Pine
SHATTERED	
by news	Star of Bethlehem, Rescue Remedy
by exhaustion	Olive
by over-work	Vervain, Oak, Centaury
by stress	Vervain, Elm, Agrimony
in crisis situation	Rescue Remedy
SHOCK	Star of Bethlehem, Rescue Remedy

Moods	Remedies

SHOW-OFF
 knows everything—big "I am" Vine
 due to insecurity Agrimony
 due to excitement/enthusiasm Vervain
 to attract attention Chicory, Heather

SHRUG
 with resignation/apathy Wild Rose
 with disinterest Clematis, Hornbeam, Olive
 with despondency Gentian, Gorse
 with self-pity Willow
 with indignation Chicory

SHYNESS Mimulus

SICKNESS
 generally Crab Apple
 through travel Scleranthus
 see also Illness and Ailments

SILENCE
 enjoys Water Violet, Clematis

SIN
 believes one has committed Pine

SINCERE Vervain, Oak, Water Violet, Red Chestnut, Centaury

SKITTISH Impatiens, Scleranthus, Mimulus, Aspen

SLEEP
 easily Clematis
 unrefreshingly Hornbeam, Wild Rose
 desires, due to exhaustion Olive

Moods	Remedies
SLEEPLESSNESS	
through worry/mental arguments/ tormented thoughts	White Chestnut
through tension	Vervain, Rock Water
through over-exhaustion	Olive
through grief	Star of Bethlehem, Honey-suckle, Rescue Remedy
through restlessness	Vervain, Agrimony, Impatiens
through anxiety	Aspen, Agrimony
through fear	Mimulus, Rock Rose
SLOW	
in learning/correcting past mistakes	Chestnut Bud
because of lack of interest	Clematis
because of indecision	Scleranthus
to get started	Hornbeam
SLOWNESS	
irritated by	Impatiens
SMILE	
covers feelings	Agrimony
finds it hard to (depressed)	Mustard, Willow, Gorse, Sweet Chestnut
SMOTHER	
with love	Chicory
SMUG	Vine, Chicory, Holly, Rock Water, Beech
SNOOTY	Vine, Rock Water, Water Violet, Beech
SNOBBISHNESS	Rock Water, Beech, Vine, Heather, Chicory

Moods	Remedies
SOCIABLE	Agrimony, Vervain, Chicory, Heather
SOLACE	
needs after bad news/shock	Star of Bethlehem
needs after disappointment	Gentian
desire for quietude	Water Violet
wants to be left alone to brood	Willow
SOLITARY	
by choice, preference for privacy	Water Violet
by choice, to work at own pace	Impatiens
strong aversion to being	Heather
by choice, for escapism	Clematis
SORROWFUL	
due to grief/loss	Star of Bethlehem
utterly forlorn/dejected	Sweet Chestnut
due to self-pity	Willow, Chicory
for unknown reason	Mustard
remembering past/good old days	Honeysuckle
easily affected by sentiment	Honeysuckle, Walnut, Red Chestnut, Chicory
SORRY	Pine
SPACED OUT	Clematis
SPELL-BOUND	Clematis, Centaury
SPIRITLESS	
due to depression	Mustard, Gorse, Sweet Chestnut
due to self-pity	Willow
de to apathy	Wild Rose
due to disinterest	Clematis, Honeysuckle
due to deep sadness	Star of Bethlehem, Sweet Chestnut

Moods	Remedies
SPIRITLESS (continued)	
due to lost direction	Wild Oat, Walnut
due to subservience	Centaury
due to fear	Mimulus, Larch
SPIRITUALITY	
to regain sense of	Walnut, Clematis, Willow, Holly, Wild Oat
SPITEFULNESS	Holly, Chicory
SPOOKED	Star of Bethlehem, Aspen, Rock Rose, Rescue Remedy
SQUEAMISHNESS	Mimulus, Crab Apple
STAGE-FRIGHT	
panic due to	Rock Rose, Cherry Plum, Rescue Remedy
worry prior to	White Chestnut, Aspen, Mimulus
due to lack of confidence	Larch
hides behind exuberance	Agrimony
STAGNATION	
due to listlessness	Wild Rose
due to disinterest	Honeysuckle, Gorse, Mustard, Willow
due to despondency	Gentian
due to inability to learn from experience	Chestnut Bud
help to move on	Walnut (*in addition to remedy for cause*)
STAMINA	
possesses	Oak, Vervain, Vine, Heather
lack of	Centaury, Gorse, Gentian, Olive, Hornbeam, Clematis, Wild Rose

Moods	Remedies
STAND-OFFISH	
due to private nature (not rudely)	Water Violet
due to suspicion	Holly
due to fear	Mimulus
STARCHY	Rock Water
STARTLED	Star of Bethlehem, Rescue Remedy
STEADFAST	Oak, Vervain, Vine, Water Violet, Chicory
STIGMA	
shame due to	Crab Apple
frustrated/angry about injustice of	Vervain
STOICISM	Water Violet
STRAIN	Impatiens, Rock Water, Vervain
STRANGE SENSATION	
unexplained apprehension	Aspen
unexplained depression	Mustard
as though on a knife edge	Aspen, Impatiens, Vervain
STRANGERS	
frightened of	Mimulus
suspicious of	Holly
searches out	Heather
STRENGTH	
of character	Vine, Vervain, Oak, Water Violet
self-disciplined	Rock Water, Water Violet
in matters of principle	Vervain
in illness/maintains against adversity	Oak

MOODS	REMEDIES

STRICT
with others

Beech, Chicory, Vervain,
Vine

with self
Rock Water

STRIVE   Oak, Vervain

STRUGGLES
on in spite of adversity   Oak
to make point understood   Vervain
to please others   Centaury
to please self   Rock Water, Pine, Crab
Apple

STUBBORNNESS
generally, by nature   Vervain, Vine, Chicory, Beech
about self-discipline   Rock Water
due to genuine courage   Oak

STUNNED   Star of Bethlehem, Clematis

STUPIDITY
intolerant of   Beech, Vine, Impatiens

SUBMISSIVE   Centaury

SUBSERVIENT   Centaury

SUCCESS
fear of   Larch
pessimistic about   Gentian, Larch, Gorse

SUDDEN
terror/panic   Rock Rose, Rescue Remedy
alarm   Star of Bethlehem
depression/dark cloud descending   Mustard
confrontation, causing fear   Mimulus, Rescue Remedy

MOODS	REMEDIES
SUFFERANCE	
willingly, as martyr	Rock Water, Chicory
endures without complaint	Oak, Centaury, Agrimony
works under, complaining	Willow
SUFFOCATION, emotional	
by possessive love	Chicory
SUICIDE	
irrational desire to commit	Cherry Plum
considers, to escape from fear	Aspen, Agrimony, Rock Rose, Mimulus
fear of committing	Cherry Plum
rationally considers, to escape boredom	Clematis
rationally considers, to escape deep depression	Sweet Chestnut
rationally considers, to join loved one	Clematis, Honeysuckle
rationally considers, for self-reproach	Pine
considered due to being over-burdened by responsibility or pressures	Elm, Larch, Centaury

NB: *White Chestnut in addition to the above is recommended.*

SULKINESS	Willow, Chicory
SULLEN	Willow, Gorse
SUPERCILIOUS	Water Violet, Vine, Beech, Rock Water
SUPERFICIAL	Agrimony
SUPERIORITY COMPLEX	Water Violet, Vine, Beech, Rock Water

Moods	Remedies
SUPERNATURAL	
defined fear of	Mimulus, Rock Rose
undefined fear of	Aspen
uncontrolled fear of	Cherry Plum, Rock Rose
feels strong but unwanted influence of	Walnut
seeks companionship with	Clematis
SUPERSTITIOUS	
generally	Rock Water, Mimulus, Rock Rose
influenced by superstition	Walnut
SUPPRESSED EMOTION	
due to shock	Star of Bethlehem
hidden behind cheerfulness	Agrimony
SURE OF THEMSELVES	Vine, Water Violet, Oak, Rock Water
SUSPICION	Holly
SYMPATHY	
wish for	Chicory, Heather, Willow
lack of, for others	Beech, Vine, Holly
SYMPTOMS	
obsessed with detail of	Crab Apple, White Chestnut
obsessed with consequences of	Heather, Mimulus, White Chestnut
unspoken fear of	Agrimony, Mimulus, Aspen, White Chestnut
TACTLESSNESS	Vine, Chicory, Impatiens, Beech, Vervain

Moods	Remedies

TALKATIVE

generally — Heather, Chicory, Cerato, Vervain, Agrimony

about self — Heather

for attention — Heather, Chicory

for reassurance/guidance — Cerato

about the past — Honeysuckle

with explanations, opinions — Vervain

nervously, about fears — Rock Rose, Mimulus, Cherry Plum

nervously, as means of masking troubles — Agrimony

impatiently — Impatiens

TALKS QUICKLY

by nature — Impatiens, Heather

because of fear/anxiety — Agrimony, Mimulus, Impatiens

due to over-enthusiasm — Vervain

TANTRUMS — Cherry Plum, Holly, Impatiens, Vervain

to ease transition in childhood — Walnut

TEARFULNESS

easily prone to, out of self pity — Chicory, Willow

through instability — Scleranthus

through despair — Sweet Chestnut

through utter exhaustion — Olive

due to sensitivity — Centaury, Mimulus, Red Chestnut, Walnut

easily moved, due to sensitivity to influence — Walnut

through sentimentality — Honeysuckle, Walnut

hidden/cries alone — Water Violet, Agrimony

see also Cries easily, Sensitivity, and Weepiness

MOODS	REMEDIES
TEDIUM	
life/work etc., seems full of	Clematis, Hornbeam, Wild Rose
irritated by	Impatiens, Vervain, Vine, Beech
TEMPER	
violent, uncontrolled	Cherry Plum
quick, fiery	Impatiens, Vervain, Vine, Holly
unstable	Scleranthus, Cherry Plum
controlled, but frustrated annoyance due to restriction or incapacity	Oak
TEMPTATION	
influenced by	Cerato, Walnut, Centaury
influenced by, due to greed	Chicory
TENSION	
suffers by nature	Beech, Impatiens, Rock Water, Vervain, Vine
due to shock	Star of Bethlehem
through fear	Mimulus, Aspen, Rock Rose, Cherry Plum
through fear for others	Red Chestnut
through concerned fretfulness over others	Chicory, Red Chestnut
TENTATIVE	Mimulus, Larch, Cerato, Scleranthus
TERROR	Rock Rose
TERSE	Impatiens, Vine
TETCHY	Impatiens, Beech, Willow
THANKS	
expects, desires	Chicory

MOODS	REMEDIES

THEATRICAL
to hide feelings/make light of   Agrimony
    situation
self-indulgent/attention seeking   Chicory, Heather, Willow
over-enthusiastic/uncontrollably   Vervain, Cherry Plum
due to jealousy/envy of others'   Holly
    success
due to panic (*see also Stage*   Rescue Remedy
    Fright)

THICK-SKINNED   Vine

THOUGHTS
persistent worrying   White Chestnut
of future   Clematis
of past   Honeysuckle
of revenge   Holly, Willow
unrealistic/irrational dread   Cherry Plum, Aspen
miserable   Willow, Gorse
frustrated   Agrimony, Walnut, Vervain

THOUGHTFUL
over (lost in thought/dreamy)   Clematis

THWARTED
frustrated   Vervain, Impatiens, Beech,
    Walnut
feels hurt when   Chicory

TIME
careless with/no sense of   Clematis, Wild Rose
impatient with   Impatiens
over-concerned with   Impatiens, Vervain, Rock
    Water, Beech

TIMIDITY   Mimulus, Centaury, Larch

MOODS	REMEDIES

TIRED
  generally — Olive, Hornbeam
  sleepy drowsy/escapist — Clematis
  with life — Sweet Chestnut
NB: Important to acknowledge and treat cause

TIRESOME
  due to negative outlook — Willow
  due to nagging — Chicory
  due to talkativeness — Heather
  due to apathetic lack of interest — Wild Rose
  of others if not listening, taking — Vervain, Vine, Impatiens,
    no notice, not obeying, being   Beech
    too slow or stupid

TIRELESS — Oak, Vervain, Rock Water, Vine

TOLERANCE
  lack of — Beech, Chicory, Vine, Vervain, Impatiens

TOMORROW
  looking forward to — Clematis
  afraid of — Mimulus, Aspen
  worried about — White Chestnut
  cannot wait to arrive — Impatiens

TONGUED-TIED
  through shyness/lack of confidence/self-consciousness — Mimulus, Larch
  through impatience/trying to talk too quickly — Impatiens, Vervain

Moods	Remedies
TORMENTED	
by hidden worries	Agrimony
by persistent thoughts	White Chestnut
by fears	Aspen, Rock Rose, Mimulus, Red Chestnut
by anguish	Sweet Chestnut
by thoughts of jealousy/envy	Holly
by fear of losing control	Cherry Plum
TOTALITARIAN	Vine
TOUGH	Vine, Vervain, Oak, Chicory
TOXICITY	
feeling of contamination by	Crab Apple
TRANQUILLITY	
enjoys/needs, by nature	Water Violet, Clematis, Wild Rose, Mimulus, Centaury
seeks, due to sensitivity	Walnut
seeks, due to troubled thoughts	White Chestnut, Agrimony, Scleranthus
seeks, due to fear of others and forced situations	Mimulus, Larch
TRANSFIXED	
in deep thought/bemused	Clematis
after shock	Star of Bethlehem, Rescue Remedy
TRANSITION	Walnut
TRAUMA	Star of Bethlehem, Rescue Remedy
TRAVEL-SICK	Rescue Remedy, Scleranthus

MOODS	REMEDIES
TREMBLE	
for no reason	Aspen
with fear	Mimulus, Aspen, Rock Rose
with effects of shock	Star of Bethlehem
TRENCHANT	Vervain, Impatiens, Vine
TRIP (hallucinatory)	
frightened by	Rock Rose, Aspen, Mimulus, Rescue Remedy
disturbed by	Honeysuckle, Walnut
shocked by	Star of Bethlehem
bemused by	Clematis
flashbacks after	Honeysuckle, Walnut
TRIVIALITIES	
obsessed with	Crab Apple, Impatiens, Beech
TRUST	
lack of, in others	Holly
lack of, in self	Cerato
TRUTH	
seeking	Wild Oat, Vervain
TRUTHFULNESS	
concerned for	Vervain
TURBULENT THOUGHTS	Agrimony, White Chestnut
TURMOIL, mental	Agrimony, White Chestnut, Scleranthus
TYRANNICAL	Vine
UBIQUITOUS	Vervain
UGLY	
believes one is	Crab Apple

Moods	Remedies
ULTERIOR MOTIVE	
to control	Vine, Chicory
to possess	Chicory
for vengeance	Holly
for sympathy	Willow, Chicory
UMBRAGE	Chicory, Willow
UNASSUMING	Mimulus, Centaury, Clematis, Wild Rose, Larch
UNAWARE	Clematis, Wild Rose
UNCERTAINTY	Scleranthus
Through self-distrust	Cerato
through lack of faith	Gentian, Cerato
through lack of hope	Gorse
through lack of strength	Hornbeam
of ambitions	Wild Oat
due to doubt of ability to cope with responsibility	Elm
due to lack of confidence	Larch
UNCLEANLINESS, feeling of	Crab Apple
UNCOMPLAINING	
through resignation	Wild Rose
through disinterest	Clematis
courage	Oak
pretended courage	Agrimony
UNCONVENTIONAL	
due to creative, futuristic tendencies	Wild Oat, Clematis
to create own standards	Vine
UNDERSTANDING	
lack of	Beech, Vine, Impatiens
at times, when against own standards	Chicory, Vervain

MOODS	REMEDIES
UNEASINESS	
vague sense of apprehensive	Aspen
in company of others	Mimulus, Larch
UNGROUNDED	Clematis
UNHAPPY	
with present	Clematis
for no reason	Mustard
due to bitterness/self pity	Willow
due to jealousy	Holly
due to longing for past	Honeysuckle
due to guilt	Pine
due to exhaustion	Olive
with self	Scleranthus, Cerato, Crab Apple, Pine, Rock Water, Larch, Centaury
UNKNOWN CAUSES	
of depression	Mustard
of fear	Aspen
UNNERVED	Mimulus, Walnut, Aspen
UNOBSERVANT	Clematis
UNPREDICTABLE	Scleranthus, Cherry Plum, Clematis, Impatiens
UNREASONABLE	
with others	Vine, Beech, Impatiens
with self	Rock Water
UNRELIABLE	
because of uncertainty	Scleranthus
because of self-distrust	Cerato
because easily influenced	Centaury, Cerato, Agrimony, Mimulus

Moods	Remedies
UNREST	
due to tension	Vervain
due to mental arguments/worry	White Chestnut, Agrimony
due to fear	Mimulus, Aspen, Rock Rose, Red Chestnut
due to agitation/irritability	Impatiens, Beech, Vervain
due to inner torment	Agrimony
due to vexatious thoughts	Holly
due to fear of losing control	Cherry Plum
due to violent imaginings	Cherry Plum
due to indecision	Scleranthus
UPTIGHT	Vervain, Impatiens, Rock Water, Beech, Vine
UNSETTLED	
Generally	Walnut
by worry	White Chestnut
by indecision	Scleranthus
by guilt	Pine
USED	
feels used by others	Centaury, Chicory, Willow
USELESSNESS, sense of	Cerato, Pine, Gentian, Gorse, Larch, Elm
VACANT EXPRESSION	Clematis, Wild Rose
VAGUE	Clematis, Cerato, Scleranthus, Wild Rose
VAIN	Beech, Rock Water, Chicory, Heather
VARIABLE MOOD	Scleranthus, Mustard, Cerato, Walnut
VEHEMENCE	Vervain, Impatiens, Cherry Plum, Holly, Beech

MOODS	REMEDIES
VEIL	
cast for privacy	Water Violet
cast as means of hiding feelings	Agrimony
VENGEFUL	
through hate/spite/revenge	Holly
fear of being	Cherry Plum
VENOMOUS	Holly
VERBOSE	Heather, Vervain
VERVE	Vervain
VEXED	Impatiens, Beech, Holly, Vervain
VICTIMISED	Centaury, Mimulus
feels, and resents being	Willow, Chicory
irrationally fears one is being	Cherry Plum, Holly
VINDICTIVE	Holly, Chicory
VIOLENT	
rage	Cherry Plum
fear of being	Cherry Plum
satisfaction from being/desire to be	Holly
to show superiority	Vine
VITALITY	
sapped by others	Agrimony, Centaury, Clematis, Mimulus, Larch
saps others	Cerato, Chicory, Heather
drained of/exhausted	Hornbeam, Olive
VIVACIOUS	Agrimony, Impatiens, Vervain

Moods	Remedies
VOCAL	
at any opportunity, about self	Heather
opinionated about beliefs	Vervain
self-opinionated	Vine
VOCATION	
uncertain of	Wild Oat, Cerato
VOLATILE	Scleranthus, Mustard, Holly
VOMIT	
fear of	Mimulus, Crab Apple
disgust of	Crab Apple
VOO-DOO	
vague apprehension about	Aspen
terrified of	Rock Rose
influenced by	Walnut
desire to rid oneself of	Crab Apple, Walnut
VULNERABILITY	Centaury, Scleranthus, Walnut, Mimulus, Larch, Chestnut Bud, Cerato
WAIL	
for attention	Chicory, Willow
with utter despair	Sweet Chestnut
with feelings of remorse	Pine
WALLOW	
in self pity	Willow, Chicory
see also Martyr	
WANDER AIMLESSLY in life	
by nature, due to apathy	Wild Rose
due to unfulfilled ambitions	Wild Oat
due to lack of interest	Clematis
due to disappointing set-backs/ hopelessness	Gentian, Gorse

MOODS	REMEDIES

WARY
    through suspicion — Holly
    through fear — Mimulus
    through reasonable caution — Oak, Vervain, Water Violet

WEAKNESS
    doubt of mental strength — Hornbeam
    weak-willed — Centaury
    exhausted — Olive

WEAK-WILLED
    by nature — Centaury
    through shyness/timidity — Mimulus
    through lack of confidence — Larch

WEARINESS
    through exhaustion — Olive
    through listlessness — Hornbeam, Wild Rose
    from over-work, but keeps going — Centaury, Oak, Rock Water

WEEP
    easily — Chicory, Heather, Willow
    unable to, due to numbness (e.g. following serious news) — Star of Bethlehem, Agrimony, Walnut
    unable to, due to self-denial — Rock Water

WEEPINESS
    out of self-pity — Chicory, Willow, Heather
    with utter despair — Sweet Chestnut
    with remorse — Pine
    with grief — Star of Bethlehem, Sweet Chestnut, Honeysuckle
    with sentimentality — Walnut, Honeysuckle
    with relief — Agrimony
    weeps alone/hides tears from others — Water Violet, Agrimony
    see also Cries easily, Sensitivity, and Tearfulness

Moods	Remedies
WEIRD FEELINGS	Cherry Plum, Clematis
WICKEDNESS	Holly
Fear of acting in	Cherry Plum
WILD	Cherry Plum
WILL	
strong	Beech, Chicory, Rock Water, Vervain, Vine
weak	Centaury
weak on occasions	Agrimony, Walnut
strength of character	Oak
WISDOM	
lacks	Chestnut Bud, Cerato
WISE	Water Violet, Oak, Vervain
WISHFUL	Clematis, Honeysuckle
with regrets	Pine, Honeysuckle
WISTFUL	Clematis, Honeysuckle
WITHDRAWAL	
from drugs/alcohol/tobacco etc.,	
—helps adjustment during	Walnut
—helps learn from experience	Chestnut Bud
—helps to cleanse mind/body	Crab Apple
—helps strengthen will to resist	Hornbeam, Centaury

NB: *Important to treat underlying cause of addiction*
see also Addiction

WITHDRAWN	
from society through shyness	Mimulus
due to desire for privacy	Water Violet
by hiding from/ignoring existence of problems	Agrimony
sulkily, due to self-pity	Willow

MOODS	REMEDIES

WITHDRAWN (continued)
  due to distrust/suspicion — Holly
  as means of escape — Clematis
  due to pre-occupation with worry — White Chestnut
  having lost all hope — Gorse, Sweet Chestnut

WONDERS
  about future event — Clematis

WORKAHOLIC
  by nature — Vervain, Oak, Rock Water
  servile — Centaury

WORRY
  generally — White Chestnut
  over other people's troubles — Red Chestnut
  over own troubles — Heather
  hidden — Agrimony
  fussily — Chicory, Vervain
  with mental arguments — White Chestnut
  welfare of others — Vervain, Red Chestnut, Chicory

WORTHINESS
  low sense of — Pine, Crab Apple, Larch

WRONG-DOING
  blames self/feels guilty, for others' mistakes — Pine
  blames others — Willow, Beech, Vine, Chicory
  condemns self for — Crab Apple, Pine, Rock Water

X-RAY
  feels contaminated by — Crab Apple
  feels need for protection from — Walnut, Crab Apple
  fear of — Mimulus, Rock Rose
  persistent worry over — White Chestnut, Crab Apple

MOODS	REMEDIES

"YES"
"yes person", cannot say "no"   Centaury
agrees against own natural   Mimulus, Larch, Centaury,
    instincts   Cerato, Walnut

YEARNING
for better times   Clematis
for past   Honeysuckle
for youth   Honeysuckle
for love   Chicory
for loved ones   Red Chestnut, Chicory
covetously/for selfish reasons   Chicory, Holly

YOGA
to calm mind of worry, prior to   White Chestnut, Agrimony,
    Walnut
to relax mind of tension, prior to   Vervain, Rock Water, Beech,
    Holly

YOUTHFULNESS
obsessive preservation of   Rock Water, Crab Apple,
    Heather, Honeysuckle
obsessed with, due to fear of   Rock Rose, Mimulus,
    ageing   Agrimony
obsessed with physical state/   Rock Water
    pushes self to over-exercise/stay
    fit

ZEALOUS   Vervain

ZEST
lack of, through exhaustion   Olive
lack of, through listlessness   Hornbeam, Wild Rose
lack of, through disinterest   Clematis, Wild Rose, Mustard
lack of, through depression   Mustard, Sweet Chestnut,
    Gorse, Gentian, Willow
lack of, through worry   White Chestnut

MOODS	REMEDIES

ZOMBIE-LIKE
    as in dream state — Clematis
    apathetic/blank — Wild Rose
    through depression — Mustard, Gorse, Sweet Chestnut

    through exhaustion — Olive
    mentally stunned, through shock — Star of Bethlehem, Rescue Remedy

Index

Boldface indicates flower remedy.
Underlining indicates negative aspect or lack of attitude/mood.

Boldface indicates flower remedy.
Underlining indicates negative aspect or lack of attitude/mood.

Boldface indicates flower remedy.
Underlining indicates negative aspect or lack of attitude/mood.

Boldface indicates flower remedy.
Underlining indicates negative aspect or lack of attitude/mood.

Boldface indicates flower remedy.
Underlining indicates negative aspect or lack of attitude/mood.

Boldface indicates flower remedy.
Underlining indicates negative aspect or lack of attitude/mood.

Boldface indicates flower remedy.
Underlining indicates negative aspect or lack of attitude/mood.

The World Economy

Growth or Stagnation?

Edited by

DALE W. JORGENSON
KYOJI FUKAO
MARCEL P. TIMMER

CAMBRIDGE
UNIVERSITY PRESS

CAMBRIDGE
UNIVERSITY PRESS

University Printing House, Cambridge CB2 8BS, United Kingdom

One Liberty Plaza, 20th Floor, New York, NY 10006, USA

477 Williamstown Road, Port Melbourne, VIC 3207, Australia

4843/24, 2nd Floor, Ansari Road, Daryaganj, Delhi – 110002, India

79 Anson Road, #06–04/06, Singapore 079906

Cambridge University Press is part of the University of Cambridge.

It furthers the University's mission by disseminating knowledge in the pursuit of
education, learning and research at the highest international levels of excellence.

www.cambridge.org
Information on this title: www.cambridge.org/9781107143340
DOI: 10.1017/9781316534502

© Cambridge University Press 2016

First published 2016

A catalogue record for this publication is available from the British Library

Library of Congress Cataloging-in-Publication Data
Names: Jorgenson, Dale W. (Dale Weldeau), 1933– editor. | Fukao, Kyōji, editor. |
    Timmer, Marcel, editor.
Title: The world economy : growth or stagnation? / edited by Dale W. Jorgenson,
    Kyoji Fukao, Marcel P. Timmer.
Other titles: World economy (Cambridge University Press)
Description: Cambridge, United Kingdom : Cambridge University Press, 2016.
Identifiers: LCCN 2015049531 | ISBN 9781107143340 (hardback)
Subjects: LCSH: Economic history – 21st century. | Economic
    development. | Economics.
Classification: LCC HC59.3 .W674 2016 | DDC 330.9–dc23
LC record available at http://lccn.loc.gov/2015049531

ISBN 978-1-316-50774-2 Paperback

Contents

Figures

Tables

Contributors

Suresh Aggarwal, Professor, Department of Business Economics, University of Delhi, South Campus, India

Claudio Aravena, Researcher, Economic Commission for Latin American and the Caribbean (ECLAC) in Santiago, Chile; Professor, USACH University, Santiago, Chile

Hyunbae Chun, Professor, Department of Economics, Sogang University

Carol Corrado, Senior Advisor and Research Director, Economics Program, The Conference Board; Senior Policy Scholar, Georgetown University Center for Business and Public Policy

Deb Kusum Das, Associate Professor, Ramjas College, University of Delhi

Juan Fernández de Guevara, Lecturer of Economic Analysis, Universitat de València; Associate Researcher, Ivie

Gaaitzen J. de Vries, Assistant Professor, Groningen Growth and Development Centre, Faculty of Economics and Business, University of Groningen

Abdul A. Erumban, Senior Economist, The Conference Board; Assistant Professor, Faculty of Economics and Business, University of Groningen

Barbara M. Fraumeni, Special-term Professor, Central University for Finance and Economics; Professor of Public Policy Emerita, University of Southern Maine; National Bureau of Economic Research

Kyoji Fukao, Professor, Institute of Economic Research, Hitotsubashi University; Faculty Fellow, Research Institute of Economy, Trade and Industry

Jonathan Haskel, Professor of Economics, Imperial College Business School; Research Fellow, Centre for Economic Policy Research; Research Fellow, Institute for the Study of Labor, Bonn

Mun S. Ho, Visiting Scholar, Resources for the Future

André Hofman, Director, Professor, UAB and USACH in Santiago, Chile

Kenta Ikeuchi, Research Fellow, First Theory-Oriented Research Group, National Institute of Science and Technology Policy

Robert Inklaar, Associate Professor of Economics, University of Groningen

Cecilia Jona-Lasinio, Senior Researcher, Econometric Studies and Economic Forecasting Division, Italian Statistical Institute; Associate Professor, LUISS Guido Carli University

Dale W. Jorgenson, Samuel W. Morris University Professor, Harvard University

YoungGak Kim, Associate Professor, School of Economics, Senshu University

HyeogUg Kwon, Professor, Nihon University College of Economics; Faculty Fellow, Research Institute of Economy, Trade and Industry

Gang Liu, Senior Adviser, Statistics Norway

Bart Los, Associate Professor, Groningen Growth and Development Centre, Faculty of Economics and Business, University of Groningen

Tatsuji Makino, Researcher, Institute of Economic Research, Hitotsubashi University

Matilde Mas, Professor of Economic Analysis, Universitat de València; International Projects Director, Ivie

Tsutomu Miyagawa, Professor, Faculty of Economics, Gakushuin University; Faculty Fellow, Research Institute of Economy, Trade and Industry

Koji Nomura, Associate Professor, KEO, Keio University; PDB Project Manager, Asian Productivity Organization

Mary O'Mahony, Professor of Applied Economics, King's College, London; Visiting Fellow, National Institute of Economic and Social Research

Hak Kil Pyo, Professor of Economics Emeritus, Seoul National University

Steven Rosenthal, Supervisory Economist, Office of Productivity and Technology, Bureau of Labor Statistics, US Department of Labor

Matthew Russell, Senior Economist, Federal Aviation Administration, US Department of Transportation

Jon D. Samuels, Research Economist, Industry Economic Accounts, Bureau of Economic Analysis, US Department of Commerce

Sreerupa Sengupta, PhD Student, Centre for Economic Studies and Planning, Jawaharlal Nehru University, India

Erich H. Strassner, Division Chief, Industry Applications Division at Bureau of Economic Analysis, US Department of Commerce

Miho Takizawa, Associate Professor, Faculty of Economics, Toyo University

Marcel P. Timmer, Professor and Director, Groningen Growth and Development Centre, University of Groningen

Konomi Tonogi, Assistant Professor, Faculty of Economics, Kanagawa University

Lisa Usher, Retired Chief, Division of Industry Productivity Studies, Office of Productivity and Technology, Bureau of Labor Statistics, US Department of Labor

Bart van Ark, Professor in Economic Development, Technological Change and Growth, University of Groningen; Chief Economist, The Conference Board

Ilya B. Voskoboynikov, Senior Research Fellow, Laboratory for Research in Inflation and Growth, National Research University Higher School of Economics

Harry X. Wu, Professor of Economics, Institute of Economic Research, Hitotsubashi University

1 | *The new world order*

DALE W. JORGENSON

This book shows that the world economy is undergoing a massive transformation. The transformation is generating a new world order that is scarcely recognizable from the perspective of the twentieth century. According to the authoritative estimates of Angus Maddison, the United States was the world's largest economy throughout the century (Maddison 2001). In the twenty-first century the balance of the world economy has shifted from the industrialized economies, led by Europe, Japan, and the US, to the emerging economies of Asia, especially China and India.

Throughout the last century a fundamental transformation of the world economy seemed a remote and unlikely prospect. However, the World Bank's 2005 International Comparison Program (ICP2005) showed that China had overtaken Japan in terms of purchasing power more than a decade earlier (World Bank 2008). By 2012 India overtook Japan and has continued to grow much more rapidly. The obvious question posed by these findings is, will China surpass the US? The World Bank's 2011 International Comparison Program (ICP2011) has revealed that in 2014 China's output achieved parity with the US in terms of purchasing power (World Bank 2014).

We find that Germany will continue to lead Russia and Russia will lead Brazil, resulting in the new economic order: China, the US, India, Japan, Germany, Russia, and Brazil. Jim O'Neill, then a Goldman-Sachs economist, originated the terminology "BRIC economies" in 2001 and published a book documenting the progress of Brazil, Russia, India, and China in 2010 (O'Neill 2011). However, we find that Brazil and Russia, as well as Germany, Japan, and the US, will grow more slowly than the world economy.

Our second major finding is that world economic growth has accelerated during the twenty-first century and that rapid growth will continue. We answer the question, "Growth or Stagnation?" in favor of growth. While Chinese economic growth has already slowed, Indian

1

growth will increase. Both giant economies will continue to grow faster than the world economy. As China and India increase in relative importance during the twenty-first century, the accelerated growth of the world economy will be maintained.

At first impression the choice of growth over stagnation may seem implausible. Recovery of the industrialized economies from the Great Recession of 2007–2009 has been slow and fitful. The US has emerged with low unemployment but reduced prospects for growth.[1] Japan has continued to languish in the torpor of the Lost Decades, awaiting the implementation of a new growth strategy.[2] The fiscal and financial burden of public debt in Europe and the inability of international institutions to cope with a financial crisis like Greece pose potential threats to the restoration of growth.[3]

The most significant impact of the Great Recession on the emerging economies of Asia was the collapse of global trade in late 2008 and early 2009. This was quickly reversed and the leading Asian economies have continued to grow more rapidly than the world economy. The challenges facing these economies are different but equally daunting. Can China cope with inflationary pressures following the vast expansion of lending in response to the economic crisis?[4] Will India succeed in dealing with fiscal consolidation and a higher inflation rate?[5]

In this book we set aside short-term threats to the world economy to focus on the potential for long-term growth. We show that the fundamentals of the world economy remain strong. Trends established in the watershed reforms of China and India more than two decades ago have produced the dramatic changes of economic leadership in the twenty-first century. We can now recognize the emergence of Asia from the underdevelopment that persisted until the middle of the twentieth century as the great economic achievement of our time.

The third major finding of this book is that replication rather than innovation is the major source of growth of the world economy. *Replication* takes place by adding identical production units with no change in technology. Labor input grows through the addition of new members of the labor force with the same education and experience.

[1] For more detail, see Chapter 2 of this volume.
[2] For discussion of Japan's Lost Decades, see Chapter 3 of this volume.
[3] See Chapter 4 of this volume for more discussion.
[4] On China see Chapter 6 of this volume.
[5] On India see Chapter 7 of this volume.

Capital input expands by providing new production units with the same collection of plant and equipment. Output expands in proportion with no change in productivity. By contrast, successful *innovation* involves the creation of new products and new processes, so that productivity increases. Of course, replication and innovation are simply analytical categories for characterizing aspects of the complex processes that generate long-term growth and structural change.

The Asian model of economic growth relies on globalization and investment in human and non-human capital, rather than innovation. This new growth paradigm places a high premium on skillful management by public and private authorities. The performance of the leading economies in developing and implementing the new growth paradigm, first Japan, then the Asian Tigers – Hong Kong, Singapore, South Korea, and Taiwan – and now China and India, has changed the course of economic development in Asia and around the world.

The growing significance of the Asian model is overturning long-established theories of economic growth and accelerating overdue revisions of the official economic statistics. The ruling theories of growth of the twentieth century put enormous weight on innovation, which has played a relatively modest role. This view neglected investments in human and non-human capital, which are much more important for advanced economies as well as emerging economies. The new economic order will help to establish an empirically based view of the balance between replication and innovation.

In Section 1 of this chapter we analyze the recent performance of the world economy. We rely on gross domestic product (GDP) as a measure of output and define productivity as output per unit of both capital and labor inputs. We present output, inputs, and productivity for the world economy and major groups like the G7 and the G20. We also consider the individual economies of the G7 – Canada, France, Germany, Italy, Japan, the United Kingdom and the United States – and the major emerging economies – Brazil, China, India, Indonesia, Mexico, Russia, and South Korea. We refer to these emerging economies as the extended BRICs.

In analyzing the growth of the world economy we utilize the Total Economy Database (TED), originally developed by Maddison at the University of Groningen and maintained by the Conference Board. This was greatly enhanced by the Conference Board in collaboration with Jorgenson and Khuong Vu.[6] The new database includes inputs and productivity as well as outputs. The Conference Board presents annual reports on the key findings. Jorgenson and Vu have published a series of international comparisons of outputs, inputs, and productivity (Jorgenson and Vu 2013).

The Conference Board's TED incorporates the advances in growth accounting summarized in Paul Schreyer's *OECD Productivity Manual* (2001) and his *OECD Capital Manual* (2009). International standards for measuring labor and capital inputs were established in Chapters 19 and 20 of the United Nations 2008 System of National Accounts (SNA), (United Nations 2009). This is the most recent revision of the United Nations' SNA, developed in collaboration with four other international organizations – the Organisation for Economic Cooperation and Development (OECD), the International Monetary Fund (IMF), the World Bank, and Eurostat.

Data on capital and labor inputs are essential in analyzing economic growth, preparing projections of future growth, and choosing among alternative economic policies. The framework for growth projections is provided by the neo-classical theory of growth (Jorgenson et al. 2008). Growth in labor inputs is based on demographic projections from the United Nations and by national statistical agencies like the US Bureau of the Census (US Census Bureau 2013). Productivity growth provides a link to innovation. Growth in capital inputs is determined endogenously by saving and investment behavior.

In Section 2 we present projections of economic growth for the major groupings of economies, including the G7, the G20, and the extended BRICs. We provide historical data for the period 1990–2012 and projections for 2012–2022. The future growth of the world economy will accelerate, relative to the historical period. The advanced economies of the G7, the OECD, and the European Union (EU) will grow more slowly, while the growth rate of the extended BRICs is almost the same. The acceleration in world economic growth is due to the rising importance of the more rapidly growing economies.

Jorgenson and Vu have adapted the methodology of Jorgenson, Ho, and Kevin Stiroh for projecting the growth of labor productivity and GDP (Jorgenson and Vu 2011). The driving forces in the future growth

---

[6] See: Conference Board (2015). Sections 1 and 2 of this chapter incorporate the results of Jorgenson and Vu (forthcoming).

of the world economy are demography and technology. Projections of labor productivity incorporate projections of improvements in capital and labor composition and total factor productivity. For the advanced economies of the G7 we assume that output and capital input will grow at the same rate. The rate of economic growth is determined by the underlying growth in hours worked, improvements in capital and labor composition, and productivity.

The fourth major finding of this book is that the contributions of individual industries are essential for understanding the sources of economic growth. The modest rates of innovation needed to maintain long-run growth are usually concentrated in a relatively small number of sectors. For example, the production of information technology equipment and software has dominated recent innovation in the US. Data on the growth of outputs, inputs, and productivity at the industry level are required for identifying the sources of growth of the US economy.

The concentration of innovation in a narrow range of industries has important implications for changes in the structure of a growing economy. Surprisingly, many of the major emerging economies have discarded the traditional pattern of movement of resources out of agriculture into industry, followed by the growth of the service industries. International comparisons of differences in productivity levels based on purchasing power parities of outputs and inputs at the industry level provide a second focus for industry-level productivity research. These comparisons are essential in assessing changes in comparative advantage and formulating strategies for economic growth.

In Section 3 we present the framework for the measurement of growth of output and productivity at the industry level used in this book. A key feature is that capital input is measured by capital services rather than capital stocks. The prices of capital inputs used in aggregating different types of capital input are rental values rather than asset values. This approach to measuring capital was incorporated into official statistical systems in 2009 by the *OECD Capital Manual* and in Chapter 20 of the *2008 System of National Accounts*. The change from capital stocks to capital services has been critical in measuring the impact of the shift in the composition of capital input toward information technology equipment and software.

The measure of labor input in the TED includes investments in human capital in the form of education. This measure of labor input incorporates differences in hours worked by workers with different levels of educational attainment. Labor quality is the ratio of labor input to hours worked, so that labor input is the product of hours worked and labor quality. Labor quality is essential for capturing the impact of investment in human capital on economic growth.

In Section 4 we outline the contents of this book. We draw on the results of the World KLEMS Initiative, a research consortium covering Europe, Latin America, and Asia, as well as major economies such as Australia, Canada, Russia, and the US. All of these countries have developed industry-level data on outputs and inputs of capital (K), labor (L), energy (E), materials (M), and services (S). Productivity is defined as output per unit of all inputs. The GDP is measured by aggregating over industries. Jorgenson and Schreyer (2013) have shown how to incorporate this industry-level productivity data into the United Nations' *2008 System of National Accounts*.

1.1 Growth of the world economy

To prepare for projections of world economic growth we analyze the sources of economic growth for the G7, the G20, and the world economy. We consider fourteen major economies – the G7 economies, including the US, and seven emerging economies of the G20, including India and China. We have sub-divided the period 1990–2012 in 1995, 2000, and 2005 in order to capture major changes in the growth rate of the world economy.

In Figure 1.1 we divide the contribution of capital services to world economic growth between information technology (IT) and non-information technology (non-IT). Figure 1.2 gives data on the world economy and seven major groups. We allocate the contribution of labor services between hours worked and labor quality, defined as labor input per hour worked. Finally, we present data on total factor productivity (TFP), defined as output per unit of both capital and labor inputs. The period 1995–2000 witnessed a major acceleration in world economic growth. The rate of world growth increased further during 2000–2005. The economic and financial crisis of 2007–2009 in the advanced economies dominated the world economy after 2005. Growth continued at a rapid pace but slowed relative to 2000–2005.

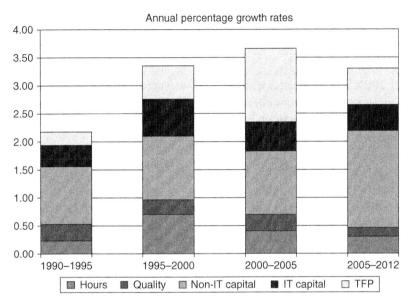

Figure 1.1 Sources of world economic growth, 1995–2012

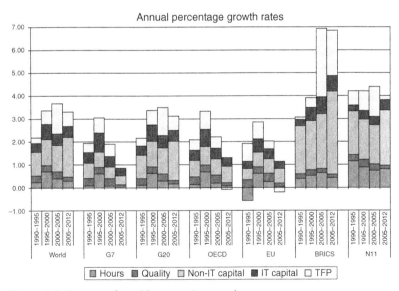

Figure 1.2 Sources of world economic growth

During 2005–2012 total factor productivity growth for the advanced economies of the G7 was negative for Canada, France, Italy, and the UK. This poses a paradox: how could innovation, reflecting changes in technology, be negative? The world-wide financial and economic crisis of 2007–2009 opened a wide gap between actual output and potential output for the G7 economies, determined by supplies of capital and labor inputs and productivity. Negative productivity growth is the difference between the positive effects of advances in technology and the negative effects of the widening output gap.

During the period 1990–2012 US economic growth has been strong, relative to growth of other advanced economies. This is due to capital deepening, increases in capital input per hour worked, especially during the information technology boom of 1995–2000. Growth in total factor productivity revived during the boom and continued at a brisk pace in the "jobless recovery" of 2000–2005. The growth of US GDP has been more rapid than that of any other economy in the G7 with Canada close behind. However, US economic growth collapsed during the period 2005–2012, largely due to the Great Recession.

The advanced economies of the G7 were strongly impacted by the Great Recession of 2007–2009. In Figure 1.3 we analyze the sources of

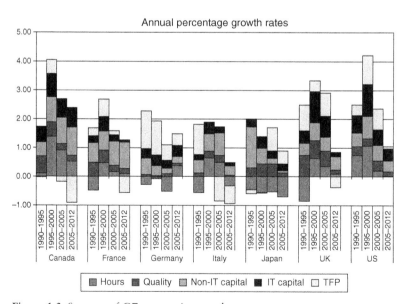

Figure 1.3 Sources of G7 economic growth

economic growth of the G7 during 1990–2012. Germany had the strongest economic performance with positive growth in total factor productivity and hours worked. Japan's productivity growth revived during the period 2000–2005 and this continued during 2005–2012. The revival of productivity growth was largely offset by a declining labor force throughout the period 1990–2012. Italy had the weakest performance during the Great Recession and was unable to maintain positive economic growth.

China sustained double-digit economic growth throughout the decade 2000–2012 with only slight deceleration during the Great Recession, as shown in Figure 1.4. India's growth rate rose steadily during the two decades 1990–2012. For both China and India capital input contributed more to economic growth than the rise in total factor productivity. Russia's economic growth was dominated by the collapse of the former Soviet Union and the gradual recovery of 1995–2005. The decline in growth of non-IT capital input from 1990 to 2005 is an unusual feature of Russian economic growth that was finally reversed after 2005.

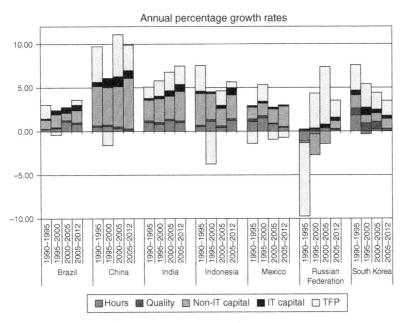

Figure 1.4 Sources of BRICs economic growth

1.2 Projecting the growth of the world economy

We consider three different scenarios for the growth of the world economy – Base Case, Pessimistic, and Optimistic. The contributions of hours worked and labor quality to potential economic growth over the next decade can be projected with little uncertainty, since most of the people entering the labor force are already in the population. Accordingly, we use the same projections in our alternative scenarios. Projections of technology are far more challenging. Our Base Case incorporates the average rate of total productivity growth for 1990–2012. Our Pessimistic Case is based on average productivity growth for the two worst sub-periods, while our Optimistic Case is based on an average for the two best sub-periods. For emerging economies like China and India we also extrapolate recent trends in the capital–output ratio.

We limit our projections to potential economic growth, leaving projections of actual growth to economic forecasters like the IMF (IMF 2015). We have incorporated differences in trends in demography and technology. For example, the growth of the Japanese population and labor force will continue to be negative and France, Germany, Italy, Russia, and South Korea will also experience negative labor force growth. The growth of the Chinese labor force will decline substantially and India's labor force will grow much more rapidly than China's.

We have represented the uncertainty in our projections of the world economy for 2012–2022 in Figures 1.5 and 1.6. The first bar in Figure 1.5 provides historical data. The average growth rate of labor productivity for 1990–2012 was 1.8 percent per year. The remaining bars give Pessimistic, Base Case, and Optimistic projections of labor productivity for the decade 2012–2022. More rapid productivity growth is associated with higher rates of growth of capital deepening, defined as the growth rate of capital per hour worked, as well as more rapid growth in total factor productivity.

Finally, we project the rate of GDP growth as the sum of the growth rate of hours worked from our demographic projections and the growth rate of labor productivity. The first bar in Figure 1.6 gives historical data for 1990–2012. The remaining three bars give Pessimistic, Base Case, and Optimistic projections.

Our Base Case projection of world economic growth for the period 2012–2022 is 3.4 percent per year. This corresponds to labor productivity growth of 2.2 percent per year and growth of hours worked of

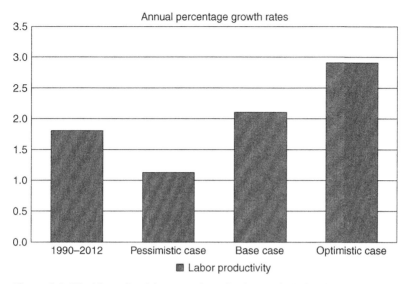

Figure 1.5 World productivity growth projections, 2012–2022

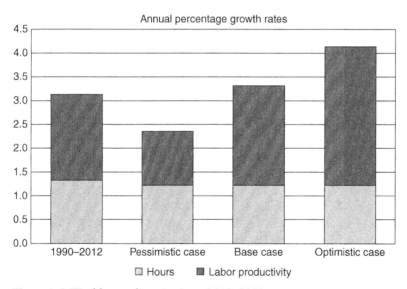

Figure 1.6 World growth projections, 2012–2022

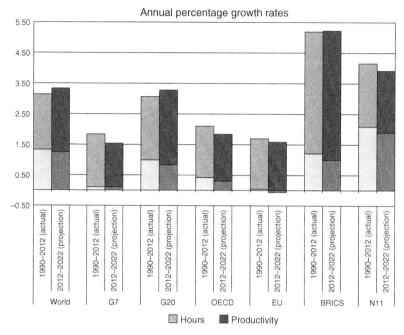

Figure 1.7 Growth projections for the world economy

1.2 percent. The Base Case reflects an acceleration of world economic growth, combining a slowdown in the growth of hours worked and a substantial acceleration in labor productivity growth. The Pessimistic projection of world growth of 2.4 percent per year incorporates a continuation of the marked slowdown in growth of total factor productivity after 2005. The Optimistic projection for world economic growth of 4.1 percent would require full recovery from the Great Recession.

Figure 1.7 gives projections for the world economy and seven major groups. Our projections for the individual economies in the G7 are given in Figure 1.8. The US will outperform the other members of the G7 due to expansion of the labor force and continued growth of labor productivity. Labor productivity growth in Germany, Japan, and the UK will be stronger than in the US, but the rate of decline in the Japanese labor force will reach almost 1 percent per year. The German labor force will also decline, but less rapidly, while the UK labor force will increase only slightly. Italy will continue to lag in economic growth among the G7

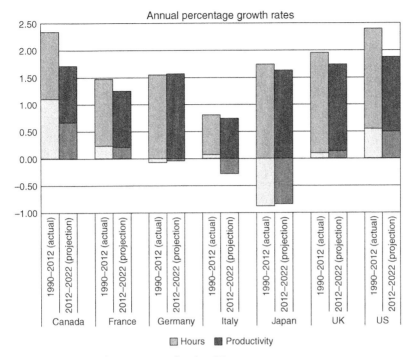

Figure 1.8 Growth projections for the G7 economy

economies. Canada's labor productivity growth will be similar to that of the US, but growth of the Canadian labor force will drop considerably.

As shown in Figure 1.9, the outlook for China and other emerging economies continues to be relatively sanguine. The Chinese growth rate will decline relative to the blistering pace of the past decades, still exceeding 6.5 percent per year. Growth in India and Mexico will accelerate, while Brazil, Indonesia, Russia, and South Korea will grow more slowly. How can the world economy grow more rapidly? This is due to the rising importance of the more rapidly growing economies, especially China and India.

Figure 1.10 summarizes the new economic order that will emerge by 2022. China has already displaced the US as the world's leading economy, but China and the US, taken together, will increase in relative importance. India's growth rate will rise to 6.5 percent, so that India will also increase in relative importance. Japan will grow more slowly than the world economy, but will retain its place as the world's fourth

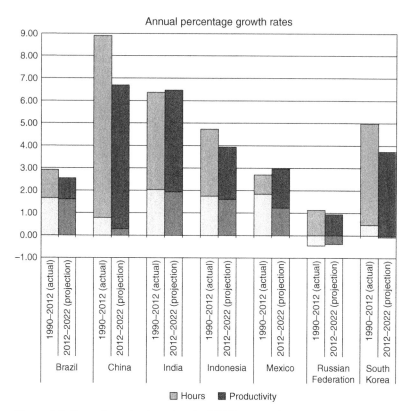

Figure 1.9 Growth projections for the BRIC economies

largest economy. Russian economic growth will continue to languish and Russia will fail to overtake Germany. Brazil will grow more rapidly than Russia, but Brazilian GDP will remain below that of Russia.

We have quantified the substantial uncertainty in our projections for the world economy, but it is important to emphasize that there are uncertainties for each of the leading economies as well. For example, China's accumulation of foreign exchange to preserve the dollar exchange rate of the Chinese currency is reaching a plateau. The real exchange rate of the yuan is rising due to a modest revaluation and a very substantial increase in production costs in China. All of this is helping to moderate the imbalances that have attracted international attention. China is moving toward slower but more sustainable growth.

Japan, the US, and other industrialized economies will remain far in advance of China and India in terms of per capita GDP. But the

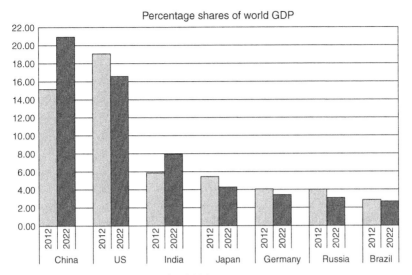

Figure 1.10 New economic order 2022

experience of Japan and the four Asian Tigers tells us that advanced economies can emerge outside Europe and North America. It is only a matter of time until these developments spread to China, India, and the other major countries of developing Asia, but this will be measured in decades rather than years. The world economy has the opportunity to accelerate the process of adjustment to the new economic order. This process will require rethinking international business, including the international trading system and international investment.

1.3 Productivity at the industry level

Jorgenson, Frank M. Gollop, and Barbara M. Fraumeni (1987) constructed the first dataset containing annual time series data on output, inputs of capital, labor, and intermediate goods, and productivity for all the industries in the US economy. This study provided the model for the methods of economy-wide and industry-level productivity measurement presented in Paul Schreyer's (2001) OECD *Productivity Manual*. The hallmarks of the new framework for productivity measurement are constant quality indexes of capital and labor services at the industry level and indexes of energy, materials, and services inputs from a time series of input–output tables. This book presents recent research on the growth of output, inputs, and productivity at the industry level for nearly forty countries.

Jorgenson *et al.* (2005) updated the US dataset and revised it to include investment in IT. This required new data on the production of hardware, telecommunications equipment, and software, as well as inputs of IT capital services. The new dataset has demonstrated the importance of industry-level productivity growth, especially in the information technology-producing industries, in understanding the US investment boom of the 1990s. Jorgenson *et al.* (2005) have provided the framework for the new datasets. International comparisons for Europe, Japan, and the US are presented by Jorgenson in *The Economics of Productivity* (2009).

The key idea underlying a *constant quality index of labor input* is to capture the heterogeneity of different types of labor inputs. Hours worked for each type of labor input are combined into a constant quality index of labor input, using labor compensation per hour as weights. Constant quality indexes of labor input for the US at the industry level are discussed in detail by Jorgenson *et al.* (2005, ch. 6, pp. 201–290).

Similarly, a *constant quality index of capital input* deals with the heterogeneity among different types of capital inputs. These capital inputs are combined into a constant quality index, using rental prices of the inputs as weights, rather than the asset prices used in measuring capital stocks. This makes it possible to incorporate differences among asset-specific inflation rates that are particularly important in analyzing the impact of investments in information technology, as well as differences in depreciation rates and tax treatments for different assets. Constant quality indexes of capital input for the US at the industry level are presented by Jorgenson *et al.* (2005, ch. 5, pp. 147–200).

The framework for industry-level productivity measurement summarized by Schreyer (2001) incorporates a time series of input–output tables in current and constant prices. Estimates of intermediate inputs of energy, materials, and services are generated from these tables. Details on the construction of the time series of input–output tables and estimates of intermediate inputs are presented by Jorgenson *et al.* (2005, ch. 4, pp. 87–146).

Jorgenson and J. Steven Landefeld (2006) have developed a new architecture for the US national income and product accounts (NIPAs) that includes prices and quantities of capital services for all productive assets in the US economy. This was published in a volume on the new architecture by Jorgenson, Landefeld, and William D. Nordhaus (Jorgenson and Landefeld 2006). The incorporation of the price and quantity of capital services into the United Nations' *2008 System of National Accounts* (United Nations 2009) was approved by the United Nations Statistical Commission at its February–March 2007 meeting.

Schreyer, then head of national accounts at the OECD, prepared a second edition of an OECD Manual, *Measuring Capital*, published in 2009. This provided detailed recommendations on methods for the construction of prices and quantities of capital services at industry and economy-wide levels. Jorgenson and Schreyer (2013) showed how to incorporate industry-level measures of outputs, inputs, and productivity into the 2008 SNA.

In Chapter 20 of SNA 2008 (United Nations 2009, p. 415), estimates of capital services are described as follows: "By associating these estimates with the standard breakdown of value added, the contribution of labor and capital to production can be portrayed in a form ready for use in the analysis of productivity in a way entirely consistent with the accounts of the System." The measures of capital and labor inputs in the prototype system of US national accounts of Jorgenson and Landefeld (2006) are consistent with the *OECD Productivity Manual*, the 2008 SNA, and the OECD Manual, *Measuring Capital*.

The first half of this book is devoted to individual country experiences in compiling and analyzing industry-level statistics on productivity and growth. Chapters 2, 3, and 4 are devoted to long-term trends in growth of the United States, Japan and Europe. Chapters 5, 6, 7, and 8 analyze trends in growth and productivity in the major emerging economies of Latin America, China, India, and Russia. We provide a more detailed summary of country experiences in Section 1.4.

The second half of this book is devoted to new and emerging sources of economic growth. Chapters 9 and 10 consider investments in software, research and development, and other intangible assets. Software and research and development have been recommended for inclusion in official systems of national accounts by the United Nations' *2008 System of National Accounts*. Chapter 11 presents industry-level data for the US on outputs, inputs, and productivity, including the investments in intellectual property recently added to the US national accounts. Chapter 12 presents international comparisons of investments in human capital, quantitatively the most important form of investment in intangible capital.

An important application of industry-level data is the comparison of industry outputs, inputs, and productivity across economies. Chapter 13 presents detailed comparisons of industries in Japan and the US. These comparisons are based on a single accounting framework for the two economies and their interactions with the world economy through trade. A more extensive accounting framework for forty economies, the World Input–Output Database (WIOD), is discussed in Chapters 14 and 15. We consider the individual contributions to Part II in more detail in Section 1.4.

1.4 World KLEMS Initiative

This book draws on the research of participants in the World KLEMS Initiative. This was established by Jorgenson, Timmer and van Ark at the First World KLEMS Conference, held at Harvard University in August 2010.[7] The purpose of the World KLEMS Initiative is to generate industry-level datasets, consisting of outputs and inputs of capital (K) and labor (L), together with inputs of energy (E), materials (M), and services (S). Productivity for each industry is defined as output per unit of all inputs. These datasets implement the new framework we have outlined in Section 1.3 for analyzing the sources of economic growth at the industry and aggregate levels for countries around the world.

The starting point for the World KLEMS Initiative is the internationally uniform methodology established by the OECD, beginning with Schreyer's OECD Manual, *Measuring Productivity*, published in 2001. This incorporated the advice and recommendations of the Statistical Working Party of the OECD Industry Committee, chaired by Edwin Dean, former Associate Commissioner for Productivity of the US Bureau of Labor Statistics.[8] The participants in the World KLEMS Initiative have adapted this methodology to industry data generated in a wide variety of settings.

The international standards for productivity measurement were greatly extended through their adoption by the United Nations

---

[7] For the program and participants see: www.worldklems.net/conference1.htm.

[8] Schreyer (2001), Annex 7, Acknowledgements, p. 146.

Statistical Commission in 2007. This was the outcome of deliberations by the Canberra II Expert Group convened by the Commission.[9]
The revised version of the OECD Manual *Measuring Capital* by
Schreyer was an important product of these deliberations. The final
development was the incorporation of the international standards
into Chapters 19 and 20 of the United Nations' *2008 System of
National Accounts*.

In the US a critical role in establishing standards for KLEMS-type
research was played by the Advisory Committee on Measuring
Innovation in the 21st Century Economy to the US Secretary of
Commerce. The Advisory Committee was chaired by Carl Schramm,
Chief Executive Office (CEO) of the Kauffman Foundation in Kansas
City.[10] The recommendations of the Advisory Committee were imple-
mented by the Bureau of Economic Analysis of the Department of
Commerce and the Bureau of Labor Statistics of the Department of
Labor.

Industry-level productivity statistics were incorporated into the
US National Income and Product Accounts in 2014. These statistics
were updated and revised to incorporate intellectual property products
in the benchmark revision of the US accounts in the same year. Official
systems of industry-level production accounts are now part of the
national accounts in Australia, Canada, Denmark, Finland, Italy,
Mexico, The Netherlands, Sweden, and the UK, as well as the US.

In Chapter 2 Jorgenson, Ho, and Samuels present an industry-level
production account for the US for the period 1947–2012. They find
that US economic growth will recover from the Great Recession period
2007–2009 through the resumption of productivity growth and the
recovery of investment in capital input. However, the long-term
growth of the US economy will depend critically on the performance
of the relatively small number of sectors where innovation takes place.

Jorgenson, Ho, and Samuels have confirmed Jorgenson's (2009)
result that the great preponderance of US economic growth since
1947 involves the replication of existing technologies through investment in equipment and software and the expansion of the labor force.
Contrary to the well-known views of Robert M. Solow (1957) and

---

[9] See: http://unstats.un.org/unsd/methods/citygroup/non-financial-assets.htm.

[10] Advisory Committee on Measuring Innovation in the 21st Century
Economy to the US Secretary of Commerce (2008).

Simon Kuznets (1971), innovation accounts for a relatively modest 20 percent. An important policy implication is that policies to maintain the growth of employment and investment will be much more effective in reestablishing consistent growth of the US economy than policies to enhance rates of innovation.

Looking into the future, Jorgenson, Ho, and Samuels find that US economic growth will slow substantially from the pace observed during 1990–2012, mainly due to a marked slowdown in labor quality growth. The educational attainment of people emerging from the education system, while high, has been nearly constant for the past several decades. As the last of the baby boomers retire changes in labor quality will slow almost to a standstill.

The Japan Industrial Productivity (JIP) database is compiled in collaboration between the Research Institute for Economy Trade and Industry (RIETI) and Hitotsubashi University.[11] This contains data on outputs, inputs, and productivity for 108 sectors of the Japanese economy. The latest JIP database is for 2014 and covers the period 1970–2011. This uses the 2000 benchmark revision of the Japanese national accounts. The JIP database has been compiled annually since 2006.[12]

In Chapter 3 Kyoji Fukao, Kenta Ikeuchi, HyeogUg Kwon, YoungGak Kim, Tatsuji Makino, and Miho Takizawa, employ the Japan Industrial Productivity Database in analyzing the slowdown in productivity growth in Japan. The initial downturn in productivity growth followed the collapse of the "bubble" in Japanese real estate prices in 1991. This gave way to a prolonged stagnation of the Japanese economy, extending into two Lost Decades.

A brief revival of Japanese productivity growth after 2000 ended with the sharp decline in Japanese exports in 2008–2009. This followed rapid appreciation of the Japanese yen, relative to the US dollar, after the adoption of a monetary policy of quantitative easing by the Federal Reserve, the US central bank. When the Bank of Japan failed to respond, Japan experienced a much more severe downturn in productivity growth and a larger decline in output than the US in the aftermath of the Great Recession of 2007–2009.

---

[11] See: www.rieti.go.jp/en/database/d05.html.

[12] See: www.rieti.go.jp/en/database/JIP2014/index.html#05.

Fukao and his co-authors first consider the causes of the Japanese stagnation from the demand side. Before the collapse of the real estate bubble in 1991 Japan had a high rate of personal saving that was largely absorbed by the high rate of private investment. Rates of investment began to decline as a consequence of the slowing growth of the labor force, which dropped to zero in the 1990s and became negative in the 2000s. In addition, the rate of growth of productivity, defined as output per unit of input, collapsed during the 1990s. Both the rate of growth of the labor force and the rate of productivity growth had begun much earlier and gradually undermined private incentives to invest.

Modes of adjustment for Japan's excess saving could have included depreciation of the yen and running a large current account surplus. Fukao and his co-authors identify the substantial obstacles to implementation of these policy measures. These obstacles revolve around "trade frictions" with Japan's leading trade partners, especially the US. Declines in the rate of growth of the labor force, the rate of productivity growth, and the rate of investment resulted in a sharp decline in Japan's rate of economic growth. Fukao and his co-authors conclude by comparing Japan's Lost Decades with the growth of other leading industrialized economies during the period since 1990.

The EU KLEMS project was initiated in 2003 and completed in 2008. This project applied international standards for productivity measurement to data for twenty-five of the (then) twenty-seven countries of the EU. These standards were incorporated into a manual written by Timmer and his colleagues at the University of Groningen and the National Institute of Social and Economic Research in London (Timmer *et al.* 2007). This manual was employed by the twenty-one participating research organizations and statistical agencies that contributed to the project.

The EU KLEMS datasets are essential for analyzing the slowdown in European economic growth that preceded the current financial and fiscal crisis.[13] The datasets and results were presented at the final EU KLEMS Conference in Groningen, The Netherlands, in June 2008.[14] Timmer *et al.* (2010) analyze the sources of economic growth in Europe

---

[13] Updated data for the EU countries are posted on the EU KLEMS website: www.euklems.net/eukNACE2.shtml.

[14] For the program and participants see: www.euklems.net/conference.html.

at the industry level in their book, *Economic Growth in Europe: A Comparative Industry Perspective.*

The EU KLEMS project also included datasets for Australia, Canada, Japan, Korea, and the US. Matilde Mas and Robert Stehrer (2012) present international comparisons within Europe and between Europe and the advanced economies in Asia and North America in their book, *Industrial Productivity in Europe: Growth and Crisis.* As European policy-makers focus on removing barriers to the revival of economic growth, international differences in the sources of growth have become central in understanding the impacts of changes in economic policy.

The EU KLEMS project identified failure to develop a knowledge economy as the most important source of the slowdown in European economic growth. A knowledge economy requires investments in human capital, information technology, and intellectual property. An important policy implication is that extension of the single market to the services industries, particularly those intensive in the use of information technology, is essential to remove barriers to the knowledge economy.

The analysis of European economic growth presented in reports on the EU KLEMS project has been updated and extended by van Ark and O'Mahony in Chapter 4 of this book. The economic and financial crisis that began in the US in 2007 was transmitted to Europe during 2008 and 2009. This produced a "double dip" recession and stagnant growth for an extended period of time. Slower growth can be attributed to deficient growth of demand or "secular stagnation," as well as to supply side factors – slower growth of productivity and employment across Europe. The overall differences between growth rates in Europe and the US have increased substantially since 2008.

Chapter 4 includes a detailed examination of factors affecting the knowledge economy, the focus of the earlier EU KLEMS study. The production of information technology hardware and software has continued to languish in Europe, relative to the US. Europe has largely caught up to the US in the deployment of information technology, but productivity growth in IT-using sectors has increased much less in Europe. On a positive note, the employment of high-skilled labor has continued to grow as a proportion of total employment in Europe. Investment in intangible assets, including research and development and human capital, has held up better than other forms of investment. The failure to create a single market in services remains a significant barrier to the revival of investment, but presents important opportunities for stimulating economic growth in the future.

The Second World KLEMS Conference was held at Harvard University on August 2012.[15] The conference included reports on progress in the development of industry-level datasets.[16] Regional organizations in Asia and Latin America have joined the EU in supporting research on industry-level datasets. Due to the growing recognition of the importance of these datasets, an effort was underway to extend the new framework to emerging and transition economies, such as Brazil, China, India, Mexico, and Russia.

The Latin American regional organization of the World KLEMS Initiative, LA KLEMS, was established in December 2009 at a conference at the Economic Commission for Latin America and the Caribbean (ECLAC), in Santiago, Chile.[17] This organization is co-ordinated by ECLAC and includes research organizations and statistical agencies in leading Latin American countries.[18] Mario Cimoli, Andre Hofman, and Nanno Mulder (2010) have summarized the results of the initial phases of the LA KLEMS project.

The current state of the LA KLEMS project is summarized by André Hofman, Matilde Mas, Claudio Arevena, and Juan Fernández de Guevara in Chapter 5 of this book. This chapter presents industry-level data on outputs, inputs, and productivity for Argentina, Brazil, Chile, Columbia, and Mexico. The most remarkable finding is that none of these Latin American economies has experienced growth in output per unit of input over the period 1990–2010. All of the growth of the five Latin American economies during these two decades is due to replication of existing technologies and none to innovation.

A detailed report on Mexico KLEMS was published in 2013 by the National Institute of Statistics and Geography (INEGI).[19] This was presented at an international seminar at the Instituto Technologico

---

[15] For the program and participants see: www.worldklems.net/conference2.htm.

[16] The conference program and presentations are available at: www.worldklems .net/conference2.htm.

[17] For the program and participants see: www.cepal.org/de/agenda/8/38158/ Agenda.pdf.

[18] Additional information about LA-KLEMS is available on the project website: www.cepal.org/cgi-bin/getprod.asp?xml=/la-klems/noticias/paginas/4/40294 /P40294.xml&xsl=/la-klems/tpl-i/p18f-st.xsl&base=/la-klems/tpl-i/top-bot tom.xsl.

[19] Instituto Nacional de Estadistica y Geografia (2013).

Autonoma de Mexico (ITAM) in Mexico City on October 2013.[20]
Mexico KLEMS includes a complete industry-level productivity database for 1990–2011 that is integrated with the Mexican national
accounts and will be updated annually. This report confirms that
productivity has not grown in Mexico since 1990. Periods of positive
economic growth have been offset by the negative impacts of the
Mexican sovereign debt crisis of 1995, the US dot-com crash in 2000,
and the US financial and economic crisis of 2007–2009.

Asia KLEMS, the Asian regional organization of the World KLEMS
Initiative, was founded in December 2010. The first Asia KLEMS
Conference was held at the Asian Development Bank Institute in
Tokyo in July 2011.[21] Asia KLEMS includes the Japan Industrial
Productivity Database,[22] the Korea Industrial Productivity Database,[23]
and the China Industrial Productivity Database.[24] Industry-level
databases have been constructed for Taiwan and work is underway
to develop a database for Malaysia. These databases were discussed at
the Second Asia KLEMS Conference, held at the Bank of Korea in
Seoul in August 2013.[25]

The Third World KLEMS Conference was held in Tokyo in May
2014.[26] This conference discussed industry-level datasets for almost
forty countries, including participating countries in the three regional
organizations that make up the World KLEMS Initiative – EU KLEMS in
Europe, LA KLEMS in Latin America, and Asia KLEMS in Asia.
The Third World KLEMS Conference included reports on new industry-
level data sets for China, India, and Russia. In addition, the conference
considered research on linking datasets for forty countries through the
WIOD.[27]

---

[20] For the program and participants see: www.inegi.org.mx/eventos/2013/contabi
lidad_mexico/presentacion.aspx.

[21] For the program and participants see: http://asiaklems.net/conferences/confer
ences.asp. Asia KLEMS was preceded by International Comparison of
Productivity among Asian Countries (ICPAC). The results were reported by
Jorgenson *et al.* (2007).

[22] See: www.rieti.go.jp/en/database/JIP2014/index.html. Data are available for
108 industries covering the period 1970–2011.

[23] See: www.kpc.or.kr/eng/state/2011_kip.asp?c_menu=5&s_menu=5_4.

[24] See: www.rieti.go.jp/en/database/CIP2011/index.html.

[25] For the program and participants see: http://asiaklems.net/conferences/confer
ences.asp.

[26] See: http://scholar.harvard.edu/jorgenson/world-klems.

[27] See: www.wiod.org/new_site/home.htm.

The China Industrial Productivity (CIP) database was released in April 2015 by the Research Institute for Economy, Trade, and Industry (RIETI). This is a key component of RIETI's East Asian Industrial Productivity Project,[28] along with the Japan Industrial Productivity Database employed by Fukao and his co-authors in Chapter 3 of this book. The CIP database has been constructed by Harry Wu of Hitotsubashi University and is reported in Chapter 6. This database covers the period 1980–2010, almost the entire period since the epoch-making reforms in China, initiated under Deng Xiaoping in 1978. During this period the Chinese economy has grown at the remarkable annual rate of 9.2 percent per year, lifting more than 600 million people out of extreme poverty and elevating China to the status of the world's leading economy in terms of purchasing power.

Wu finds that 7.1 percentage points of China's GDP growth of 9.2 percent per annum during this period can be attributed to increases in labor productivity and 2 percentage points to growth in hours worked. Further decomposition of labor productivity growth shows that 5.6 percentage points are explained by capital deepening, 0.4 by percentage points by labor quality improvements, and 1.2 percentage points by TFP growth. Thus, capital deepening was the main engine of economic growth, but TFP growth also made a non-negligible contribution.

Comparing industries, Wu shows that industries subject to less government intervention, such as agriculture and semi-finished and finished goods manufacturing industries, have enjoyed faster productivity growth than those subject to more government intervention, such as the energy industries. He also finds large positive factor reallocation effects, particularly with regard to labor. These findings suggest that there is room for stimulating productivity growth by disentangling government from business and allowing market forces to improve the cost structures of regulated and government-owned industries.

The India KLEMS database was released in July 2014 by the Reserve Bank of India.[29] This database covers twenty-six industries for the period 1980–2011. The India KLEMS database is presented by Deb Kusum Das, Abdul A. Erumban, Suresh Aggarwal, and Sreerupa Sengupta in Chapter 7. Beginning in the 1980s, liberalization of the

[28] See: www.rieti.go.jp/en/projects/program/pg-05/008.html.
[29] See: www.rbi.org.in/scripts/PublicationReportDetails.aspx?UrlPage=&ID=785.

Indian economy has resulted in a gradual and sustained acceleration in economic growth. The stagnant share of manufacturing in the GDP and the rapid growth in the share of services is a surprising feature. Given the shrinking proportion of agriculture in the GDP and the size of the Indian agricultural labor force, another surprise is that growth of capital input has been the most important source of growth in manufacturing and services, as well as more recently in agriculture.

Russia KLEMS was released in July 2013 by the Laboratory for Research in Inflation and Growth at the Higher School of Economics in Moscow.[30] This is discussed in detail by Marcel P. Timmer and Ilya B. Voskoboynikov in Chapter 8 of this book. Russia's recovery from the sharp economic downturn that followed the dissolution of the Soviet Union has been very impressive. Surprisingly, increases in productivity growth widely anticipated by observers inside and outside Russia have characterized only the service industries, which were underdeveloped under central planning. Mining industries have attracted large investments without corresponding gains in efficiency. The recent collapse in world oil prices poses an important challenge for the future growth.

An important theme of the Third World KLEMS Conference was the extension of the measurement of capital inputs to include intangible assets, such as human capital and intellectual property, as well as tangible assets – plant, equipment, and inventories. Carol Corrado, Jonathan Haskel, and Cecilia Jona-Lasinio present results for European economies in Chapter 9. Hyunbae Chun, Miyagawa Tsutomu, Hak Kil Pyo, and Tonogi Konomi compare these investments in Japan and Korea in Chapter 10. Finally, Gang Liu and Barbara M. Fraumeni consider investment in human capital in Chapter 12.

In Chapter 9 Corrado, Haskel, and Jona-Lasinio combine a new dataset on investment in intangible assets with data on growth and productivity from the EU KLEMS study for fourteen European countries over the period 1995–2010. Intangible investments include research and development, as well as non-research and development expenditures. Investment in research and development is taken from Eurostat, while non-research and development includes expenditures included in the national accounts, such as software, minerals exploration, and some forms of intellectual property such as artistic originals.

---

[30] See: www.hse.ru/en/org/hse/expert/lipier/ruklems.

The authors make imputations for own-account investments in intangibles not included in the national accounts.

Expanded growth accounts for Europe, including investments in intangibles, are dominated by the service industries. For these industries non-research and development investment greatly predominates. Growth of output per unit of input in the service industries is very low in Europe and negative in Italy and Spain. In the manufacturing industries both tangible and intangible forms of investment are important sources of growth with research and development playing an important role. Chapter 9 concludes with an investigation of the relationship between intangibles and information technology. These capital inputs are complementary, since the impact of intangibles in economic growth is greater for industries and countries with greater information technology intensities.

Using the Japan Industrial Productivity (JIP) database, the Korea Industrial Productivity (KIP) database, and other primary statistics for Japan and Korea, Chun, Miyagawa, Pyo, and Tonogi estimate and compare intangible investment in Japan and Korea at the industry-level for the period 1980–2010. Employing growth accounting with intangibles, they find that the contribution of intangible investment to economic growth in Japan decreased significantly after 1995.

The contribution of intangibles to productivity growth in Japan after 1995 is lower than in Korea and also in Europe and the US. There is no positive cross-sectional correlation between information technology assets and intangibles. Unlike other industrialized economies, Japan has been unable to fully exploit the synergies of investments in information technology and intangibles. An important policy implication is that policies to promote intangible investment in Japan should be accompanied by policies to stimulate investment in information technology.

The 2014 benchmark revision of the US industry accounts is presented in Chapter 11 by Steven Rosenthal, Matthew Russell, Jon D. Samuels, Erich H. Strassner, and Lisa Usher, "BEA/BLS industry-level production account for the US: integrated sources of growth, intangible capital, and the US recovery." The chapter covers the period 1997–2012 for the sixty-five industrial sectors used in the US National Income and Product Accounts (NIPAs). The capital and labor inputs are provided by the Bureau of Labor Statistics, while output and intermediate inputs are generated by Bureau of

Economic Analysis.[31] This industry-level production account is included in the NIPAs and is updated annually.

Quantitatively, investment in human capital is the most important form of investment in intangible assets. In Chapter 12 Gang Liu and Barbara Fraumeni review the recent empirical literature on this significant form of investment. They compare four different approaches and present detailed results from Liu's OECD study of sixteen countries plus China and India, based on the lifetime income approach of Jorgenson and Fraumeni (Liu 2014). They also summarize the expanded growth accounts for the US by Fraumeni, Christian, and Samuels, treating investment in human capital as an output of the economy and from human capital as an input (Fraumeni, Christian, and Samuels 2015). The role of total factor productivity as a source of growth of the expanded concept of output is much below the proportionate contribution to the market-based concept of output used in the studies that comprise the rest of this book.

Linked datasets for two or more countries are essential for analyzing the role of international trade and investment in economic growth. In Chapter 13 Dale W. Jorgenson, Koji Nomura, and Jon D. Samuels have compiled linked KLEMS-type databases for thirty-six industries in Japan and the US. The database covers the entire economy in each of the two countries, as well as trade links among the two countries and the rest of the world. The data are presented in current and constant prices, using purchasing power parities (PPPs) for outputs and inputs as well as imports and exports.

Jorgenson, Nomura, and Samuels present a detailed analysis of the relative competitiveness of industries in the two countries over the period 1955–2012. They find that the wide Japan–US productivity gap that existed in 1955 shrank over the following three decades, so that Japan came close to parity with the US in 1991. After the collapse of the "bubble economy" in Japan, the Japan–US productivity gap widened again and in 2012 only a few industries in Japan retained a productivity advantage over their US counterparts.

Jorgenson, Nomura, and Samuels find that industries sheltered from international competition offer the greatest opportunities for improvement in productivity performance. The US could reinvigorate productivity growth in medical care or at least avert further decline. This would relieve much of the budgetary pressure from the rapidly rising

[31] An earlier "prototype" was published by Susan Fleck *et al.* (2014).

cost of health care at every level of the US government. In the case of Japan, large opportunities remain to improve productivity by removing barriers to entry and eliminating regulations that limit price competition in five sheltered industries – real estate, electricity and gas, construction, other services, finance and insurance, and wholesale and retail trade.

The final two chapters of this book, Chapter 14 by Robert Inklaar and Chapter 15 by Marcel P. Timmer, Bart Los, and Gaaitzen J. de Vries, employ the World Input–Output Database (WIOD), a unified accounting framework for thirty industries in forty countries for the period 1995–2011. The WIOD includes a time series of input–output tables containing inputs and outputs of intermediate goods for each country in current and constant prices. The prices of inputs and outputs are expressed in terms of purchasing power parities and separate price indexes are used to deflate trade flows among the forty economies and the rest of the world.[32]

The WIOD is especially valuable in analyzing the development of global value chains in Asia, North America, and Europe. International trade is decomposed by tasks performed at each link of the value chain. Trade in tasks can be compared with trade in commodities, which involves "double-counting" of intermediate goods as products pass through the value chain. The WIOD is augmented by measures of capital and labor inputs. As Inklaar points out, an important limitation is that capital input is identified with capital stocks, rather than capital services. However, labor input includes three types of labor – unskilled, medium-skilled, and high-skilled – so that changes in labor quality can be quantified for all industries and all economies.

In Chapter 14 Inklaar uses the WIOD to study one of the most striking of the recent changes in the world economy. More than a century of divergence in levels of aggregate output per capita and productivity among countries ended in around 2000. Inklaar shows that most of the subsequent convergence has taken place in manufacturing. The relative decline in the share of agriculture in GDP, especially in emerging economies, provides a modest contribution to convergence. A second aim of the chapter is to examine the possible explanations of convergence by testing their impact on productivity growth and proximity to

---

[32] The WIOD is described in detail by Timmer *et al.* (2015). The WIOD is available online at: www.wiod.org/new_site/home.htm.

the productivity frontier. The results are largely negative, creating an agenda for future research.

Using the WIOD in Chapter 15, Timmer, Los, and de Vries have analyzed changes in global value chains, the set of activities needed to generate the value of final goods, from 1995 to 2011. They find increasing international fragmentation in the production of manufactures, indicated by the growing share of foreign value added in production. This has been accompanied by a rapid shift towards higher-skilled activities in advanced economies. Emerging economies are increasing their shares in global value chain incomes with much of the increase driven by rapid growth in China. One of the central findings is that regional value chains are now merging into global value chains involving economies around the world (Timmer *et al.* 2014).

Timmer, Los, and de Vries find that tasks performed in global value chains are increasingly carried out in the service sectors. This intertwining of manufacturing and services implies that trade policy should focus on activities or tasks in global value chains rather than the industrial sectors in which they are carried out. A myopic focus on job creation in manufacturing or countering fears of deindustrialization should be avoided. The WIOD is providing a model for an expanded version at the OECD with support from the WTO.[33]

References

Advisory Committee on Measuring Innovation in the 21st Century Economy to the US Secretary of Commerce. 2008. *Innovation Measurement: Tracking the State of Innovation in the American Economy.* Washington, DC: Economics and Statistics Administration, US Department of Commerce, January. See: www.esa.doc.gov/sites/defaul t/files/innovation_measurement_01-08.pdf.

Christian, Michael S. 2014. "Human Capital Accounting in the United States: Context Measurement, and Application," in Dale W. Jorgenson, J. Steven Landefeld, and Paul Schreyer (eds.), *Measuring Economic Sustainability and Progress.* University of Chicago Press, See: http://papers.nber.org/books/jorg12-1.

Cimoli, Mario, Andre Hofman, and Nanno Mulder. 2010. *Innovation and Economic Development: The Impact of Information and*

[33] See: www.oecd.org/sti/ind/measuringtradeinvalue-addedanoecd-wtojointinitia tive.htm. An overview is provided by OECD (2013).

Communication Technologies in Latin America. Northamption, MA: Edward Elgar.

Conference Board. 2015. *Total Economy Database: Key Findings*. New York: The Conference Board. See: www.conference-board.org/data/economy database.

Fleck, Susan, Matthew Russell, Erich Strassner, and Lisa Usher. 2014. "A Prototype BEA/BLS Industry-level Production Account for the United States," in Dale W. Jorgenson, J. Steven Landefeld, and Paul Schreyer (eds.), *Measuring Economic Sustainability and Progress*. University of Chicago Press, 323–372. See: http://papers.nber.org/books/jorg12-1.

Instituto Nacional de Estadistica y Geografia. 2013. *La Contabilidad de Crecimiento y la Productividad Total in Mexico*. Aguascalientes, MX: Instituto Nacioal de Estadistica y Geografia, October. See: www.inegi .org.mx/eventos/2013/contabilidad_mexico/presentacion.aspx.

International Monetary Fund (IMF). 2015. *World Economic Outlook*. Washington, DC: International Monetary Fund, April. See: www.imf .org/external/pubs/ft/weo/2015/01.

Jorgenson, Dale W. 2009. (ed.) *The Economics of Productivity*. Northampton, MA: Edward Elgar.

Jorgenson, Dale W., Frank M. Gollop, and Barbara M. Fraumenti. 1987. *Productivity and US Economic Growth*. Cambridge, MA: Harvard University Press.

Jorgenson, Dale W., Mun S. Ho, and Kevin J. Stiroh. 2005. *Information Technology and the American Growth Resurgence*. Cambridge, MA: The MIT Press.

Jorgenson, Dale W., Masahiro Kuroda, and Kazuyuki Motohashi. 2007. *Productivity in Asia*. Northampton, MA: Edward Elgar. See: http://sch olar.harvard.edu/jorgenson/publications/productivity-asia.

Jorgenson, Dale W. and J. Steven Landefeld. 2006. "Blueprint for Expanded and Integrated US Accounts: Review, Assessment and Next Steps," in Dale W. Jorgenson, J. Steven Landefeld, and William D. Nordhaus (eds.), *A New Architecture for the US National Accounts*. University of Chicago Press, 13–112.

Jorgenson, Dale W. and Paul Schreyer. 2013. "Industry-level Productivity Measurement and the 2008 System of National Accounts," *Review of Income and Wealth*, 59(2, June): 185–211.

Jorgenson, Dale W. and Khuong Minh Vu. 2011. "The Rise of Asia and the New World Order," *Journal of Policy Modeling*, 33(5, September–October): 698–751. See: http://scholar.harvard.edu/jorgenson/publica tions/rise-developing-asia-and-new-economic-order.

2013. "The Emergence of the New Economic Order: Economic Growth in the G7 and the G20," *Journal of Policy Modeling*, 35(3, May–June):

389–399. See: http://econpapers.repec.org/article/eeejpolmo/v_3a35_
3ay_3a2013_3ai_3a3_3ap_3a389-399.htm.

Forthcoming. "Australia and the Growth of the World Economy,"
Economic Analysis and Policy.

2008. "A Retrospective Look at the US Productivity Growth Resurgence,"
Journal of Economic Perspectives, **22**(1, Winter): 3–24. See: http://scho
lar.harvard.edu/files/jorgenson/files/retrosprctivelookusprodgrowthre
surg_journaleconperspectives.pdf.

Kuznets, Simon. 1971. *Economic Growth of Nations: Total Output and
Production Structure*. Cambridge, MA: Harvard University Press.

Liu, Gang. 2014. "Measuring the Stock of Human Capital for International
and Intertemporal Comparisons," in Dale W. Jorgenson, J. Steven
Landefeld, and Paul Schreyer (eds.), *Measuring Economic Sustainability
and Progress*. University of Chicago Press, 493–544. See: http://papers
.nber.org/books/jorg12-1.

Maddison, Angus. 2001. *The World Economy: A Millennial Perspective*.
Paris: OECD. See: http://theunbrokenwindow.com/Development/MA
DDISON%20The%20World%20Economy-A%20Millennial.pdf.

Mas, Matilde and Robert Stehrer. 2012. (eds.), *Industrial Productivity in
Europe: Growth and Crisis*. Northampton, MA: Edward Elgar.

O'Neill, Jim. 2011. *The Growth Map: Economic Opportunity in the BRICs
and Beyond*. New York: Penguin.

Organization for Economic Co-operation and Development (OECD).
2013. *Interconnected Economies: Benefiting from Global Trade*.
Paris: OECD.

Schreyer, Paul. 2001. *Measuring Productivity*. Paris: OECD. See: www.oecd
.org/std/productivity-stats/2352458.pdf.

2009. *Measuring Capital*, 2nd edn. Paris: OECD. See: www.oecd.org/std/
productivity-stats/43734711.pdf.

Solow, Robert M. 1957. "Technical Change and the Aggregate Production
Function," *Review of Economics and Statistics*, **39**(3, November):
312–320.

Timmer, Marcel P., Erik Dietzenbacher, Bart Los, Robert Stehrer, and
Gaaitzen J. de Vries. 2015. "An Illustrated User Guide to the World
Input–Output Database: The Case of Automobile Production," *Review
of International Economics*, **23**:pp. 575–605.

Timmer, Marcel, Robert Inklaar, Mary O'Mahony, and Bart van Ark. 2010.
Growth of the European Economy: A Comparative Industry Perspective.
Cambridge Unversity Press.

Timmer, Marcel P., Bart Los, and Gaaitzen de Vries. 2014. "How Global Are
Global Value Chains? A New Approach to Measure International
Fragmentation," *Journal of Regional Science*, **55**(1, January): 66–92.

Timmer, Marcel, Ton van Moergastel, Edwin Stuivenwold, Gerard Ypma, Mary O'Mahony, and Mari Kangasniemi. 2007. *EU KLEMS Growth and Productivity Accounts, Part I. Methodology,* March. See: www .euklems.net/data/EUKLEMS_Growth_and_Productivity_Accounts_ Part_I_Methodology.pdf.

United Nations. 2009. *The 2008 System of National Accounts.* New York: United Nations. See: http://unstats.un.org/unsd/nationalaccount/sn a2008.asp.

US Census Bureau. 2013. *International Database: Population Estimates and Projections Methodology.* Washington, DC: Population Division, International Programs Center, December. See: www.census.gov/popu lation/international/data/idb/estandproj.pdf.

World Bank. 2008. *2005 International Comparison Program*, February. See: http://siteresources.worldbank.org/ICPINT/Resources/ICP_final-results.pdf.

　2014. *2011 International Comparison Program*, October. See: http://siter esources.worldbank.org/ICPEXT/Resources/ICP_2011.html.

2 | US economic growth – retrospect and prospect: lessons from a prototype industry-level production account for the US, 1947–2012

DALE W. JORGENSON, MUN S. HO, AND
JON D. SAMUELS

2.1 Introduction

In order to analyze the long-term growth of the US economy we have constructed a new dataset on the growth of US output and productivity by industry for 1947–2012. This includes the output for each of the sixty-five industries represented in the US national accounts, as well as the inputs of capital (K), labor (L), energy (E), materials (M), and services (S). The key indicator of innovation is productivity growth for each industry, where productivity is the ratio of output to input.

We build on the work of Jorgenson, Ho, and Stiroh (2005), who have presented a less detailed industry-level dataset for the US economy for 1977–2000. Data for 1947–1977 capture the development of the telecommunications services and equipment industries before the commercialization of semiconductor technology. Data for 2000–2012 highlight the slowdown in productivity growth and the drop in investment during and after the Great Recession of 2007–2009.

We project the future growth of the US economy by adapting the methodology of Jorgenson, Ho, and Stiroh (2008).[1] We aggregate over industries to obtain data on the sources of US economic growth and project the future growth of hours worked and labor productivity.

In the next section we incorporate our industry-level data set into the US National Income and Product Accounts (NIPAs). Paul Schreyer's (2001) Organisation for Economic Development and Cooperation (OECD) manual, *Measuring Productivity*, has established international

---

[1] Jorgenson and Vu (2013) employ this methodology to project the growth of the US and the world economy.

standards for economy-wide and industry-level productivity measurement, exemplified by Jorgenson, Gollop, and Fraumeni (1987). The methodology for our new dataset is consistent with the OECD standards.

Our dataset comprises a prototype production account within the framework of the US national accounts. Over the 1998–2012 period, our industry-level production account is consistent with industry-level production accounts presented by Rosenthal, Russell, Samuels, Strassner, and Usher (Chapter 11, this volume). We aggregate industries by means of the production possibility frontier employed by Jorgenson *et al.* (2005) and Jorgenson and Schreyer (2013). This links industry-level data with the economy-wide data reported by Harper, Moulton, Rosenthal, and Wasshausen (2009).[2]

In the following section of the chapter we analyze the changing sources of postwar US economic growth. We divide the postwar period into three broad sub-periods: the Postwar Recovery, 1947–1973, the Long Slump following the 1973 energy crisis, 1973–1995, and the recent period of Growth and Recession, 1995–2012. We focus more narrowly on the period of Growth and Recession by considering the sub-periods 1995–2000, 2000–2007, and 2007–2012 – the Investment Boom, the Jobless Recovery, and the Great Recession.

We show that the great preponderance of US economic growth since 1947 involves the replication of existing technologies through investment in equipment and software and expansion of the labor force. Contrary to the well-known views of Robert M. Solow (1957) and Simon Kuznets (1971), innovation accounts for a relatively modest 20 percent of US economic growth. This is the most important empirical finding from the extensive recent research on productivity measurement summarized by Jorgenson (2009).

The predominant role of replication of existing technologies in US economic growth is crucial to the formulation of economic policy. During the protracted recovery from the Great Recession of 2007–2009, US economic policy should focus on maintaining the growth of employment and reviving investment. Policies for enhancing the rate of innovation would have a very limited impact in the medium term.

---

[2] The most recent data set is available at: www.bea.gov/national/integrated_prod .htm. Our data for individual industries could also be linked to firm-level data employed in the micro-economic research reviewed by Syverson (2011).

We next consider the future growth of the US economy for the period 2012–2022. We project future growth of the US labor force from demographic projections. We project the future growth of the quality of labor input from the educational attainment of age cohorts that have recently entered the labor force. We find that US economic growth will slow substantially from the period 1990–2012, mainly due to a marked slowdown in labor quality growth.

Labor quality growth represents the upgrading of the labor force through higher educational attainment and greater experience. While much attention has been devoted to the aging of the labor force and the ongoing retirement of the baby boomers, the looming plateau in average educational attainment of US workers has been overlooked. The educational attainment of people emerging from the educational system, while high, has been nearly constant for the past decade. Rising average educational attainment is about to become part of US economic history.

We find that US economic growth will recover from the Great Recession period 2007–2012 through the resumption of productivity growth and the recovery of investment in capital input. However, the long-term growth of the US economy will depend critically on the performance of the relatively small number of sectors where innovation takes place.

2.2 A prototype industry-level production account for the US, 1947–2012

In December 2011 the Bureau of Economic Analysis (BEA) released an integrated industry-level dataset. This combines three separate industry programs – benchmark input–output tables released every five years, annual input–output tables, and gross domestic product (GDP) by industry, also released annually. The input–output tables provide data on the output side of the national accounts along with intermediate inputs in current and constant prices. This account forms the foundation of our industry-level production account. The BEA's industry-level dataset is described in more detail by Mayerhauser and Strassner (2010).

McCulla, Holdren, and Smith (2013) summarize the 2013 benchmark revision of the NIPAs. A particularly significant innovation is the addition of intellectual property products such as research and development and entertainment, artistic, and literary originals. Investment in intellectual property is treated symmetrically with other types of capital expenditures. Intellectual property products are included in the official national product and the capital services generated by these products are included in the national income in our integrated production account. Kim, Strassner and Wasshausen (2014) discuss the 2014 benchmark revision of the industry accounts, including the incorporation of intellectual property.

BEA's annual input–output data are employed in the industry-level production accounts presented by Rosenthal *et al.* (Chapter 11, this volume). This covers the period 1998–2012 for the sixty-five industrial sectors used in the NIPAs. The capital and labor inputs are provided by the Bureau of Labor Statistics (BLS), while output and intermediate inputs are generated by the BEA.[3] Labor quality estimates are based on the methodology in Jorgenson *et al.* (2005) and are broadly consistent with the labor quality estimates in our prototype account.

Our estimates of nominal output and intermediate input for 1998–2012 are consistent with the BEA/BLS industry-level production accounts. For the period 1947–1997 we begin with a time series of input–output tables in current prices on a North American Industry Classification System (NAICS) basis constructed by Mark Planting, former head of the input–output accounts at BEA, and adjust them to reflect the 2013 benchmark revision of the NIPAs and industry accounts. This time series incorporates all earlier benchmark input–output tables for the US, including the first benchmark table for 1947.

The Planting estimates for 1947–1962 consisted of only forty-six industries and we expanded them to the sixty-five sectors in the current BEA accounts using the work in Jorgenson *et al.* (1987) for 1948–1979. We deflated these nominal data using the BEA industry prices for 1998–2012 and prices estimated in Jorgenson *et al.* (1987), Jorgenson *et al.* (2005) for 1977–2000, and Jorgenson, Ho, and Samuels (2012) for 1960–2007. We have revised, extended, and updated the data on capital and labor inputs in constant prices from the same sources.[4] Finally, we

---

[3] Earlier data are presented by Fleck, Rosenthal, Russell, Strassner, and Usher (2014). For current data, see: www.bea.gov/industry/index.htm#integrated.

[4] A detailed description of the data construction is given in "Data Appendix to US Economic Growth: Retrospect and Prospect" which is available at www.worldklems.net/data.htm. We are grateful to the BEA Industry Division for sharing their labor quality estimates for 2010–2012 with us.

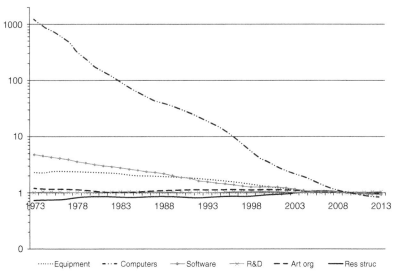

Figure 2.1 Price of investment relative to GDP deflator (log scale)

obtain an industry-level production account for the US, covering the period 1947–2012 in current and constant prices. This KLEMS-type dataset is consistent with the BEA's annual input–output tables for 1998–2012.

2.2.1 Changing structure of capital input

Swiftly falling information technology (IT) prices have provided powerful economic incentives for the rapid diffusion of IT through investment in hardware and software. Figure 2.1 presents price indices for 1973–2012 for asset categories included in our measures of capital input – equipment, computers, software, research and development, artistic originals, and residential structures. A substantial acceleration in the IT price decline occurred in 1995, triggered by a much sharper acceleration in the price decline for semiconductors. The IT price decline after 1995 signaled even faster innovation in the main IT-producing industries – semiconductors, computers, communications equipment, and software – and ignited a boom in IT investment.

The price of an asset is transformed into the price of the corresponding capital input by the *cost of capital*, introduced by Jorgenson

(1963). The cost of capital includes the nominal rate of return, the rate of depreciation, and the rate of capital loss due to declining prices. The distinctive characteristics of IT prices – high rates of price decline and rates of depreciation – imply that cost of IT capital input relative to the IT asset price is very large by comparison with non-IT capital input.

Schreyer (2009) provides recommendations for the construction of prices and quantities of capital services. In the *System of Natioonal Accounts 2008* (United Nations 2009, 415), estimates of capital services are described as follows: "By associating these estimates with the standard breakdown of value added, the contribution of labor and capital to production can be portrayed in a form ready for use in the analysis of productivity in a way entirely consistent with the accounts of the System."

To capture the impact of the rapid decline in IT equipment prices and the high depreciation rates for IT equipment we distinguish between the flow of capital services and the stock of capital. Figure 2.2 gives the share of IT in the value of total capital stock and the share of IT capital services in total capital input. The IT stock share rose from 1.4% in

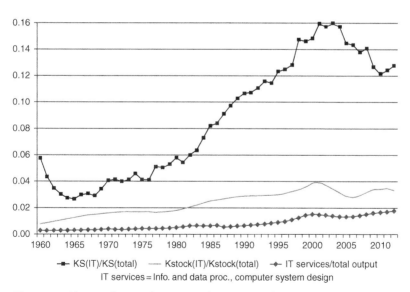

Figure 2.2 Shares of IT stock, IT capital services, and IT service output in total economy

1960 to 5.3% in 1995 on the eve of the IT boom and reached a high of 6.4% in 2001 after the dot-com bubble burst. This share fell to 5.1% during the Jobless Recovery when there was a plunge in IT investment and only a partial recovery.

The share of the IT service flow in total capital input is much higher than the IT share in total capital stock. The share of the IT service flow in total capital input was 5–7% during 1960–84 and rose with the rapid growth in IT investment during 1995–2000, reaching a peak of 15.8% in 2000. The IT service flow then declined with the fall in the IT stock, ending with a sharp plunge in the Great Recession.

By contrast with the production of IT equipment, the IT services industries – information and data processing and computer system design – increased steadily between 2005 and 2012. The share of the gross output of these two industries in the value of total gross output, shown in Figure 2.2, declined slightly from 1.45% in 2000 to 1.29% in 2005 and then continued to rise, hitting a high of 1.60% in 2012. This reflects the displacement of in-house hardware and software by the growth of IT services like cloud computing.

Investment in intellectual property products (IPP) since 1973 is shown in Figure 2.3. This proportion grew during the Investment

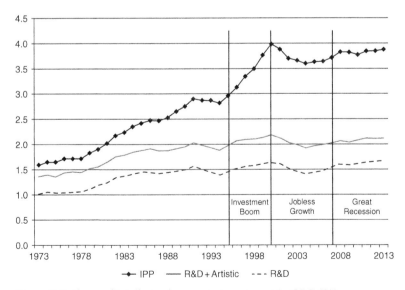

Figure 2.3 Share of intellectual property investment in GDP (%)

Boom of 1995–2000 to 4 percent of US GDP and has declined only slightly since the peak around 2000. Investment in research and development also peaked around 2000, but has remained close to 2 percent through the Great Recession of 2007–2012.

The intensity of the use of IT capital input differs substantially by industry. Figure 2.4 shows the share of IT in total capital input for

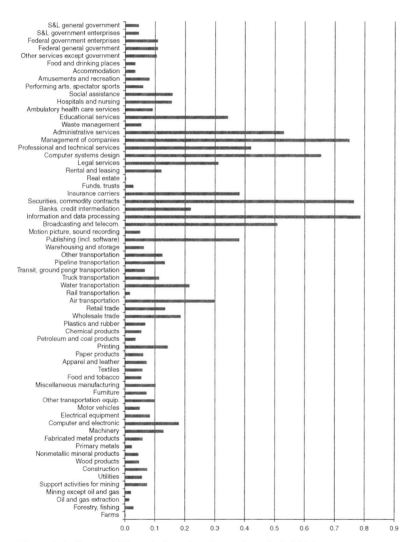

Figure 2.4 Share of IT capital services in total capital, 2005

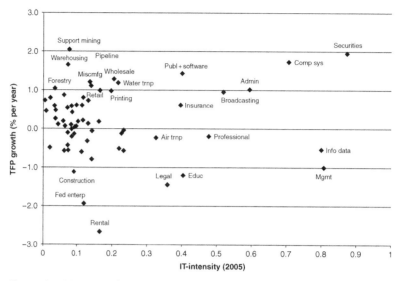

Figure 2.5 TFP growth 1995–2012 versus IT-intensity

each of the sixty-five industries on the eve of the Great Recession in 2005. There is an enormous range from less than 0.5% in farms and real estate to about 80% for computer system design and information and data processing. The sectors with the higher-valued added growth have mostly high IT shares – the two IT service industries just noted – as well as publishing (72%), broadcasting and telecommunications (61%), securities (76%), and administrative services (59%). The high growth industries with low IT shares are petroleum products (3.9%), truck transportation (12%), rental and leasing (12%), and social assistance (17%).

In Figure 2.5 we give a scatter plot of factor productivity (TFP) growth during 1995–2012 and the 2005 share of IT capital services in total capital. The positive correlation here is weak; the industries with the high IT intensity and high productivity growth are computer products, securities and commodities, computer system design, publishing, broadcasting and telecommunications, and administrative services. Industries with moderate IT intensity and high TFP growth include wholesale trade, water transportation, air transportation, and miscellaneous manufacturing. The sectors with moderate IT intensity and negative TFP growth are educational services and legal services.

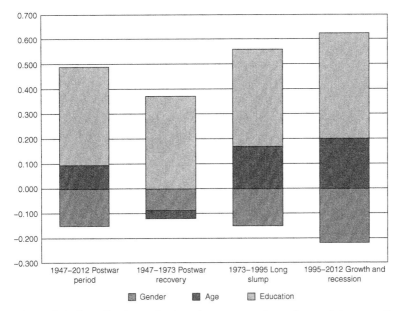

Figure 2.6 Contribution of education, age and gender to labor quality, 1947–2012

2.2.2 *Changing structure of labor input*

Our labor input index recognizes differences in labor compensation for workers of different ages, educational attainment, and gender, as described in detail by Jorgenson *et al.* (2005, ch. 6). Labor quality growth is the difference between the growth of labor input and the growth of hours worked. For example, shifts in the composition of labor input toward more highly educated workers, who receive higher wages, contribute to the growth of labor quality. Of the 1.45 percent annual growth rate of labor input over 1947–2012, hours worked contributed 1.01 points and labor quality 0.43 points. Figure 2.6 shows the decomposition of changes in labor quality into age, education, and gender components.

During the Postwar Recovery of 1947–1973 the massive entry of young, lower wage, workers contributed –0.04 percent annually to labor quality change, while increasing female work force participation contributed –0.10 percent, reflecting the lower average wages of female workers. The improvement in labor quality is due to rising educational

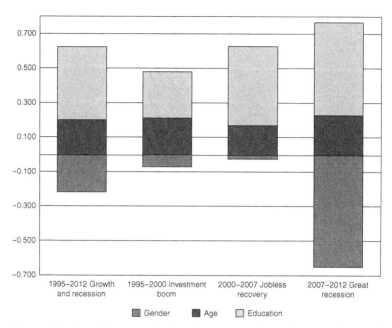

Figure 2.7 Contribution of education, age and gender to labor quality, 1995–2012

attainment, which contributed 0.37 percent. During the Long Slump of 1973–1995, the rise of female workers accelerated and the gender composition change contributed –0.15 points, while the aging of the work force contributed 0.17 points and education 0.40.

The contribution of higher educational attainment to labor quality growth accelerated to 0.48 percent during the period of Growth and Recession, 1995–2012. As workers gained in experience, aging of the work force also rose to 0.20, but this was more than offset by the drop in the contribution of gender to –0.22, capturing increased female labor force participation. Considering the period of Growth and Recession in more detail in Figure 2.7, we see that labor quality growth rose steadily during the period, but declined slightly in 1995–2000 relative to the Long Slump of 1973–1995 as a consequence of a jump in labor force participation. The drastic decline in the gender contribution during the Great Recession period 2007–2012, reflects the fact that unemployment rates rose much more sharply for men than for women.

The change in the educational attainment of workers is the main driver of changes in labor quality and this is plotted in Figure 2.8. In

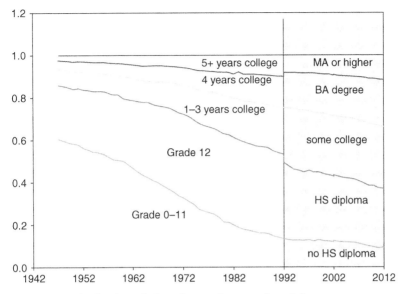

Figure 2.8 Distribution of education attainment of work force

1947 only 6.6% of the US work force had completed four or more years of college. By 1973 this proportion had risen to 14.5% and by 1991 to 24.8%. There was a change in classification in 1992 from years enrolled in school to years of schooling completed.

By 2012 32.7% of US workers had a BA degree or higher. The fall in the share of workers with lower educational attainment accelerated during the Great Recession.

The increase in the "college premium," the difference between wages earned by workers with college degrees and wages of those without degrees, has been widely noted. In Figure 2.9 we plot the compensation of workers by educational attainment, relative to those with a high school diploma (four years of high school). We see that the four-year college premium was stable at about 1.4 in the 1960s and 1970s, but rose to 1.6 in 1995 and 1.8 in 2000. The college premium stalled throughout the 2000s. The Masters-and-higher degree premium rose even faster than the BA premium between 1980 and 2000 and continued to rise through the mid-2000s.

A possible explanation for the rise in relative wages for college workers with a rising share of these workers is that they are complementary to the use of information technology. The most rapid growth of the college

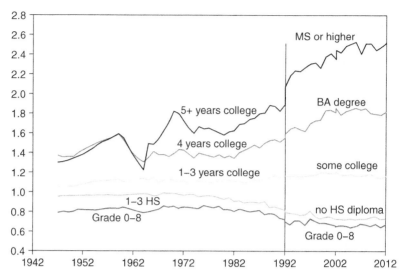

Figure 2.9 Compensation by education attainment (relative to those with HS diploma)

premium occurred during the 1995–2000 boom when IT capital made its highest contribution to GDP growth. Our industry-level view of postwar US economic history allows us to also consider the role of changing industry composition in determining relative wages.

Table 2.1 gives the work force characteristics by industry for 2010. The industries with the higher share of college-educated workers are also those that expanded rapidly –industries that produce computer and electronic products, publishing (including software), information and data processing, and computer systems design, as well as industries that use these IT products and services – securities and commodity contracts, legal services, professional and technical services, and educational services. Not all sectors that expanded faster than average, such as retail trade and truck transportation, are dominated by highly educated workers. However, in declining sectors like mining, primary metals, and textiles the work force consists predominantly of less educated workers.

After educational attainment the most important determinant of labor quality is the age of the worker. We have noted that the entry of the baby boomers into the labor force contributed negatively to labor quality growth during 1947–1973 and that the aging of these

Table 2.1 *Labor characteristics by industry, 2010*

		% workers college educated	compensation ($/hour)	% of total hours; aged 16–35	% total hours; females	% females college educated	% males college educated
1	Farms	15.1	19.5	20.3	14.7	18.6	14.3
2	Forestry fishing and related activities	16.4	16.6	30.8	15.3	30.6	13.3
3	Oil and gas extraction	38.6	79.5	14.6	22.2	44.4	36.7
4	Mining except oil and gas	11.8	39.2	20.2	8.8	28.0	10.1
5	Support activities for mining	26.0	37.6	25.8	13.8	39.4	23.4
6	Utilities	24.0	64.0	22.0	23.4	28.6	22.6
7	Construction	14.0	31.6	33.9	8.9	24.8	12.8
8	Wood products	12.2	26.0	32.9	15.1	17.3	11.1
9	Non-metallic mineral products	18.1	32.3	26.0	19.7	21.6	17.2
10	Primary metals	17.7	39.7	26.0	13.5	24.8	16.6
11	Fabricated metal products	15.2	32.2	27.7	17.7	15.9	15.0
12	Machinery	24.5	38.7	25.6	19.4	24.2	24.6
13	Computer and electronic products	62.3	56.7	31.0	30.3	54.2	66.0
14	Electrical equipment appliances	44.2	52.5	26.4	30.9	33.6	49.2
15	Motor vehicles bodies and parts	23.6	37.9	28.4	21.8	20.8	24.4
16	Other transportation equipment	31.4	50.6	22.6	17.3	30.9	31.7
17	Furniture and related products	15.6	26.3	31.5	24.3	17.4	15.0
18	Miscellaneous manufacturing	32.1	40.7	26.8	35.6	26.3	35.7

Table 2.1 (*cont.*)

		% workers college educated	compensation ($/hour)	% of total hours; aged 16–35	% total hours; females	% females college educated	% males college educated
19	Food, beverage, and tobacco	23.8	27.2	24.3	31.5	23.2	24.2
20	Textile mills and textile product mills	14.0	25.6	26.5	45.2	11.9	15.8
21	Apparel and leather products	17.6	27.0	27.4	55.9	15.4	20.9
22	Paper products	18.8	37.3	23.9	20.7	18.5	18.9
23	Printing and related support activities	22.0	29.5	28.7	32.2	23.1	21.4
24	Petroleum and coal products	32.9	81.5	17.7	17.4	45.2	30.0
25	Chemical products	49.5	54.1	27.4	35.2	49.1	50.3
26	Plastics and rubber products	16.4	30.7	30.2	28.5	11.4	18.5
27	Wholesale trade		41.2	29.1	26.0	32.6	31.7
28	Retail trade	15.8	23.0	35.4	42.0	14.4	17.3
29	Air transportation	38.2	49.5	28.6	35.9	36.7	39.1
30	Rail transportation	13.2	50.7	14.0	8.3	28.7	11.7
31	Water transportation	31.1	51.6	19.1	19.6	32.6	30.6
32	Truck transportation	8.6	28.0	24.6	11.1	14.4	7.8
33	Transit, ground passenger transportation	16.3	22.8	18.4	23.5	11.5	18.1
34	Pipeline transportation	32.8	65.6	17.5	18.4	45.6	29.6

35	Other transportation and support	19.7	33.5	34.1	20.7	22.3	19.0
36	Warehousing and storage	12.6	29.2	35.6	26.3	13.2	12.4
37	Publishing industries (includes software)	60.2	52.5	38.1	42.8	59.7	60.5
38	Motion picture and sound recording	45.9	46.4	47.9	31.6	48.8	44.3
39	Broadcasting and telecommunications	39.5	46.7	37.9	39.0	42.4	37.7
40	Information and data processing services	55.4	55.0	47.7	40.8	50.8	59.1
41	Federal Res banks, credit intermediation	42.4	42.1	36.5	60.1	30.3	62.8
42	Securities, commodity contracts	71.9	120.6	38.3	35.2	58.0	80.7
43	Insurance carriers	46.6	48.7	28.5	56.4	33.9	65.0
44	Funds, trusts, and other financial vehicles	71.0	99.4	40.7	37.3	57.1	80.4
45	Real estate	40.6	31.1	18.6	46.6	36.1	45.1
46	Rental, leasing, and lessors of intangibles	25.4	31.1	45.0	28.8	24.1	26.0
47	Legal services	65.5	57.5	29.0	53.1	46.3	90.6
48	Computer systems design	68.6	56.7	41.1	28.5	67.0	69.3
49	Misc. professional and technical services	65.3	46.9	31.1	42.3	58.9	70.6
50	Management of companies	53.4	62.2	28.9	51.4	39.8	69.4

Table 2.1 (*cont.*)

		% workers college educated	compensation ($/hour)	% of total hours; aged 16–35	% total hours; females	% females college educated	% males college educated
51	Administrative and support services	20.1	24.8	37.7	40.4	23.2	17.9
52	Waste management	10.2	32.5	33.9	14.3	16.1	9.2
53	Educational services	64.2	28.8	27.5	65.9	64.2	64.2
54	Ambulatory health care services	38.8	39.2	27.5	74.2	30.8	66.6
55	Hospitals, nursing and residential care	30.4	28.4	28.1	79.5	29.4	34.4
56	Social assistance	30.0	18.8	36.1	86.7	28.9	37.4
57	Performing arts, spectator sports	48.7	53.8	29.1	43.8	55.1	43.1
58	Amusements, gambling and recreation	21.7	20.1	39.4	41.0	22.2	21.4
59	Accommodation	18.6	22.1	35.8	52.7	16.3	21.3
60	Food services and drinking places	11.1	14.8	53.5	47.9	9.9	12.2
61	Other services except government	17.9	25.7	26.7	64.8	18.8	19.3
62	Federal general government	52.0	63.3	19.5	54.6	49.6	54.9
63	Federal government enterprises	19.6	42.0	14.5	34.6	20.0	19.3
64	S&L government enterprises	29.9	40.9	25.4	40.2	28.9	30.7
65	S&L general government	48.6	36.3	23.5	61.2	48.6	50.6

Note: "College educated" workers are those with BA or BA+.

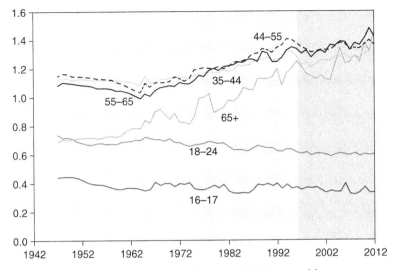

Figure 2.10 Compensation by age relative to 25–34-year-olds

workers contributed positively after 1973. We show the relative wages of the different age groups, relative to the wages of the 25–34 age group, in Figure 2.10. The wages of the prime age group, 45–54, rose steadily relative to the young from 1.11 in 1970 to 1.41 in 1994. During the peak of the information age, the wages of the younger workers surged and the prime-age premium fell to 1.32.

The wage premium of the 35–44 and 55–64 groups show the same pattern as the premium of prime age workers, first rising relative to the 25–34 year olds, then falling or flattening out during the IT boom. The wage premium of the oldest workers is the most volatile but showed a general upward trend throughout the postwar period 1947–2012. The share of workers aged 65+ has been rising steadily since the mid-1990s during a period of large swings in the wage premium. The relative wages of the very young, 18–24, has been falling steadily since 1970, reflecting the rising demand for education and experience.

2.3 Sources of US economic growth

In *Information Technology and the American Growth Resurgence,* Jorgenson *et al.* (2005) analyzed the economic impact of IT at the Standard Industrial Classification (SIC) industry level for 1977–2000 and provided a concise history of the main technological innovations in information technology during the postwar period, beginning with the invention of the transistor in 1947. Jorgenson *et al.* (2012) have converted the industrial classification to NAICS and updated and extended the data to cover seventy industries for the period 1960–2007.

The NAICS industry classification includes the industries identified by Jorgenson, Ho, and Samuels (2014) as IT-producing industries, namely, computers and electronic products and two IT services industries, information and data processing and computer systems design. We have classified industries as IT-using the IT-intensity index of Jorgenson *et al.* (2014). We classify all other industries as non-IT.

Value added in the IT-producing industries during 1947–2012 is only 2.5 percent of the US economy, in the IT-using industries about 47.5 percent, and the non-IT industries the remaining 50 percent. The IT-using industries are mainly in trade and services and most manufacturing industries are in the non-IT sector. The NAICS industry classification provides much more detail on services and trade, especially the industries that are intensive users of IT. We begin by discussing the results for the IT-producing sectors, now defined to include the two IT-service sectors.

Figure 2.11 reveals a steady increase in the share of IT-producing industries in the growth of value added since 1947. This is paralleled by a decline in the contribution of the non-IT industries, while the share of

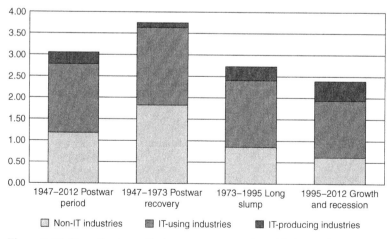

Figure 2.11 Contributions of industry groups to value added growth, 1947–2012

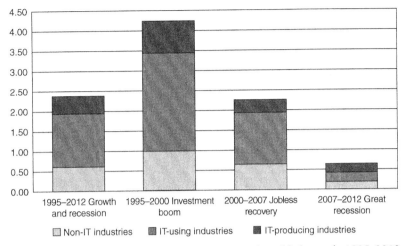

Figure 2.12 Contributions of industry groups to value added growth, 1995–2012

IT-using industries has remained relatively constant. Figure 2.12 decomposes the growth of value added for the period 1995–2012. The contributions of the IT-producing and IT-using industries peaked during the Investment Boom of 1995–2000 and have declined since then. However, the contribution of the non-IT industries also revived during the Investment Boom and declined substantially during the Jobless Recovery and the Great Recession.

Figure 2.13 gives the contributions to value added for the sixty-five individual industries over the period 1947–2012. In order to assess the relative importance of productivity growth at the industry level as a source of US economic growth, we express the growth rate of aggregate productivity as a weighted average of industry productivity growth rates, using the ingenious weighting scheme of Evsey Domar (1961)[5]. The Domar weight is the ratio of the industry's gross output to aggregate value added and they sum to more than one. This reflects the fact that an increase in the rate of growth of the industry's productivity has a direct effect on the industry's output and a second indirect effect via the output delivered to other industries as intermediate inputs.

The rate of growth of aggregate productivity also depends on the reallocations of capital and labor inputs among industries. The rate

[5] The formula is given in Jorgenson *et al.* (2005), equation 8.34.

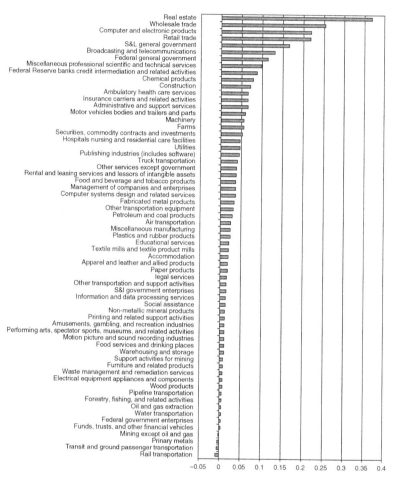

Figure 2.13 Industry contributions to value added growth, 1947–2012

of aggregate productivity growth exceeds the weighted sum of industry productivity growth rates when these reallocations are positive. This occurs when capital and labor inputs are paid different prices in different industries and industries with higher prices have more rapid input growth rates. Aggregate capital and labor inputs then grow more rapidly than weighted averages of industry capital and labor input growth rates, so that the reallocations are positive.

Figure 2.14 shows that the contributions of IT-producing, IT-using, and non-IT industries to aggregate productivity growth are similar in

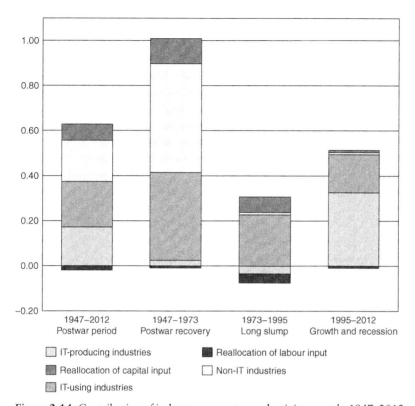

Figure 2.14 Contribution of industry groups to productivity growth, 1947–2012

magnitude for the period 1947–2012.[6] The non-IT industries greatly predominated in the growth of value added during the Postwar Recovery, 1947–1973, but this contribution became negative after 1973. The contribution of IT-producing industries was relatively small during the Postwar Recovery, but became the predominant source of US productivity growth during the Long Slump, 1973–1995, and increased considerably during the period of Growth and Recession, 1995–2012.

The IT-using industries contributed substantially to US economic growth during the Postwar Recovery, but this contribution disappeared during the Long Slump, 1973–1995, before reviving after 1995. The reallocation of capital input made a small but positive contribution to growth of the US economy for the period 1947–2012

[6] The contribution of an industry is its annual TFP growth multiplied by its Domar weight, and then averaged over the sub-period.

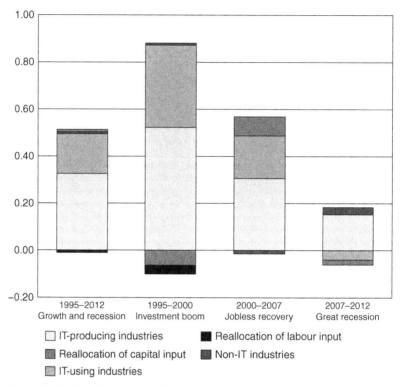

Figure 2.15 Contribution of industry groups to productivity growth, 1995–2012

and for each of the sub-periods. The contribution of reallocation of labor input was negligible for the period as a whole. During the Long Slump and the period of Growth and Recession, the contribution of the reallocation of labor input was slightly negative.

Considering the period of Growth and Recession in more detail in Figure 2.15, the IT-producing industries predominated as a source of productivity growth during the period as a whole. The contribution of these industries remained substantial during each of the sub-periods – 1995–2000, 2000–2007, and 2007–2012 – despite the sharp contraction of economic activity during the Great Recession of 2007–2009. The contribution of the IT-using industries was slightly greater than that of the IT-producing industries during the period of Jobless Growth, but dropped to nearly zero during the Great Recession. The non-IT industries contributed positively to productivity growth during the Investment Boom of 1995–2000, but these contributions were

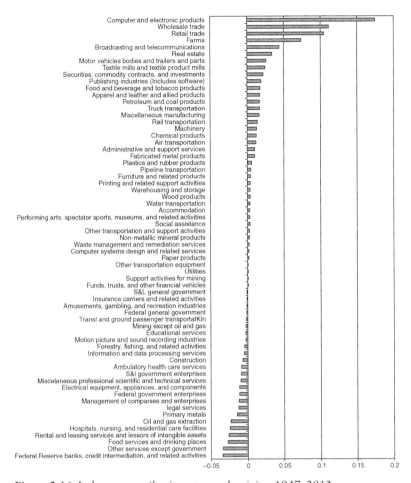

Figure 2.16 Industry contributions to productivity, 1947–2012

almost negligible during the Jobless Recovery and became substantially negative during the Great Recession.

Figure 2.16 gives the contributions of each of the sixty-five industries to productivity growth for the postwar period. Wholesale and retail trade, farms, computer and peripheral equipment, and semiconductors and other electronic components were among the leading contributors to US productivity growth during the postwar period. About half the sixty-five industries made negative contributions to aggregate productivity. These include non-market services, such as health and education, as well as resource industries, such as oil and gas extraction and mining,

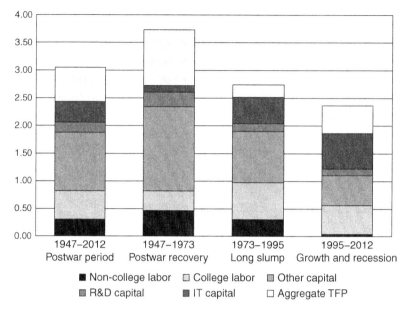

Figure 2.17 Sources of US economic growth, 1947–2012

affected by resource depletion. Other negative contributions reflect the growth of barriers to resource mobility in product and factor markets due, in some cases, to more stringent government regulations, but may also reflect measurement challenges.

Figure 2.17 gives the sources of US growth. The contributions of college-educated and non-college-educated workers to US economic growth are given by the relative shares of these workers in the value of output, multiplied by the growth rates of their labor input. The contribution of college-educated workers predominated in the growth of labor input during the postwar period 1947–2012. This contribution jumped substantially from the Postwar Recovery period 1947–1973 to the period 1973–1995 of the Long Slump. The contribution of non-college workers predominated during the Postwar Recovery, but declined steadily and almost disappeared during the period 1995–2012 of Growth and Recession.

Capital input was the predominant source of US economic growth for the postwar period 1947–2012, accounting for 1.62 percent of US economic growth of 3.05 percent. Capital input was also predominant during the Postwar Recovery, the Long Slump, and the period of

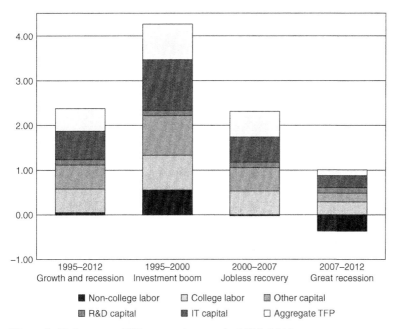

Figure 2.18 Sources of US economic growth, 1995–2012

Growth and Recession. Considering the period of Growth and Recession in greater detail, Figure 2.18 reveals that the contribution of capital input was about half of US economic growth during the Investment Boom and increased in relative importance as the growth rate fell in the Jobless Recovery and again in the Great Recession.

Figure 2.17 provides more detail on important changes in the composition of the contribution of capital input. For the postwar period as a whole the contribution of research and development (R&D) to US economic growth was considerably less than the contribution of IT, but other forms of capital input greatly predominated. While the contribution of R&D exceeded that of IT during the Postwar Recovery, the contribution of IT grew rapidly during the Long Slump and jumped to nearly half the contribution of capital input during the period of Growth and Recession. By contrast, the contribution of R&D shrank during both periods and became relatively insignificant.

Figure 2.18 reveals that all of the sources of economic growth contributed to the US growth resurgence between 1995 and 2000, relative to the Long Slump represented in Figure 2.17. Both IT and non-IT investment contributed substantially to growth during the Jobless Recovery of 2000–2007, but the contribution of labor input dropped precipitously and the contribution of non-college workers became slightly negative. The most remarkable feature of the Jobless Recovery was the continued growth in productivity, indicating an ongoing surge of innovation.

Both IT and non-IT investment continued to contribute to US economic growth during the Great Recession period 2007–2012, while the contribution of R&D investment remained insignificant. Productivity growth almost disappeared, reflecting a widening gap between actual and potential growth of output. The contribution of college-educated workers remained positive and substantial, while the contribution of non-college workers became strongly negative.

2.4 Future US economic growth

Byrne, Oliner, and Sichel (2013) provide a recent survey of contributions to the debate over prospects for future US economic growth. Tyler Cowen (2011) presents a pessimistic outlook and his views are supported by Robert Gordon (2012, 2014), who analyzes six headwinds facing the US economy, including the end of productivity growth in IT-producing industries. Cowen (2013), expresses a more sanguine view.

Gordon's pessimism about the future of IT is forcefully countered by Erik Brynjolfsson and Andrew McAfee (2014).[7] Martin Baily, James Manyika, and Shalabh Gupta (2013) summarize an extensive series of studies of technological prospects for American industries, including IT, conducted by the McKinsey Global Institute (Manyika, *et al.* 2011) and also provide a more optimistic view.

John Fernald (2012) analyzes the growth of potential output and productivity before, during, and after the Great Recession and reaches the conclusion that half the shortfall in the rate of growth of output, relative to pre-recession trends, is due to slower growth in potential output. Byrne *et al.* (2013) present projections of future US

---

[7] Brynjolfsson and Gordon have debated the future of information technology on the Total Economy Database (TED). See: http://blog.ted.com/2013/02/26/debat e-erik-brynjolfsson-and-robert-j-gordon-at-ted2013.

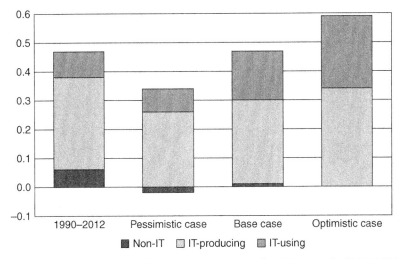

Figure 2.19 Contribution of industry groups to productivity growth, 2012–2022

productivity growth for the non-farm business sector and compare their results with others, including Fernald and Gordon. They show that there is substantial agreement among the alternative projections.

Byrne, Oliner and Sichel provide detailed evidence on the recent behavior of IT prices. This is based on research at the Federal Reserve Board to provide deflators for the Index of Industrial Production. While the size of transistors has continued to shrink, performance of semiconductors devices has improved less rapidly, severing the close link that had characterized Moore's Law as a description of the development of semiconductor technology.[8] This view is supported by Unni Pillai (2011) and by the computer scientists John Hennessey and David Patterson (2012).[9]

We present base case, pessimistic, and optimistic projections of future growth in potential US GDP for the period 2012–2022 in Figures 2.19, 2.20 and 2.21. Appendix 2.1 describes our projection methods. Our base case projections are based on the average

---

[8] Moore's Law is discussed by Jorgenson *et al.* (2005), ch. 1.

[9] See Hennessey and Patterson (2012), Figure 1.16, p. 46. An excellent journalistic account of the turning point in the development of Intel microprocessors is presented by John Markoff (2004) in the *New York Times* for May 17, 2004.

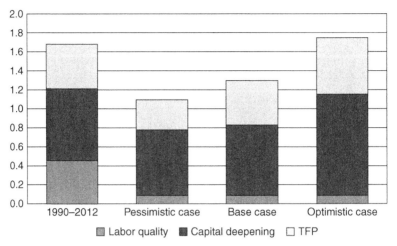

Figure 2.20 Range of labor productivity projections, 2012–2022

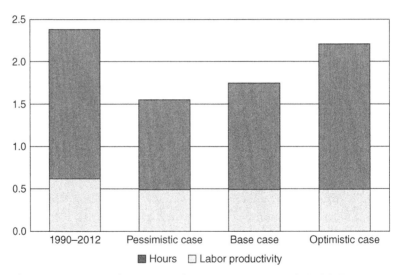

Figure 2.21 Range of US potential output projections, 2012–2022

contributions of total factor productivity growth for the IT-producing, IT-using, and non-IT industries for the period 1995–2012. Our optimistic projections omit the Great Recession period of 2007–2012, while our pessimistic projections take account the final five years of the Great Recession and the Long Slump. We compare our projections with actual growth for 1990–2012.

Our base case projection of growth in potential GDP in 2012–2022 is 1.75 percent per year, compared with growth for 1990–2012 of 2.38 percent. The difference is due mainly to the projected slowdown in the growth of labor quality. Labor quality growth is driven mainly by increases in average educational attainment, and rising educational attainment has been a major driver of US economic growth throughout the postwar period. However, educational attainment will reach a plateau early in our projection period 2012–2022. Labor quality growth will fall from 0.46 percent per year during 1990–2012 to only 0.087 percent per year in 2012–2022.

Our optimistic projection for potential US GDP growth is 2.2 percent per year during 2012–2022, short of actual growth of 2.38 percent per year in 1990–2012. The contributions of IT-using and non-IT industries, along with more rapid growth in capital quality, are mainly responsible for the higher projected growth. Our pessimistic projection for potential growth is only 1.56 percent per year. The difference from our base case is due mainly to a reduction in the projected growth of productivity in IT-producing and IT-using sectors and slower improvement in capital quality.[10]

2.5 Conclusions

Our industry-level dataset reveals that replication of established technologies through growth of capital and labor inputs, recently through the growth of college-educated workers and investments in both IT and non-IT capital, explains by far the largest proportion of US economic growth. International productivity comparisons reveal similar patterns for the world economy, its major regions, and leading industrialized, developing, and emerging economies.[11] Studies are now underway to extend these comparisons to individual industries for the countries included in the World KLEMS Initiative.[12]

Conflicting interpretations of the Great Recession can be evaluated from the perspective of our new dataset. We do not share the technological pessimism of Cowen (2011) and Gordon (2014), especially for the IT-producing industries. Careful studies of developments of

---

[10] These projections are not directly comparable with those summarized by Byrne *et al.* (2013), which are limited to non-farm business.
[11] See Jorgenson and Vu (2013).   [12] See Jorgenson (2012).

semiconductor and computer technology show that the accelerated pace of innovation that began in 1995 reverted to the lower, but still substantial, rates of innovation in IT. This accounted for almost all of productivity growth during the Great Recession.

Our findings also contribute to an understanding of the future potential for US economic growth. Our new projections corroborate the perspective of Jorgenson *et al.* (2008), who showed that the peak growth rates of the US Investment Boom of 1995–2000 were not sustainable. However, our projections are less optimistic, due mainly to the slowing growth of the US labor force and the virtual disappearance of improvements in labor quality. Low productivity growth during the Great Recession is transitory, but productivity growth is unlikely to return to the high rates of the Investment Boom and the Jobless Recovery.

Finally, we conclude that the new findings presented in this chapter have important implications for US economic policy. Maintaining the gradual recovery from the Great Recession will require a revival of investment in IT equipment and software and non-IT capital as well. Enhancing opportunities for employment is also essential, but this is likely to be most successful for college-educated workers. These measures will contribute to closing the substantial remaining gap between potential and actual output.

Appendix 2.1: projections

We adapt the methodology of Jorgenson *et al.* (2008) to utilize data for the sixty-five industries included in the US National Income and Product Accounts. The growth in aggregate value added (Y) is an index of the growth of capital (K) and labor (L) services and aggregate growth in productivity (A):

$$\Delta \ln Y = \bar{v}_K \Delta \ln K + \bar{v}_L \Delta \ln L + \Delta \ln A \tag{A1}$$

To distinguish between the growth of primary factors and changes in composition, we decompose aggregate capital input into the capital stock (Z) and capital quality (KQ), and labor input into hours (H) and labor quality (LQ). We also decompose the aggregate productivity growth into the contributions from the IT-producing industries, the IT-using industries, and the non-IT industries. The growth of aggregate output becomes:

$$\Delta \ln Y = \bar{v}_K \Delta \ln Z + \bar{v}_K \Delta \ln KQ + \bar{v}_L \Delta \ln H + \bar{v}_L \Delta \ln LQ$$

$$+ \bar{u}_{ITP} \Delta \ln A_{ITP} + \bar{u}_{ITU} \Delta \ln A_{ITU} + \bar{u}_{NIT} \Delta \ln A_{NIT} \quad (A2)$$

where the $\Delta \ln A_i$'s are productivity growth rates in the IT-producing, IT-using and non-IT groups and the u's are the appropriate weights. Labor productivity, defined as value added per hour worked, is expressed as:

$$\Delta \ln y = \Delta \ln Y - \Delta \ln H \quad (A3)$$

We recognize the fact that a significant component of capital income goes to land rent. In our projections we assume that land input is fixed, and thus the growth of aggregate capital stock is:

$$\Delta \ln Z = \bar{\mu}_R \Delta \ln Z_R + (1 - \bar{\mu}_R) \Delta \ln LAND = \bar{\mu}_R \Delta \ln Z_R \quad (A4)$$

where Z_R is the reproducible capital stock and $\bar{\mu}_R$ is the value share of reproducible capital in total capital stock.

We project growth using equation (A2), assuming that the growth of reproducible capital is equal to the growth of output, $\Delta \ln Y^P = \Delta \ln Z_R^P$, where the P superscript denotes projected variables. With this assumption, the projected growth rate of average labor productivity is given by:

$$\Delta \ln y^P = \frac{1}{1 - \bar{v}_K \bar{\mu}_R} \times [\bar{v}_K \Delta \ln KQ - \bar{v}_K (1 - \bar{\mu}_R) \Delta \ln H + \bar{v}_L \Delta \ln LQ$$

$$+ \bar{u}_{ITP} \Delta \ln A_{ITP} + \bar{u}_{ITU} \Delta \ln A_{ITU} + \bar{u}_{NIT} \Delta \ln A_{NIT}] \quad (A5)$$

We emphasize that this is a long-run relationship that removes the transitional dynamics related to capital accumulation.

To employ equation (A5) we first project the growth in hours worked and labor quality. We obtain population projections by age, race, and sex from the US Census Bureau and organize the data to match the classifications in our labor database (eight age groups, two sexes).[13] We read the 2010 Census of Population to construct the

---

[13] The projections made by the US Census Bureau in 2012 are given on their website: www.census.gov/population/projections/data/national/2012.html. In that projection the resident population is projected to be 420 million in 2060. We make an adjustment to give the total population including armed forces overseas.

educational attainment distribution by age, based on the 1 percent sample of individuals. We then use the micro-data in the Annual Social and Economic Supplement (ASEC) of the *Current Population Survey* to extrapolate the educational distribution for all years after 2010 and to interpolate between the 2000 and 2010 Censuses. This establishes the actual trends in educational attainment for the sample period. Educational attainment derived from the 2010 Census shows little improvement for males compared to the 2000 Census with some age groups showing a smaller fraction with professional degrees. There was a higher fraction with BA degrees for females.

We assume that the educational attainment for men aged 39 or younger will be the same as the last year of the sample period; that is, a man who becomes 22 years old in 2022 will have the same chance of having a BA degree as a 22-year-old man in 2012. For women, this cut-off age is set at 33. For men over 39-years-old, and women over 33, we assume that they carry their education attainment with them as they age. For example, the educational distribution of 50-year-olds in 2022 is the same as that of 40-year-olds in 2012, assuming that death rates are independent of educational attainment. Since a 50-year-old in 2022 has a slightly higher attainment than a 51-year-old in 2020, these assumptions result in a smooth improvement in educational attainment that is consistent with the observed profile in the 2010 Census.

The next step after constructing the population matrix by sex, age and education for each year in the projection period is to calculate the employment and hours worked matrices by these dimensions. The employment rate fell significantly during the Great Recession and we assume that the employment rate rises gradually from the observed 2010 levels back to the 2007 rates. We also assume that the annual hours worked per worker gradually recover to 2007 levels. We assume there are no further changes in the relative wages for each age–sex–education cell and thus calculate the effective labor input in the projection period by multiplying these projected hours per year by the projected population in each cell, and then weighting by the 2010 compensation matrix. The ratio of labor input to hours worked is the labor quality index.

The growth rate of capital input is a weighted average of the stocks of various assets weighted by their shares of capital income. The ratio of total capital input to the total stock is the capital quality index which rises as the composition of the stock moves towards short-lived assets with high rental costs. The growth of capital quality during the period 1995–2000 was clearly unsustainable. For our base case projection we assume that capital quality grows at the average rate observed for 1995–2012. For the optimistic case we use the rate for 1995–2007. Finally, we use the rate for 1990–2012 for the pessimistic case.

References

Baily, Martin, James Manyika, and Shalabh Gupta. 2013. "US Productivity Growth: An Optimistic Perspective," *International Productivity Monitor*, 25: 3–12.

Brynjolfsson, Erik, and Andrew McAfee. 2014. *The Second Machine Age: Work, Progress, and Prosperity in a Time of Brilliant Technologies*. New York: W. W. Norton.

Byrne, David, Steven Oliner, and Dan Sichel. 2013. "Is the Information Technology Revolution Over?" *International Productivity Monitor*, 25: 20–36.

Cowen, Tyler. 2011. *The Great Stagnation: How America Ate All the Low-Hanging Fruit, Got Sick, and Will (Eventually) Feel Better*. New York: Dutton.

2013. *Average is Over: Powering America Beyond the Age of the Great Stagnation*. New York: Dutton.

Domar, Evsey. 1961. "On the Measurement of Technological Change," *Economic Journal* 71(284): 709–729.

Fernald, John. 2012. *Productivity and Potential Output Before, During, and After the Great Recession*. San Francisco: Federal Reserve Bank of San Francisco, September.

Fleck, Susan, Steven Rosenthal, Matthew Russell, Erich H. Strassner, and Lisa Usher. 2014. "A Prototype BEA/BLS Industry-level Production Account for the United States." In Dale W. Jorgenson, J. Steven Landefeld, and Paul Schreyer (eds.), *Measuring Economic Stability and Progress*. University of Chicago Press, 323–372.

Gordon, Robert. 2012. *Is US Economic Growth Over? Faltering Innovation and the Six Headwinds*. Cambridge, MA: National Bureau of Economic Research, Working Paper No 18315, August.

2014. *The Demise of US Economic Growth: Restatement, Rebuttal, and Reflections*. Cambridge, MA: National Bureau of Economic Research, Working Paper No 19895, February.

Harper, Michael, Brent Moulton, Steven Rosenthal, and David B. Wasshausen. 2009. "Integrated GDP-Productivity Accounts," *American Economic Review*, 99(2): 74–79.

Hennessey, John L., and David A. Patterson. 2012. *Computer Organization and Design*, 4th edn. Waltham, MA: Morgan Kaufmann.

Jorgenson, Dale W. 1963. "Capital Theory and Investment Behavior," *American Economic Review*, **53**(2): 247–259.

2009. (ed.) *The Economics of Productivity*. Northampton, MA: Edward Elgar.

2012. "The World KLEMS Initiative," *International Productivity Monitor*, Fall: 5–19.

Jorgenson, Dale W., Frank M. Gollop, and Barbara M. Fraumeni. 1987. *Productivity and US Economic Growth*. Cambridge MA: Harvard University Press.

Jorgenson, Dale W., Mun S. Ho, and Jon Samuels. 2012. "Information Technology and US Productivity Growth," in Matilde Mas and Robert Stehrer (eds.), *Industrial Productivity in Europe*. Northampton, MA: Edward Elgar, 34–65.

2014. "What Will Revive US Economic Growth?" *Journal of Policy Modeling*, **36**(4): 674–691.

Jorgenson, Dale W., Mun S. Ho, and Kevin J. Stiroh. 2005. *Information Technology and the American Growth Resurgence*. Cambridge, MA: The MIT Press.

2008. "A Retrospective Look at the US Productivity Growth Resurgence," *Journal of Economic Perspectives*, **22**(1): 3–24.

Jorgenson, Dale W. and Paul Schreyer. 2013. "Industry-level Productivity Measurement and the 2008 System of National Accounts," *Review of Income and Wealth*, **58**(4): 185–211.

Jorgenson, Dale W., and Khuong M. Vu. 2013. "The Emergence of the New Economic Order: Economic Growth in the G7 and the G20," *Journal of Policy Modeling*, **35**(2): 389–399.

Kim, Donald D., Erich H. Strassner, and David B. Wasshausen. 2014. "Industry Economic Accounts: Results of the Comprehensive Revision Revised Statistics for 1997–2012," *Survey of Current Business*, **94**(2): 1–18.

Kuznets, Simon. 1971. *Economic Growth of Nations: Total Output and Production Structure*. Cambridge, MA: Harvard University Press.

Manyika, James, David Hunt, Scott Nyquest, Jaana Remes, Vikrram Malhotra, Lenny Mendonca, Byron August, and Samantha Test. 2011. *Growth and Renewal in the United States*, Washington, DC: McKinsey Global Institute, February.

Markoff, John. 2004. Intel's Big Shift after Hitting Technical Wall. *New York Times*, **153** (52, 888). See: www.nytimes.com/2004/05/17/business/technology-intel-s-big-shift-after-hitting-technical-wall.html.

Mayerhauser, Nicole M., and Erich H. Strassner. 2010. "Preview of the Comprehensive Revision of the Annual Industry Accounts: Changes in Definitions, Classification, and Statistical Methods," *Survey of Current Business*, **90**(3): 21–34.

McCulla, Stephanie H., Alyssa E. Holdren, and Shelly Smith. 2013. "Improved Estimates of the National Income and Product Accounts: Results of the 2013 Comprehensive Revision," *Survey of Current Business*, **93**(9): 14–45.

Pillai, Unni. 2011. "Technological Progress in the Microprocessor Industry," *Survey of Current Business*, **91**(2): 13–16.

Schreyer, Paul. 2001. *OECD Manual: Measuring Productivity: Measurement of Aggregate and Industry-Level Productivity Growth*. Paris: OECD.

  2009. *OECD Manual: Measuring Capital*. Paris: OECD.

Solow, Robert M. 1957. "Technical Change and the Aggregate Production Function," *Review of Economics and Statistics*, **39**(3): 312–320.

Syverson, Chad. 2011. What Determines Productivity? *Journal of Economic Literature*, **49**(2): 325–365.

United Nations, Commission of the European Communities, International Monetary Fund, Organisation for Economic Cooperation and Development, and World Bank. 2009. *System of National Accounts 2008*. New York: United Nations. See: http://unstats.un.org/unsd/natio nalaccount/sna2008.asp.

3 | The structural causes of Japan's Lost Decades

KYOJI FUKAO, KENTA IKEUCHI, HYEOG UG
KWON, YOUNGGAK KIM, TATSUJI
MAKINO, AND MIHO TAKIZAWA

3.1 Introduction

Since the burst of the "bubble economy" in 1991, Japan has experienced sluggish growth in the economy overall as well as in total factor productivity (TFP).[1] The first ten years of this stagnation – the "Lost Decade" – have been the subject of a considerable body of research. Studies have focused on financial problems such as banks' non-performing loans, firms' damaged balance sheets, and deflation as the main causes of Japan's stagnation.[2] By the early 2000s, Japan had largely resolved the non-performing loan problem as well as the problem of damaged balance sheets, but economic growth hardly accelerated, resulting in what now are "Two Lost Decades." The argument put forward in this study is that Japan's Two Lost Decades are not a transient problem of sluggish economic growth as a result of inappropriate fiscal and monetary policies but need to be seen from a more long-term and structural perspective, reflecting a chronic lack of demand and a long-term decline in productivity.

It is certainly true that during the past two decades, Japan has persistently suffered from deflation or inflation that has remained below the central bank's target. And there is no question that Japan needs to resolve the problem of deflation and escape from its liquidity trap in order to restore the effectiveness of conventional monetary policy. However, it seems very unlikely that Japan will be able to resolve its structural problems simply by stoking sufficient inflation to keep real interest rates negative or at least extremely low. In fact, maintaining very low or negative real interest rates for a prolonged period may give rise to bubbles like those in Japan during the late 1980s

---

[1] This chapter comes from a study conducted as a part of the project "East Asian Industrial Productivity" undertaken at the Research Institute of Economy, Trade and Industry (RIETI).

[2] See, for example, Saxonhouse and Stern (2004) and Ito *et al.* (2005).

or the United States in the 2000s. Moreover, stimulating final demand will not be sufficient to accelerate Japan's productivity growth.

Against this background, the aim of this chapter is to examine the causes of Japan's economic stagnation from a long-term, structural perspective and investigate whether it will be possible to resolve the causes of stagnation. Taking a long-term perspective that compares the two decades from the early 1990s onward with the preceding two decades and, at the same time, taking advantage of databases such as the Japan Industrial Productivity (JIP) Database and the EU KLEMS Database, we will compare Japan's performance with that of the US and other advanced economies.[3]

The remainder of this study is organized as follows. Section 3.2 considers the causes of Japan's economic stagnation from a demand perspective. Next, Section 3.3, using a growth accounting framework, examines Japan's economy over the past forty years from the supply side and conducts various comparisons with other developed economies. The section also examines why capital accumulation and increases in labor input – the determinants of supply capacity – came to a standstill. Section 3.4 then investigates why TFP growth slowed in the last two decades. The section mainly focuses on the low level of investment in information and communication technology (ICT) and the slowdown in human capital accumulation. Finally, Section 3.5, based on the analysis in the preceding sections, examines what kind of research and policies are necessary to find a solution to Japan's long-term economic stagnation.

3.2 Insufficient demand

Like most developed economies, Japan experienced a severe drop in final demand in the wake of the global financial crisis that started in autumn

---

[3] The JIP Database has been compiled by the six authors of this chapter and other scholars of Gakushuin, Keio, and other universities as a part of a joint project of RIETI and Hitotsubashi University. The most recent version of the database (JIP 2014) contains annual information on 108 sectors from 1970 to 2011. These sectors cover the whole Japanese economy. The database includes detailed information on factor inputs, annual nominal and real input–output tables, and some additional statistics, such as intangible assets, Japan's international trade by trade partner, inward and outward FDI, etc. at the detailed sectoral level.
An Excel file version of the JIP 2014 is available at www.rieti.go.jp/en/database/JIP2014/index.html.

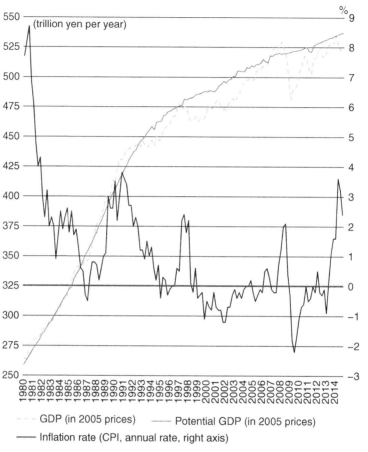

Figure 3.1 Japan's real GDP, potential GDP, and inflation rate (%), 1980Q1–2014Q4

2008. Unlike most other economies, however, Japan was already suffering from a lack of demand even before the crisis. Figure 3.1 shows the trend in Japan's real gross domestic product (GDP), estimated potential GDP, and inflation rate (in terms of the CPI). The figure indicates that in the wake of the global financial crisis Japan experienced a huge negative GDP gap of –8%. However, even in 1993–95 and 1998–2003 it already experienced a GDP gap of more than –2%. Moreover, these were periods during which Japan also experienced deflation.

Despite the Bank of Japan's massive stimulus measures and various fiscal policy measures undertaken by the government, Japan still had a GDP gap of –2.3% in the fourth quarter of 2014 and suffers from very low inflation rates (when excluding the impact of the consumption tax hike).

3.2.1 *Japan's excess saving problem*

Reasons for the insufficient effective demand in the 1990s include not only temporary factors such as a decline in investment due to a decline in the appetite for investment as a result of deflation (Hamada and Horiuchi 2004), the disruption of financial intermediation (Bayoumi 2001, Horie 2002), damaged corporate balance sheets (Koo 2003, Ogawa 2011), a downturn in consumption based on asset effects and precautionary motives (Ishii 2009, Iwaisako and Okada 2009), or the downturn in exports as a result of the yen appreciation of 1994–1995, and so on, but also due to the problem of chronic excess saving since the 1980s, as pointed out by Krugman (1998) and Fukao (2001).

Despite Japan's exceptionally high private gross saving rate when compared with other advanced economies, it did not experience any excess saving until the 1970s due to extremely high investment during the high speed growth era. However, as can be seen in Figure 3.2, from the beginning of the 1970s, Japan's economy started to experience chronic excess saving.[4] This is due to the large decline in private investment, for which there are the following reasons.

First, after the 1960s, when the first baby boomer generation reached adulthood, the growth rate of the working age population slowed considerably. Looking at the average growth rate of the working age population (those aged 15–64) by decade, we find a steady decline in the growth rate from 1.9% in the 1950s to 1.8% in the 1960s, 1.0% in the 1970s, 0.9% in the 1980s, 0.0% in the 1990s, and −0.6% in the 2000s (Statistics Bureau, Ministry of Internal Affairs and Communications 2014). The decline in the growth rate of the working age population reduced the need to invest in capital equipment for new workers, thus exerting a negative impact on capital investment.

Second, the process of catching up with manufacturing technologies in the United States and Europe and increases in TFP driven by this

---

[4] It should be noted that the saving–investment balance depends not only on structural factors but also on the business cycle. However, the basic picture given by Figure 3.2 does not change much when adjusting for the business cycle. See Cabinet Office (2009) for more details.

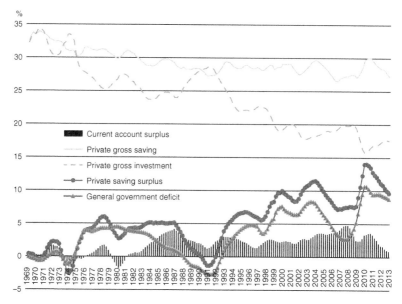

Figure 3.2 Japan's savings–investment balance: relative to nominal GDP (four-quarter moving average)

process had more or less run their course by the early 1970s, and probably as a result of this, TFP growth started to slow down from the 1970s onward.[5] Kuroda and Nomura (1999), for example, estimate that the TFP growth rate in 1972–1992 was 2.8 percentage points lower than in 1960–1972. This decline in TFP growth, by lowering the rate of return on capital, likely reduced private investment.

These two structural factors explain the largest part of the decline in private investment. For example, assuming balanced growth and Harrod-neutral (labor-saving) technical change in a Solow-type neo-classical growth model, and further assuming a capital–GDP ratio of 3

---

[5] For a long-term comparison of TFP levels by industry between Japan and the US, see Jorgenson *et al.* (1987) and Jorgenson *et al.* (2015). Jorgenson *et al.* (2015) is based on a KLEMS-type database for the US and Japan. Compared with the JIP Database, the industry classification of their database is more aggregated (about thirty-five sectors). There are many other differences in the estimation procedure employed by us (for the JIP Database) and Jorgenson *et al.* (2015). They explicitly treat land as a production factor, while we omitted land input. The inclusion of land lowers the cost share of other inputs. This difference usually makes their estimate of TFP growth higher than ours. They also include consumer durables in capital input, which we did not.

and a labor and capital cost share ratio of 2 to 1, a 2 percentage point decline in the growth rate of the working age population and a 2 percentage point decline in TFP growth reduce Japan's economic growth rate by 2 and 3 percentage points respectively (for a total of 5 percentage points) and lower the investment–GDP ratio by 6 and 9 percentage points (for a total of 15 percentage points) respectively.[6] In addition to these two factors, as will be discussed in detail in Section 3.3, while in the immediate postwar period Japan was able to achieve high speed growth by raising the capital stock per worker, the increase in the capital ratio lowered the rate of return on capital through the accumulation of excess capital, likely making the reduction in investment more severe than otherwise would have been the case.

The saving–investment balance of the private sector (private saving surplus) will be either invested abroad (current account surplus) or borrowed by the government (general government deficit). Moreover, according to Keynesian economics, if intended private saving is greater than the intended current account surplus plus the intended government deficit, there arises an excess supply of goods. In this case, a reduction in GDP, through a reduction in excess private saving, restores balance in the goods market.

The lower part of Figure 3.2 shows how much of the private saving surplus was used for investment abroad (current account surplus) or for financing of the government (general government deficit). The figure shows that during most of the period the largest part of excess saving went to the government deficit. The only exceptions are the mid-1980s, when Japan recorded large current account surpluses as a result of "Reaganomics," the late 1980s to early 1990s, when there was active private investment during the bubble economy, and the export-driven boom during 2006–2008.

3.2.2 *The equilibrium exchange rate and trade friction*

Open economy macroeconomics (see, e.g., Obstfeld and Rogoff 1996) suggests that when there is a large private saving excess in an economy with free international capital flows, then – assuming neo-classical

---

[6] Hayashi and Prescott (2002), like the analysis here, use a neo-classical growth model and point out that it is very likely that the decline in the TFP growth rate and in labor input from the 1990s onward reduced capital investment.

adjustment mechanisms where goods and factor prices as well as the real exchange rate adjust flexibly to achieve full-employment equilibrium – the excess supply of domestic goods should be resolved through a large depreciation of the domestic currency and an increase in the current account surplus. In this situation, the exchange rate that achieves full-employment equilibrium can be called the "equilibrium real exchange rate" in the same sense that the "equilibrium real interest rate" is the interest rate that achieves full employment in a closed economy.

However, there are a number of examples in which Japan's current account surplus did not expand sufficiently to bring about such equilibrium during a recession, such as that of the time of the Japan–Germany "locomotive theory" of 1977, the recession brought about by yen appreciation following the 1985 Plaza Agreement, and the recession following the collapse of the bubble economy in 1991. Why did the yen not depreciate sufficiently and the current account surplus increase sufficiently to achieve full employment? The following two factors can be pointed out.

First, Japan, which for a long time persistently had the largest current account surplus in the world, did not have sufficient bargaining power vis-à-vis the US, which for a long time has been the country with the largest current account deficit in the world and which urges surplus countries to expand domestic demand. Compared with China, which has subsequently taken on the role of largest surplus country, the reasons for the lack of bargaining power are that Japan probably was not important as an export base for American firms and Japan's security considerations. Moreover, in contrast with China, which continues with strict controls on capital movements, it was difficult for Japan to maintain a weak yen through foreign market interventions, since by the early 1970s, as a result of joining the Organisation for Economic Cooperation and Development (OECD), and acceding to Article 8 status of the International Monetary Fund (IMF) in 1964, it had already greatly liberalized international capital transactions. Whenever Japan recorded a large current account surplus in transactions with the US, protectionism reared its head in the US as can be seen around the time of the "locomotive theory" and the Plaza Agreement, pushing Japan to expand domestic demand by increasing government expenditure and to reduce the current account surplus through an appreciation of the yen.

Second, compared with the golden era of the gold standard before the First World War, even from the 1980s onward, when international capital liberalization had advanced, international capital movements were not sufficiently smooth to absorb Japan's huge excess savings.

In contrast with the era of the gold standard, in today's environment, in which many countries having adopted a flexible exchange rate regime, international lending and borrowing typically involves exchange rate risk. Because most of the investment in the US is in bonds denominated in US dollars, institutional and other investors in Japan suffer exchange rate losses as result of a depreciation of the dollar vis-à-vis the yen. If there are fears of exchange rate risk and there are not sufficient actors willing to shoulder this risk (that is, residents willing to hold foreign currency-denominated assets and non-residents willing to shoulder liabilities denominated in yen), a large current account surplus will sooner or later cause an appreciation of the yen and a reduction in the current account surplus, and foreign investment as a result will fall. This kind of phenomenon could be observed during the strong-yen periods of 1978 and 1995. Moreover, in the golden era of the gold standard, capital flowed mainly from the UK to the New World through the issuance of bonds, and the claims were often preserved through gunboat diplomacy. In contrast, in the case of international borrowing and lending from and to developing countries in the postwar era, it was difficult to seize those assets even if debtor countries reneged on repayments. For this reason, debtor countries have an incentive to renege on repayments, making the debt accumulation of developing countries more serious and, at the same time, making new international lending and borrowing difficult.

Meltzer (1999) and Hamada and Okada (2009) argue that in the 1990s the Japanese government should have carried out more determined polices to effect a depreciation of the yen.[7] However, given that the effect of yen-selling interventions not accompanied by an interest rate cut are weak, and that policy interventions to weaken the yen through a cut in real interest rates were difficult because of limitations through deflation and the liquidity trap, it is doubtful that it would have been possible to induce a large yen depreciation. Moreover, even if there had been room to effect large negative real interest rates in Japan in the 1990s, because of trade frictions with the US, it is highly unlikely that Japan could have continued with yen depreciation and a current account surplus large enough to cancel out the huge savings surplus for a prolonged period. In fact, as seen above, the yen appreciation

---

[7] On this issue, also see Jorgenson *et al.* (2015).

following the Plaza Agreement and the recession that followed it arose
before the deflation period.

3.2.3 *The unresolved excess saving problem*

Let us return to considering how Japan's excess savings are used. When
a saving surplus country cannot achieve sufficient capital exports and
a sufficient current account surplus, then, under neo-classical conditions,
real interest rates will fall as a result of the excess supply of goods and full
employment will be maintained through an expansion of private investment. The policy of monetary easing pursued by the Bank of Japan
during the second half of the 1980s gave rise to this kind of situation,
but it had the adverse effect of giving rise to the bubble economy with
negative consequences such as inefficient capital formation, as became
clear through the subsequent non-performing loan crisis.

Finally, as already seen, the majority of Japan's private saving excess
has been put into compensating for the government deficit, but as the
economic measures conducted by the Obuchi government in the late
1990s typify, government expenditure was not necessarily used for
efficient purposes.

For example, public investment by the Japanese government was
concentrated in low income regions of Japan. Figure 3.3 shows the

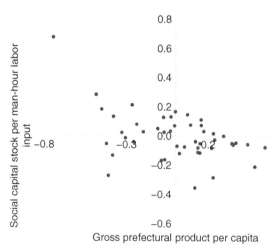

Figure 3.3 The relationship between per capita gross prefectural product and
social capital stock per man-hour labor input, 2008

cross-prefectural relationship between per capita gross prefectural product and social capital stock (non-toll roads and bridges, harbor facilities, dikes, etc.) per man-hour labor input in 2008. There is a statistically significant negative correlation (at the 1 percent level) between the two variables. Japan has constructed many roads used by no one and bridges to nowhere.

Many of the researchers arguing that the main cause of Japan's prolonged economic stagnation since the 1990s is insufficient demand assert that the stagnation was caused by the increase in real interest rates as a result of deflation and the liquidity trap, the impairment of financial intermediation as a result of the non-performing loan problem, and impediments to investment due to damaged balance sheets. Certainly, as researchers such as Ogawa (2003) and Miyao (2006), among others, show, part of the downturn in investment in the 1990s was caused by these factors. However, as Ogawa (2009) also indicates, only part of the downturn in investment can be explained by the impairment of balance sheets.

As seen in Figure 3.2, from the mid-1970s to the 1980s, when the factors impeding investment such as deflation and the non-performing loan problem did not exist and TFP growth was relatively strong, Japan experienced large excess saving except during the period of the bubble economy. As explained earlier, reasons for the decline in investment relative to GDP include not only the above-mentioned temporary factors observed in the 1990s and the 2000s, but also structural factors such as excess capital as a result of demographic trends and the decline in the return on capital due to economic growth relying on capital accumulation. Japan should have eliminated early on the factors impeding investment such as deflation and the non-performing loan problem. However, it would be rather too optimistic to assume that if this had been achieved the chronic lack of demand could have been overcome. If, hypothetically, investment had been stimulated sufficiently through, for example, negative real interest rates to absorb the huge excess savings, there would have been a real danger of another bubble economy.[8]

---

[8] Using various methods, Kamata (2009) estimated how the level of the equilibrium real interest rate that would have eliminated the GDP gap through an expansion in investment, would have moved, and finds that in the latter half of the 1990s, when the equilibrium real interest rate was lowest, it would have been more or less 0 percent or around −1 percent.

Moreover, as Section 3.3 will show, in contrast with the US, where the capital coefficient remained more or less unchanged during the same period, the capital coefficient in Japan increased rapidly from the 1990s onward. Looking at the average of the capital coefficient over the past two decades, it certainly cannot be said that investment has been impeded in Japan; instead, it would be more correct to regard capital accumulation in Japan as having continued apace – despite the demographic trends and the decline in the return on capital – as a result of a low interest rate policy and loan guarantees by the government.

As we have seen above, any of the three outlets for excess saving, namely, a current account surplus, an acceleration in private investment, or a government deficit, would at any rate have given rise to problems. However, if there is no outlet for intended excess saving, this will cause a recession through insufficient demand. This danger of insufficient demand has been a chronic presence in Japan since the latter half of the 1970s. As also pointed out in Fukao (2001), looking at the period since 1980, we find that Japan experienced a recession in 1982, 1986, 1992, 1997, 2000, and 2008, and many of these recessions coincided with periods in which the outlet for excess saving changed. Put simply, it could be said that when the main outlet for excess saving in a particular period became unsustainable – for example, as a result of changes in the international environment or concerns about the fiscal deficit getting out of hand – and a smooth transition to a new alternative outlet was not possible, the economy dived into a recession. This can be seen by looking at the changes in the main outlet for excess saving, which until 1982 had been government deficits, followed by current account surpluses until 1986, private investment until 1992, government deficits until 1997, current account surpluses and government deficits until 2000, and current account surpluses again until 2008.

Krugman (1998), examining deflation in Japan in the 1990s, compared Japan's high private saving rate and the US' extremely low saving rate, and similarly pointed out that following the end of Japan's high speed growth Japan was constantly in danger of falling into deflation.

Another way to resolve Japan's excess saving problem would be to increase private consumption or lower the saving rate. The Maekawa Report (The Study Commission on Adjustment of Economic Structure for International Cooperation 1986) published in April 1986 emphasized that desirable policies would be to promote private consumption and housing investment.

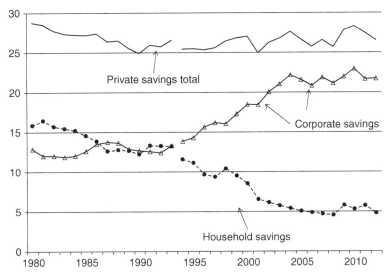

Figure 3.4 Household and corporate saving relative to nominal GDP (%)

Setting aside temporary consumption stimuli as part of antirecession policies, lowering the private saving rate for a prolonged period through government intervention is probably not that easy. However, many economists, based on the life cycle hypothesis, thought that with the aging of the population, Japan's saving rate inevitably would fall rapidly and the excess saving problem would before long be resolved.[9] For example, Horioka (2008) expected that Japan's household saving rate would rapidly fall to zero or even turn negative by around 2010. As can be seen from Figure 3.4, the actual household saving rate, more or less in line with Horioka's prediction, has fallen considerably. However, as if to offset that decline, the corporate saving rate has increased rapidly, and as a result the private saving rate has remained unchanged at around 25 percent. Overall, therefore, it can be said that the problem of excess private saving has still not been resolved.

An important issue regarding Japan's excess saving problem is to what extent household and corporate saving are substitutes for each other and, moreover, to what extent household and government saving are substitutes for each other. A considerable number of studies have

---

[9] However, the experience of the US indicates that the private saving rate moves in a way that cannot necessarily be explained by changes in demographic structure (Auerbach and Kotlikoff 1989).

examined this issue, including Poterba (1987), Auerbach and Hassett (1989), Iwaisako and Okada (2009), and Matsubayashi (2009), and many of them find that the substitutability between the three types of saving is not very high.

While there are many empirical studies on the determinants of household saving, there has been relatively little research on the determinants of corporate saving. If household and corporate saving are not close substitutes for each other, more research on why firms in Japan have been saving as much as they have in recent years is necessary. What we do know is that major corporations account for a large part of corporate saving.[10] As will be shown in Sections 3.3 and 3.4, given that large corporations – despite their high productivity – do not actively invest domestically, it is likely that they use their surplus funds not for capital investment but for debt repayment (see Schaede 2008 on the rapid deleveraging of corporations) and the accumulation of liquid assets.[11] Whether this kind of corporate saving behavior is desirable, and whether governance in major corporations functions properly, is an important research topic for the future.[12]

3.3 Examining Japan's prolonged stagnation from the supply side

As seen in the previous section, in most of the period since 1991, Japan has suffered from a lack of demand. The reason is huge excess saving as a result of structural causes such as a high saving rate and the decline in

---

[10] Approximating firms' gross saving by subtracting corporation and municipal taxes, interim dividends, and dividends from their current profits using data from the Financial Statements Statistics *of Corporations by Industry (Yearbook)*, we find that, in 2008, corporations with 1 billion yen of paid-in capital, which produce 30.3% of value added of all for-profit corporations (excluding finance and insurance), accounted for 41.5% of saving by all corporations. On the other hand, saving by corporations with less than 20 million yen of paid-in capital, which produce 31.4% of value added, only accounted for 13.5% of saving by all corporations.

[11] Large corporations are actively expanding employment not within their own company but in domestic subsidiaries (Kwon and Kim 2010) and are engaging in foreign direct investment abroad. It is likely that part of large corporations' saving is used for these purposes.

[12] Recently, the Japanese government introduced new policies to reform Japan's corporate governance (Benes 2015). This reform might change corporate saving behavior in the future.

investment due to demographic change. This huge excess saving has made it difficult to overcome deflation and has produced a situation in which even with a very active fiscal policy Japan has continued to register a large negative GDP gap throughout most of the last two decades.

However, even if Japan has suffered from insufficient demand for a long time, this does not necessarily mean that there is no point in analyzing the economy from the supply side. For example, understanding the structural reasons for the decline in investment – such as the increase of the capital coefficient and the decline in the return on capital – and determining whether the decline in investment is a temporary or a structural phenomenon is important for understanding the lack of demand. Moreover, understanding the impact of population aging and trends on the macro-economy is indispensable when considering Japan's future growth prospects.

3.3.1 Supply-side sources of Japan's economic growth

Based on these considerations, this section attempts to look at Japan's prolonged stagnation from the supply side using growth accounting.[13] Figure 3.5, using the JIP 2014 Database, shows the results of the growth accounting for ten-year intervals.

Figure 3.5 shows that the annual average growth rate of Japan's real GDP (shown by the solid line in the figure) fell by 3.5 percentage points from 4.4% in 1970–1990 to 0.9% in 1990–2011. Decomposing this 3.5 percentage point decline in the growth rate shows that it is due to a decline in TFP growth from 1.5% to 0.2%, a decline in the contribution of capital accumulation from 1.8% to 0.7%, a decline in the contribution of labor quality improvements from 0.8% to 0.5%, and a reversal in the contribution of man-hour growth from +0.4% to –0.5%.[14] The sum of the contribution of labor quality improvements and of man-hour growth in 1990–2011 was almost zero (0.5%–0.5% = 0.0%), meaning that

---

[13] The productivity analyses in this section and in Section 4 are partly based on Fukao (2012).

[14] Preceding studies on the deceleration in TFP growth from the 1990s onward include Hayashi and Prescott (2002), Jorgensen and Motohashi (2003), and Fukao and Kwon (2006). The estimated decline in TFP growth differs across these studies. An analysis of the reasons for these differences is provided by Inui and Kwon (2005) and Fukao and Kwon (2006).

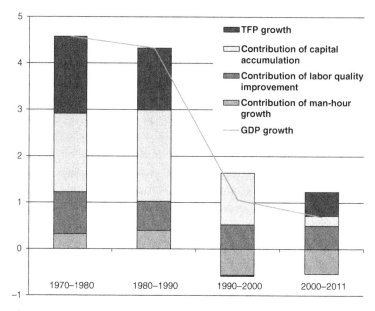

Figure 3.5 Decomposition of Japan's GDP growth (annual rate, %)

labor service input (man-hour growth plus labor quality improvement) did not increase in this period.

With regard to TFP, it should be noted that there is the danger that because of labor hoarding and a decline in the capital utilization rate during a recession, the contribution of increases in factor inputs to output may be overestimated and TFP growth as a result underestimated. However, as pointed out by Shioji (2009), the decline in TFP growth from the 1990s onward is so large that it cannot be explained by such temporary factors. Moreover, comparing different points in time when the GDP gap was very similar, such as 1983, 1992, and 2006 (Figure 3.1), we can easily confirm that TFP growth after 1990 was much lower than until 1990.

As seen above, notable characteristics of Japan's prolonged economic stagnation from the 1990s onward include the following: (1) labor service input growth was negative; and (2) TFP growth declined sharply. In addition, (3) capital accumulation became markedly slower after 2000. The remainder of this section discusses the third and the first of these issues in greater detail, while Section 3.4 focuses on the deceleration in TFP growth.

3.3.2 The increase in the capital coefficient and the decline in the rate of return on capital

As seen in the growth accounting in the preceding sub-section, the contribution of capital accumulation continued to be positive in the 1990s and the 2000s, although labor service input did not increase in the 1990s and after. This means that the capital service/labor service input ratio rose substantially during the period 1990–2011.

As a result of this rise, Japan achieved some increases in labor productivity even during the 1990s and after despite very low TFP growth. Annual average labor productivity (real GDP/man-hour) growth from 1990 to 2011 was 1.7%. Using growth accounting, labor productivity growth can be decomposed into the following three factors: increases in the capital input–labor input ratio, improvements in labor quality, and TFP growth. The contribution of each of these to the 1.7% annual average increase in labor productivity from 1990 to 2010 was 0.9, 0.5, and 0.3 percentage points respectively. Thus, labor productivity growth was mainly accomplished by physical and human capital deepening, not by TFP growth. However, due to the decreasing marginal productivity of capital, economic growth relying on capital accumulation lowers the rate of return on capital and sooner or later reaches a limit. Let us examine this issue in more detail.

Figures 3.6(a) and 3.6(b) show the capital coefficient (capital stock/ GDP) as well as the gross rate of return on capital for Japan and the US. Figure 3.6(a) shows that although the increase in Japan's capital coefficient decelerated somewhat from the end of the 1990s, on the whole it continued to rise relatively strongly. Comparing the periods before and after 1990, we find that between 1975 and 1990, the capital coefficient rose at an average annual rate of 1.6%. However, between 1990 and 2009, the rate of increase then accelerated to 2.2% per year, while, at the same time, the gross rate of return on capital fell at a rate of 2.1% per year.[15]

---

[15] In a country like Japan, that imports natural resources and exports manufacturing goods, if the relative price of natural resources rises and the terms of trade deteriorate, the return on capital falls in the relatively short term in which capital stock does not change much. The fall in the return on capital in the 1970s and the increase in the 1980s to a considerable extent can be understood as the result of these kinds of movements in the terms of trade.

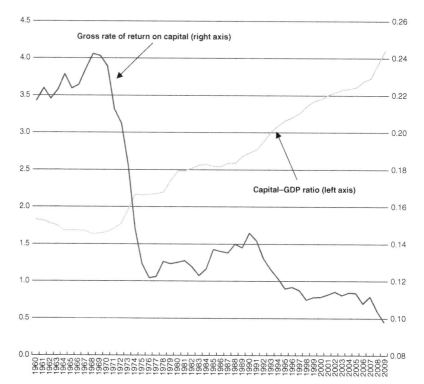

Figure 3.6a Japan's capital coefficient and return on capital

In contrast with Japan, the US, as shown in Figure 6(b), experienced a substantial decline in the capital coefficient and an increase in the rate of return on capital from the first half of the 1980s onward.[16,17]

---

[16] As will be seen in the next section, the ICT investment/non-ICT investment ratio in the US is higher than that in Japan; the capital formation deflator for ICT capital continued to decline; and the depreciation rate of ICT capital and capital losses from ICT capital holdings are larger than those of non-ICT capital. It should be noted that the decline in the capital–GDP ratio and the high rate of return on capital in the US are probably partly caused by these factors. However, when using the capital–GDP ratio and the rate of return on capital in real terms, that is, real capital stock/real GDP, and gross operating surplus/ (GDP deflator × real capital stock), similar differences between Japan and the US as in Figures 3.6(a) and 3.6(b) can be found.

[17] Using the EU KLEMS database, we also constructed a similar figure for Germany after unification. We find that, like the US, Germany also registered a decline in the capital coefficient for the total economy.

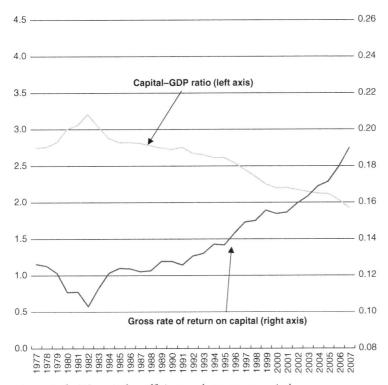

Figure 3.6b US capital coefficient and return on capital

As highlighted by Kaldor in one of his stylized facts (Kaldor 1957), in advanced economies in a situation of balanced growth where sufficient capital has been accumulated, the capital coefficient does not increase. In contrast with the US, this rule of thumb does not hold for Japan, particularly in the 1990s. Economic growth relying on capital accumulation is not necessarily bad per se; however, the question is whether it can be sustained.[18]

[18] Ando (2002) and Saito (2008) point out that it is possible that protracted inefficient investment in the corporate sector may have imposed large capital losses on the household sector. Hayashi (2006) and Saito (2008) try to explain Japan's excess investment using a macro-economic model in which corporate governance does not work well and in which firms, other than making the bare minimum dividend payments, invest all profits and for this reason conduct excess investment above the optimal level determined by households' time preference rate and return on capital. However, as seen in Section 3, from the 2000s, we find huge corporate saving especially by major firms, while capital

Reasons why Japan's capital coefficient increased from the 1990s onward despite low returns on capital likely are the prolonged low interest rate policy and active investment in the public sector. However, it is very likely that even with very low interest rates, investment-led growth will reach its limits due to the decline in the return on capital and government deficits. In Japan, the private gross investment/GDP ratio (Figure 3.2), the contribution of increases in the capital service input to GDP growth (Figure 3.5) and the speed of the increases in the capital coefficient (Figure 3.6(a)) have diminished since the early 2000s, signaling that growth driven by capital accumulation may be coming to an end.[19]

As seen above, in Japan, unlike in the US, the capital coefficient increased substantially, particularly in the 1990s. At the same time, the return on capital deteriorated and it is very likely that this was not due to a credit crunch, the disruption of financial intermediation, or a lack of demand, but mainly due to the increase in the capital coefficient. If we assume a Cobb-Douglas production function, we would expect the gross rate of return on capital multiplied by the capital–GDP ratio to be constant over time. Under this assumption, the 2.2% annual growth in the capital–GDP ratio in the period 1990–2009 is large enough to fully explain the 2.1% annual decline in the gross rate of return on capital during this period.

The low rate of TFP growth and the low rate of return on capital found above are of considerable relevance in the debate on the policy mix pursued by the present government. Japan has been suffering from a lack of final demand for the last two decades. Despite the recovery from the recession following the global financial crisis, Japan still had a negative GDP gap of 2.3% in the fourth quarter of 2014 (Figure 3.1). The government is pursuing policies to overcome

accumulation by major firms was relatively lacklustre. It is highly likely that major firms used surplus funds not only for investment in plant and equipment (including in subsidiaries at home and abroad), but also for the repayment of liabilities and the accumulation of liquid assets. Therefore, at least with regard to the 2000s, it is difficult to say that firms have been investing all available funds in capital equipment.

[19] Although Figure 3.6(a) suggests that the speed of increase in the capital coefficient accelerated between 2007 and 2009, this is due not to substantial changes in the rate of capital accumulation but to the considerable decline in the numerator (GDP) as a result of the global financial crisis. It is therefore likely that, with the recovery in GDP, the capital coefficient has fallen since 2009.

deflation and seems to be aiming to stimulate private investment through a reduction in real interest rates. However, since investment opportunities are limited and the rate of return on capital is very low, extremely low or negative real interest rates are required, but maintaining very low or negative real interest rates, a positive inflation rate, and full employment without causing bubbles is likely to be extremely difficult to achieve. Therefore, for sustainable growth, it is necessary to raise the rate of return on capital through productivity growth and to stimulate private consumption through job creation and higher wage incomes.

3.3.3 Causes of the decline in labor input and future prospects

One of the main causes of the slowdown of Japan's economic growth from the 1990s is the sharp drop in labor service input growth. As we saw in Figure 3.5, the contribution of labor quality improvements declined from 0.8% in 1970–1990 to 0.5% in 1990–2011, while the contribution of man-hour growth switched from +0.4% to −0.5%.

In this sub-section, we examine the causes of this decline in labor input as well as the future prospects. Man-hour growth in the macroeconomy can be decomposed into the following three factors: changes in the working age population (those aged 15–64), changes in average working hours per worker, and other factors such as changes in the labor force participation rate. Figure 3.7 shows the results of this decomposition for the period 1970–2010. In addition, the figure shows projections by the National Institute of Population and Social Security Research (2012) for changes in the working age population until 2030.

As can be seen in Figure 3.7, the sharp drop in Japan's man-hour input after 1990 was mainly caused by the decline in the working-age population as well as the decline in the average working hours per worker. The shrinking of the working-age population, which is caused by Japan's low birthrate and population aging, is expected to continue in this and the next decade. The expected decline of the working-age population is particularly large in this decade because of the retirement of the baby boomers.

Regarding the decline in working hours per worker, the following can be pointed out. As highlighted by Hayashi and Prescott (2002),

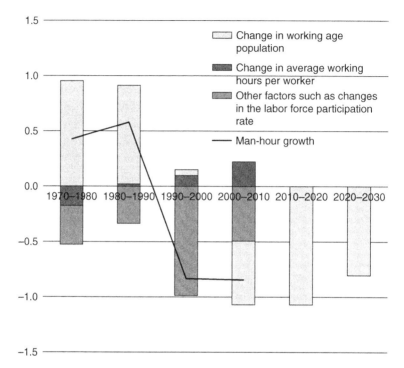

Figure 3.7 Decomposition of Japan's man-hour growth (annual rate, %)

Japan's Labor Standards Act was amended in 1987 and "a 40 hour, five day week" was introduced. Working hours gradually declined until the full implementation of the amendment in 1997. However, even after that, the average working hours of employees continued to decline because of the increase in part-time workers. As shown in Figure 3.8, if we assume that the percentage of part-time workers had remained constant after 1988, there would have been almost no decline in working hours until the onset of the global financial crisis in 2008.

Next, let us examine why improvements in labor quality have slowed down. Figure 3.9 decomposes changes in the labor quality index into the contribution of changes in the labor quality of different types of workers, namely full-time workers, the self-employed (including unpaid family workers), and part-time workers. We measure the quality of labor in terms of the wage rate. The wage rates of full-time workers tend to be higher than those of part-time workers and the estimated labor income per hour of the self-employed. Therefore, an

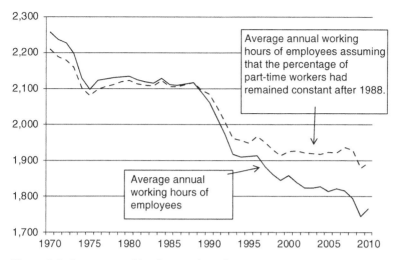

Figure 3.8 Average working hours of employees

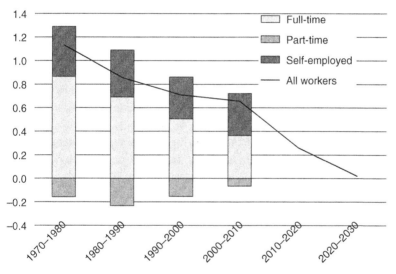

Figure 3.9 Decomposition of growth in the labor quality index by employment status

increase in the percentage of full-time workers contributes to an improvement in labor quality.

In the 1970s and the 1980s, the contribution of full-time workers takes large positive values, because the percentage of full-time workers in total workers increased, the average education level of full-time workers increased, and the average age of full-time workers increased (older full-time workers tend to earn higher wages than younger workers). However, in the 1990s, the percentage of full-time workers in total workers started to decline, while the other two trends almost came to a halt, so that the contribution of full-time workers became smaller.

The contribution of the self-employed took positive values, because their labor income per hour is low and the percentage of self-employed in total workers declined over time. Finally, the contribution of part-time workers took negative values, because their wage rates are low and the percentage of part-time workers in total workers increased over time.

Figure 3.9 also shows projections of labor quality changes in this and the next decade by Kawaguchi *et al.* (2007). They assume that the following four sets of values will take the same value as in 2004: (1) the wage rate and working hours per worker by age, education, sex, and employment status; (2) the percentage of each category of education level for each sex among new workers; (3) the percentage of full-time workers, of part-time workers, and of the self-employed in each category (age, sex, and education) of workers; and (4) the labor force participation rate by age, sex, and education. Under these assumptions, they estimated how demographic changes will affect Japan's labor quality in the future.

The results indicate that the growth rate of the labor quality index will decline substantially in the 2010s as most of the baby boomers retire. Moreover, in the 2020s, with the children of the baby boomers reaching their 50s, the growth rate of the labor quality index will decline further, since wage rates no longer increase by age for workers in their 50s.

The two projections of the working age population (Figure 3.7) and labor quality (Figure 3.8) and the increasing share of part-time workers suggest that it will be difficult for Japan to maintain positive labor service input growth (man-hour growth plus labor quality growth) in this and the next decade, even if the Japanese government were to embark on a full range of policies to address this issue such as raising the labor force participation rates of the elderly and women, raising the education level of new workers, and reducing the share of part-time workers.

3.3.4 TFP growth is indispensable for sustainable growth of Japan's economy

Considering the potential contribution of the three engines of economic growth (labor input growth, capital accumulation, and TFP growth), the discussion above showed that the contribution of labor input growth, if anything, is likely to be negative in Japan. Moreover, as also discussed, for capital accumulation to be sustainable, it is necessary to raise the rate of return on capital through productivity growth and to stimulate private consumption through job creation and higher wage incomes. This means that future economic growth in Japan will have to come mainly from TFP growth. Let us consider Japan's growth prospects in more detail.

The Japanese government now has a target of 2% annual GDP growth. But is this goal realistic? Assume that the production function of the macro-economy is constant returns to scale, technological progress is Harrod-neutral, the economy is in a situation of balanced growth, and the cost share of labor is two-thirds. Then, the long-run growth rate will be labor input growth plus Harrod-neutral technological change, which is equal to TFP growth times 1.5 under our assumptions. Even if we are optimistic about labor supply and assume that labor service input does not decline, Japan needs annual average TFP growth of 1.33% (2/1.5=1.33). Under this scenario, 2% GDP growth can be accomplished if TFP growth contributes 1.33%, labor service input growth contributes 0%, and capital accumulation contributes 0.67%. Since this capital accumulation is induced by TFP growth, 2% GDP growth will be sustainable. Thus, whether Japan can achieve sustainable GDP growth in the long run – and hence whether the growth target of 2% is realistic – crucially depends on whether it can substantially accelerate TFP growth from the rates seen since the 1990s.

3.4 Why Japan's TFP growth has been so low from the 1990s

In this section, we study why Japan's TFP growth has slowed down from the 1990s onward. We examine this issue using two approaches. We start by analyzing Japan's TFP growth from the 1970s using sectoral data.

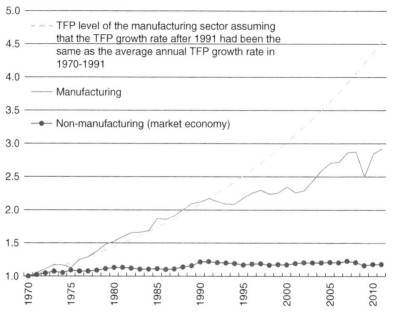

Figure 3.10 TFP level of the manufacturing and the non-manufacturing sector (market economy), 1970–2011 (1970 = 1)

3.4.1 TFP growth by sector

Figure 3.10 shows how TFP (on a value added basis) in Japan's manufacturing and non-manufacturing sectors changed over time. Since inter-temporal changes in TFP in non-market activities such as public administration, education, and health and social services are difficult to measure, our data for the non-manufacturing sector cover only the market economy.

In the case of the manufacturing sector, TFP growth declined sharply after 1991. The dotted line in the figure shows the TFP level of the manufacturing sector when assuming that the TFP growth rate from 1992 onward had remained the same as the average annual TFP growth rate in 1970–1991. TFP growth in the manufacturing sector accelerated again from 2002 to 2007. However, since the stagnation of TFP growth in the 1990s, the early 2000s, and the late 2000s was so pronounced, there is a huge gap between the trend line based on earlier TFP growth rates and the actual TFP level. If Japan's manufacturing sector had been able to maintain TFP growth as high as that in 1970–1991 after 1991, the manufacturing sector's real value added now would be more than 50% higher (without increasing factor inputs) than the actual current level.

In the case of the non-manufacturing sector, TFP growth in Japan, like in other countries, has been much lower than that of the manufacturing sector. Nevertheless, there is also a distinct difference before and after 1991. Until 1991, the non-manufacturing sector achieved slow but steady TFP growth and the TFP level in 1991 was 27% higher than that in 1970. However, after 1991, TFP growth came to a complete halt and – depending on the period examined – even turned slightly negative.

Comparing the 1970–1991 period with the 1991–2011 period, average annual TFP growth in the manufacturing sector declined by 2.2 percentage points from 3.7% to 1.5%, while average annual TFP growth in the non-manufacturing sector (market economy) fell by 1.4 percentage points from 1.1% to –0.2%. Since the nominal value added share of the non-manufacturing sector (market economy) is more than twice as large as that of the manufacturing sector (in 1991, the shares were 54% and 26%, respectively), the contribution of the slowdown of TFP growth in the non-manufacturing sector (market economy) to the slowdown of TFP growth in the macro-economy (approximated by multiplying the TFP growth decline by the value added share) was 30% greater than that of the manufacturing sector. Overall, both the manufacturing and the non-manufacturing sector dragged down macro-TFP growth after 1991.

Comparing Japan's TFP growth with that of the US helps to more clearly understand the stagnation of TFP growth in Japan after 1991. Before 1991, Japan was rapidly catching up with the US. Partly because of low productivity growth in the US in the late 1970s and early 1980s, Japan's TFP level relative to that of the US in 1977–1991 increased by 45% in the manufacturing sector and by 24% in the non-manufacturing sector. After 1991, both the slowdown in productivity growth in Japan and the acceleration in productivity growth in the US reversed this trend. In 1991–2007, Japan's TFP level relative to that of the US declined by 19% in the manufacturing sector and 8% in the non-manufacturing sector.[20]

---

[20] This calculation is based on the EU KLEMS Database and the Rolling Updates as well as Inklaar and Timmer (2008). On this issue, also see Jorgenson *et al.* (2015).

Why has TFP growth in the US accelerated? And why was Japan left behind? One important factor is the ICT revolution in the US. This can be confirmed by comparing Japan's TFP growth with that of the US and other developed countries at a more disaggregated level.[21] In Figure 3.11, the market economy is divided into six sectors and average annual TFP growth rates in each sector before and after 1995 are compared across six major developed economies.

The figure shows that the US experienced an acceleration of TFP growth not only in the ICT-producing sector (electrical machinery, post, and communication), but also in ICT-using sectors, such as distribution services (retail, wholesale, and transportation) and in the rest of the manufacturing sector (i.e., excluding electrical machinery). Japan also experienced relatively high TFP growth in the ICT-producing sector. The problem for Japan, however, is that TFP growth in ICT-using service sectors, such as distribution services and the rest of the manufacturing sector, declined substantially after 1995. Moreover, these ICT-using sectors are much larger than the ICT-producing sector: the average labor input share (hours worked) of the ICT-producing sector in Japan's total labor input in 1995–2007 was only 4.1% (similar to the corresponding share in the US of 3.8%). On the other hand, the labor input shares of distribution services and the rest of the manufacturing sector in 1995–2007 were 22.8% and 16.5%, respectively.[22]

3.4.2 ICT investment in Japan

Why did an ICT revolution of the magnitude observed in the US not occur in Japan? Figures 3.12 and 3.13 provide an answer to this question.

In Japan, the ICT investment–GDP ratio in IT-using service sectors, such as distribution services and total manufacturing excluding the

---

[21] For more details on the industry classification and the ICT intensity of each sector, see Timmer *et al.* (2007).

[22] Basu *et al.* (2003) find that TFP growth of the retail and wholesale sector accounted for more than 70% of TFP growth of the US total economy during 1995–2003. Fukao *et al.* (2008), on the other hand, report that TFP growth of the electrical and optical machinery sector accounted for about 70% of TFP growth of the Japanese total economy during 2000–2005.

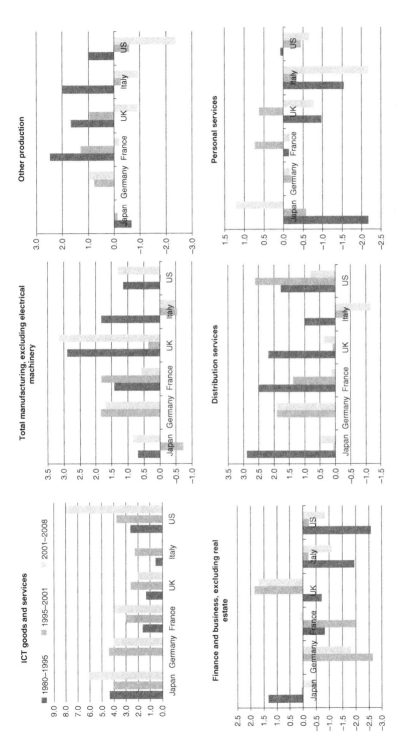

Figure 3.11 TFP growth in the market economy, by sector and country, 1980–1995, 1995–2001, and 2001–2008 (annual rate, %)

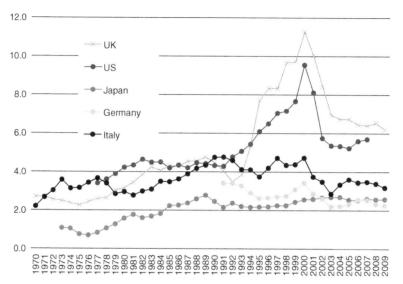

Figure 3.12 ICT investment–GDP ratio in major developed economies: distribution services

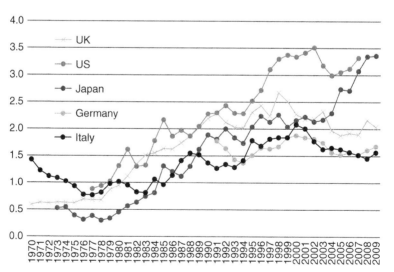

Figure 3.13 ICT investment–GDP ratio in major developed economies: total manufacturing, excluding electrical machinery

electrical machinery sector, is very low in comparison with the US.[23] It appears that the ICT revolution did not happen in Japan simply because Japan has not accumulated sufficient ICT capital.

The next question that needs to be addressed is why ICT investment in some sectors is so small in Japan. It is interesting to note that Japan's ICT investment in these sectors has been low in comparison with other countries since the 1970s. It therefore cannot be argued that the economic slump after 1991 has been the main cause of Japan's low ICT investment. Several structural impediments to ICT investment in Japan can be pointed out.

First, one of the main contributions of the introduction of ICT is that it allows firms to save unskilled labor input. However, because of the high job security in Japan, it may be difficult for firms to actually cut jobs, preventing them from introducing ICT in the first place.

Second, the benefits from ICT investment seem to be closely related to management practices (Bloom *et al.* 2012) and corporate strategies. Miyagawa *et al.* (2014), for example, show that Japanese firms are far behind US firms in terms of their incentive management. Moreover, Motohashi (2010) finds that, unlike US firms, Japanese firms tend to introduce ICT not as strategic tools to enhance firms' total competitiveness but to increase the efficiency of specific divisions. Probably reflecting such weaknesses of Japanese firms, computer network use has a much smaller positive impact on firms' performance in Japan than in the US (Atrostic *et al.* 2008).

Third, in order to introduce ICT, firms need to incur certain initial fixed costs, such as those associated with the revision of organizational structures and training of workers. Some of these expenditures are one shot, and it seems that once firms have adjusted their organizational structures to new ICT and have accumulated a certain mass of ICT-literate workers, they can expand their scale later without substantial additional costs. Probably because of this characteristic of ICT technology, younger and growing firms tend to be more active in ICT investment. Using micro-data of the *Basic Survey of Japanese Business Structure and Activities* by the Ministry of Economy, Trade

---

[23] As Figure 3.13 shows, the ICT investment–GDP ratio in the manufacturing sector excluding electric machinery has increased substantially in recent years. An interesting question therefore is whether TFP growth in this sector will accelerate in the near future.

and Industry (METI), Fukao *et al.* (2012) find that, in Japan's non-manufacturing sector, after controlling for firm size, industry, etc., younger firms have a significantly higher software stock–sales ratio. However, because of the low entry and exit rates in Japan, firms that have been around for forty-five years or more have a majority of market share in all industries except transportation, communication, and public services. This low metabolism has probably impeded ICT investment in Japan.

Fourth, Japan's retail sector is characterized by small shops, whereas the US retail sector is characterized large chain stores (Haskel *et al.* 2007). Moreover, in service sectors, Japanese listed firms are of a much smaller scale on a consolidated basis than their counterparts in the US (Fukao and Miyagawa 2010), and these smaller firms in Japan probably have found it more difficult to introduce ICT because of their small scale.

Fifth, Japan's ICT sector has been suffering from a shortage of software engineers for a considerable time. For example, according to Arora *et al.* (2011), inflows to the ICT labor pool in the US in 1995 were 68 percent greater than those in Japan, and by 2001, inflows in the US were almost three times larger than in Japan. This slow human capital accumulation may also have hindered ICT investment by Japanese firms.

Sixth, since it is too costly for small firms to have their own ICT service division providing a full range of ICT services, having access to efficient vendors of ICT services is a key factor for procuring ICT inputs at a reasonable price; however, in Japan, the market for business process outsourcing (BPO), which includes outsourcing of ICT processes, is not well developed (Fukao *et al.* 2015). The underdevelopment of the BPO market in Japan is closely related with the rigidity of the labor market. Since it is difficult for firms to lay off workers, firms hesitate to restructure costly internal business processing divisions. Moreover, even when they restructure such divisions, they often relocate workers in such divisions to affiliates or firms in the same business group and procure business process services from the firms to which they transferred former employees. Because of these constraints, Japanese firms cannot procure business services from the most productive vendors, reducing the benefit of BPO and keeping the BPO market underdeveloped.

It is also important to note that in order to avoid changes in corporate structure, employment adjustment, and training of workers,

Japanese firms tend to choose custom software rather than packaged software, making ICT investment more expensive and network externality effects smaller, because each firm uses different custom software.

The impediments to ICT investment mentioned above may be closely related with intangible investment in Japan. Intangible investment is defined as expenditures by firms for future production and profits and includes training of workers and the revision of firms' organizational structure. ICT capital and intangible assets may be close complements, economic competencies and computerized information has stagnated (Fukao *et al.* 2009). It seems that the decline in the accumulation of economic competencies was caused by the harsh restructuring resulting from the long-term economic stagnation. For example, many firms increased the percentage of part-time workers in total workers and did not provide intensive training in the case of part-time workers. This change reduced training expenditure substantially (Fukao 2013).

3.5 Conclusion

This study examined the causes of Japan's economic stagnation from a long-term, structural perspective and investigated whether it will be possible to resolve the causes of stagnation. We took a long-term perspective that compares the two decades from the early 1990s onward with the preceding two decades. In addition, taking advantage of databases such as the JIP Database and the EU KLEMS Database, we compared Japan's performance with that of the US and other advanced economies. The main findings are as follows.

(1) Japan has been suffering from a large negative GDP gap since the 1970s. Underlying this large negative GDP gap is an excess-saving problem caused by the persistently high private saving rate and the decline in private investment. Moreover, the declining trend in private investment from the 1970s is due not only to temporary financial factors such as banks' non-performing loans, firms' damaged balance sheets, and deflation, but also structural factors such as the slowdown in the growth of the working age population and the decline in TFP growth.

(2) The saving–investment balance of the private sector (private saving surplus) can be either invested abroad (current account surplus) or borrowed by the government (general government deficit). If there

is no outlet for intended excess saving, this will cause a recession through insufficient demand. This danger of insufficient demand has been a chronic presence in Japan since the latter half of the 1970s.

(3) Consistent with the life cycle hypothesis, Japan's household saving rate has fallen considerably with the aging of the population. However, as if to offset that decline, the corporate saving rate has increased rapidly, so that the private saving rate has remained unchanged at around 25 percent.

(4) The largest part of Japan's excess private saving has gone toward covering the government deficit, but government expenditure was not necessarily used for efficient purposes. For example, public investment by the Japanese government was concentrated in low income regions of Japan.

(5) Open economy macro-economics suggests that when there is a large private saving excess in an economy with free international capital flows, the excess supply of domestic goods should be resolved through a large depreciation of the domestic currency and an increase in the current account surplus. However, Japan's current account surplus did not expand sufficiently to bring about such equilibrium because of three factors: trade friction with the US, insufficient international capital movements to absorb Japan's huge excess saving, and deflation, which made it difficult for Japan to reduce real interest rates further. In addition to these factors, excess saving in other Asian countries such as China and major ASEAN members probably also contributed to making it difficult for Japan to expand its current account surplus.

(6) Japan's TFP growth declined substantially after 1991 both in the manufacturing and the non-manufacturing sector. Before 1991, Japan's TFP was rapidly catching up with that of the US, but after 1991, Japan's TFP level relative to that of the US declined by 19 percent in the manufacturing sector and 8 percent in the non-manufacturing sector. It seems that this large and prolonged drop in TFP growth cannot be fully explained by labor hoarding and the idling of capital stock caused by a scarcity of final demand.

(7) Japan's capital accumulation continued apace after 1990, especially when taking the slow rate of GDP growth and the decline in the working age population into account. Japan's capital–GDP ratio continued to increase after 1991, and this increase in the

capital–GDP ratio must have contributed to the decline in the rate of return on capital in Japan by decreasing the marginal productivity of capital.

(8) From 1995, the US experienced an acceleration of TFP growth in ICT-using sectors such as distribution services and the rest of the manufacturing sector. It appears that a similar ICT revolution did not occur in Japan simply because Japan did not accumulate sufficient ICT capital. Japan's accumulation of intangible capital was also very slow. Since ICT capital and intangible assets may be close complements, it seems that the stagnation of these two types of investment mutually reinforced each other.

(9) The low levels of ICT and intangible investment are closely related with labor market problems. For example, one of the main contributions of the introduction of ICT is that it allows firms to save unskilled labor input. However, because of the high job security in Japan, it may be difficult for firms to actually cut jobs. Moreover, many firms have increased the percentage of part-time workers in total workers and do not provide intensive training for part-time workers. This change has substantially reduced training expenditure, which is an important part of intangible investment.

The above findings yield the following policy implications for Japan. First, the present government is taking steps to overcome deflation and appears to be aiming to stimulate private investment through a reduction in real interest rates. However, since investment opportunities are limited and the rate of return on capital is very low, extremely low or negative real interest rates are required, but maintaining very low or negative real interest rates, a positive inflation rate, and full employment without causing bubbles is likely to be extremely difficult to achieve. Therefore, for sustainable growth, it is necessary to raise the rate of return on capital through productivity growth.

Second, more empirical research is needed to judge for certain whether Japan's low growth rates of ICT capital and intangible assets are sub-optimal. However, if it is indeed desirable to enhance ICT and intangible investment, labor market reforms (such as improving the social safety net, enhancing labor market flexibility, and reducing the unfair gap between regular and part-time workers) and support for ICT and intangible investment by small and medium-sized enterprizes (SMEs) will be important issues. Labor market reform is also important from the perspective of human capital accumulation. Firms pay a premium to part-time workers in order to obtain flexibility of employment. Such behavior by firms is quite rational in the context of slow economic growth and Japan's system of high job security. However, at the same time it may also be creating a huge economic loss by reducing human capital accumulation.

Since the outbreak of the global financial crisis, most developed economies have suffered from insufficient final demand. According to recent estimates by the IMF, the combined negative GDP gap of thirty-seven developed economies in 2014 was about 1.9 percent of their GDP (IMF World Economic Outlook Database April 2015). In a world characterized by "secular stagnation" (Summers 2013), what lessons can we derive from Japan's experience of the lost decades?

First, although it is important not to fall into a deflationary trap, keeping real interest rates very low or negative through a zero nominal interest rate plus moderate inflation is not sufficient to resolve the underlying fundamental problems. It is probably possible for economies to keep on growing by maintaining high investment rates through low real interest rates. However, as capital accumulation continues, the rate of return on capital will eventually decline, so that extremely low or even negative real interest rates will be required. Yet, maintaining very low or negative real interest rates, a positive inflation rate, and full employment carries the danger of leading to new bubbles. Therefore, for growth to be sustainable, it is necessary to raise the rate of return on capital through productivity growth. Japan's fundamental structural problem was not its deflation but the continuation of capital accumulation under a zero interest rate policy and the lack of political will or courage to introduce policies to bring about structural change to accelerate TFP growth.

Second, at least in the case of Japan, the TFP slowdown seems to be caused not by an exogenous drying up of innovation (on this issue, see Gordon 2013), but by structural factors such as low intangible and ICT investment by small and medium-sized firms, an inflexible labor market, the overseas relocation of production by productive firms (Fukao 2013), the inefficient use of public investment, the increase in part-time workers, etc., most of which could have been fixed through sensible policies. In other words, it appears that productivity growth in Japan slowed as a result of impediments that could have been removed, and most other developed economies probably are similarly characterized by obstacles to productivity growth that can be overcome if the necessary will is there. We need sensible and courageous policy-makers, not fatalists.

Third, in the case of Japan, the decline in household saving was cancelled out by an increase in saving by large corporations. Large corporations – despite their high productivity – do not actively invest domestically and use their surplus funds not for capital investment or paying dividends but for debt repayment and the accumulation of liquid assets. Whether this kind of corporate saving behavior is desirable, and whether governance in major corporations functions properly, is an important research topic for the future.

Fourth, some countries, such as China and Germany, seem to be enjoying low real exchange rates and huge current account surpluses, and other economies suffer from that. On the other hand, many low-income economies still want capital inflows. We need a fundamental reform of the international monetary system which will mitigate the scarcity of final demand in developed economies.

References

Ando, Albert. 2002. "Missing Household Saving and Valuation of Corporations," *Journal of Japanese and International Economies*, **16**: 147–176.

Arora, Ashish, Lee G. Branstetter, and Matej Drev. 2011. "Going Soft: How the Rise of Software Based Innovation Led to the Decline of Japan's IT Industry and the Resurgence of Silicon Valley," *Global COE Hi-Stat Discussion Paper Series*, no. 199, Institute of Economic Research, Hitotsubashi University.

Atrostic, B. K., Kazuyuki Motohashi, and Sang V. Nguyen. 2008. "Computer Network Use and Firms' Productivity Performance: The United States vs. Japan," *US Census Bureau Center for Economic Studies Paper*, No. CES-WP-08-30.

Auerbach, Alan J. and Kevin Hassett. 1989. "Corporate Savings and Shareholder Consumption," *NBER Working Paper Series*, no. 2994, National Bureau of Economic Research, Cambridge, MA.

Auerbach, Alan J. and Laurence J. Kotlikoff. 1989. "Demographics, Fiscal Policy, and US Saving in the 1980s and Beyond," *NBER Working Paper Series*, no. 3150, National Bureau of Economic Research, Cambridge, MA.

Basu, Susanto, John G. Fernald, Nicholas Oulton, and Sylaja Srinivasan. 2003. "The Case of the Missing Productivity Growth: Or, Does

Information Technology Explain why Productivity Accelerated in the United States but not in the United Kingdom?" *NBER Macroeconomics Annual*, **18**: 9–82.

Bayoumi, Tamim. 2001. "The Morning After: Explaining the Slowdown in Japanese Growth in the 1990s," *Journal of International Economics*, 53(2): 241–259.

Benes, Nicholas. 2015. "Corporate Governance Reform in Japan," *Ethical Boardroom*. See: http://ethicalboardroom.com/leadership/corporate-governance-reform-in-japan, April 15.

Bloom, Nicholas, Raffaella Sadun, and John Van Reenen. 2012. "Americans do IT Better: US Multinationals and the Productivity Miracle," *American Economic Review*, **102**(1): 167–201.

Cabinet Office. 2009. *Annual Report on the Japanese Economy and Public Finance 2009: Overcoming Financial Crisis and Vision for Sustained Recovery*. Tokyo: Government Cabinet Office.

Fukao, Kyoji. 2001. "Japan's Excess Saving and the Outbreak of the 'Bubble.'" In Michio Muramatsu and Masahiro Okuno (eds.), *Heisei baburu no kenkyu (The Research on Bubble Economy in Heisei Era* [author's translation]). Tokyo: Toyo Keizai Shinposha (in Japanese).

2012. *The Structural Causes of Japan's "Two Lost Decades": Forging a New Growth Strategy*. Tokyo: Nikkei Publishing Inc. (in Japanese).

2013. "Explaining Japan's Unproductive Two Decades," *Asian Economic Policy Review*, **8**: 193–213.

Fukao, Kyoji, Kenta Ikeuchi, YoungGak Kim, and Hyeog Ug Kwon. 2015. "Why was Japan Left Behind in the ICT Revolution?" *RIETI Discussion Paper Series*, No. 15-E-043, Research Institute of Economy, Trade and Industry.

Fukao, Kyoji, YoungGak Kim, and Hyeog Ug Kwon. 2012. "Intangible Investment in Japan," *PPT prepared for the OECD Workshop on Productivity*, OECD Conference Centre, Paris, November 5–6, 2012.

Fukao, Kyoji and Hyeog Ug Kwon. 2006. "Why Did Japan's TFP Growth Slow Down in the Lost Decade? An Empirical Analysis Based on Firm-level Data of Manufacturing Firms," *Japanese Economic Review*, 57(2): 195–228.

Fukao, Kyoji and Tsutomu Miyagawa. 2010. "Service Sector Productivity in Japan: The Key to Future Economic Growth." In MoonJoong Tcha (ed.), *The Service Sector Advancement: Issues and Implications for the Korean Economy*. Sejong-si, Korea: KDI Publishing, ch. 2–2, pp. 92–109.

Fukao, Kyoji, Tsutomu Miyagawa, Kentaro Mukai, Yukio Shinoda, and Konomi Tonogi. 2008. "Intangible Investment in Japan: New Estimates and Contribution to Economic Growth," *Global COE Hi-Stat*

Discussion Paper Series, gd08-015, Institute of Economic Research, Hitotsubashi University.

Fukao, Kyoji, Tsutomu Miyagawa, Kentaro Mukai, Yukio Shinoda, and Konomi Tonogi. 2009. "Intangible Investment in Japan: Measurement and Contribution to Economic Growth, *The Review of Income and Wealth*, 55(3): 717–736.

Gordon, Robert J. 2013. "Is US Economic Growth Over? Faltering Innovation Confronts the Six Headwinds," *NBER Working Paper*, no. 18315, National Bureau of Economic Research, Cambridge, MA.

Hamada, Koichi and Akiyoshi Horiuchi. 2004. "Wrap-up Comments: Why Did Japan Experience Long-Term Stagnation?" In Koichi Hamada, Akiyoshi Horiuchi and Economic and Social Research Institute, Cabinet Office (eds.), *Debates on the Economic Crisis in Contemporary Japan*. Tokyo: Nihon Keizai Shinbun (in Japanese).

Hamada, Koichi and Yasushi Okada. 2009. "Monetary and International Factors behind Japan's Lost Decade," *Journal of the Japanese and International Economies*, 23: 200–219.

Haskel, Jonathan, Ron S. Jarmin, Kazuyuki Motohashi, and Raffaella Sadun. 2007. "Retail Market Structure and Dynamics: A Three Country Comparison of Japan, the UK and the US," Harvard Business School Working Paper.

Hayashi, Fumio. 2006. "The Over-investment Hypothesis." In Lawrence R. Klein (ed.) *Long-run Growth and Short-run Stabilization: Essays in Memory of Albert Ando*. Cheltenham, UK: Edward Elgar.

Hayashi, Fumio, and Edward C. Prescott. 2002. "The 1990s in Japan: A Lost Decade," *Review of Economic Dynamics*, 5(1): 206–235.

Horie, Yasuhiro. 2002. "Economic Analysis of the 'Credit Crunch' in the Late 1990s," *Discussion Paper Series*, no. 2002–1, Faculty of Economics, Kyushu University.

Horioka, Charles Yuji. 2008. "The Flow of Household Funds in Japan," *Public Policy Review*, Policy Research Institute, Japan Ministry of Finance, 4(1): 37–52.

Inklaar, Robert and Marcel P. Timmer. 2008. "GGDC Productivity Level Database: International Comparison of Output, Inputs and Productivity at the Industry Level," a paper prepared for the 30th General Conference of The International Association for Research in Income and Wealth, Portoroz, Slovenia, August 24–30, 2008, Groningen Growth and Development Centre, University of Groningen, The Netherlands.

Inui, Tomohiko and HyeogUg Kwon. 2005. "Survey: Did the TFP Growth Rate in Japan Decline in the 1990s?" *Economic Analysis*, 176:138–167, Economy and Social Research Institute, Cabinet Office (in Japanese).

Ishii Tatsuya. 2009. "Changes in Households' Precautionary Saving Behavior from the Bubble Economy Period to the Deflation Period." In Kyoji Fukao (ed.), *The Japanese Economy in the Bubble/Deflation Periods and Economic Policy. Vol. 1: Macro Economy and Industrial Structure*. Keio University Press (in Japanese).

Ito, Takatoshi, Hugh Patrick, and David E. Weinstein. 2005. (eds.) *Reviving Japan's Economy: Problems and Prescriptions*, Cambridge, MA: MIT Press.

Iwaisako, Tokuo and Keiko Okada. 2009. "Overview of the Consumption and the Saving in the Japanese Economy from the 1980s." In Kyoji Fukao (ed.), *The Japanese Economy in the Bubble/Deflation Period and Economic Policy. Vol. 1: Macro Economy and Industrial Structure*. Keio University Press (in Japanese).

Jorgenson, Dale W., Masahiro Kuroda and Mieko Nishimizu. 1987. "Japan–US Industry-level Productivity Comparisons, 1969–1979," *Journal of the Japanese and International Economies*, 1(1): 1–30.

Jorgenson, Dale W. and Kazuyuki Motohashi. 2003. "The Role of Information Technology in Economy: Comparison between Japan and the United States," *prepared for RIETI/KEIO Conference on Japanese Economy: Leading East Asia in the 21st Century?* Keio University, May 30.

Jorgenson, Dale W., Koji Nomura, and Jon D. Samuels. 2015. "A Half Century of Trans-pacific Competition: Price Level Indices and Productivity Gaps for Japanese and US Industries, 1955–2012." In Dale W. Jorgenson, Kyoji Fukao, and Marcel P. Timmer (eds.), *Growth and Stagnation in the World Economy*. Cambridge University Press.

Kaldor, Nicholas. 1957. "A Model of Economic Growth," *The Economic Journal*, **67**: 591–624.

Kamata, Koichiro. 2009. "Japan's Equilibrium Real Interest Rate," in Kyoji Fukao (ed.), *The Japanese Economy in the Bubble/Deflation Period and Economic Policy. Vol. 1: Macro Economy and Industrial Structure*. Keio University Press (in Japanese).

Kawaguchi, Daiji, Ryo Kambayashi, YoungGak Kim, HyeogUg Kwon, Satoshi Shimizutani, Kyoji Fukao, Tetsuji Makino, and Izumi Yokoyama. 2007. "Are Wage-tenure Profiles Steeper than Productivity-tenure Profiles? Evidence from Japanese Establishment Data from the *Census of Manufacturers* and the *Basic Survey of Wage Structure*," *Economic Review*, 58(1): 61–90 (in Japanese).

Koo, Richard C. 2003. *Balance Sheet Recession: Japan's Struggle with Uncharted Economics and its Global Implications*. Singapore: John Wiley and Sons (Asia).

Krugman, Paul. 1998. "It's BAAACK! Japan's Slump and the Return of the Liquidity Trap," *Brookings Papers on Economic Activity*, **2**: 137–205.

Kuroda, Masahiro and Koji Nomura. 1999. "Japan's Growth Potential," Keizai Kyoshitsu column, Nihon Keizai Shimbun, January 27 (in Japanese).

Kwon, HyeogUg and YoungGak Kim. 2010. "Ownership Structure and TFP: Evidence from Japanese Firms," *RIETI Discussion Paper Series*, no. 10-J-050, Research Institute of Economy, Trade and Industry.

Matsubayashi, Yoichi. 2009. "Substitutability of Savings by Sectors in Japan and the United Sates," *The Economic Analysis*, 181:46–77, Economy and Social Research Institute, Cabinet Office (in Japanese).

Meltzer, Allan H. 1999. "Comments: What More Can the Bank of Japan Do?" *Monetary and Economic Studies*, 17(3): 189–191.

Miyagawa, Tsutomu, Kazuma Edamura, Kim YoungGak, and Jung Hosung (2014) "Management Practice and R&D Activity: Empirical Analysis Based on Japan-Korea Interview Surveys," *Bank of Japan Working Paper Series*, No. 14-J-4, Bank of Japan (in Japanese).

Miyao, Ryuzo. 2006. "Causes of Fluctuations in the Japanese Economy: The Role of Productivity Shocks," *Bank of Japan Working Paper Series*, No. 06-J-1, Bank of Japan (in Japanese).

Motohashi, Kazuyuki. 2010. "Empirical Analysis of IT and Productivity: Comparisons between Japan and the US," *RIETI Policy Discussion Paper Series*, no. 10-P-008, Research Institute of Economy, Trade and Industry (in Japanese).

National Institute of Population and Social Security Research. 2012. "Population Projections for Japan (January 2012)." See: www.ipss.go.jp/site-ad/index_english/esuikei/gh2401e.asp, accessed April 28, 2014.

Obstfeld, Maurice and Kenneth S. Rogoff. 1996. *Foundations of International Macroeconomics*. Cambridge, MA: The MIT Press.

Ogawa, Kazuo. 2003. *Economic Analysis of the Great Recession: Investigation into the Long-term Stagnation of the Japanese Economy*. Nihon Keizai Shinbun-sha (in Japanese).

——— 2009. "Balance Sheet Deterioration and the Real Economy: Empirical Analysis of the Japanese Economy sincethe 1990s." In Kazuto Ikeo (ed.), *The Japanese Economy in the Bubble/Deflation Period and Economic Policy. Vol. 4: Non-performing Loans and the Financial Crisis*. Keio University Press (in Japanese).

——— 2011. "Balance Sheet Deterioration and Credit Allocations: Japanese Evidence from the Short-Term Economic Survey of Enterprises," *Japan and the World Economy*, 23(2): 86–96.

Poterba, James M. 1987, "Tax Policy and Corporate Saving," *Brookings Papers on Economic Activity*, 18(2): 455–516.

Saito, Makoto. 2008. "On Substitution Between Household Consumption and Equipment Investment." In Shinsuke Ikeda, Kazumi Asako,

Hidehiko Ichimura, and Hideshi Ito (eds.), *Recent Developments in Economics 2008*. Tokyo: Toyo Keizai Shinpo-sha (in Japanese).

Saxonhouse, Gary and Robert Stern. 2004. (eds.) *Japan's Lost Decade: Origins, Consequences and Prospects for Recovery*. Oxford, UK: Blackwell Publishing.

Schaede, Ulrike. 2008. *Choose and Focus: Japanese Business Strategies for the 21st Century*. Cornell University Press.

Shioji, Etsuro. 2009. "Productivity Fluctuations and the Japanese Economy Since the 1990s." In Kyoji Fukao (ed.) *Japanese Economy in the Period of Bubble/Deflation and Economic Policy. Vol. 1: Macro Economy and Industrial Structure*. Keio University Press (in Japanese).

Statistics Bureau, Ministry of Internal Affairs and Communications. 2014. *Population Estimates*. See: www.stat.go.jp/english/data/jinsui/index .htm, accessed April 13, 2014.

Summers, Lawrence H. 2013. "Speech at IMF Fourteenth Annual Research Conference in Honor of Stanley Fischer." For transcript, see: http://larry summers.com/imf-fourteenth-annual-research-conference-in-honor-of-stanley-fischer, accessed May 10, 2014.

The Study Commission on Adjustment of Economic Structure for International Cooperation. 1986. *Report of the Study Commission on the Adjustment of Economic Structure for International Cooperation* (the so-called Maekawa Report, in Japanese). Tokyo: Cabinet Secretariat, Government of Japan.

Timmer, Marcel, Ton van Moergastel, Edwin Stuivenwold, Gerard Ypma, Mary O'Mahony, and Mari Kangasniemi. 2007. *EU KLEMS Growth and Productivity Accounts, Part I. Methodology*, March. See: www .euklems.net/data/EUKLEMS_Growth_and_Productivity_Accounts_ Part_I_Methodology.pdf.

4 Productivity growth in Europe before and since the 2008/2009 economic and financial crisis

BART VAN ARK AND MARY O'MAHONY

4.1 Introduction

The economic and financial crisis which started in 2008/2009 has thrown the European economy into a "double-dip" recession with overall stagnant growth for a lengthy period of time, in terms of significantly slower growth, a decline in employment, and a negative growth rate in total factor productivity (TFP).[1] However, the perils that the crisis inflicted on the European economy can by no means be seen independently from the pre-crisis period. Well before the crisis hit, most European countries exhibited a significant slowdown in their long-term trend growth, driven primarily by slowing productivity growth, especially in the "original" EU-15 economies and the Euro Area.

The long-term structural weaknesses of Europe's economy have been well documented in our earlier work (van Ark, O'Mahony, and Timmer 2008; 2012; Timmer *et al.* 2010). First, a remarkable recovery in employment growth in Europe since the mid-1990s went together with slowing productivity growth. Second, the weak productivity performance could be largely attributed to a low contribution of information and communication technology (ICT) to productivity growth. And third, much of the weakness in productivity growth seemed concentrated in the services sector of the economy, while manufacturing was relatively strong in terms of productivity growth, at least compared to the United States.

To better understand how the economic landscape has changed, this chapter revisits our earlier work on the growth drivers of Europe's

[1] We are grateful to Abdul Erumban (The Conference Board and University of Groningen), Klaas de Vries (The Conference Board), and Kirsten Jäger (The Conference Board) for their statistical support.

economies until the mid-2000s, and places it in the light of the experiences since the beginning of the crisis. Since the onset of the crisis, European economies experienced a drastic decline in employment growth whereas productivity growth showed no signs of recovery. Clearly a significant part of the employment slowdown and the rise in unemployment related to cyclical factors. However, beyond some short-lived pro-cyclical improvements in 2010, there have been virtually no signs of a significant recovery in productivity growth, especially not in TFP. This suggests that medium-term factors remain predominant in explaining the productivity slowdown. The emergence of negative TFP growth rates across countries and sectors points to the possibility of a long-term (or "secular") stagnation due to a persistent shortfall in demand and an erosion of supply side factors as established by the long-term slowdown of potential output growth (Teulings and Baldwin 2014). However, it is also possible that there is a lull in the emergence of productive technology applications or that the negative productivity impact of the regulatory environment is playing a larger role than before the crisis.

In Section 4.2 of this chapter, we look at the most recent evidence on the sources of growth in Europe from a growth accounting perspective, updating our earlier work from Van Ark, O'Mahony, and Timmer (2008, 2012) and Timmer *et al.* (2010). In a comparison with the US, we find that, in the eight years before the crisis (1999–2007), the gross domestic product (GDP) growth shortfall of Europe, and especially the Euro Area, relative to the US, was largely driven by slower growth in ICT investment and weaker TFP growth. In contrast, employment growth was slightly faster in Europe than in the US. Since the crisis hit, both employment and TFP growth in the EU-28 as a whole were more strongly impacted than in the US, even though the contribution of ICT capital dropped off more in the US. Overall, the growth differential between Europe and US increased substantially between 2008 and 2014, although the patterns differed widely between countries.

In Section 4.3, we look at the latest updates on labor productivity estimates by industry from Eurostat, and provide a sector decomposition of growth, using the latest updates on labor productivity from the *EUKLEMS Growth and Productivity Accounts* (November 2012). The analysis confirms our earlier observations that the pre-crisis weakness in Europe's productivity performance was strongly concentrated in market services while the manufacturing sector enjoyed a productivity advantage in Europe over the US, with the ICT sector as the major exception. When digging more deeply, we roughly find a 50–50 split between European economies that showed weaker TFP growth in market services than in the US, including the largest economies (Germany, France, Spain, and Italy, and also Belgium), and a smaller group of economies (Austria, Finland, Sweden, and the Netherlands) as well as the UK, which showed faster productivity growth rates in market services. Since the crisis, the productivity crisis in Europe has quickly spread to the manufacturing sector, although cyclical elements related to the double dip recession have clearly played a role as well.

In the second half of the chapter we focus on how much the crisis has impacted on the rise of the knowledge economy, resulting from an increased utilization of ICT, improvements in labor force skills, and a shift from investments in tangible assets (machinery, equipment, and structures) to intangible assets (software, databases, research and development, other innovative property, marketing and branding, and organizational improvements).

In Section 4.4, we zoom in on the impact of the digital economy on Europe's productivity growth. The analysis shows that both the production and use of ICT in Europe grew much slower than in the US before the crisis. The growth contribution from the ICT-producing sector weakened considerably in European economies, while it remained relatively strong in the US. However, beyond ICT manufacturing, the contribution of ICT capital services to growth in Europe declined only moderately since the crisis. In particular, we find that ICT capital intensity in Europe caught up rapidly with the US in recent years. In contrast, TFP growth emerging from ICT utilization has declined in Europe since 2008 at a much faster rate than in the US. The discussion in Section 4.4 suggests that weaker network effects from ICT are a key explanation for the overall slow-down in TFP growth.

In Section 4.5 we look at two key drivers behind the knowledge economy. First, we find that despite the sharp drop in employment since the recession, the increase in human capital measured as the share of workers with a college degree and above continued. Therefore human capital has not been as much of a constraining factor for the growth recovery as other types of investment or productivity. The obvious flipside of this strengthening in the share of high-skilled workers since the recession is that, with a decline in overall employment, layoffs weighed heavier on those workers below college-education level. Second, this section discusses how the shift from investments in tangible assets (machinery, equipment, and structures) to intangible assets (software, databases, research and development, other innovative property, marketing and branding, and organizational improvements) has proceeded since the crisis. The latter are not included on a standard basis in the growth accounts, but according to recent research have become a more important source of growth in the past decades also in Europe (Corrado *et al*. 2013). While the investment in human capital and intangible assets have held up much better than other growth sources since the recession, the intensity level of intangible assets is still much lower across Europe than in the US. Intangible investment could become a more important driver to the recovery of productivity, providing an important catalyst for Europe's future growth.

In the final section of the chapter we draw some conclusions on how Europe's investment agenda enables Europe to revive long-term productivity growth. Despite the focus on short-term cyclical and crisis-related policy management since 2008/2009, the structural weaknesses in Europe's growth performance have also remained a long-standing concern. In addition to policy actions which support the creation of knowledge and other intangible assets, we stress the accumulating evidence that the failure to generate productivity-enhancing scale effects from creating a larger single market in services could seriously inhibit Europe's future growth performance.

4.2 The aggregate sources of growth revisited

As elsewhere in the advanced world, the global economic and financial crisis significantly affected the economic performance of European economies. Especially the Euro Area suffered from two recessions within three years (2008/2009, 2011/2012). Outside the Euro Area, the UK also experienced a very deep recession, and several Central and Eastern European economies not in the Euro Area, especially the Baltic States, suffered from the slowdown in external markets and the exposure of their own financial sectors to the crisis.

To understand how the recovery has evolved and how it might change the global and European economic landscape in the longer term, it is important to distinguish between cyclical recession and recovery effects, and the structural impact of the crisis. All growth sources (labor, capital, and productivity) have strong cyclical features. Labor growth, however, has been also very dependent on policy reactions and on the state of the labor markets in individual countries before the crisis hit.

We therefore adopt a comparative view, focusing on the pre- and post-crisis trends in economic growth and the sources of growth in the longer term. We first review GDP estimates decomposed into their sources of growth (hours worked, labor composition, ICT and non-ICT capital, and total factor productivity) for 1999–2007 and 2008–2014 from *The Conference Board Total Economy Database* (May 2015). Hence for the first period we look at the growth performance roughly between the pre-peaks in the business cycle, and for the second period we take the year in which the crisis started (by the end of 2008) until the year for which the latest data are available (2014 at the time of writing).

4.2.1 *Output, employment, and labor productivity performance*

When looking at the impact of the global economic and financial crisis on Europe's growth, the aggregate GDP, employment, and labor productivity (GDP per hour worked) metrics capture the first order effects of the response to the crisis (see the first three columns of Table 4.1). GDP growth in the European Union (EU) was 2.6% between 1999 and 2007, only 0.2 percentage point below the US growth rate over the same period.[2] In the Euro Area, growth was 0.5 percentage points slower than in the US during the pre-crisis period.[3] Strikingly, employment performance, measured as total hours worked, in Europe was relatively strong, with the EU-28 (0.8%) and the Euro Area (0.9%), on the one hand, and the US on the other (0.6%). Overall productivity growth in Europe was between 0.4 percentage points (EU-28) and 0.8 percentage points (Euro Area) lower than in the US.

---

[2] Measures are for the EU-28, excluding Croatia, which has been an EU member since July 1, 2013.

[3] Measures are the for Euro Area, excluding Latvia, which became a member of Euro Area on January 1, 2014.

Table 4.1 *Output, hours, and labor productivity growth, and growth contributions by major input, 1999–2007 and 2008–2014 (log growth)*

	Growth rate of GDP	Hours worked[1]	Labor productivity (GDP per hour)
1999–2007			
EU-28*	2.6	0.8	1.8
Euro Area**	2.3	0.9	1.4
EU-15***	2.4	0.9	1.5
EU-12****	4.4	−0.1	4.5
United States	2.8	0.6	2.2
2008–2014			
EU-28*	0.2	−0.4	0.5
Euro Area**	−0.2	−0.6	0.5
EU-15***	0.0	−0.3	0.3
EU-12****	1.5	−0.4	1.9
United States	1.1	0.0	1.2

Following the near-decade long period of fairly solid growth in GDP in Europe, the emergence of the crisis in 2008 and the two recessions in 2008/2009 and 2011/2012 caused a drop in GDP growth. EU-28 growth dropped to 0.2%, while US GDP growth slowed to 1.1%, leaving a much larger growth gap between the two regions. In eleven of the twenty-seven EU member states included in the analysis, GDP growth contracted over the six-year period. Greece showed the largest drop at –4.3% per year between 2008 and 2014 (see Appendix Tables 4.1a and 4.1b).[4] Also, several large economies such as Italy (–1.3%) and Spain (–0.7%) showed a contraction. While the Euro Area as a whole saw a decline in GDP at –0.2% since the onset of the crisis, some countries within the Euro Area fared comparatively well, such as Germany at 0.7% GDP growth on average. In the broader EU, Sweden still grew its economy at 0.8% on average, and Poland showed the fastest GDP growth at 3.1% per year on average from 2008–2014.

---

[4] The EU-28 aggregate excludes Croatia which became a member of the European Union on July 1, 2013.

Table 4.1 (*cont.*)

Contributions to GDP growth from				
Hours worked (weighted)[2]	Labor composition	Non-ICT capital	ICT capital	Total Factor Productivity growth
0.5	0.2	0.8	0.5	0.6
0.6	0.2	0.7	0.4	0.4
0.6	0.2	0.7	0.5	0.4
−0.1	0.3	1.2	0.8	2.2
0.4	0.2	0.7	0.7	0.9
−0.2	0.2	0.5	0.3	−0.5
−0.4	0.2	0.3	0.3	−0.6
−0.2	0.1	0.4	0.3	−0.6
−0.3	0.2	1.1	0.7	−0.2
0.0	0.1	0.3	0.4	0.3

Notes

[1] Refers to actual log growth rate of total hours worked.

[2] Refers to the contribution of total hours worked, weighted by the share of labor in total compensation, to the log growth rate of GDP.

* Excludes Croatia, which became member of EU on July 1, 2013.

** Refers to pre-2014 membership of eighteen members, excluding Latvia, which became a member on January 1, 2014.

*** Refers to pre-2004 membership of EU.

**** Refers to new membership of EU since 2004, excluding Croatia, which became member of EU on July 1, 2013.

Source: The Conference Board Total Economy Database™, May 2015. See: www
.conference-board.org/data/economydatabase. See Appendix Tables 4.1a and 4.1b for country details.

The slowdown in labor productivity growth in the EU was much more moderate than for GDP, dropping from 1.8% between 1999 and 2007 to a still positive 0.5% growth between 2008 and 2014. This is accounted for by the strong decline in total hours worked beyond the slowdown in GDP, which has resulted from a combination of higher unemployment and lower labor force participation. In fact, the growth rate in total hours declined at −0.4% per year between 2008 and 2014. Underlying the EU-wide slowdown in productivity growth are stark differences between countries. The biggest declines in labor productivity growth in Euro Area countries were seen in Greece (–0.9%) and Finland (–0.3%). These productivity declines were related to the large decline in GDP growth in those economies. In Germany, despite a rise in GDP and per capita income growth at 0.7%, labor productivity increased at only 0.4% between 2008 and 2014, suggesting strong labor hoarding effects as a result of short-time working programs. In contrast, labor productivity growth in Poland increased by 2.8% per year between 2008 and 2014 periods, which resulted from an expansionary growth process adding to both output and employment. Strikingly, Spain also saw an acceleration in labor productivity growth at 1.7%, but, in contrast to Poland, it resulted from cutting hours even more than GDP.

4.2.2 A sources-of-growth analysis

Using a standard growth accounting framework, as used by Jorgenson, Ho and Stiroh (2005), the remaining columns of Table 4.1 decompose the growth of aggregate GDP into the contributions of labor, capital, and TFP. While Europe and the Euro Area saw a faster increase in the contribution of working hours to growth from 1999 to 2007 than the US, hours have contributed negatively since the beginning of the crisis, in contrast to a zero contribution in the US. Cyclical factors played some role in hitting Europe's labor market harder than the US as domestic demand was more heavily affected, although this largely depends on the degree of labor hoarding that took place in different European countries. Indeed growth in total hours still contributed as much as 0.5 percentage points to growth in the UK (although offset by a small decline in labor productivity growth – see Barnett *et al.* 2014) and 0.2 percentage points in Germany (together with a moderate increase in labor productivity growth – see Bellmann *et al.* 2016). Country details are provided in Appendix Tables 4.1a and 4.1b.

Capital services, split between ICT and non-ICT capital, have been the main driver of GDP growth in the aggregate EU and the US. Before the crisis, non-ICT capital accounted for about 0.8 percentage points of GDP growth in the EU, but declined to 0.5 percentage points as the crisis happened. In the Euro Area the contribution of non-ICT capital dropped from 0.7 to 0.3 percentage points, which was comparable to the drop-off in the US. In contrast to most European economies, the Polish economy showed the biggest deviation from the European average: it saw the non-ICT capital contribution increase from 0.9 percentage points from 1999–2007 to 1.6 percent from 2008–2014 (Piatkowski 2013).

The contribution of ICT capital in Europe, which had already slowed in the early 2000s relative to the late 1990s, only slowed modestly more during the crisis. During the 1995–2007 period, the US advance in the ICT capital contribution was faster (at 0.7 percentage points) than in Europe (at 0.5 percentage points and the Euro Area as 0.4 percentage points). Much of the faster investment pace in the "new economy" during the late 1990s in the US was driven by the scale effects from larger US markets, especially in market services such as trade and transportation (Inklaar *et al.* 2008). However, since 2008 the ICT capital contribution to growth slowed down a lot in both regions, but slightly more in the US (from 0.7 to 0.4 percentage points) than in the EU-28 (from 0.5 to 0.3) or the Euro Area (from 0.4 to 0.3). The ICT capital contributions strengthened in Nordic economies (Denmark, Finland, and Sweden), but weakened most strongly in France, Italy, Spain, and the UK.

In Section 4.4 we will address in more detail how much investment in ICT has helped to strengthen the economies' productivity performance. First it is necessary to address the aggregate TFP performance, which has emerged as the Achilles' heel of Europe's growth performance. Between 1999 and 2007, TFP growth in the EU-28 was 0.6% (two-thirds of the US growth rate at 0.9%) and only 0.4% in the Euro Area (less than half of that in the US). Central and Eastern European economies mostly exhibited much faster TFP growth, as they still benefited from "catchup growth" during the 1990s and most of the 2000s.

Since 2008, Euro Area TFP growth has turned negative for all Euro Area economies. Even relatively strong economies like Germany could not maintain TFP growth at positive rates, showing a decline of 0.2% (See Appendix Tables 4.1a and 4.1b). The continuation of the slowing trend in TFP growth points to a range of possible explanations. Beyond the temporary cyclical impact from the recession related to weak demand, it can be a sign of weakening innovation and technological change as companies hold back on new investment due to longer-term concerns about demand and investment (Teulings and Baldwin 2014). But for the TFP growth rate to turn negative, additional explanations are needed. First, it could signal the greater force of rigidities in labor, product, and capital markets during the crisis, causing increased misallocation of resources to low-productive firms. This is especially so in times during which scale-dependent technologies such as communication technology require flexibility across a larger economic space (see Section 4.4). Limited scale effects in Europe, related to fragmented markets and limited impacts from ICT utilization, might have played a larger role than in the US (see Section 4.6). Finally, and related to the previous explanation, there might be a negative reallocation effect, with more resources going to the less productive sectors in the economy.

4.3 An industry perspective on the productivity slowdown in Europe

The major industry sectors of the European economies have been affected quite differently by the crisis. Table 4.2 presents the average yearly growth rates of labor productivity for eight major Euro Area economies (Austria, Belgium, Finland, France, Germany, Italy, the Netherlands, and Spain), the UK, and the US for 1999–2007 and 2008–2013. The productivity measures are divided between three main sectors: (1) ICT goods and services, including manufacturing in electronics and telecommunication equipment and IT and other information services (which will be discussed separately in the next section); (2) other goods production, comprising manufacturing (excluding ICT), agriculture, mining, utilities, and construction; and (3) market services, which includes distribution, financial and business services, and personal services.[5]

Table 4.3 presents the growth decomposition by major sector for the average of the eight Euro Area economies and the US. The estimates are based on the latest updates of the *EUKLEMS Growth and Productivity Accounts* (November 2012). For the Euro Area aggregate, current

---

[5] The analysis does not include non-market services, which comprises education, health care and public administration, and real estate services. Measurement problems with regard to output in non-market services are large and we therefore refrain from showing those separately. Real estate activities are also included with non-market services, as the output measure includes imputed rents on owner-occupied dwellings, making the interpretation of the productivity measure problematic.

Table 4.2 *Output per hour by major sector, 1999–2007 and 2008–2013 (%)*

	ICT goods and services*	Goods production, excl. electrical machinery*	Market services, excl. information and telecom
1999–2007			
Euro Area	4.4	1.9	0.7
Finland	10.0	2.7	1.4
Netherlands	5.0	2.9	1.9
Austria	3.6	3.1	1.5
Belgium	2.5	2.8	1.4
France	4.8	2.6	1.1
Germany	4.8	2.5	0.7
Italy	3.3	0.9	−0.1
Spain	2.3	0.1	−0.2
United Kingdom	6.1	2.5	2.6
United States	10.5	1.7	2.1
2008–2013*			
Euro Area	2.1	0.5	−0.1
Finland	−3.4	−0.7	−0.2
Netherlands	0.3	−0.4	0.2
Austria	1.1	−1.0	0.8
Belgium	−0.4	0.7	−0.3
France	2.5	−0.1	0.2
Germany	3.6	0.6	−0.6
Italy	1.2	−0.1	−0.7
Spain	1.2	2.9	0.8
United Kingdom	1.1	−1.9	−0.2
United States	5.0	0.7	0.9

Notes: (1) ICT goods and services includes manufacturing in electronics and telecommunication equipment and IT and other information services; goods production includes manufacturing excluding ICT, agriculture, mining, utilities, and construction); market services excludes ICT services, including distribution, financial and business services, and community, personal and social services. (2) The Euro Average refers to Austria, Belgium, Finland, France, Germany, Italy, Netherlands and Spain.

* ICT goods could not be separated for 2013, so that ICT goods and services, and goods (excluding ICT) refers to 2008–2012, rather than 2008–2013.

Sources: Eurostat, Bureau of Labor Statistics (BLS), and Bureau of Economic Analysis (BEA).

Table 4.3 *Output, hours and labor productivity growth, and growth contributions by major sector and major input, 1999–2007 and 1999–latest year available (log growth)*

	Growth rate of real value added	Hours worked (weighted)	Labour composition	Non-ICT capital	ICT capital	Total Factor Productivity growth
			Contributions to real value added growth from			
Euro Area						
ICT goods and services						
1999–2007	5.4	0.6	0.2	0.7	0.8	3.1
2008–2009	−1.3	−0.8	0.5	0.2	0.3	−1.4
1999–2009	4.2	0.3	0.3	0.6	0.7	2.3
Goods production, excl. electrical machinery						
1999–2007	1.7	−0.3	0.3	0.2	0.4	1.1
2008–2009	−6.8	−2.9	0.5	0.1	0.4	−4.9
1999–2009	0.1	−0.8	0.3	0.1	0.4	0.0
Market services, excl. information and telecom						
1999–2007	2.4	1.0	0.2	0.5	0.7	−0.1
2008–2009	−1.6	−0.4	0.3	0.3	0.4	−2.3
1999–2009	1.7	0.8	0.2	0.5	0.7	−0.5

		Contributions to GDP growth from				
	Growth rate of real value added	Hours worked (weighted)	Labour composition	Non-ICT capital*	ICT capital*	Total Factor Productivity growth
United States						
ICT goods and services						
1999–2007	9.1	-0.7	0.5		2.0	7.3
2008–2010	4.3	-1.4	0.2		1.0	4.6
1999–2010	7.9	-0.8	0.4		1.8	6.6
Goods production, excl. electrical machinery						
1999–2007	0.6	-0.4	0.2		0.6	0.1
2008–2010	-3.5	-4.1	0.5		0.6	-0.6
1999–2010	-0.5	-1.3	0.3		0.6	0.0
Market services, excl. information and telecom						
1999–2007	3.0	0.5	0.3		1.7	0.5
2008–2010	-0.8	-1.6	0.3		0.2	0.2
1999–2010	2.1	0.0	0.3		1.4	0.4

Notes: (1) ICT goods and services includes manufacturing in electronics and telecommunication equipment and IT and other information services; goods production includes manufacturing excluding ICT, agriculture, mining, utilities, and construction); market services excludes ICT services, including distribution, financial and business services, and community, personal and social services. (2) The Euro Average refers to Austria, Belgium, Finland, France, Germany, Italy, Netherlands, and Spain. * Non-ICT capital and ICT capital combined.
Source: EUKLEMS industry-level productivity accounts (www.euklems.net), November 2012. See Appendix Table 4.2 for country.

EUKLEMS estimates are available up to 2009, so that only the immediate crisis effects can be analyzed.[6]

4.3.1 Productivity in the goods sectors excluding ICT production

The most important observation from the sector data is that before the 2008/2009 crisis, the goods sector was the relative stronghold of productivity growth in Europe. In seven of the nine European economies (all except Italy and Spain) productivity growth in goods production, which was largely dominated by manufacturing, excluding ICT production, but including agriculture, utilities, and construction, was higher than in the US.[7] The average growth rate of labor productivity in the Euro Area goods production sector was 1.9% from 1999–2007 versus 1.7% in the US (Table 4.2). The Europe–US productivity gap in goods production before the crisis was even higher for TFP growth, namely 1.1% in the Euro Area) versus only 0.1% in the US from 1999–2007 (Table 4.3).

Clearly, the differences in goods productivity performance reflect the specialization of goods production. For example, the US and Nordic economies strongly concentrated in high-tech ICT sectors (which are separate from the estimates for the goods producing sector – see Table 4.2, Appendix Table 4.2 and Section 4.4). In contrast, European continental economies saw a broader range of specializations across manufacturing sectors, such as Germany's stronghold in investment goods and high-end specialized manufactured products, France's specialization in infrastructure and transportation equipment, and Belgium and the Netherlands' concentration on chemicals and related industries.

In the early aftermath of the recession, labor productivity growth for European goods producing sectors dropped off significantly to 0.5% from 2008–2012, to a large extent because of the cyclical impact which typically hit the tradeable goods harder than less-tradeable services, and fell slightly below the US growth rate (at

---

[6] See Appendix Table 4.2 for the results for the eight individual Euro Area economies, as well as Sweden and the UK. The country series have different end-years for the various countries between 2009 and 2012, requiring caution in the interpretation of the comparative growth effects since the crisis.

[7] For a discussion of the ICT sector, see Section 4.4 of this chapter.

0.7%) for the same period. With the exception of Spain, none of the European economies saw faster productivity growth than the US in goods production (even excluding ICT) after 2008. The more moderate decline in US productivity growth was largely achieved by a rapid layoff of manufacturing and construction workers. In most European countries employment growth rates didn't decline as much, with the notable exception of Spain and Italy, where they fell dramatically (see Appendix Tables 4.2a and 4.2b). In several countries, in particular Germany, temporary employment subsidy programs supported labor hoarding in manufacturing (Bellmann *et al.* 2016). More recent estimates of manufacturing output show that the cyclical recovery effects on manufacturing have largely played out. Still, by 2014 manufacturing value added levels were still below the pre-2008 level.

4.3.2 *Productivity in the market services sectors excluding ICT production*

The market services sector (excluding ICT services) showed the opposite relative productivity performance between Europe and the US compared to goods production (excluding ICT goods). On average, labor productivity growth in market services was 0.7% for the eight Euro Area economies from 1999–2007, well below the 1.9% in the goods producing sector. In the US, we saw the opposite, with market services productivity at 2.1% from 1999–2007, ahead of the 1.7% labor productivity growth rate in goods production (excluding ICT) (Table 4.2). The TFP growth advantage of the US market services sector over Europe was much smaller, at 0.5% compared to -0.1% for the eight Euro Area countries (Table 4.3). This demonstrates that growth in US market services was largely investment-driven, as attested by the higher growth contributions of capital services in the US (see Appendix Tables 4.2a and 4.2b).

There are large differences between European countries, though, with regard to market services productivity growth. Labor productivity growth was lower than in the US in all eight Euro Area economies from 1999–2007, but higher (at 2.6%) in the UK, mainly reflecting faster productivity growth in financial services. In the UK the contribution of capital intensity, especially in ICT, was among the highest in Europe. Still, in half of the ten European economies (Finland, Austria, the UK, the Netherlands, and Sweden) TFP growth in market services productivity was higher than in the US from 1999–2007, whereas it was flat in Belgium, France, and Germany, and negative in Italy and Spain.

The weak productivity performance in market services (excluding ICT) has been extensively documented in our earlier work (Van Ark *et al.* 2008, 2012; Inklaar *et al.* 2008; Timmer 2010), but it has significantly worsened since the crisis – although it weakened in the US as well. The average labor productivity growth rate for the eight economies approximating the Euro Area dropped from 0.7% in 1999–2007 to –0.1% in 2008–2013 (Table 4.2). To some extent, the European slowdown can be attributed to lower investment in ICT– albeit with large differences across economies. However, more importantly, average TFP growth in Euro Area market services dropped dramatically from already –0.1% from 1999–2009 to –2.3% in 2008–2009, the first crisis years (Table 4.3). Factors related to market structure, competition, and lack of a European single market for services were also playing a role in Europe's weak productivity performance in market services.

Overall, the sectoral growth accounts for European countries show considerable declines in labor productivity and TFP growth across the board over the past two decades, even though productivity in goods production (excluding ICT) has remained relatively strong compared to market services. The short-term impact of the crisis has unmistakably affected the years immediately following 2008.

However, the discussion in this section also shows that several trends have longer-term characteristics. Slow productivity growth in services partly results from slower adjustments and misallocations of inputs, which may point to the need for continued structural reforms in labor and product markets. There are also many indications that the failure to effectively adopt new technologies and innovation over a significant period of time is an important factor in understanding Europe's relative performance, which may be related to institutions and regulations (van Ark 2014, see also Section 4.6). The remainder of this chapter will focus on the role of technology and innovation, in particular the slow ICT pickup in Europe, and investment trends in human capital and intangible assets.

4.4 Recent developments on ICT's impact on productivity growth

The important and long-lasting productivity effects of the production and use of ICT and digital content is a key factor in recent productivity research.[8] ICT production, investment, and the digitalization of production has had visible effects on economic growth, especially in mature economies. From the mid-1990s to the mid-2000s, most of the economic effects of digitalization were reflected in rising labor productivity resulting from larger investment in ICT hardware and software. More recently, however, the contribution of ICT has become more widely diffused, but also less visible – and so more complex when it comes to its impact on productivity. Especially the combined rise of broadband and the production of evermore powerful mobile devices are among the biggest enablers of productivity gains from the economy's digitalization (see, for example, Greenstein 2000; Röller and Waverman 2001; van Ark 2011).

However, detailed analysis shows that the effects of digitalization on growth were more muted in Europe than in the US. This is best understood when decomposing the different effects of ICT on growth. As with the rise of any general purpose technology (Crafts 2010), one can distinguish three different impacts from ICT over a prolonged period of time:

(1) A technology effect through the ICT-producing sector

Firms in the technology producing sector often experience very strong productivity gains. Before the onset of the crisis, US productivity growth in the ICT producing sector (including hardware, software, and telecommunications) grew at 10.5% for labor productivity and 7.3% in terms of TFP growth in 1999–2007 (Table 4.2 and Table 4.3). Only Finland posted productivity growth rates in the same range as the US, whereas in other Euro Area countries productivity growth rates in ICT production were mostly less than half of that.[9] Even though ICT-producing industries only represent a small part of the economy (about 8% of total GDP in Europe), they

---

[8] This section is largely based on van Ark (2014), with data and estimates obtained from Corrado and Jäger (2014).

[9] See also Appendix Table 4.2 for growth decomposition on Sweden, which also showed relatively strong performance in ICT products and services.

accounted for more than 40% (or 0.28 percentage points) of aggregate TFP growth in the market sector (See Table 4.4; Corrado and Jäger 2014).[10] Even though European countries continued to grow employment in the ICT sector since the emergence of the crisis, productivity growth stayed well behind the US, which hardly showed any decline in productivity. Only Sweden continued to match US TFP growth numbers, while Finland saw its average productivity growth rates in the ICT sector more than half when comparing 1999–2007 to 1999–2012 (Appendix Table 4.2). The TFP contribution of the ICT-producing sector remained positive at a modest 0.16% from 2008 to 2011 (Table 4.4).

Table 4.4 *Contributions from digitalization to average annual GDP growth for eight major EU economies, 2001–2011 (%)*

	2001–2007	2008–2011
Technology effect through the ICT-producing sector		
ICT hardware TFP	0.12	0.05
Sofware MFP	0.04	0.05
Telecom MFP	0.12	0.06
Investment effect from ICT-using industries through capital deepening		
IT investment	0.33	0.12
CT and spectrum investment	0.11	0.09
Network effects on productivity from ICT use in non-ICT sectors		
TFP from ICT returns to scale in non-ICT sector	0.16	−0.31
TFP from ICT adaptions in non-ICT sector	0.09	0.07
Total effects from ICT production, investment, and use	0.97	0.14

Note: EU-8 refers to the weighted average contributions for eight EU economies: Austria, Finland, France, Germany, Italy, Netherlands, Spain, and the UK.
Source: Corrado and Jäeger (2014), van Ark (2014), The Conference Board.

[10] The estimates in Corrado and Jäger (2014) are for 2001–2007 and for only eight European countries (Austria, Finland, France, Germany, Italy, the Netherlands, Spain, and the UK).

(2) An investment effect from ICT-using industries through capital deepening

Investment in digital technology takes place through the spending on ICT and telecom hardware, software, networks, databases, and user platforms across the economy. As documented above, the investment effects from ICT in Europe already slowed during the ten years before the 2008–2009 crisis, and only declined moderately further since 2008. Table 4.3 shows that the ICT contribution (including investment in spectrum) to growth, was 0.44 percentage point from 2001–2007 and 0.21 percentage point from 2008–2011, slightly lower than the aggregate ICT investment effect in Table 4.2 for 2008–2014.

Other evidence on the amount of capital relative to GDP shows that the US has made a faster adjustment from non-ICT to ICT capital than Europe. Figure 4.1 shows that the ICT capital output ratio in the US increased more than five-fold from 0.02 to 0.1 in just over thirty years. In Europe, growth was historically much less capital-intensive, and while the ICT capital output ratio also increased, it remained about 20–25% below that of the US during the late 1990s and 2000s. However, ICT capital output ratios caught up rapidly on the US since 2008. This suggests that despite the big hit of the crisis on output, ICT investment has become a relatively more important source of growth in Europe, although still less than in the US.

(3) Network effects on productivity from ICT use

While supportive for labor productivity growth in Europe, the rise in capital output ratios in ICT investment does not necessarily lead to greater efficiency in the economy, as measured by TFP growth. Indeed TFP growth in ICT production in the Euro Area turned negative on average –1.4% in 2008–2009, while it remained strong in the US at 4.6% on average (Table 4.3).

The productivity effects of using new technology are not easy to identify, quantify, and disentangle from other (related) factors impacting on productivity. For example, investment booms in new technology can, temporarily, cause a slowdown or even a decline in TFP (Basu, Fernald, and Shapiro 2001). Changing degrees of utilization of the new capital installed, especially after the creation of new networks, can impact significantly on productivity.

While significant progress has been made in measuring the contribution of ICT production and investment to productivity, traditional

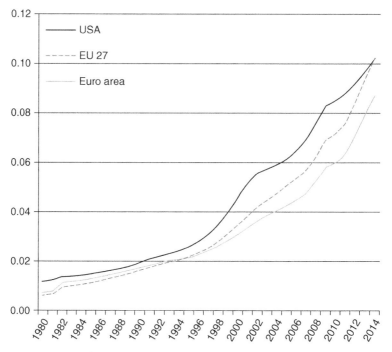

Figure 4.1 Level of ICT capital stock per unit of output, in 2014 US$ (PPP-converted)

standard growth accounts do not suffice to nail down which part of TFP growth can be linked to spillover effects and externalities from ICT. Increasingly network effects from *digitalization*, including higher returns to scale due to more connectivity between businesses and innovative adaptations from ICT across the economy, are key to generating productivity growth.

Network externalities come in two parts: (1) a return-to-scale effect, which directly relates to Metcalfe's law, which states that the value of a network increases with the square of the number of users of the network; and (2) the productivity effects from innovative adaptations from the use of, for example, the internet and wireless technologies. The productivity impact of the two network effects, which was obtained from an econometric analysis for eight European countries, shows these effects to be quite low.[11] For example, between 2001 and

[11] See Corrado and Jäger (2014) for a fuller explanation of the dataset, the sources-of-growth analysis and the econometric estimates on ICT externalities.

2007, the returns-to-scale (Metcalfe) effect accounted for as little as 0.16% of TFP growth in the eight European countries. During the 2008–2011 period, the returns-to-scale effect detracted 0.3% of TFP growth. The effect of innovative adaptation on TFP growth – at less than 0.1% throughout the 2001–2011 period – is even smaller than returns to scale but more sustainable.

Table 4.4 shows that the combined impacts of ICT production, investment, and use accounted for about one percentage point of output growth in the eight European economies from 2001 to 2007, which is substantial given the overall market sector output growth rate of just over 2%. Close to half of the ICT effect comes from investment and the other two quarters from productivity of ICT producers and ICT users. While the productivity contribution from ICT producers and ICT capital was largely sustained since the onset of the crisis, especially the returns-to-scale part of TFP by the non-ICT sector contracted sharply and became negative, bringing the overall contribution of ICT to output growth in the 2008–2011 period to 0.1%, down from 1% in the 2001–2007 period.

4.5 The role of labor force skills and intangible investments

Human capital has long been seen as an important factor in determining economic growth and the ability of countries to adopt and utilize technologies, depending on their skill endowments (Acemoglu 1998). Much research effort has been devoted to the issue of whether technical change is skill-biased and on the impact of ICT on the demand for skilled labor (Autor *et al.* 1998). This literature especially focuses on workers with university or equivalent qualifications, as the evidence suggests that the skills and competencies acquired are those needed to effectively adopt the new technology.

A severe recession can therefore have serious long-term consequences beyond the immediate drop in output if the extent of human capital accumulation becomes affected. However, Table 4.5 shows that the percent of those employed in the highest skill group (ISCED levels 5–6, college education), the education group which the previous literature referred to above suggests are most in demand in adopting new technologies, kept increasing for the whole period from 1995 to 2011. For most of the EU-15 countries the rate of increase in the high skill proportion was faster between 1995 and 2002 than in

Table 4.5 *High skilled employment as a proportion of total employment, aggregate economy (%)*

	1995	2002	2007	2011
EU-15*				
Austria	12.9	17.1	18.3	19.7
Finland	31.6	33.8	36.5	39.8
France	21.3	27.2	30.2	34.0
Germany	21.5	24.2	25.7	29.0
Italy	9.2	13.1	16.2	17.9
Netherlands	21.6	25.1	30.8	32.6
Spain	23.5	29.6	33.1	38.5
Sweden	18.2	26.4	30.9	34.7
UK	23.1	31.0	33.3	38.4
EU-12**				
Czech Republic	11.5	13.2	15.0	20.1
Hungary	16.4	17.7	21.7	25.7
Poland	14.0	17.2	23.8	28.6
Slovakia	12.3	13.2	16.4	21.4

Note: Percent of those employed in the highest skill group (ISCED levels 5–6, college education).
* Refers to pre-2004 membership of the EU.
** Refers to new membership of the EU since 2004; excludes Croatia, which became a member of the EU on July 1, 2013.
Source: EU Labor Force Survey.

the subsequent period, 2003–2007. New member states showed a faster increase in the share since the early 2000s, reflecting that these countries were still catching up in terms of university education during the past decade.

Since the crisis in 2008/2009, the upskilling of the work force has continued in all countries, and has even accelerated in some of Europe's largest economies, including France, Germany, the UK, and even Spain. In all new EU-10 countries the growth in high-skilled relative to overall employment also strengthened during the crisis. The obvious flipside of this strengthening in the share of high-skilled workers since the recession is that, with a decline in overall employment, layoffs weighed heavier on those workers below college-education level.

Table 4.6 presents the same information as in Table 4.5 but broken down into three broad sectors, including the goods producing sector, the

Table 4.6 *High skilled employment as a proportion of total employment, by major sector (%)*

		1995	2002	2007	2011
EU-15*					
Austria	Goods	6.1	9.9	13.1	14.2
	Market services	9.3	12.6	15.5	16.7
	Non-market services	32.7	37.1	31.4	33.7
Finland	Goods	20.8	23.0	24.3	27.3
	Market services	30.7	31.2	33.6	37.1
	Non-market services	47.4	50.6	54.7	57.1
France	Goods	12.2	15.0	19.6	21.9
	Market services	20.5	26.5	29.8	35.0
	Non-market services	34.3	40.9	40.2	42.6
Germany	Goods	17.3	20.0	20.7	22.7
	Market services	17.8	20.2	21.3	24.6
	Non-market services	34.8	36.9	39.5	43.6
Italy	Goods	3.3	4.5	5.4	6.8
	Market services	7.2	12.1	15.5	16.4
	Non-market services	23.2	28.7	36.2	38.9
Netherlands	Goods	9.8	11.6	16.5	18.4
	Market services	18.1	21.9	26.6	28.1
	Non-market services	39.4	40.9	47.6	47.3
Spain	Goods	11.5	17.8	20.9	26.9
	Market services	18.1	27.1	30.7	33.4
	Non-market services	55.3	60.4	62.6	63.7
Sweden	Goods	7.0	10.8	13.7	14.6
	Market services	14.7	21.7	26.0	30.5
	Non-market services	32.9	44.7	49.8	54.2
United Kingdom	Goods	16.3	22.5	25.3	27.7
	Market services	18.7	24.6	26.8	32.7
	Non-market services	38.4	48.6	49.3	52.9
EU-12**					
Czech Republic	Goods	5.6	6.5	7.3	9.6
	Market services	11.8	13.3	15.4	20.6
	Non-market services	26.4	28.7	31.8	41.5
Hungary	Goods	7.3	7.2	9.3	11.5
	Market services	14.0	16.9	21.0	25.8
	Non-market services	37.1	38.7	44.1	47.4

Table 4.6 (*cont.*)

		1995	2002	2007	2011
Poland	Goods	5.6	6.0	9.6	12.7
	Market services	12.9	17.2	25.5	31.0
	Non-market services	37.9	42.2	51.9	58.8
Slovakia	Goods	6.4	5.4	7.5	10.1
	Market services	13.2	13.9	17.1	21.4
	Non-market services	26.3	29.0	34.8	42.2

Note: Percent of those employed in the highest skill group (ISCED levels 5–6, college education). Goods-producing sector includes manufacturing, agriculture, mining, utilities and construction; market services include distribution, financial and business services, and personal services; non-market services include community, personal and social services, education, health care and public administration, and real estate services.
* Refers to pre-2004 membership of the EU.
** Refers to new membership of the EU since 2004; excludes Croatia, which became a member of the EU on July 1, 2013.
Source: EU Labor Force Survey, 2013.

market services sector, and the non-market services sector.[12] The table shows that in all countries the high-level skill proportions are largest in non-market services and lowest in goods production. In market services the rate of increase in high skill levels accelerated the most during the post 2008/2009 period, especially in Finland, France, Germany, and the UK, but less so in the goods producing sector.

These differences might reflect the impacts of job polarization that emphasises the substitution of routine tasks by computers (Autor *et al.* 2003; Acemoglu and Autor 2011). Goods production is likely to be more prone to such substitution, as well as to offshoring of jobs, whereas the more intensive ICT-using industries in market services increased employment for workers with complex non-routine tasks that are less easily substituted for by ICT. Still, even in goods

---

[12] Goods production includes agriculture, mining, manufacturing, utilities, and construction. Market services include wholesale and retail trade, transportation and warehousing, and community, personal and social services. Non-market services include, education, health care and public administration, and real estate services.

production the high-skill proportion of employment increased in Germany, Finland, Italy, and Spain. Non-market services are typically much less prone to the impact of technology, as the high-skilled shares of employment remained relatively stable throughout the period.

Overall the evidence on the impacts of the early aftermath (2008–2011) of the recession on human capital in Europe appears reasonably positive, suggesting that skilled labor, on the whole, might not have been as much of a constraining factor for the growth recovery as other types of investment or productivity. Indeed the growth decompositions in Table 4.1 (and Appendix Tables 4.1a and 4.1b) suggest that the post-crisis period shows very little weakening in the aggregate growth contribution from labor composition during the period since the crisis.[13]

In a similar vein as for human capital, research has highlighted that organizational changes and other forms of intangible investment such as work force training are necessary to gain significant productivity benefits from using ICT (Brynjolfsson, Hitt, and Yang 2002; Black and Lynch 2001). ICT and intangible assets are connected in many ways. Some ICT assets such as software and databases are themselves classified as an intangible asset. ICT can facilitate the deployment of other intangible assets and enable innovations across the economy, such as the reorganization of production emphasized by Bertschek and Kaiser (2004) and Bresnahan, Brynjolfsson, and Hitt (2002). It can also involve streamlining of existing business processes, for example order tracking, inventory control, accounting services, and the tracking of product delivery. At the same time, capital deepening in intangible assets also provides the foundation for ICT to impact on productivity. For example, the internal organization of a firm plays a role in its ability to use ICT more efficiently, in particular through managerial and other organizational changes. Indeed, there is a strong relationship between intangible capital deepening (excluding ICT) and TFP growth, which is consistent with the possibility of TFP spillovers from intangible investments beyond GDP (Corrado *et al.* 2013).

---

[13] The data in Table 4.1 run up to 2014, suggesting that the slow recovery in employment growth might have been a detrimental factor in leveraging a positive effect from the upskilling of the aggregate labor force.

Following the pioneering work by Corrado, Hulten and Sichel (2005, 2009), internationally comparable estimates of private sector investment in intangibles have been put together by the Intan-Invest project and discussed in Corrado *et al.* (2013) and in Chapter 9 of this volume. This work divides intangibles into three broad categories: computerized information (software and databases), innovative property (scientific research and development [R&D], design, financial innovations), and economic competencies (work force training, improvements in organizational structures, marketing and branding).

Figures 4.2a and 4.2b show that Europe (here the EU-15 aggregate) has a much lower investment intensity in intangibles than the US. The share of all measured private intangible investment in the EU-15 has increased by 2 percentage points from 8.5% of GDP in the market sector in 1995 to 10.5% in 2012, by which time it was about two-thirds of the US share.[14] Within the EU-15, the Scandinavian countries, France, and the UK have the highest intangibles intensity, even for those countries the gap with the US remains significant. Many EU-15 countries currently invest less than half that

4.2a EU–15

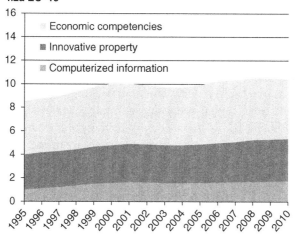

Figure 4.2a Investment intensity of intangible assets as a % of value added in the market sector, EU-15 and the US, 1995–2010 (EU-15)

---

[14] The estimates refer to the 'market' economy, excluding education, health, and public administration.

4.2b US

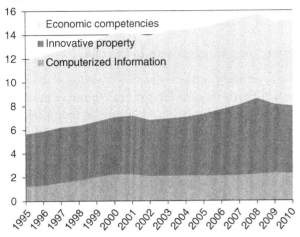

Figure 4.2b Investment intensity of intangible assets as a % of value added in the market sector, EU-15 and the US, 1995–2010 (US)

in the US – these include Italy, Greece, and Portugal (see Chapter 9 for details).

The US saw sharper increases than Europe in intangibles intensity, rising by 2.3 percentage points over the same period from 12.9% to 15.2% of market sector value added. While the EU-15 retained its intangibles during the recession, the intangible capital intensity in the US declined by almost almost 0.6 of a percentage point in 2009, although this may primarily have been an impact of the crisis.[15]

The division between the three main categories is fairly similar between the two main regions, but the US showed stronger growth over the entire period in all three asset types, and saw sharper increases especially in computerized information and economic competencies (especially organizational capital) during the late 1990s. The intensity of intangibles is in part related to the structure of the economy, which explains the relatively high intangible shares for the UK and the US, which have large shares of GDP in service sectors. These economies have relatively large shares of their intangibles concentrated in economic competencies, notably organizational investments, and in ICT.

[15] The latest updates for the US show that by 2013 the share of intangibles in total GDP had recovered to the pre-recession level. Updated by Carol Corrado and Kirsten Jäger in Van Ark *et al.* (2015).

In Germany, which has a share of GDP in manufacturing, the role of innovative property, including R&D, is relatively more important.

4.6 Towards reviving long-term growth in Europe

This chapter has amply demonstrated the need for a medium- to long-term focus on growth in Europe, especially the need to revive productivity growth. Cyclical factors play an important role in the recovery, but structural factors are clearly present translating into slower potential output growth. Policy attention needs to shift to a more medium-term focus on reigniting growth, especially now that it turns out that we may have entered a longer period of moderate growth, sometimes referred to as "secular stagnation" (Teulings and Baldwin 2014).

At face value, it makes much sense to direct our attention to investment as a key policy tool to revive growth. For example, in a recent report the German Institute for Economic Research, DIW, has claimed that since the crisis a large investment gap has emerged across Europe (DIW, 2014). In this chapter, we have put much emphasis on one specific component of investment in knowledge assets, including ICT, human capital, and intangible capital. While Europe has held up relatively well during the crisis, and even exhibited some catching up on the US, for example in ICT capital, the translation of those investments into faster productivity remains a major constraint. Investment in intangible assets can drive innovation and organizational change, which should translate to stronger productivity. Innovation and educational policies should focus on supporting the productivity effects from those investments, partly through focusing on public investment in areas with positive externalities, and partly through providing the business sector with platforms to connect and reduce information asymmetries.

The productivity of investment and the way it translates into TFP growth in Europe depends strongly on the ability to strengthen static effects (focused primarily on cost reductions and allocative efficiency) as well as dynamic effects (related to competition in product, labor and capital markets, and innovation) from a large single market in the EU. Recent analysis shows that the creation of a single digital market and a single market for services across the EU could contribute significantly to unleash the productivity gains from larger market size (van Ark 2014; Mariniello *et al.* 2015).

Appendix Table 4.1a Output, hours, and labor productivity growth, and growth contributions by major input, 1999–2007 (log growth)

	Average growth of 1999–2007			Contributions to GDP growth				
	Growth rate of GDP	Hours worked[1]	Labor productivity	Hours worked (weighted)[2]	Labor composition	Non-ICT capital	ICT capital	Total factor productivity growth
EU-28*	2.6	0.8	1.8	0.5	0.2	0.8	0.5	0.6
Euro Area**	2.3	0.9	1.4	0.6	0.2	0.7	0.4	0.4
EU-15***	2.4	0.9	1.5	0.6	0.2	0.7	0.5	0.4
Ireland	5.9	3.3	2.6	1.8	0.4	2.4	1.0	0.4
Luxembourg	4.7	3.4	1.3	1.9	0.2	2.6	0.0	0.0
Greece	3.9	1.2	2.7	0.7	0.7	1.8	0.7	0.1
Spain	3.8	3.4	0.3	2.2	0.4	1.5	0.5	-0.8
Finland	3.5	1.1	2.4	0.7	0.1	0.4	0.8	1.5
Sweden	3.3	0.8	2.6	0.5	0.3	0.7	0.4	1.4
United Kingdom	3.0	0.7	2.3	0.5	0.4	0.7	0.7	0.7
Netherlands	2.5	0.9	1.6	0.6	0.2	0.4	0.5	0.8
Austria	2.5	0.6	1.9	0.4	0.2	0.5	0.4	1.0
Belgium	2.4	1.1	1.3	0.7	0.2	0.7	0.5	0.2
France	2.2	0.5	1.7	0.3	0.3	0.8	0.3	0.5
Denmark	2.0	0.7	1.3	0.5	0.1	0.5	0.7	0.2
Portugal	1.8	0.4	1.3	0.3	0.8	0.9	0.6	-0.9
Germany	1.6	0.0	1.6	0.0	0.0	0.3	0.3	1.0
Italy	1.5	1.0	0.4	0.7	0.2	0.7	0.2	-0.3

Appendix Table 4.1a (*cont.*)

	Average growth of 1999–2007			Contributions to GDP growth				
	Growth rate of GDP	Hours worked[1]	Labor productivity	Hours worked (weighted)[2]	Labor composition	Non-ICT capital	ICT capital	Total factor productivity growth
EU-12****	*4.4*	*-0.1*	*4.5*	*-0.1*	*0.3*	*1.2*	*0.8*	*2.2*
Latvia	7.6	-0.4	7.9	-0.2	0.2	5.1	0.0	2.5
Estonia	6.8	0.9	5.9	0.5	0.2	2.7	0.0	3.4
Lithuania	6.4	0.4	6.0	0.2	0.1	2.8	0.0	3.3
Romania	4.9	-1.7	6.6	-1.2	0.3	-0.2	0.7	5.3
Slovak Republic	4.9	0.1	4.7	0.0	0.2	1.1	1.0	2.5
Slovenia	4.3	0.6	3.7	0.4	0.7	1.4	0.6	1.3
Bulgaria	4.3	0.8	3.4	0.4	0.3	3.6	1.5	-1.5
Poland	4.1	0.1	4.0	0.0	0.3	0.9	0.7	2.3
Czech Republic	4.1	-0.4	4.5	-0.2	0.3	1.6	0.6	1.8
Cyprus	4.1	2.3	1.8	1.5	0.4	0.8	0.0	1.4
Hungary	3.6	0.1	3.5	0.0	0.5	1.1	1.5	0.4
Malta	3.0	0.6	2.4	0.4	0.0	0.8	0.0	1.8
United States	2.8	0.6	2.2	0.4	0.2	0.7	0.7	0.9

Note: Countries are ranked by their GDP growth rate for 1999–2007.

[1] Refers to actual log growth rate of total hours worked.

[2] Refers to the contribution of total hours worked, weighted by the share of labor in total compensation, to the log growth rate of GDP.

* Excludes Croatia, which became member of the EU on July 1, 2013.

** Refers to pre-2014 membership of eighteen members, excluding Latvia, which became a member on January 1, 2014.

*** Refers to pre-2004 membership of the EU.

**** Refers to new membership of the EU since 2004, and excludes Croatia, which became a member of the EU on July 1, 2013.

Source: The Conference Board Total Economy Database™, May 2015. See: www.conference-board.org/data/economydatabase.

Appendix Table 4.1b *Output, hours, and labor productivity growth, and growth contributions by major input, 2008–2014 (log growth)*

	Average growth of 2008–2014			Contributions to GDP growth				
	Growth rate of GDP	Hours worked[1]	Labor productivity	Hours worked (weighted)[2]	Labor composition	Non-ICT capital	ICT capital	Total factor productivity growth
*EU-28**	0.2	-0.4	0.5	-0.2	0.2	0.5	0.3	-0.5
*Euro Area***	-0.2	-0.6	0.5	-0.4	0.2	0.3	0.3	-0.6
*EU-15****	0.0	-0.3	0.3	-0.2	0.1	0.4	0.3	-0.6
Ireland	-0.3	-1.9	1.6	-1.2	0.2	0.8	0.6	-0.6
Luxembourg	0.9	0.5	0.3	0.3	0.2	2.0	0.0	-1.5
Greece	-4.3	-3.4	-0.9	-2.1	0.3	0.4	0.7	-3.6
Spain	-0.7	-2.4	1.7	-1.4	0.3	0.7	0.3	-0.6
Finland	-0.8	-0.5	-0.3	-0.3	0.2	0.2	0.9	-1.8
Sweden	0.8	0.6	0.2	0.4	0.1	0.5	0.7	-0.9
United Kingdom	0.6	0.7	-0.1	0.5	0.1	0.5	0.2	-0.8
Netherlands	0.0	-0.2	0.2	-0.1	0.1	0.3	0.2	-0.4
Austria	0.6	0.1	0.5	0.0	0.1	0.3	0.3	-0.1
Belgium	0.5	0.6	0.0	-0.1	0.2	0.4	0.5	-0.4
France	0.3	-0.1	0.4	0.0	0.2	0.6	0.1	-0.5
Denmark	-0.5	-0.7	0.2	-0.5	0.1	0.0	0.8	-0.8
Portugal	-0.9	-2.0	1.0	-1.3	0.6	0.1	0.7	-1.0
Germany	0.7	0.3	0.4	0.2	0.1	0.2	0.4	-0.2
Italy	-1.3	-1.2	-0.1	-0.8	0.1	0.0	0.1	-0.7

Appendix Table 4.1b (*cont.*)

	Average growth of 2008–2014			Contributions to GDP growth				
	Growth rate of GDP	Hours worked[1]	Labor productivity	Hours worked (weighted)[2]	Labor composition	Non-ICT capital	ICT capital	Total factor productivity growth
EU-12****	1.5	-0.4	1.9	-0.3	0.2	1.1	0.7	-0.2
Latvia	-0.8	-2.3	1.5	-1.3	0.1	0.9	0.0	-0.4
Estonia	-0.4	-1.9	1.5	-1.3	0.2	0.9	0.0	-0.1
Lithuania	0.6	-1.9	2.4	-1.1	0.2	1.3	0.0	0.1
Romania	1.1	-1.6	2.7	-1.0	0.2	0.6	0.1	1.2
Slovak Republic	1.8	0.1	1.7	0.0	0.1	0.7	1.5	-0.5
Slovenia	-0.6	-0.6	0.0	-0.5	0.3	0.3	0.7	-1.4
Bulgaria	0.9	-1.3	2.2	-0.7	0.3	2.3	1.3	-2.2
Poland	3.1	0.3	2.8	0.1	0.1	1.6	0.7	0.5
Czech Republic	0.3	-0.1	0.4	0.0	0.1	1.1	0.3	-1.2
Cyprus	-1.0	-1.6	0.6	-1.0	0.3	0.9	0.0	-1.2
Hungary	0.0	-1.0	1.0	-0.6	0.2	0.3	0.0	-1.5
Malta	2.2	1.4	0.8	0.8	0.2	-0.1	1.5	1.2
United States	1.1	0.0	1.2	0.0	0.1	0.3	0.4	0.3

Note: Countries are ranked by their GDP growth rate for 2008–2014.

[1] Refers to actual log growth rate of total hours worked.

[2] Refers to the contribution of total hours worked, weighted by the share of labor in total compensation, to the log growth rate of GDP.

* Excludes Croatia, which became member of EU on July 1, 2013.

** Refers to pre-2014 membership of eighteen members, excluding Latvia, which became a member on January 1, 2014.

*** Refers to pre-2004 membership of the EU.

**** Refers to new membership of the EU since 2004, and excludes Croatia, which became a member of the EU on July 1, 2013.

Source: The Conference Board Total Economy Database™, May 2015. See: www.conference-board.org/data/economydatabase.

Appendix Table 4.2 *Output, hours, and labor productivity growth, and growth contributions by major sector and major input, 1999–2007 and 1999–latest year available (log growth)*

	Growth rate of Real Value Added	Hours worked (weighted) [2]	Contributions to real value added growth			
			Labour composition	Non-ICT capital	ICT capital	Total factor productivity growth
Austria					Article I.	
ICT goods and services						
1999–2007	4.1	0.7	0.3	0.0	1.0	2.2
2008–2009	-1.9	-0.7	0.5	-0.3	0.5	-2.0
1999–2009	3.0	0.4	0.3	-0.1	0.9	1.4
Goods production, excl. electrical machinery						
1999–2007	2.7	-0.3	0.3	-0.2	0.2	2.6
2008–2009	-6.5	-1.8	0.1	-0.1	0.1	-4.9
1999–2009	1.0	-0.5	0.2	-0.1	0.2	1.3
Market services, excl. information and telecom						
1999–2007	3.1	0.9	0.2	0.4	0.6	1.0
2008–2009	0.2	-0.6	0.5	0.2	0.4	-0.3
1999–2009	2.6	0.6	0.3	0.4	0.5	0.8
Belgium						
ICT goods and services						
1999–2007	3.9	0.8	0.3	0.6	2.1	0.1
2008–2011	0.6	0.1	0.2	0.5	1.3	-1.5
1999–2011	2.9	0.6	0.3	0.6	1.8	-0.3

Appendix Table 4.2 (*cont.*)

	Growth rate of Real Value Added	Hours worked (weighted) [2]	Contributions to real value added growth			
			Labour composition	Non-ICT capital	ICT capital	Total factor productivity growth
Goods production, excl. electrical machinery						
1999–2007	1.7	-0.2	0.2	0.7	0.3	0.8
2008–2011	-0.1	-0.8	0.2	0.8	0.2	-0.5
1999–2011	1.2	-0.4	0.2	0.7	0.2	0.4
Market services, excl. information and telecom						
1999–2007	2.7	0.7	0.2	0.9	0.8	0.0
2008–2011	0.7	0.5	0.1	0.6	0.4	-0.8
1999–2011	2.1	0.7	0.2	0.8	0.7	-0.2
Finland						
ICT goods and services						
1999–2007	12.8	1.1	0.5	1.2	1.0	8.9
2008–2012	-5.2	-0.5	0.4	0.6	-0.5	-5.3
1999–2012	6.3	0.5	0.5	1.0	0.5	3.9
Goods production, excl. electrical machinery						
1999–2007	2.9	0.1	0.1	0.2	0.2	2.1
2008–2012	-2.7	-1.2	0.2	0.1	0.2	-2.0
1999–2012	0.9	-0.3	0.1	0.2	0.2	0.7
Market services, excl. information and telecom						
1999–2007	2.9	1.3	0.0	0.4	-0.2	1.4

2008–2012	0.3	0.5	0.1	0.0	0.0	−0.4
1999–2012	2.0	1.0	0.0	0.3	−0.2	0.8
France						
ICT goods and services						
1999–2007	5.7	0.5	0.4	0.5	0.6	3.7
2008–2009	−1.7	−0.4	0.7	0.5	0.2	−2.8
1999–2009	4.3	0.4	0.4	0.5	0.5	2.5
Goods production, excl. electrical machinery						
1999–2007	1.6	−0.4	0.4	0.3	0.1	1.3
2008–2009	−4.6	−1.5	0.6	0.4	0.1	−4.2
1999–2009	0.5	−0.6	0.4	0.3	0.1	0.3
Market services, excl. information and telecom						
1999–2007	2.5	1.1	0.3	0.7	0.4	0.0
2008–2009	−1.8	−0.3	0.5	0.4	0.2	−2.5
1999–2009	1.7	0.8	0.4	0.6	0.4	−0.5
Germany						
ICT goods and services						
1999–2007	5.5	0.5	0.0	0.3	0.4	4.2
2008–2009	1.0	−1.5	0.5	0.1	0.1	1.9
1999–2009	4.7	0.1	0.1	0.3	0.4	3.8
Goods production, excl. electrical machinery						
1999–2007	1.3	−1.3	0.1	0.1	0.1	2.3
2008–2009	−9.5	−2.2	0.6	0.1	0.2	−8.3
1999–2009	−0.6	−1.4	0.2	0.1	0.2	0.4

Appendix Table 4.2 (*cont.*)

	Growth rate of Real Value Added	Hours worked (weighted) [2]	Contributions to real value added growth				
			Labour composition	Non-ICT capital	ICT capital	Total factor productivity growth
Market services, excl. information and telecom							
1999–2007	1.9	0.4	0.0	0.6	0.7	0.1
2008–2009	-1.3	-0.3	0.3	0.4	0.5	-2.0
1999–2009	1.3	0.3	0.0	0.6	0.7	-0.3
Italy							
ICT goods and services							
1999–2007	4.5	0.8	0.2	1.9	0.5	1.1
2008–2009	-4.1	-1.0	0.1	0.7	0.1	-4.0
1999–2009	2.9	0.5	0.2	1.7	0.4	0.2
Goods production, excl. electrical machinery							
1999–2007	1.1	0.3	0.4	0.7	0.1	-0.4
2008–2009	-7.7	-3.4	0.4	0.1	0.0	-4.8
1999–2009	-0.5	-0.4	0.4	0.6	0.1	-1.2
Market services, excl. information and telecom							
1999–2007	1.7	1.2	0.2	0.8	0.3	-0.9
2008–2009	-3.1	-0.9	0.1	0.2	0.0	-2.6
1999–2009	0.8	0.8	0.2	0.7	0.3	-1.2

Netherlands

ICT goods and services

1999–2007	6.0	0.7	0.5	0.5	1.1	3.3
2008–2010	-0.4	0.0	0.0	-0.1	0.4	-1.2
1999–2010	4.4	0.5	0.4	0.3	0.9	2.1

Goods production, excl. electrical machinery

1999–2007	1.9	-0.3	0.4	0.0	0.2	1.6
2008–2010	-0.7	-0.3	0.0	0.3	0.1	-1.5
1999–2010	1.3	-0.3	0.3	0.1	0.2	0.9

Market services, excl. information and telecom

1999–2007	3.0	0.7	0.3	0.4	0.5	1.0
2008–2010	-0.7	-0.2	0.1	0.1	0.1	-1.2
1999–2010	2.0	0.5	0.3	0.3	0.4	0.4

Spain

ICT goods and services

1999–2007	4.3	0.3	0.4	2.1	1.1	0.3
2008–2009	-0.9	-0.2	0.6	0.6	0.2	-2.0
1999–2009	3.3	0.2	0.4	1.8	0.9	-0.1

Goods production, excl. electrical machinery

1999–2007	2.8	1.2	0.3	1.5	0.2	-0.4
2008–2009	-5.2	-6.6	0.8	1.0	0.1	-0.5
1999–2009	1.3	-0.2	0.4	1.4	0.2	-0.4

Market services, excl. information and telecom

1999–2007	4.3	2.7	0.4	1.4	0.6	-0.8
2008–2009	-0.8	-0.2	0.5	1.3	0.3	-2.6
1999–2009	3.4	2.2	0.4	1.4	0.6	-1.1

Appendix Table 4.2 (*cont.*)

	Growth rate of Real Value Added	Hours worked (weighted)[2]	Contributions to real value added growth			
			Labour composition	Non-ICT capital	ICT capital	Total factor productivity growth
Sweden						
ICT goods and services						
1999–2007	10.0	0.2	1.2	0.9	7.7	
2008–2011	6.1	0.2	0.2	1.5	4.1	
1999–2011	8.8	0.2	0.9	1.1	6.6	
Goods production, excl. electrical machinery						
1999–2007	3.5	0.2	0.2	0.6	2.6	
2008–2011	-2.2	-0.4	-0.3	0.4	-1.8	
1999–2011	1.8	0.0	0.0	0.5	1.2	
Market services, excl. information and telecom						
1999–2007	4.0	0.7	0.8	1.6	0.9	
2008–2011	1.6	1.1	0.1	1.2	-0.8	
1999–2011	3.2	0.8	0.5	1.5	0.4	
United Kingdom						
ICT goods and services						
1999–2007	6.3	0.3	0.5	1.2	1.3	3.0
2008–2009	-3.1	-2.9	0.4	0.2	-0.2	-0.5

1999–2009	4.6	-0.3	0.5	1.0	1.0	2.4

Goods production, excl. electrical machinery

1999–2007	0.7	-1.2	0.4	0.2	0.2	1.1
2008–2009	-6.7	-2.6	0.4	0.0	0.1	-4.6
1999–2009	-0.7	-1.5	0.4	0.2	0.2	0.0

Market services, excl. information and telecom

1999–2007	4.0	1.0	0.4	0.6	1.0	1.0
2008–2009	-4.0	-1.3	0.5	-0.1	0.3	-3.4
1999–2009	2.6	0.6	0.4	0.5	0.9	0.2

Notes: (1) ICT goods and services include manufacturing in electronics and telecommunication equipment and IT and other information services; (2) goods production includes manufacturing excluding ICT, agriculture, mining, utilities, and construction; (3) market services excludes ICT services and includes distribution, financial and business services, and community, personal, and social services. Non-market services include education, health care and public administration, and real estate services.

Source: EUKLEMS industry-level productivity accounts, November 2012. See: www.euklems.net.

References

Acemoglu, D. 1998. "Why do New Technologies Complement Skills? Directed Technical Change and Wage Inequality," *Quarterly Journal of Economics*, **113**(4): 1055–1089.

Acemoglu, D. and D. H. Autor. 2011. "Skills, Tasks and Technologies: Implications for Employment and Earnings." In Orley Ashenfelter and David Card (eds.) *Handbook of Labor Economics*, Vol. 4B. Dan Diego, CA: North Holland, Ch. 12, 1043–1171.

Autor, D. H., L. F. Katz, and A. B. Krueger. 1998. "Computing Inequality: Have Computers Changed the Labour Market?' *Quarterly Journal of Labour Economics*, **113**(4): 1169–1213.

Autor D. H., F. Levy, and R. Murnane. 2003. "The Skill Content of Recent Technological Change: An Empirical Exploration," *Quarterly Journal of Economics*, **118**(4): 1279–1333.

Barnett, A., S. Batten, A. Chiu, J. Franklin, and M. Sebastia-Barriel. 2014. "The UK Productivity Puzzle," *Bank of England Quarterly Bulletin*, Q2.

Basu, S., J. G. Fernald, and M. D. Shapiro. 2001. "Productivity Growth in the 1990s: Technology, Utilization, or Adjustment?" *Carnegie-Rochester Conference Series on Public Policy*, **55**: 117–165.

Bellmann, L., H-D. Gerner, and M.-C. Laible. 2016. "The German Labour Market Puzzle in the Great Recession." In P. Askenazy, (ed.), *Productivity Puzzles in Europe*. Paris: CEPREMAP. See: www.cepremap.fr/depot/201 5/ProductivityPuzzle/BellmannGerner.pdf.

Bertschek, I., and U. Kaiser. 2004. "Productivity Effects of Organisational Change: Microeconometric Evidence," *Management Science*, **50**(3): 394–404.

Black, S. E. and L. M. Lynch. 2001. "How to Compete: The Impact of Workplace Practices and Information Technology on Productivity," *The Review of Economics and Statistics*, **83**(3): 434–445.

Bresnahan, T. F., E. Brynjolfsson, and L. M. Hitt. 2002. "Information Technology, Workplace Organization, and the Demand for Skilled Labor: Firm-Level Evidence," *Quarterly Journal of Economics*, **117**(1): 339–376.

Brynjolfsson, E., L. M. Hitt, and Shinkyu Yang. 2002. "Intangible Assets: Computers and Organisational Capital," *Brookings Papers on Economic Activity: Macroeconomics*, (1): 137–199.

Corrado, C., Jonathan Haskel, Cecilia Jona-Lasinio, and Massimiliano Iommi. 2013. "Innovation and Intangible Investment in Europe, Japan, and the United States," *Oxford Review of Economic Policy*, **29**(2): 261–286.

Corrado, C., C. Hulten, and D. Sichel. 2005. "Measuring Capital and Technology: An Expanded Framework." In C. Corrado, J. Haltiwanger and D. Sichel (eds.) *Measuring Capital in the New Economy*. University of Chicago Press, 11–46.

2009. "Intangible Capital and US Economic Growth," *Review of Income and Wealth*, 55(3): 661–685.

Corrado, C. and K. Jäger. 2014. *"Communication Networks, ICT and Productivity Growth in Europe,"* Economics Program Working Paper, no. 14–04, The Conference Board, New York.

Crafts, Nicholas. 2010. "The Contribution of New Technology to Economic Growth: Lessons from Economic History," *Revista de Historia Economica*, **28**: 409–440.

DIW. 2014. "Economic Impulses in Europe," *DIW Economic Bulletin*, No. 7, Berlin.

Greenstein, S. 2000. "Building and Delivering the Virtual World: Commercializing Services for Internet Access." *Journal of Industrial Economics*, **48**(4): 391–411.

Inklaar, R. C., M. P. Timmer, and B. van Ark. 2008. "Market Services Across Europe and the US," *Economic Policy*, **23**(53, January): 139–194.

Jorgenson, Dale W., Mun S. Ho, and Kevin J. Stiroh. 2005. *Information Technology and the American Growth Resurgence*. Cambridge, MA: The MIT Press.

Mariniello, M., A. Sapir, and A. Terzi. 2015. "The Long Road Towards the European Single Market," *Bruegel Working Paper*, Brussels, Belgium, March 16.

Piatkowski, M. 2013. "Poland New Golden Age. Shifting for Europe's Periphery to Its Center," *Policy Research Working Paper*, No. 6639, Washington DC.

Röller, L. H. and L. Waverman. 2001. "Telecommunications Infrastructure and Economic Development: A Simultaneous Approach," *American Economic Review*, **91**(4): 909–923.

Teulings, C. and R. Baldwin. 2014. *Secular Stagnation: Facts, Causes and Cures*. London: VoxEU, Centre for Economic Policy Research.

Timmer, Marcel P., Robert Inklaar, Mary O'Mahony, and Bart van Ark. 2010. *Economic Growth in Europe. A Comparative Industry Perspective*. Cambridge University Press.

van Ark, Bart. 2011. (Exec. ed.) *The Linked World: How ICT is Transforming Societies, Cultures and Economies*. New York: The Conference Board, Report for Fundación Telefonica.

2014. *Productivity and Digitalisation in Europe: Paving the Road to Faster Growth*. Brussels/New York: The Lisbon Council and The Conference Board.

van Ark, Bart, Mary O'Mahony, and Marcel Timmer. 2008. "The Productivity Gap between Europe and the US: Trends and Causes," *Journal of Economic Perspectives*, **22**(1, Winter): 25–44.

    2012. "Europe's Productivity Performance in Comparative Perspective: Trends, Causes and Recent Developments." In M. Mas and R. Stehrer (eds.), *Industrial Productivity in Europe, Growth and Crisis*. Cheltenham, UK: Edward Elgar Publishing, pp. 65–91.

van Ark, Bart, Ataman Ozyildirim, Prajakta Bhide, Elizabeth Crofoot, Abdul Erumban, and Gad Levanon. 2015. "Prioritizing Productivity to Drive Growth, Competitiveness and Profitability," *Research Report, R-1580-KBI*, The Conference Board, New York, May.

5 | LA-KLEMS: *economic growth and productivity in Latin America*

ANDRÉ HOFMAN, MATILDE MAS, CLAUDIO ARAVENA, AND JUAN FERNÁNDEZ DE GUEVARA

Introduction

In the last two decades, the comparatively poor performance of economic growth in Latin America (LA) masks significant changes in both its sources and growth patterns.[1] This chapter examines economic growth, productivity, and its determinants in five countries in Latin America for the period 1990–2010 for the aggregate economy as well as for nine economic sectors. In our analysis we use a new database, LA-KLEMS, which serves as a fundamental tool for research in the area of economic growth and productivity. The variables are organized around the growth accounting methodology, which provides a clear conceptual framework for analyzing interaction between variables in a consistent manner. LA-KLEMS is part of the World KLEMS initiative led by Professor Dale W. Jorgenson. An overview of this initiative can be found in Jorgenson (2016). The countries participating in LA-KLEMS are Argentina, Brazil, Chile, Colombia, and Mexico, and the project will continue to expand to include other countries in the region.[2] Information provided on these countries is broken down into nine industries.

---

[1] The authors are thankful for the comments and suggestions made by Dale Jorgenson, Kyoji Fukao, and Marcel Timmer to earlier versions of this chapter. We would like to acknowledge Juan Carlos Robledo for his research assistance, and Matilde Mas and Juan Fernández de Guerara thank the Spanish Ministry of Economy and Competitiveness (ECO2015-70632-R and ECO2013-43959-R).

[2] The LA-KLEMS project was coordinated by the United Nations Economic Commission for Latin America and the Caribbean (ECLAC). The project started with four countries, Argentina, Brazil, Chile, and Mexico, which were later joined by Colombia, Costa Rica, and Peru. See also Cimoli, Hofman, and Mulder (2010) with the results on the aggregate level, of the first phase of the LA-KLEMS project in ECLAC.

Although the main objective of generating the KLEMS database is to identify comparative productivity trends, the data collected are also useful for a large number of other purposes because of the database's comprehensive and detailed coverage. The data series follow the format of EU-KLEMS (see Timmer, Inklaar, O'Mahony and van Ark 2010) including measures of production and growth factors and variables in various categories of capital (K), labor (L), energy (E), materials (M), and service inputs (S).[3] The LA-KLEMS database is largely built upon the information provided by the national statistical institutes (INE) and/or central banks, and is processed according to internationally standardized procedures. These procedures have been developed to ensure international comparability of data and generate coherent series.

The KLEMS data are based both on national accounts statistics for each country and on the concepts and conventions of the System of National Accounts. Employment statistics, labor information coming from household and/or employment surveys, and, in some cases, social security registers, are also used to obtain the most consistent series for hours worked.

This brand new database is particularly relevant for Latin America countries, as comparable studies on economic growth and productivity have been hampered by the lack of standard databases covering a wide range of countries. The KLEMS methodology allows for comparable cross-country series of the main variables associated with economic growth and productivity. The comparative analysis of gross domestic product (GDP) growth by industry, capital, and labor productivity obtained from the KLEMS data provides an extremely useful starting point for identifying the sources of growth. However, growth accounting applied in this study does not explicitly take into account institutional factors, the external context, etc. that is, the ultimate factors in explaining economic development (see Hsieh and Klenow 2010).

Examining productivity figures with LA-KLEMS clearly reveals the differences between countries and gives a new perspective for understanding the evolution of the series over time. This coherent structure allows researchers to observe whether Latin America is in the process of 'catching up' with Europe and the United States, and in what industries

---

[3] E, M, and S are included in the LA-KLEMS database but the analysis of this chapter is based upon value added data of the database.

progress or setbacks occur. The possibilities opened up to researchers with the LA-KLEMS database are relevant as homogeneous series detailed by industry can be observed, allowing for analysis of how each country evolves over time, and subsequent comparison both among Latin American countries and with developed economies.

The aim of this chapter is twofold: first, to use the KLEMS homogeneous database to discern and discover patterns in both value added (VA) and labor productivity growth in Argentina, Brazil, Chile, Colombia, and Mexico over the period 1990–2010; and second, to present the LA-KLEMS database and disseminate information about it. The remainder of the chapter is organized as follows. Section 5.1 provides a brief overview of the literature dealing with the patterns of growth in Latin American countries. Section 5.2 presents the theoretical framework. Section 5.3 describes the data sources and methodology used in developing the database. Section 5.4 starts by placing the five countries in the LA context and describes the main facts and trends that emerge from this new database. Section 5.5 presents the growth accounting results. Section 5.6 decomposes aggregated productivity growth and capital deepening by means of a shift-share analysis to assess the relevance of both individual industry evolution and the consequences of structural change (changes in specialization). Finally, Section 5.7 concludes.

5.1 Background

Productivity is defined as the ratio between what a company produces and the resources used for production. However, productivity is the result of business decisions about the choice of quantity and quality of productive inputs, the type, quantity, and quality of production, the technology used, and how these elements change (organizational structure, business models) as well as their innovative activity. In each of these aspects there may be important differences between industries and even between companies in the same industry. Differences in productivity depend on the volume and characteristics of production, the choice of production factors and the combination of these. Therefore, productivity differentials may be due to multiple factors, including the type of production processes of product innovation, quality factors (capital and labor), process innovations, organizational structure, capacity to adapt to the environment, etc. In this chapter the

behavior of productivity at the aggregate level of the economy as well as
the industry (sector) level in Argentina, Brazil, Chile, Colombia, and
Mexico were studied from 1990 to 2010.

Several studies have examined, at the aggregated level, whether
differences in output per worker are due to the differences in physical
and human capital or to total factor productivity (TFP) in Latin
America.[4] However, Elías (1992) is the first systematic application of
the *Sources of Growth* (*Growth Accounting*) methodology in seven LA
countries, namely Argentina, Brazil, Chile, Colombia, Mexico, Peru,
and Venezuela, for the period 1940–1985. He makes a detailed study of
the composition of labor and capital inputs, establishing links between
growth and development analysis. His main conclusion is that for all
countries and decades, capital made the highest contribution to output
growth (45.6%), while the contribution of labor was similar to that of
TFP. Capital's greatest contribution lay in the growth of both its
quantity (3.8%) and its weight (60%), higher than in developed economies. Quality improvements also played an important role in the
growth of labor input and through it, in output growth. See also
Hofman (2000) for a careful application of the growth accounting
methodology with data for six countries in Latin America.[5]

De Gregorio (2006) decomposes differences in output per capita (not
output per worker) comparing Latin American countries to the US in
a more recent period. He finds that TFP is the most important factor in
explaining differences with the US, followed by human capital.
Physical capital, on the other hand, accounts for only a small part of
the difference between Latin America and the US. A similar finding is
presented in Cole *et al.* (2005), who find that both capital output and
the level of education in Latin America are relatively similar to those of
the US. Therefore, according to their results, differences in TFP mainly
explain differences in GDP per worker.

Using capital per worker, Blyde and Fernández-Arias (2006) found
that the Latin America TFP gap with respect to developed countries

---

[4] Among the first authors were Bruton (1967), Correa (1970), and Langoni (1974).
[5] Hofman (2000) also compares the Latin American performance with three
other groups of countries: (a) two rapidly growing Asian countries (Korea and
Taiwan), whose economic growth in the past decades has been remarkably fast;
(b) Portugal and Spain, whose institutional heritage had a good deal in common
with Latin America; and (c) six advanced capitalist countries (France, Germany,
Japan, the Netherlands, the UK, and the US), whose levels of income and
productivity are among the highest in the world.

widened between 1960 and 1999. They estimate that the gap in TFP in Latin America increased from about 84% in 1960 to 58% in the 1990s. In contrast, the human capital gap with respect to developed countries decreased slightly from 76% to 80%, and the gap of physical capital increased marginally from 58% to 53%. Thus, TFP in Latin America was the key factor behind the fall in productivity growth in this area as compared to the US.

Few authors have studied sectoral differences in productivity in Latin America. Restuccia (2013) compares the sectoral productivity performance of Latin American countries to that of the US. He finds that productivity growth in the agricultural, industrial, and services sector was below that in the US during 1950–2000. The exception is the agricultural sector in Chile, which has been catching up since the 1980s. In addition, the fall in relative productivity was more marked in the services sector than in the agricultural and industrial sector. As Restuccia (2013) uses the Groningen Growth and Development Centre (GGDC) ten-sector database which does not include information on capital stock by sector, the comparison is not possible in terms of capital/output ratio or in terms of TFP.

Szirmai *et al.* (2013) summarize the literature on the importance of the manufacturing sector in the development process and emphasize its role in the nineteenth and twentieth century. Szirmai and Verspagen (2010) find that the manufacturing sector has a particularly important role during periods of accelerated growth. However, Timmer and de Vries (2009) point out that the manufacturing sector has become less important in recent periods.

Vergara and Rivero (2006) extended existing sectoral capital data at the Banco Central de Chile, and examined industry TFP growth in Chile during the period 1986–2001. They found that the average annual TFP growth was highest in the wholesale and retail sector and lowest in the manufacturing industry. According to Vergara and Rivero (2006) the high TFP growth in the commercial sector could be related to the benefits of adopting information and communications technology (ICT), which are relatively large in this sector. Fuentes and Garcia (2014) describe patterns of productivity growth in nine sectors in Chile in order to explain recent lower TFP growth. They present evidence that aggregate shocks like the increase in the minimum wage, especially for industries intensive in labor like manufacturing, construction, and retail, and the increase in energy costs, explain lower TFP growth. A special mention is made of the mining sector and the lower copper grade and its effect on mining productivity and on the increase in energy costs. In his analysis of the problem of development in Latin America, Restuccia (2013) emphasizes that both low labor productivity and TFP growth explain much of the poor performance in terms of GDP growth.

In Aravena and Fuentes (2013), value added growth is decomposed into the change in hours worked and in labor productivity (value added per hour worked) for a set of sixteen Latin American countries. The average growth of 2.8% of value added between 1981 and 2010 for the sample countries is explained by the increase in hours worked, while labor productivity had a negative contribution. Regarding the time profile, the results show that in the 1980s value added increased by only 1.3% on average, and only two countries, Colombia and Honduras, experienced increases in labor productivity. During the nineties there was an improvement in both value added and labor productivity, and seven countries recorded increases in labor productivity. Argentina, Chile, and Uruguay stood out for their large contribution of labor productivity. In the period 2001–2010, when the value added grew by 3.8%, thirteen of the sixteen countries increased in labor productivity, particularly Chile, but without regaining the productivity levels that existed in the early 1980s in several cases. On the other hand, eight countries ended up with lower labor productivity than that observed thirty years ago, with a sharp decline in the first decade that was not compensated for by the productivity gains in later years.

5.2 Theoretical framework

The methodology for measuring the sources of value added growth must consider the heterogeneity in each of the inputs used in the production of goods and services. Our analysis considers the two traditional sources of economic growth – capital and labor – with emphasis on the importance of both the amount of the factor used and its composition in terms of quality. Different types of assets are considered in the case of capital. For labor eight characteristics are used: three levels of education, gender, and three age groups. The methodology applied to measure its contribution to economic growth is known as growth accounting, which originated in the work of Solow (1956 and 1957), Denison (1967), Jorgenson and

Griliches (1967), Jorgenson, Gollop, and Fraumeini (1987), and Jorgenson, Ho and Stiroh (2005).

Elías's (1992) approach – based on the procedure developed by Jorgenson and Griliches (1967) – accounts for the sources of growth. Y represents the goods produced; l is the types of intermediate inputs $(X_1, X_2, \ldots X_l)$; m is the different worker characteristics $(L_1, L_2, \ldots L_m)$; n is the types of capital inputs $(K_1, K_2, \ldots K_n)$. The value of total output in a given period is equal to the sum of payments for all inputs used during the same period. This is expressed by the following equation:

$$p_Y Y = \sum_{h=1}^{l} x_h X_h + \sum_{i=1}^{m} w_i L_i + \sum_{j=1}^{n} r_j K_j \tag{1}$$

where p is the price of goods produced, and x, w, and r are the prices of services for each type of intermediate input, labor, and capital, respectively. This relationship is defined for a given period t, which in this case is one year. Equation (1) is the basic expression to identify the role of each variable in the growth of gross output (GO). In this case, we will work with two simultaneous postings: one explaining changes in the GO by changes occurring in the goods produced. The other, the right hand side of equation (1), explains the sources of these changes.

Differentiating equation 1 with respect to time, the following expression is obtained:

$$p_Y \dot{Y} + Y \dot{p}_Y = \sum_{h=1}^{l} x_h \dot{X}_h + \sum_{i=1}^{m} w_i \dot{L}_i + \sum_{j=1}^{n} r_j \dot{K}_j$$
$$+ \sum_{i=1}^{m} L_i \dot{w}_i + \sum_{j=1}^{n} K_j \dot{r}_j + \sum_{h=1}^{l} X_h \dot{x}_h \tag{2}$$

If we rewrite the terms of equation (2), leaving all derivative quantities of output and inputs for a period on the left hand side of the equation, and those derived from the production input prices for the same period on the right of the equation, we obtain:

$$p_Y \dot{Y} - \sum_{h=1}^{l} x_h \dot{X}_h - \sum_{i=1}^{m} w_i \dot{L}_i - \sum_{j=1}^{n} r_j \dot{K}_j$$
$$= \sum_{i=1}^{m} L_i \dot{w}_i + \sum_{j=1}^{n} K_j \dot{r}_j + \sum_{h=1}^{l} X_h \dot{x}_h - Y \dot{p}_Y \tag{3}$$

Equation (3) presents the duality between prices and quantities, the term used in the theory of production and cost function. This expression suggests that the difference between changes in the production input values for given prices of output and inputs is equal to the difference between price changes of output and inputs for given inputs and outputs. If we consider only the left hand side of equation (3) under conditions of cost minimization, we have:

$$p_Y \dot{Y} = \sum_{h=1}^{l} x_h \dot{X}_h + \sum_{i=1}^{m} w_i \dot{L}_i + \sum_{j=1}^{n} r_j \dot{K}_j \qquad (4)$$

Expressing the relationship in terms of percentage changes, dividing and multiplying each derivative by the corresponding variable:

$$p_Y Y (\dot{Y}/Y) = \sum_{h=1}^{l} x_h X_h (\dot{X}_h / X_h) + \sum_{j=1}^{m} w_i L_i (\dot{L}_i / L_i)$$
$$+ \sum_{h=1}^{n} r_j K_j (\dot{K}_j / K_j) \qquad (5)$$

Then, if both sides of (5) are divided by $P_Y Y$, which is expressed for each side of equation (1), and defined

$$\beta_h = (x_h X_h / GO)$$
$$\beta_i = (w_i L_i / GO)$$
$$\beta_j = (r_j K_j / GO)$$
$$\beta_X = \sum_h \beta_h$$
$$\beta_L = \sum_i \beta_i$$
$$\beta_K = \sum_j \beta_j$$

we obtain,

$$\dot{Y}/Y = \sum_{h=1}^{l} \beta_h (\dot{X}_h / X_h) + \sum_{i=1}^{m} \beta_i (\dot{L}_i / L_i) + \sum_{j=1}^{n} \beta_j (\dot{K}_j / K_j) \qquad (6)$$

Equation (6) states that the exchange rates of the goods produced is equal to the weighted average exchange rates for all types of intermediate inputs, labor, and capital. The weight represents the proportion of these factors in GO. All components of equation (6), the variation rates and the weights average, refer to the time period t, which is not included as a subscript in order to simplify the notation. We define the gross concept of each input as the sum of all types of labor and capital:

$$X = \sum_{b} X_b$$

$$L = \sum_{i} L_i$$

$$K = \sum_{j} K_j$$

and the weighted average unit price of intermediate inputs, labor and capital:

$$x = \sum_{b} x_b X_b / X$$

$$w = \sum_{i} w_i L_i / L$$

$$r = \sum_{j} r_j K_j / K$$

If we substitute these concepts and averages in equation (6) and rearrange some terms, we find:

$$\dot{Y}/Y = \sum_{b=1}^{l} \beta_b (\dot{X}_b / X_b - \dot{X}/X) + \sum_{i=1}^{m} \beta_i (\dot{L}_i / L_i - \dot{L}/L)$$

$$+ \sum_{j=1}^{n} \beta_j (\dot{K}_j / K_j - \dot{K}/K) + \beta_X (\dot{X}/X) + \beta_L (\dot{L}/L) \beta_K (\dot{K}/K)$$

$$= \beta_X (\dot{X}/X) + \beta_X \sum_{b=1}^{l} \dot{x}_b / x (\dot{X}/X) + \beta_L (\dot{L}/L)$$

$$+ \beta_L \sum_{i=1}^{m} \dot{w}_i / w (\dot{L}_i / L) + \beta_K (\dot{K}/K) + \beta_K \sum_{j=1}^{n} \dot{r}_j / r (\dot{K}_j / K) \tag{7}$$

In equation (7) the weighted sum of the rates of change of intermediate inputs, labor, and capital have been decomposed into two terms for each type of input. The first is the growth rate of the gross component of intermediate inputs, labor, and capital (X, L, and K), weighted by the proportion of the total income of each type of input. The second component for each type of input is the rate of change in the quality of intermediate inputs, labor, and capital.

This approach considers changes in technology and changes in the quality of inputs. The best way to capture these changes is through a definition of input price indices to incorporate the changes in its accounting quality.

$$\dot{Y}/Y - \beta_X(\dot{X}/X) - \beta_X\sum_{b=1}^{l} \dot{x}_b/x(\dot{X}/X)$$

$$= \beta_L(\dot{L}/L) + \beta_L\sum_{i=1}^{m} \dot{w}_i/w(\dot{L}_i/L) + \beta_K(\dot{K}/K)$$

$$+\beta_K\sum_{j=1}^{n} \dot{r}_j/r(\dot{K}_j/K)$$

$$\dot{V}A/VA = \beta_L(\dot{L}/L) + \beta_L\sum_{i=1}^{m} \dot{w}_i/w(\dot{L}_i/L) + \beta_K(\dot{K}/K)$$

$$+\beta_K\sum_{j=1}^{n} \dot{r}_j/r(\dot{K}_j/K) \tag{8}$$

However, as the calculation of the quality of both capital and employment cannot capture all changes resulting from TFP, we include as an element the rate of change in TFP.

5.3 Data and sources

This section describes the main sources and data used in constructing the LA-KLEMS database for five LA countries (Argentina, Brazil, Chile, Colombia, and Mexico). Overall, the database uses the national accounts of each country, which are prepared using homogeneous classifications and definitions. This ensures that the resulting database will be consistent and uniform across countries. Furthermore, capital accounts were homogenized according to the asset classification of national accounts, also including the capital good "software." The data sources come from the official statistical institutes and/or central banks of each of the countries included in the database. The project provides information for most of the variables from 1990 to 2010.

Additionally, the LA-KLEMS database includes variables for growth accounting at the industry level. Although the industry disaggregation available varies across countries due to data limitations, the LA-KLEMS database was created in a way that meets the minimum standards set by KLEMS. More precisely, it uses a standard minimum level disaggregation of nine industries, as shown in Table 5.1. Given data availability for some of the countries analyzed it is not possible to achieve the thirty-one industry disaggregation proposed by KLEMS.

Table 5.1 *Industries in LA-KLEMS*

Description KLEMS	Congo Democratic Republic KLEMS
Total economy	TOT
Agriculture, hunting, forestry, and fishing	AtB
Mining and quarrying	C
Total manufacturing	D
Electricity, gas, and water supply	E
Construction	F
Wholesale, retail trade, and hotels and restaurants	GtH
Transport and storage and communication	I
Finance, insurance, real estate, and business services	JtK
Community social and personal services	LtQ

Table 5.2 *Gross fixed capital formation by type of asset*

Total construction
   Residential structures
    Total non-residential investment
Transport equipment
Machinery and equipment
Other products
Products information technology and communications
   Computing equipment
   Communications equipment
   Software

One of the major challenges in creating the database is how to calculate capital services. This requires a series of gross fixed capital formation (GFCF) broken down into the type of asset included in the KLEMS database (Table 5.2). The required breakdown does not necessarily coincide with the GFCF classifications published by the national statistical institutes and/or central banks of the countries studied. The main difficulties arise because of the lack of disaggregation in some assets and/or methodological changes throughout the period (changes in the reference years of national accounts, for example).

The database is divided into three sections by type of data: *Module 1: Production accounts by industries*, which gathers basic production variables; *Module 2: Labor accounts*, which gathers information about employment variables; and *Module 3: Capital accounts*, which gathers information about investment series.

Module 1: Production accounts by industries. This module includes the economic variables that make up the production accounts and generation of income from the economic activity, expressed at current and constant prices. The macro-economic variables were obtained from the national accounts of each member country. Three types of intermediate consumption are considered: energy, materials, and services. Energy comprises International Standard Industrial Classifier (ISIC) energy products in mining (10–12), refined petroleum products (23), and products of electricity, gas, and water (40). Services contain all products (50–99). The remaining intermediate consumption is classified as materials.

Data for Argentina were taken from the National Institute of Statistics and Census (INDEC). In Brazil economic data for thirty industries were obtained from the Instituto Brasileiro de Geografia e Estatística (IBGE). The production accounts for Chile were constructed from national accounts data for different reference years. Series for Colombia came from the Administrative Department National Statistics (DANE). Series for Mexico were provided by the National Institute of Statistics and Geography (INEGI), through the accounts of goods and services (CBYS). INEGI is, so far, the only LA institution providing very detailed KLEMS data on a regular basis as part of its official statistics.[6]

Module 2: Labor accounts. Labor accounts information is mostly provided by the statistical agencies in the labor force surveys and other statistics operations. In these surveys the labor force can be disaggregated by sex, age, industry, and education level, as detailed in Table 5.3.

Data for Argentina came from the Permanent Household Survey (EPH), which contains information on all urban areas and Gran Buenos Aires (Buenos Aires and Greater Buenos Aires) for the period 1990–2008. Employment data for Brazil were taken from the National Household Sample Survey (PNAD), which is the statistic that best

---

[6] See: www.inegi.org.mx/est/contenidos/proyectos/cn/ptf/default.aspx.

Table 5.3 *Classification by characteristics*

Industries	Agriculture, hunting, forestry, and fishing
	Mining and quarrying
	Total manufacturing
	Electricity, gas, and water supply
	Construction
	Wholesale, retail trade, and hotels and restaurants
	Transport and storage and communication
	Finance, insurance, real estate, and business services
	Community social and personal services
Gender	Female
	Male
Age range	Aged 15–29
	Aged 30–49
	Aged 50 and over
Skilled range	Low skilled
	Medium skilled
	High skilled

represents the employed population in terms of coverage, comparability, disaggregation, and history. An annual report on social information (RAIS) was also used. For Chile, employment figures were drawn from the National Employment Survey (ENE), which provides information about the number of employees and hours worked, and from the Supplementary Survey of Income (ESI), which provides information about income earned by the employed population. For Colombia, the National Household Survey (ENH), the Continuous Household Survey (ECH), and the Large Integrated Household Survey (GEIH) provide information on the number of employees, hours worked, and income for the period 1990–2010. Employment information for Mexico was obtained from the National Occupation and Employment Survey (ENEO) and the National Employment Survey (ENE).

Module 3: Capital accounts. Capital accounts for all countries require information on GFCF in eight KLEMS assets: residential construction, non-residential construction, machinery and equipment, transport equipment, other equipment, computer equipment, telecommunications equipment, and software. The main sources of information for Argentina were National Accounts, input–output matrix (IPM), the

Monthly Industrial Survey (EIM) and construction industry statistics compiled by the INDEC.

Estimates for GFCF for Brazil are based on official data available for 298 domestic and imported products. Data for the construction of civil, residential, and non-residential construction are based on the Annual Survey of Construction Industry (PAIC). Because the data available are not broken down by industry, the annual surveys of IBGE (PIAPAIC, PAC and PAS) must be used, which contain information up to a three-digit level about investment and production value. Chilean GFCF series are constructed from data published by the Central Bank of Chile, which provides disaggregated information on industry and assets. Because the series are published with different reference base years it is necessary to homogenize these series using growth rates. The Colombian investment series correspond to three different base years, 1994, 2000, and 2005. The distribution of investment by economic activity from 2000–2010 is based on the financial statements collected by superintendents who oversee the various sectors of the economy, on information from the General Accounting Office, on surveys of trade, services, and industry produced by DANE, and on import records from 2003 to 2009. For the period 1990–1999 the investment series were retropolated. For the capital accounts in Mexico data from CBYSSCNM, particularly data on GFCF by type of economic activity, were used for 2003–2009 (available at two-digit level of industry classification). For the period 1990–2004 the information is available at a one-digit level. These two datasets were homogenized to obtain a series of 1990–2012.

5.3.1 ICT capital formation

National accounts today include investment series in computer and telecommunications equipment, but this is only a recent change. A particular case of ICT assets is software; information on it is scarce as it is not usually estimated in Latin American countries, and it requires a methodology in accordance with the standards lineaments of the Organisation for Economic Cooperation and Development (OECD) and Bureau of Economic Analysis (BEA).

For countries and periods where there are no official series, the assets of telecommunications and computer equipment are estimated with the "commodity flow method." This method follows the product from origin or import to its final destination: production, consumption, or investment. This method cannot be used for investment in software, since this is not explicitly recorded in the input–output matrices of the countries.

In order to transform current investment into real terms a number of possible deflators are proposed, but given the availability of data, its construction becomes complicated particularly when differentiating by type of software. The alternative used here is the harmonized process as described by Schreyer (2002), which allows the software series to be deflated.

$$P_{Soft-country} = \frac{P_{GDP-country}}{P_{GDP-USA}} P_{soft-USA} \tag{9}$$

Historical data for hardware and software in the countries analyzed are scant, so backward projection is applied using their elasticity in OECD countries (Vries de, Mulder, dal Borgo, and Hofman 2010). The methodology used for the breakdown of the series is provided by the System of National Accounts, which uses the acquisitions of new and existing fixed assets in line with OECD and BEA methodologies.

5.4 Main trends

In Table 5.4 the five countries analyzed – Argentina, Brazil, Chile, Colombia, and Mexico – are placed in a more general context, providing information for eighteen LA countries during the period 1990–2010. The main messages that can be drawn from this table are as follows. First, there are very marked differences among the eighteen countries. In 2010 GDP per capita was almost five times higher in Chile, the highest, than in Nicaragua, the lowest. In terms of labor productivity per hour worked the differences were of the same magnitude: in Chile, again the highest, it was almost five times that of Bolivia, now the lowest. Second, the differences among the countries – as measured by the three dispersion statistics appearing at the bottom of the table – increased for both variables between 1990 and 2010. Third, Brazil and Mexico are by far the two countries with the largest weight in the sample, both in terms of GDP and of hours worked. In 2010 GDP in Brazil amounted to 36.5% of the GDP generated by the eighteen countries, and 38.4% of the hours worked. In Mexico the corresponding figures were 23.9% and 16.4%. Thus, those two countries alone

Table 5.4 *GDP per capita and labor productivity in Latin America, 1990–2010*

	Levels (2011 US$ PPP)						Percentage structure							Annual growth rates (percentage), 1990–2010[2]	
	GDP per capita		Labor productivity per hour worked		GDP			Hours worked				GDP per capita	Labor productivity per hour[2]
	1990	2010	1990[1]	2010	1990	2010		1991	2010					
Argentina	9,942	17,484	11.3	17.3	8.0	9.2		8.4	8.0				2.8	2.1
Bolivia	3,795	5,364	6.2	4.5	0.6	0.7		1.3	2.3				1.7	-1.6
Brazil	10,228	14,371	11.9	14.4	37.7	36.5		38.8	38.4				1.7	0.9
Chile	9,224	19,272	11.7	22.4	3.0	4.3		3.2	2.9				3.7	3.3
Colombia	7,729	10,806	7.0	10.9	6.3	6.5		11.2	9.0				1.7	2.4
Costa Rica	7,544	12,642	8.9	12.9	0.6	0.8		0.7	0.9				2.6	1.9
Ecuador	7,571	9,359	11.2	11.8	1.9	1.8		2.2	2.4				1.1	0.2
El Salvador	4,454	7,237	6.4	8.2	0.6	0.6		1.1	1.1				2.4	1.3
Guatemala	5,319	6,858	7.4	7.4	1.2	1.3		1.9	2.6				1.3	0.0
Honduras	3,205	4,271	6.2	4.7	0.4	0.4		0.9	1.4				1.4	-1.3

Mexico	12,680	15,944	17.6	22.1	26.7	23.9	18.4	16.4	1.1	1.1
Nicaragua	3,000	3,944	4.9	4.6	0.3	0.3	0.8	1.0	1.4	-0.4
Panama	7,054	14,111	11.1	17.5	0.4	0.7	0.5	0.6	3.5	2.3
Peru	5,518	10,433	11.2	13.5	3.0	4.0	3.4	4.4	3.2	0.9
Paraguay	6,045	7,009	7.1	6.9	0.6	0.6	1.0	1.3	0.7	-0.1
Dominican Republic	5,086	10,686	7.3	13.3	0.9	1.4	1.5	1.6	3.7	3.1
Uruguay	9,454	16,208	11.6	16.4	0.7	0.7	0.7	0.7	2.7	1.7
Venezuela	14,539	16,539	22.0	18.9	7.1	6.3	4.0	5.0	0.6	-0.8
Standard deviation	3,116	4,670	4.2	5.6	9.9	9.3	9.3	8.9	1.0	1.4
Coefficient of variation	0.42	0.42	0.42	0.44	1.78	1.68	1.67	1.60	0.47	1.48
Ratio max/min	4.8	4.9	4.5	4.9	123.3	122.3	81.5	65.9	5.8	-2.1
Total 18 countries	9,756	13,713	12.4	15.1	100.0	100.0	100.0	100.0	1.7	1.0

[1] Total, Colombia and Dominican Republic, 1991.
[2] Total, Colombia and Dominican Republic, 1991–2010.

Source: Elaborated by Aravena and Fuentes (2013) from data of ECLAC and International Labor Organization (ILO).

represented 60.4% in terms of GDP and 54.8% of hours worked. Fourth, in 2010 the five countries analyzed represented 80.4% of the GDP of the area and 74.7% of the hours worked. Therefore, the five LA-KLEMS countries cover a very high percentage of the Latin America economy. Fifth, there were also striking differences in growth rate of GDP per capita and labor productivity among countries, with differences being higher than for labor productivity. For the average of the eighteen countries, and the period 1990–2010, GDP per capita annual rate of growth was 1.7%, and 1.0% for labor productivity. The fastest growing countries – over 3% per year – were, in terms of GDP per capita, Chile (3.7%), Dominican Republic (3.7%), Panama (3.5%), and Peru (3.2%); and in terms of labor productivity Chile (3.3%) and Dominican Republic (3.1%). The countries with the lowest – below 1% – annual GDP per capita rate of growth were Paraguay (0.7%) and Venezuela (0.6%), while five countries experienced negative labor productivity growth: Bolivia (–1.6%), Honduras (–1.3%), Venezuela (–0.8%), Nicaragua (–0.4%), and Paraguay (–0.1%).

Figure 5.1 provides information for the annual rates of growth of four key macro-economic variables for the five countries analyzed using LA-KLEMS data. A general picture emerges: the high degree of volatility throughout the 1990–2010 period. This volatility is higher for GFCF, as expected, but it is also very marked in the other three variables. However, GDP growth rates were consistently higher for the five countries during the period from 2003 to 2008, a period characterized by the boom years of commodity prices, ending with the Great Recession of 2008–2009 generated by the "sub-prime" crisis in the US. Chile and Brazil showed a longer period of positive growth after 1999, and Mexico a somewhat shorter period, from 2003 to 2008. Argentina presents the highest volatility of the five countries analyzed.

Thus, volatility is an important characteristic of growth patterns in LA countries. In order to state its importance Table 5.5 displays the standard deviation of the annual growth rates of the four variables plotted in Figure 5.1. For the sake of comparison with other economies it also considers five big European countries (France, Germany, Italy, Spain, and the UK), the US and Japan. As can be seen in the table, the standard deviation in the five LA countries is higher than in the rest of the countries for GDP, labor productivity, and GFCF. In terms of hours worked volatility is also very high in Spain, similar to Mexico and higher than Brazil and Chile. Overall, Brazil is the LA country showing

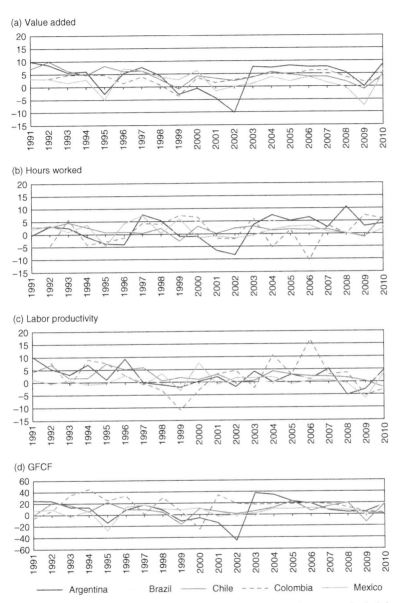

Figure 5.1 Growth rate of value added, employment, hours worked, labor productivity, and GFCF, 1990–2010 (%)
Source: LA-KLEMS database, INEGI Mexico and own elaboration.

Table 5.5 *GDP, hours worked, labor productivity, and GFCF: standard deviation of the annual growth rates, 1990–2010*

	GDP	Hours worked	Labor productivity per hour worked	GFCF
Argentina	5.7	4.8	4.3	18.9
Brazil	2.3	1.5	2.2	8.4
Chile	3.0	2.0	2.7	10.6
Colombia	2.4	5.0	6.5	16.0
Mexico	3.3	2.8	2.4	9.4
France	1.5	1.2	1.2	4.4
Germany	2.1	1.3	1.3	4.7
Italy	1.9	1.4	1.5	4.9
Spain	2.2	2.8	1.0	7.2
United Kingdom	2.3	1.7	1.7	6.4
Japan	2.1	1.4	1.1	3.4
United States	1.8	1.8	0.8	9.1

Source: Elaborated by Aravena and Fuentes (2013) from data of ECLAC and World Labor Organization (WLO); The Conference Board (TCB), Eurostat, LA-KLEMS, and OECD.

the lowest levels of volatility – as measured by the standard deviation – whereas Argentina and surprisingly Colombia present the highest levels.

The high volatility of macro-economic variables has traditionally been blamed on the price of commodities. What is known as the "natural resources curse" or the "paradox of plenty" highlights the problems faced by countries with rich endowments of natural non-renewable resources such as minerals and fuels, and also agricultural products like soya, which are highly dependent on their export markets.[7] The main explanations for this curse include the decline in competitiveness of other economic sectors, caused by appreciation of the real exchange rate as resource revenues enter an economy – a phenomenon known as the *Dutch disease* – volatility of revenues from the natural resource sector due to exposure to global commodity market swings, or the lack of adequate financial regional institutions to cope with the turbulences coming from outside (Machinea and Titelman 2007).

---

[7] Auty (1994) appears to have coined the term "natural resources curse" and Sachs and Warner (1995) the "paradox of plenty."

The relation between volatility and growth has attracted a great deal of research attention. The empirical evidence seems to support the existence of a negative relation between the two. This is the case of Ramey and Ramey (1995), who present evidence that countries with highly volatile GDP grow at a lower rate, particularly so in a reduced sample of OECD countries. Their results are largely confirmed in Martin and Rogers (2000), who use European regional data and a slightly different international sample. However, Imbs (2007) points out that even though growth and volatility correlate negatively across countries, they correlate positively across sectors. He argues that cross-country estimates identify the detrimental effects of macro-economic volatility on growth, but they cannot be used to dismiss theories implying a positive growth–volatility coefficient, which appear to hold in sectoral data since volatile sectors command high investment rates.

The high volatility observed for LA countries should not hinder the long-term perspective since, after all, it is long-run performance that really matters for the wealth of nations. This is the perspective we take in the rest of the chapter, which will concentrate on the main sources of economic growth, namely, the contribution of capital, in terms of quantity and asset composition; labor, also in terms of both quantity and quality; and technological progress measured by the TFP, as described in Section 5.2.

Latin American countries have traditionally been characterized by low levels of investment in comparison with developed countries, and with other emerging regions. In the 1990–2010 period the investment effort (GFCF/value added) in Latin American countries was 19%, while for developing countries in Asia this figure was 28% on average (Figure 5.2a).[8] Figure 5.2b shows the evolution of this variable during the period analyzed for the five LA countries considered. Overall, like the rest of the region, the five countries underwent a process of decreasing their investment effort in the late nineties and early 2000s, partly because of the Asian crisis of 1998–1999 and/or the slowdown in 2001–2002, but ending 2010 with a high investment effort. Argentina and Brazil show the highest rates at 25.4% and 24.7%, while the rest are around 23%.

---

[8] The gap increases considerably when gross capital formation is used, with an average for Latin America of 20% and 37% for East Asia and the Pacific.

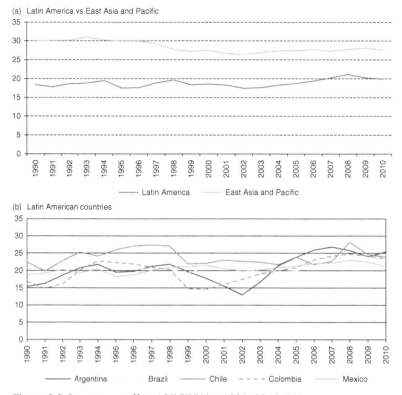

Figure 5.2 Investment effort (GFCF/VA), 1990–2010 (%)
Source: ELAC, WB, LA-KLEMS database, INEGI Mexico and own elaboration.

One of the advances of the database presented in this chapter is its ability to calculate gross fixed capital formation by types of assets. The LA-KLEMS database distinguishes between ICT capital – which consolidates three assets: *Office machinery and computer equipment, Telecommunications equipment*, and *Software* – and non-ICT capital. Within the latter it distinguishes between *Residential, Non-residential, Transport equipment*, and *Other machinery* GFCF. Table 5.6 reports the share of each of these assets in total GFCF for 1990 and 2010 and the average share for the 1990–2010 period.

As for other variables, there are important differences among countries. For the average of 1990–2010, Chile had the lowest share of ICT investment over total GFCF (4.2%) and Brazil the highest (18.7%).

Table 5.6 *Distribution of GFCF by type of assets, 1990–2010 (%)*

| | ICT | | | Non-ICT | | | | | | | | | | | | | | |
| | | | | Total non-ICT | | | Residential | | | Other constructions | | | Transport equipment | | | Other machinery and equipment | | |
	1990	2010[1]	1990–2010[2]	1990	2010[1]	1990–2010[2]	1990	2010[1]	1990–2010[2]	1990	2010[1]	1990–2010[2]	1990	2010[1]	1990–2010[2]	1990	2010[1]	1990–2010[2]
Argentina	7.3	5.5	6.9	92.7	94.5	93.1	35.5	38.1	37.2	25.0	19.4	22.9	11.8	13.2	11.5	20.4	23.7	21.5
Brazil	–	19.9	18.7	–	80.1	81.3	–	20.3	23.4	–	15.9	18.4	–	15.3	12.5	–	28.6	27.0
Chile	–	8.6	4.2	100.0	91.4	95.8	21.6	15.8	21.5	36.0	39.5	38.0	9.5	7.2	8.0	32.9	29.0	28.2
Colombia	9.4	8.7	10.2	90.6	91.3	89.8	8.7	17.3	13.2	49.1	44.0	47.5	6.4	9.2	7.5	26.4	20.8	21.6
Mexico	5.8	7.6	6.7	94.2	92.4	93.3	24.6	28.7	28.0	29.0	31.8	30.2	12.2	8.4	10.6	28.5	23.5	24.5

[1] Mexico 2009.

[2] Brazil 1995–2010, Mexico 1990–2009.

Source: LA-KLEMS database and own elaboration.

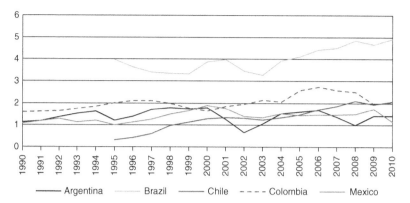

Figure 5.3 Investment effort in ICT (GFCF/VA), 1990–2010 (%)
Source: LA-KLEMS database, INEGI Mexico and own elaboration.

Within the non-ICT assets *Residential* and *Other constructions* represented the highest shares, over 55% in all countries except Brazil (41.8%). Investment in *Transport equipment* ranges from 7.5% in Colombia to 12.5% in Brazil, and *Other machinery and equipment* represents around 20% to 30% in all countries.

The availability of ICT investment data allows us to observe the evolution throughout the period of the ICT investment effort depicted in Figure 5.3. In 1995, the first year shown for all countries, Brazil was the leading country in share of ICT investment in VA (4%), doubling that of Colombia (2%), the second country with the highest share. Despite being last in the ratio ICT investment/VA in 1995 (0.3%), Chile increased its participation faster than Argentina, Mexico, and Colombia to become the second country with the highest share in 2010.

The composition of gross fixed capital formation by industry (Table 5.7) in the period 1990–2010 for the five countries is relatively homogeneous between Argentina and Brazil on one side and Chile, Colombia, and Mexico on the other. The first group concentrates investment more in *Manufacturing* and *Community social and personal services*. The rest of the countries center investment in *Manufacturing* and *Mining*, and also invest more heavily in *Electricity, gas, and water*. The percentage of investment in *Transport and communication* industries is high in the five countries, but especially in Argentina. Chile stands out for its high share of *Financial and business services*, and Argentina for the relatively high share in the *Agriculture, hunting, forestry, and fishing* sector.

Table 5.7 *Distribution of GFCF by industry, 1990–2010 (%)*

	Argentina			Brazil			Chile			Colombia			Mexico		
	1990	2010	1990–2010	1995	2010	1995–2010	1990	2010	1990–2010	1990	2010	1990–2010	1990	2009	1990–2009
Agriculture, hunting, forestry, and fishing	6.6	9.4	9.3	7.4	6.9	7.6	10.3	3.6	6.2	8.0	3.9	5.7	5.9	4.6	5.8
Mining and quarrying	1.2	3.4	2.0	2.9	3.1	3.6	18.1	25.2	17.4	19.5	16.3	15.7	17.1	11.2	12.2
Total manufacturing	27.9	27.6	27.9	34.6	33.9	33.9	19.0	11.3	16.4	18.0	16.9	15.7	22.2	17.8	22.7
Electricity, gas, and water supply	0.6	0.4	0.5	2.6	2.7	2.8	9.1	8.6	9.3	14.8	15.1	16.3	10.3	10.2	10.2
Construction	4.5	1.6	2.8	6.3	7.3	6.4	2.4	1.0	1.8	1.7	2.0	1.7	4.3	5.2	5.3
Wholesale, retail trade, and hotels and restaurants	14.4	11.8	13.8	6.3	5.6	5.8	6.5	8.1	7.9	3.6	6.6	5.0	5.7	10.5	8.0
Transport and storage and communication	20.3	17.7	17.9	11.7	11.9	11.2	10.7	15.5	13.5	12.7	17.0	15.7	15.0	11.1	13.8
Finance, insurance, real estate, and business services	5.7	4.6	5.7	3.7	2.8	3.1	5.0	9.8	8.2	3.5	4.2	4.5	5.1	4.2	5.3
Community social and personal services	18.9	23.5	20.0	24.6	25.8	25.6	19.0	16.9	19.4	18.2	18.0	19.7	14.4	25.3	16.5
Total	100.0	100.0	100.0	100.0	100.0	100.0	100.0	100.0	100.0	100.0	100.0	100.0	100.0	100.0	100.0

Source: LA-KLEMS database and own elaboration.

Table 5.8 *Hours worked per year and per worker, 1990–2010*

	1990	1995	2000	2010[1]
Argentina	2,261	2,189	2,179	1,980
Brazil	–	2,212	2,158	2,068
Chile	2,347	2,354	2,300	2,098
Colombia	2,505	2,403	2,691	2,383
Mexico	2,118	2,156	2,160	2,244

[1] Brazil and Mexico 2009.
Source: LA-KLEMS database and own elaboration.

Concerning the second source of growth, employment, in 1990 an average worker in Colombia accumulated 2,505 hours worked per year (Table 5.8), while in Chile, Argentina, and Mexico the hours worked were 7%, 10%, and 16% lower, respectively. The average hours per worker decreased over the years in all countries, except in Mexico, in this last case probably due to changes in labor laws. Between 1990 and 2010 Mexico showed an increase of 0.3%, from 40.7 hours a week on average in 1990 to 43.3 hours per week in 2010, while in Argentina hours fell from 47.2 to 42.3 hours per week, and in Chile from 45.1 to 40.3 hours per week.

The impact of labor on growth not only depends on the quantity of labor used (people employed and hours worked), but also on its quality. That is, labor contribution is also related to human capital embodied in the labor force, characterized by level of education and experience. Table 5.9 shows total employment broken down by level of education (high, medium, and low) from 1990 to 2010. The first thing that stands out is how in just twenty years, the workers' educational levels in the five countries have risen significantly. Argentina's share of highly educated workers increased by more than 18 percentage points; in Chile this share increased by more than 15 percentage points, and in Brazil – in a shorter period – and Colombia between 6 and 7 percentage points. Only in Mexico did the percentage of highly educated employees fall, although the increase in the share of employees with a medium level of education increased notably (by 19 percentage points) and the share of low educated employees fell sharply. The share of employment of less educated workers also fell dramatically in all five countries. However, in the medium segment three groups of countries can be

Table 5.9 *Share of employment by levels of education, 1990–2010 (%)*

| | High | | | | Medium | | | | | Low | | | | |
	1990	1995[1]	2000[2]	2010[3]	1990	1995[1]	2000[2]	2010[3]	1990	1995[1]	2000[2]	2010[3]
Argentina	18.0	21.2	23.9	36.5	37.3	41.6	41.1	39.3	44.7	37.2	35.0	24.1
Brazil	–	7.4	8.4	14.3	–	29.5	34.8	47.3	–	63.1	56.8	38.4
Chile	12.6	20.2	22.9	28.2	56.2	54.3	57.6	47.7	31.1	25.5	19.5	24.1
Colombia	15.4	15.6	14.6	21.5	49.7	50.4	40.6	42.8	34.9	34.0	45.2	35.6
Mexico	12.2	12.2	12.1	11.5	27.6	31.7	34.6	46.7	60.2	56.1	53.3	41.8

[1] Brazil 1996.
[2] Colombia 2001.
[3] Brazil and Mexico 2009.

Source: LA-KLEMS database and own elaboration.

identified. On one side are Argentina and Colombia with a stable share, then Brazil and Mexico where this segment is growing, and finally Chile, where it decreased.

5.5 Growth accounting in Latin American countries: LA-KLEMS results

This section uses the growth accounting methodology described in Section 5.2 to analyze the patterns of growth of the five countries included in the first version of the LA-KLEMS database. The growth of value added in the period 1990–2010 in the five countries was on average just over 3%, with Chile having the best performance (4.5%) and at the other extreme Mexico showing the smallest growth rate, 1.8%. Figure 5.4 shows the decomposition of VA growth into its sources for the period 1990–2010. The figure distinguishes between labor contributions – in terms of both hours worked and quality, capital (ICT and non-ICT contributions), and TFP. Total labor (the sum of hours worked and labor composition) accounted for 1.8 (Mexico) and 2.7 (Chile) percentage points of the total observed growth rate. In Brazil, labor explains a greater proportion of VA growth, 2.9 percentage points of an observed value added growth of 2.6%, while in Argentina total capital (ICT and non-ICT) is more important, with a contribution of 3.5 percentage points, substantially higher than the contribution of total labor (1.2 percentage points).

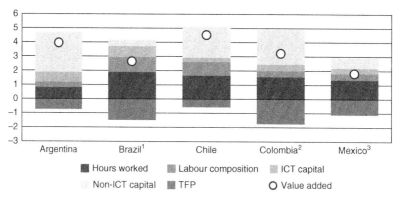

Figure 5.4 Value added growth determinants, 1990–2010 (% and contribution to growth)
1 Brazil 1995–2009
2 Colombia 1991–2010
3 Mexico 1990–2009
Source: LA-KLEMS database and own elaboration.

The contribution of hours worked is notable for its similarity across countries, and is always positive and sizable. Brazil, Chile, and Colombia show contributions slightly lower than 2 percent and Argentina and Mexico around 1 percent (0.8 and 1.4 percentage points, respectively). The contribution of changes in the composition of employment by levels of education (quality effect) is also positive in all countries. However, this contribution is less homogeneous across countries than that of hours worked. On the one hand in Brazil and Chile human capital explained one percentage point of the increase in value added, but in Argentina, Colombia, and Mexico it is less than half a percentage point. Capital accounts for about 50% of VA growth in Brazil (42%) and Chile (54%). This contribution is higher in Mexico (62%), Argentina (88%), and Colombia (92%). In Brazil almost two-thirds of the contribution of capital is explained by ICT assets, and non-ICT capital one third. In Argentina, Chile, and Colombia, less than a fifth of total capital contribution is due to ICT capital. In Mexico, the contribution of ICT assets lies at an intermediate point. A common thread running through all five countries in the database is that the TFP component is negative. Hence, the growth model of these Latin American countries was based on the accumulation of factors of production, both labor and capital – particularly non-ICT capital – and not on the efficiency gains in the production process.

Table 5.10 presents the same growth accounting decomposition at the industry level. The fastest growing industry in four countries, and the second fastest in Colombia, was *Transport and communications*. The slowest growth was experienced in *Manufacturing* in Brazil and *Mining and quarrying* in Colombia and Mexico. *Community social and personal services* was the slowest growing sector in Argentina and Mexico, whereas in Colombia it was *Agriculture and fishing*. On average, the service industries grew at a higher rate than primary and secondary industries, except in Brazil where the average growth of *Agriculture and fishing* and *Mining and quarrying* was the largest after *Transport and communications*.

Analyzing the contribution of capital as a source of growth in the fastest growing industry, *Transport and communications*, it is important to notice that total capital accumulation was above the average contribution of capital in all countries, but only in Brazil and Colombia did ICT and non-ICT asset accumulation go hand in hand, pointing to growth based on technical progress incorporated in communication

Table 5.10 *Value added growth determinants by economic industry, 1990–2010 (% and contribution to growth)*

Argentina (1990–2010)	Value added	Hours worked	Labor composition	ICT capital	Non-ICT capital	TFP
Total economy	**3.9**	0.8	0.4	0.7	2.8	-0.7
Agriculture and fishing	3.0	0.0	0.8	0.0	3.5	-1.5
Mining and quarrying	3.0	2.2	-0.4	0.2	10.6	-9.5
Manufacturing	3.5	0.0	0.4	0.5	3.1	-0.5
Electricity, gas, and water supply	5.3	-0.9	-0.3	0.9	3.9	1.7
Construction	5.6	2.1	0.5	0.2	1.3	1.5
Wholesale and retail trade; hotels and restaurants	4.0	2.1	0.2	1.1	1.9	-1.3
Transport and communications	6.9	0.5	0.4	0.4	3.6	2.1
Finance, insurance, real estate, and business services	4.2	0.8	0.1	1.6	3.9	-2.2
Community social and personal services	2.9	1.0	0.8	0.4	0.5	0.3

Brazil (1995–2009)	Value added	Hours worked	Labor composition	ICT capital	Non-ICT capital	TFP
Total economy	2.6	1.9	1.0	0.8	0.4	-1.5
Agriculture and fishing	3.5	-0.6	1.0	0.3	0.6	2.2
Mining and quarrying	3.9	1.1	0.9	2.8	1.6	-2.4
Manufacturing	1.1	1.4	0.8	1.0	0.2	-2.3

	Value added	Hours worked	Labor composition	ICT capital	Non-ICT capital	TFP
Electricity, gas, and water supply	2.9	0.3	0.6	1.4	1.2	-0.7
Construction	2.0	2.3	0.8	0.2	0.8	-2.2
Wholesale and retail trade; hotels and restaurants	2.5	2.4	1.1	0.2	0.1	-1.3
Transport and communications	4.0	1.4	0.7	1.2	0.7	0.1
Finance, insurance, real estate, and business services	3.5	4.1	0.6	0.5	0.0	-1.8
Community social and personal services	2.6	1.5	1.6	0.8	0.5	-1.8

Chile (1990–2010)	Value added	Hours worked	Labor composition	ICT capital	Non-ICT capital	TFP
Total economy	4.5	1.7	1.0	0.3	2.2	-0.6
Agriculture and fishing	4.3	-0.6	0.9	0.1	-0.7	4.6
Mining and quarrying	4.1	0.1	0.7	0.3	4.5	-1.5
Manufacturing	3.4	0.4	1.1	0.2	2.1	-0.4
Electricity, gas, and water supply	4.3	0.4	0.1	0.4	6.3	-2.8
Construction	4.2	3.0	1.1	0.1	0.4	-0.4
Wholesale and retail trade; hotels and restaurants	6.0	2.1	1.1	0.3	1.1	1.4
Transport and communications	6.5	1.8	0.9	0.4	3.7	-0.2
Finance, insurance, real estate, and business services	6.0	4.3	0.6	0.5	1.9	-1.4
Community social and personal services	3.4	1.5	1.5	0.3	1.2	-1.0

Table 5.10 (*cont.*)

Colombia (1991–2010)	Value added	Hours worked	Labor composition	ICT capital	Non-ICT capital	TFP
Total economy	3.2	1.6	0.4	0.5	2.5	-1.8
Agriculture and fishing	1.7	-1.3	-1.9	0.0	2.5	2.4
Mining and quarrying	4.0	1.3	0.1	0.7	9.4	-7.4
Manufacturing	2.0	0.7	1.0	0.1	3.1	-2.8
Electricity, gas, and water supply	3.0	-0.5	-0.9	0.0	10.4	-6.0
Construction	2.7	2.9	-1.0	0.0	1.4	-0.5
Wholesale and retail trade; hotels and restaurants	2.6	2.6	1.8	0.3	1.4	-3.4
Transport and communications	4.6	1.9	1.8	4.1	3.4	-6.6
Finance, insurance, real estate, and business services	3.4	3.7	1.4	0.3	1.1	-3.1
Community social and personal services	5.0	-0.4	-1.1	0.1	1.7	4.7

Mexico (1990–2009)	Value added	Hours worked	Labor composition	ICT capital	Non-ICT capital	TFP
Total economy	1.8	1.4	0.4	0.4	0.7	-1.1
Agriculture and fishing	1.0	-0.1	0.3	0.1	-0.7	1.4
Mining and quarrying	0.4	-0.4	0.6	0.1	1.1	-1.0
Manufacturing	1.6	-0.1	0.4	0.2	1.0	-0.1
Electricity, gas, and water supply	2.9	0.3	0.1	0.2	1.0	1.4

Construction	1.6	2.3	1.0	0.4	1.3	-3.3
Wholesale and retail trade; hotels and restaurants	1.6	2.1	0.9	0.6	0.8	-2.9
Transport and communications	3.9	1.1	0.9	0.3	1.1	0.5
Finance, insurance, real estate, and business services	2.9	3.0	0.1	0.8	0.3	-1.3
Community social and personal services	0.5	1.2	-0.2	0.2	0.7	-1.4

Source: LA-KLEMS database and own elaboration.

equipment in these two countries. ICT capital also made a large contribution in Brazil in other sectors, apart from the aforementioned *Transport and communications,* such as *Electricity, gas, and water* and *Mining and quarrying.* The latter two industries were also characterized by strong VA growth. On the other hand, *Manufacturing* VA growth in Brazil was noticeably low despite the robust contribution of ICT capital due to the low non-ICT capital contribution.

The contribution to growth of total capital in *Mining and quarrying* was high in all countries, with the exception of Mexico. This industry is also characterized by high VA growth. *Agriculture* grew relatively quickly in Argentina, Brazil, and Chile but with small – and in Chile even negative – contributions of capital. In Chile and Colombia the VA growth rate of *Electricity, gas, and water* was clearly less than the contribution of total non-ICT capital. In Chile this is explained by a particular set of contingencies that have to do with water availability for hydroelectric energy and cuts of gas imports from Argentina, starting in 2004, representing a major increase in costs for the gas and electricity industry. In Mexico the contributions of ICT capital, and to a lesser extent non-ICT capital, were important in *Finance, insurance, and real estate* or *Wholesale and retail trade and hotels.*

The highest contributions of total labor (quantity and quality) to value added growth are observed in *Construction*, especially the quantity term, and in some service industries such as *Commerce* and *Financial services.* In contrast, hours worked grew very little in *Manufacturing* in the five countries and even declined in Mexico. Quality of labor improved across all industries and countries. Colombia, Argentina, and Mexico showed negative contributions in a limited number of industries. In *Agriculture and fisheries* hours worked contributed in small measure – or even negatively – to VA growth, but with an improvement in the quality of labor. This means that in all five countries, as the economy grew the labor force moved from the primary sector to other sectors in the economies.

Interestingly, the results presented in Table 5.10 support the idea mentioned above that in these Latin American countries there is a problem in terms of total factor productivity, as in almost all the sectors considered the TFP contribution is negative. This fact suggests that the growth model of these countries in the last twenty years has been based on the accumulation of productive factors (capital and labor) and on the improvements in human capital. They have failed to use the improvements in productive efficiency brought by technical progress as the engine of growth. However, it is important to note that in the case of *Transport and communications* TFP is positive in Argentina, Brazil, and Mexico.

Finally, it is interesting to note a negative correlation between TFP and capital deepening, particularly when non-ICT capital is considered. That is, in the industries where TFP growth is lower, capital made its greatest contribution to value added growth. This relationship is particularly evident in the *Mining* industry in Argentina, Brazil, and Colombia, and *Electricity, gas, and water* in Chile and Colombia. This could indicate that the problem of lower growth in value added in the region's countries was not driven by a lack of investment, but basically by the allocation of this investment among sectors and assets. In other words, this negative correlation might indicate the existence of a problem of excess capacity due to a strong accumulation of underutilized capital. The two sectors where this problem is most evident usually need large amounts of capital – linked to specific projects – which require a minimum threshold. This might result in underutilization, at least at the beginning of setting up. Correcting the capital figures to take into consideration the degree of capital utilization is an alternative that was explored in the sixties by Jorgenson and Griliches (1967, 1972) and questioned by Denison (1969, 1972) in a well-known debate.

5.6 Structural change

This section aims to disentangle the performance of the five Latin American countries over time into the effect of the changes in the industry specialization (structural change) and the ones due to the dynamic behavior within each industry. It therefore analyzes whether the poor aggregated performance of LA countries, particularly in terms of TFP, is driven by the evolution of structural change (specialization in less TFP growing industries) or by the evolution within individual industries. To this end, the algebraic shift-shares decomposition is proposed for a set of variables. In the case of labor productivity (VA_t / L_t) it will take the form given by equation (10):

$$\frac{VA_t}{L_t} - \frac{VA_0}{L_0} = \sum_j \theta_{j0} \left(\frac{VA_{jt}}{L_{jt}} - \frac{VA_{j0}}{L_{j0}} \right) + \underbrace{\sum_j (\theta_{jt} - \theta_{j0}) \frac{VA_{j0}}{L_{j0}}}_{}$$

$$\underbrace{\phantom{\frac{VA_t}{L_t}}}_{\text{Within component}} \qquad \text{Structural change} \atop \text{component}$$

$$+ \sum_j (\theta_{jt} - \theta_{j0}) \left(\frac{VA_{jt}}{L_{jt}} - \frac{VA_{j0}}{L_{j0}} \right) \qquad (10)$$

$$\text{Dynamic component}$$

where θ_{jt} is the weight of the hours worked (L) in sector j in total hours worked in year t. The subscript 0 refers to the initial year, 1990. The within component proxies the effect on the aggregated labor productivity of the evolution of productivity on individual industries assuming that the weight of each industry in total employment remains constant at the initial year level. On the other hand, the structural change component measures the changes in aggregated labor productivity associated to the evolution of the rearrangement of labor across sectors, assuming that industry labor productivity remains constant at the initial year levels. Finally, the dynamic component measures the effect on the aggregated labor productivity growth of the two joint effects. That is, whether sectors whose productivity increases are those that also gain weight in the economy by increasing their share in employment.

The shift-share decomposition is calculated for the five variables included in the previous sections: labor productivity, ratios of total, ICT and non-ICT per hour worked, and TFP. The calculations require the availability of values of each variable. In the case of TFP the growth accounting methodology presented earlier can only calculate its growth rate. Hence, levels of TFP – and not only growth rates – need to be calculated. To this end Hulten and Schwab (1993) use a reference country, or aggregation of countries, to obtain a transitive indicator which allows comparisons across sectors, countries, and years. The reference used here is the aggregation of the five Latin American countries in the first year available for all of them (1995). TFP is calculated according to the following expression:

$$\ln TFP_{itk} = (\ln Y_{itk} - \ln Y_0) - \sum_j \frac{1}{2} \left(s_{jitk} + s_{j0} \right) \left(\ln X_{jitk} - \ln X_{j0} \right)$$

$$(11)$$

where i is sector; t year; and k country. Subscripts 0 refer to the values of each variable in the total aggregated five Latin American economies in 1995. Y is value added; s_j, factor shares of labor – quantity and quality – and capital – ICT and non-ICT; X_j, production factors (labor quantity and quality, K ICT and K non-ICT). TFP is calculated as the $exp(lnTFP)*100$ and takes the value 100 for aggregated Latin American countries in 1995.

Table 5.11 presents the shift-share decomposition of the compound growth rate into the *within*, the *structural change* and the *dynamic* components for the five variables analyzed, namely labor productivity, capital per hour worked – distinguishing between ICT and non-ICT capital – and TFP.[9]

The main results of the shift-share analysis are the following. First, in terms of labor productivity there is no one-size-fits-all explanation for the evolution of labor productivity. In Argentina and Chile the main contribution was the *within* component, meaning that the main source of aggregated labor productivity growth is the evolution of productivity in each sector. In Brazil the *structural change* component clearly dominated, explaining 126% of aggregated labor productivity evolution. In Colombia and Mexico both the *within* and *structural change* components were quite significant, although the *dynamic* component shows that there was a negative interaction between these two effects. The five countries partially reallocate their resources to more productive sectors in relative terms (positive structural change component), but at the same time to sectors where relative productivity gains during the period are more moderate (dynamic component). That is, these economies reallocate their resources to sectors where labor productivity is growing more slowly than the rest. However, as the structural change component is greater than the dynamic component, the final result is a reallocation of total hours worked to sectors with higher productivity, except for Argentina which reassigned to sectors with lower relative labor productivity.

In the case of the capital/labor ratio – total, non-ICT and ICT – and TFP the picture is quite similar across countries. In all cases the main determinant of the evolution is the *within* component. Hence, the process of capital deepening in the five Latin American countries is

---

[9] Labor productivity growth rates are different from those offered in Table 5.1 due to the different datasets used for the calculations: ECLAC and ILO (Table 5.1) vs LA-KLEMS (Table 5.11).

Table 5.11 *Shift-share decomposition of the compound annual growth rate, 1990–2010*

	Argentina	Brazil	Chile	Colombia	Mexico
Labor productivity growth	**2.28**	**0.57**	**2.90**	**2.19**	**0.47**
Total variation	100.00	100.00	100.00	100.00	100.00
Within	107.31	18.34	87.41	68.43	69.19
Structural change	14.01	125.96	15.37	56.07	95.83
Dynamic component	−21.32	−44.31	−2.79	−24.50	−65.03
Capital/labor ratio growth	**4.75**	**2.09**	**5.23**	**14.68**	**1.76**
Total variation	100.00	100.00	100.00	100.00	100.00
Within	109.50	86.10	97.87	108.79	123.15
Structural change	−0.63	15.40	−3.16	0.83	−7.13
Dynamic component	−8.87	−1.50	5.29	−9.62	−16.02
Non-ICT capital/labor growth	**3.95**	**−0.31**	**4.59**	**14.85**	**1.10**
Total variation	100.00	100.00	100.00	100.00	100.00
Within	112.75	143.35	100.13	112.60	149.90
Structural change	−0.72	−108.16	−3.88	0.42	−13.98
Dynamic component	−12.02	64.81	3.75	−13.02	−35.92
ICT capital/labor growth	**11.86**	**9.43**	**25.39**	**12.89**	**10.78**
Total variation	100.00	100.00	100.00	100.00	100.00
Within	100.91	91.62	–	59.19	87.49
Structural change	−0.41	3.48	–	6.22	2.01
Dynamic component	−0.51	4.90	–	34.60	10.50
TFP growth	**−0.46**	**−1.23**	**−0.51**	**−2.35**	**−1.14**
Total variation explained	100.00	100.00	100.00	100.00	100.00
Within	43.93	102.96	100.34	116.20	102.68
Structural change	−0.98	−12.86	−93.48	−117.14	−27.27
Dynamic component	57.05	9.89	93.15	100.94	24.59

Note: The initial and final values for Brazil are 1995 and 2009, for Colombia 1991 and 2010, and for Mexico 1990 and 2009.

Source: LA-KLEMS database and own elaboration.

almost entirely explained by the increase of the stock of capital per hour worked in every sector, and not by the reassignment of labor from the less to the more capital intensive industries. The same picture emerges regardless of whether we focus on ICT or non-ICT capital. The dynamic component is small in all cases except for ICT capital in Colombia, where is positive and relevant.

All five countries in the sample performed poorly in terms of TFP, with highly negative growth rates between 1990 and 2010. The shift-share decomposition complements this vision with the fact that this performance is again basically driven by the *within* component. In Brazil, Chile, Colombia, and Mexico what happened inside the sectors, the *within* component, explains more than 100 percent of the decrease in labor productivity. In all these countries the *structural change* component is negative, and in some cases (Colombia and Chile) is quite relevant. Given the fact that TFP growth is negative, a negative structural component shows that the sluggish TFP observed in all sectors of the economy has been offset to a certain extent by a positive reassignment of labor from less to more total factor productive growing sectors. Furthermore productivity gains associated with reallocation of factors (capital and labor) across sectors with higher TFP growth, as measured by the dynamic component, are positive and especially significant.

From the shift-share analysis, a common thread emerges in the five large Latin American economies, namely the difficulties of increasing TFP within the sectors. However, as Aravena *et al.* (2014) point out, these results should be taken with caution as the level of disaggregation is relevant. The LA-KLEMS database only offers disaggregation for nine industries. More detailed information at industry level will be useful to verify whether the results obtained for Mexico – for which a very high level of industry disaggregation is available – are also shared by the rest of the countries. For Mexico, the *structural change* component increases sharply when moving from a nine-industry level of disaggregation (27.5% of total) to thirty-one industries (32.4%) and up to 45.8% when sixty-five industries are considered.

5.7 Concluding remarks

Economic growth in Latin America has been relatively low in the last twenty years. This chapter seeks to identify factors that explain this performance through the use of growth accounting at the industry level in five Latin American countries. To this end, a new database is presented: the LA-KLEMS database, the Latin American chapter of the World-KLEMS Initiative. It is built under the framework of national accounts, and is homogeneous with other KLEMS databases available for other world regions. For the moment it only includes five countries – Argentina, Brazil, Chile, Colombia, and Mexico – although more countries are expected to be included in the near future. It is also expected that most countries, if not all, will follow the example of Mexico. Mexico KLEMS, produced by INEGI, includes a complete industry-level productivity database that is integrated with the Mexican national accounts and is updated annually within this framework.

In this chapter we use the database to analyze the patterns of growth of the five initial LA-KLEMS countries. It starts by placing the five countries in a more general perspective, noting that these five countries are highly representative of Latin America, since in 2010 they accounted for 80.4% of GDP and 74.7% of the hours worked. Chile (3.3%) was the fastest growing country in terms of labor productivity of the eighteen countries for which information is available, followed by the Dominican Republic (3.1%), Colombia (2.4%), Panama (2.3%), and Argentina (2.1%). Growth performance in the two largest countries in the sample was slower: 0.9% in Brazil and 1.1% in Mexico. However, from the time perspective, the most noticeable fact is the high volatility showed by the annual rates of growth of four main variables: GDP, hours worked, labor productivity, and GFCF. This volatility is higher than for more developed economies. It is especially high in Argentina, while Brazil shows a more stable path.

The available evidence usually recognizes that volatility is not beneficial for economic growth. Once this is recognized, the chapter adopts a long-term perspective since, in the end, long-term growth is what is relevant for societies' wellbeing. Growth accounting methodology is adopted, which allows the growth of GDP or labor productivity to be decomposed into the contributions of capital, labor, and total factor productivity. The evolution over time of the two factors of production presented the following features throughout the period 1990–2010.

Regarding capital, the five LA countries' investment effort was lower than that observed in Asian countries with similar levels of development. Most of the countries experienced a downturn in the

GFCF/VA ratio by the late nineties and the beginning of the new century, to recover by the end of the period. As for most countries, investment is highly concentrated in real estate assets – *Residential and other constructions* – followed by *Other machinery and equipment* and *Transport and equipment.* One important feature of the LA-KLEMS is the provision of information for the distribution of GFCF by industry and information for ICT assets. Investment is mainly directed to service sectors in general, which are non-tradable and, in many cases, are regulated sectors. The fact that investment is concentrated in protected or non-tradable and regulated sectors implies that it has less potential for long-term growth and that, in general, these sectors have less incentive to innovate due to the lower competition. For ICT assets, the available information points to important differences among the five countries, with Brazil presenting the highest share and Chile the lowest.

From the labor perspective the most notable facts are the reduction of the hours worked in all countries except Mexico, and improvements in workers' educational attainment in all countries without exception.

The most remarkable fact in the results from the growth accounting perspective is the negative contribution of total factor productivity in all countries and in almost all industries. Thus, Latin America – or at least the countries analyzed – faces a genuine problem of productivity. Almost all sectors of the economy, including those in which capital contributes the most to the productive process, show negative TFP on average during the last twenty years. This suggests there are problems in the efficient functioning of these economies and in the lack of capacity to achieve technical progress. It also points to the possibility that they are facing a dual problem of low capital accumulation – at least for their level of development – together with a misallocation among the different industries.

The shift-share decomposition of TFP shows that these problems are not specific to any particular sector, but, on the contrary, affect the whole economy. The fact that the evolution of TFP in each sector – the *within* component – is the most relevant factor to explain the growth of aggregated productivity suggests that LA countries face a genuine problem of productivity. It is therefore important to identify the barriers and obstacles that hinder the increase of the efficiency in the productive sector. Of course there is also room for *structural change*, that is the reallocation of productive factors from low to high TFP sectors, in these economies, but it should not divert the focus from the problem of a lack of more general efficiency.

Appendix

Appendix Table 5.1 gives an overview of all variables including the LA-KLEMS database, which are arranged into three groups: basic variables, growth accounting variables, and additional variables. The basic variables contain all the information needed to build the various measures of productivity and are estimated at current and constant prices; they are obtained from the national accounts of each country. These series are constructed according to the theoretical model of production described above. Finally, additional variables were constructed for use in the calculation of growth accounting as they are considered relatively important for ICT.

Appendix Table 5.1 *Basic table*

Values	
GO	Gross output at current basic prices (in millions of national currency)
II	Intermediate inputs at current purchasers' prices (in millions of national currency)
VA	Gross value added at current basic prices (in millions of national currency)
COMP	Compensation of employees (in millions of national currency)
EMP	Number of persons engaged (thousands)
EMPE	Number of employees (thousands)
H_EMP	Total hours worked by persons engaged (millions)
H_EMPE	Total hours worked by employees (millions)
Prices	
GO_P	Gross output, price indices, 1995=100
II_P	Intermediate inputs, price indices, 1995=100
VA_P	Gross value added, price indices, 1995=100
Volumes	
GO_QI	Gross output, volume indices, 1995=100
II_QI	Intermediate inputs, volume indices, 1995=100
VA_QI	Gross value added, volume indices, 1995=100

Appendix Table 5.1 (*cont.*)

LP_I	Gross value added per hour worked, volume indices, 1995=100

Growth accounting

LAB	Labor compensation (in millions of national currency)
CAP	Capital compensation (in millions of national currency)
LAB_QI	Labor services, volume indices, 1995=100
CAP_QI	Capital services, volume indices, 1995=100
VA_Q	Growth rate of value added volume (% per year)
VAConH	Contribution of hours worked to value added growth (percentage points)
VAConLC	Contribution of labor composition change to value added growth (percentage points)
VAConKIT	Contribution of ICT capital services to value added growth (percentage points)
VAConKNIT	Contribution of non-ICT capital services to value added growth (percentage points)
VAConTFP	Contribution of TFP to value added growth (percentage points)
TFPva_I	TFP (value added based) growth, 1995=100

Additional variables

CAPIT	ICT capital compensation (share in total capital compensation)
CAPNIT	Non-ICT capital compensation (share in total capital compensation)
CAPIT_QI	ICT capital services, volume indices, 1995=100
CAPNIT_QI	Non-ICT capital services, volume indices, 1995=100
CAPIT_QPH	ICT capital services per hour worked, 1995 reference
CAPNIT_QPH	Non-ICT capital services per hour worked, 1995 reference
LAB_QPH	Labor services per hour worked, 1995 reference
LAB_AVG	Labor compensation per hour worked
H_AVG	Average number of hours worked

References

Aravena C. and J. A. Fuentes. 2013. "El desempeño mediocre de la productividad laboral en América Latina: una interpretación neoclásica," *Serie Macroeconomía del Desarrollo*, No. 140, November (LC/L.3725).

Aravena C., J. Fernández, A. A. Hofman, and M. Mas. 2014. "Structural Change in Four Latin American Countries: An International Perspective," *ECLAC Macroeconomics of Development Series*, No. 150.

Auty, R. 1994. "Industrial Policy Reform in Six Large Newly Industrializing Countries: The Resources Curse Thesis," *World Development*, **22** (1, January): 11–26.

Blyde, J. and E. Fernández-Arias. 2006. "Why Does Latin America Grow More Slowly?" In J. Blyde, E. Férnandez-Arias, and R. Manuelli (eds.), *Sources of Growth in Latin America: What is Missing?* Washington, DC: Inter-American Development Bank.

Bruton, H. 1967. "Productivity Growth in Latin America," *American Economic Review*, **57**: 1099–1116.

Cimoli, M., A. A. Hofman, and N. Mulder (eds.) 2010. *Innovation and Economic Development – The Impact of Information and Communication Technologies in Latin America*. Northampton, MA: Edward Elgar.

Cole, H. L., L. E. Ohanian, A. Riascos, and J. A. Schmitz, Jr. 2005. "Latin America in the Rearview Mirror," *Journal of Monetary Economics*, **52**: 69–107.

Correa, H. 1970. "Sources of Economic Growth in Latin America," *The Southern Economic Journal*, **37**(1, July): 17–31.

Denison, E. F. 1967. *Why Growth Rates Differ*. Washington, DC: The Brookings Institution.

    1969. "Some Major Issues in Productivity Analysis: An Examination of Estimates by Jorgenson and Griliches," *Survey of Current Business*, **49**(5, pt. II): 1–27.

    1972. "Reply to Jorgenson and Griliches," *Survey of Current Business*, **52**(5, pt. II): 37–63.

de Gregorio, J. 2006. "Economic Growth in Latin America: From the Disappointment of the Twentieth Century to the Challenges of the Twenty-First," *Working Paper*, No. 377, Central Bank of Chile.

de Vries, G., N. Mulder, M. dal Borgo, and A. A. Hofman. 2010. "ICT Investment in Latin America: Does it Matter for Economic Growth?" In M. Cimoli, A. A. Hofman, and N. Mulder (eds.) *Innovation and Economic Development – The Impact of Information and Communication Technologies in Latin America*. Northhampton, MA: Edward Elgar.

Elías, V. J. 1992. *Sources of Growth: A Study of Seven Latin American Economies*. San Francisco: ICS Press.

Fuentes, J. and G. García. 2014. "Una Mirada Desagregada al Deterioro de la Productividad en Chile: ¿Existe un Cambio Estructural?" *Economía Chilena*, **17**(1, April): 4–36.

Hofman, A. A. 2000. *The Economic Development of Latin America in the Twentieth Century*. Cheltenham: Edward Elgar Publishers.

Hsieh, C. T. and P. J. Klenow. 2010. "Development Accounting," *American Economic Journal: Macroeconomic*, **2**(1): 207–223.

Hulten, Charles R. and Robert M. Schwab. 1993. "Infrastructure Spending: Where Do We Go from Here?" *National Tax Journal*, **46**(3, September): 261–273.

Imbs, J. 2007. "Growth and Volatility," *Journal of Monetary Economics*, **54**(7, October): 1848–1862.

Jorgenson, D. W., F. M. Gollop, and B. M. Fraumeni. 1987. *Productivity and US Economic Growth*. Cambridge, MA: Harvard University Press.

Jorgenson, D. W. and Z. Griliches. 1967. "The Explanation of Productivity Change," *Review of Economic Studies*, **34**: 249–283.

1972. "Issues in Growth Accounting: A reply to Edward F. Denison," *Survey of Current Business*, **52**(5, pt II): 65–94.

Jorgenson, D. W., M. S. Ho, and K. J. Stiroh. 2005. *Information Technology and the American Growth Resurgence*. Cambridge, MA: MIT Press.

Langoni, C. G. 1974. *As Causas do Crescimiento Económico do Brasil*. Rio de Janeiro: APEC.

Machinea, J. L. and D. Titelman. 2007. "¿Un crecimiento volátil? El papel de las instituciones financieras regionales," *Revista de la CEPAL*, **91**(April): 7–26.

Martin, P. and C. A. Rogers. 2000. "Long-term Growth and Short-term Economic Instability," *European Economic Review*, **44**(2): 359–381.

Ramey, V. and G. Ramey. 1995. "Cross Country Evidence on the Link between Volatility and Growth," *American Economic Review*, **85**(5): 1138–1159.

Restuccia, D. 2013. "The Latin American Development Problem: An Interpretation," *Economía*, **13**(2, Spring): 69–100.

Sachs, J. and A. M. Wamer. 1995. "Natural Resources Abundance and Economic Growth," *NBER Working Paper*, No. 5398, National Bureau of Economic Research, Cambridge, MA.

Schreyer, P. 2002. "Computer Price Indices and International Growth and Productivity Comparisons," *Review of Income and Wealth*, **48**(1, March): 15–31.

Solow, R. M. 1956. "A Contribution to the Theory of Economic Growth," *The Quarterly Journal of Economics*, **70**(1, February).

1957. "Technical Change and the Aggregate Production Function," *Review of Economics and Statistics*, **39**: 312–320.

Szirmai, A., W. A. Naudé, and L. Alcorta. 2013. *Pathways to Industrialization in the 21st Century*. Oxford University Press.

Szirmai, A. and B. Verspagen. 2010. "Is Manufacturing Still an Engine of Growth in Developing Countries?" Paper prepared for the 31st General

Conference of The International Association for Research in Income and Wealth, St. Gallen, Switzerland.

Timmer, M. and G. de Vries. 2009. "Structural Change and Growth Accelerations in Asia and Latin America: A New Sectoral Data Set," *Cliometrica*, 3(2): 165–190.

Timmer, M. P., R. Inklaar, M. O'Mahony, and B. van Ark. 2010. *Economic Growth in Europe. A Comparative Industry Perspective*. Cambridge University Press.

Vergara, R. and R. Rivero. 2006. "Productividad Sectorial en Chile: 1986–2001," *Cuadernos de Economía*, 43(May): 143–168.

6 On China's strategic move for a new stage of development – a productivity perspective

HARRY X. WU

6.1 Introduction

Despite a series of reforms over the past three decades, China's economic growth is still heavily government-engineered. However, unlike in the planning period that relied on centralized, comprehensive, and mandatory controls through state ownership, local governments have been playing an important role in the reform era under a "regional decentralized authoritarian" regime (Xu 2011). The driving force is growth competition among localities. Since all efforts made by local governments are indexed by the rate of local gross domestic product (GDP) growth and assessed by upper authorities as political performance, officials are highly motivated to engage in "growth tournament" with their peers of other localities (Li and Zhou 2005). Consequently, their restless search for new growth engines has resulted in increasing government interventions in resource allocation and business decisions (Huang 2012; Wu and Shea 2008; Xu 2011).

There have been several important investment waves in which local governments played a very important role. China's accession to the World Trade Organization (WTO) at the end of 2001 found an outlet for China's huge surplus capacity of labor-intensive manufacturing industries that was built up in the growth race between local governments to attract foreign direct investment (FDI) in the 1990s. Since the early 2000s, led by coastal provinces, new growth contests began with local urbanization and industrialization concentrating on heavy machinery and chemicals (J. Wu 2008). Government dominance in resource allocation was further enhanced in the wake of the global financial crisis in 2008–2009 with a 4-trillion-yuan stimulus package from the central government accompanied by 18-trillion-yuan projects financed by local governments.

The central authorities were caught in between two distinct policy choices with one emphasizing the speed of growth and the other underlining the quality of growth. In the ninth "Five-Year Plan" (1996–2000), convinced by the seriousness of resource misallocation and structural distortion caused by such local governments-promoted "extensive growth model," the central government urged a strategic shift to a "more balanced intensive growth model." Nevertheless, in the wake of rising unemployment due to the deepening reforms of state-owned enterprises and the Asian financial crisis (1997–1998), the tenth "Five-Year Plan" (2001–2005) stressed that "despite the need for the restructuring of the economy a fast growth should be maintained," which in fact endorsed local governments-engineered ambitious urbanization and heavy industrialization projects (see J. Wu 2013).

Academics, economists of policy think tanks, and mainstream medias have been divided in the debate over the importance of the speed of growth and hence the role of government in promoting growth, though both sides criticize repetitious industrial projects and widespread "window-dressing constructions" across localities due to local governments' heavy involvement in resource allocation. The new Xi-Li administration since 2013 has appeared to be willing to allow the market to play a fundamental role in resource allocation and transform the Chinese economy from an input-driven to a more productivity and innovation-led growth model in the next decade via deepening structural reforms albeit still emphasizing "the dominance of the public ownership" and "the leadership of the state economy" (CPCCC 2013).

However, what has been missing in the debate is a proper analysis of the sources of growth and productivity trends. The government's heavy involvement has (so far) successfully solved China's growth problem, but it remains unclear to what extent and in which sectors this has taken its toll on the economy's efficiency and productivity growth. Ultimately, productivity improvements are the key to efficient and sustainable long-run growth in any economy. Therefore, this policy debate could benefit from an in-depth industry-level productivity analysis, which we will provide in this chapter.

To analyze China's productivity performance in the light of the role of government, it is essential not only to find an appropriate methodological framework that is able to examine productivity performances of individual industries and their contribution to the aggregate productivity performance of the economy, but also to have industry production accounts that are constructed as coherent parts of the national input and output accounts. This "industry perspective" is indispensible because government interventions are often made through industry-specific policies and "upstream" industries (those that deliver intermediate goods and services, such as energy and telecommunications) may affect downstream industries through the input-output linkages of the economy.

The present study benefits from a newly constructed economy-wide industry-level dataset that follows the KLEMS principles in data construction.[1] It is part of the ongoing China Industry Productivity (CIP) Database Project. Methodology-wise, following Jorgenson, Ho and Stiroh (2005a) this study adopts the Jorgensonian aggregate production possibility frontier framework, incorporating Domar weights, to account for contributions of individual industries to the growth of aggregate inputs and output. This approach relaxes most of the restrictive assumptions of the widely used aggregate production function approach in growth accounting that all industries are homogenous, subject to the same value added function, and facing the same input and output prices.

The rest of the chapter is organized as follows. Section 6.2 discusses the role of government in the Chinese economy from an industry perspective. Section 6.3 introduces the aggregate production possibility frontier framework incorporating Domar weights for aggregation. Section 6.4 briefly explains the features of the CIP database. This is followed by Section 6.5 which reports and interprets the empirical results. Finally, Section 6.6 concludes this study.

6.2 Productivity growth in sectors and the role of the government

We are interested in how government involvement in resource allocation has affected the productivity performance of the Chinese economy. This is challenging because policy or institutional factor is not an inherent part of the standard theory of production, hence difficult to measure.

---

[1] KLEMS is used as an acronym for K(C)apital, Labor, Energy, Materials, and Services that are used to produce any product. By the same token, the gross output of an industry equals the total costs of "KLEMS" and the gross output of an economy equals the sum of the costs of KLEMS of all industries. See O'Mahony and Timmer (2009) for an introduction of the EU-KLEMS database.

However, we will use the fact that government policy is industry-specific and industries are connected through vertical input–output links. Therefore, to explore the role of government we may consider distinguishing industries subject to different types of government interventions, directly and indirectly through their use of output from other regulated industries.

One important change since the reform is that government interventions are no longer all-encompassing as in the central planning era that completely ignored the market. They have, however, become more industry-specific through either subsidization or administrative interference or some combination of both. Subsidies can be made in direct or indirect form. Indirect subsidies intend to reduce the producer cost of inputs including energy, land, environment, labor, and capital (Huang and Tao 2010). By contrast, direct subsidies come with administrative interferences aiming to compensate for output losses. Administrative interferences serve the state interests or government strategic plans by controlling or influencing output prices and business operations ranging from managerial personnel to the choice of technology.

Whether or to what extent the government uses administrative interference or different types of subsidization depends on the distance of an industry from the final demand, especially the international market. Indirect subsidies have been mainly used by local governments to promote export-oriented manufacturers that make semi-finished and finished goods. Most of these downstream industries are labor-intensive and therefore crucial for China to timely reap its demographic dividend. However, the government tends to directly get involved in upstream industries such as energy and primary input materials that are deemed strategically important to support downstream industries.

Considering the behavior of enterprises in such a policy environment and its implications for efficiency improvement and productivity growth, we may conjecture that industries that are mainly supported by indirect subsidies could be more efficient and productive than those receiving direct subsidies for losses with administrative interferences. In the former case, enterprises may still behave like true market competitors although their competitiveness is arbitrarily enhanced.[2] Upstream industries are traditionally dominated by state-owned

---

[2] This is conditional on whether they can repeatedly negotiate for benefits regardless of their true performance. Here we assume that this is not the case.

enterprises and do not conform to China's comparative advantage. Their assumed "strategic importance" gives them strong bargaining power in negotiating for government support. In return they have to accept controls from the authorities. This distorts their behavior and disincentivizes their effort for efficiency and innovation.

The nature of the government interventions and subsidies is a kind of "cross subsidization." The key to sustaining it is that downstream industries must be able to grow faster and relatively more efficient than upstream industries and the public revenues generated from downstream industries must be able to cover direct subsidies. However, the cost of negative externalities, i.e. the cost that cannot be internalized due to subsidies, has to be borne by the public. On the other hand, negative externalities also play a role in resource misallocation.

To investigate the total factor productivity (TFP) performance of industries, we categorize the thirty-seven industries in the CIP database into eight groups (see Appendix Table 6.1). This grouping is guided by our desire to study differences across industries that vary in the degree of government intervention, either directly or indirectly.[3] We first divide twenty-four industries of the industrial sector into three groups, namely "energy" including coal mining, petroleum, and utilities, "commodities and primary input materials (C&P)" such as basic metals, chemicals, and building materials, and "semi-finished and finished goods (SF&F)" such as wearing apparel, electrical equipment, and machinery. C&P and SF&F in particular have been the key drivers of China's post-reform growth. According to their "distances" from the final demand, the energy group is located upstream, followed by C&P and SF&F being the closest to the final consumer market. The SF&F group will thus as conjectured be most inclined to indirect effects of government interventions in addition to any direct effect.

The non-industrial industries are divided into five groups though their "location" of the production chain cannot be easily defined. Agricultural sector not only serves the final demand but also provides intermediate inputs to food processing and manufacturing industries and as such can be an important channel for indirect policies. Construction also delivers

---

[3] Strictly speaking, as suggested by Marcel Timmer, the effect of government interventions or regulations on individual industries should be examined by some policy proxies and its impact should be investigated through input–output table analysis.

both investment and consumer goods. Services are divided into three groups with Services I consisting of state-monopolized services of important intermediate input industries such as financial intermediaries, transportation, and telecommunication services; Services II covering the rest of market services which are mainly final demand providers; and Services III denoted by "non-market services" including government administration, education, and health care.

This grouping aims to examine group-level productivity performance that may be affected by different types and degrees of government intervention. Taking the three industrial groups as examples, the "energy" group is monopolized, if not completely owned, by large, central government-owned enterprises due to its "strategic importance." It can easily access public resources but subject to strong administrative interferences. The C&P group is also considered important for downstream industries and hence heavily influenced though not completely owned by the government. Finally, the SF&F group consists of all downstream industries including not only private enterprises and foreign invested enterprises, but also state-owned enterprises particularly in heavy machinery industries. However, its competitive nature makes it difficult for the government to directly interfere in business decisions. On average, SF&F is more labor-intensive than the other groups, hence more in line with China's comparative advantage. Therefore, we may conjecture that the productivity growth of SF&F is faster than that of energy and C&P.

6.3 Measuring the sources of growth

The widely used aggregate production function approach to TFP analysis is implicitly subject to very stringent assumptions that for all (underlying) industries "value-added functions exist and are identical across industries up to a scalar multiple" and "the aggregation of heterogeneous types of capital and labor must receive the same price in each industry" (Jorgenson *et al.* 2005a). Given heavy government interventions and institutional set-ups that cause market imperfections in China, this approach is inappropriate for the growth accounting exercise of the Chinese economy. This study adopts Jorgenson's aggregate production possibility frontier (APPF) framework instead, incorporating Domar weights to account for contributions of individual industries to the growth of aggregate inputs and output.

The APPF approach in growth accounting relaxes the strong assumption that all industries are subject to the same value added production function to account for the industry origin of aggregate growth (Jorgenson 1966). The Domar-weighted aggregation was introduced into the APPF framework in Jorgenson, Gollop, and Fraumeni (1987) to exercise direct aggregation across industries to account for the role of American industries in the changes of aggregate inputs. It has been used in Jorgenson and Stiroh (2000), Jorgenson (2001) and Jorgenson, Ho, and Stiroh (2005a, 2005b) to quantify the role of information technology (IT)-producing and IT-using industries in the US economy. This approach has become the international standard and has also been applied to the Chinese economy in Cao *et al.* (2009).

To illustrate this methodology, let us begin with a production function where industry gross output is a function of capital, labor, intermediate inputs, and technology indexed by time. We use individual industries as building blocks which allow us to explicitly trace the sources of the aggregate productivity growth and input accumulation to the underlying industries. Focusing on an industry-level production function given by equation (1), each industry, indexed by *j*, purchases distinct intermediate inputs, capital and labor services to produce a set of products:

$$Y_j = f_j(K_j, L_j, M_j, T) \tag{1}$$

where Y is output, K is an index of capital service flows, L is an index of labor service flows and M is an index of intermediate inputs, purchased from domestic industries and/or imported. Note that all input variables are indexed by time but this is suppressed for notational convenience.

Under the assumptions of competitive factor markets, full input utilization and constant returns to scale, the growth of output can be expressed as the cost-weighted growth of inputs and technological change, using the translog functional form:

$$\Delta \ln Y_j = \overline{v}_j^K \Delta \ln K_j + \overline{v}_{jt}^L \Delta \ln L_j + \overline{v}_j^M \Delta \ln M_j + v_j^T \tag{2}$$

where $\overline{v}_j^K$, $\overline{v}_j^L$ and $\overline{v}_j^M$ are two-period averages of nominal weights of input $v_j^K = \frac{P_j^K K_j}{P_j^Y Y_j}$, $v_j^L = \frac{P_j^L L_j}{P_j^Y Y_j}$ and $v_j^M = \frac{P_j^M M_j}{P_j^Y Y_j}$, respectively. Note that under constant returns to scale $v_j^K + v_j^L + v_j^M = 1$, which is controlled by industry production accounts in nominal terms. Each element in the right-hand side of equation (2) indicates the proportion of output growth accounted for respectively by the growth of capital services ($\bar{v}_j^K \Delta \ln K_j$), labor services ($\bar{v}_j^L \Delta \ln L_j$), intermediate materials ($\bar{v}_j^M \Delta \ln M_j$) and total factor productivity (v_j^T).

One of the advantages of equation (2) is that it can better account for each input services by different types. For example, it can account for labor services provided by different types of labor with specific demographic, educational, and industrial attributes, as shown in pioneering studies by Griliches (1960), Denison (1962) and Jorgenson and Griliches (1967). It has relaxed the usual strong assumption that treats numbers employed or hours worked as a homogenous measure of labor input. The growth of total labor input is thus defined as a Törnqvist quantity index of individual labor types as follows:

$$\Delta \ln L_j = \sum_h \bar{v}_{h,j} \Delta \ln H_{h,j} \tag{3a}$$

where $\Delta \ln H_{h,j}$ indicates the growth of hours worked by each labor type h (with specific gender, age, and educational attainment) and its cost weights $\bar{v}_{h,j}$ given by two-period average shares of each type in the nominal value of labor compensation controlled by the labor income of industry production accounts.

The same user-cost approach is also applied to K and M to account for the contribution of different types of capital asset (Z_k) and intermediate input (M_m) in production with type-specific, two-period average cost weight defined as $\bar{v}_{k,j}$ and $\bar{v}_{m,j}$, respectively:

$$\Delta \ln K_j = \sum_k \bar{v}_{k,j} \Delta \ln Z_{k,j}, \text{and} \tag{3b}$$

$$\Delta \ln M_j = \sum_m \bar{v}_{m,j} \Delta \ln M_{m,j} \tag{3c}$$

It should be noted that the equations from (2) through the whole set of (3) also explicitly express the methodological framework for the CIP industry-level data construction that is linked to and controlled by the national production and income accounts. This point will be discussed again when we discuss the data issues in the following section.

Using the value added concept, equation (2) can be rewritten as:

$$\Delta \ln Y_j = \overline{v}_j^V \Delta \ln V_j + \overline{v}_j^M \Delta \ln M_j \tag{4}$$

where V_j is the real value added in j and v_j^V is the nominal share of value added in industry gross output.

By rearranging equations (2) and (4), we can obtain an expression for the sources of industry value added growth (i.e. measured in terms of input contributions):

$$\Delta \ln V_j = \frac{\overline{v}_j^K}{\overline{v}_j^V} \Delta \ln K_j + \frac{\overline{v}_j^L}{\overline{v}_j^V} \Delta \ln L_j + \frac{1}{\overline{v}_j^V} v_j^T \tag{5}$$

Growth of aggregate value added by the APPF approach is expressed as weighted industry value added in a Törnqvist index:

$$\Delta \ln V = \sum_j \overline{w}_j \Delta \ln V_j \tag{6}$$

where w_j is the share of industry value added in aggregate value added. By combining equations (5) and (6), we can have a new expression of aggregate value added growth by weighted contribution of industry capital growth, industry labor growth and TFP growth:

$$\Delta \ln V \equiv \sum_j \overline{w}_j \Delta \ln V_j = \sum_j \left(\overline{w}_j \frac{\overline{v}_j^K}{\overline{v}_j^V} \Delta \ln K_j + \overline{w}_j \frac{\overline{v}_j^L}{\overline{v}_j^V} \Delta \ln L_j + \overline{w}_j \frac{1}{\overline{v}_j^V} v_j^T \right) \tag{7}$$

Through this new expression, we have introduced the well-known Domar weights in our aggregation (Domar 1961), i.e. a ratio of each industry's share in total value added (w_j) to the proportion of the industry's value added in its gross output (v_j^V).

If we maintain the stringent assumption that capital and labor inputs have the same marginal productivity in all industries we can define aggregate TFP growth as:

$$v^T \equiv \sum_j \overline{w}_j \Delta \ln V_j - \overline{v}^K \Delta \ln K - \overline{v}^L \Delta \ln L \tag{8}$$

However, this assumption is not likely to hold, in particular in China, as argued above. It is therefore interesting to look at the difference of the two measurement approaches. By subtracting equation (7) from equation (8) and rearranging, we can show how the aggregate TFP growth relates to the sources of TFP growth at the industry level and to the effect of factor mobility across industries (Jorgenson *et al.* 2005a):

$$
v^T = \left(\sum_j \frac{\overline{w}_j}{\overline{v}_j^V} v_j^T \right) + \left(\sum_j \overline{w}_j \frac{\overline{v}_j^K}{\overline{v}_j^V} \Delta \ln K_j - \overline{v}_K \Delta \ln K \right)
$$

$$
+ \left(\sum_j \overline{w}_j \frac{\overline{v}_j^L}{\overline{v}_j^V} \Delta \ln L_j - \overline{v}_L \Delta \ln L \right) \tag{9}
$$

in which the *reallocation* terms in the second and third brackets can be simplified as:

$$
v^T = \sum_j \frac{\overline{w}_j}{\overline{v}_j^V} v_j^T + \rho^K + \rho^L \tag{9}
$$

Equation (9) expresses the aggregate TFP growth in terms of three sources: Domar-weighted industry TFP growth, reallocation of capital and reallocation of labor across industries. This Domar weighting scheme $(\overline{w}_j/\overline{v}_j^V)$, originated by Domar (1961), plays a key role in the direct aggregation across industries under the Jorgensonian growth accounting framework. A direct consequence of the Domar-aggregation is that the weights do not sum to unity, implying that aggregate productivity growth amounts to more than the weighted average of industry-level productivity growth (or less, if negative). This reflects the fact that productivity change in the production of *intermediate inputs* do not only have an "own" effect but in addition they lead to reduced or increased prices in downstream industries, and that effect accumulates through vertical links. As elaborated by Hulten (1978), the Domar aggregation establishes a consistent link between the industry level productivity growth and the aggregate productivity growth. Productivity gains of the aggregate economy may exceed the average productivity gains across industries because flows of intermediate inputs between industries contribute to aggregate productivity by allowing productivity gains in successive industries to augment one another. The same logic can explain productivity losses.

The next two terms reflect the impact on aggregate TFP growth of the reallocation effect of capital (ρ^K) and labor (ρ^L) across industries, respectively. Each of the reallocation term is obtained by subtracting cost-weighted aggregate factor (capital or labor) input growth from the

Domar-weighted input growth across industries. It should be noted that both theoretically and methodologically, when these terms are not negligible, it indicates that industries do not face the same factor costs, which suggests a violation of the assumption of the widely used aggregate approach. However, one should not expect a significant reallocation effect in an economy where there is a well developed market system. This is a very useful analytical tool for the Chinese case where strong government interventions in resource allocation may have caused severe market distortions.

6.4 Data issues and periodization

Data issues

This study has benefited from a newly constructed economy-wide, industry-level dataset in the ongoing CIP Project. It is beyond the scope of this study to go through a long history of separate database studies.[4] We refer the interested reader for details to three working papers (Wu 2015; Wu and Ito 2015; Wu, Yue, and Zhang 2015) as well as earlier versions of this work if one wants to trace the development of data construction ideas (e.g. Wu 2008 and 2013a; Wu and Xu 2002; Wu and Yue 2003, 2010, and 2012).

In the CIP Project the principles of industry data construction adhere to the underlying theory and data constraints as expressed in equation (2) and the set of equations (3a, 3b, and 3c). This implies that the industry-level data are linked to and made consistent with the national production and income accounts of China.

Some features of the CIP data should be noted. For the classification of industries, we in principle adopt the 2002 version of the Chinese Standard Industrial Classification (CSIC/2002) and reclassify the economy into thirty-seven industries (see Appendix Table 6.1). The reconstruction of the Chinese national accounts is based on different versions of official national accounts compiled under the Material

---

[4] The CIP project is based on Wu's China Growth and Productivity Database project, self-initiated in 1995 and heavily involved in Angus Maddison's work on China's aggregate economic performance from 1912 and manufacturing, mining, and utility industries from 1949 (see Maddison 1998 and 2007; Maddison and Wu 2008). The CIP project began in 2010 aiming to extend Wu's earlier work to all non-industrial sectors under the KLEMS framework.

Product System (MPS) prior to 1992 and the United Nations System of National Accounts (SNA) afterwards. China's SNA input–output accounts that are available for every five years since 1987 and a MPS input–output table for 1981 that is converted to a SNA-type table, are used to construct a time series of Chinese input–output accounts for the period 1981–2010 (Wu and Ito 2015). It should be noted that in the CIP project we do not challenge the official national accounts data except for consistency adjustment. However, the widely discussed data problems should be born in mind when interpreting the results.[5]

The nominal accounts are deflated by industry-level producer price index (PPI), constructed using official PPIs for the agricultural and industrial sectors and consumer price index (CPI) or its components for service industries (Wu and Ito 2015). However, the work reported in this chapter still uses the single deflation approach assuming changes in input prices are the same as changes in output prices, similar to the Chinese national accounts, rather than the double-deflation approach which would be preferred, due to lack of price data.[6]

For the required labor data, following earlier studies by Wu and Yue (2003, 2010, and 2012) which analyzed the industrial sector only, CIP has established economy-wide employment series (in both numbers of workers employed and hours worked) and compensation matrices for thirty-seven industries. Workers include both employees as well as self-employed workers, which is important as a majority of workers in for example agriculture and retail is still self-employed. Workers are cross-classified by gender, seven age groups, and five educational levels (Wu *et al.* 2015).

The construction of net capital stock at the industry-level proved to be most challenging. CIP has constructed annual flows of investment

---

[5] China's official estimates of GDP growth have long been challenged for upward bias (see Wu 2013 and 2014a for reviews). Alternative estimates have indeed shown slower growth rates than the official estimates, which inevitably also have level effects. The most affected sectors are identified as manufacturing and so-called "non-material services" (including non-market services). Wu (2013) shows that the official industrial output index has substantially moderated the impact of all external shocks. Besides, Wu (2014a) also shows that the 5–6 percent annual growth of labor productivity in "non-material services" based on official data appears to be too fast to be true if considering the international norm in history between –1 and +1 percent per annum (Griliches 1992; van Ark 1996).

[6] See Wu and Ito (2015) for very preliminary growth estimates at industry level using the double deflation approach, although our work on prices is still ongoing.

for the industrial sectors using official gross stock data at historical costs. But it has to adopt the official investment series estimates for the non-industrial sectors. The results are yet to be reconciled with the national accounts gross fixed capital formation data. Industry-specific investment deflators are constructed using PPIs of investment goods industries and nominal wage index of construction workers (Wu and Xu 2002; Wu 2008 and 2015). Industry-specific depreciation rates are estimated based on asset service lives and declining balance values used in the US national accounts, following the approach developed by Hulten and Wykoff (1981).

Periodization

To better examine the productivity impact of major policy regime shifts on the Chinese economy, we divide the entire period 1980–2010 covered by the current version of the CIP data into four sub-periods, namely 1980–1991, 1992–2001, 2002–2007, and 2008–2010. In most cases, the empirical findings are reported in line with this periodization. The first sub-period 1980–1991 is characterized by decollectivization in agriculture and planning-market double track price reform with more operational autonomy in the industrial sector. It ended with rising inflation that triggered the 1989 Tiananmen political turmoil.

The second sub-period 1992–2001 began with Deng's call for bolder and deeper reforms in 1992 and the official adoption of the so-called "socialist market economy" in 1993. Wider opening-up to western technology and FDI drove a new wave of investment in export-oriented manufacturing capacities. Meanwhile, due to deregulations of private activities, new private firms absorbed a huge number of the state industrial employees who lost their jobs in the state-owned enterprise reforms of the 1990s. However, it also resulted in overinvestment. In the wake of the Asian financial crisis (1997–1998), which hit the economy hard, China entered a four-year-long deflation period.[7]

The third sub-period 2002–2007 began with China's WTO entry at the end of 2001. It is characterised by counteracting forces. On one hand, WTO-entry induced a further opening up to foreign trade and

---

[7] China's retail price index (RPI) declined from 380.8 in 1997 (1978=100) to 346.7 in 2003 and meanwhile producer price index (PPI) declined from 315.0 to 299.3 (NBS 2014, p. 123).

direct investment. This directed the Chinese economy further towards the market system. On the other hand, consolidated and enlarged state corporations resurged in the name of protecting national interests in a time of accelerating globalization. Meanwhile, growth-motivated local governments were pressured to race for rapid urbanization and heavy industrialization.

We separately identify the period from 2008 to 2010 as the last sub-period, though rather short, to examine the aftermath of the global financial crisis. The unprecedented fiscal stimulus package from both the central and local governments substantially enhanced the role of state-owned enterprises (SOEs). Separating this period from others also helps examine differences in productivity performance between state and non-state dominated industries at the time of crisis.

6.5 Empirical results

Sources of gross output growth by industry group

We start with an examination of industry-level sources of growth as reported in Table 6.1 for sub-periods and Figure 6.1 for indices based on a gross output production function expressed in equation (2). This is a necessary starting point because industries are building blocks of the national economy and the originators of aggregate productivity growth.

China's agriculture achieved the best TFP performance of all groups. It maintained a strong positive productivity growth throughout the three decades and since the 2000s its TFP growth was the fastest (Table 6.1). This was accompanied by a rapid decline in labor input in the more recent periods: –2.4 percent per year in 2001–2007 and –2.1 afterwards. In assessing agricultural performance, three factors should be considered. First, although agriculture still received various subsidies in the 2000s, unlike in the planning era it was no longer subject to administrative controls. Second, we adopt the official broad measure of labor compensation that defines the income of self-employed (including all farmers) as "labor income" rather than "capital income" as suggested by the SNA. Third, we are not yet able to measure the contribution by land. Since we do not include rent-weighted land growth as an input, which would be negative as more and more land is

Table 6.1 *Decomposition of gross output growth in China by industry Group*

1980–1991

	GO	L	K	M	TFP
Agriculture	6.7	0.8	1.0	2.8	2.2
Construction	7.4	2.0	0.6	5.1	-0.3
Energy	0.9	0.5	3.5	1.9	-5.0
C&P	7.9	0.4	2.4	5.9	-0.9
SF&F	13.6	0.2	2.1	10.0	1.2
Services I	11.0	0.9	5.2	3.3	1.6
Services II	11.0	1.5	2.7	5.4	1.4
Services III	5.5	1.8	1.2	1.9	0.7

1991–2001

	GO	L	K	M	TFP
Agriculture	7.3	0.6	0.7	3.5	2.4
Construction	12.5	1.1	1.4	9.3	0.7
Energy	7.0	-0.1	3.4	4.7	-1.0
C&P	11.0	-0.1	1.4	8.0	1.6
SF&F	14.8	0.1	1.7	10.9	2.2
Services I	7.3	0.6	6.5	3.9	-3.7
Services II	9.9	1.5	6.0	4.7	-2.3
Services III	9.1	2.4	1.0	5.4	0.3

2001–2007

	GO	L	K	M	TFP
Agriculture	3.7	-2.4	0.8	1.4	3.9
Construction	13.6	0.3	1.4	10.7	1.2
Energy	15.0	0.7	3.2	11.7	-0.5
C&P	15.2	0.4	2.1	12.3	0.4
SF&F	20.1	0.7	2.2	16.2	1.0
Services I	13.5	1.1	4.9	6.7	0.8
Services II	10.3	1.3	6.9	4.3	-2.2
Services III	11.4	4.5	2.3	4.8	-0.2

2007–2010

	GO	L	K	M	TFP
Agriculture	4.6	-2.1	0.6	1.9	4.2
Construction	14.1	0.8	1.7	10.8	0.8
Energy	2.4	0.4	2.6	1.5	-2.1
C&P	8.9	0.1	2.8	6.9	-0.9
SF&F	14.8	0.2	2.8	11.9	-0.1
Services I	10.0	1.2	6.1	4.2	-1.4
Services II	12.8	0.5	8.1	5.9	-1.6
Services III	10.0	6.4	2.2	4.9	-3.5

Source: Author's calculation based equation (2) using CIP 2.2 data.

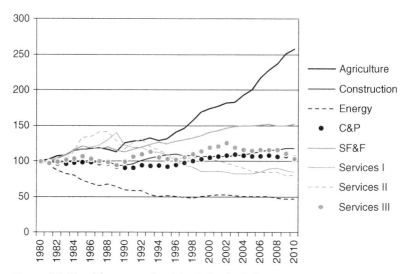

Figure 6.1 Total factor productivity index by industry group

taken out of agricultural production, while exaggerating the weight on labor, the bias in TFP could be in either direction.

The SF&F and C&P groups are well-known as China's growth engines and the backbone of the "world factory." Compared to C&P, as discussed earlier, SF&F received much less direct government interference due to its competitive nature and greater exposure to the international market. We find that SF&F in general experienced faster productivity growth than C&P. Before the global financial crisis, despite significant increase in input materials both groups showed positive TFP growth, except for C&P in the 1980s. Nonetheless, in the wake of the crisis, both suffered from TFP decline but the case of "C&P" was much worse than that of SF&F.

The performance of the "energy" group presents a sharp contrast to the "SF&F" group. It experienced heavy TFP loss in the 1980s and continuous TFP decline till the end of the period. Indeed, there appeared to be a significant post-WTO improvement that substantially slowed down TFP decline to –0.5 percent per annum compared to –5.0 in 1980–1991 and –1.0 in 1991–2007. However, the most recent post-crisis period has made it worse again (–2.1). Figure 6.1 shows that in level terms energy has never been able to resume its initial level of TFP in 1980. This may not be a big surprise because this group consists of industries almost completely monopolized by SOEs and are subject to heavy government interventions.[8]

We find that since the 1990s China's construction industry has maintained positive though slow TFP growth which is not often seen in many other economies. Most market services (I and II) show exceptional acceleration of TFP growth in the 1980s following deregulations after a long period of suppressed service development under central planning. One has to acknowledge though that these estimates are only preliminary: overestimation of output and underestimation of output prices due to political incentives of local governments lead to major measurement problems that complicate productivity measurement in all Chinese services industries (Wu 2014). Compared to Services II (market), there are more state subsidies as well as administrative controls in Services I (market monopolies) and III (non-market): these factors could be translated into different TFP growth rates but are not easy to disentangle. Nevertheless, from the indices presented in Figure 6.1, we can see that TFP in Services I and II has been declining since the late 1980s, whereas Services III have experienced nearly zero TFP growth on average.

Sources of growth in the APPF framework

From the above analysis, we have seen that industries (groups) perform very differently in the growth of factors and productivity over time. In this sub-section we examine China's aggregate TFP performance in the APPF framework taking into account that industries (groups) may have different value added functions. The results are summarized in Table 6.2.

The Chinese economy achieved a real output growth of 9.16 percent per annum in 1980–2010. The SF&F group was the top contributor before the global financial crisis. It was followed by Services II (market). In the wake of the crisis, SF&F was marginally overtaken by Services II. On average over the entire period 1980–2010, agriculture, C&P and Services I (state monopoly) made similar contributions to real output growth. The estimated aggregate TFP growth is 1.24 percent per annum. However, the TFP performance was highly unstable over

---

[8] Here I would like to acknowledge Mun S. Ho's important comment that the negative TFP may also indicate some data issues caused by conceptual problems such as how to properly measure the depreciation of pipelines and exploration costs, which may result in poor capital measurement.

Table 6.2 *Growth in aggregate value added and sources of growth in China*

	1980–1991	1991–2001	2001–2007	2007–2010	1980–2010
		Industry contributions to value added growth			
Value-added growth due to (%)	7.72	9.15	11.23	10.30	9.16
Agriculture	1.75	1.18	0.50	0.48	1.18
Construction	0.38	0.64	0.68	0.89	0.58
Energy	-0.06	0.33	0.74	0.37	0.27
Commodities & primary materials	0.90	1.49	1.57	1.21	1.26
Semi-Finished & finished goods	1.91	2.69	2.83	2.54	2.42
Services I (market)	0.93	0.66	1.61	1.36	1.02
Services II (market monopolies)	1.50	1.78	2.37	2.66	1.89
Services III (non-market)	0.39	0.37	0.94	0.80	0.53
		Factor contributions to value added growth			
Value-added growth due to (%)	7.72	9.15	11.23	10.30	9.16
Capital input:	4.95	6.11	8.49	10.57	6.61
Stock	4.94	6.18	8.56	10.55	6.64
Capital quality (composition)	0.01	-0.06	-0.07	0.02	-0.03
Labor input:	1.39	1.26	1.19	1.53	1.32
Hours	1.34	0.88	0.71	0.36	0.96
Labor quality (composition)	0.05	0.38	0.48	1.17	0.35
Aggregate TFP	1.39	1.79	1.57	-1.80	1.24

Source: Author's estimates.

time with the highest growth achieved in 1991–2001 and the worst in 2007–2010.[9]

Of the 9.16% annual output growth rate for the entire period, the contribution of capital input was 6.61, labor input 1.32 and TFP 1.24. This means that the Chinese economy relied for 72.5% of its real value added growth on capital input, 14% on labor input, and 13.5% on TFP growth. The contribution of capital input increased from 64% in the 1980s to 76% post-WTO and even more than 100% in the wake of the global financial crisis. On the other hand, the contribution of labor input declined from 18% in the 1980s to 11% post-WTO. This trend reversed following the crisis and the contribution of labor input rose back to 15%, largely attributed to quality improvement (11.4%) rather than hours worked (3.4%). The contribution of the quality of capital was insignificant on average.[10]

If these annual aggregate TFP growth rates are translated into an index as shown in Figure 6.2, we observe a volatile TFP performance

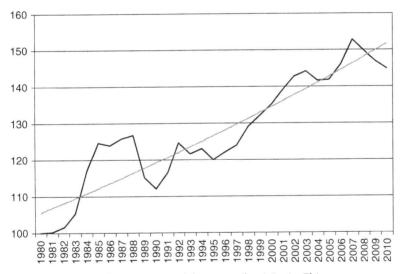

Figure 6.2 Index of aggregate total factor productivity in China

[9] Appendix Table 6.2 reports the details for individual industries.
[10] This might be due to the limited set of asset types ("structures" and "equipment") that is available in the current CIP database. If a distinction between ICT and non-ICT assets could be made, a higher measured contribution is to be expected, see Jorgenson and Vu (2013).

around its underlying trend. The first TFP drive was clearly observed in the early 1980s associated with China's agricultural reform. As a result the Chinese productivity performance stayed well above the trend until its collapse following the 1989 political crisis. TFP growth recovered in the early 1990s but this was short-lived. It began to accelerate again from the late 1990s and exceeded the trend in the early 2000s. China's post-WTO period, nonetheless, only observed the resurgence of TFP growth in 2006–2007 before its sharp drop in the wake of the global financial crisis. The most recent significant slowdown in the official GDP growth rate from above 10 percent to around 7.5 percent per year in 2011–2013 seems to suggest that China is facing serious challenges to turn productivity growth back to positive again after 2010.

Table 6.3 presents the results of a decomposition of China's aggregate value added per hour worked into changes in capital deepening, labor quality, and TFP. This enables us to separate the contribution of hours worked from the contribution of genuine labor productivity improvement and its sources. The Chinese economy benefited significantly from the increase in hours worked as the so-called "demographic dividend." This has, however, declined overtime as shown in Table 6.3 from 2.83% per annum in 1980–1991 to 0.83% per annum in 2007–2010. Although value added per hour worked increased from 4.89% to 9.47% per annum, it appeared to be increasingly relying on capital deepening from 3.46% to 10.10% per annum. More importantly, the growth of TFP was not necessarily in line with the pace of capital deepening if comparing the results for 2007–2010 with those for 2001–2007, suggesting misallocation of resources that was likely caused by overinvestment, which will be examined below.

The industry origin of aggregate TFP growth

In order to explicitly account for differences across industries and their impact on China's aggregate TFP performance we now introduce Domar weights in the exercise, following the studies on the US economy by Jorgenson *et al.* (2005a and 2005b). The results presented in the first line of Table 6.4 are estimated with the stringent assumption that marginal productivities of capital and labor are the same across all industries, which are the same as

Table 6.3 *Decomposition of aggregate labor productivity growth in China*

	1980–1991	1991–2001	2001–2007	2007–2010	1980–2010
			Growth rates		
Value-added growth (APPF)	7.72	9.15	11.23	10.30	9.16
Value added per hour worked	4.89	7.40	9.67	9.47	7.14
Hours	2.83	1.75	1.57	0.83	2.02
			Factor contributions		
Value-added per hour worked	4.89	7.40	9.67	9.47	7.14
Capital deepening	3.46	5.23	7.62	10.10	5.55
Labor quality	0.05	0.38	0.48	1.17	0.35
TFP growth	1.39	1.79	1.57	-1.80	1.24

Source: Author's estimates.

Table 6.4 Domar-weighted TFP growth and reallocation effects in the Chinese economy

	1980–1991	1991–2001	2001–2007	2007–2010	1980–2010
Aggregate TFP growth	1.39	1.79	1.57	-1.80	1.24
(1) Domar-weighted TFP growth	0.74	1.81	0.98	-2.31	0.84
Agriculture	0.99	0.75	0.82	0.76	0.85
Construction	-0.05	0.12	0.29	0.22	0.10
Energy	-0.76	-0.24	-0.33	-0.57	-0.48
Commodities and primary materials	-0.50	0.77	0.21	-0.61	0.05
Semi-finished and finished goods	0.35	1.39	0.59	-0.27	0.68
Services I (market monopolies)	0.30	-0.58	0.55	-0.03	0.02
Services II (market)	0.36	-0.37	-0.76	-1.10	-0.25
Services III (non-market)	0.06	-0.03	-0.40	-0.71	-0.14
(2) Reallocation of K (ρ^K)	0.30	-0.03	-1.15	-0.30	-0.16
(3) Reallocation of L (ρ^L)	0.35	0.01	1.73	0.81	0.56

Source: Author's estimates following equation (9).

those presented in Table 6.2 and Table 6.3. As expressed in equation (9), using Domar weights the aggregate TFP growth rate can be decomposed into three additive components, i.e. (1) the change of Domar-weighted aggregate TFP; (2) the change of capital reallocation; and (3) the change of labor reallocation. Let us first focus on the first component in Table 6.4 which is the most important finding of the study.

On average, of the entire period 1980–2010, China's TFP growth estimated with Domar weights is 0.84% per annum, much slower than the aggregate TFP growth of 1.24%, implying a net factor reallocation effect of 0.40 which will be discussed later. Table 6.4 also shows the contribution of each industrial group to the Domar-weighted annual TFP growth (see Appendix Table 6.2 for the results of individual industries). The highest contributor to the Domar-weighted aggregate TFP growth was agriculture that contributed 0.85 percentage points (ppts). The SF&F group also did rather well over time (0.68) and then construction (0.10). The worst performer was the energy group (–0.48), followed by Services II (–0.25) and Services III (–0.14). Such a sharp contrast across industry groups in TFP performance can also be observed over different sub-periods, which clearly suggests that treating individual industries homogenous in the growth accounting can substantially distort our view of the productivity performance of the Chinese economy.

A closer examination through sub-periods with the background of policy regime shifts may shed important light on the role of the government. The agricultural sector benefited most from reforms in the 1980s especially the decollectivization in farming and deregulations on township and village enterprises. It contributed 0.99 ppts to the Domar-weighted TFP growth at 0.74% per annum. Even in the latest period that was affected by the global financial crisis it was still the most important contributor (0.76 ppts) to the Domar-weighted TFP growth (–2.31% per annum), which might come as a surprise. While its share in nominal GDP was declining over time (see Table 6.2), its contribution to the Domar-weighted TFP growth remained high throughout the period. This is suggestive of a process in which the agricultural sector is still releasing capital (including land) and labor that have a marginal productivity below the sector's average. By shedding these "surplus" factors, the average productivity with which factors are used is still growing. But clearly this cannot be a long-run source of growth as this structural shift is temporary. Future growth must come from the manufacturing and services sectors.[11]

The period 1991–2001 experienced the most rapid TFP growth at 1.81% per annum by Domar weights albeit the impact of the Asian financial crisis (1997–1998) and the subsequent deflation period (1998–2003; see footnote 7). The SF&F group was the most important contributor (1.39 ppts), followed by the C&P group (0.77), thanks to unprecedented state sector reforms and opening up to foreign trade and direct investment, which allowed the market to play a significant role in resource allocation. The productivity performance of the construction industry also turned positive for the first time (0.12 ppts) and even the productivity decline of the energy group substantially slowed down to –0.24 from –0.76 in the previous period (1980–1991).

Nevertheless, we find that China's accession to the WTO at the end of 2001 was accompanied by a slowdown rather than an acceleration of TFP growth which was 0.98% per annum in 2001–2007, only about the half of the rate of 1.81 achieved in 1991–2001. This puzzling result may support observed increasing interventions by local governments throughout the 2000s aiming to promote local urbanization and heavy industrialization (J. Wu 2008). Table 6.4 shows that in 2001–2007 while the contribution of SF&F (0.59) and C&P (0.21) to TFP growth was considerably reduced, the contribution of related industries in particular construction (0.29) and state monopolized Services I (transportation, telecommunications, and financial services) (0.55) significantly increased.

In the wake of the global financial crisis, despite a 4-trillion-yuan stimulus package from the central government that was further accompanied by 18-trillion-yuan projects financed by local governments, China's TFP growth turned to negative, declining considerably by –2.31 percent per year in 2007–2010. Since most of the projects concentrated on infrastructural development, construction continued to enjoy a positive TFP growth (0.22). Perhaps for the same reason, Services I was the least suffered (–0.03) among those suffering from productivity decline. However, the most recent development shows

---

[11] I am indebted to Marcel Timmer for the discussion of the role of Chinese agriculture in the productivity performance of the aggregate economy.

that while the effect of the unprecedented government injection on growth has quickly abated after 2010, there are increasing signs indicating that China's surplus capacity in manufacturing is worsening and may take many years to solve.

The effect of factor reallocation

The slower Domar-weighted TFP growth (0.84) compared to the aggregate TFP growth (1.24) implies that about 70% of the aggregate TFP growth is attributable to the productivity performances of individual industries while 30% to the reallocation of capital and labor. Following equation (9), in Table 6.4 we show that this effect consists of a positive labor reallocation effect (ρ^L) of 0.56 percentage points and a negative capital reallocation effect (ρ^K) of –0.16 percentage points.

It should be noted that such a magnitude of reallocation effect is typically not observed in market economies. Based on their empirical work on the US economy in 1977–2000, Jorgenson *et al.* (2005a) showed that first, the reallocation effect was generally negligible and second, if it was non-negligible for some sub-periods, the capital and labor reallocation effects generally moved in opposite directions. Jorgenson *et al.* (1987) also reported the reallocation of capital that was typically positive and the reallocation of labor that was typically negative for the US economy for the period 1948–1979. This is because capital grew more rapidly in industries with high capital service prices, hence high returns on capital, whereas labor grew relatively slowly in industries with high marginal compensation.

In the case of China, the large magnitude and unexpected sign of capital and labor reallocation effects have two important implications. First, individual industries indeed face significantly different marginal factor productivities suggesting that there are barriers to factor mobility which cause misallocation of resources in the economy. The flipside of this finding is that corrections to the distortions can potentially be productivity-enhancing, which is good news in terms of much talked about and long awaited structural reforms.

We find that the effect of labor reallocation remained generally positive over time. This suggests that labor market was much less distorted than the capital market benefitting from increasing labor mobility along with reforms. Notably, the post-WTO period experienced the most significant gain from labor reallocation (1.73 in 2001–2007) which could be driven by the rapid expansion of export-oriented, labor-intensive industries that was in line with China's comparative advantage. Besides, the effect of labor reallocation was also strong in the wake of the global financial crisis (0.81 in 2007–2010) reflecting that labor responded more quickly to the changes of market conditions.

The case of capital reallocation is different. The early reform period was the only period that saw a positive effect of capital reallocation (0.30 percentage points in 1980–1991) due to partial removal of distortions inherited from the central planning period. However, the effect of capital reallocation turned negative substantially following China's WTO entry in 2001–2007 (–1.15 percentage points) because of the enhanced role of the government that supported the state sector resurging in upstream industries. During the global financial crisis period, it remained negative but less so than before (–0.30) despite unprecedented fiscal injection benefitting mainly state-owned enterprises and state-controlled industries.

6.6 Concluding remarks

Using the newly constructed CIP database, this study adopts the aggregate production possibility frontier approach in the Jorgensonian growth accounting framework incorporated with the Domar aggregation approach to examine the sources of growth in the Chinese economy for the reform period 1980–2010. This approach provides a highly appropriate analytical tool for investigating the industry origin of aggregate productivity and the effect of resource reallocation across industries in the Chinese economy.

Our preliminary results show that China achieved a TFP growth of 0.84% per annum for the entire period 1980–2010. This means that compared to an industry-weighted value added growth of 9.16% per annum, TFP growth accounted for about 9.2% of the average GDP growth. This is a result that is much smaller than all previous productivity studies on the Chinese economy based on the aggregate approach, e.g. about 40% contribution by Bosworth and Collins (2008) and by Perkins and Rawski (2008). However, compared to the only work in the literature that applied the same approach for the period 1982–2000 by Cao *et al.* (2009), our finding of 0.84% is only about one-third of their result of 2.51%. The differences in data construction and measurements, classification, and coverage could be the main reason, e.g. we have eleven service sectors instead of one as in Cao *et al.*

At the industry group level, as conjectured, we do find that, in general, industries less prone to government intervention, such as agriculture and the SF&F manufactures, tended to have higher TFP growth rates than those industries subject to direct government interventions, such as the energy group. The fact that the SF&F group maintained a positive TFP growth while the energy group experiencing persistent TFP decline suggests the existence of "cross-subsidization" between upstream and downstream industries in which the government plays different roles to serve its strategy.

We also found strong effects of factor input reallocation across industries which significantly address the key issue of resource misallocation in the ongoing policy debate. This large magnitude of the reallocation effect on the one hand reflects barriers to factor mobility in the economy and on the other hand also suggests potential gain from market-driven reallocation. Institutional deficiencies in the Chinese economy that allow the government at all levels to intervene resource allocation at their discretion are responsible for resource misallocation. Therefore, disentangling government from business and allowing market to correct the cost structure of industries is the key to solving China's "structural problems." Indeed, "restructuring" for healthy and sustainable growth is the most crucial and challenging pillar of the Liconomics. Nevertheless, there is no such thing as the "right structure" without allowing more market-based resource allocation.

The present work is more sophisticated in data and methodology than studies so far. Nevertheless further work needs to be done to address some limitations. The top priority of the CIP/China KLEMS data construction work is to improve measures on China's factor income by identifying the contribution of land and accordingly adjusting capital and labor compensation in the national accounts. This will improve in particular our measure of agricultural TFP.

Second, we need to reconstruct the time series of the input–output accounts using the forthcoming Chinese input–output table for 2012 and strictly integrate the present analysis in an input–output framework. In principle this will also allow for a truly double-deflation of value added if more price series become available. Double deflation is important to correctly identify the sources of productivity growth (see Triplett 1996). While it will not change the estimate of aggregate TFP, it might change the industry sources. In particular, when we want to consider the knock-on effects of regulations and government interventions in upstream industries on downstream industries this becomes an important issue.

Last but not least, we also need to improve our measure of capital stock by reconciling industry accounts with national accounts and by decomposing equipment into ICT and non-ICT equipment such that a better measure of capital input will be derived. With the increasing upgrading of the Chinese economy and diffusion of ICT technologies, capital input is likely to grow faster than is measured now. Given that our current data is already suggesting severe overinvestment in the Chinese economy with capital input growth being responsible for all output growth since 2008, more accurate accounting for capital input will not only further improve our understanding of China's productivity performance but also better address the policy dilemma in facing increasing surplus capacity in production but weakening capacity in consumption.

Appendix

Appendix Table 6.1 *CIP/China KLEMS industrial classification and code*

CIP code	EU-KLEMS code	Grouping	Industry	
1	AtB	Agriculture	Agriculture, forestry, animal husbandry, fishery	AGR
2	10	Energy	Coal mining	CLM
3	11	Energy	Oil and gas excavation	PTM
4	13	C&P	Metal mining	MEM
5	14	C&P	Non-metallic minerals mining	NMM
6	15	Finished	Food and kindred products	F&B
7	16	Finished	Tobacco products	TBC
8	17	C&P	Textile mill products	TEX

Appendix Table 6.1 (*cont.*)

CIP code	EU-KLEMS code	Grouping	Industry	
9	18	Finished	Apparel and other textile products	WEA
10	19	Finished	Leather and leather products	LEA
11	20	SF&F	Saw mill products, furniture, fixtures	W&F
12	21t22	C&P	Paper products, printing, publishing	P&P
13	23	Energy	Petroleum and coal products	PET
14	24	C&P	Chemicals and allied products	CHE
15	25	SF&F	Rubber and plastics products	R&P
16	26	C&P	Stone, clay, and glass products	BUI
17	27t28	C&P	Primary and fabricated metal industries	MET
18	27t28	SF&F	Metal products (excluding rolling products)	MEP
19	29	Semi-finished	Industrial machinery and equipment	MCH
20	31	SF&F	Electric equipment	ELE
21	32	SF&F	Electronic and telecommunication equipment	ICT
22	30t33	SF&F	Instruments and office equipment	INS
23	34t35	Finished	Motor vehicles and other transportation equipment	TRS
24	36t37	Finished	Miscellaneous manufacturing industries	OTH
25	E	Energy	Power, steam, gas, and tap water supply	UTL
26	F	Construction	Construction	CON
27	G	Services II	Wholesale and retail trades	SAL
28	H	Services II	Hotels and restaurants	HOT
29	I	Services I	Transport, storage, and post services	T&S
30	71t74	Services I	Telecommunication and post	P&T
31	J	Services I	Financial intermediations	FIN

Appendix Table 6.1 (*cont.*)

CIP code	EU-KLEMS code	Grouping	Industry	
32	K	Services II	Real estate services	REA
33	71t74	Services II	Leasing, technical, science, and business services	BUS
34	L	Services III	Public administration and defense	ADM
35	M	Services III	Education services	EDU
36	N	Services III	Health and social security services	HEA
37	O&P	Services II	Other services	SER

Source: See the text.

Note: This is based on Wu's series of works to reclassify official statistics reported under different CSIC systems adopted in CSIC/1972, CSIC/1985 and CSIC/1994 (see Wu and Yue 2012; Wu and Ito 2015). The current Chinese classification system CSIC/2011 largely conforms to the two-digit level industries of the ISIC (Rev. 4) and can be reconciled with the EU-KLEMS system of classification (see Timmer *et al.*, 2007).

Appendix Table 6.2 *Industry contributions to value added and total factor productivity growth*

	Value-added			Total factor productivity		
	VA weight	VA growth	Contribution to aggregate VA growth	Domar weight	TFP growth	Contribution to aggregate TFP growth
AGR	0.204	5.42	1.18	0.319	2.83	0.85
CLM	0.016	7.21	0.11	0.031	1.03	0.02
PTM	0.018	−3.07	−0.05	0.026	−10.20	−0.26
MEM	0.005	10.66	0.06	0.013	1.59	0.02
NMM	0.006	9.35	0.05	0.012	2.15	0.03
F&B	0.027	10.89	0.29	0.121	0.25	0.03
TBC	0.012	8.07	0.09	0.018	−4.97	−0.11
TEX	0.027	7.84	0.21	0.113	−0.02	−0.03
WEA	0.009	12.74	0.11	0.034	0.64	0.03
LEA	0.004	11.48	0.05	0.019	0.39	0.01
W&F	0.007	12.83	0.09	0.024	1.22	0.03

Appendix Table 6.2 (*cont.*)

	Value-added			Total factor productivity		
	VA weight	VA growth	Contribution to aggregate VA growth	Domar weight	TFP growth	Contribution to aggregate TFP growth
P&P	0.011	10.26	0.12	0.038	0.42	0.02
PET	0.011	1.10	0.00	0.043	−3.88	−0.13
CHE	0.036	10.27	0.37	0.131	0.39	0.05
R&P	0.012	12.56	0.15	0.048	0.61	0.03
BUI	0.025	9.46	0.23	0.073	0.47	0.05
MET	0.031	7.38	0.22	0.128	−0.58	−0.08
MEP	0.012	12.03	0.15	0.049	0.99	0.04
MCH	0.035	11.03	0.39	0.116	1.78	0.19
ELE	0.015	14.82	0.21	0.062	1.09	0.05
ICT	0.016	24.87	0.36	0.075	3.17	0.13
INS	0.003	14.07	0.04	0.010	1.88	0.02
TRS	0.018	15.78	0.30	0.073	1.86	0.13
OTH	0.014	13.10	0.19	0.040	1.95	0.11
UTL	0.027	7.06	0.20	0.103	−1.23	−0.11
CON	0.054	10.60	0.58	0.206	0.44	0.10
SAL	0.077	12.15	0.89	0.143	2.00	0.22
HOT	0.019	11.88	0.22	0.053	−0.36	−0.02
T&S	0.052	8.61	0.45	0.100	−1.05	−0.10
P&T	0.012	15.15	0.18	0.021	4.03	0.07
FIN	0.040	11.35	0.39	0.059	2.57	0.05
REA	0.038	9.22	0.33	0.052	−8.03	−0.44
BUS	0.022	10.95	0.27	0.051	1.09	0.00
ADM	0.032	11.02	0.36	0.061	0.33	−0.01
EDU	0.025	3.71	0.10	0.043	−2.31	−0.09
HEA	0.011	6.02	0.07	0.031	−1.10	−0.04
SER	0.016	9.82	0.18	0.035	−1.29	−0.01
Sum	*1.000*		*9.16*	*2.575*		*0.84*

Source: Author's calculations.

Notes: See Appendix Table 6.1 for industry abbreviation. Value added and TFP growth rates are annualized raw growth rates in percent. Industry contribution to VA and TFP growth is weighted growth rate in percentage points. See equation (9) for Domar aggregation.

References

Bosworth, Barry and Susan M. Collins. 2008. "Accounting for Growth: Comparing China and India," *Journal of Economic Perspectives*, **22**(1): 45–66.

Cao, Jing, Mun S. Ho, Dale W. Jorgenson, Ruoen Ren, Linlin Sun, and Ximing Yue. 2009. "Industrial and Aggregate Measures of Productivity Growth in China, 1982–2000," *The Review of Income and Wealth*, **55**, Special Issue 1, July.

CPCCC (Communist Party of China Central Committee). 2013. CPCCC on Deepening Reforms of Major Issues. *Third Plenary Session of the Eighteenth Central Committee*, November 12, 2013.

Denison, Edward F. 1962. *The Sources of Economic Growth in the United States and the Alternative before Us*. New York: Committee on Economic Development.

Domar, Evsey. 1961. "On the Measurement of Technological Change", *Economic Journal*, **71**.

Griliches, Zvi. 1960. "Measuring Inputs in Agriculture: A Critical Survey," *Journal of Farm Economics*, **40**(5): 1398–1427.

1992. "Introduction." In Zvi Griliches (ed.), *Output Measurement in the Service Sectors*. University of Chicago Press.

Huang, Yasheng. 2012. "How Did China Take Off?" *Journal of Economic Perspectives*, **26**(4): 147–170.

Huang, Yiping and Kunyu Tao. 2010. "Factor Market Distortion and the Current Account Surplus in China," *Asian Economic Papers*, **9**(3).

Hulten, Charles. 1978. "Growth Accounting with Intermediate Inputs," *Review of Economic Studies*, **45**.

Hulten, Charles R., and Frank C. Wykoff. 1981. "The Measurement of Economic Depreciation." In Charles R. Hulten (ed.), *Depreciation, Inflation, and the Taxation of Income from Capital*. Washington DC: The Urban Institute Press, 81–125.

Jorgenson, Dale W. 1966. "The Embodiment Hypothesis." *Journal of Political Economy*, **74**(1): 1–17.

2001. "Information Technology and the US Economy," *American Economic Review*, **91**(1): 1–32.

Jorgenson, Dale W., Frank Gollop, and Barbara Fraumeni. 1987. *Productivity and US Economic Growth*. Cambridge, MA: Harvard University Press.

Jorgenson, Dale W. and Z. Griliches. 1967. "The Explanation of Productivity Change," *Review of Economic Studies*, **34**(3): 249–283.

Jorgenson, Dale W., M. S. Ho, and K. J. Stiroh. 2005a. *Information Technology and the American Growth Resurgence*, Productivity vol 3. Cambridge, MA: MIT Press.

Jorgenson, Dale W. and Kevin J. Stiroh. 2000. "Raising the Speed Limit: US Economic Growth in the Information Age," *Brookings Papers on Economic Activity, Economic Studies Program, The Brookings Institution*, 31(1): 125–236.

Jorgenson, Dale W., and Khuong Vu. 2013. "The Emergence of the New Economic Order," *Journal of Policy Modeling*, 35(3): 389–399.

2005b. "Growth of US Industries and Investments in Information Technology and Higher Education." In Carol Corrado, John Haltiwanger, and Daniel Sichel (eds.), *Measuring Capital in a New Economy*. University of Chicago Press.

Li, Hongbin, and Li-An Zhou. 2005. "Political Turnover and Economic Performance: The Incentive Role of Personnel Control in China." *Journal of Public Economics*, 89(9–10): 1743–1762.

Maddison, Angus. 1998. *Chinese Economic Performance in the Long Run*. Paris: OECD Development Centre. See www.ggdc.net/Maddison.

2007. *Chinese Economic Performance in the Long Run, 960–2030*. Paris: OECD.

Maddison, Angus and Harry X. Wu. 2008. "Measuring China's Economic Performance," *World Economics*, 9(2, April–June).

National Bureau of Statistics (NBS), China. 2014. *China Statistical Yearbook*. Beijing: China Statistical Press.

O'Mahony, Mary and Marcel P. Timmer. 2009. "Output, Input and Productivity Measures at the Industry Level: The EU KLEMS Database," *The Economic Journal*, 119(June), F374–F403.

Perkins, Dwight H. and Thomas G. Rawski. 2008. "Forecasting China's Economic Growth to 2025." In Loren Brandt and Thomas G. Rawski (eds.), *China's Great Economic Transformation*. Cambridge University Press, ch. 20.

Timmer, Marcel, Ton van Moergastel, Edwin Stuivenwold, Gerard Ypma, Mary O'Mahony, and Mari Kangasniemi. 2007. *EU-KLEMS Growth and Productivity Accounts*, Version 1.0, PART I Methodology. Paris: OECD.

Triplett, J. 1996. "High Tech Industry Productivity and Hedonic Price Indices." In OECD, *Industry Productivity. International Comparison and Measurement Issues*. Paris: OECD Proceedings, 119–142.

van Ark, Bart. 1996. "*Sectoral Growth Accounting and Structural Change in Postwar Europe*." In B. van Ark and N. Crafts (eds.), *Quantitative*

Aspects of Post-war European Economic Growth. Cambridge University Press, pp. 84–164.

Wu, Harry X. 2008. "Measuring Capital Input in Chinese Industry and Implications for China's Industrial Productivity Performance, 1949–2005," *Presented at the World Congress on National Accounts and Economic Performance Measures for Nations,* Washington DC.

2013a. "Measuring Industry Level Employment, Output, and Labor Productivity in the Chinese Economy, 1987-2008," *Economic Review, Hitotsubashi University,* **64**(1, January): 42–61.

2013b. "How Fast Has Chinese Industry Grown? – The Upward Bias Hypothesis Revisited," *China Economic Journal,* 6(2–3): 80–102.

2014. "The Growth of 'Non-material Services' in China – Maddison's 'Zero-labor-productivity-growth' Hypothesis Revisited," *The Economic Review,* **65**(3).

2015. "Constructing China's Net Capital Stock and Measuring Capital Service in China," *RIETI Discussion Papers,* 15-E-006. See: www.rieti .go.jp/en/publications/summary/15010007.html.

Wu, Harry X. and Keiko Ito. 2015. "Reconstruction of China's National Output and Income Accounts and Supply–Use and Input–Output Accounts in Time Series," *RIETI Discussion Papers,* 15-E-004. See: www.rieti.go.jp/en/publications/summary/15010005.html.

Wu, Harry X. and Esther Y. P. Shea. 2008. "China: Institutions, Domestic Financial Architecture and Macro Volatility." In José M. Fanelli (ed.), *Macroeconomic Volatility, Institutions and Financial Architecture.* London: Palgrave Macmillan, 125–156.

Wu, Harry X. and Xianchun Xu. 2002. *"Measuring the Capital Stock in Chinese Industry – Conceptual Issues and Preliminary Results,"* Presented at the 27th General Conference of International Association for Research in Income and Wealth, Stockholm, Sweden.

Wu, Harry X. and Ximing Yue. 2003. *"Sources of Quality Change in the Labour Input of Chinese Industry, 1955–2000,"* Presented at Western Economic Association International Pacific Rim Conference, Taipei.

2010. *"Accounting for Labor Input in Chinese Industry,"* Presented at the 31st IARIW General Conference, St. Gallen, Switzerland.

2012. "Accounting for Labor Input in Chinese Industry, 1949–2009," *RIETI Discussion Papers,* 12-E-065.

Wu, Harry X., Ximing Yue, and George G. Zhang. 2015. "Constructing Employment and Compensation Matrices and Measuring Labor Input in China," *RIETI Discussion Papers,* 15-E-005. See: www.rieti.go.jp/e n/publications/summary/15010006.html.

Wu, Jinglian. 2008. *The Choice of China's Growth Model* (Zhongguo zengzhang moshi jueze). Shanghai: Yuandong Book Press.

    2013. "Towards a Proper Analytical Framework for Studying the Engine of China's Growth." In Boyuan Foundation (ed.), *China's Opportunities and Challenges in the Next Ten Years*. China Economy Press: 3–7.

Xu, Chenggang. 2011. "The Fundamental Institutions of China's Reforms and Development," *Journal of Economic Literature*, **49**(4): 1076–1151.

7 | Productivity growth in India under different policy regimes

DEB KUSUM DAS, ABDUL A. ERUMBAN,
SURESH AGGARWAL, AND SREERUPA
SENGUPTA

7.1 Introduction

Following the substantial liberal market reforms, the Indian economy
has been growing at a spectacular rate in the last decade and this
has attracted much attention in the literature (e.g. Bhagwati and
Panagariya 2013; Eichengreen *et al.* 2010; Panagariya 2008;
Bosworth and Collins 2008).[1] In 1991, when India started liberalizing
the economy, its size was only 3% of global gross domestic product
(GDP), while in 2013 it was almost double at 6% (The Conference
Board 2014), definitely suggesting a faster growth compared to most
other emerging economies, except China. The Indian economy grew
at an average annual rate of 7% since 1996 for a period of fifteen
years, with little deviation from the mean growth rate. Even when the
global economy was suffering from recession in 2008 and 2009, the
Indian economy grew at about 6–8%, although the rate of growth
slowed down significantly to an average of 5% after 2012.[2]

---

[1] This chapter is from a paper presented at the 3rd world KLEMS conference held
in Tokyo, Japan on May 16–17, 2014, organized by REITI (Japan). The authors
would like to thank REITI for travel and other support for Deb Kusum Das and
Suresh Aggarwal, and all conference participants especially Barbara Fraumeni
and Harry Wu for useful comments. Detailed comments by Marcel Timmer and
Dale Jorgenson on the first draft are also acknowledged. The authors thank
K. L. Krishna and B. N. Goldar for advisory support in discussions relating to the
construction of India KLEMS dataset. Financial support from Reserve Bank of
India in building the India KLEMS dataset is gratefully acknowledged. The usual
disclaimers apply.
[2] The recent set-backs, particularly after 2012, are sometimes attributed partly to
the global financial crisis (Mohan and Kapur 2015). However, multiple factors
played a substantial role in dragging down India's growth. These include both
internal and external factors including soaring inflation, increased fiscal and
current account deficit, and a weakening of Indian Rupee.

Concerns, however, have been raised about the underlying dynamics of the Indian growth process, in particular whether growth is trickling down to reduce poverty and inequality and whether fast growth can be sustained in the longer term. In particular the question of sustainability, which has been raised in the past in the context of East Asian economies as well, gains importance, as economic growth in emerging economies are often driven heavily by capital accumulation, which owing to diminishing returns would stall the long-term growth momentum. For instance, China has been able to maintain high growth rates by consistently high investment rates over the past decades but is already experiencing a slowdown in its economic growth (see for instance Dorrucci *et al.* 2013). For India, given its still unexploited demographic dividend and underdeveloped infrastructure, potential for investment-driven growth might still be existing, though productivity growth will remain the most important source for sustaining the return over capital in the longer term.

An important factor that is argued to play a significant role in enhancing productivity growth is appropriate policy atmosphere. Trade and investment liberalization are often considered to be major policy aspects in this context. Lowering of trade barriers could lead to increased productivity via increased import competition, better access to foreign technology, and improved managerial efficiency, innovation, and exploitation of economies of scale (Bernard *et al.* 2003; Melitz 2003). With the aim of improving its manufacturing competitiveness, Indian policy-makers initiated a number of trade and industrial policy reforms as part of the broader economic policy reforms since the mid-1980s. Studies that analyzed productivity performances in India's (organized) manufacturing suggest a positive impact of these policy reforms on productivity growth through directly impacting the sector and through inter-sectoral linkages with the overall economy (Das 2004; Balakrishnan *et al.* 2000; Krishna and Mitra 1998). However, these studies are mostly confined to the formal manufacturing sector, which constitutes only a minor part of the economy, particularly in terms of employment generation.[3]

---

[3] Kathuria *et al.* (2010) is an exception, which looks into the productivity performance of both organized and unorganized manufacturing, but for the provincial aggregate manufacturing.

This chapter takes a broader perspective on the empirical association between liberal market policy reforms and productivity. We analyze the productivity performance of the entire economy divided into twenty-six sub-sectors, using a recently developed KLEMS (capital, labor, energy, material, and services) database, and relate it to various liberal policy reforms that have been initiated in Indian economy during the last three decades. Previous studies, which are conducted using aggregate economy data, suggest relatively better productivity growth in the post-liberalization period (Bosworth and Maertens 2010; Bosworth and Collins 2008). Bosworth and Collins (2008) and Jorgenson and Vu (2005) suggest a total factor productivity (TFP) growth of above 2% in the 1990s through early 2000s. Taking account of a number of heterogeneities – both in terms of differences in factor inputs across assets and worker categories, as well as in industries – our results suggests a lower TFP of 1.2% for the aggregate economy during 1980–2011, without much deviation over the three decadal averages (1980s, 1990s, and 2000s). Excluding 1992 from the analysis, our study suggests 1.4% TFP growth during the 1990s, which is slightly higher than the other two decades.

Even though we do not find acceleration in aggregate economy productivity growth, this aggregate picture masks several industry dynamics. Our detailed industry analysis, which clearly documents the structural shift in the Indian economy, indeed suggests a positive impact of economic reforms on productivity growth in several industries, but it does not appear to be broad-based. In particular, our sectoral analysis suggests that the driver of aggregate productivity growth is the market services sector. We find both the agriculture and market services sectors have gained substantial productivity growth during the 1990s, whereas the manufacturing sector has weakened significantly.[4] The manufacturing sector – inclusive of formal and informal sectors – however, has regained its 1980s TFP growth rates in the 2000s. Nevertheless, even while improving its overall efficiency in using labor and capital, there is no substantial expansion in the manufacturing sector in terms of employment and investment, compared to the previous decades. This points to several hurdles,

---

[4] This weak performance of manufacturing in the 1990s has been acknowledged by several studies in the context of formal manufacturing (Goldar 2014; Trivedi *et al.* 2011; Kathuria *et al.* 2010). There is also limited evidence on the unorganized sector (Kathuria *et al.* 2010).

particularly in the formal sector, such as labor market rigidities, that hampers expansion of formal sector activities.

Market services had the most impressive TFP growth in the 2000s, being the main driver of India's economic growth. In general the market economy has been performing substantially better than the non-market economy, which reflects the impact of several pro-market reforms. This becomes particularly clear as this study distinguishes between market and non-market segments, in contrast to earlier studies such as Bosworth and Collins (2008) which only considered all services sectors together.[5] A breakdown of the services sector is of high importance given that public administration, education, and health do not follow the market principles, such that output and productivity is hard to measure and not particularly meaningful.

The rest of the chapter is organized as follows. Section 7.2 documents the economic growth and associated structural changes that have taken place in the Indian economy under different policy regimes. In Section 7.3 the data and methodology used for analyzing India's sources of growth are detailed. In Section 7.4, the empirical analysis of the sources of growth is provided with emphasis on the contributions of input versus productivity. Industry origins of aggregate productivity growth are also discussed. Section 7.5 presents results on sectoral productivity using a gross output production function approach, and an analysis of the pattern of productivity growth across industries. In Section 7.6, we provide a discussion on sectoral productivity dynamics under policy reforms, by comparing productivity growth in the 1990s and 2000s, and discuss some future policy perspectives. The final section concludes the study.

7.2 Economic growth and structural change: an overview

The first set of postcolonial economic policies in India was characterized by the "License and Permit Raj" with substantial emphasis on public

---

[5] Verma (2012), while analyzing India's service sector growth during 1980–2005, distinguishes between trade, transportation, and communication services; financial and business services; and community, social, and personal services. We analyze the services sector for a longer period, 1980–2011, at further disaggregation, considering nine sub-sectors, five of which are market service sectors (see Appendix Table 7.1).

Table 7.1 *Growth rates of GDP and labor productivity in the Indian economy – pre- and post-1980s*

Total economy	1951–1980	1981–2011	1981–1990	1992–1999	2000–2011
GDP	3.5	6.3	5.4	5.9	7.4
GDP per worker	1.8	3.4	2.1	3.7	4.4

Note: All growth rates are measured in log differences. Growth rates in GDP and labor productivity for 1980–2011 are based on weighted growth rates of sectoral employment and GDP.
Source: 1950 to 1980 are from the Conference Board Total Economy Database (2014); all others are author's calculation using India KLEMS data.

sector investment.[6] Import substitution, control on the private sector and large domestic firms, resistance to foreign direct investment, technology transfer, and interventions in factor markets were notable features of these policies. Arguably, these strict policy measures led to a stifling of market forces, resulting in a low rate of economic growth. In Table 7.1, we provide the average growth rates of GDP and labor productivity in India since 1950.[7] The Indian economy grew at an annual average rate of around 3.5 percent (also known as the "Hindu rate" of growth, a term to rationalize the sluggish economic growth) during 1950–1980 period.

The process of reforms continued during the 1980s, during which a mix of industry-specific and more generic policies aimed to reduce the license barriers and to ease restrictions on imports were introduced.[8] However, the tariff rates remained by and large high. GDP growth has increased in the post-1980 period from the "Hindu rate" of about 3.5% during 1950–1980 to 6.3% during 1980–2011, with 1980–1990 period registering an average growth of 5.4% per annum. Indeed, there has

[6] The elaborate system of licenses, regulations, and accompanying red-tapes required to set up and run businesses in India between 1947 and the 1990s is often called "License Raj."

[7] Indian economic statistics are generally available for a financial year, starting from April 1 to March 31. For instance data for 1980–1981 refers to the period of April 1, 1980 to March 31, 1981. Since it covers three quarters from the first year and one quarter from the second year, for ease of use throughout this chapter, we refer to the first three quarters. I.e. 1980–1981 is generally referred to as 1980.

[8] See Panagariya (2008) and Bhagwati and Panagariya (2013) for discussions on various policy reforms in India.

been a marked increase in both GDP and labor productivity growth in the post-1980 period compared to the previous period. However, the growth acceleration could not be sustained, and the economy witnessed a serious balance of payment crisis in the early 1990s. It is often argued that the policy reforms in the 1980s were pro-business supporting the incumbent firms rather than pro-market or pro-liberalization, thus limiting the entry of new firms to encourage healthy competition (Rodrik and Subramanian 2005).

However, as argued by Srinivasan and Tendulkar (2003), they did help change the political perspective on liberalization, which made it easier for the government to introduce widespread liberalization policies in the aftermath of the balance of payments crisis. In 1991, India introduced substantial structural reforms, characterized by the increased role attributed to the private sector, massive delicensing, easing of quantitative controls, and increased integration with the global market.[9] However, the growth performance of the Indian economy in the first decade after did not show any sharp upward trend, being 5.9% during 1992–2000, compared to 5.4% during 1980–1990.[10] The economy grew at 7.4% during 2000–2011 period. As is clear from Table 7.1, labor productivity growth acceleration had already started in the 1980s, it gained further momentum in the 1990s, and increased substantially in the 2000s, owing to the liberal market reforms in the early 1990s (Balakrishnan and Parameswaran 2007; Rodrik and Subramaniam 2005).

While there is a reasonable degree of agreement on growth acceleration in the 1980s there exist divergent views on what caused this growth turnaround. While Rodrik and Subramanian (2005) attribute growth acceleration in the 1980s to manufacturing sector productivity gain, Balakrishnan and Parameswaran (2007) and Bosworth *et al.* (2007) also assign a substantial role to the reallocation of resources from low productive sectors like agriculture to high productive sectors

---

[9] Both the level and dispersion of tariffs were lowered and tariff rates were reduced across the board. The peak rate of customs duty was lowered to around 65% from over 200%. The non-tariff barriers in the form of quantitative restrictions (QR) on intermediate and capital goods import were completely withdrawn. Moreover, the economy has moved from a fixed and overvalued exchange rate to a market-determined flexible exchange rate (see Das 2004).

[10] We exclude 1991 while averaging productivity and output growth in the 1990s throughout this chapter, because it was a year of extreme turbulence in the Indian economy due to severe external imbalances and the consequent balance of payments crisis.

like manufacturing and services. A recent study by De Vries *et al.*
(2012) also signifies the important role of structural change in the
Indian economy both in the 1980s and in 1990s.

In Table 7.2 we provide the sectoral composition of the Indian economy in order to see how economic structure has been evolving over time.
The table shows that the value added share of the agriculture, hunting,
and fishing sector has declined steadily from 35.6% in 1980 to 17.5% in
2011. This decline, however, is not mirrored by an increase in the
manufacturing share, which declined from 17.4% to 14.4%. Within
manufacturing we distinguish between labor intensive and non-labor
intensive segments (See Appendix Table 7.1 for the sector classifications). As is evident from the table, the GDP share of the most labor-
intensive sectors has declined rapidly, while that of others increased only
marginally. Thus manufacturing did not absorb the release of agricultural labor. Sen and Das (2014) attributes this decline in labor intensive
manufacturing to increasing substitution of labor by capital, facilitated
by reforms in capital goods and falling import tariffs on capital goods.
Yet another possibility is that the rigid labor market regulations provided fewer or no incentives for formal firms to create more jobs.[11]
The value added share of non-manufacturing industries, which includes
utilities (electricity, gas, and water supply), mining, and construction,
has increased from 7.9% in 1980 to 12.4% in 2011.

The most important feature of structural transformation in the
Indian economy is the emergence of the service sector, which makes
India defy the conventional structural change hypothesis of moving
from primary to secondary and then to services (Erumban *et al.* 2012).
The service sector remains the single largest contributor to value added
in the post-1980 period. The share of the service sector increased
rapidly from 39.1% in 1980 to 55.7% in 2011, with greater acceleration since 1990 being observed in market services share in value
added.[12] The distinction of market and non-market services is of high

---

[11] See Moreno-Monroy *et al.* (2014), for an analysis of increasing outsourcing of
formal sector activities to informal sector in order to avoid many rigidities in the
formal labor market.

[12] Market services includes trade, transport services, financial services, post and
telecommunications, and hotels and restaurants. Ideally it should also include
business services, which is a fast-growing segment in the Indian economy.
However, it was almost impossible to split this sector from other services for
investment data – an essential variable in our productivity analysis – making us
keep it under "other services."

Table 7.2 *Gross value added and employment shares in GDP,*
1980–2011 (%)

Sector	Value added				Employment			
	1980	1990	2000	2011	1980	1990	2000	2011
Agriculture	35.6	29.4	23.0	17.6	69.8	64.7	59.8	48.1
Industry	25.3	26.6	26.0	26.8	13.2	15.2	16.5	22.7
Manufacturing	17.4	16.4	15.3	14.4	10.4	10.7	11.1	11.4
High labor intensive	10.2	7.5	7.1	5.3	8.5	8.4	8.3	8.3
Medium labor intensive	4.2	5.2	4.2	4.5	1.2	1.4	1.7	1.9
Low labor intensive	3.0	3.7	4.0	4.6	0.8	0.9	1.0	1.1
Non-manufacturing	7.9	10.3	10.7	12.4	2.8	4.5	5.4	11.3
Services	39.1	44.0	51.0	55.7	16.9	20.0	23.7	29.2
Market services	18.6	22.6	27.6	30.9	8.9	11.5	14.6	16.8
Non-market services	20.4	21.4	23.4	24.7	8.0	8.5	9.1	12.4

Note: Agriculture is inclusive of hunting and fishing activities.
Source: Authors calculations using India KLEMS database.

significance, as most reforms were oriented towards the development of a solid private market sector in Indian economy.

The observed high value added share of the service sector, however, does not appear to have translated into an increasing employment generation of similar magnitude. The primary sector remains the leading contributor to employment in all three decades, although its share has declined steadily over time by about 20 percentage points from 69.8% in 1980 to about 48.1% in 2011. The employment share of the manufacturing sector has been rather stagnant over the years, whereas there is a sharp rise in the employment share in non-manufacturing industries in the 2000s due to large employment generation in the construction sector. Services, on the other hand, see an employment gain of 12%, while its output share increased by 17%.

The increasing share of services in GDP has clear implications for its role in driving growth in the Indian economy, and several studies have attributed economic growth in India to the service sector (Eichengreen and Gupta 2009; Gorden and Gupta 2003 among others). The declining share of manufacturing, and the increasing role of the service sector in the Indian economy, however, raises the question of what is the impact of economic reforms, which were primarily aimed at increasing efficiency and competitiveness of the manufacturing sector, on boosting productivity and economic growth? Many studies assert that for a developing country like India, it is important to maintain a high manufacturing growth without which the pace of growth of the service sector cannot be sustained (Rodrik 2013; Panagariya 2008; Acharya *et al.* 2003). Except for a few countries with abundant natural resources, almost all countries that sustained high growth did so with the help of the manufacturing sector (Rodrik 2013). This chapter is the first to deal with this issue in a satisfactory way by providing detailed, industry-level data, and as such makes an important contribution to the discussion of Indian economic growth policies.

7.3 Data and methodology

7.3.1 Methodology

In order to analyze sources of India's economic growth, this chapter uses the standard growth accounting approach as outlined in Jorgenson *et al.* (1987, 2005). We decompose total output growth into the contributions from growth rates of primary inputs (capital and labor) and TFP growth as:

$$\Delta ln Y_t = \Delta ln A_t + \overline{v}_{K,t} \Delta ln K_t + \overline{v}_{L,t} \Delta ln L_t \tag{1}$$

where Y is the real output, measured by value added, K is the capital input, L is the labor input, $\overline{v}_{K,t}$ is the compensation share of capital in value added averaged across current and previous period, and $\overline{v}_{L,t}$ is the compensation share of labor. Under constant returns to scale the income shares of labor and capital sum to unity. A is the measure of TFP.

Equation (1) has been widely used in the literature, including in studies on productivity in the Indian economy (Bosworth and Collins 2008). In several previous studies in the Indian context, K is represented by capital stock measured using standard perpetual inventory method (PIM) often not even allowing for depreciation of older vintages, and L is measured by number of employees. We, however, differ from these in terms of the treatment of factor inputs K and L, and consequently the measured TFP growth. Following the theoretical arguments (Jorgenson 1963), and international practices (see for instance Timmer *et al.* 2010; OECD 2001), in this chapter aggregate capital and labor inputs are measured as the flow of services from these inputs to the production process. Since aggregate capital and aggregate labor inputs consist of different types of capital assets (e.g. machinery, computers, buildings etc.) and labor types (low skilled, high skilled etc.), it is important to account for the possible heterogeneity while measuring these inputs, as their marginal productivities may differ. In order to take account of asset heterogeneity of capital and skill heterogeneity of labor, we distinguish between five types of labor and three types of capital assets (see section 7.3.2 on data). Our approach to measuring capital and labor input will be discussed in detail subsequently.

Equation (1) is a value added function, which is appropriate for measuring productivity for the aggregate economy. We also measure productivity at detailed sectoral level, for which a more appropriate approach would be to use a gross output function (Jorgenson *et al.* 1987). As in equation (1) we can decompose the growth rate of gross output into L, K and TFP, but also to the contributions of intermediate inputs, energy (E), material (M), and services (S):

$$\Delta lnQ_{j,t} = \Delta lnA_{j,t}^* + \overline{v}_{K,j,t}^* \Delta lnK_{j,t} + \overline{v}_{L,j,t}^* \Delta lnL_{j,t} + \overline{v}_{E,j,t}^* \Delta lnE_{j,t}$$
$$+ \overline{v}_{M,j,t}^* \Delta lnM_{j,t} + \overline{v}_{S,j,t}^* \Delta lnS_{j,t} \tag{2}$$

where Q is the real gross output, $\overline{v}_{X,t}^*$ is the compensation share of input x (capital, labor, energy, material, and services) in nominal gross output averaged across current and previous period – all for any given industry j. As before, under constant returns to scale the income shares of all inputs sums to unity. A^* is the measure of TFP based on gross output function, which is different from, but related to A in equation (1). Hulten (1978) shows that there is an accounting relationship between A and A^* such that A is the product of A^* and the ratio of gross output to gross value added. This relationship can be expressed to obtain A^* from A as:

$$\Delta lnA_{j,t}^* = \frac{VA}{GO} * \Delta lnA_t \tag{3}$$

While A, which is indicative of improvements in the productivity of factor inputs, labor and capital, is more interesting from an aggregate economy and welfare perspective, A^*, which accounts for the efficiency of all inputs, is important from a technological change point of view. Therefore, in our industry growth accounting analysis we focus on A^* and in our aggregate analysis we use A.

7.3.2 Data and variables

The data used in the empirical analysis of this study is from the India KLEMS data compiled from various sources, and cover the period 1980–2011. Though the primary source of India KLEMS data is the National Accounts Statistics (NAS), published annually by the Central Statistical Organization (CSO), various other sources have been used to construct variables that are not often available in national accounts. This includes input–output (IO) tables, and various rounds of National Sample Survey Organizations (NSSO) surveys on employment and unemployment. Our analysis requires industry-wide data on nominal and real value added, investment by asset type, number of workers and labor compensation by type of worker, and intermediate inputs.[13] In what follows we discuss these sources more specifically with regard to each of the variables used in our analysis.

Gross output (GO): National Accounts provides data on gross output in agriculture, hunting, forestry and fishing, mining and quarrying, construction, and fourteen manufacturing sectors at current and constant prices. However, NAS does not provide gross output series for other sectors in our twenty-six industry classification. Moreover, the manufacturing sectors available in NAS classification were not fully consistent with our KLEMS classification. Therefore, to estimate output in our KLEMS sectors, additional information is used from Annual Survey of Industries (ASI) for registered manufacturing sectors, NSSO quinquennial surveys for unregistered manufacturing sectors, and input–output transaction tables for the service sectors. For seven manufacturing industries, for which the sectoral data is not available from NAS, the output data for a higher level aggregation from NAS is split using output distribution from ASI and NSSO rounds to arrive at desired KLEMS sector estimate.[14] We aggregate registered and unregistered manufacturing data to obtain KLEMS consistent total manufacturing sector.

---

[13] See Appendix Table 7.1 for a list of twenty-six industries in the India KLEMS database (also see Table 7.4).

[14] These sectors are wood and wood products, coke refined petroleum and nuclear fuel, rubber and plastic products, basic metals and fabricated metal products, machinery not elsewhere classified, electrical and optical equipment, and other manufacturing.

For service sectors, except public administration and defense, and electricity, gas, and water supply, output estimates are constructed using information from IO tables.[15] We take the benchmark year gross output to value added ratio for the relevant sector from IO tables for years 1978–1979, 1983–1984, 1989–1990, 1993–1994, 1998–1999, 2003–2004, and 2007–2008. These ratios are linearly interpolated for intervening years and applied to the gross value added series obtained from national accounts to derive the output estimates consistent with NAS at current prices.

For constant price series, the NAS estimates are directly used wherever the sector classification matches the KLEMS classifications. For the seven KLEMS manufacturing industries where direct NAS estimates are not available, the nominal estimates constructed are deflated with suitable wholesale price deflators. For services sectors and utilities, for which the wholesale price deflators are not available, the nominal estimates are deflated with implicit value added deflators from NAS to arrive at constant price series.

Intermediate inputs: Time series of intermediate inputs, energy, material, and services, are constructed using the methodology developed by Jorgenson *et al.* (1987) and extended by Jorgenson (1990). This approach involves extensive use of IO tables from where we can obtain the flows of all commodities in the economy (Jorgenson *et al.* 2005; Timmer *et al.* 2010). For constructing the current price series, proportions of energy, material, and service inputs in total intermediate inputs are calculated from the benchmark IO tables for years mentioned before, and for intervening years these are linearly interpolated. This interpolation involves an implicit assumption that for each IO sector input–output coefficients change progressively between the benchmark years. For years after 2007, the last IO table, a similar assumption is made; we assume that the input–output coefficients vary at a similar rate as in between 2003 and 2007. In order to ensure consistency of final estimates with published National Accounts series, the projected input vector has been proportionately adjusted to match the gap between gross output and value added of NAS sectors.

---

[15] Public administration and defense is a special case where no intermediate inputs are given in IO tables. In this case, we use value added to output ratio from System of National Accounts tables, available from the CSO.

For constructing the constant price series, the nominal values of intermediate inputs are deflated using weighted intermediate input deflators, constructed for each of the three inputs – energy, material, and services.[16] For any given intermediate input (energy, material, or services), the intermediate input price for any industry is obtained as the weighted sum of wholesale prices of each commodity used by that industry, with the weights being the share of these commodities in the total basket of the intermediate inputs. For instance, the intermediate price deflator for energy input in the agricultural sector is the weighted sum of wholesale prices of all energy inputs (e.g. electricity, gas) used by the agricultural sector, with weights being the share of each of these inputs in total energy consumed by this sector. These weights are obtained from IO tables and the wholesale prices are obtained from the Ministry of Commerce and Industry, Government of India.

Gross value added (GVA): NAS provides estimates of GVA by industries at both current and constant prices since 1950. We use the GDP data since 1980 from the most recent National Accounts series which is based on 2004–2005 prices. GDP estimates are adjusted for Financial Intermediation Services Indirectly Measured (FISIM). The value of such services forms a part of the income originating in the banking and insurance sector and, as such, is deducted from the GVA. The KLEMS sectors for which value added are directly taken from NAS are the agriculture sectors, mining, electricity, construction, manufacturing, and the service sectors. For manufacturing sectors, registered and unregistered segments from NAS are added. As in the case of output, for sectors where no KLEMS industry classification was available, we use additional information from ASI and NSSO to arrive at desired KLEMS sector estimates. The estimates of real value added for each industry are arrived at by subtracting real intermediate input from real gross output, i.e. using a double deflation approach.

Employment and labor composition: National Accounts does not provide data on employment. Therefore, we rely on Employment and Unemployment Surveys (EUS) published by NSSO every five years.

---

[16] This approach is similar to Balakrishnan and Pushpangadan (1994), who were the first to use a double deflated value added function to estimate productivity growth in India's organized manufacturing sector.

EUS provides estimates of work participation rates by sectors classified on the basis of National Industrial Classification (NIC), which are used to derive number of employees in each sector using population estimates from various population censuses. However, EUS provides more than one definition of employment based on activity status, which are usual principal status (UPS), usual principal and subsidiary status (UPSS), current weekly status (CWS), and current daily status (CDS). Since UPSS is the most liberal and widely used of these concepts, we estimate the number of employed persons using UPSS definition (Aggarwal 2004).[17]

We obtain numbers of all persons employed including self-employed in each industry, using UPSS assumption from the EUS. However, our measure of labor input also takes account of worker heterogeneity in terms of educational attainment and therefore, following Jorgenson *et al.* (1987) we define labor input in any industry j (Lj) as a Tornqvist volume index of workers by individual labor types '*l*' categorized on the basis of educational attainment:

$$\Delta \ln L_j = \sum_1^5 \overline{v}_{l,j}^L \Delta \ln L_{l,j} \tag{4}$$

We use five education categories (l=5 in the above equation) namely: up to primary, primary, middle, secondary and higher secondary, and above higher secondary. The weights $\overline{v}_{l,j}^L$ are obtained as the compensation share of worker category *l* in total wage bill of industry j, averaged through current and previous year i.e.

$$\overline{v}_{l,j}^L = \frac{P_{l,j}^L L_{l,j}}{\sum_l^5 P_{l,j}^L L_{l,j}} \tag{5}$$

The EUS also provides statistics on compensation received by regular and casual workers in each industry, and can be directly used. However, it does not provide any information on wages of self-employed. To obtain a complete picture of wage composition, we supplement the

---

[17] However, UPSS definition suffers from limitations such as: (1) it seeks to place as many persons as possible under the category of employed by assigning priority to work; (2) there is no single long-term activity status for many as they move between statuses over a long period of one year; and (3) it requires a recall over a whole year of what the person did, which is not easy for those who take whatever work opportunities they can find over the year or have prolonged spells out of the labor force.

wage data directly obtained from EUS for casual and regular workers by econometrically estimated self-employed compensation (see Aggarwal and Erumban 2013).

Note that equation (4) can be decomposed into pure employment growth, measured by the growth rate of aggregate employment (sum of all workers, disregarding their skill differences), say $\Delta \ln H = \Delta \ln \sum_l L_l$ and a labor composition effect $\Delta \ln LC$. If the proportion of highly educated workers is increasing, the later component will be positive, suggesting an improving quality of work force. Thus, subtracting $\Delta \ln H$, the growth rate of aggregate employment from (4), we obtain the labor composition growth rates. In our growth accounting equations (1) and (2) we divide our labor input L, into the contributions of pure labor quantity, $\Delta \ln H$ and that of labor composition $\Delta \ln LC$.

Capital services: As in the case of labor input we measure capital input in any given sector j (K_j) as a Tornqvist volume index of individual capital assets as follows:

$$\Delta ln K_j = \sum_k \bar{v}_{k,j}^K \Delta ln K_{k,j} \tag{6}$$

where $\Delta ln K_j$ is the growth rate of aggregate capital services in any given industry j, $\Delta ln K_{k,j}$ is the growth rate of capital stock in asset k (we distinguish between three types of capital assets: construction, machinery, and transport equipment) and the weights $\bar{v}_{k,j}^K$ are given by the period average shares of each type of asset in the total value of capital compensation, such that the sum of shares over all capital types adds to unity. The asset shares in total capital compensation are calculated as:

$$v_{k,j}^K = \frac{P_{k,j}^K K_{k,j}}{\sum_k P_{k,j}^K K_{k,j}} \tag{7}$$

where individual capital stocks K_K are estimated using standard perpetual inventory method (PIM) with geometric depreciation rates:

$$K_{k,j,t} = K_{k,j,t-1}(1 - \delta_k) + I_{k,j,t} \tag{8}$$

and the rental prices of capital $p_{k,j}^K$ are computed as

$$P_{k,j,t}^K = P_{k,tj,-1}^I i_t^* + \delta_k P_{k,j,t}^I \tag{9}$$

where p_k^I is the investment price of asset k, i^* is real external rate of return and δ_k is the assumed geometric depreciation rate of asset k.[18] We assume a depreciation rate of 2.5% for construction, 8% for machinery, and 10% for transport equipment, based on a double declining balance rate derived using the average lifetimes of these assets used in the National Accounts. We measure the real external rate of return, i^* by a long-run average of real bond rate and market interest rate, obtained from Reserve Bank of India. Nominal investment and investment deflators by asset type (I_k) and industries are obtained from National Accounts, and therefore are consistent with our measure of output and value added.

As in the case of labor, one can also add up the capital stock measured in (8) across assets to obtain the growth rate of aggregate capital stock (K^s) in any given industry j as:

$$\Delta ln K_j^s = \Delta ln \sum K_{k,j} \tag{10}$$

The difference between (6), the growth rate of capital services, and (10), the growth rate of capital stock, reflects the compositional changes in the capital stock. This composition effect will be positive if the share of fast depreciating assets such as information and communication technology increases compared to slow depreciating assets such as buildings.

Labor Income: For empirically evaluating the relative roles of factor inputs and productivity in driving growth using growth accounting approach (equations 1 and 2) we also need the nominal compensation shares of factor inputs in value added and output. There are no published data on factor income in Indian economy at a detailed disaggregate level. The NAS publishes the net domestic product (NDP) series comprising of compensation of employees (CE), operating surplus (OS), and mixed income (MI) for the NAS sectors. However, this series does not separate the income of the self-employed persons, rather it is included in the mixed income (MI) category, which also includes

---

[18] In the present version of the India-KLEMS database, we use an external rate of return. However, one can also use an internal rate of return, which will ensure consistency with NAS (see Jorgenson and Vu 2005). Oulton (2007) suggests a hybrid approach, where both external and internal rates are used in the measurement of capital services and productivity. See Erumban (2008) for a discussion on the empirical implications of alternative approaches to the measurement of rental prices.

a capital component of the income. Therefore, to compute the labor incomes, one has to take the sum of the compensation of employees and the part of the mixed income that is wages for labor.

We delineate the self-employed income component from mixed income as: $CS_{j,t}^* = \eta_j MI_{j,t}$, where $CS_{j,t}^*$ is the estimated self-employed income, MI is the mixed income in industry j in year t obtained from National Accounts, and η_j is the fraction of mixed income attributed to self-employed workers. η_j, which is assumed to be a fixed parameter for each industry, is obtained as an average of two alternate measures of self-employed to mixed income ratio.

In the first case, the wages of the self-employed are estimated using a Mincer equation with Heckman two step regression procedure (see Aggarwal and Erumban 2013). Wages for regular and casual workers are regressed on workers' properties in terms of gender, age, education, location, socio-economic group, marital status, and industry dummies – all obtained from employment surveys. The estimated coefficients are applied to worker properties of self-employed, in order to estimate self-employed labor compensation. We estimate income of self-employed workers for each industry for six benchmark years of employment and unemployment surveys (i.e. t = 1983–1984, 1987–1988, 1993–1994, 1999–2000, 2004–2005, and 2009–2010). The ratio of thus obtained self-employed income to the NAS estimates of mixed income is considered as the first estimate of self-employed to mixed income ratio ($\eta 1_{j,t}$) in industry j. In other words, in this case, self-employed income is a direct estimate from NSSO employment surveys, based on income of regular and casual workers.

In the second approach, the proportion of self-employed income to mixed income is computed as: $\eta 2_{j,t} = \frac{CE_{j,t} \cdot j,t}{MI_{j,t}}$, where CE is the compensation of employees from national accounts, θ is the ratio of estimated labor income of self-employed (CS^* in approach 1) and the labor income of regular and casual workers (CR) also from employment surveys ($_{j,t} = CS_{j,t}^*/CR_{j,t},$). The numerator $CE\,\theta$ provides self-employed income consistent with NAS. However, in this case, it is possible that the estimated $\eta 2_j$ exceeds one, in which case, we assumed it to be unity.[19]

---

[19] This has been the case for industries mining (in 2004–2005), electricity, gas, and water supply (in 1993–1994 and 2004–2005), and construction (in 1983–1984, 1987–1988, 1993–1994, and 1999–2000).

Finally, η_j is obtained as an average of $\eta1_{j,t}$ and $\eta2_{j,t}$, over the five benchmark years for which employment surveys are available. For industries for which estimates of CE and MI are available directly from NAS, η_j has been computed and applied directly.[20] For the remaining industries, the ratio of the higher industry aggregate has been applied.

Income shares of capital and intermediate inputs: Following constant returns to scale assumption, the capital income share in value added is obtained as a residual: it is defined as one minus labor income over gross value added (GDP). Shares of intermediate inputs in gross output are directly obtained from their nominal cost divided by nominal gross output, and again the residual after adjusting for intermediate and labor shares in gross output, we obtain capital income share in gross output.

7.4 Sources of economic growth: results

7.4.1 Productivity growth in major sectors of the economy

Using equation (1) we decompose the growth rate of GDP into contribution of capital services (capital stock and capital composition), labor input (employment and labor composition), and TFP growth. In Figure 7.1 we depict GDP growth along with input and productivity contributions in agriculture, manufacturing, and market services sectors of the economy in the 1980s, 1990s, and 2000s.[21] The overall economy-wide productivity shows a moderate increase in the 1990s compared to the 1980s. However, aggregate productivity growth fell marginally from 1.4% during 1992–1999 to 1.2% during 2001–2011, thus being back to the rate at which it grew during 1981–1990. The stagnant productivity growth even while the economy is growing faster suggests a decline in the relative share of TFP growth in aggregate

---

[20] These are industries agriculture, mining and quarrying, total manufacturing (but not by sub-sectors), electricity, construction, trade, hotels and restaurants, transport and storage, communication, financial services, public administration, and all other services (available separately for real estate and business services, ownership of dwelling, social and personal services, and other services).

[21] Results for non-manufacturing industries and non-market services are not discussed here, but are available in the detailed industry results section.

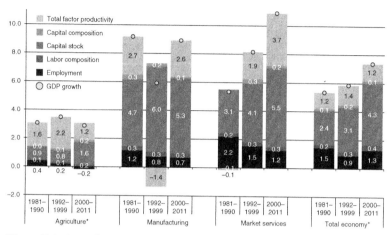

Figure 7.1 Contribution of factor inputs and total factor productivity growth to GDP growth, 1980–2011

growth. Whereas TFP growth contributed 22% of output growth (1.2 percentage points out of 5.4%) during 1981–1990, and 24% (1.4 out of 5.9%) during 1992–1999, it declined by almost 8% to 16% (1.2 out of 7.4%) during 2000–2011. In the subsequent analysis we will see this decline has been largely driven by the non-market economy. Almost 45% to 60% of output growth during the entire period of analysis has been due to capital, whereas the contribution of workers (excluding the contribution of labor quality) declined from 27% in the 1980s to 16% in the 1990s and increased only marginally to 18% during the 2000s.

Productivity growth in agriculture: TFP growth appears to be an important driver of output growth in the agricultural sector throughout the period. The 1980s was a period of a widespread green revolution in Indian agriculture across different crops, which is often argued to have impacted agricultural growth positively (Binswanger-Mkhize 2013).[22] Our results suggest that more than half of the output growth in the 1980s was due to productivity gain in the sector, whereas one-third of the growth was due to increased capital services (sum of capital

---

[22] Indeed the green revolution in the 1980s also helped to improve the rural income and create a market for non-agricultural products and services which might also have helped growth in other sectors in the 1980s.

stock and capital composition). In the 1990s, almost 65% of total value added growth is due to increased TFP, which grew at 2.2% per annum. Certainly, the surge in TFP growth from 1.6% in the 1980s to 2.2% has been clearly the source of acceleration in value added growth, while the contribution from capital services has remained the same at 0.9 percentage point. However, capital services increased its contribution substantially during the 2000s, while that of TFP growth declined. The increased contribution of capital in the agricultural sector is, perhaps, due to increased mechanization of the sector. This is also evident from the declining contribution of employment, even dragging output growth down during the 2000s with a contraction in employment. However, the labor composition contribution has been increasing, though marginally, over time.

The observed acceleration in agricultural productivity growth in the 1990s, however, seems to defy previous findings. A strict comparison of our results with previous studies is less feasible due to both methodological differences and the time period covered by previous studies. However, we provide a broad comparison for the 1980s, 1990s, and 2000s using select studies on sectoral productivity in Indian economy. Fuglie (2012) reports TFP growth of 2% during 1981–1990 in agriculture, which declined by almost half a percentage point during 1991–2000. Our estimate for the 1980s is lower by 0.4 percentage points at 1.6%, and moreover, it suggests an increase during 1992–1999. This opposing trend is driven by the fact that we exclude 1991 from our analysis of the 1990s (see footnote 10). Therefore, for comparison purposes we recalculated the average TFP growth using our data for comparison.[23] In 1991, agricultural TFP growth fell by – 3.2%, and if we include it in our estimates, our TFP growth estimates for the 1990s will be 1.2%, which is 0.6 percentage point lower than the TFP growth in the 1980s. Our estimates for 2000–2007 is 1.5% compared to their estimate of 1.9%, both suggesting an increase over the 1990s, whereas in the post-2007 years TFP growth has fallen, thus causing our estimate for the entire 2000s decade to decline. Thus the trends in our results are comparable to that of Fuglie (2012), though the growth rates are lower.

Bosworth and Collins (2008) also see a decline in productivity growth from 1.0% during 1978–1993 to 0.5% during 1993–2004,

---

[23] This has been done for all studies compared in subsequent sections.

which is a trend that is consistent with our results, as well for the same period (a decline from 1.4% to 0.9%).[24] However, our estimate is higher by 0.4 percentage point in both periods. Bosworth and Maertens (2010) report a productivity growth of 1.9% compared to 1.6% in our estimate, in the 1980s, which declines drastically to 0.7% during the 1990s, which is again primarily due to a massive decline in 1992. Our estimate also suggests a decline in the 1990s (if the same period is considered), but not to the same magnitude. This clearly suggests that the agricultural productivity decline in the 1990s, reported by previous studies, is primarily driven by the sharp decline in 1991, a year of severe economic imbalances in Indian economy.

Productivity growth in manufacturing: While the agricultural sector registered the highest growth in the 1990s, the golden period of India's *manufacturing* seems to be the 1980s, during which it registered nearly 10% growth rate with about 30% coming from increased TFP growth. Nevertheless, capital remains the single largest contributor to growth in manufacturing throughout the period. Its contribution averaged around 73%, varying from 55% (5 out of 9.2 percentage points) in the 1980s to more than 100% (6.2 out of 5.9 percentage points) in the 1990s, though declined to about 60% in the 2000s (Figure 7.1).

TFP growth has been substantial in driving manufacturing growth in the 1980s, with 2.7% of TFP growth.[25] However the 1990s, the period of massive liberalization focusing on manufacturing, has seen a deceleration in TFP growth, registering −1.4%, being the primary cause of a declining value added growth. During this period, contribution of capital services increased while that of labor composition remained the same as in the previous period. Even though employment contribution declined, the main source of growth deceleration was the deceleration in TFP growth. A turnaround in productivity is seen in the 2000s, arguably suggesting the lagged effect of substantial liberal

---

[24] As in Bosworth and Collins (2008), we also include land as part of our capital input in agricultural sector, though we do not present its contribution separately. Bosworth and Collins (2008) have shown that the role of land, however, is negligible in explaining aggregate growth.

[25] Ahluwalia (1991) has argued that there has been a turnaround in productivity growth in the organized manufacturing sector in the mid-1980s, owing to the economic policies of the 1980s. Such conclusions, however, are often contested on methodological grounds (Hulten and Srinivasan 1999; Balakrishnan and Pushpangadan 1994).

market reforms in the 1990s, registering 2.6% (almost 30% of total value added growth). The contribution of employment growth has declined in the 1990s, and remained at about 0.7 percentage point in the 2000s, while labor quality maintained a contribution of 0.3 percentage point.

This sluggish productivity performance in the Indian manufacturing sector in the 1990s is largely confirmed by previous studies that looked at the productivity growth in the registered manufacturing (Goldar 2004; Kathuria *et al.* 2010). There is hardly any study that looks into the manufacturing sector as a whole which makes a strict comparison of our results less possible. A recent study by Kathuria *et al.* (2010), which looks into the productivity performance of both organized and unorganized manufacturing, suggests a large and increasing gap in TFP growth between the two segments, with the unorganized productivity growth being substantially lower than the organized.[26] Clearly the productivity differences between organized and unorganized sector reflects in the aggregate manufacturing productivity. They also confirm a negative productivity growth in the manufacturing sector – both in organized and unorganized – in the 1990s, which is in conformity with our finding. A weighted average of their registered and unregistered manufacturing results, using relative shares of value added, suggests a negative TFP growth in the 1990s, which is close to our estimate of –1.4%. However, if we stick to their periodization, our results are even worse, at about –2% for 1994–2001 period. For the 2000s, our results are quite impressive for the entire 2000–2011 period, and for 2000–2007 it is just 0.5% compared to almost –4% in their estimates.

Even after several improvements in data and measurement, our results confirm that manufacturing – inclusive of formal and informal – has not performed well in the 1990s in terms of productivity growth. Clearly the sector has been pursuing a capital intensive growth path, accompanied by considerable productivity growth in the 1980s, while

---

[26] Their results suggest that the unorganized sector TFP growth has been negative and 4% lower than the organized sector during 1994–2001, while it deteriorated further to 19% lower than formal productivity growth during 2001–2005.
A strict comparison of our results with Kathuria *et al.* (2010) is not feasible, as they provide a simple average of regional manufacturing TFP growth by registered and unregistered separately. What we compare here is an average of the registered and unregistered regional averages, to obtain a comparable national TFP growth, which is what we are interested in.

the 1990s was a period of productivity slow down. Both investment growth and job creation has declined in the 2000s, whereas the sector's overall efficiency in using these resources has improved, even though output growth has not surpassed its performance in the 1980s. Certainly, the sector needs further boost for rapid expansion both in terms of employment and output. Nevertheless, it is worth mentioning that the policies in the 1980s and 1990s seem to have paid off in terms of productivity gain in the sector, though after a time lag.

Productivity in services: While the 1990s was a period of productivity slowdown in manufacturing, interestingly it has been a period of rapid productivity growth in the market services sector. TFP grew at an annual average rate of 1.9% during 1992–1999, as compared to a decline at –0.1% during the previous decade. The contribution of capital services also increased substantially, while that of employment declined. Thus, clearly the increased service sector growth in India in the 1990s can be largely attributed to productivity growth (also see Verma 2012) and capital accumulation. Market service sector productivity growth continued to be high and positive in the 2000s, and it grew at a much faster rate compared to the 1990s. It registered a 3.7 average TFP growth during 2000–2011, which is higher than the TFP growth in manufacturing and agriculture. Contribution of capital to output growth also increased during this period, while that of employment declined marginally and that of labor composition remained the same. The growth acceleration in the Indian economy is therefore largely due to accelerated productivity and capital accumulation in the market service sector, while the manufacturing sector still needs to raise the speed at which it grows.

A broad comparison of our results with those of Bosworth and Collins (2008), which is one of the very few studies that looks into productivity growth in the entire economy, suggests the trend in our results are quite comparable for the service sector. They report a TFP growth of 1.4% during 1978–1993, whereas our estimate for the entire services economy (including market and non-market segments) suggests 1.1% productivity growth during the same period, which in our case increased to 2.4% during 1993–2004, whereas their estimate increased to 3.9%. Indeed, both suggest acceleration in productivity growth in the 1990s, though the acceleration in our estimates for the entire service sector is much less.

A major part of the differences between our results and previous studies can be attributed to several methodological and data improvements. If factor inputs are not properly accounted for their compositional differences, which is the case with several previous studies on the Indian economy, it is likely that TFP growth will be overstated. For instance, if we add labor and capital composition effects to our measured TFP growth, we will have a TFP growth closer to 2% in both the 1990s and the 2000s. Our analysis also relaxes the assumption of constant factor income share in GDP, which is the case in several studies in the context of aggregate economy growth accounting. Bosworth and Collins (2008), for instance, assume a constant wage share of 0.6 over time and across sectors, whereas our data – which includes estimated income of self-employed workers – suggests that on average during 1980–2011 wage share in GDP varied from 9% in the petroleum sector to 77% in construction and 85% in public administration. We allow factor income share to vary across years and industries, which will also have an impact on measured productivity growth. For instance, if we assume a wage share of 0.6, as in Bosworth and Collins (2008), our TFP growth estimates for the 1990s and 2000s approximates to about 2%, which is closer to their estimate.

7.4.2 *Sectoral contributions to aggregate productivity growth*

Given that the service sector is expanding and manufacturing sector is shrinking in terms of their relative size in the overall economy, productivity growth in the service sector would be decisive in driving aggregate productivity growth. In Table 7.3, we provide the contribution of various sectors of the economy to aggregate TFP growth. These are arrived at using their relative shares in nominal GDP as weights.

The aggregate TFP growth in the 1980s was driven by both manufacturing and non-manufacturing sectors (also see Balakrishnan and Parameswaran 2007), primarily by non-market services and agriculture. Other industries which include market services and non-manufacturing industries (utilities and construction) pulled productivity growth down, with high negative contribution from non-manufacturing industries, and almost no contribution from market services. Within manufacturing low labor intensive sectors had a relatively larger TFP growth contribution, though the differences between low and high

Table 7.3 *Sectoral contribution to aggregate total factor productivity*

	1981–1990	1992–1999	2000–2011
Agriculture	0.52	0.60	0.23
Industry	0.09	–0.28	0.12
Manufacturing	0.44	–0.21	0.39
High labor intensive	0.15	–0.16	0.14
Medium labor intensive	0.10	0.11	–0.04
Low labor intensive	0.19	–0.16	0.29
Non-manufacturing industries	–0.35	–0.07	–0.27
Services	0.51	1.06	0.92
Market services	–0.02	0.48	1.09
Non market services	0.53	0.58	–0.17
Market Economy	0.59	0.81	1.45
Total economy	**1.15**	**1.39**	**1.21**

Note: Market economy consists of all sectors excluding non-market services. Non-manufacturing industries are utilities (electricity gas and water) and construction. For manufacturing sector classification based on labor intensity and details on other industry aggregations, see Appendix Table 7.1.
Source: Author calculation using India KLEMS data.

labor intensive manufacturing sectors in terms of TFP growth contribution are not large.

However, the picture started changing in the 1990s, as market services started picking up substantially, and manufacturing, in particular high- and low-labor intensive manufacturing sectors, witnessed productivity slowdown. Agriculture and non-market services continued to grow faster in the 1990s, each contributing approximately 40 percent of aggregate productivity growth. This clearly suggests that immediately after the market reforms in the 1990s, productivity gains in the manufacturing sector were less evident, while the accompanied information and communications technology (ICT) revolution might have helped India's market service sector gain productivity growth.

In the 2000s, the period of high growth in India, most of the productivity gains are due to market services. Even though manufacturing contribution has increased in the 2000s, primarily due to low-labor intensive segments within the manufacturing sector, more than 90 percent of productivity gain was from market services. Interestingly, contribution of high-labor intensive manufacturing also increased during this period, while medium labor intensive segments witnessed a slowdown. Productivity contribution from agricultural as well as non-market services declined significantly during this period.

Also, there is a large difference in the productivity pattern in the 2000s compared to the 1980s and 1990s. In the 1980s 53% (0.6 out of 1.2% TFP growth) of aggregate productivity was driven by the market sector (both manufacturing and services) and 47% was driven by the non-market economy. In the 1990s the market economy increased its productivity contribution to 58% (0.8 out of 1.4) and in the 2000s its contribution has gone up to 114% (1.4 out of 1.2), during which the non-market economy witnessed a deceleration in productivity, thus pulling down aggregate productivity by almost 14%. The non-manufacturing industries, which are largely utilities and construction, had a negative productivity contribution throughout. The utilities sector in India largely operates under administrative control. If this sector is also excluded from the market economy, then the contribution of the market economy to aggregate productivity growth increases to 135% (i.e. 1.7 percentage points out of 1.2% TFP growth) in the 2000s. Indeed, the market economy has taken over the productivity drive, which is suggestive of the impact of policy reforms aimed at promoting market principles. TFP growth in the market economy grew at an annual rate of about 2% in the 2000s, compared to 0.8% during 1980s and 1% during the 1990s. Below we will examine which sectors within and outside of market services that gained productivity acceleration in 2000s.

7.5 TFP growth in India using aggregate production function

Using equation (2) we computed the output growth decomposition of all the twenty-six industries in the KLEMS database. The results for the three sub-periods are given in Figure 7.2. Also, in Table 7.4, we provide the sectoral TFP growth obtained using a value added function (equation 1), along with value added/output ratio, the product of which provides the gross output based TFP growth presented in Figure 7.2. Capital is the main driver of growth in the mining and education sectors in the 1980s, while intermediate inputs drive output growth in almost all other sectors. In the manufacturing industries contribution of intermediate inputs is substantial in driving output growth, which is in conformity with many previous studies on organized manufacturing in Indian economy (Banga and Goldar 2007).

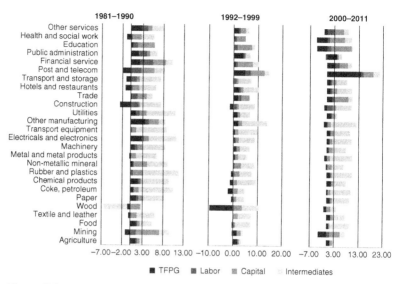

Figure 7.2 Decomposition of output growth into contribution from factor inputs and TFP growth, twenty-six industries, 1980–2011

Industries such as rubber and plastics, transport equipment, chemical products, and electrical and optical equipment were ranked high in terms of material contribution. TFP growth played an important role in some sectors, which includes electrical and optical equipment, chemical and chemical products, food products, beverages and tobacco, financial services, and agriculture. In particular, the first three industries registered 8 to 10 percent productivity growth in the 1980s.

The picture changed substantially in the 1990s, where TFP growth almost vanished in a large number of manufacturing sectors, while some service sectors like post and telecom showed high productivity growth. There was no industry that registered a TFP growth of the similar magnitude that was witnessed in fast growing sectors like electrical and optical equipment and chemical and chemical products in the 1980s. Moreover, the role of capital also increased substantially across all the service sectors, while manufacturing output growth was largely material driven. Electrical and optical manufacturing, transport equipment, wood and wood products, and chemical and chemical products had the highest material contribution among the twenty-six industry groups.

Table 7.4 *Sectoral total factor productivity using value added function and value added/output ratio*

	Total factor productivity growth (value added based)			Value added/output ratio		
	1981–1990	1992–1999	2000–2011	1981–1990	1992–1999	2000–2011
Agriculture, hunting, forestry, and fishing	1.6	2.2	1.2	0.72	0.75	0.76
Mining and quarrying	-1.5	2.3	-4.5	0.75	0.74	0.77
Food products, beverages, and tobacco	8.0	-1.8	5.2	0.19	0.19	0.15
Textiles, textile products, leather, and footwear	-1.5	0.3	6.1	0.31	0.29	0.25
Wood and products of wood	-2.2	-20.3	-2.5	0.43	0.47	0.39
Pulp, paper, paper products, printing, and publishing	5.0	-2.6	5.7	0.28	0.26	0.24
Coke, refined petroleum products, and nuclear fuel	7.5	-16.0	1.9	0.09	0.14	0.14
Chemicals and chemical products	9.8	-6.3	7.5	0.19	0.22	0.22
Rubber and plastic products	-0.6	-4.8	8.6	0.23	0.20	0.17
Other non-metallic mineral products	1.7	1.0	-0.9	0.36	0.33	0.31
Basic metals and fabricated metal products	-1.1	2.7	-5.0	0.23	0.22	0.19
Machinery, nec.	3.7	4.7	1.8	0.27	0.24	0.26
Electrical and optical equipment	10.1	2.8	4.7	0.27	0.22	0.21

Table 7.4 (*cont.*)

	Total factor productivity growth (value added based)			Value added/output ratio		
	1981–1990	1992–1999	2000–2011	1981–1990	1992–1999	2000–2011
Transport equipment	0.0	4.7	7.2	0.21	0.17	0.18
Manufacturing, nec; recycling	7.8	5.0	−6.5	0.46	0.36	0.21
Electricity, gas, and water supply	3.0	4.5	4.5	0.39	0.36	0.38
Construction	−7.5	−4.4	−3.5	0.34	0.34	0.34
Wholesale and retail trade	0.4	2.4	2.6	0.71	0.79	0.84
Hotels and restaurants	−4.3	6.6	4.3	0.30	0.34	0.33
Transport and storage	−2.2	−0.2	3.2	0.48	0.45	0.42
Post and telecommunication	−2.2	5.5	17.7	0.83	0.84	0.78
Financial services	2.7	1.1	4.0	0.81	0.81	0.80
Public administration and defense	2.6	5.3	5.4	0.73	0.73	0.74
Education	0.6	0.1	−4.8	0.86	0.88	0.89
Health and social work	−2.5	0.6	−7.0	0.38	0.51	0.62
Other services	3.4	2.4	−1.7	0.80	0.81	0.79

Note: TFP growth in this table is based on value added function (equation 1). The gross output based TFP growth presented in Figure 7.2 is the product of TFP growth presented in the first three columns here, and the value added/output ratio given in the last three columns (see equation 3).
Source: Author calculation using India KLEMS data.

In the 2000s, the economy started regaining productivity growth in some sectors, with market services being the largest recipient. In particular, post and telecom and financial intermediation sectors had registered high TFP growth, while non-market sectors education, health, and other services had negative TFP growth. The manufacturing sector seemed to be moving out of the negative TFP growth territory in the 2000s, with most sectors except wood and wood products, other non-metallic minerals, and other manufacturing, registering a positive TFP growth. Nevertheless, the relative role of materials in driving output growth is dominant, and the role of capital is less than what is seen in the service sector. In general employment contributions were larger in the financial service, post and telecom, public administration, education, and construction sectors during all the three periods.

Thus, in general, output growth in the Indian economy, particularly in goods producing sectors, is heavily material driven. This is not surprising, given the material intensity of these sectors, compared to, for instance, most services sectors. There is, nevertheless, clear indication that the market economy in general has witnessed an improvement in TFP in the post-2000 period. Moreover, the increasing intermediates' contribution could also be a reflection of increased outsourcing and vertical specialization of trade. As is shown by the recent World Input–Output Database (Timmer *et al.* 2015, see also Chapter 15 in this volume), the imported intermediate content of India's export has been increasing steadily since 1995, and in particular in the 2000s, which might suggest the increased use of intermediate inputs to increase output and exports. This aspect, however, requires further examination, which is beyond the scope of this chapter.

While the sectoral productivity growth rates provided in Table 7.4 and Figure 7.2 are insightful and informative on the performance of individual industries, it is hard to get a visual image of the pattern of productivity growth across industries – whether it is concentrated in some specific sectors or widespread across the board. To understand how widespread productivity growth and its changes are within the Indian economy during the last three decades, we use the Harberger diagram (Harberger 1998). The Harberger diagram, which plots the cumulative contribution of industries to aggregate productivity growth against the cumulative share of these industries, provides a graphical

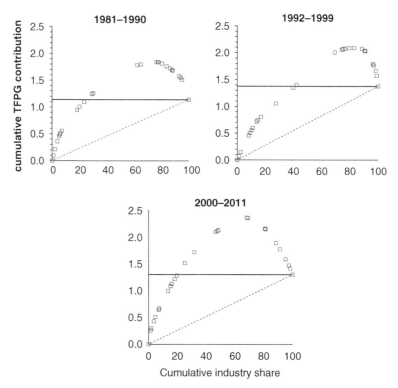

Figure 7.3 Harberger diagrams of aggregate total factor productivity growth in the Indian economy

summary of the industry pattern of productivity growth (Timmer *et al.* 2010).[27]

Figure 7.3 provides the Harberger diagrams for the three periods. Further, in Table 7.5 we provide the pattern of aggregate economy TFP growth over the three sub-periods, using useful summary statistics from Harberger diagram (see Inklaar and Timmer 2007). The first row of the table suggests a picture of stagnant productivity growth in

---

[27] To plot the Harberger diagrams, we first rank the industries according to their TFP growth. Then the cumulative contribution of industries (i.e. the share weighted TFP growth of each sector) is plotted against the cumulative shares of these industries (Timmer *et al.* 2010; Harberger 1998). The resulting curve, which is concave in shape, tells us how equal the distribution of productivity growth across industries is. The area under the curve will be less if growth is broad-based ("yeast-like" pattern), and it will be larger if the growth is concentrated in a few sectors ('mushroom-like" pattern).

Table 7.5 *Pattern of aggregate economy TFP growth, 1981–2011*

	1981–1990	1992–1999	2000–2011
Aggregate TFP growth	1.2	1.4	1.2
Percentage of industries with positive TFP growth	61.5	69.2	65.4
Value added share of industries with positive TFP growth	77.7	83.1	68.1
Relative area under Harberger	0.55	0.59	0.55

Note: Value added-based TFP growth aggregated using value added shares. Relative area under Harberger is the curvature measured by the area between the diagram and the diagonal line (dotted line in Figure 7.3) divided by the total area below the diagram.
Source: Author calculation using India KLEMS data.

the Indian economy over years, which stayed at a range of 1.2% to 1.4%. However, the number of industries with positive TFP growth has increased in the post-liberalization period. Before the liberalization regime, there were about 62% of industries with positive TFP growth, which has increased to 69% during the 1990s (also see the next section). However, in the 2000s, this declined again to 65%, still being higher than the 1980s. Thus even when more industries were registering positive TFP growth, aggregate TFP growth does not seem to be increasing faster. This is because the relative size of these industries in aggregate GDP in the 2000s is lower than it was in the 1980s, though it was about 5% higher in the 1990s. As evident from the figure, while the positive contributions from industry TFP growth to aggregate TFP growth added up to 1.8 percentage points in 1980s, it added up to 2.1 and 2.4 percentage points respectively in the 1990s and 2000s. The negative contributions added up to –0.7 percentage point in both the 1980s and 1990s and up to –1.1 percentage points in the 2000s, pulling down aggregate TFP growth.

The last row of the table shows the area under Harberger – the area between the curve and the dotted line in the figure – which will take a value between 0 and 1, with it being zero when all industries have equal growth. The closer the relative area to one, the more divergent the growth rates across industries. The relative area did not change in the 2000s compared to the 1980s, whereas it increased marginally in 1990s. Even though there is no substantial difference in the relative area statistics between three decades, this pattern is suggestive of a relatively more uneven growth in the 1990s compared to the 1980s and 2000s. TFP growth was not broad-based, rather it seem to have become more "mushroom-like" (i.e. being concentrated in a few industries), rather than "yeast-like" (i.e. being spread across all industries).

7.6 Productivity under policy regimes: a discussion

India's economic policy regime since independence to the present time has been a mix of socialism and market experimentation followed by an open economy (see Virmani 2004). Out of the several policy reforms initiated, two stand out in the context of productivity improvements. They are the domestic industrial deregulations and the external trade reforms, as these potentially allow firms a level playing ground to face international competition and in turn become globally competitive. In Figure 7.4, we look into the specific industries which performed better in 2000s compared to the 1990s. We distinguish between: (1) positive TFP growth in the 1990s as well as the 2000s; (2) positive TFP growth in 2000 only; (3) negative TFP growth in both the 1990s and the 2000s; and (4) positive TFP growth in the 1990s only.

We find that nine out of twenty-six industries had positive productivity growth both in the 1990s and the 2000s, with five of them being in the service sector, and within which post and telecommunication being the best performer. The telecommunication sector has been a national development priority since the 1980s. Whereas the 1980s was a period of state dominance and administrated prices, telecom services (and the service sector in general) in India witnessed massive liberalization with increased role for private sector and foreign participation in the post-1990s. Significant reforms took place in 1984, 1999, and the 2000s, including delicensing of telecom equipment manufacturing.[28] The sector seems to have benefitted from these policies; we see a productivity growth that outpaces many other sectors.

---

[28] These reforms include: allowing foreign collaboration, setting up of a national telecom policy in 1994, opening up of value added services to private and foreign players, setting up of the Telecom Regulatory Authority of India in 1997 to separate regulatory functions from policy-making, allowing multiple fixed services operator and opening domestic long distance services to private operators in 1999, a broad band policy initiative in 2004, regulation on quality of service introduced in 2006, and allowing increased FDI participation in telecom services in 2012.

Other industries that registered positive productivity growth in both periods include financial services, trade, hotels and restaurants (all service sectors), electrical and optical equipment, transport equipment and machinery (manufacturing), and agriculture (Figure 7.4). Though the core of economic reforms of 1991 centered on trade and industrial policy changes, significant changes were also introduced aiming to create a competitive and efficient financial sector.[29] The reforms put in place envisaged to take care of the fiscal deficit issues through augmenting revenues by removing anomalies in the tax structure through restructuring, simplification, and rationalization of both direct and indirect taxes. Aiming to create a competitive as well as efficient financial sector, several reforms were also introduced in the debt and securities markets as well as in the banking and insurance sectors. Historically, banking sector in India has been highly state dominated, ever since the banks were nationalized in 1969. This picture started changing drastically, as several reforms, varying from liberalization of the sector in the mid-1990s to allowing increased foreign participation in the early 2000s, were introduced to enhance competition in the sector. Similar reforms were also introduced in the insurance sector, even though at a slower pace. Indeed, these policies have helped the sector gain substantial productivity improvement. However many issues still remain for policy advocacy, which includes promoting competition, bringing financial stability, and strengthening inter-regulatory coordination (Krishnan 2011).

Apparently, the manufacturing industries that gained productivity growth in the post-reform period are primarily equipment producing industries, including the ICT goods producing sector. It is important to point out here that these sectors were beneficiaries of delicensing, broad banding, capacity reendorsements, and scale expansions announced in the India's industrial policy reforms of the mid-1980s and further liberalization in the 1990s.[30] The delicensing announced in the mid-1980s encompassed industries such as machinery and machine tools, electronics, electronic components, iron and steel, automotive components, and drugs and chemicals.

---

[29] See Mohan (2006) for a list of several policy measures advocated for reforms in banking, the government securities market, and foreign exchange markets as well as a monetary policy framework.

[30] See Government of India (1986).

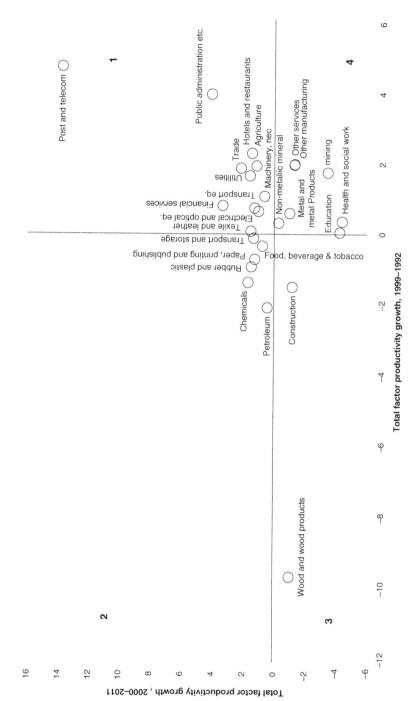

Figure 7.4 Productivity performance and policy regimes: 1990s versus 2000s

In terms of trade policy, the tariff levels in the 1980s remained high across all product groups. Indeed, the substantial tariff reforms in the 1990s along with removal of import restrictions on many of these industries have paved the way for productivity improvements in both the 1990s and 2000s.

The sectors in category 2, with positive productivity growth in 2000s, even though they had negative growth in the 1990s, include petroleum, chemicals, rubber and plastics, paper and paper products, and the only service sector in this group, transport and storage. Transport services, in particular air transportation, were opened to private players in the late 1990s, and apparently its impact on productivity seems to have appeared in the 2000s. India's airline industry has been predominantly a government monopoly until 1986, the year in which private participation was allowed in the sector and a limited number of players entered the market. With the Air Corporation Act 1994, and the subsequent massive entry of several low-cost service providers in 2003, the industry has seen fierce competition, which might have also helped the transport sector in general to acquire better productivity growth in 2000s.

Despite being in the list of industries subjected to delicensing, and exposed to trade liberalization, sectors like chemicals did not even see a positive productivity growth in the 1990s. It often seems that trade liberalization takes time to result in efficiency of firms as benefits of tariff reductions and import restrictions facilitates access to technology embodied in imported inputs as well as better imported inputs themselves (Das 2005).[31] Indeed these industries, which moved out of the negative territory in 1990s to positive TFP growth in the 2000s, along with transport equipment, electrical and optical equipment, and machinery and textiles, which maintained their positive TFP growth in both decades, helped the overall manufacturing sector register an improved productivity growth in the 2000s.

Two sectors that have witnessed negative productivity growth in both the 1990s and the 2000s (category 3) are construction and wood products. The construction sector is particularly interesting, because this is the sector that absorbed a large chunk of workers moving out of agriculture. The share of construction in total employment has

---

[31] Also see Topalova and Khandelwal (2011) and Chand and Sen (2002) for evidence on a lagged impact of policy changes on productivity growth.

increased from a mere 2% in 1980 to 3% in 1990, to 5% in 2000, and further to 10% in 2011. In contrast, its output share has increased from 5% in 1980 to only 8% in 2011, thus suggesting that its employment share has surpassed its output share. On average nearly half of the additional employment generated in the Indian economy between 2000 and 2011 is in the construction sector. There have been about 73 million more workers in the Indian economy in 2011, compared to 1999, out of which 32 million jobs were created in construction sector, thus driving down average productivity.[32]

The industries in group 4, registering positive productivity growth in the 1990s, but negative TFP growth in the 2000s are non-metallic minerals, basic metals and metal products, other manufacturing, and all non-market sectors except public administration and defense. Interestingly, one of the manufacturing sectors that lost the productivity momentum in the 1990s – basic metals and metal products – is one to which the post-independence policy reforms have given substantial importance, though it was not given any special importance in the later liberal policy reforms. Since a productivity analysis in the non-market sectors may not be very helpful, one may not give significant importance to the observed decline in its productivity in the 1990s. Yet, it may be noted that two major sectors within this group – health and education – in India needs to be enhanced in order to improve India's human capital, and thereby to improve productivity in other sectors (see our discussion below).

Thus, defying the growth path followed by countries like China, Japan, or South Korea, much of the growth and productivity in India has been in the service sector. This service output expansion, however, did not generate proportional employment growth. Given a large demographic dividend and a vast majority of its population still not high-skilled, one may doubt the ability of the Indian economy to sustain this service-led economic growth in the longer run.[33] This warrants particular attention, as most service sector industries that witnessed acceleration in productivity and growth

---

[32] Other notable sectors where jobs were created are other services (17 million) and trade (10 million), with agriculture losing about 14 million jobs. The entire manufacturing sector added only 10 million jobs, with the highest being in other manufacturing (2.7 million) and textiles (2 million).

[33] India's working age population is projected to increase while that of China will stagnate in the next two decades (UN population division).

are skill-intensive sectors such as telecommunication, financial services, and non-market sectors like public administration. The share of tertiary educated working age population in India is a mere 6 percent in 2010, which has increased only by 1 percent over a decade (Barro and Lee, 2013). In fact, several recent quality and accessibility indicators of education are suggesting mixed results. Most recent economic surveys (2014–2015) acknowledge that the overall standard of the Indian education system is well below global standards, and the learning levels have not improved. Even though the overall school enrolment ratio has gone up, the survey suggests stagnation in rural enrolment, decline in teacher–student ratios and in student attendance in rural areas. Moreover, the share of the formally skilled work force in India is as small as 2 percent, which is substantially lower compared to 80–95 percent in countries like Japan and South Korea (Government of India 2015). Therefore, if India does not invest substantially in improving both quality of and accessibility to education, it may fail in translating its demographic dividend into growth.

Another possible consequence of the service-led growth, with a shrinking manufacturing sector, would be a rise in wage inequality across sectors, as the service sector pushes up wages of high skilled workers, while a major chunk of (uneducated) work force still remains at primary and secondary sectors (Drèze and Sen 2013). There is a huge and increasing gap between the market services wage rate and the manufacturing wage rate; the latter has steadily declined from 75 percent of the former's wage rate in 1980 to 55 percent in 2011. On the contrary, if the increasing wages in the service sector lead to faster wage growth in the manufacturing sector, it might affect India's manufacturing competitiveness. Indeed, the impact of raising wages on competitiveness could be overcome only by achieving faster productivity growth, and thereby reducing unit labor cost.

However, rigidities in the (formal) labor market, the presence of a large informal sector, a weak infrastructure and insufficient energy availability are adding challenges to achieving higher productivity growth and job creation, particularly in the manufacturing sector. The lack of job creation even within the labor intensive sectors (Sen and Das 2014), along with the shrinking the organized manufacturing sector, clearly calls for substantial labor market reforms in India, to reduce rigidities in the labor market that make formal firms shy away from expanding their activities. The inflexible labor regulations, indeed, foster faster expansion of the informal sector of the economy at the cost of a more productive and stable formal sector.[34] Another major supply side constraint on India's productivity growth is its weak infrastructure and insufficient energy availability. India's infrastructure spending has been relatively low at about 5 percent (with private sector spending even lower at 1 percent) of GDP (Planning Commission 2014; Mohan and Kapur, 2015), which is only half of Chinese spending. Therefore, policies that would help firms grow in size, modernization, and formalization of the informal sector, better environment for foreign investment, and better infrastructure, are among measures that would help the sector perform better in terms of productivity, growth, and employment generation.

7.7 Conclusions

This chapter attempted to explore the link between different policy regimes prevalent in India and productivity performance of the economy. In particular, the productivity dynamics for the period 1980–2011 – a crucial period of substantial policy changes – was examined from a policy perspective. Three different policy regimes were identified: (1) 1980–1990, a phase of piecemeal and ad hoc policy changes; (2) 1992–2000, a phase of major changes in economic policy; and (3) 2001–2011, a period of consolidation of economic reforms. The study was conducted at detailed industry level – dividing the entire economy into twenty-six subsectors – thus trying to understand the dynamics of policy effects at sectoral level. Using the India KLEMS database and a growth accounting methodology,

---

[34] As of 2011, within manufacturing, more than three-quarters of total employment is generated in the unregistered sector, whereas it produces less than only one-quarter of output (residual estimates based on India KLEMS total manufacturing and Annual Survey of industries registered manufacturing data). The story is not any different in the services sector. Depending upon the definition one uses, the informal employment share in services varies from 74–90 percent in 2006 (Ghani *et al.* 2013). Moreover the informality of the Indian economy has not shown any declining tendency. Rather, existing estimates are suggestive of moderate increase over time (Joddar and Sakthivel 2006).

we assessed the productivity performance of each of the individual industrial as well as broad sectors during the different policy regimes. Our analysis suggests that, indeed, the policy changes had substantial impact on productivity and economic growth in India, though it is still debatable whether the sectors that were intended to benefit from the reforms have really gained or not. The underlying data used in this study – the India KLEMS – is an important contribution to empirical research and policy-making, as it can help researchers better investigate India's economic growth and the underlying dynamics since the 1980s.

Overall, the Indian economy registered a moderate TFP growth rate of 1.2 percent during 1980–2011 without much deviation from the last three decadal averages. Market services seem to be the main driver of productivity growth both in the 1990s and 2000s, whereas agriculture, non-market services, and manufacturing all contributed to productivity growth in the 1980s. However, the productivity performance of the manufacturing sector, which showed a TFP growth of 2.6 percent in the 2000s as against a negative TFP growth in the 1990s, is commendable in the light of widespread consolidation of economic reforms initiated in the 1990s. For the manufacturing sector, the 1990s was a decade of factor accumulation and gradual diffusion of technology. The widespread reforms in industrial and trade policies in that period, however, seem to have contributed to a surge in productivity growth in the 2000s. Yet, its declining share in overall value added has reduced its overall role in boosting aggregate productivity growth. While the manufacturing sector still appears to be suffering from many policy constraints, several liberalization policies in the 2000s seem to have helped market services gain faster productivity growth. In particular, the telecom and financial services sectors, which have witnessed several market enhancing reforms, have shown impressive productivity performance.

Indeed, the removal of policy barriers in the mid-1980s and early 1990s in the form of bans, controls, and restrictions on production, investment, and trade, have helped firms improve TFP growth as well as factor input accumulation, especially capital input in several sectors of the Indian economy. However there still remain many barriers to overcome. While India's agriculture is yet to be integrated fully with the world markets, its manufacturing sector witnesses many factor market inflexibilities and supply side constraints.

As Bhagwati and Panagariya (2013) point out there is a clear need for reforming the labor market in India, in order to promote manufacturing jobs, production, and export, by creating a competitive product and factor market. Moreover, focusing on infrastructure and energy efficiency is essential to ease many supply side constraints.

Recently, there has been some discussion in the context of India's economic growth and its policy challenges, centering on whether to focus on social sector spending first or on growth first. Drèze and Sen (2013) advocate investment in social infrastructure to improve the quality of life and also to raise productivity and growth, whereas Bhagwati and Panagariya (2013) argue that growth can bring necessary resources to improve the social sector, and therefore policies should focus on achieving faster growth. It is quite obvious from our results that India needs a balanced policy approach. Given that the growth is concentrated in the services sector (of relatively high skill intensity), which can ultimately push the overall wages up, it is unlikely that India will be able to step into the Chinese style of low-cost manufacturing. Focusing on productivity is essential to maintain competitiveness and also create more jobs in the manufacturing sector. Even though it is highly acknowledged that the reallocation of workers from primary to secondary and tertiary sectors are beneficial for aggregate growth, reallocation of the labor force from primary to other sectors in India will be highly constrained by the lack of appropriate skill, which makes workers with low marginal productivity stay in the farm sector or move to less skill intensive sectors like construction. The only way to raise productivity and growth is therefore to improve quality of and accessibility to education, and thereby improve its human capital, which, however, should not be at the cost of policies aimed at achieving economic growth. Improved human capital would ultimately facilitate the availability of appropriate skills required by the rapidly expanding service sector as well. Most of today's advanced economies benefitted from better human capital endowment, and most countries that sustained long-term high growth were supported by a solid manufacturing sector. It is clear that what India needs is a balanced policy perspective, which focuses on improving its human capital, and creating opportunities for its younger population by focusing on economic growth, particularly in the manufacturing sector.

Appendix Table 7.1 *Classification of industries*

KLEMS description	ISIC 3.1
Agriculture, hunting, forestry, and fishing	**A to B**
Manufacturing*	**D**
High labor intensive	
Food products, beverages, and tobacco	15 to 16
Textiles, textile products, leather, and footwear	17 to 19
Wood and products of wood	20
Other non-metallic mineral products	26
Manufacturing, nec; recycling	36 to 37
Medium labor intensive	
Rubber and plastic products	25
Basic metals and fabricated metal products	27 to 28
Machinery, nec.	29
Electrical and optical equipment	30 to 33
Low labor intensive	
Pulp, paper, paper products, printing, and publishing	21 to 22
Coke, refined petroleum products, and nuclear fuel	23
Chemicals and chemical products	24
Transport equipment	34 to 35
Non-manufacturing industries	
Mining and quarrying	C
Electricity, gas, and water supply	E
Construction	F
Services	
Market services	
Wholesale and retail trade	G
Hotels and restaurants	H
Transport and storage	60 to 63
Post and telecommunication	64
Financial services	J
Non-market services	
Public administration and defense	L
Education	M
Health and social work	N

Appendix Table 7.1 (*cont.*)

KLEMS description	ISIC 3.1
Other services**	K+O+P
Total economy	

* Classification of manufacturing industries is done on the basis of percentile of employment to capital stock ratio (L/K). Low labor intensive are sectors with below 33.3 percent K/L of the entire data range; medium labor intensive are sectors with K/L between 33.6 and 66.6; and high labor intensive are those with K/L above 66.6 percent of the entire data range.

** Other services include real estate, renting, and business services (K), other community, social, and personal services (O), and activities of private households (P). Ideally, business services should be part of market economy, which however, was hard to separate from other services in the investment data.

References

Acharya, S., I. J. Ahluwalia, K. L. Krishna, and I. Patnaik. 2003. *India: Economic Growth, 1950–2000, Global Research Project On Growth.* New Delhi: Indian Council for Research on International Economic Relations.

Aggarwal, S. C. 2004. "Labor Quality in Indian Manufacturing: A State Level Analysis," *Economic and Political Weekly*, **39**(50): 5335–5344.

Aggarwal, S. C. and A. A. Erumban. 2013. "Labor Input for Measuring Productivity Growth in India: Methodology and Estimates," Presented at the Second India KLEMS Annual Workshop, April 26, 2012, ICRIER, New Delhi.

Ahluwalia, I. J. 1991. *Productivity and Growth in Indian Manufacturing.* Delhi/New York: Oxford University Press.

Balakrishnan, P. and M. Parameswaran. 2007. "Understanding Economic Growth in India, Further Observations," *Economic and Political Weekly*, **42**(44): 117–119.

Balakrishnan, P. and K. Pushpangadan. 1994. "Total Factor Productivity Growth in Manufacturing Industry: A Fresh Look," *Economic and Political Weekly*, **29**: 2028–2035.

Balakrishnan, P., K. Pushpangadan, and M. S. Babu. 2000. "Trade Liberalisation and Productivity Growth in Manufacturing: Evidence from Firm Level Panel Data," *Economic and Political Weekly*, **35**(41): 3679–3682.

Banga, R. and B. Goldar 2007. "Contribution of Services to Output Growth and Productivity in Indian Manufacturing: Pre- and Post-reforms," *Economic and Political Weekly*, **42**(26): 2769–2777.

Barro, R. and J-W. Lee. 2013. "A New Data Set of Educational Attainment in the World, *1950–2010," Journal of Development Economics*, **104**: 184–198.

Bernard, A. B., J. Eaton., J. B. Jensen, and S. S. Kortum. 2003. "Plants and Productivity in International Trade," *American Economic Review*, **93**(4): 1268–1290.

Bhagwati, J. and A. Panagariya. 2013. *Why Growth Matters: How Economic Growth in India Reduced Poverty and the Lessons for Other Developing Countries*. New York: Public Affairs.

Binswanger-Mkhize, H. P. 2013. "The Stunted Structural Transformation of the Indian Economy: Agriculture, *Manufacturing and the Rural Non-farm Sector," Economic and Political Weekly*, **48**(26–27): 5–13.

Bosworth, B. and S. M. Collins. 2008. "Accounting for Growth: Comparing China and India," *Journal of Economic Perspectives*, **22**(1): 45–66.

Bosworth, B., S. M. Collins and A. Virmani. 2007. "Sources of Growth in Indian Economy," *NBER Working Paper*, No. 12901.

Bosworth, B., and A. Maertens. 2010. "The Role of the Service Sector in Economic Growth and Employment in South Asia." In E. Ghani and H. Kharas (eds.), *The Service Revolution in South Asia*. Oxford University Press.

Chand, S., and K. Sen. 2002. "Trade Liberalization and Productivity Growth: Evidence from Indian Manufacturing," *Review of Development Economics*, **6**(1): 120–132.

Das, D. K. 2004. Manufacturing Productivity under Varying Trade Regimes, 1980–2000," *Economic and Political Weekly*, **39**(5), 423–433.

2005. "Improving Industrial Productivity – Does Trade Liberalization Matter? Evidence from Indian Intermediate and Capital Goods Industries." In S. D. Tendulkar *et al.* (eds.), *India: Industrialization in a Reforming Economy*. New Delhi: Academic Foundation.

De Vries, G. J., A. A. Erumban, M. P. Timmer, I. Voskoboynikov, and H. X. Wu. 2012. "Deconstructing the BRICs: Structural Transformation and Aggregate Productivity Growth," *Journal of Comparative Economics*, **40**(2): 211–227.

Dorrucci, E., G. Pula, and D. Santabarbara 2013. "China's Economic Growth and Rebalancing," *European Central Bank Occasional Paper, Series #142*.

Drèze, J., and A. Sen. 2013. *An Uncertain Glory: India and its Contradictions*. London: Allen Lane.

Eichengreen, B. and P. Gupta. 2009. "The Service Sector as India's Road to Economic Growth," *ICRIER Working Paper, #249*.

Eichengreen, B., P. Gupta, and R. Kumar. 2010. *Emerging Giants: China and India in the World Economy*. Oxford University Press.

Erumban, A. A. 2008. "Rental Prices, Rates of Return, Capital Aggregation and Productivity: Evidence from EU and US," *CESifo Economic Studies*, **54**(3): 499–533.

Erumban, A. A., D. K. Das, and S. C. Aggarwal. 2012. "Industry Origins of Aggregate Productivity Growth in India," Paper presented at the 32nd General Conference of the International Association for Research in Income and Wealth, Boston.

Fuglie, K. O. 2012. "Total Factor Productivity in the Global Agricultural Economy: Evidence from FAO data." In J. Alston, B. Babcock, and P. Pardey (eds.), *The Shifting Patterns of Agricultural Production and Productivity Worldwide*. Midwest Agribusiness Trade and Research Information Center (MATRIC), Iowa State University.

Ghani, E., W. R. Kerr, and S. D. O'Connell. 2013. "The Exceptional Persistence of India's Unorganized Sector," *The World Bank Working Paper, WPS6454*.

Goldar, B. N. 2004. "Indian Manufacturing: Productivity Trends in Pre- and Post-reform Periods," *Economic and Political Weekly*, **39**(46/47): 5033–5043.

2014. "Productivity in Indian Manufacturing in the Post-reform Period." In V. Kathuria *et al.* (eds.), *Productivity in Indian Manufacturing - Measurements, Methods and Analysis*. New Delhi/UK: Routledge.

Gorden, J. and P. Gupta. 2003. "Understanding India's Services Revolution," *IMF Working Paper*, WP/04/171.

Government of India. 1986. *Economic Survey (1985–1986)*.

2015. *Economic Survey (2014–2015)*.

Harberger, A. C. 1998. "A Vision of the Growth Process," *American Economic Review*, **88**(1): 1–32.

Hulten, C. R. 1978. "Growth Accounting with Intermediate Inputs," *Review of Economic Studies*, **45**: 511–518.

Hulten, C. R. and S. Srinivasan. 1999. "Indian Manufacturing Industry: Elephant or Tiger? New Evidence on the Asian Miracle," *NBER Working Paper*, No. 7441.

Inklaar, R. and M. P. Timmer. 2007. "Of Yeast and Mushrooms: Patterns of Industry-level Productivity Growth," *German Economic Review*, 8(2): 174–187.

Joddar, P. and S. Sakthivel. 2006. "Unorganised Sector Workforce in India," *Economic and Political Weekly*, **41**(21).

Jorgenson, D. W. 1963. "Capital Theory and Investment Behavior," *American Economic Review*, **53**(2): 247–259.

1990. "Productivity and Economic Growth." In E. R. Berndt and J. Triplett (eds.), *Fifty Years of Economic Development*. University of Chicago Press.

Jorgenson, D. W., F. Gollop, and B. Fraumeni. 1987. *Productivity and US Economic Growth*. Cambridge, MA: Harvard University Press.

Jorgenson, D. W., M. S. Ho, and K. J. Stiroh. 2005. *Information Technology and the American Growth Resurgence*. Cambridge, The MIT Press.

Jorgenson, D. W. and K. Vu. 2005. "Information Technology and the World Economy," *Scandinavian Journal of Economics*, 107(4): 631–650.

Kathuria, V., S. N. R. Raj, and K. Sen. 2010. "Organised Versus Unorganised Manufacturing Performance in the Post-reform Period," *Economic and Political Weekly*, 45(24): 55–64.

Krishna, P. and D. Mitra. 1998. "Trade Liberalization, Market Discipline and Productivity Growth: New Evidence from India," *Journal of Development Economics*, 56(2): 447–462.

Krishnan, K. P. 2011. "Financial Development in Emerging Markets: The Indian Experience," *Asian Development Bank Institute Working Paper*, 276.

Melitz, M. 2003. "The Impact of Trade on Intra-industry Reallocations and Aggregate Industry Productivity," *Econometrica*, 71(6): 1695–1726.

Mohan, R. 2006. "Economic Growth, Financial Deepening and Financial Inclusion," Annual Bankers' Conference, Hyderabad, India.

Mohan, R. and M. Kapur. 2015. "Pressing the Indian Growth Accelerator: Policy Imperatives," *IMF Working Paper*, WP/15/53.

Moreno-Monroy, A. I., J. Pieters, and A. A, Erumban. 2014. "Formal Sector Subcontracting and Informal Sector Employment in Indian Manufacturing," *IZA Journal of Labor and Development*, 3(22): 1–17.

OECD. 2001. *OECD Productivity Manual: A Guide to the Measurement of Industry-level and Aggregate Productivity Growth*. Paris: OECD.

Oulton, N. 2007. "Ex Post versus Ex Ante Measures of the User Cost of Capital," *Review of Income and Wealth*, 53(2): 295–317.

Panagariya, A. 2008. *India the Emerging Giant*. New York: Oxford University Press.

Planning Commission. 2014. "Data-book Compiled for use of Planning Commission." See: http://planningcommission.nic.in/data/datatable/03 06/Databook_June2014.pdf, accessed May 4, 2015.

Rodrik, D. 2013. "The Past, Present, and Future of Economic Growth," *Global Citizen Foundation Working Paper*, 1. See: www.sss.ias.edu/fil es/pdfs/Rodrik/Research/GCF_Rodrik-working-paper-1_-6-24-13.pdf.

Rodrik, D., and A. Subramanian. 2005. "From 'Hindu Growth' to Productivity Surge: The Mystery of the Indian Growth Transition," *IMF Staff Papers*, 52(2).

Sen, K. and D. K. Das. 2014. "Where Have all the Workers Gone? The Puzzle of Declining Labour Intensity in Organized Indian Manufacturing," *Development Economics and Public Policy Working Paper Series*, WP

No. 35/2014. Institute for Development Policy and Management, University of Manchester, UK.

Srinivasan, T. N. and S. D. Tendulkar. 2003. *Reintegrating India with the World Economy*. New Delhi: Oxford University Press.

The Conference Board. 2014. "The Conference Board Total Economy Database™." See: www.conference-board.org/data/economydatabase, January.

Timmer, M. P., E. Dietzenbacher., B. Los., R. Stehrer, and G. J. de Vries. 2015. "An Illustrated User Guide to the World Input–Output Database: The Case of Global Automotive Production," *Review of International Economics*, **23**: 575–605.

Timmer, M. P., R. Inklaar., M. O'Mahony, and B. van Ark. 2010. *Economic Growth in Europe: A Comparative Industry Perspective*. Cambridge University Press.

Topalova, P. and A. Khandelwal. 2011. "Trade Liberalization and Firm Productivity: The Case of India," *The Review of Economics and Statistics*, **93**(3): 995–1009.

Trivedi, P., L. Lakshmanan, R. Jain, and Y. K. Gupta. 2011. "Productivity, Efficiency and Competitiveness of the Manufacturing Sector," *Development Research Group Study, No. 37*, Reserve Bank of India, Mumbai.

Verma, R. 2012. "Can Total Factor Productivity Explain Value Added Growth in Services?", *Journal of Development Economics*, **99**(1): 163–177.

Virmani, A. 2004. "Sources of India's Economic Growth," *ICRIER Working Paper*, No. 131.

8 Is mining fuelling long-run growth in Russia? Industry productivity growth trends in 1995–2012

MARCEL P. TIMMER AND ILYA B.
VOSKOBOYNIKOV

8.1 Introduction

GDP per capita growth in Russia has been among the highest in the world since the mid-1990s, averaging 3.7 percent annually between 1995 and 2012.[1,2] For this reason it is occasionally clubbed together with other fast growing economies such as Brazil, China, and India into BRIC, and set against the European Union, Japan and the United States where growth is sluggish. As such, Russian economic development today is seen as yet another successful transition from a command to a market

---

[1] The Conference Board Total Economy Database™, January 2013. See: www.conference-board.org/data/economydatabase.

[2] This chapter is an adaptation of our paper "Is Mining Fuelling Long-run Growth in Russia? (Timmer and Voskoboynikov 2014). The original paper has been shortened, results updated, and new information on the educational attainment level of workers added. Acknowledgement to Dale Jorgenson and Rostislav Kapeliushnikov for their useful comments and suggestions.

This chapter is the outcome of six years of working on Russia KLEMS project. Many economists and statisticians contributed to the development of the dataset. The system of real added value indicators is based on the industrial production indices, which have been developed since the early 1990s by Eduard Baranov and Vladimir Bessonov. At all stages of working on this chapter the project has been professionally supported by Vladimir Gimpelson and Rostislav Kapelyushnikov from the HSE Centre for Labour Market Studies, leading experts in the Russian labor market and Russian labor statistics with strong international backgrounds. They helped to reveal and solve many questions on the dynamics of labor costs in industry. The project wouldn't have been realized without organizational and methodical support from the Federal State Statistics Service on different levels – from management to ordinary staff members, responsible for calculating certain indicators. We would like to specially mention statisticians who have worked in the National Accounts Office – Mikhail Gordonov, Liudmila Kochneva, Irina Masakova, and Galina Romashkina. They explained the specifics of official statistics of investment and capital assets, and made a big contribution to solving the most difficult tasks of the project. Last, but not least, we thank our colleagues from Groningen Growth and Development Centre, in particular Robert Inklaar and Reitze Gouma.

economy. This is a dramatic change of fortune. In the past Soviet economic performance was highlighted as a typical example of extensive growth, driven by high investment and labor input growth, with little improvements in technology and efficiency (Ofer 1987; Krugman 1994). But with the introduction of a market economy in early 1990s, it was expected that growth would become intensive, relying on improvements in productivity rather than input growth. Through the elimination of multiple price distortions of the planned economy, a better allocation of inputs among industries and increasing incentives for firms to diminish real costs of production, productivity should become the main driver of growth (Campos and Coricelli 2002). These benefits were not realized immediately, and as is well known the Russian transition triggered a deep crisis that finally bottomed out in the mid-1990s (see Figure 8.1). But since then, the trend in growth picked up and the benefits from the market economy seem to be finally realized, akin to the success of various other formerly planned economies in Eastern Europe (Fernandes 2009; Havlik, Leitner, and Stehrer 2012) and China.

Recent growth accounting studies of Russia confirm this view and find that growth was mainly driven by improvements in the efficiency of input

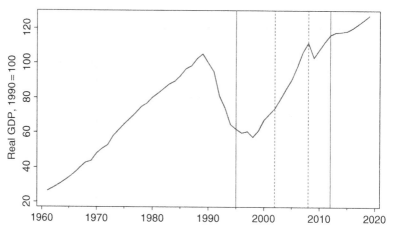

Figure 8.1 Long-run growth of the Russian economy, 1961–2019
Source: 1961–1990 – (Ponomarenko 2002); 1991–2013 – the Russian statistical office (*Rosstat*), 2014–2019 – Projection of International Monetary Fund, World Economic Outlook Database, October 2014.
Note: Vertical lines correspond to the following years : 1995, 2002, 2008, and 2012.

use, as measured by multi-factor productivity (MFP) growth, rather than growth in labor and capital inputs. Entov and Lugovoy (2013), Jorgenson and Vu (2013) and Kuboniwa (2011) all find that MFP growth was (much) higher than input growth in the period from about 1995 to 2008. Izyumov and Vahaly (2008) find that input growth is even negative in this period, and all output growth is due to MFP growth. These findings are consistent, despite the wide variety of methods and data used (as will be discussed in more detail below). And compared to a large set of developed and developing countries, Russian MFP growth of around 5 percent annually since the mid 1990s appeared to be among the highest in the world (Jorgenson and Vu 2011). This supports the view that Russia managed to switch from an extensive input-driven to an intensive productivity-driven growth trajectory.

There is another strand of the literature however, that emphasizes the important role of tradable natural resources in Russian growth. It suggests that Russian growth is mainly driven by the windfall profits made through soaring oil and gas prices in the past fifteen years.[3] These profits fuelled an investment boom in sectors such as mining and ancillary services, which were considered to be neither particularly innovative nor efficient. These more qualitative studies refer to the increasing share of the mining sector in total investments and gross domestic product (GDP) and maintain that Russian growth is still extensive, rather than driven by productivity improvements.

In this study we aim to contribute to this debate and analyze for the first time the drivers of Russian growth at a detailed industry-level. We develop a new and consistent set of output and input measures for thirty-four industries for the period 1995 to 2012, taking into account revisions in the National Accounts Statistics, changes of industrial classifications, measurement issues of labor and capital, and estimates of factor shares in value added. We pay in particular attention to derive a proper measure of capital services in the tradition of Jorgenson, Gollop, and Fraumeni (1987), instead of using stock measures that dominate previous research, and discuss the importance of properly accounting for depreciation and rental prices. We show that the use of the capital services concept is not only theoretically to be preferred, but also empirically matters, as it qualifies the previous growth accounting findings.

---

[3] See e.g. Connolly (2011).

Based on these improved input measures, we find that Russian growth since 1995 is driven as much by input growth as by MFP growth. As such our study is comparable in spirit to the studies by Alwyn Young on East Asia (1995) and on China (2003) where he showed that a proper accounting for quantity and quality of inputs leads to considerably lower estimates of MFP growth compared to analysis based on raw unadjusted series. Our second contribution is that we trace the slow productivity performance to a limited set of industries, namely mining and retailing, where growth was particularly driven by capital inputs. These industries increased shares in GDP, and the mining sector accounted for more than a quarter of GDP in 2012. On the other hand, intensive growth took place in many manufacturing industries, but their share in GDP declined. Russian high-tech production was well developed before transition but did not survive the competition from high-quality imported products, while low-tech manufacturing suffered from low-cost competition from Asia. Various modern market services expanded in Russia and showed high MFP growth. These sectors were particularly underdeveloped in the 1990s, and much of this growth was through catching-up.

The rest of the chapter is organized as follows. In the next section we briefly outline the growth accounting methodology used in this study and discuss our reasons to opt for an ex post external rate of return approach to capital measurement. In Section 8.3 we discuss the various data challenges to be faced when attempting a growth account based on official Russian statistics. We highlight deficiencies in the official data and how we dealt with those. Comparisons with previous studies are made as well. Growth accounting results at the aggregate and industry levels are discussed in Section 8.4. Section 8.5 concludes.

8.2 Growth accounting method

To analyze the sources of Russian growth we will use the standard growth accounting methodology which allows a breakdown of output growth rates into a weighted average of growth in various inputs and productivity change (see Schreyer 2001 for an overview). We follow the representation of value added-based industrial growth accounting of Jorgenson, Ho and Stiroh (2005, ch. 8).

The quantity of value added (Z_j) in industry j may be represented as the function of capital services, labor services and technology as

$$Z_j = g_j(K_j, L_j, T). \tag{1}$$

Assuming a translog production function, competitive markets for inputs and constant returns to scale the change in multifactor productivity (A_j) is defined as

$$\Delta \ln A_j \equiv \Delta \ln Z_j - \bar{v}_{K,j}^Z \Delta \ln K_j - \bar{v}_{L,j}^Z \Delta \ln L_j \tag{2}$$

where $\bar{v}_{\circ,j}^Z$ is the period-average share of the input in the nominal value added. The value shares of capital and labor are defined as follows:

$$v_{K,j}^Z = \frac{p_j^K K_j}{p_j^Z Z_j}; v_{L,j}^Z = \frac{p_j^L L_j}{p_j^Z Z_j} \tag{3}$$

such that they sum to unity. Rearranging equation (2), industry value added growth can be decomposed into the contributions of capital, labor and MFP:

$$\Delta \ln Z_j = \bar{v}_{K,j}^Z \Delta \ln K_j + \bar{v}_{L,j}^Z \Delta \ln L_j + \Delta \ln A_j. \tag{4}$$

This decomposition is performed at the industry level and aggregate results are derived by using the direct aggregation across industries approach (Jorgenson *et al.* 2005). Then the volume growth of GDP is defined as a Törnqvist weighted average of value added growth in industries as follows

$$\Delta \ln Z \equiv \sum_j \bar{v}_{Z,j}^{GDP} \cdot \Delta \ln Z_j \tag{5}$$

where $\bar{v}_{Z,j}^{GDP}$ is the average share of value added of industry j in GDP. Substituting (4) in (5) gives

$$\Delta \ln Z = \sum_j \bar{v}_{Z,j}^{GDP} \cdot \bar{v}_{K,j}^Z \cdot \Delta \ln K_j + \sum_j \bar{v}_{Z,j}^{GDP} \cdot \bar{v}_{L,j}^Z \cdot \Delta \ln L_j$$
$$+ \sum_j \bar{v}_{Z,j}^{GDP} \cdot \Delta \ln A_j \tag{6}$$

This equation allows decomposition of GDP growth rates by contributions of factors and MFP growth in industries.

In this chapter we pay particular attention to the measurement of capital, given the various difficulties and uncertainties in deriving a proper empirical measure in the Russian context. Here we outline our theoretical approach and in the next section the empirical implementation. Following the growth accounting tradition, we measure capital input as a flow of capital services which takes into account the different marginal productivities of various asset types. Aggregate capital input in industry j (K_j) is defined as a Törnqvist volume index of individual capital assets stocks as:

$$\Delta \ln K_j = \sum_k \bar{v}_{k,j}^K \Delta \ln K_{k,j} \tag{7}$$

where $\Delta \ln K_{k,j}$ indicates the volume growth of capital stock of asset k. Assets are weighted by the period average shares of each type in the value of capital compensation given by

$$v_{k,j}^K = \frac{p_{k,j}^K K_{k,j}}{p_j^K K_j} \tag{8}$$

such that the sum of shares over all capital types add to unity. The estimation of the compensation share of each asset is related to the user cost of each asset. The rental price of capital services $p_{k,t}^K$ reflects the price at which the investor is indifferent between buying and renting the capital good for a one-year lease in the rental market. In the absence of taxation the familiar cost-of-capital equation is given by:

$$p_{k,j,t}^K = p_{k,j,t-1}^I i_{j,t} + \delta_k p_{k,j,t}^I - \left(p_{k,j,t}^I - p_{k,j,t-1}^I \right) \tag{9}$$

with $i_{j,t}$ representing the nominal rate of return in industry j, δ_k the depreciation rate of asset type k, and $p_{k,t}^I$ the investment price of asset type k. This formula shows that the rental fee is determined by the nominal rate of return, the rate of economic depreciation and an asset-specific capital gain.[4]

The literature is divided on the question of how to measure the rate of return, both on theoretical and empirical grounds. Following the neo-classical theory underlying growth accounting, the nominal rate of return is determined ex-post in the so-called endogenous approach (Jorgenson *et al.* 2005). It is assumed that the total value of capital services for each industry equals its compensation for all assets. This procedure yields an internal rate of return that exhausts capital income and is consistent with constant returns to scale. This nominal rate of

---

[4] Ideally taxes should be included to account for differences in tax treatment of the different asset types and different legal forms (household, corporate and non-corporate). However this refinement would require data on capital tax allowances and rates which is beyond the scope of this study.

return is the same for all assets in an industry, but is allowed to vary across industries, and is derived as a residual as follows:

$$
i_{j,t} = \frac{p^K_{j,t} K_{j,t} + \sum_k \left(p^I_{k,j,t} - p^I_{k,j,t-1} \right) K_{k,j,t} - \sum_k p^I_{k,j,t} \delta_{k,j} K_{k,j,t}}{\sum_k p^I_{k,j,t-1} K_{k,j,t}}
\tag{10}
$$

where the first term $p^K_{j,t} K_{j,t}$ is the capital compensation in industry j, which is derived as value added minus the compensation of labor.

The theoretical basis for the Jorgenson-type implementation of user cost is fairly restrictive though, relying among others on perfect foresight of investment returns. Balk (2010) provides a defense of the ex-ante approach which is considered to be independent of neo-classical theory. Also Oulton (2007) argues that the ex-post approach which assumes a single appropriate rate of return for all assets does not do full justice to a world with many assets.[5] For a proper empirical implementation of the ex-post approach all assets in the economy have to be covered and capital income should be accurately measured. Measurement error in any of these will in part show up in variation of the internal rate of return, and hence impact MFP measures.[6] The main reason to opt for an ex-post rate of return nevertheless is that it provides a method to take into account changes in capital utilization rates, which is of particular importance for an analysis of Russian growth from 1995 to 2012 which was a typical boom period. In 1998, Russia was at the trough of a severe crisis (see Figure 8.1) and obviously utilization rates increased rapidly afterwards. This increase should be accounted for in our input measures as we are interested in MFP as a measure of technological change, and almost all previous growth accounting studies attempt to deal with this one way or the other (see next section).[7]

---

[5] He ends up advocating a hybrid approach that uses an external rate of return to aggregate across different capital assets and an internal rate of return to determine the overall output elasticity of capital in the calculation of MFP.

[6] See Diewert (2008) and Schreyer (2009) for a more extensive discussion of these topics.

[7] Schreyer (2009) notes that if one is interested in MFP as a measure of real cost reduction, improvements in the utilization of capital capacity might be considered as a part of MFP growth and not capital input growth. An ex-ante approach would fit this interpretation.

We opt to deal with this through the ex-post approach. Berndt and Fuss (1986) showed that by treating capital as a quasi-fixed input, the income accruing to it is correctly measured in the approach outlined above, which would make a separate adjustment to the capital input measure superfluous. Hulten (1986) elucidated this theoretical result and highlights the conceptual problems of defining and measuring capital utilization rates as opposed to capacity utilization. He also shows that the theoretical result of Berndt and Fuss (1986) was derived under rather strict assumptions which do not necessarily hold in practice. Therefore our MFP measure might still (partially) include the effects of improved capacity utilization and only an econometric approach will be able to separate it out, see Hulten (1986) for further discussion.[8] Timmer and Voskoboynikov (2014) also provide some growth accounting results based on an ex-ante approach and show that the main conclusions of this study are not dependent on this choice of method.

Finally, aggregate labor input L_j is defined as a Törnqvist volume index of hours worked by individual labor types as follows:

$$\Delta \ln L_j = \sum_l \bar{v}_{l,j}^L \Delta \ln H_{l,j} \tag{11}$$

with weights given by

$$v_{l,j}^L = \frac{p_{l,j}^L H_{l,j}}{p_j^L L_j} \tag{12}$$

where $\Delta \ln H_{l,j}$ shows the hours worked growth by labor type l and weights are given by the period average shares of each type in the value of labor compensation, such that the sum of shares over all labor types add to unity. Because of the assumption that marginal revenues are equal to marginal costs, the weighting procedure guarantees that inputs which have a higher price also have a larger contribution to the input index. So for example a doubling of hours worked by a high-skilled worker gets a bigger weight than a doubling of hours worked by a low-skilled worker.

---

[8] Examples of such work include Beaulieu and Mattey (1998) or Basu and Fernald (2001).

8.3 Data sources and choices

This chapter is based on a newly developed detailed dataset of real value added, labor, and capital for thirty-four industries for the period from 1995 to 2012 in the international classification NACE 1.0 (Voskoboynikov 2012). The dataset includes longer and more detailed time series of industrial output and labor than available both in the literature and in the official statistics. Detailed data of output for industries in an international industrial classification, which cover the total economy, has become available in official publications of the Russian statistical office (Rosstat) only recently, whereas detailed series of labor and capital have never been issued.[9] In comparison with the extant literature, our measures of capital and labor are more detailed, cover a longer period, and have a better theoretical foundation. In this section we discuss our choices for the data sources and methods, and compare those with the previous growth accounting literature on Russia. In section 8.3.1 we discuss sources for value added and labor input, and in section 8.3.2 capital input. In general, our choices lead to higher estimates of the contribution of capital to growth and consequently lower estimates of MFP than the extant literature.

Although we use this new database for a growth accounting exercise, it serves many other application of economic analysis, in particular when used in conjunction with comparable data for other countries.[10]

8.3.1 Output and labor input series

A key concern when dealing with statistics from formerly centrally planned economies is the quality of the official data. Canonical prerequisites for industry growth accounting are a set of consistent data on labor and capital inputs and outputs within the System of National Accounts (SNA) framework.[11] SNA is the international standard of

---

[9] For convenience all sources published by the Russian statistical office are referenced as Rosstat in spite of the fact that the official name of the Russian/Soviet statistical office has been changing over time.

[10] The first release of Russia KLEMS data was issued in July 2013, covered the period from 1995 to 2009, and is available on the World KLEMS website (www.worldklems.net). This study is based on a preliminary version of the second release, posted in September 2016. In this release the series are extended until 2012 and the index of labor composition is added.

[11] Schreyer 2001; Jorgenson *et al.* 2005.

measures of economic activity, which amounts to a coherent and consistent set of macro-economic accounts of sources and uses of national income. However, in case of Russia some of these elements are not consistent with each other, whereas others only recently exist in the official statistics. SNA was introduced in Russia in early 1990s, substituting for the old Soviet national income accounting called the Material Product System (MPS).[12] But this process was slow and even nowadays some rudiments of the MPS have survived in the system of national statistics. This coexistence creates conceptual inconsistencies between different blocks of the Russian statistical system.[13] In contrast with the National Accounting Statistics (NAS), such primary sources as regular firms and households surveys in many aspects are well developed and have been collected for decades. Detailed data of primary sources in many cases is published and may be used to fill gaps in NAS statistics, improving official data for the purpose of detailed industrial growth accounting. The industrial classification was changed in 2003. The old industrial classification was introduced in the period of planned economy and made up within MPS, and inconsistent with any international classification (Masakova 2006). It was supplanted by a new classification in 2003, but Rosstat did not revise industry-level series in NAS back before 2002 in the new classification. We briefly discuss how we dealt with three major data hurdles issues and relegate interested readers for more details to Voskoboynikov (2012). These are: linking of industries across the old and new classification, measuring labor input, and measuring the labor share in value added.

To construct real value added series we had to bridge the change in industrial classification. For years before 2003 the NAS industrial data is available only in the old Soviet industrial classification, which is inconsistent with the new one, or any other international one.[14]

---

[12] In Soviet and Russian literature this system is called the Balance of National Economy (*Balans narodnogo khoziaĭstva*). We use term *the* Material Product System to provide consistency with the bulk of the literature in English.

[13] Ivanov 1987, 2009; Ivanov, Rjabushkin, and Homenko 1993; Masakova 2006. See also Entov and Lugovoy (2013) for a discussion in the context of growth accounting.

[14] The all-union classification of industries of the national economy is OKONKh (*Obshchesoiuznyĭ klassifikator "Otrasli narodnogo khoziaĭstva"*) (Rosstat 1976). From now on the OKONKh classification will be mentioned as "the old classification." The new industrial classification, OKVED (*Obshcherossiĭskiĭ klassifikator vidov ėkonomicheskoĭ deiatel'nosti*), coincides with NACE 1.0 to

Nominal gross output values by industries in the new classification before 2003 were obtained from Rosstat and were created within the Russia KLEMS feasibility study project (Bessonov *et al.* 2008). This dataset is an unpublished backcast estimation, which is based on the detailed bridge between the old classification and the new one. The bridge was compiled by Rosstat for 2003–2004, when primary data were collected in the two classifications at the same time.[15] To obtain nominal value added in industries we multiply the gross output of an industry to the corresponding value added – gross-output ratio. These ratios were calculated for the industries in the old classification, which were the closest counterparts of the industries in the new classification with published data. The volume indices of gross output until 2002 are based on output volume indices for detailed products with nominal gross output weights fixed in the new classification. The volume indices of value added until 2002 are assumed to be equal to the volume indices of output. This approach is justified by the fact that official volume indices of values added are calculated on the basis of the same set of physical volume indices of products as the indices of gross output. The only difference between official gross output and value added volume indices is in a different set of product weights.

Labor input is measured as hours worked and the labor composition effect. For compilation of the hours worked series we use series from the *Balance of Labour Inputs* which is consistent with the value added numbers from NAS.[16] It is available from 2005 onwards but only at an aggregate one-digit industry level. To breakdown to a finer industry detail and backcast the series before 2005 we rely on a combination of data from the *Balance of Labour Force* (BLF),[17] and reports of organizations of "*the Full Circle*" (FC),[18] which include large, medium, and small firms as well as various public administration

the four-digit level. OKVED/NACE 1.0 is mentioned as "the new industrial classification."

[15] Corresponding methodology was developed by Eduard Baranov and Vladimir Bessonov and implemented for backcast estimations of industrial output for the Ministry of Economic Development of the Russian Federation (Bessonov *et al.* 2008). Detailed description of this methodology is available in (Bessonov 2005).

[16] In Russian – *Balans zatrat truda*. Its description and methodology is available in Rosstat (2006).

[17] In Russian – *Balans trudovykh resursov*.

[18] In Russian – *Polnyĭ krug organizatsiĭ*. Its comprehensive definition and description is available in Vishnevskaya *et al.* (2002).

organizations. The BLF is the oldest system of labor accounts and used to be part of the MPS. It is based on FC with additional estimations for self-employed and workers engaged in commercial production in husbandries (Rosstat 1996; Rosstat 2003). FC contains more detailed data than the BLF. For 2003 and later detailed industry shares from BLF, and if necessary from FC, were applied to the aggregate series from the Balance of Labor Inputs. Before 2003, trends in BLF and FC at the corresponding industries were applied. BLF and FC measure number of employees and we have to assume that employee growth proxies for growth in hours. Details on the construction of labor series can be found in Voskoboynikov (2012, section 4).

Previous studies use estimations of the number of workers from BLF. But before 2003, the BLF is inconsistent with the NAS as it does not cover self-employment in agricultural husbandries. This mostly informal activity in agriculture is about one-fifth of the total amount of FTE jobs in the Russian economy. An imputation for value added made in the NAS GDP such that any measure of aggregate productivity based on official statistics, is biased. Following Poletayev (2003), we assume zero productivity growth rates in non-market households. Since data on output growth rates of non-market households are available, it is possible to impute employment growth.[19]

The index of labor composition (11)-(12) was calculated with the following data. Following Timmer *et al.* (2010), we use eighteen types of labor, breaking it down by gender (male and female), age (15–29; 30–49; 50 and older), and education (low, medium, and high skills levels) following the EU KLEMS framework: low skills level corresponds to International Standard Classification of Education (ISCED) levels 0–2 and 3 C; medium skills – 3 and 4, excluding 3 C; and high skills – 5 and 6 (Timmer *et al.* 2010, tab. 3A.4). In turn, the bridge between ISCED levels and levels of the Russian educational system was suggested by Kapeliushnikov (2008, tab. 1).

Hours worked by individual labor types were obtained by breaking down the total amount of hours worked in an industry with shares of

---

[19] Detailed description of the model is available in Appendix of Voskoboynikov (2012). Kapeliushnikov (2006) suggested an alternative approach for imputations of labor costs in non-market households for years before 1999 on the basis of changes of the area of plowing.

hours worked by a particular labor type. In turn, these shares were calculated on the basis of the Labor Force Survey.[20] Next, we used two sources of data on relative wages by type of labor. The first one is the National Survey of Household Welfare and Participation in Social Programs,[21] conducted by Rosstat in 2003 within the assistance program of the World Bank. The second one is the Survey of Wages by Occupations,[22] provided by Rosstat in 2005, 2007, 2009, and 2011. Relative wages for years between the surveys and before 2003 were assumed to be equal to ones in the nearest upcoming year, for which data is available.

The shares of labor and capital in value added are used as weights in the growth accounting methodology and reflect the output elasticity of the inputs. The labor share should reflect the total cost of labor from the perspective of the employer and hence include wages but also non-wage benefits for employees and an imputed wage for self-employed workers. In Russia there is a long standing tradition of non-wage payments. This is well known and Rosstat does make estimates which are included in the total economy series of the NAS, but not in the industry statistics. This is why industry-level NAS series on labor compensation in industries underestimate labor costs share. For total economy in 1995–2008 this underestimation is substantial and varies between 11 and 17% (Voskoboynikov 2012, A.T11). Bessonov (2004) argued that given the low accuracy of official imputations of hidden wages, using these shares would not make growth accounting estimations more precise. Previous studies therefore resorted to an alternative share, mostly taking a fixed 0.6 or 0.7 as the labor share, which is assumed to be typical for developed economies (Gollin 2002) or get them from econometric estimations (Kuboniwa 2011). Instead we develop new measures of labor compensation at a detailed industry level by using official imputations on shadow wages and value added made by Rosstat. These are added to official labor compensation of employees and value added from the NAS. For 2002 and consecutive years the overall amount of hidden wages at the overall economy level has been allocated among industries in proportion to the industry value

---

[20] In Russian – *Obsledovanie naseleniia po problemam zaniatosti (ONPZ).*
[21] In Russian – *Natsional'noe obsledovanie biudzhetov domashnikh khoziaĭstv (NOBUS).*
[22] In Russian – *Obsledovanie zarabotnykh plat po professiiam (OZPP).*

added share of shadow activities taken from official imputations.[23] For years before 2002 the hidden wages were allocated in proportion to the industry distribution of shadow value added of 2002. Finally our estimate of labor income of self-employed is added. For all industries except agriculture it was assumed that the hourly earnings of self-employed are the same as of employees. For agriculture, with a high share of low educated workers, we imputed with the total economy average wage for low educated employees based on data from the RLMS survey.[24] Further details can be found in Voskoboynikov (2012, section 6).

8.3.2 Capital input series

One of the most difficult problems in doing growth accounting for economies that were formerly centrally planned is the measurement of capital input. The present chapter uses the concept of capital services, which is superior to the concept of capital stocks used in recent literature for Russia. In contrast with capital stocks, capital services take into account variations in productivity of different types of assets. For example, one rouble of investment in buildings generates much less capital services per year than the same rouble invested in software, because buildings are much longer in operation. We constructed detailed capital stocks by eight asset types to measure capital input based on the perpetual inventory method (PIM): computing equipment, communication equipment and software, residential structures, non-residential structures, machinery and equipment, transport, and other assets.[25] For each individual asset, stocks have been estimated on the basis of investment series using the PIM with geometric

---

[23] Data is available in official publications – see (Rosstat 2010, tab. 2.3.46–2.3.53).

[24] Qualification of workers was identified in RLMS with the code of International Standard Classification of Occupations ISCO 88. Workers were considered as low qualified if the corresponding code varied between 6000 and 7000. "Russia Longitudinal Monitoring survey, RLMS-HSE," conducted by Higher School of Economics and ZAO "Demoscope" together with Carolina Population Center, University of North Carolina at Chapel Hill and the Institute of Sociology of the Russian Academy of Science.

[25] In Russian – *vychislitel'naia tekhnika; informatsionnye mashiny, ne vkliuchaia vychislitel'nuiu tekhniku; nematerial'nye aktivy; zhilishcha; zdaniia, sooruzheniia i peredatochnye ustroĭstva; transportnye sredstva; silovye i rabochie mashiny;* and *prochie aktivy*.

depreciation profiles. According to the PIM, the capital stock (S) is defined as a weighted sum of past investments with weights given by the relative efficiencies of capital goods at different ages:

$$S_{k,T} = \sum_{t=0}^{\infty} \partial_{k,t} I_{k,T-t} \tag{13}$$

with $S_{k,T}$ the capital stock (for a particular asset type k) at time T, $\partial_{k,t}$ the efficiency of a capital good k of age t relative to the efficiency of a new capital good, and $I_{k,T-t}$ the investments in period T-t. The geometric depreciation pattern δ_k is assumed constant over time, but different for each asset type, so we get $\partial_{k,t} = (1 - \delta_k)^{t-1}$, and:

$$S_{k,T} = \sum_{t=0}^{\infty} (1 - \delta_k)^{t-1} I_{k,T-t} = S_{k,T-1}(1 - \delta_k) + I_{k,T} \tag{14}$$

If it is assumed that the flow of capital services from each asset type k (K_k) is proportional to the average of the stock available at the end of the current and the prior period ($S_{k,T}$ and $S_{k,T-1}$), capital service flows can be aggregated from these asset types as a translog quantity index by weighting growth in the stock of each asset by the average shares of each asset in the value of capital compensation, as in equation (7) above.

In order to estimate capital stocks in Russia there are three particular issues that need to be addressed. First, the measures have to deal with so-called "communist capital." The term "communist capital" was suggested by Campos and Coricelli (2002) and refers to equipment and buildings put into operation before transition but becoming idle after transition due to the changing patterns of production and consumption. This stock has no market value anymore but is however still present in official capital stock statistics. Related to this is the questions of whether and how capital input measures should be adjusted for changes in capital utilisation rates, as Russia experienced some major fluctuations in growth after transition (see Figure 8.1). And third, given that the official NAS investment deflator appears to be highly overestimated, a proper choice of alternative investment deflators need to be made.

There are two main sources for official data on investment and capital stock in constant prices in Russia. The first is the Balance of Fixed Assets (BFA) which covers the total economy (Bratanova

2003).[26] This provides capital stocks based on direct observations of firm balance sheets in the current year based on previous year stocks plus new acquisitions minus discards. Also imputations for firms without a balance sheet are made. It should be noted that this stock measure does not account for depreciation of assets, unless scrapped as reported by firms. Volume indices of capital stocks are also published by deflating nominal stocks with an investment price index (Rosstat 2006, section 2.1); see below for more on deflation of BFA. Much of the communist capital is likely to be included in this stock measure and its growth rate is particularly low. Nevertheless, it is used by Entov and Lugovoy (2013).

Most other studies prefer to build up their own estimates through the perpetual inventory method and use the stock estimate only as a benchmark estimate for the initial year of the series. Investments series are taken from the series of gross fixed capital formation (GFCF) from the NAS which are available in current and constant prices. This is the approach followed by Kuboniwa (2011) and Izyumov and Vahaly (2008), both using aggregate investment data with a depreciation rate of 1.8 and 5% respectively. Izyumov and Vahaly (2008) pay particular attention to the communist capital problem and correct for "market quality" of the capital stock in 1991. They estimate that only about half of the stock was useful for production after transition and use this to initiate the PIM estimate. The problem with the NAS investment series however is that the implicit deflator appears to be highly overestimated. Bessonov and Voskoboynikov (2008) provide a comparison with other price indices and show that especially in the period 1991–1996 prices on investment goods grew much faster than the overall level of prices in the economy. However, this is very unlikely because typically investment price indices are falling relative to the overall price levels (Greenwood, Hercowitz, and Krusell 1997). Also Bratanova (2003, 4.40) has pointed out the overestimation of prices on investment in Russian statistics. This is clearly shown in Figure 8.2 which provides the developments of a number of Russian price series. As prices changes are overestimated real investments are underestimated and likewise the growth rate of capital stocks.

---

[26] In Russian – *balans osnovnykh fondov po polnoĭ stoimosti v postoiannykh tsenakh*. The Russian statistics also develops the Net Balance of Fixed Assets (*balans osnovnykh fondov po ostatochnoĭ stoimosti v tekushchikh tsenakh*), which includes net capital stocks and depreciation. However, data on net capital stocks in constant prices is not available.

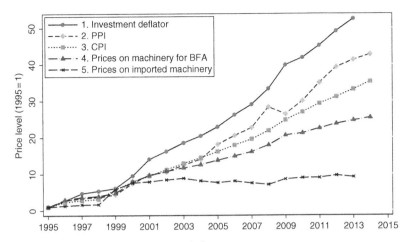

Figure 8.2 Alternative investment deflators
Source: 1–4 Rosstat (see details in Section 3); 5 – own calculations.
Note: Price level measured by investments deflator from NAS(1); producer price index in manufacturing(2); consumer price index(3); price index on machinery and equipment from BFA(4); price index on imported machinery and equipment(5); the price index on imported machinery and equipment captures price changes on imported machinery from the perspective of a Russian domestic purchaser. It has been calculated on the basis of the series of imported machinery and equipment in U.S. dollars (*Import po tovaram; tovarnym gruppam v razreze TN VED Rossii; Mashiny i oborudovanie*) available in (Rosstat 2014), producer price index on machinery and equipment of the U.S. Bureau of Labor Statistics (BLS 2014) and yearly averaged exchange rates of U.S. dollars to Russian rubles of the Central Bank of Russia. This approach is based on the assumption that prices on imported equipment in a foreign currency change in the same way as corresponding prices in the U.S.

Our solution to deal with the particular problems posed is by building up stocks from 1995 with a PIM using new investment deflators and asset-specific depreciation rates. Our approach tries to improve previous estimates by combining NAS investment series with deflators used in the BFA. We start with the GFCF series given in the NAS which are available by industry, but not by asset type for the whole period under consideration.[27] For the breakdown by asset type we use shares derived from detailed information on new acquisitions by industry and asset type from

[27] Formally, Rosstat publishes series of GFCF for total economy only. For industries only investments to fixed assets are available. However, the official

the annual survey of large and medium firms called "Form F11" which is part of the BFA.[28] Instead of using the NAS investment price indices we use the underlying asset type deflators used by Rosstat to deflate overall capital stocks in the BFA.[29] We use the price index of construction works for deflation of investments in residential and non-residential structures; the overall investments price index is used for other assets and the index on machinery and equipment as part of investments to fixed capital for the remaining types of assets (Rosstat 2002; Rosstat 2014). Asset deflators are assumed to be the same for each industry. The trend of these price series appear to be much more plausible (see Figure 8.2), and they explicitly take into account changes on prices of imported equipment and varies for different types of assets. These deflated investment series are used in a PIM building up from the net capital stock estimate in 1995 from the BFA and using asset specific depreciation rates from Fraumeni (1997).[30] Transformation of initial stocks and investment series from the old to the new classification was accomplished with the detailed official (unpublished) bridge for investments.

Summarizing, in contrast with recent growth accounting literature, which deals with the Russian economy, the present study develops a more detailed dataset, focusing on the following measurement issues of inputs.[31] First, we use alternative deflators that seem more in line with other price developments in the Russian economy. Second, we implement more flexible depreciation rates. Unlike the most previous literature, where depreciation was fixed at the level of 5% (e.g. Iradian 2007; Izyumov and Vahaly 2008), in this study we implement the BEA depreciation rates

methodology acknowledges that the conceptual difference between the two measures of investments is minor (Rosstat 2009).

[28] Detailed data of survey F11 is issued by Rosstat in yearly internal publications *Otchet o nalichii i dvizhenii osnovnykh sredstv i drugikh nefinansovykh aktivakh (f. №11)* (Statement of inventories and flows of fixed assets and other non-financial assets (form 11)). The full list of sources for various years is available in (Voskoboynikov and Dryabina 2009). A detailed description of the survey in Russian statistics of capital in English is given by (Bratanova 2003).

[29] Russian terms: *indeks tsen proizvoditelei v stroitel'stve; indeks tsen na stroitel'no-montazhnye raboty; indeks tsen na mashiny i oborudovanie v sostave investitsii v osnovnoi kapital.*

[30] However, for sensitivity analysis we also used rates on the basis of a survey of services lives, provided by Rosstat in 2008. Results of the growth accounts appear to be barely affected.

[31] A more detailed quantitative assessment of the influence of each of these measurement issues on growth accounting results is provided by Timmer and Voskoboynikov (2014).

Table 8.1 *Value added decomposition for market economy growth, 1995–2012*

	1995–2002	2002–2008	2008–2012	1995–2012
Growth rates				
Value added	2,78	6,85	1,03	3,74
Hours worked	1,22	1,57	–0,04	0,98
Labor composition	0,43	0,30	0,34	0,37
Capital	0,43	6,88	5,61	3,76
ICT capital	9,91	11,92	0,92	10,16
Machinery and equipment	–0,65	12,37	9,08	5,75
Non-residential buildings	0,38	2,90	3,79	2,13
MFP	1,63	2,85	–1,61	1,16
Contributions to value added				
Value added	2,78	6,85	1,03	3,74
Hours worked	0,46	0,91	–0,10	0,52
Labor composition	0,25	0,18	0,22	0,22
Capital	0,43	2,92	2,53	1,84
ICT capital	0,21	0,26	0,09	0,16
Machinery and equipment	–0,01	1,68	1,19	0,89
Non-residential buildings	0,22	0,99	1,25	0,79
MFP	1,63	2,85	–1,61	1,16

Notes: Market economy excludes public administration, education, health care and real estate industries.
Sources: Authors' calculations based on value added and labor from Voskoboynikov (2012); alternative official deflators from (Rosstat 2014); depreciation rates from Fraumeni (1997) and the ex-post rate of return.

(Fraumeni 1997), which vary from 3% for buildings and construction to 33% for information and communication technology (ICT) and software. Third, we calculate capital input growth not as the growth of aggregate stock, but of capital services. This does not affect the growth in individual asset stocks, but gives larger weight to assets with higher rental prices (such as machinery) in the capital input index. Fourth, we take into account changes in labor composition, considering variations in productivity in eighteen types of labor. As can be seen in Table 8.1, this effect explains almost 0.4 percentage points (pp) of growth, which was attributed in previous studies to MFP. Finally, the assumption of a labor share of 0.7% is common for developed economies, but not necessarily valid for a transition economy like Russia. We use a labor share in value added in industries calculated as employee wages from the NAS, adjusted for shadow wages from the NAS and our imputation of self-employed and household workers' income (see Section 8.3.1). We find that the share of labor is much lower and at 52% of value added. Hence the output elasticity of capital is estimated to be higher and given that capital inputs is growing faster than labor inputs, estimated MFP is falling.

8.4 Growth accounting results

In this section we describe the main results from the industry-level growth accounting using the constructed data set discussed above.

8.4.1 Aggregate economy growth accounting alternatives

We study the period from 1995 to 2012 in which Russia has undergone major shocks. As can be seen in Figure 8.1, it includes two economic crises, 1998 and 2009, as well as the inter-crises period of rapid resurgence. How did the growth structure change in these periods? The advantage of using the KLEMS data is that we cover a long time period up to the recent financial crisis, allowing for simple dynamic analysis. We split the data into three periods, 1995–2002, 2002–2008, and 2008–2012. In this split we put peaks and troughs of business cycles into the periods to minimize errors of growth accounting decomposition because of short-term demand effects. Indeed, in case of a sharp output fall, which happened in 1998 and 2009, a decrease of capital utilization might not be fully captured by capital input measures and may partially be attributed to MFP slowdown.[32] Moreover, in the following recovery years the opposite might occur.

Traditionally it has been argued that growth in post-transition economies, including Russia, is driven by multi-factor productivity (e.g. Campos and Coricelli 2002; Entov and Lugovoy 2013). In contrast, our results for the Russian economy shown in Table 8.1 reveal that MFP contributed only

---

[32] Although implementation of the ex-post rate of return reduces this type of error (see Section 8.3.2).

1.2pp of 3.7% of the yearly average growth of the total economy in 1995–2012, or less than one-third. Indeed, Table 8.1 demonstrates that over time, growth becomes more extensive. During the period 1995–2002 MFP provided 1.6pp of 2.8, or almost 60%, but in the following years the contribution of MFP declined to about 42%. In years of the global crisis MFP growth turns to be negative. At the flip-side, these results indicate that Russia has become ever more dependent on investment for driving growth.[33] While in the first period the contribution of capital services growth was relatively low, in the following years its role was increasing dramatically. In years of recovery, it accounted for 2.7 p.p., or almost 40% of output growth, while in the last global crisis it became the dominant source of growth, growing faster than value added. The growth accounting results in Table 8.1 show for the first time also the contribution of changes in the labor composition. This data was not available before. The main finding here is that in post-transition Russia, the quality of labor continues to grow. Interestingly, Table 8.1 demonstrates a stable positive contribution of labor composition for the Russian economy in all three periods, including years of crisis. This indicates that with general labor-shedding in a crisis firms shed mainly low skilled workers, while retaining high skilled ones.

8.4.2 Changing structure of the Russian economy

To understand the deeper sources of growth of the Russian economy, it is useful to look at changes at a more detailed sectoral level. The literature, which deals with structural change of the Russian economy, typically explores a traditional division of activities into agriculture, industry, and services. This partition of the economy is useful for analyzing structural change in developing economies where the majority of workers are still in primary industries, but is unsuited for studies of Russian development. Russia passed the first stage of industrialization in the first half of the twentieth century and had a sizable industrial complex at the end of the 1980s (Ofer 1987, table 4). Market services on the other hand were relatively underdeveloped and it is useful to distinguish them from non-market services. O'Mahony and van Ark (2003) proposed a classification of industries based on the skill-intensity of production, distinguishing between high-skilled and low-skilled

---

[33] See also Voskoboynikov and Solanko (2014) about this.

goods production and services, and we follow this. Finally, we separate out the mining industry which is important for the Russian economy. In Table 8.2 we show the shares of these sectors in nominal GDP and their real growth rates over the period 1995–2012.

Particular attention should be given to the definition and measurement of the mining industry in Russia. Mining activities are covered in the Russian statistical system in the industry *Mining*, but also in some sub-industries of *Wholesale Trade, Inland Transport,* and *Fuel*. For example, the World Bank report (2005), Gurvich (2004), and Kuboniwa, Tabata, and Ustinova (2005) pointed out that separate performance measures of each of these industries on the basis of SNA data are misleading because of non-market pricing of transactions between establishments of the vertically integrated holdings, such as *Gazprom*. These firms have establishments in various industries and are known to use transfer pricing in order to minimize tax payments. Due to a lack of detailed data, we approximate the size of the mining sector by clubbing together the mining and wholesale distribution industries and find that its share has been growing from around one-fifth of total GDP in 1995 to more than a quarter in 2012.

Other goods production, on the other hand, declined rapidly in importance from 26% to 16% in 2012. While high-skill intensive manufacturing industries such as chemicals and electrical equipment remained relatively stable but small (just above 3%), value added in agriculture, textiles, metal, and plastics declined rapidly. The share of market services remained more or less constant at 40% of GDP, but structural change within this sector was high. Low-skill intensive services such as utilities and construction lost shares, while high-skill intensive services such as financial intermediation and business services increased their share in GDP to over 10% in 2012. This is a reflection of the catching up process of certain services sectors which were underdeveloped in planned economy (Fernandes 2009). Also the share of non-market services (especially public administration and education) increased somewhat but is still much lower than in advanced nations (Jorgenson and Timmer 2011).

Table 8.2 also unveils changes in the Russian economy after the global financial crisis of 2008. Three distinctive features of this are worthy of discussion. First, high skilled intensive services shrank for the first time since 1995, in particular the financial sector. Second, non-market services expanded by 3 percentage points, which is more than for the whole previous period in question. This can be the outcome of efforts of the government to keep unemployment under control, hiring

Table 8.2 *Sectoral shares of value added and contribution to real growth, 1995–2012 (%)*

	Value added share (%)				Annual real growth rates (%)			
	1995	2002	2008	2012	1995–2002	2002–2008	2008–2012	1995–2012
Total economy	100.0	100,0	100,0	100.0	2,78	6,85	1,03	3.7
Mining and distribution	20.1	23,5	24,7	26.9	2,64	7,74	2,52	4.3
Goods	25.6	21,9	18,3	15.5	1,80	4,40	–0,60	2.1
High-skill intensive	3.6	2,9	3,6	3.3	0,91	7,35	–1,63	2.6
Low-skill intensive	22.0	19,0	14,8	12.2	1,94	3,83	–0,33	2.1
Services	40.4	39,1	41,0	38.6	3,19	8,97	0,50	4.5
High-skill intensive	5.1	8,4	11,2	10.7	9,65	12,07	1,70	8.7
Low-skill intensive	35.3	30,7	29,8	27.9	1,88	7,97	0,05	3.5
Non-market services	13.9	15,5	16,0	19.0	3,43	3,26	1,62	3.1

Source: Authors' calculations, see main text.

more workers for public services. Finally, we observe shrinking of high skill-intensive goods by 0.3 percentage points relative to 2008, and only mining and distribution continued to expand. As will be discussed in the following sub-section, all these trends led to a slowdown in aggregate multi-factor productivity growth.

8.4.3 *Sectoral contribution to aggregate input and productivity growth*

The productivity performance of the various sectors has been quite diverse. In Table 8.3 we provide the annual growth rates of labor and capital input and MFP growth for the main sectors in Russia from 1995–2012. This is shown in the left-hand side of the table. MFP is calculated by subtracting weighted input growth from value added growth as shown in equation (4). Capital input has been measured by our preferred method, the ex-post approach. In the right hand side of the table the contribution of each sector to aggregate growth in inputs and MFP is shown. This is derived by weighting industry growth by its share in value added as in equation (6). The contributions of all industries add up to aggregate market economy growth by definition.

The fastest MFP growth rates are found in the skill-intensive sectors, in particular in finance and business services. While labor and capital input grew at rates comparable to the market economy as a whole, MFP growth was more than 6% annually, which is more than 4 p.p. higher than the aggregate. This is a remarkable high level of improvement compared to what has been found for advanced countries, but much of this is catch-up growth as the level of development of these services was particularly low before and during transition, as suggested by Fernandes (2009).[34] Using industry specific purchasing power parities (PPPs) it is possible to compare the level of productivity in Russia with other countries in the same industries. Based on the industry output PPPs for 2005, derived from expenditure PPPs as described in Inklaar and Timmer (2012), we find that MFP in high-skilled services in Russia in 1995 was only about 12% of the level in Germany. This was by far the lowest relative level of all sectors considered here, confirming the retarded state of these sectors. Even after

---

[34] For Russia the pre-transition underdevelopment of trade, banking, and insurance in comparison with "normal" for a corresponding level of GDP per capita is discussed in Gregory and Stuart (2001, p. 368).

Table. 8.3 *Average annual growth rates of inputs and MFP during 1995–2012*

	Annual real growth rates (%)				Contribution to total (percentage points)			
	Hours worked	Cap. input	MFP	Lab. com-pos.	Hours worked	Cap. input	MFP	Lab. com-pos.
Market economy	0.91	3.55	1.30	0.39	0.91	3.55	1.30	0.39
Goods	-1.01	0.86	1.90	0.67	-0.25	0.21	0.46	0.16
High skill intensive	-2.52	0.44	3.70	0.38	-0.10	0.02	0.15	0.02
Low skill intensive	-0.71	0.94	1.54	0.73	-0.14	0.19	0.31	0.15
Services	1.51	4.79	1.52	0.20	0.72	2.27	0.72	0.09
High skill intensive	1.37	4.35	6.15	0.44	0.13	0.42	0.59	0.04
Low skill intensive	1.55	4.91	0.36	0.14	0.58	1.85	0.14	0.05
Mining and wholesale trade	1.56	3.80	0.43	0.45	0.44	1.08	0.12	0.13

Sources: Authors' calculations, see main text.

the period of rapid growth, in 2007 the gap with Germany is still 49% leaving plenty of room for further catching-up.

MFP growth was also fast for high-skilled manufacturing with 3.7 percent annually and this could potentially be a major source of growth for Russia. But it appeared that MFP growth was mainly due to a severe rationalization of the sector in the wake of increased competition from advanced nations as Russia gradually opened up to international trade in high-tech in the 1990s. Capital input growth was negative and labor especially declined rapidly such that this sector is now less than 4% GDP (Table 8.2) and ceased to be an important source of growth.

In contrast labor and in particular capital inputs gravitated towards low-skill intensive services and the mining sector. Together these two sectors more than fully "explain" aggregate labor input growth. But while input growth rates were high, MFP growth rates were far below average. Both in low-skill intensive services and mining average MFP growth rates were 0.4%, such that together they are responsible for only less than 0.3 percentage points out of 1.3 percent aggregate MFP growth.

Retail is one of the industries that is growing fast in terms of inputs, but MFP growth is only slow. The retail sector in Russia has a strong dual nature. One part is represented by new modern capital-intensive supermarkets with up-to-date retail technologies, whereas the other is made up of labor-intensive, mostly informal, family-run retail shops. The retail sector in the Soviet Union was lagging for a long time and McKinsey (1999, p. 5), reported that modern high-productivity for-mats were almost entirely absent, with less than 1% of market share. Starting from the middle of 1990s Russia experienced an explosive growth of modern retail centers and in 2009 they had captured 35% of total retail sales (McKinsey 2009, p. 65), through both foreign direct investment (FDI) and expansion of domestic retail chains. But this expansion has not yet lead to increased MFP.

Interestingly, the quality of the labor force in goods grew twice as fast as in services, being strongest in low-skills intensive goods. Given the massive downsizing of this industry, in particular in the low-tech industries, this suggests a pattern where firms mainly shed low-skilled workers while retaining high-skilled ones. Redundant manufacturing workers might have to find new jobs in low-skill intensive services in which the quality of the labor force grew only slowly.

Finally, it is worth mentioning the influence of the global financial crisis on aggregate MFP growth rates. Since all sectors-contributors to the aggregate MFP growth started shrinking, aggregate growth would slow down in the long run. For example, fast growth in skills-intensive services was likely to slow down as most of the catch-up potential was realized. At the same time, the sectors with the fastest productivity growth until 2008 started shrinking, bringing down aggregate MFP growth even more. This makes perspectives of long-run sustained growth of the Russian economy even more uncertain.

To illustrate the industry concentration of Russian growth in more detail, we turn to the detailed growth account results for the thirty-one detailed industries listed in the Appendix and present the diagrams suggested by Harberger (1998), known as Harberger diagrams. These diagrams provide an intuitive way of identifying whether an aggregate growth rate is caused by a few industries or whether growth is widespread. This diagram is a graphical representation of the industrial growth pattern with the Y-axis showing growth contributions and X-axis the cumulative value added shares. The industries are ranked by growth rates, so the fastest growing industry is to be found near the origin. Inklaar and Timmer (2007) have suggested three useful descriptive indices for these diagrams, which are the aggregate growth, the cumulative share of growth with positive contributions, and curvature. The aggregate growth is the sum of industry contributions, whereas the other two measures indicate pervasiveness of growth. The cumulative share is the summed share of value added of all industries which demonstrate positive growth rates. The curvature is defined as the ratio of the area between the diagram and the diagonal line, and the total area beneath the diagram. The value of curvature lies between 0 and 1, with the value being lower when the growth pattern is more broad-based and observed in many industries. On the other hand, if growth is more concentrated in few industries, the value will be higher. The Harberger diagrams for MFP are given in Figure 8.3. They represent three sub-periods, 1995–2002, 2002–2008, and 2008–2012. In years before the global crisis of 2008, MFP growth was widely spread across industries. The value added share of industries with positive growth rates was almost 75% in the first sub-period and 80% in the second one. However, after the crisis the MFP decline became widespread. Only around one-fifth of the economy remained on the positive area.

A more scrupulous analysis unveils interesting details concerning the nature of this MFP growth pattern. First, the role of manufacturing industries was positive for the whole period. Table 8.3 provides some

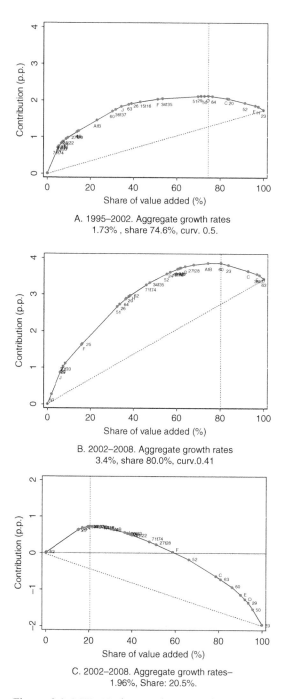

A. 1995–2002. Aggregate growth rates
1.73% , share 74.6%, curv. 0.5.

B. 2002–2008. Aggregate growth rates
3.4%, share 80.0%, curv.0.41

C. 2002–2008. Aggregate growth rates–
1.96%, Share: 20.5%.

Figure 8.3 MFP Harberger diagrams for multi-factor productivity growth, 1995–2012 (See the list of codes and industries in the Appendix Table 8.1.)

evidence of this at the aggregate level, reporting MFP growth rates 1.9% per year for goods. This is the highest value in comparison with the other aggregate sectors of the market economy. The Harberger diagrams show a more detailed picture of this. Almost all manufacturing industries contributed to MFP growth positively before 2008, five of which (leather and footwear, chemicals, rubber and plastics, and transport equipment) continuing growth in the following period.[35] Moreover, two high-skill intensive industries, machinery and electrical and optical equipment, were among leaders in 2002–2008, demonstrating 11.1% and 7.8% MFP annual growth rates correspondingly. Taking into account the initial technology backwardness in Russian manufacturing this matches the story of global convergence in manufacturing, reported by Rodrik (2013) and also observed in other Central and East European post-transition economies (Havlik *et al.* 2012).

Second, along with manufacturing, financial intermediation and business services were powerful drivers of aggregate MFP growth until 2008. Starting from a very low initial MFP level of 12% of Germany in 1995 for high-skill intensive services, they grew with soaring rates of 8.2% and 9.3% in 1995–2008 correspondingly, contributing 0.7 p.p.

Third, two of the three industries of the oil and gas sector, mining and fuel, were stagnant in all sub-periods. They demonstrated negative MFP growth rates along with plentiful capital inflow (Table 8.3). This confirms inability of the Russian oil and gas sector to diminish real costs of production both in years of high and low world oil prices, well known also in the literature (Ahrend and Tompson 2004). However, these data must be interpreted with caution because the performance of industry with the largest value added share in the oil and gas sector, wholesale trade, is unclear, because some share of valued added of mining, fuel and inland pipeline transport can be shifted to wholesale trade because of transfer pricing.

Finally, comparing the diagrams for years before and after the crisis, it is possible to highlight the influence of the last crisis on the Russian productivity pattern. The crisis hit manufacturing, especially such high-skills intensive industries as machinery and optical equipment. As can

[35] Exceptions are wood in 1995–2002 and other manufacturing in 2002–2008.

be seen, both have shifted to the negative territory in 2008–2012. In addition other manufacturing industries – food, textiles, non-metallic minerals – also stopped minimizing real costs of production. The last period was harmful for market services, which are financial intermediation and business services as well as construction and retail. Comparing the first and the last periods it is obvious that the Russian economy after 2008 is in a worse position in comparison with the period of stagnation and initial recovery in 1995–2002. Probably, this could be explained deterioration of the institutional environment, which amplified negative shocks from global markets and the stagnation of oil prices growth. Difficulties with the access to domestic and foreign capital were harmful for manufacturing industries with a long production cycle, while the slowdown of consumption growth hit market services. This illustrates a general observation from Table 8.1 that because of the crisis Russian growth has become more dependent on capital inflow than before, which makes its growth perspective uncertain.

8.5 Concluding remarks

GDP per capita growth rates in Russia have been among the highest in the world since the mid-1990s. In contrast to previous growth accounting studies we do not find that this is mainly driven by MFP growth. Rather, labor and capital input growth explain more of the value added growth during the period 1995–2012 than MFP. The greater measured contribution of capital input is due to the fact that we derived a proper measure of capital services input that distinguishes various capital types with asset-specific depreciation and investment deflators. Using the new industry-level dataset on inputs and outputs, we also found that the (extended) mining sector was not a driver of growth. Together with wholesale and retail trade, the mining sector absorbed an increasing share of labor and capital inputs, but had only poor MFP performance. The mining sector expanded to more than a quarter of GDP in 2012, up from one-fifth in 1995. MFP growth was high in goods industries but this sector's GDP share declined as it could not cope with increased foreign competition. Finance and business services were the only industries that performed well in terms of MFP growth and were expanding. But as their MFP levels were extremely low in the mid-1990s much of this growth is because of basic catching-up rather than an indication of dynamism and innovativeness. Given that the reallocation of inputs to more productive activities is a hallmark of growth in successful economies (McMillan and Rodrik 2011), these trends in Russia do not provide hopeful signs for future economic development.

Although we believe that the dataset developed for this chapter is of a higher quality than is currently available from official sources or otherwise, there is still much to be improved upon. This includes the development of better price indices for value added in the NAS. Many of the value added volume series in the NAS are still based on gross output quantity indicators (weighted with value added) and should be gradually replaced by properly (double) deflated value added series. The development of a new supply and use table (SUT) for 2011 that is currently under way should be helpful in that respect (the most recent one is of 1995), as is the development of new price deflators that take quality change into account. With respect to capital, new investment price indices should be used in the NAS that properly account for imported equipment and quality changes (e.g. for ICT capital). As shown, some of these indices are used by Rosstat in deflation of capital stocks, but not for investment series. Better measurement of labor costs and profits by industry where activities of large vertically integrated firms are allocated to the various industries would also be useful for any analysis of changes in industrial structures. Finally, the new benchmark SUTs create a possibility for formation of official KLEMS series by Rosstat, which would be a great leap forward to the SNA 2008 framework and, in addition, create more opportunities for the analysis of the Russian economy.

As a final note, we would like to stress that the growth accounting based on index numbers used in this study relies on stringent neo-classical assumptions that are likely to be violated for the case of Russia where market competition is still limited. Also the issue of how to deal with capital utilization variation cannot be completely resolved within this neo-classical non-parametric framework. We hope that the database developed for this study will be a fertile breeding ground for other studies into the sources of growth in Russia, relying on other non-parametric or parametric approaches.

Appendix Table 8.1 *List of sectors and industries*

NACE 1.0 code	Name of sector/industry used in the paper
	TOTAL ECONOMY
	Market economy
	Goods
	High skill-intensive
24	Chemicals and chemical products
29	Machinery, nec
30t33	Electrical and optical equipment
	Low skill-intensive
AtB	Agriculture, hunting, forestry, and fishing
15t16	Food, beverages, and tobacco
17t18	Textiles and textile products
19	Leather, leather, and footwear
20	Wood and products of wood and cork
21t22	Pulp, paper, paper, printing, and publishing
25	Rubber and plastics
26	Other non-metallic mineral
27t28	Basic metals and fabricated metal
34t35	Transport equipment
36t37	Manufacturing, nec; recycling
	Market services
	High skill-intensive
J	Financial intermediation
71t74	Renting of machinery and equipment and other business activities
	Low skill-intensive
E	Electricity, gas, and water supply
F	Construction
H	Hotels and restaurants
50	Sale, maintenance and repair of motor vehicles and motorcycles; retail
52	Retail trade, except of motor vehicles and motorcycles; repair of personal and household goods
60t63	Transport and transport services
64	Post and telecommunications
O	Other community, social, and personal services

Appendix Table 8.1 (*cont.*)

NACE 1.0 code	Name of sector/industry used in the paper
	Extended mining
23	Fuel
C	Mining and quarrying
51	Wholesale trade
	Non-market economy
70	Real estate activities
L	Public administration and defence; compulsory social security
M	Education
N	Health and social work

References

Ahrend, Rudiger and William Tompson. 2004. "Russia's Gas Sector: The Endless Wait for Reform?" *OECD Economic Department Working Papers*, ECO/WKP(2004)25 (402).

Balk, Bert M. 2010. "An Assumption-free Framework for Measuring Productivity Change." *Review of Income and Wealth*, 56: S224–S256.

Basu, Susanto and John Fernald. 2001. "Why is Productivity Procyclical? Why do we Care?" In Charles R. Hulten, Edwin R. Dean, and Michael J. Harper (eds.) *New Developments in Productivity Analysis*. Chicago and London: University of Chicago Press, ch. 7,225–301.

Beaulieu, John J. and Joseph Mattey. 1998. "The Workweek of Capital and Capital Utilization in Manufacturing," *Journal of Productivity Analysis*, 10(2): 199–223.

Berndt, Ernst R. and Melvyn A. Fuss. 1986. "Productivity Measurement with Adjustments for Variations in Capacity Utilization and Other Forms of Temporary Equilibrium," *Journal of Econometrics*, 33(1–2): 7–29.

Bessonov, Vladimir A. 2004. "O Dinamike Sovokupnoĭ Faktornoĭ proizvoditel'nosti v Rossiĭskoĭ Perekhodnoĭ Ėkonomike [on Dynamics of Total Factor Productivity in the Russian Economy in Transition]," *HSE Economic Journal*, 8(4): 542–587.

2005. *Problemy Analiza Rossiĭskoĭ Makroėkonomicheskoĭ Dinamiki Perekhodnogo Perioda [Problems of the Analysis of Macroeconomic Dynamics of the Russian Economy in Transition]*. Moscow: Institut Ėkonomiki Perekhodnogo Perioda.

Bessonov, Vladimir A. and Ilya B. Voskoboynikov. 2008. "Fixed Capital and Investment Trends in the Russian Economy in Transition," *Problems of Economic Transition*, 51(4): 6–48.

Bessonov, Vladimir A., Ilya B. Voskoboynikov, Elena V. Dryabina, Igor A. Kim, and Aleksey N. Ponomarenko. 2008. "On Findings of Preliminary Study of RU-KLEMS," Background Paper for the RU KLEMS Workshop in Higher School of Economics, Moscow, *March* 31.

BLS. 2014. "Producer Price Index Commodity Data. Group 11. Item 11. Machinery and Equipment," *Bureau of Labor Statistics*. See: www.bls .gov/data/#prices (accessed September 17, 2014).

Bratanova, Lidia. 2003. *Measurement of Capital Stock in Transition Economies*. Occasional Paper 2003/1. United Nations Economic Commission for Europe. Statistical division.

Campos, Nauro F. and Fabrizio Coricelli. 2002. "Growth in Transition: What we Know, What we Don't, and What we Should," *Journal of Economic Literature*, 40(3): 793–836.

Connolly, Richard. 2011. "Financial Constraints on the Modernization of the Russian Economy," *Eurasian Geography and Economics*, 52(3): 428–459.

Diewert, Erwin W. 2008. "What is to be Done for Better Productivity Measurement," *International Productivity Monitor*, 16: 40–52.

Entov, Revold M. and Oleg V. Lugovoy. 2013. "Growth Trends in Russia After 1998." In Michael Alexeev and Shlomo Weber (eds.) *The Oxford Handbook of the Russian Economy*. Oxford University Press.

Fernandes, Ana M. 2009. "Structure and Performance of the Service Sector in Transition Economies," *Economics of Transition*, 17(3): 467–501.

Fraumeni, Barbara. 1997. "The Measurement of Depreciation in the US National Income and Product Accounts," *Survey of Current Business*, July.

Gollin, Douglas. 2002. "Getting Income Shares Right," *The Journal of Political Economy*, 110(2): 458–474.

Greenwood, Jeremy, Zvi Hercowitz, and Per Krusell. 1997. "Long-run Implications of Investment-specific Technological Change," *The American Economic Review*, 87(3): 342–362.

Gregory, Paul R. and Robert C. Stuart. 2001. *Russian and Soviet Economic Performance and Structure*, 7th edn. Boston (MA): Addison-Wesley.

Gurvich, Evsey. 2004. "Makroèkonomicheskaia Otsenka Roli Rossiĭskogo Neftegazovogo Kompleksa [Macroeconomic Role of Russia's Oil and Gas Sector]," *Voprosy Èkonomiki*, 10: 4–31.

Harberger, Arnold C. 1998. "A Vision of the Growth Process," *The American Economic Review*, 88(1): 1–32.

Havlik, Peter, Sebastian Leitner, and Robert Stehrer. 2012. "Growth Resurgence, Productivity Catching-up and Labor Demand in Central and

Eastern European Countries." In Matilde Mas and Robert Stehrer (eds.), *Industrial Productivity in Europe. Growth and Crisis*, ch. 8, 219–263.

Hulten, Charles R. 1986. "Productivity Change, Capacity Utilization and the Sources of Efficiency Growth," *Journal of Econometrics*, **33**: 31–50.

Inklaar, Robert and Marcel P. Timmer. 2007. "Of Yeast and Mushrooms: Patterns of Industry-level Productivity Growth," *German Economic Review*, 8(2): 174–187.

2012. "The Relative Price of Services," *GGDC Research Memorandum*, **124**: 23.

Iradian, Garbis. 2007. "Rapid Growth in Transition Economies: Growth-Accounting Approach," *IMF Working Paper*, WP/07/164.

Ivanov, Youri. 1987. "Possibilities and Problems of Reconciliation of the SNA and the MPS," *Review of Income and Wealth*, 33(1): 1–18.

2009. "Experiences and Problems of the CIS Countries in Transition from the MPS to the SNA," *Review of Income and Wealth*, 55: 466–484.

Ivanov, Youri, Boris Rjabushkin, and Tatjana Homenko. 1993. "Introduction of the SNA into the Official Statistics of the Commonwealth of Independent States," *Review of Income and Wealth*, 39(3): 279–294.

Izyumov, Alexei and John Vahaly. 2008. "Old Capital vs. New Investment in Post-Soviet Economies: Conceptual Issues and Estimates," *Comparative Economic Studies*, 50 (1): 111–157; 111.

Jorgenson, Dale W., Frank M. Gollop, and Barbara Fraumeni. 1987. *Productivity and US Economic Growth*. Amsterdam: North-Holland.

Jorgenson, Dale W., Mun S. Ho, and Kevin J. Stiroh. 2005. *Information Technology and the American Growth Resurgence. Productivity*, Vol. **1**. Cambridge: The MIT Press.

Jorgenson, Dale W. and Marcel P. Timmer. 2011. "Structural Change in Advanced Nations: A New Set of Stylised Facts," *Scandinavian Journal of Economics*, 113(1): 1–29.

Jorgenson, Dale W. and Khuong M. Vu. 2011. "The Rise of Developing Asia and the New Economic Order," *Journal of Policy Modeling*, 33(5): 698–716.

2013. "The Emergence of the New Economic Order: Growth in the G7 and the G20," *Journal of Policy Modeling*, 35(3): 389–399.

Kapeliushnikov, Rostislav I. 2006. "Zaniatost' v Domashnikh Khoziaĭstvakh Naseleniia [Employment in Households]." In Vladimir E. Gimpelson and Rostislav I. Kapeliushnikov (eds.), *Nestandartnaia Zaniatost' v Rossiĭskoĭ Ėkonomike [Atypical Employment in the Russian Economy]*. Moscow: Gosudarstvennyĭ universitet – Vysshaia shkola ėkonomiki, 224–280.

2008. "Zapiska Ob Otechestvennom Chelovecheskom Kapitale [Russia's Human Capital: An Assessment]," *HSE Working Paper*, WP3/2008/01.

Krugman, Paul. 1994. "The Myth of Asia's Miracle," *Foreign Affairs*, 73(6): 62–78.

Kuboniwa, Masaaki. 2011. "The Russian Growth Path and TFP Changes in Light of Estimation of the Production Function using Quarterly Data," *Post-Communist Economies*, 23(3): 311–325.

Kuboniwa, Masaaki, Shinichiro Tabata, and Nataliya Ustinova. 2005. "How Large is the Oil and Gas Sector of Russia? A Research Report," *Eurasian Geography and Economics*, 46(1): 68–76.

Masakova, Irina D. 2006. *Recalculation of the Russian GDP Series in Connection with the Transition to New Classifications.* Joint UNECE/Eurostat/OECD Meeting on National Accounts and Update of SNA. 8th Meeting, April 25–28, 2006. ECE/CES/GE.20/2006/3. See: www.unece.org/fileadmin/DAM/stats/documents/ece/ces/ge.20/2006/mtg2/3.e.pdf.

McKinsey. 1999. *Unlocking Economic Growth in Russia.* Brussels: McKinsey Global Institute.

——— 2009. *Lean Russia: Sustaining Economic Growth through Improved Productivity.* Brussels: McKinsey Global Institute.

McMillan, Margaret and Dani Rodrik. 2011. "Globalization, Structural Change, and Productivity Growth," *NBER Working Paper Series*, 17143.

Ofer, Gur. 1987. "Soviet Economic Growth: 1928–1985," *Journal of Economic Literature*, 25(4): 1767–1833.

O'Mahony, Mary and Bart van Ark. 2003. *EU Productivity and Competitiveness: An Industry Perspective*, European Commission.

Oulton, Nicholas. 2007. "Ex Post Versus Ex Ante Measures of the User Cost of Capital," *Review of Income and Wealth*, 53(2): 295–317.

Poletayev, Andrei V. 2003. "Èffektivnost' Funktsionirovaniia Rossiĭskogo Rynka Truda [Efficiency of Labor Market in Russia]," *HSE Working Paper*, WP3/2003/06.

Rodrik, Dani. 2013. "Unconditional Convergence in Manufacturing," *Quarterly Journal of Economics*, 128(1): 165–204.

Rosstat. 1976. *Otraslevaia Klassifikatsiia Otraslei Narodnogo Khoziaĭstva [Statistical Classification of Industries of the National Economy].* Moscow: Gosudarstvennyĭ komitet SSSR po statistike.

——— 1996. *Metodicheskie Polozheniia Po Statistike, vyp. 1 [Methodological Regulations on Statistics, vol. 1].* Moscow: Gosudarstvennyĭ komitet Rossiĭskoĭ Federatsii po statistike.

——— 2002. *Metodicheskie Rekomendatsii Po Nabliudeniiu Za Tsenami Proizvoditelei v Stroitel'Stve [Manual for Measurement of Producer's Prices in Construction].* Moscow: Gosudarstvennyĭ komitet Rossiĭskoĭ Federatsii po statistike.

2003. *Metodicheskie Polozheniia Po Statistike, vyp. 4 [Methodological Regulations on Statistics, vol. 4].* Moscow: Gosudarstvennyĭ komitet Rossiĭskoĭ Federatsii po statistike.

2006. *Metodicheskie Polozheniia Po Statistike, vyp. 5 [Methodological Regulations on Statistics, vol. 5].* Moscow: Federal'naia sluzhba gosudarstvennoĭ statistiki.

2009. *Investitsii v Rossii 2009 [Investments in Russia 2009].* Moscow: Federal'naia sluzhba gosudarstvennoĭ statistiki.

2010. *Natsional'nye Scheta Rossii v 2002–2009 Godakh [National Accounts of Russia in 2002–2009].* Moscow: Federal'naia sluzhba gosudarstvennoĭ statistiki.

2014. *"Tsentral'naia Baza Statisticheskikh Dannykh [The Central Database of Statistical Data]."* Federal'naia sluzhba gosudarstvennoĭ statistiki.

Schreyer, Paul. 2009. *Measuring Capital. OECD Manual. Measurement of Capital Stock, Consumption of Fixed Capital and Capital Services*, 2nd edn. Paris: OECD.

2001. *OECD Productivity Manual: A Guide to the Measurement of Industry-level and Aggregate Productivity Growth.* Paris: OECD.

Timmer, Marcel P., Robert Inklaar, Mary O'Mahony, and Bart van Ark. 2010. *Economic Growth in Europe.* Cambridge University Press.

Timmer, Marcel P. and Ilya B. Voskoboynikov. 2014. "Is Mining Fuelling Long-run Growth in Russia? Industry Productivity Growth Trends since 1995," *Review of Income and Wealth*, 60, S398–S422.

Vishnevskaya, Natal'ia T., Vladimir E. Gimpelson, S. V. Zaharov, Rostislav I. Kapeliushnikov, T. Iu Korshunova, P. M. Kudiukin, T. M. Maleva, and Andrei V. Poletayev. 2002. *Obzor Zaniatosti v Rossii, vyp. 1 (1991–2000 Gg.) [Employment Survey in Russia, Issue 1, 1991–2000].* Moscow: TEIS.

Voskoboynikov, Ilya B. 2012. "New Measures of Output, Labor and Capital in Industries of the Russian Economy," *GGDC Research Memorandum*, GD-123.

Voskoboynikov, Ilya B. and Elena V. Dryabina. 2009. "Otraslevaia Istoricheskaia Statistika Osnovnykh Fondov Rossiĭskoĭ Promyshlennosti (1970–2004). Dannye i Istochniki [Historical Time Series Data of Fixed Capital of the Russian Economy. Manufacturing (1970–2004). Data and Sources]," *HSE Working Paper*, WP2/2009/03.

Voskoboynikov, Ilya B. and Laura Solanko. 2014. "When High Growth is Not Enough: Rethinking Russia's Pre-crisis Economic Performance," *BOFIT Policy Brief*, 6.

World Bank. 2005. *Russian Federation: From Transition to Development.* A Country Economic Memorandum for the Russian Federation, March.

Young, Alwyn. 1995. "The Tyranny of Numbers: Confronting the Statistical Realities of the East Asian Growth Experience," *The Quarterly Journal of Economics*, **110**(3): 641–680.

    2003. "Gold into Base Metals: Productivity Growth in the People's Republic of China during the Reform Period," *Journal of Political Economy*, **111**(6): 1220–1261.

9 | Intangibles, ICT and industry productivity growth: evidence from the EU

CAROL CORRADO, JONATHAN HASKEL,
AND CECILIA JONA-LASINIO

Using intangible investment data by industry for fourteen EU countries in 1995–2010 we investigate industry growth accounting and complementarities between intangibles and ICT.[1] We find: (a) intangible investment has grown in manufacturing and services, but most strongly in services; (b) the contribution of intangibles to labor productivity growth is similar in both manufacturing and services and in the high growth economies (Austria, Germany, Finland, France, Netherlands, UK) exceeds the contribution of labor quality; (c) the very large size of the service sector means that countries with good manufacturing but poor service productivity growth (Germany and France) have done relatively badly overall and those with good service sector growth (UK, Netherlands) have performed well; (d) Spain and Italy have very low labor productivity growth due to very low total factor productivity (TFP) growth; and (e) we find evidence of complementarities between intangible capital and information and communications technology (ICT).

Empirical evidence shows that once intangible capital is included in a sources-of-growth analysis it accounts for 20–33 percent of labor productivity growth in the market sector of the United States and European Union economies.[2] As a consequence, the measurement of

---

[1] The authors thank Massimiliano Iommi for methodological and data support and participants at the 3rd World KLEMS (RIETI, Tokyo, May 2014) conference for helpful discussions on earlier versions of this chapter. Errors and opinions are our own. For financial support we thank the EU FP-7 SPINTAN grant No. 612774.

[2] The most recent report of this accounting is in Corrado, Haskel, Jona-Lasinio, and Iommi (2013). Corrado, Hulten, and Sichel (2009) and Marrano, Haskel, and Wallis (2009) first reported results of about one-fourth for the US and UK, respectively. The contribution in Japan and many EU countries is lower (Fukao, Miyagawa, Mukai, Shinoda, and Tonogi 2009) and (van Ark, Hao, Corrado, and Hulten 2009).

intangible investment is a potentially important addition to both sources-of-growth analysis and national accounting practice.

Following the work of Corrado *et al.* (2005, 2009) and Nakamura (1999), building in turn on the work of Machlup (1962), among others, major research efforts were undertaken to measure intangible investment and intangible capital for the business sector of European countries (INNODRIVE and COINVEST FP7 European funded projects). This led to the development of the INTAN-Invest harmonized framework for measuring intangible investment in these countries.[3] At the same time, estimates for many other countries (not necessarily harmonized) have emerged, e.g., for Japan (Fukao *et al.* 2009), Australia (Barnes and McClure 2009), Canada (Baldwin, Gu, and Macdonald 2012), and Korea (Pyo, Chun, and Rhee 2012).

Sources-of-growth analyzes that feature ICT (e.g., Jorgenson, Ho, and Stiroh 2005), as well as those that analyze intangible capital and economic growth, demonstrate that better measurement of different types of capital allows for the identification of productivity change due to composition shifts to higher performing asset types. The macro literature on the impact of ICT on productivity change usually does not consider the possibility of synergies between ICT and intangible capital, although Basu, Fernald, Oulton, and Srinivasan (2004) is a notable exception. This may seem surprising given the body of micro-economic evidence that suggests ICT capital and intangible capital are complements in production (e.g., Brynjolfsson and Hitt 2000; Brynjolfsson, Hitt, and Yang 2002). But it is in fact *un*surprising given that key intangible asset types, e.g., investments in firm-specific training and organizational change, are not capitalized in national accounts.

In this chapter, we focus on identifying synergies between intangible capital and ICT capital after first remedying the lack of cross-country harmonized sectoral investment data covering all intangible assets. Our main hypothesis is that the interaction between ICT and co-investment in intangible capital is a relevant omitted effect in a conventional industry or sector-level production function. As shown by Brynjolfsson and Hitt (2000) in a firm-level fixed effects productivity model, estimates of the return to ICT are 50 percent lower than in an ordinary least square

---

[3] See www.intan-invest.net. "Harmonized" means that, to the extent possible, the same concepts, methods, and data sources are applied and used for each country. INTAN-Invest contains harmonized estimates of intangible investment for the EU plus Norway and the US.

regression, while the coefficients of other inputs change only marginally. Their results suggest that unmeasured organizational practices (intangible investments) significantly affect the returns to ICT investment. Thus if the interaction between ICT and intangible capital is left out of the production function, estimates will be biased.

To investigate these issues, we merge newly produced INTAN-Invest *industry-level* measures of intangible investment for fourteen EU economies in 1995–2010 (Corrado, Haskel, Jona-Lasinio, and Iommi 2014) with EUKLEMS industry data on output, and labor and tangible inputs. Next, we conduct a sources-of-growth analysis using a Divisia index approach to computing TFP (Caves, Christensen, and Diewert 1982). The approach is consistent with an underlying translog production function, which encompasses substitutability/complementarity between inputs but is silent on whether such relations exist. Therefore, we also estimate industry-level production functions with interacted inputs to examine the linkages between ICT and intangibles.

Our major findings are as follows. First, intangible investment has grown in both manufacturing and services, but most strongly in services. Second, the contribution of intangibles to labor productivity growth is similar in both manufacturing and services (about 25 percent of labor productivity growth) and in the high growth economies (Austria, Germany, Finland, France, Netherlands, UK) exceeds the contribution of labor quality (about 20 percent). Finally, we find evidence of intangible/ICT complementarity in our macro-economic productivity data.

The chapter is organized as follows. Section 9.1 illustrates the theoretical framework of our analysis and Section 9.2 provides a description of the new INTAN-Invest data and methodology to measure intangible investments by industry. Section 9.3 reviews both the dynamics of intangible investment across European country-industries and the industry growth accounting results. Section 9.4 investigates ICT-intangible capital complementarity and Section 9.5 concludes.

9.1 Framework and sectoral accounting

9.1.1 Input and output payment flows with and without capitalization

In conventional national accounts, spending on many intangibles, such as organizational capital, training, and design, is treated as an intermediate good, i.e., such expenditures are assumed to be fully used up in annual production. This implies that *purchases* of intangible services are considered intermediate costs and subtracted from gross output to obtain value added. The treatment also implies that *own account* production of intangibles are not included in the value of output, because the statistical authorities will only look at the value of sales as output and ignore the production of intangible assets on own-account.

Consider an industry j selling gross output $P_S S_j$ using intermediates and labor of value $P_M M, P_L L$, and the implicit value of capital inputs measured as $P_K' K$ (industry subscripts ignored). Assume now that part of the intermediate inputs are in fact purchases of long-lived intangible assets $P_N N^{PUR}$ (e.g., expenditure on product design provided by a design firm) and that the industry also produces intangible assets (e.g., it conducts research and development (R&D)) valued as $P_N N^{OA}$ in the current period. Then measured value added of industry j, $P_V V_j'$, is written as

$$
\begin{aligned}
P_V V_j' &= P_S S_j - P_M M_j = P_S S_j - (P_{OM} OM_j + P_N N_j^{PUR}) \\
&= P_L L_j + P_K K_j'
\end{aligned}
\tag{1}
$$

where $P_{OM} OM_j$ is the value of intermediate inputs *other* than purchased intangibles and the value of inputs used to produce $P_N N_j^{OA}$ are subsumed in conventional inputs.

Suppose now one decides to treat intangibles as capital. The purchases of intangibles are no longer intermediates but purchases of knowledge capital, in which case they are no longer subtracted from gross output to obtain value added. Own-account production of intangibles leads to the creation of additional output by the industry. Both types of intangibles lead to the creation of newly owned capital inputs with implicit rental payments $P_R R^{PUR}$ and $P_R R^{OA}$, which sum to $P_R R, R^{PUR}, R^{OA}$ and R are the corresponding accumulated stocks. Thus nominal value added of an industry rises both because intermediate inputs are lower and because the recognized value of production is higher. This overall increase in nominal value added of industry j is equal to the additional nominal investment. Income generated by industry j rises by the additional rental payment, which follows implicitly. Thus we may write new value added, $P_V V_j$ as

$$P_V V_j = P_S S_j + P_N N_j^{OA} - (P_M M_j - P_N N_j^{PUR})$$
$$= P_L L_j + P_K K_j + P_R R_j^{OA} + P_R R_j^{PUR} \tag{2}$$

Subtracting (1) from (2) shows the adjustment we must make to measured industry value added to get industry value added on the output and factor payments side, which is

$$P_V V_j = P_V V_j' + (P_N N_j^{OA} + P_N N_j^{PUR})$$
$$= P_L L_j + P_K K_j + P_R R_j^{OA} + P_R R_j^{PUR} \tag{3}$$

i.e. we must add total intangible investment and total payments to intangible assets. Because the latter are implicit, the capitalization of intangibles revalues $P_K K_j'$ to $P_K K_j$.

To measure whole economy value added, we sum value added in all the sectors. The output of some sectors, such as intermediates, tangible capital, and intangible capital are then inputs into other sectors.

9.1.2 Inputs and outputs

Because capital and labor are made up of many types, following Jorgenson and Griliches (1967) we may write down labor and capital services in industry j as rental share-weighted aggregates over asset or labor types, where the rental shares are averages over adjacent years. For the inputs $X = K, L, R$, $\Delta lnX = \Sigma \bar{s}_a^X \Delta lnX_a$ where $\bar{s}_{X,a} = P_a^X X / (\Sigma P_a^X X)$ where the sum is over asset or labor inputs a, and the overline indicates averaged over two years.

Suppose now that industry value added depends on primary inputs of labor and capital services where capital is both tangible and intangible (Corrado *et al.* 2009; Corrado *et al.* 2013).

$$Q_{c,i,t} = A_{c,i,t} F_{c,i}(L_{c,i,t}, K_{c,i,t}, R_{c,i,t}) \tag{4}$$

where A is an industry TFP index. As Jorgenson, Ho, and Stiroh (2003) and Stiroh (2002) discuss, such a production function is a special case of a more general gross output production function. In our data, however, we do not yet have consistent disaggregated gross output measures and so cannot work with gross output (but see Borgo, Goodridge, Haskel, and Pesole 2013 for an implementation on UK data). Thus for each industry, we have the following where $\Delta lnTFP_j$ is defined residually:

$$\Delta ln(Q/H)_j = \bar{v}_j^L \Delta ln(L/H)_j + \bar{v}_j^K \Delta ln(K/H)_j + \bar{v}_j^R \Delta ln(R/H)_j$$
$$+ \Delta lnTFP_j \qquad (5)$$

The $\bar{v}$ are shares of factor costs in industry nominal value added, $P^Q Q_j$, averaged over two periods.

The results we present for each country are defined as above, although we on occasion break out K into ICT and nonICT capital and R into nonR&D and R&D intangibles, in which case for each industry we have

$$\Delta ln(Q/H)_j = \bar{v}_j^L \Delta ln(L/H)_j + \bar{v}_j^{K^{ICT}} \Delta ln(K^{ICT}/H)_j$$
$$+ \bar{v}_j^{K^{nonICT}} \Delta ln(K^{nonICT}/H)_j + \bar{v}_j^{R^{R\&D}} \Delta ln(R^{R\&D}/H)_j$$
$$+ \bar{v}_j^{R^{nonR\&D}} \Delta ln(R^{nonR\&D}/H)_j + \Delta lnTFP_j \qquad (6)$$

In what follows we refer to the terms on the right-hand side as *contributions*, i.e. $\bar{v}_j^X \Delta ln(X/H)_j$ which are of course each the product of a share and a *deepening* term, i.e. $\Delta ln(X/H)_j$. All such terms are weighted by their value added share of the aggregate. Note that aggregation to the market sector level presents a set of issues set out in Reinsdorf and Yuskavage (2010).

9.2 Data

We develop harmonized measures of intangible investment across countries and sectors that are (a) consistent with national accounts principles and (b) aligned with existing INTAN-Invest market sector estimates of intangible capital for the following non-national accounts intangible assets: brand, organizational capital, firm-specific training, and design and other new product development costs.[4] We then merge these estimates with national accounts measures of new investment in software, mineral exploration, and entertainment, artistic and literary originals. Although R&D has been recently capitalized in the national accounts of most European countries, at the time of writing national

---

[4] This section draws from Corrado *et al.* (2014).

accounts data on R&D investment by industry are not available for many countries.

The estimates cover fourteen European countries (Austria, Belgium, Germany, Denmark, Finland, France, Greece, Netherlands, Italy, Ireland, Portugal, Spain, Sweden, and UK) at the NACE Rev2 sector level (sectors A through N [excluding real estate] plus sectors R and S). Thus the industry coverage is: agriculture, mining, manufacturing, utilities, construction, trade, financial services, and other services, i.e, eight (8) major sectors of economic activity.

To obtain industry-level data on intangibles, we use the framework for estimating nominal expenditure set out in Corrado, Haskel, Jona-Lasinio, and Iommi (2012) and we adopt two different empirical approaches depending on data availability. When industry-level information is not available, we use a top-down approach where the economy-wide market sector data from INTAN-Invest are scaled down to the industry level. If industry-level information and data are available, we follow a bottom-up approach.

National accounts intangibles are of course gathered from individual country websites or from Eurostat. R&D expenditure is based on BERD surveys, also gathered from Eurostat. For assets not measured in national accounts, we need to further distinguish between own account and purchased intangible investment. Own account estimates usually require detailed employment data by type of occupation and by industry (e.g., from the Structure of Earning survey or the Labor Force survey). Available information allows us to readily identify occupations related with organizational capital, and this is the sole asset for which we newly produce own-account measures at the industry level. See Corrado *et al.* (2012) for how occupational information was used to measure spending on new product development in the financial services industry.

Purchased intangibles are estimated from industry expenditure data gathered from use tables compiled according to the new classification system (NACE Rev2/CPA 2008) and available from 2008 onwards. The use tables provide the industry distribution of expenditure for: brand (proxied by advertising and market research expenditure), design (purchases of architecture, engineering, and design services), and organizational capital (purchases of management consulting services). For these assets, we first produced a detailed benchmark estimate of intangible investment in 2008 and then we built time series for the period 1995 to 2010 applying the rate of change of value added by industry to the level of the estimated intangible gross fixed capital formation in 2008.

Total training investment expenditure (i.e., the sum of purchased and own account components) is calculated following a bottom-up approach based on the information provided by Continuing Vocational Training Survey; see Corrado *et al.* (2013) for an explanation. Finally, because our benchmark is the INTAN-invest business sector estimate of intangibles, we rescale the estimated value for each industry, in each country, for every year, to the total provided by INTAN-invest. Intangible investment in real terms and measures of net capital stock used in the sources of growth analysis are obtained as in Corrado *et al.* (2012, 2013).

9.3 Intangible investment and growth in EU countries and industries

9.3.1 Intangible investment by country and industry

Using the newly developed data described in the previous section, we first provide an overview of the dynamics of intangible investment and the average intensity of R&D, nonR&D intangible and ICT investments in manufacturing and services across fourteen European economies.[5] Figure 9.1 shows that the average annual rate of growth of intangible investment is relatively higher in the service sectors (5.4 percent) than in manufacturing (3.0 percent) in all sample countries. Finland is the sole country where intangible capital accumulation is more dynamic in manufacturing than services.

ICT, R&D and nonR&D intangibles average intensity for manufacturing and services in all sample countries in 1995–2010 is reported in Figure 9.2. Notice that while ICT intensity is higher in services, R&D intensity is highly skewed towards manufacturing, as expected. NonR&D intangible investment, by contrast, looks much more like ICT: more evenly distributed than R&D but sometimes more intensive in manufacturing and sometimes in services. Looking at the countries in more detail, some interesting patterns emerge. For ICT, Portugal and

---

[5] NonR&D intangible investments include: design, advertising and market research, organizational capital, training and entertainment, and artistic originals.

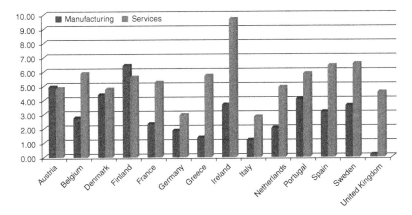

Figure 9.1 Intangible investments (chain linked volumes): compounded average rates of growth, 1995–2010

Belgium are obvious laggards, but there is no very clear north/south divide. For R&D, the southern countries such as Spain, Italy, and Portugal are, as had been documented, rather lagging with intensity particularly high in the Nordic countries. For nonR&D intangibles, Spain is somewhat of a laggard, but the Nordic countries are by no means leaders.

9.3.2 Growth accounting by country and industry

Because there are many industries we proceed here by reducing the industries to three: other goods producers (including agriculture, mining, and construction); manufacturing; and services (which cover utilities, trade, financial services, and other services). The service sector is between 60 percent (Finland) and 80 percent (UK) of value added and so dominates in most of our countries (including Spain and Italy). Other goods producers is rather small and so in the interests of readability we omit it from Table 9.1.

The growth accounting results are summarized in Table 9.1, where each panel refers to a macro sector (manufacturing, services, and value added share weighted manufacturing plus services) by each country. Each panel has a panel summary which consists of: (a) a value added weighted total (and the share of $\Delta ln(V/H)$) of that panel; (b) a simple average of the panel (and its shares of $\Delta ln(V/H)$); and (c) a value added

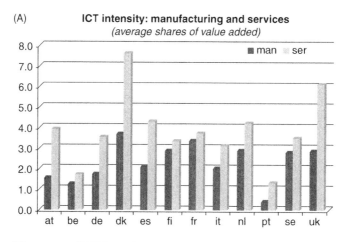

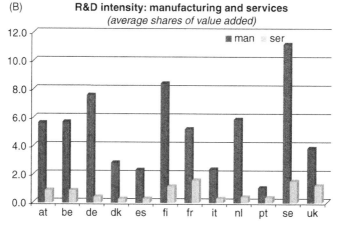

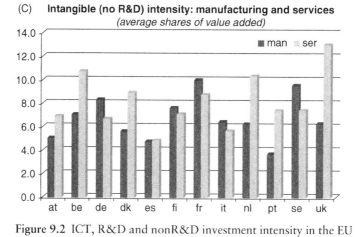

Figure 9.2 ICT, R&D and nonR&D investment intensity in the EU

Figures show average values from 1995 to 2010. Darker columns are manufacturing, lighter columns are services.

Source: Authors' calculations from the INTAN-Invest and EUKLEMS databases.

Table 9.1 Sources of industry labor productivity growth

Manufacturing

Country	Labor productivity growth	Labor composition	Tangible capital deepening	ICT	NonICT	Intangible capital deepening	R&D	NonR&D	TFP
						Contributions of components			
Austria	2.82	0.26	0.32	0.26	0.06	0.77	0.52	0.24	1.47
Germany	1.98	0.23	0.52	0.17	0.34	0.58	0.31	0.27	0.66
Spain	1.49	0.51	1.24	0.28	0.97	0.33	0.16	0.17	-0.59
Finland	4.28	0.30	0.59	0.40	0.19	1.39	0.93	0.46	2.00
France	2.98	0.60	0.84	0.33	0.51	0.63	0.22	0.42	0.91
Italy	0.34	0.45	0.80	0.19	0.60	0.23	0.07	0.16	-1.13
Netherlands	2.50	0.30	0.62	0.34	0.28	0.54	0.27	0.28	1.03
UK	3.09	0.64	0.78	0.37	0.41	0.40	0.14	0.26	1.27
Weighted total	2.03	0.40	0.71	0.25	0.46	0.51	0.24	0.27	0.41
Share of w't total (%)		20	35	12	23	25	12	13	20
Average	2.44	0.41	0.71	0.29	0.42	0.61	0.33	0.28	0.70
Share of average (%)		17	29	12	17	25	13	12	29
Weighted total, nonMed	2.51	0.38	0.63	0.26	0.37	0.60	0.29	0.31	0.91
Share w't total, nonMed (%)		15	25	10	15	24	12	12	36

Table 9.1 (*cont.*)

Services

Country	Labor productivity growth	Labor composition	Contributions of components						
			Tangible capital deepening	ICT	NonICT	Intangible capital deepening	R&D	NonR&D	TFP
Austria	1.90	0.26	0.58	0.46	0.12	0.28	0.07	0.21	0.77
Germany	1.24	0.04	0.86	0.45	0.42	0.16	0.04	0.13	0.17
Spain	0.35	0.34	1.11	0.46	0.65	0.13	0.05	0.08	-1.22
Finland	1.55	0.08	-0.22	0.35	-0.57	0.30	0.09	0.20	1.39
France	1.31	0.42	0.59	0.32	0.27	0.37	0.08	0.29	-0.07
Italy	0.14	0.21	0.48	0.24	0.24	0.09	0.01	0.08	-0.64
Netherlands	2.17	0.33	0.78	0.54	0.24	0.38	0.05	0.33	0.68
UK	2.68	0.35	1.40	0.90	0.49	0.53	0.07	0.46	0.40
Weighted total	1.31	0.25	0.83	0.47	0.36	0.27	0.05	0.22	-0.04
Share of w't total (%)		*19*	*63*	*36*	*27*	*21*	*4*	*17*	*-3*
Average	1.42	0.25	0.67	0.50	0.16	0.34	0.07	0.27	0.56
Share of average (%)		*17*	*47*	*36*	*11*	*24*	*5*	*19*	*39*
Weighted total, nonMed	1.69	0.25	0.87	0.52	0.35	0.33	0.06	0.27	0.25
Share w't total, nonMed (%)		*15*	*51*	*31*	*20*	*19*	*4*	*16*	*15*

Manufacturing plus services

Country	Labor productivity growth	Labor composition	Tangible capital deepening	Contributions of components		Intangible capital deepening			
				ICT	NonICT	deepening	R&D	NonR&D	TFP
Austria	2.18	0.26	0.50	0.40	0.10	0.43	0.21	0.22	0.99
Germany	1.50	0.11	0.74	0.35	0.39	0.31	0.13	0.18	0.34
Spain	0.66	0.38	1.15	0.41	0.74	0.18	0.08	0.11	-1.05
Finland	2.63	0.17	0.10	0.37	-0.27	0.73	0.42	0.30	1.64
France	1.71	0.46	0.65	0.32	0.33	0.43	0.11	0.32	0.17
Italy	0.20	0.28	0.58	0.23	0.35	0.13	0.03	0.11	-0.79
Netherlands	2.24	0.32	0.75	0.49	0.25	0.42	0.10	0.32	0.76
UK	2.76	0.41	1.27	0.80	0.48	0.51	0.09	0.42	0.58
Weighted total	1.52	0.29	0.80	0.41	0.39	0.34	0.11	0.23	0.09
Share of w't total (%)		*19*	*52*	*27*	*26*	*22*	*7*	*15*	*6*
Average	1.73	0.30	0.72	0.42	0.30	0.39	0.15	0.25	0.33
Share of average (%)		*17*	*41*	*24*	*17*	*23*	*8*	*14*	*19*
Total	1.92	0.29	0.80	0.45	0.35	0.41	0.13	0.28	0.44
Share w't total, nonMed (%)		*15*	*42*	*23*	*18*	*21*	*7*	*15*	*23*

Notes: (1) Data are for manufacturing and services: services are a value added weighted aggregate of utilities, trade, financial services, and other services. (2) Labour quality contribution: compensation-weighted growth in person-hours per hour. Tangible capital deepening (TCD) contribution: rental-price weighted growth in real capital stocks per hour of commercial buildings, vehicles, plant, and computer hardware and software. Then we split TCD into ICT and NonICT capital deepening, where ICT includes software. Intangible capital deepening (ICD) contribution: rental-price weighted growth in real capital stocks per hour of R&D, mineral exploration, artistic originals, design, new financial products, branding, training, and organizational capital, split into R&D and NonR&D contributions. (3) Countries are Austria (at), France (fr), Finland (fi), Germany(de), Italy (it), Netherlands (nl), Spain (es), and UK (uk).

weighted total of the non-Mediterranean countries (and their shares of $\Delta ln(V/H)$).

The columns are $\Delta ln(V/H)$ and the contributions of $\Delta ln(L/H)$ (labor composition), tangible capital ($\Delta ln(K/H)$), which consists of ICT and nonICT tangible capital ($\Delta ln(K^{ICT}/H)$ and $\Delta ln(K^{NonICT}/H)$), intangible capital ($\Delta ln(R/H)$), which consists of R&D and nonR&D intangible capital and $\Delta ln TFP$, which is a residual. The numbers may not add up exactly due to rounding.

With this in mind, what do we learn from these findings? First, the low growth economies of Spain and Italy may be grouped together. Their labor productivity is the lowest, in manufacturing and services, and it is driven by negative TFP in both sectors. In both countries, in both sectors, the contribution of intangibles is the lowest and the contribution of tangibles among the highest. So these are tangible intensive economies, with small intangible contributions, all of which are outweighed by negative $\Delta ln TFP$.

Second, turning to the high growth economies, all have higher $\Delta ln(V/H)$ in manufacturing rather than services. $\Delta ln TFP$ is 36% of $\Delta ln(V/H)$ in manufacturing and 15% in services. $\Delta ln(R/H)$ is 15% in manufacturing but 21% in services. Tangible capital contributes 25% of $\Delta ln(V/H)$ in manufacturing and 51% in services (made up of 10% and 31% from ICT tangible capital). So on average, about 20% of productivity growth in both sectors comes from intangibles while the rest is driven by TFP in manufacturing and ICT in services.

To summarize, we have three sets of countries. First, Spain and Italy show high contributions of $\Delta ln(K/H)$, little contribution from $\Delta ln(R/H)$, and very poor $\Delta ln TFP$. Second, Germany and France show relatively high contributions of $\Delta ln(K/H)$, modest $\Delta ln(R/H)$, and low $\Delta ln TFP$. Third, Austria, Finland, Netherlands, and the UK show high contributions of $\Delta ln(K/H)$ and $\Delta ln(R/H)$ and high $\Delta ln TFP$.

To get an overall view, the lower panel of the table sets out, for each country, the weighted sum of manufacturing and services. As that panel shows, Spain and Italy have low $\Delta ln TFP$ and $\Delta ln(V/H)$. The panel summary shows the weighted and unweighted averages corresponding therefore to the performance of a synthetic Europe (composed of manufacturing and services in these countries) and average country in that synthetic Europe. Note that even in the Mediterranean countries, services are more than 60 percent of total employment (including agriculture and minerals) and 80 percent in the UK. So when weighting all the sectors together, country performance is dominated by services.

What do we find? First, in both cases, intangible capital, $\Delta ln(R/H)$ accounts for 23% of $\Delta ln(V/H)$, where 7% and 15% are due to R&D and nonR&D intangibles respectively. Second, tangible capital, $\Delta ln(K/H)$, accounts for around 50% of $\Delta ln(V/H)$, split roughly equally between ICT and non ICT tangible capital. Third, labor quality accounts for about 20% of $\Delta ln(V/H)$. Finally, TFP is zero in the synthetic country, due to the large negative TFPs in Spain and Italy and relatively poor services sector TFPs elsewhere, but about 19% of $\Delta ln(V/H)$ on average.

9.3.3 Section summary

We have the following. First, to understand economy productivity one has to understand the service sector – what drives service sector productivity in Europe? Intangibles accounts for about 25% of it, most of which is not from R&D but nonR&D intangibles. ICT accounts for about 35% of it and nonICT about 30%. Labor composition contributes about 20%. Over this period, TFP growth in European services has been very poor: contributing around 15% in non-Mediterranean countries and negative in Mediterranean countries. Second, what drives manufacturing productivity in Europe? About 25% is due to intangibles, half of which is due to R&D. Around 20–30% is due to TFP and 25–35% due to tangible capital, of which about one-third is ICT. Overall, ICT and intangibles are relevant drivers of growth both in services and manufacturing even if to a different extent across countries. These findings suggest a deeper investigation of the joint contribution of ICT and intangible capital might further deepen our understanding of productivity.

9.4 Exploring complementarity between intangibles and ICT

As Caves *et al.* (1982) show, the TFP calculation shown in equation 5 is consistent with any pattern of substitution/complementarity between inputs up to a translog form. However, this does not shed light on just what patterns exist and so in this section we explore how adding intangibles and their interactions with ICT might affect production function estimates. Figure 9.3 provides a schematic representation of

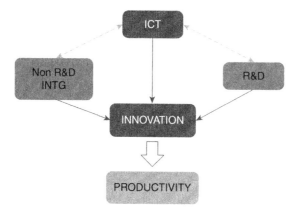

Figure 9.3 Complementary assets, innovation, and productivity growth

the main linkages between ICT and knowledge based capital potentially at work in a production process. Besides the direct growth contribution of each single capital asset (solid arrows) there may be
synergies between them (dashed arrows) that affect productivity
growth.

Micro-economic evidence suggests that the link from firm-level ICT
adoption to productivity growth depends on co-investments in intangible capital, e.g. training and organizational change (e.g. Bresnahan,
Brynjolfsson, and Hitt 2002; Brynjolfsson *et al*. 2002). On the other
hand, macro-economic evidence on the joint/disjoint contribution of
ICT and intangibles to industry productivity growth is still scant,
mainly because of lack of industry data on intangibles. Some key
macro-economic productivity studies have nonetheless suggested that
the returns to ICT and productivity growth are higher once proxies for
intangibles are included, e.g., Basu *et al*. (2004) and Acharya and Basu
(2010). Corrado, Haskel, and Jona-Lasinio (2014) found the estimated
output elasticities of ICT capital in a production function are reduced
when intangibles are introduced, suggesting that, as conjectured in
much of the pre-intangible *data* literature, returns to ICT depend
crucially on the presence of "unmeasurable" intangibles. They found
that productivity growth in ICT intensive industries is relatively higher
in countries with fast growing intangible capital accumulation thus
corroborating the assumption that ICT and intangibles are complements in production.

9.4.1 Econometric approach

Starting from equation 4 we might explore complementarities by writing down a full translog specification with all inputs interacted and/or estimate a system of factor demands. This would be stretching our data too far, and so we opted for a simpler approach, following (Rajan and Zingales 1998) who evaluate the extent to which the growth contribution of intangible capital is conditional on the intensity of ICT capital.

Thus we estimate the following specification:

$$\Delta ln(Q_{i,c,t}/H_{i,c,t}) = a_1 \Delta ln(K_{i,c,t}^{ICT}/H_{i,c,t}) + a_2 \Delta ln(K_{i,c,t}^{NonICT}/H_{i,c,t})$$

$$+ a_3 \Delta ln(R_{i,c,t}/H_{i,c,t}) + a_4 \Delta ln(R_{i,c,t}/H_{i,c,t}) * \overline{ln(K^{ICT}/H)_{i,c}}$$

$$+ a_5 \overline{ln(K^{ICT}/H)_{i,c}} + a_6 \Delta ln(L/H)_{i,c,t} + \lambda_i + \lambda_c + \lambda_t + \eta_{i,c,t}. \tag{7}$$

where Q denotes value added adjusted to include intangible capital (as in Corrado *et al.* 2005, 2009), H is total hours worked, $\overline{ln(K^{ICT}/H)_{i,c}}$ denotes country-industry's average (log) ICT intensity, and Ł is labor quality.[6] Notice that a relevant characteristic of the multiplicative interaction models is that they are symmetric with respect to the interacted terms. That is the interaction term in equation (7) does not say anything about the causality between ΔlnK and ΔlnR (Brambor, Clark and Golder 2006).[7] Thus we take a pragmatic approach and we assume that ICT is our conditional variable affecting the impact of co-investment in intangibles on productivity growth. Put differently, we assume that the output elasticity of intangible capital depends on ICT intensity.[8]

A number of points are worth making. First, the term we use to capture the differential impact of intangibles on productivity growth in ICT intensive sectors is the time average of ICT intensity of all industries interacted with the rate of growth of intangible capital in industry *i*, country *c* at time *t*. Second, we have modelled $\Delta lnA_{c,i,t}$ in equation 4

---

[6] See Corrado, Haskel, Jona Lasinio (2014).

[7] In equation(7) we cannot distinguish if ΔlnK modifies the effect of ΔlnR on ΔlnQ, or if it is ΔlnR that modifies the effect of ΔlnK on ΔlnQ.

[8] We have tested also the extent to which the output elasticity of ICT depends on intangible intensity but with less statistically robust results.

as $\Delta lnA_{c,i,t} = \lambda_c + \lambda_i + \lambda_t + \eta_{c,i,t}$ where the λ's are unobserved country, industry, and time effects.

Third, we use $\overline{ln(K^{ICT}/H)}_{i,c}$, that is, the average of the log of intensity, since it gave much better determined results than interactions with the unlogged intensity (such interactions were statistically insignificant): note that there is some economics in this restriction, since it bounds the output elasticity of R as ICT intensity rises.

Fourth, note that the industry dummies control for the possible correlation between specific industry characteristics and our measure of ICT intensity. If our proxy for ICT intensity in equation (7) is at all correct, we should find $\alpha_4 > 0$, indicating that each countries industries that are more ICT intensive grow faster when ICT stocks are complemented by higher intangible capital accumulation. Industry dummies also ensure the results are invariant to the measurement scale of ICT-intensity.[9]

9.4.2 ICT and intangibles: complementary or substitutes?

Figure 9.4 shows the relationship between ICT and intangible capital in eight EU countries.[10] The Y-axis of Figure 9.4 plots the rate of growth of per hour intangible capital accumulation, for R&D and nonR&D intangibles; the X-axis shows $\Delta lnK^{ICT}/H$. The figure shows a positive relation between intangible and ICT capital accumulation across the countries and industries in our sample, suggesting complementarity between the two types of capital.

Table 9.2 shows the cross correlations between long differences of $\Delta lnK^{ICT}/H$, $\Delta lnK^{R\&D}/H$, and $\Delta lnK^{NonR\&D}/H$.

ICT is strongly correlated with nonR&D intangible capital and less correlated with R&D (0.3). Decomposing nonR&D intangibles into its

[9] Chen, Niebel, and Saam (2014) use very similar data and approach but they find a negative interaction between ICT-intensity and $\Delta ln(K^{ICT}/L)_{i,c}$ (which is statistically significant at OLS, but not so with IV). Their implied output elasticity of R is 0.30 at the ninetieth percentile of ICT-intensity. We differ from their work by (a) we do not interact ICT-intensity with all intangible capital because we are not sure of the theoretical rationale for an interaction with e.g. buildings; (b) we add *both* interacted *and also* uninteracted terms as controls in all specifications which is more econometrically appropriate (Brambor *et al.* 2006); and (c) our intensity variable is in log form, which gives no negative signs and a lower (perhaps more plausible) output elasticity (0.16 at the ninety-fifth percentile of ICT-intensity, see below.)

[10] The econometric analysis covers a smaller number of countries because of lack of data availability for tangible capital stock in EUKLEMS.

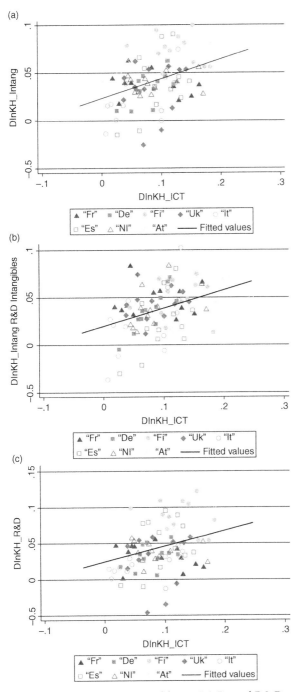

Figure 9.4 ICT versus intangible nonR&D, and R&D capital stocks
Note. Figure shows first differences, country/industries, 1995–2010.

Table 9.2 Correlations between ICT, R&D, nonR&D intangibles: long differences (1995–2007)

	$\Delta\ln (K(ICT)/H)_{i,c,t}$	$\Delta\ln (R(R\&D)/H)_{i,c,t}$	$\Delta\ln (R(Non\ R\&D)/H)_{i,c,t}$	$\Delta\ln (R^{train}/H)_{i,c,t}$	$\Delta\ln (R^{(org)}/H)_{i,c,t}$	$\Delta\ln (R^{mkt}/H)_{i,c,t}$	$\Delta\ln (R^{des}/H)_{i,c,t}$	$\Delta\ln (L/H)_{i,c,t}$
$\Delta\ln (K(ICT)/H)_{i,c,t}$	1.000							
$\Delta\ln (R(R\&D)/H)_{i,c,t}$	0.338	1.000						
$\Delta\ln (R(Non\ R\&D)/H)_{i,c,t}$	0.566	-0.192	1.000					
$\Delta\ln (R^{train}/H)_{i,c,t}$	0.362	-0.042	0.485	1.000				
$\Delta\ln (R^{(org)}/H)_{i,c,t}$	0.449	-0.279	0.821	0.235	1.000			
$\Delta\ln (R^{mkt}/H)_{i,c,t}$	0.557	0.031	0.635	0.286	0.571	1.000		
$\Delta\ln (R^{des}/H)_{i,c,t}$	0.519	0.024	0.723	0.344	0.682	0.668	1.000	
$\Delta\ln (VA/H)_{i,c,t}$	0.569	-0.226	0.833	0.427	0.797	0.460	0.566	1.000

main components reveals that organizational capital, brands, and design are all strongly correlated with ICT as suggested by the above-cited literature.

9.4.3 Estimation results

Table 9.3 reports estimates of equation (7). The dependent variable is the rate of growth of value added per hours worked $\Delta lnQ/H$. All regressions contain country, industry, and time fixed effects and are estimated by robust regression methods to guard against outliers. Column 1 estimates equation (7) but excluding the interaction terms. In all regressions, $\Delta ln(L/H)$ is lagged one period. As column 1 shows, each of the standard inputs, $\Delta ln(L/H)_{t-1}$, ΔlnK^{NonICT}, and ΔlnK^{ICT} are positive and statistically significant, and $\Delta ln(R/H)$ is positive, but statistically insignificant.

For the purposes of understanding the data, columns 2 and 3 replace $\Delta ln(R/H)$, which includes all intangibles with nonR&D intangibles (column 2) and just R&D (column 3). The former are statistically significant, but the latter not: of course, strictly these regressions might be biased since $\Delta ln(Q/H)$ would have to be recalculated to capitalize these restricted intangible assets.

Column 4 tries the interaction terms, $ln(\overline{K^{ICT}/H}) * \Delta ln(R/H)$ and $\overline{ln(K^{ICT}/H)}$ is positive and statistically significant (i.e., $\hat{a}_4 > 0$) as expected and supports the assumption that each countries industries that are more ICT intensive grow faster when ICT stocks are complemented by higher intangible capital accumulation (we show the resulting marginal effects below).

The remaining columns try similar interaction effects but with each individual intangible asset; so for example column 5 enters $\overline{ln(K^{ICT}/H)} * \Delta ln(R/H)$ but where R excludes R&D. The other columns test just R&D, organizational capital (ΔlnR^{ORG}),training (ΔlnR^{TRAIN}), design (ΔlnR^{DES}), and market research (ΔlnR^{MKT}).[11]

---

[11] Note that in all columns when inserting individual intangible assets we add *both* interacted *and all* un-interacted terms as controls, so for example, column 7 enters $\overline{ln(K^{ICT}/H)} * \Delta ln(R(org)/H), \overline{ln(K^{ICT}/H)}, \Delta ln(R(org)/H)$, and $\Delta ln(R(Non - org)/H)$, where $\Delta ln(R(Non - org)/H)$ are all intangibles except organizational capital.

Table 9.3 Augmented production function (dependent variable: $\Delta ln(Q/H)_{i,c,t}$)

	(1)	(2)	(3)	(4)	(5)	(6)	(7)	(8)	(9)	(10)
VARIABLES										
$\Delta ln(L/H)_{i,c,t-1}$	0.16*	0.20**	0.34***	0.32***	0.28***	0.34***	0.28***	0.40***	0.29***	0.26***
	(1.92)	(2.40)	(4.77)	(3.90)	(3.45)	(4.72)	(3.35)	(5.06)	(3.59)	(3.13)
$\Delta ln(K^{Non-ICT}/H)_{i,c,t}$	0.18***	0.12**	0.28***	0.12**	0.11**	0.27***	0.14***	0.06	0.22***	0.15***
	(3.49)	(2.46)	(6.62)	(2.24)	(2.31)	(6.09)	(2.74)	(1.14)	(4.00)	(2.87)
$\Delta ln(K^{ICT}/H)_{i,c,t}$	0.12***	0.08***	0.11***	0.18***	0.12***	0.12***	0.15***	0.13***	0.13***	0.15***
	(4.76)	(3.14)	(5.24)	(6.84)	(4.73)	(5.03)	(5.84)	(5.28)	(5.14)	(5.77)
$\Delta ln(R/H)_{i,c,t}$	0.07			0.04						
	(1.37)			(0.76)						
$\Delta ln(R^{NonR\&D}/H)_{i,c,t}$		0.27***			0.20***					
		(5.94)			(4.05)					
$\Delta ln(R^{R\&D}/H)_{i,c,t}$			-0.01							
			(-0.50)							
$\overline{ln(K^{ICT}/H)}_{i,c}$				0.01**	0.01*	-0.00	0.01***	0.01***	0.00	0.01***
				(2.47)	(1.83)	(-0.17)	(2.68)	(3.91)	(0.72)	(2.76)
$\Delta ln(R/H)_{i,c,t} * \overline{ln(K^{ICT}/H)}_{i,c}$				0.06**						
				(2.49)						
$\Delta ln(R^{NonR\&D}/H)_{i,c,t} * \overline{ln(K^{ICT}/H)}_{i,c}$					0.04*					
					(1.78)					

	(1)	(2)	(3)	(4)	(5)	(6)	(7)	(8)	(9)	(10)	(11)
$\Delta ln(R^{R\&D}/H)_{i,c,t} * \overline{ln(K^{ICT}/H)}_{i,c}$							0.00 (0.44)				
$\Delta ln(R^{ORG}/H)_{i,c,t} * \overline{ln(K^{ICT}/H)}_{i,c}$								0.04* (1.93)			
$\Delta ln(R^{TRAIN}/H)_{i,c,t} * \overline{ln(K^{ICT}/H)}_{i,c}$									0.05** (2.35)		
$\Delta ln(R^{DES}/H)_{i,c,t} * \overline{ln(K^{ICT}/H)}_{i,c}$										0.09*** (4.14)	
$\Delta ln(R^{MKT}/H)_{i,c,t} * \overline{ln(K^{ICT}/H)}_{i,c}$											0.09* (2.79)
$\Delta ln(R^{ORG}/H)_{i,c,t}$								0.09* (1.74)			
$\Delta ln(R^{TRAIN}/H)_{i,c,t}$									0.35*** (6.09)		
$\Delta ln(R^{DES}/H)_{i,c,t}$										0.08 (1.37)	
$\Delta ln(R^{MKT}/H)_{i,c,t}$											0.09* (1.79)
Observations	528	528	440	528	528	528	440	528	528	517	528
R-squared	0.34	0.38	0.46	0.40	0.42	0.46	0.41	0.48	0.43	0.43	0.43

Article II

Notes: T-statistics in brackets.

*** p<0.01, ** p<0.05, * p<0.1. Final four columns also include $\Delta ln(R - R^a /H)_{i,c,t}$ where $R(a)$ is the column asset.

In all cases, except R&D, the interactive term, $\overline{ln(K^{ICT}/H)}$ and ΔlnR^{ORG}, ΔlnR^{TRAIN}, ΔlnR^{DES}, and ΔlnR^{MKT} are robustly statistically significant suggesting complementarities between ICT and individual nonR&D intangible assets.

The positive interaction effects between $\overline{ln(K^{ICT}/H)}$ and $\Delta lnR/H$ suggests that labor productivity growth in above-average ICT intensive countries-industries was faster in countries-industries experiencing higher increases in intangible capital accumulation ΔlnR, or that ICT capital and intangible capital are complements in production. This result is represented in Figure 9.5 which shows the marginal effect of $\Delta lnR/H$ between the fifth and ninety-fifth percentiles of the distribution of $\overline{ln(K^{ICT}/H)}$, with shading representing the 95 percent confidence interval where the conditions under which intangible capital accumulation has statistically significant effect on productivity growth are met.

As expected, in all cases the marginal effect is increasing as the degree of ICT intensity increases. In fact, the confidence intervals show that the marginal effect of $\Delta lnR/H$ is only statistically positive at quite high

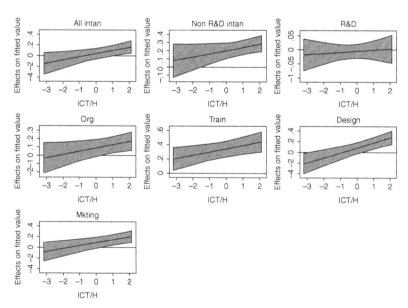

Figure 9.5 Marginal effect of intangible capital assets on productivity growth

levels of $\overline{ln(K^{ICT}/H)}$ (with the exception of training, where the marginal effect is positive throughout).

To get some idea of the numbers involved, the top left panel shows the marginal effect of $\Delta lnR/H$ when $\overline{ln(K^{ICT}/H)} > 1$. This turns out to be above the sixtieth percentile in the distribution of $ln(K^{ICT}/H)$. At the sixtieth percentile the elasticity is 0.10 whereas at the ninety-fifth percentile it is is 0.16.

Note finally that the interaction with the log of ICT intensity suggests the marginal effect is bounded from becoming very high at high levels of intensity. The marginal effect thus has diminishing returns in the level of ICT-intensity, which makes economic sense.

9.5 Conclusions

This chapter merges international EUKLEMS industry data on output and labor and tangible inputs with newly produced intan-invest industry-level measures of intangible investment for fourteen EU economies in 1995–2010. We document intangible investment by industry in fourteen European economies over this period, and then we undertake growth accounting and look for complementarity between ICT and intangible inputs restricting the sample to eight European countries.

Our major findings are as follows. First, intangible investment has grown in manufacturing and services, but most strongly in services. Second, the contribution of intangibles to labor productivity growth is similar in both manufacturing and services (about 25 percent of labor productivity growth) and in the high growth economies (Austria, Germany, Finland, France, Netherlands, UK) exceeds the contribution of labor quality (about 20 percent). Third, the very large size of the service sector means that countries with good manufacturing but poor service productivity growth (Germany and France) have done relatively badly overall, and those with good service sector growth (UK, Netherlands) have performed well. Fourth, Spain and Italy have very low labor productivity growth due to very low TFP growth.

Finally, we find evidence of intangible/ICT complementarity in that the marginal impact of intangible capital on productivity is greater in industries/countries with higher ICT-intensity, a relation that also holds for sub-classes of intangible assets.

As ever in this area, these findings would clearly benefit from better data, not only on investment, but also for asset price deflators and depreciation rates. Nonetheless, these first steps suggest that further development of intangible capital measures would be a worthwhile investment.

References

Acharya, R. and S. Basu. 2010. "ICT and TFP Growth: Intangible Capital or Productive Externalities?" *Industry Canada Working Paper 2010–1*, Industry Canada.

Baldwin, J. R., W. Gu, and R. Macdonald. 2012. "Intangible Capital and Productivity Growth in Canada," *The Canadian Productivity Review* (29).

Barnes, P. and A. McClure. 2009. "Investments in Intangible Assets and Australia's Productivity Growth. Staff Working Paper, Productivity Commission, Canberra.

Basu, S., J. G. Fernald, N. Oulton, and S. Srinivasan. 2004. "The Case of the Missing Productivity Growth: Or, Does Information Technology Explain why Productivity Accelerated in the United States but not in the United Kingdom?" In M. Gertler and K. Rogoff (eds.), *NBER Macroeconomics Annual 2003*. Cambridge, MA: The MIT Press, 9–82.

Borgo, M. D., P. Goodridge, J. Haskel, and A. Pesole. 2013. "Productivity and Growth in UK Industries: An Intangible Investment Approach," *Oxford Bulletin of Economics and Statistics*, 75(6): 806–834.

Brambor, T., W. R. Clark, and M. Golder. 2006. "Understanding Interaction Models: Improving Empirical Analyses," *Political Analysis*, 14: 63–82.

Bresnahan, T. F., E. Brynjolfsson, and L. M. Hitt. 2002. "Information Technology, Workplace Organization, and the Demand for Skilled Labor: Firm-level Evidence," *Quarterly Journal of Economics*, 117(1), 339–376.

Brynjolfsson, E. and L. M. Hitt. 2000. "Beyond Computation: Information Technology, Organizational Transformation and Business Performance," *Journal of Economic Perspectives*, 14: 23–48.

Brynjolfsson, E., L. M. Hitt, and S. Yang. 2002. "Intangible Assets: Computers and Organizational Capital," *Brookings Papers on Economic Activity*, 1: 137–198.

Caves, D. W., L. R. Christensen, and W. E. Diewert. 1982. "The Economic Theory of Index Numbers and the Measurement of Input, Output, and Productivity," *Econometrica*, 50(6): 1393–1414.

Chen, W., T. Niebel, and M. Saam. 2014. "Are Intangibles More Productive in ICT-intensive Industries? Evidence from EU Countries," *ZEW Discussion Papers*, 14(070).

Corrado, C., J. Haskel, and C. Jona-Lasinio. 2014. "Knowledge Spillovers, ICT, and Productivity Growth." The Conference Board, CEPR, and IZA Working Paper, The Conference Board, Imperial College, LUISS and ISTAT.

Corrado, C., J. Haskel, C. Jona-Lasinio, and M. Iommi. 2012. "Intangible Capital and Growth in Advanced Economies: Measurement and Comparative Results." *Working Paper*, available at www.intan-invest.net.

2013. "Innovation and Intangible Investment in Europe, Japan, and the United States," *Oxford Review of Economic Policy*, **29**(2): 261–286.

2014. "Intangibles and Industry Productivity Growth: Evidence from the EU." *Working Paper*, available at www.intan-invest.net.

Corrado, C., C. Hulten, and D. Sichel. 2005. "Measuring Capital and Technology: An Expanded Framework." In C. Corrado, J. Haltiwanger, and D. Sichel (eds.), *Measuring Capital in the New Economy, Volume 66 of NBER Studies in Income and Wealth*. University of Chicago Press, 11–46.

2009. "Intangible Capital and US Economic Growth," *Review of Income and Wealth*, **55**(3): 661–685.

Fukao, K., T. Miyagawa, K. Mukai, Y. Shinoda, and K. Tonogi. 2009. "Intangible Investment in Japan: Measurement and Contribution to Economic Growth," *Review of Income and Wealth*, **55**(3): 717–736.

Jorgenson, D. W. and Z. Griliches. 1967. "The Explanation of Productivity Change," *The Review of Economic Studies*, **34**(3), 249–283.

Jorgenson, D. W., M. S. Ho, and K. J. Stiroh. 2003. "Lessons from the US Growth Resurgence," *Journal of Policy Modeling*, **25**(5): 453–470.

2005. *Productivity. Volume 3: Information Technology and the American Growth Resurgence*. Cambridge, MA: The MIT Press.

Machlup, F. 1962. *The Production and Distribution of Knowledge in the United States*. Princeton University Press.

Marrano, M. G., J. Haskel, and G. Wallis. 2009. "What Happened to the Knowledge Economy? ICT, Intangible Investment and Britain's Productivity Record Revisited," *Review of Income and Wealth*, **55**(3): 686–716.

Nakamura, L. 1999. "Intangibles: What Put the New in the New Economy?" *Techreport, Federal Reserve Bank of Philadelphia Business Review*, July/August.

Ponomarenko, Aleksey N. 2002. "Retrospektivnye National'Nye Scheta Rossii: 1961–1990" [Retrospective Russian National Accounts in 1961–1990]. Moscow: Finansy i statistika.

Pyo, H. K., H. Chun, and K. Rhee. 2012. "Intangible Capital and Economic Growth: A Theoretical Model and Further Evidences." Paper Prepared for the 2nd World KLEMS Conference, Harvard University (August).

Rajan, R. G. and L. Zingales. 1998. "Financial Dependence and Growth," *American Economic Review*, **88**(3): 559–586.

Reinsdorf, M. and R. Yuskavage. 2010. "Exact Industry Contributions to Labor Productivity Change." In W. Diewert, B. Balk, D. Fixler, K. Fox, and A. Nakamura (eds.), *Price and Productivity Measurement: Index Number Theory*, vol. 6. Bloomington, IN: Trafford Press, ch. 5, pp.77–102.

Stiroh, K. J. 2002. "Are ICT Spillovers Driving the New Economy?" *Review of Income and Wealth*, **48**(1): 33–57.

van Ark, B., J. Hao, C. Corrado, and C. Hulten. 2009. "Measuring Intangible Capital and its Contribution to Economic Growth in Europe," *European Investment Bank Papers*, **14**(1): 62–93.

10 Do *intangibles contribute to productivity growth in East Asian countries? Evidence from Japan and Korea*

HYUNBAE CHUN, TSUTOMU MIYAGAWA,
HAK KIL PYO, AND KONOMI TONOGI

10.1 Introduction

The information and communications technology (ICT) revolution in the 1990s and the productivity growth it caused in the United States have inspired new interest among economists in exploring sources of growth.[1] Table 10.1 shows the standard growth accounting in Korea and Japan. In the manufacturing sector in both countries, total factor productivity (TFP) growth accelerated after 1995, while the contribution of capital to economic growth declined. This has led economists to look for new sources of economic growth. Hall (2000, 2001), Bresnahan, Brynjolfsson, and Hitt (2002), and Basu *et al.* (2003) emphasized intangible assets – that are complementary to ICT assets – and play a crucial role in productivity improvement. However, they had to indirectly

[1] This chapter is written based on our presentation at the 3rd World KLEMS Conference. We thank Professor Jorgenson (Harvard University), Professor Timmer (University of Groningen), and Professor Fukao (Hitotsubashi University) and the participants at the 3rd World KLEMS Conference at Tokyo on May 19–20, 2014 for their helpful comments and discussions. We also thank Dr. Fujita, President of RIETI, and Dr. Morikawa, Vice-president of RIETI, for their helpful suggestions. Excellent research assistance by Professor Hisa (Kanagawa University) and Mr. Makino (Hitotsubashi University) is also appreciated. This study is conducted as a part of the project "Study on Intangible Assets in Japan" undertaken at Research Institute of Economy, Trade, and Industry (RIETI) and supported in part by a Grant-in-Aid for Scientific Research from the Ministry of Education, Culture, Sports, Science and Technology (No. 22223004) of Japan. The study on Korea was conducted through the KIP project at Korea Productivity Center supported by the Korean Ministry of Trade, Industry, and Energy.

Table 10.1 *Traditional growth accounting in Japan and Korea (%)*

	Japan		Korea	
	1985–95	1995–2010	1985–95	1995–2010
Market economy				
GDP growth	3.13	0.43	9.29	4.23
Labor input	0.44	–0.39	2.13	0.70
Capital input	1.64	0.44	5.14	1.84
TFP growth	1.05	0.38	2.02	1.68
Manufacturing				
GDP growth	2.80	1.30	10.90	6.40
Labor input	–0.28	–0.94	2.12	0.05
Capital input	1.56	0.45	5.67	2.27
TFP growth	1.52	1.80	3.11	4.07
Service				
GDP growth	3.57	0.12	10.04	3.36
Labor input	0.86	–0.18	3.42	1.65
Capital input	1.70	0.45	5.56	1.76
TFP growth	1.00	–0.16	1.05	–0.05

estimate the role of intangible assets due to the challenges in measuring intangibles.[2]

Corrado, Hulten, and Sichel (2009) (hereafter referred to as CHS) overcame this challenge and measured intangible investment at the aggregate level in the US for the first time. Based on their estimation, they found that the ratio of intangible investment to gross domestic product (GDP) exceeded the ratio of tangible investment to GDP in the early 2000s. After their success in measuring intangible assets, many economists followed their method and estimated intangible investment in their own countries.[3]

One of the major contributions of CHS's work was to show the contribution of intangibles (which have been hidden in the contributions of capital assets and TFP) to economic growth. CHS argued that

---

[2] Miyagawa and Kim (2008) also considered the role of intangible assets on productivity improvement through the indirect measurement in intangible assets by using firm-level data.

[3] Barnes and McClure (2009) for Australia; Corrado *et al.* (2013) for the EU countries; Fukao *et al.* (2009) for Japan; and Pyo, Chun, and Rhee (2010) for Korea.

one-third of the productivity growth in the late 1990s and the early 2000s is attributable to the growth in intangible assets, and the OECD (2013) emphasized that the effects of intangibles on productivity growth are greater than those of tangibles.

The framework constructed by CHS has been developed further, mainly in two directions. One is to measure intangible investment by industry. Aggregated data does not provide enough detailed information to conduct a productivity analysis. As Jorgenson, Ho, and Stiroh (2005), Inklaar, O'Mahony and Timmer (2005), and Fukao *et al.* (2011) suggested, there is a significant productivity gap between ICT industries and non-ICT industries. In addition, even in ICT-intensive service industries, there is a productivity gap between the US and Japan. To understand the above gaps, we require intangible investment data at the industry level. Moreover, the aggregate series also constrains our analysis. The measured time series intangible investment data are available for at most thirty years. This size of data is not sufficient for several econometric analyses.

As a result, economists started measuring intangible investment at the industry level in a few countries. Chun *et al.* (2012) estimated intangible investment by industry in Japan and Korea using the Japan Industrial Productivity (JIP) database and the Korea Industrial Productivity (KIP) database, and following the framework developed by CHS (2009). In their paper, they found that although the ratio of intangible investment to GDP in Japan is higher than in Korea, the gap in the ratios between two countries has contracted in many industries. Using the same data in Korea, Chun and Nadiri (2016) conducted growth accounting including intangibles. They divided twenty-seven industries into intangible-intensive industries and non-intangible-intensive industries and found that the productivity growth in the former industries was higher than in the latter. They also showed that intangibles are key drivers in productivity growth in the intangible-intensive industries. Miyagawa and Hisa (2013) examined the effects of intangible investment on productivity growth by using data on intangibles in Japan. They found positive and significant effects of intangible investment on productivity in ICT intensive industries. Their results imply there are complementarities between ICT technology and intangibles.

In Europe, Niebel *et al.* (2013) estimated intangible investment by eleven sectors in ten EU countries by using in INTAN-Invest database.

They found that the contributions of intangibles to productivity growth are highest in the manufacturing and financial sectors. Following the CHS approach, Crass *et al.* (2015) also estimated intangible investment by six sectors in Germany. They also supported the view that the manufacturing and financial and business service sectors are intangible-intensive sectors. In these sectors, innovative capital contributes to labor productivity growth. Comparing this with intangible investment in the UK developed by Gil and Haskel (2008), they found that the UK invests more in software, firm-specific human capital, and organizational structure than Germany, while Germany invests more in research and development (R&D) and advertising than the UK.

The second direction this framework was developed towards is to reformulate CHS's components of intangibles. When CHS started to measure intangibles, only software investment was included as capital formation in the United Nations System of National Accounts (SNA), based on the 1993 SNA manual. However, the 2008 SNA manual recommends including R&D investment as capital formation and it has been accounted for as capital formation in many advanced countries. Therefore, Corrado *et al.* (Chapter 9, this volume) measure intangible investment in the EU countries, reclassifying tangibles and intangibles: non-ICT tangibles, ICT, R&D, and non-R&D intangibles. Based on these new classifications, they examine complementarities between capital assets, in particular ICT assets and R&D, and ICT assets and non-R&D intangibles.

Following the two developments of CHS's study, we examine intangible investment by industry in Japan and Korea, and contributions of intangibles to productivity growth. Although Japan and Korea are the most advanced countries in East Asia, the growth paths in the recent past of the two are different. The Japanese economy has suffered from the long-term stagnation of the economy since the collapse of the bubble economy in 1990. On the other hand, the Korean economy has recorded higher economic growth than other advanced economies – even though it experienced a serious downturn due to the financial crisis in 1997. Therefore, we expect that we will find the different effects of intangibles to economic growth in the two countries.[4]

---

[4] Using the framework developed by McGrattan and Prescott (2005, 2010), Miyagawa and Takizawa (2011) showed that the contribution of intangibles to economic growth in Korea is lareger than that in Japan.

In the Section 10.2, we introduce new asset classifications developed by Corrado *et al.* (2014) and explain how to measure these assets in Japan and Korea. In Section 10.3, we show some features of intangible investment at the industry level in Japan with some comparisons with estimates in Korea. As our industry classification is more sophisticated than those in previous literature, we are able to provide useful information for the composition of capital assets by industry. In the Section 10.4, using growth accounting with intangibles, we examine the contributions of intangible assets to productivity improvement. In Section 10.5, we examine the correlations between ICT assets and intangibles. In Section 10.6, we summarize our results.

10.2 Classification and measurement of capital assets

Economists have also developed classifications of intangibles. In Korea, Pyo (2002) defined intangibles as computer software, mineral exploration, cultural products such as entertainment, literature, and original fine arts, and unproduced intangible assets such as patents and licensing of mobile communication etc. Van Ark (2004) argued that human capital, knowledge-based capital, organizational capital, marketing of new products, and social capital, in addition to ICT capital, should be taken into account in the knowledge economy.

The category of intangibles developed by CHS that we use to measure intangibles is broader than Pyo (2002) and narrower than van Ark (2004). Intangible assets in CHS consist of computerized information, innovative property, and economic competencies. However, as Corrado *et al.* (2014) integrate tangibles and intangibles and reclassify it into four types of assets: non-ICT tangibles, ICT, R&D, and non-R&D intangibles, we will explain how we measure these assets by industry. Our measurement depends mainly on the JIP database for Japan and the KIP database for Korea and we adjust industry classifications in both countries to twenty-seven industry classifications because both industry classifications are slightly different between Japan and Korea.[5]

---

[5] In the JIP and KIP databases, we measure capital stock that firms own and do not count capital stock that firms rent. In the measurement of intangible investment by industry, we take the same approach as the capital account in the JIP and KIP databases.

10.2.1 Measurement of ICT investment and non-ICT tangibles investment

As Fukao *et al.* (2011) showed, ICT assets consist of computing equipment, communication equipment, and software. We obtain the data for the first two assets from the JIP database and the KIP database. The last asset defined by CHS, computerized information, consists of custom and packaged software and own account software. In Chun *et al.* (2012), the data in custom and packaged software in Japan were obtained from the Japanese SNA. However, since 2012, the Japanese government has published own account software investment as well as custom and packaged software investment. Therefore, for the aggregate software investment, not only Korea but also Japan follows the SNA data. To measure software investment by industry, we allocate the total software investment into each industry by using the Fixed Capital Formation Matrix (FCFM) in each country. Non-ICT tangibles are all tangibles except computing equipment and communication equipment. We also obtain this data by industry from the JIP database and the KIP database.

10.2.2 Measurement of R&D investment

Innovative property defined in CHS consists of science and engineering R&D, mineral exploitation, copyright and license costs, and other product development, design, and research expenses. Corrado *et al.* (2014) defined the first two components of innovative property as R&D investment, which has been already counted in SNA in advanced countries. In Japan, we estimate science and engineering R&D costs by using the *Survey of Research and Development* published by the Statistical Bureau of the Ministry of Internal Affairs and Communications. In Korea, we estimate science and engineering R&D costs by using the *Survey of Research and Development* published by Ministry of Education, Science, and Technology. In both countries we focus only on R&D expenditures by the private sector. We obtain the data for investment in mineral exploitation from the SNA in Japan and Korea.

10.2.3 Measurement of non-R&D intangibles

Intangibles except software and R&D are considered to be non-R&D intangibles in Corrado *et al.* (2014). Non-R&D intangibles consist of copyright and license costs, other product development, design, and research expenses, brand equity, firm specific human capital, and organizational structure.

Copyright and license costs are constructed from the input–output (IO) tables in each country. They consist of the intermediate inputs from the publishing industry and the video picture, sound information, character information, production, and distribution industry. In the new estimates by Corrado *et al.* (2013), expenditures in entertainment and artistic originals are measured instead of copyright and license costs. However, we use only intermediate inputs from the video picture, sound information, character information, production, and distribution industry.

As for the estimation of product development in financial services, the estimation method by CHS was very controversial because they assumed that 20 percent of intermediate inputs produced by financial services can be assumed to be expenditures in intangible assets. Recently, Corrado *et al.* (2013) suggested that the cost of new product development in financial services was almost 8 percent of the compensation of high skilled workers in the financial industry, to harmonize their estimate with estimates in EU countries by COINVEST and INNODRIVE projects. Thus, following Corrado *et al.* (2013)'s suggestions, we also assume that 8 percent of the compensation of college graduates in the financial and the insurance industries can be regarded as expenditures in intangible assets in these industries.

Brand equity, firm specific human capital, and organizational structure is categorized as economic competencies in CHS. To measure brand equity, we obtain the output data of the advertising industry and allocate it into twenty-seven industries by using the IO table in the JIP and KIP databases.

In estimating firm specific human capital, we focus on off-the-job-training costs. In Japan, we estimate the ratio of off-the-job training costs to total labor costs from the *General Survey on Working Conditions* by industry published by the Ministry of Health, Labor, and Welfare. We estimate off-the-job training costs by firms by industry by multiplying this ratio by total labor costs in the JIP database. For the opportunity cost of off-the-job training in terms of working hours lost, we use the results obtained by Ooki (2003). Ooki calculated the average ratio of the opportunity cost of off-the-job training to direct firm expenses for training in 1998 for the entire business sector using micro-data of the Survey on Personnel

Restructuring and Vocational Education/Training Investment in the Age of Performance-based Wage Systems (*Gyoseki-shugi Jidai no Jinji Seiri to Kyoiku/Kunren Toshi ni Kansuru Chosa*) conducted by the Japan Institute for Labor Policy and Training. The value was 1.51 and we use this same value to estimate the opportunity cost.

In Korea, employer-provided training costs are obtained from the Report on Labor Cost of Enterprise Survey published by the Ministry of Labor. The survey includes training costs only for establishments with thirty or more employees. We assume that establishments with fewer than thirty employees spend 50 percent (relative to the total labor costs) less than those with thirty or more employees, and we estimate the employer-provided training costs for all establishments in each industry. Total training costs are defined as the sum of the direct costs and the opportunity costs of training. As the opportunity costs of training are not available, we assume that the direct costs of training are equal to the opportunity costs.

To estimate expenditures into organizational structure, CHS assumed that 20% of the remuneration of executives can be considered intangible assets for an organizational structure. However, in Japan, we believe 9% is a more accurate number, because only 9% of the total working time of executives is spent on organizational reform and the restructuring of organization, according to Robinson and Shimizu (2006). We calculate the ratio of the remuneration of executives to value added using *the Financial Statements Statistics of Corporations by Industry* published by the Ministry of Finance. Then, we find the expenditure for the organizational structure by industry by multiplying this ratio to value added in the JIP database.

In Korea, consulting costs are considered to be firm-specific investments in organizational resources. To obtain expenditures on consulting at the aggregate level, we use the gross output of consulting industry. The industry-level consulting costs are also estimated from the IO tables.[6]

10.3 Intangible investment in Japan and Korea

Our measure of intangible investment (excluding hardware ICT investment) in Japan and Korea is shown in Figures 10.1a and b.[7] In Japan,

[6] The measurement of each component in intangible assets are explained in Chun *et al.* (2012) and Chun and Nadiri (2016).
[7] The industry-level intangible investment data in Japan is available at: www.rieti.go.jp/jp/database/JIP2013/index.html#04-6.

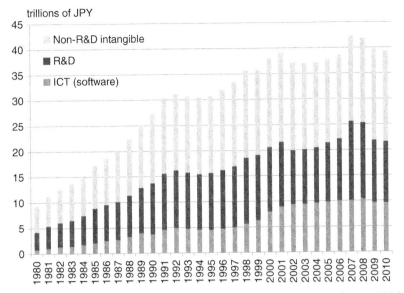

Figure 10.1a Intangible investment by industry and component in Japan, 2010

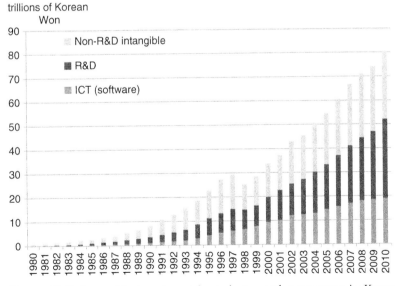

Figure 10.1b Intangible investment by industry and component in Korea, 2010

the amount of intangible investment was about 40 trillion yen in 2010. It peaked in 2007, after which it declined due to the depression caused by the global financial crisis that occurred in 2008. On the other hand, intangible investment in Korea has not been affected by business cycles except the Asian financial crisis in 1997. Growing rapidly, it reached about 80 trillion won in 2010. While growth in ICT investment is the highest (5% per annum from 1995 to 2010) among the three components in Japan, growth in R&D investment is the highest (11% per annum from 1995 to 2010) in Korea. R&D investment in Japan has not increased in the past fifteen years. We also find a gap in the growth rate in investment in non-R&D intangibles between Japan and Korea. In the past fifteen years, its annual growth rate in Korea was 6.5%, while its growth rate in Japan was only 1.1%. However, the ratio of intangible investment to GDP in Japan (7.5%) is still higher than in Korea (7.4%) in the 2000s.

In Figures 10.2a and b, we compare intangible investment by industry and by asset between Japan and Korea in 2010. In the manufacturing sector, the composition of the assets in Japan is similar to Korea in the sense that the share of R&D investment is the largest. However, in the service sector, software investment in Korea is greater than in Japan in some industries such as information and communication and business service industries. In the non-market sector such as education and health and social work industries, software investment in Korea is also larger than in Japan. In addition, in business service, education, and culture and entertainment services industries, investment in economic competencies in Korea is greater than in Japan.

We also compare intangible investment in Japan and Korea with Germany and the UK in Table 10.2.[8] Table 10.1 shows the intangible investment/gross output ratio by sector in four countries. The intangible investment/output ratios in European countries are higher than those in Japan and Korea. In particular, intangible investment/output ratios in the service sector are much higher than those in other countries.[9]

---

[8] The data in European countries are obtained from Crass *et al.* (2015).

[9] The intangible investment/output ratios in the manufacturing sector in Korea seem to be very low. These low ratios in Korea are caused by low value added/ gross output ratio in the manufacturing sector. When we look at the intangible investment/gross value added ratio in the manufacturing sector in Figure 10.2, the ratios in machinery industries are very high.

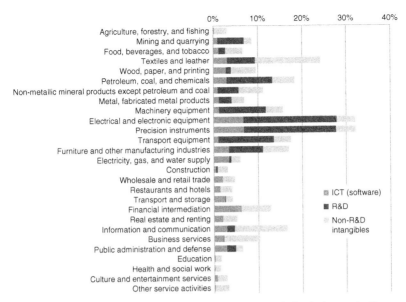

Figure 10.2a Ratio of intangible investment to GVA by industry in Japan, 2010

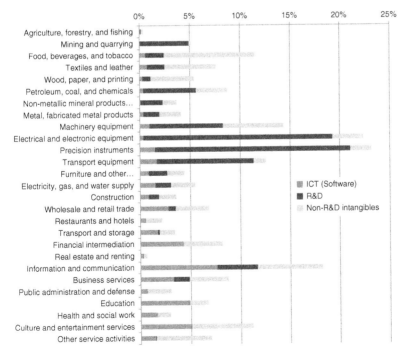

Figure 10.2b Ratio of intangible investment to GVA by industry in Korea, 2010

Table 10.2 *Comparison of intangible investment/gross output ratio (%)*

	2000		2004			2010	
	Japan	Korea	Germany	UK	Japan	Japan	Korea
Agriculture and mining	1.6	0.3	2.8	3.0	1.6	1.6	0.4
Manufacturing	6.0	2.4	6.1	8.3	6.4	6.4	2.8
Utility	2.8	2.5	3.1	2.9	2.6	2.6	1.5
Construction	1.8	1.2	2.1	3.6	1.6	1.6	1.4
Retail, hotel, and transportation	2.8	2.0	3.5	6.4	2.7	2.7	2.1
Financial and business services	6.2	5.8	7.8	8.4	8.0	8.0	5.6

We estimate capital stock in intangible assets based on the measurement of expenditures in intangible assets. The capital formation series in intangible investment is measured in nominal terms. Using the deflator by assets in the JIP and KIP databases, we construct a real capital formation series in intangible assets. Then, we generate the capital formation series by using the perpetual inventory method to find real capital stock in intangible assets. To measure capital stock in intangibles, we use the depreciation rates used in Corrado *et al.* (2013).

To find the composition of capital assets by industry, we have the share of each asset by industry in Figures 10.3a and b. The share of non-ICT tangibles for most industries is the largest among the four types of assets in both countries, but we find some differences in the shares of other assets between Japan and Korea. In the manufacturing sector, Japanese machinery industries such as machinery equipment, electrical

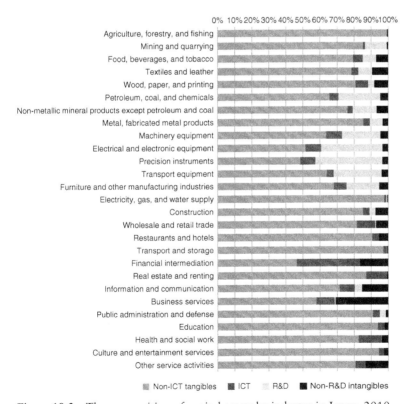

Figure 10.3a The composition of capital assets by industry in Japan, 2010

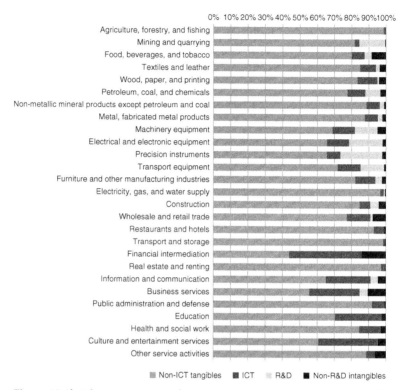

Figure 10.3b The composition of capital assets by industry in Korea, 2010

and electric equipment, precision instruments, and transportation equipment are more R&D-intensive than Korean machinery industries. On the other hand, most Korean service industries such as information and communication, business service, education, and culture and entertainment are more ICT-intensive than Japanese service industries.

10.4 The role of intangible assets on productivity improvement

Using our estimates on intangibles, we conduct a growth accounting including intangible assets to examine their impacts on productivity growth. A feature of the new growth accounting is that we can break down the contribution of capital assets into four types of assets as shown in Figures 10.3a and b. Based on the asset classification in Figures 10.3a and b, the production function in industry i for value added, V_{it}, can be expressed as

$$V_{t,i} = A_{t,i}F(L_{t,i}, K_{t,i}, C_{t,i}, R_{t,i}, Z_{t,i}), \tag{1}$$

where $L_{t,i}$ is labor input, $K_{t,i}$, $C_{t,i}$, $R_{t,i}$, $Z_{t,i}$ are non-tangible assets, ICT assets, R&D assets, and non-R&D intangible assets, respectively. A is TFP. Value-added (V) is adjusted for intangibles as $P_{t,i}^V V_{t,i} \equiv P_{t,i}^Y Y_{t,i} + P_{t,i}^H H_{t,i}$, Y is value added before considering intangible assets, H is intangible investment that is not included in the SNA. Then, we may express a growth accounting relation from equation (1) as,

$$\Delta v_{t,i} = \frac{\partial F}{\partial L_{t,i}}\frac{L_{t,i}}{V_{t,i}}\Delta l_{t,i} + \frac{\partial F}{\partial K_{t,i}}\frac{K_{t,i}}{V_{t,i}}\Delta k_{t,i} + \frac{\partial F}{\partial C_{t,i}}\frac{C_{t,i}}{V_{t,i}}\Delta c_{t,i}$$

$$+ \frac{\partial F}{\partial R_{t,i}}\frac{R_{t,i}}{V_{t,i}}\Delta r_{t,i}\frac{\partial F}{\partial Z_{t,i}}\frac{Z_{t,i}}{V_{t,i}}\Delta z_{t,i} + \Delta a_{t,i} \tag{2}$$

where $\quad \Delta x_i = \frac{\dot{X}_i}{X_i} = \sum_{j=1}^{N} \frac{w_{Xj}X_{j,i}}{\sum_{j=1}^{N} w_{Xj}X_{j,i}}\frac{\dot{X}_{j,i}}{X_{j,i}} \ (X = L, K, C, \ R, \ or \ Z)$

$X_{j,i}$ represents an input factor that has the character j in industry i and $w_{j,i}$ represents the price of an input factor which has the character j in industry i.

As for the estimation strategy for growth accounting, we can estimate the production function in equation (1) using the growth rates of the value added and inputs, while interpreting coefficients on each input as a share. Alternatively, we can calculate the share of its input using the data on labor income and capital spending, and use the growth rates of value added and input to conduct the above growth accounting exercise. In our growth accounting, we take the alternative approach. To measure the share of capital income in the alternative approach and capital service, we calculate the cost of capital for asset j as follows,

$$CC_{t,j} = p_{t,j}(i_t + \delta_{t,j} - \pi_{t,j})/(1 - u_t), \tag{3}$$

where p_j is the price of investment goods for capital j, i is the nominal interest rate (calculated as the weighted sum of the bond rate and long-term prime rate).[10] δ_j is the depreciation rate of capital j, π_j is the expected rate of increase in the price of investment goods. We assume

---

[10] The weights used here are the ratios of debt to total assets by industry.

perfect foresight for the expected rate of increase in the price of investment goods and use the growth rate of the price between this period and the next period. We can calculate the cost of capital (CC) for each type of tangible and intangible assets.[11]

Table 10.3 shows the results of growth accounting based on equation (2) in Japan and Korea. In Table 10.3, we find that the growth rate in the market economy slowed down drastically after 1995 in both countries due to the financial crises in the late 1990s. While all production factors including intangibles induced the slowdown in the growth rate after 1995 in Japan, the contribution rate of R&D assets to value added growth in Korea has kept a constant rate from 1985 to 2010.

When we compare the manufacturing and the service sectors in Japan, the growth rate of value added in the service sector has slowed more than in the manufacturing sector. While both the non-ICT tangibles and R&D assets and TFP growth are major contributors to value added growth in the manufacturing sector, we find a low contribution of non-R&D assets and a negative contribution of TFP growth to value added growth in the service sector after 1995.

In Korea, value added growth in both sectors has declined dramatically after 1995. However, the contribution rate of R&D assets to value added growth has kept the same pace since 1980. While TFP growth rate in the manufacturing sector accelerated after 1995, TFP growth rate in the service sector turned to be negative after 1995, as shown in the growth accounting in Japan.

Next, we compare a growth accounting with intangibles to a traditional growth accounting shown in Table 10.1 in both countries. The value added growth in a traditional growth accounting is different from in the growth accounting with intangibles, as spending in intangibles is treated as investments rather than intermediate expenses, and thus are part of value added. Due to the inclusion of intangibles into capital input, the contribution of capital input in the growth accounting with intangibles is greater than in the traditional growth accounting. In contrast, TFP growth in the growth accounting in Table 10.3 is smaller than that in Table 10.1 except for the case of the service sector after 1995 in Korea. In particular, TFP growth substantially decreased

---

[11] We take the effects of capital income tax on cost of capital into account only in the case of computerized information, because other intangibles are treated as intermediate inputs in the current financial statement.

Table 10.3 *Growth accounting with intangibles (%)*

	Japan		Korea	
	1985–95	1995–2010	1985–95	1995–2010
Market economy				
GDP growth	3.03	0.62	9.46	4.32
Labor input	0.38	−0.37	2.00	0.60
Capital input	2.09	0.61	5.61	2.11
Non-ICT tangibles	1.00	0.22	3.88	1.33
ICT	0.54	0.29	1.04	0.36
R&D	0.29	0.08	0.30	0.29
Non-R&D intangibles	0.26	0.02	0.38	0.12
TFP growth	0.56	0.38	1.86	1.61
Manufacturing				
GDP growth	2.51	1.53	11.14	6.55
Labor input	−0.29	−0.77	1.87	−0.18
Capital input	2.49	0.70	6.40	2.84
Non-ICT tangibles	0.90	0.28	3.61	1.74
ICT	0.46	0.17	1.60	0.25
R&D	0.85	0.23	0.74	0.72
Non-R&D intangibles	0.28	0.02	0.45	0.13
TFP growth	0.31	1.59	2.87	3.88
Service				
GDP growth	3.57	0.25	10.14	3.38
Labor input	0.80	−0.18	3.27	1.54
Capital input	2.02	0.67	5.92	1.84
Non-ICT tangibles	1.03	0.19	4.58	1.19
ICT	0.62	0.37	0.84	0.47
R&D	0.04	0.02	0.08	0.06
Non-R&D intangibles	0.34	0.09	0.42	0.12
TFP growth	0.74	−0.23	0.94	−0.01

in Japanese manufacturing during the 1985–1995 period, when intangibles were rapidly accumulated.

Lastly, we compare our growth accounting results with those for the US and Europe in Corrado *et al.* (2013) that also incorporates

intangible assets. Corrado *et al.* (2013) broke down the labor productivity growth rate, which was measured using hours worked, into
tangible assets, capital deepening rate of intangible assets, change in
labor composition, and TFP growth rate. We follow their method in
breaking down the labor productivity growth rate by using our data.

Table 10.4 shows the international comparison of growth accounting after taking intangible assets into account. We find that Japanese
capital deepening rate of intangible assets is 0.2% and lower than the
average international standard. On the other hand, the capital deepening rate of intangibles in Korea is 0.6%, and is slightly higher than the
average rate in European countries.

The share of capital deepening of intangible assets in the labor productivity growth rate is 9.5% in Japan and 13% in Korea, compared to
33.7% in the US and 19.9% in the EU respectively. After 1995, the
accumulation of intangible assets played a key role in productivity growth
in developed countries. On the other hand, the labor productivity growth
in Japan after 1995 has been attributed to a compositional shift in the
labor market – an increase in higher quality labor due to a higher demand
for higher education. However, there is a limit to this trend and once the
number of people pursuing higher education hits the ceiling, this compositional effect would be muted. In that sense, it is necessary to accumulate
intangible assets up to the level comparable to other developed countries.
In the case of Korea, tangible capital deepening and TFP growth are two
main contributors to labor productivity growth. The source of labor
productivity growth in the Korean economy has changed from massive
tangible capital investments in the rapid growth period of 1970s and
1980s, toward intangible investment and TFP growth after the 1990s.
However, the contribution of intangibles to labor productivity growth in
Korea is still relatively small compared to those in the US and European
countries.

10.5 Correlations between ICT and R&D, and ICT and non-R&D intangibles

Bresnahan *et al.* (2002) and Basu *et al.* (2003) argued that intangibles play
a complementary role on the effects of ICT assets on productivity growth.
Our growth accounting in Table 10.3 also suggests that ICT assets and
non-R&D assets moved together. However, the growth accounting exercise only captures the independent contribution of each asset. Then, we

Table 10.4 *International comparison of labor productivity growth, 1995–2007 (%)*

	Labor productivity growth	Capital deepening	Tangible assets	Intangible assets	Labor composition	TFP growth
Japan	2.1	0.9	0.7	0.2	0.8	0.5
Korea	4.6	2.3	1.7	0.6	0.7	1.7
Austria	2.4	0.8	0.3	0.5	0.2	1.4
Belgium	1.8	0.7	0.2	0.5	0.1	0.9
Czech Republic	4.2	2.4	1.9	0.5	0.3	1.5
Denmark	1.4	1.2	0.7	0.5	0.2	-0.1
Finland	3.8	0.9	0.2	0.7	0.2	2.6
France	1.9	1.0	0.4	0.6	0.4	0.4
Germany	1.7	1.0	0.7	0.3	0.0	0.7
Ireland	3.8	1.4	0.8	0.6	0.1	2.2
Italy	0.6	0.7	0.5	0.2	0.2	-0.4
Netherlands	2.3	0.9	0.4	0.5	0.7	2.8
Slovenia	5.3	1.7	1.2	0.5	0.7	2.8
Spain	0.8	1.0	0.7	0.3	0.5	-0.6
Sweden	3.7	1.9	1.1	0.8	0.3	1.4
UK	2.9	1.5	0.8	0.7	0.4	1.1
US	2.7	1.7	0.8	0.9	0.2	0.8

Note: In Japan and Korea, labor productivity growth from 1995 to 2010 is decomposed and the decomposition of labor productivity growth conducted by Corrado *et al.* (2013).

examine the correlations between ICT and R&D, and ICT and non-R&D intangibles in this section. We take the five-year moving average growth of ICT assets, R&D assets, and non-R&D intangibles in Japan and Korea from 1990 to 2010, and examine correlations among these assets. Figures 10.4a and b show the correlations between growth in ICT and R&D assets in Japan and Korea. We find positive correlations between the two assets in Japan and Korea, however, as shown in Table 10.5, these positive correlations are affected by the strong positive correlations between the two assets in the 1990s. The correlations in Japan turned out to be negative in the 2000s. In Korea, although the positive correlations were kept in the 2000s, they were not significant.

Figures 10.5a and b show the correlations between ICT and non-R&D intangibles. As shown in Table 10.4, ICT is positively and significantly correlated with non-R&D intangibles only in the 1990s in both countries. In the 2000s, the negative correlations between ICT and non-R&D intangibles in both countries were found. Although these figures do not show any causalities among assets, low productivity growth in the 2000s in Japan may be partly caused by the lack of synergy effects among ICT assets, R&D assets, and non-R&D assets.

We also examine the cross-sectional correlations between ICT and intangibles. Figures 10.6a and b show cross-sectional correlations

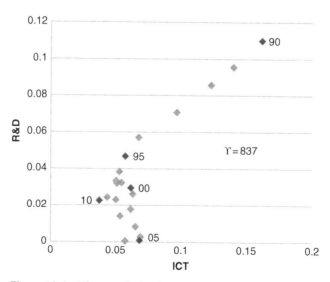

Figure 10.4a The correlation between ICT and R&D in Japan

Table 10.5 *Correlations between ICT and intangibles*

	ICT and R&D		ICT and non-R&D	
	Japan	Korea	Japan	Korea
1990–2010	0.837	0.930	0.886	0.809
	(0.065)	(0.030)	(0.047)	(0.075)
1990–1999	0.986	0.995	0.964	0.830
	(0.009)	(0.003)	(0.022)	(0.098)
2000–2010	−0.499	0.225	−0.223	−0.710
	(0.226)	(0.286)	(0.287)	(0.150)

Note: Standard deviations are shown in parenthesis.

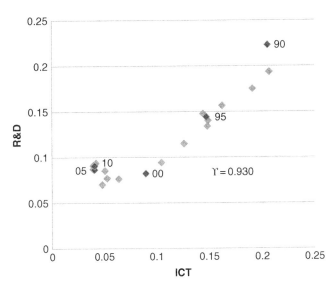

Figure 10.4b The correlation between ICT and R&D in Korea

between ICT and R&D in Japan and Korea.[12] The correlation between two assets in Japan is very week (r=0.06) while we find the high positive

---

[12] In Figures 10.6a and b, we examine the cross-sectional correlation in the manufacturing sector, because R&D investment is not conducted in some industries in the service sector. The numbers in Figures 10.6 and 10.7 correspond to each industry. The corresponding Table between numbers in Figures 10.6 and 10.7 and industry classification is shown in Appendix Table 10.1.

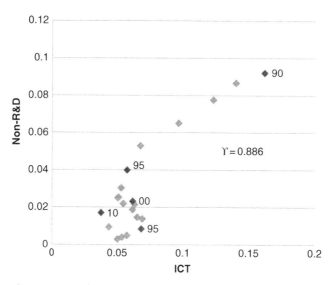

Figure 10.5a The correlation between ICT and non-R&D in Japan

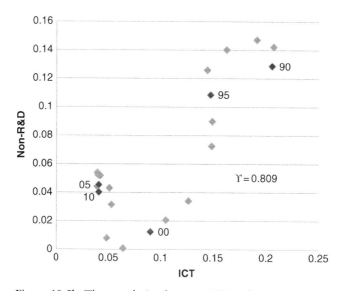

Figure 10.5b The correlation between ICT and non-R&D in Korea

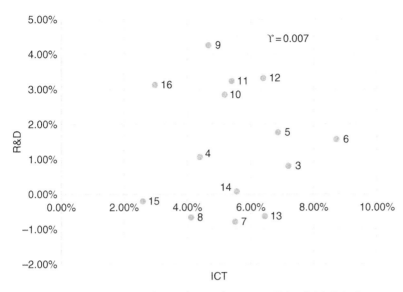

Figure 10.6a Cross-sectional correlations between ICT and R&D in Japan

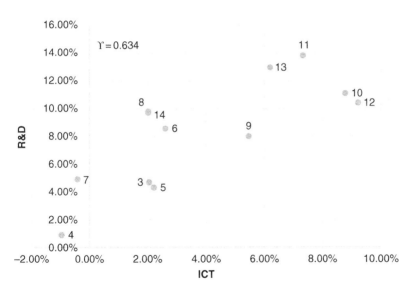

Figure 10.6b Cross-sectional correlations between ICT and R&D in Korea

correlation (r=0.77) in Korea. This finding implies that ICT intensive industries invest in R&D aggressively in Korea. On the other hand, ICT investment is conducted independently from R&D investment.

Figures 10.7a and b, which show the complementarity between ICT and non-R&D intangibles, are similar to Figures 10.6a and b. In Korea, ICT intensive industries invest in non-R&D intangibles aggressively.

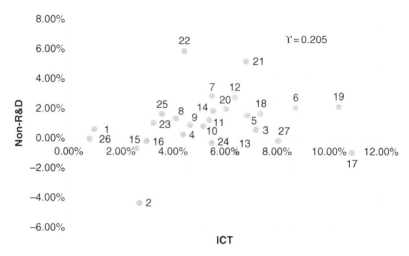

Figure 10.7a Cross-sectional correlations between ICT and non-R&D in Japan

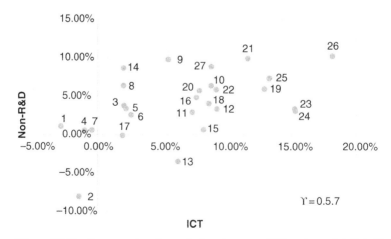

Figure 10.7b Cross-sectional correlations between ICT and non-R&D in Korea

On the other hand, growth in ICT assets is not associated with growth in non-R&D assets.

10.6 Concluding remarks

Based on the framework of Corrado, Hulten, and Sichel (2005, 2009) and Corrado *et al.* (2014), we estimated intangible investment by industry in Japan and Korea using the JIP and KIP databases. Comparing intangible investment in Japan with that in Korea, we find that Japanese growth in intangible investment slowed due to the financial crisis that occurred in 1997, and turned to be negative after the world financial crisis, while Korean intangible investment has grown at a high pace. While only software investment grew after 1995 in Japan, both R&D and software investments in Korea have rapidly grown. As a result, the gap in the ratio of intangible investment to GVA between Japan and Korea substantially reduced in the 2000s. When we examine intangible investment by industry, the ratio of intangible investment to GVA in Japan is higher than in Korea in many machinery industries because R&D investment to GVA ratios in these industries in Japan is higher than in Korea. However, in the service sector, the ratios in Korea are greater than those in Japan, because the Korean service sector is more ICT-intensive than the Japanese service sector.

Using intangible investment data, we construct capital stock in Japan and Korea by industry using the perpetual inventory method. Examining the composition of tangible and intangible capital, we find that machinery industries are R&D-intensive and the service industries are more ICT-intensive, although non-ICT tangibles dominate and take up the largest share in most industries in both countries.

We conducted growth accounting analysis with intangibles. Our results in growth accounting showed that the contributions of intangible assets to economic growth after 1995 are lower than those before 1995 in Japan. In particular, the non-R&D intangibles have not contributed to economic growth after 1995 in Japan, because expenditures in off-the-job training has decreased rapidly due to the harsh restructuring. On the other hand, the contributions of R&D assets to economic growth are constant from 1985 to 2010 in Korea. The Korean economic growth rate decreased after 1995, but the role of R&D assets to economic growth has increased.

Comparing growth accounting with traditional accounting, we find that the contribution of capital assets to economic growth and TFP growth in the traditional growth accounting includes the contributions of accumulation in intangible assets. We also find that the contribution of intangible capital accumulation to productivity growth is weaker in Japan than in other developed countries. On the other hand, the contribution of intangibles to productivity growth in Korea is similar to those in European countries.

Finally, we examine the correlation between ICT assets and intangibles. While we find positive correlations between ICT assets and intangibles in the 1990s, ICT is not positively correlated with intangibles in Japan in the 2000s. Low productivity growth in Japan in the 2000s may be due to the lack of the synergy effects of ICT assets and intangibles. This implication is confirmed by cross-sectional correlations between ICT and intangibles. However, to examine causalities among ICT assets and intangibles, more sophisticated analysis is required.

Our study suggests two important policy implications for the long-term productivity growth of the Japanese and Korean economies. First, since the contributions of intangibles to economic growth in both countries are not higher than those in other advanced countries, there is room to improve labor productivity through intangible investment. Second, our results shed light on complementarities among ICT assets and intangibles suggested by Basu *et al.* (2003), Corrado *et al.* (2013), Miyagawa and Hisa (2013), and Chun and Nadiri (2016). In the case of Japan, the lack of these complementarities may be a factor in the low productivity growth in the 2000s. Therefore, policies promoting intangible investment should be accompanied by policies promoting ICT investment.

Appendix Table 10.1 *Industry classification of the paper*

1   Agriculture, forestry, and fishing
2   Mining and quarrying
3   Food, beverages, and tobacco
4   Textiles and leather
5   Wood, paper, and printing
6   Petroleum, coal, and chemicals
7   Non-metallic mineral products except petroleum and coal
8   Metal and fabricated metal products
9   Machinery equipment
10 Electrical and electronic equipment
11 Precision instruments
12 Transport equipment
13 Furniture and other manufacturing industries
14 Electricity, gas, and water supply
15 Construction
16 Wholesale and retail trade
17 Restaurants and hotels
18 Transport and storage
19 Financial intermediation
20 Real estate and renting
21 Information and communication
22 Business services
23 Public administration and defense
24 Education
25 Health and social work
26 Culture and entertainment services
27 Other service activities

References

Barnes, Paula, and Andrew McClure. 2009. "Investments in Intangible Assets and Australia's Productivity Growth," *Productivity Commission Staff Working Paper*.

Basu, Susanto, John G. Fernald, Nicholas Oulton, and Sylaja Srinivasan. 2003. "The Case of the Missing Productivity Growth: Or, Does Information Technology Explain Why Productivity Accelerated in the United States but not in the United Kingdom?" In Mark Gertler and

Kenneth Rogoff (eds.), *NBER Macroeconomics Annual*. Cambridge, MA: MIT Press, 9–63.

Bresnahan, Timothy, Erik Brynjolfsson, and Lorin Hitt. 2002. "Information Technology, Workplace Organization, and the Demand for Skilled Labor: Firm-Level Evidence," *Quarterly Journal of Economics*, 117(1), 339–376.

Chun, Hyunbae, Kyoji Fukao, Shoichi Hisa, and Tsutomu Miyagawa. 2012. "The Measurement of Intangible Investment by Industry and its Role in Productivity Improvements with some Comparative Studies between Japan and Korea," *RIETI Discussion Paper Series* 12-e-037.

Chun, Hyunbae and M. Ishaq Nadiri. 2016. "Intangible Investment and Changing Sources of Growth in Korea," *Japanese Economic Review*, 67(1): 50–76.

Corrado, Carol, Jonathan Haskel, Cecilia Jona-Lasinio, and Massimiliano Iommi. 2013. "Innovation and Intangible Investment in Europe, Japan and the US," *Discussion Paper 2013/1*, Imperial College Business School.

Corrado, Carol, Charles Hulten, and Daniel Sichel. 2005. "Measuring Capital and Technology: An Extended Framework." In Carol Corrado, John C. Haltiwanger, and Daniel E. Sichel (eds.), *Measuring Capital in the New Economy*. University of Chicago Press, 11–46.

2009. "Intangible Capital and US Economic Growth," *Review of Income and Wealth*, 55(3): 658–660.

Crass, Dirk, Georg Licht, and Bettina Peters. 2015. "Intangible Assets and Investments at the Sector Level – Empirical Evidence for Germany." In Ahmed Bounfour and Tsutomu Miyagawa (eds.), *Intangibles, Market Failure, and Innovation Performance*. Switzerland: Springer International Publishing.

Fukao, Kyoji, Tsutomu Miyagawa, Kentaro Mukai, Yukio Shinoda, and Konomi Tonogi. 2009. "Intangible Investment in Japan: Measurement and Contribution to Economic Growth," *Review of Income and Wealth*, 55(3): 717–736.

Fukao, Kyoji, Tsutomu Miyagawa, Hak K. Pyo, and Keun Hee Rhee. 2011. "Estimates of Multi-factor Productivity, ICT Contributions and Resource Reallocation Effects in Japan and Korea." In Matilde Mas and Robert Stehrer (eds.), *Industrial Productivity in Europe: Growth and Crisis*. Cheltenham, UK: Edward Elgar Publishing.

Gil, Valentina and Jonathan Haskel. 2008. "Industry-level Expenditure on Intangible Assets in the UK." See: www.coinvest.org.uk/pub/CoInvest/ CoinvestGilHaspaper/Intang_Report_for_DTI_Nov08-1.pdf.

Hall, Robert. 2000. "E-Capital: The Link between the Stock Market and the Labor Market in the 1990s," *Brookings Papers on Economic Activity*, 73–118.

   2001. "The Stock Market and Capital Accumulation," *American Economic Review*, **91**(5): 1185–1202.

Inklaar, Robert, Mary O'Mahony, and Marcel Timmer. 2005. "ICT and Europe's Productivity Performance: Industry-level Growth Account Comparisons with the United States," *Review of Income and Wealth*, **51**(3): 505–536.

Jorgenson, Dale, Mun Ho, and Kevin Stiroh. 2005. *Information Technology and the American Growth Resurgence.* Cambridge, MA: MIT Press.

McGrattan, Ellen, and Edward C. Prescott. 2005. "Expensed and Sweat Equity," *Federal Reserve Bank of Minneapolis, Working Paper*, no. 636.

   2010. "Unmeasured Investment and the Puzzling US Boom in the 1990s," *American Economic Journal: Macroeconomics*, **2**(1): 88–123.

Miyagawa, Tsutomu, and Shoichi Hisa. 2013. "Estimates of Intangible Investment by Industry and Productivity Growth in Japan," *Japanese Economic Review*, **64**(1): 42–72.

Miyagawa, Tsutomu, and YoungGak Kim. 2008. "Measuring Organizational Capital in Japan: An Empirical Assessment Using Firm-Level Data," *Seoul Journal of Economics*, **21**(1): 171–193.

Miyagawa, Tsutomu, and Miho Takizawa. 2011. "Productivity Differences between Japan and Korea and the Role of Intangible Assets." In Kazumi Asako, Nobuo Iiduka, and Tsutomu Miyagawa (eds.), *Great Recessions in the Global Economy and Business Cycle Analysis.* The University of Tokyo Press (in Japanese).

Niebel, Thomas, Mary O'Mahony, and Marianne Saam. 2013. "The Contribution of Intangible Assets to Sectoral Productivity Growth in the EU," *ZEW Discussion Paper*, No. 13–062.

OECD. 2013. *New Sources of Economic Growth.* Paris: OECD Publishing.

Ooki, Eiichi. 2003. "Performance-based Wage Systems and Vocational Education/Training Investment (Gyoseki-shugi to Kyoiku Kunren Toshi)." In K. Konno (ed.), *Implications of Performance-based Wage Systems for Individuals and Organizations (Ko to Soshiki no Seikashugi).* Tokyo: Chuo Keizai Sha (in Japanese).

Pyo, Hak K. 2002. *A Study on Indirect Estimation of Intangible Assets.* Korea National Statistical Office Report (in Korean).

Pyo, Hak K., Hyunbae Chun, and Keun Hee Rhee. 2010. "The Productivity Performance in Korean Industries (1990–2008): Estimates from KIP Database." Presented at RIETI/COE Hi-Stat International Workshop on Establishing Industrial Productivity Database for China (CIP), India (IIP), Japan (JIP), and Korea (KIP), October 22.

Robinson, Patricia, and Norihiko Shimizu. 2006. "Japanese Corporate Restructuring: CEO Priorities as a Window on Environmental and Organizational Change," *The Academy of Management Perspectives*, **20**(3): 44–75.

van Ark, Bart. 2004. "The Measurement of Productivity: What Do the Numbers Mean?" In George Gelauff, Luuk Klomp, Stephan Raes, and Theo Roelandt (eds.), *Fostering Productivity: Patterns, Determinants and Policy Implications*. Amsterdam: Elsevier.

11 BEA/BLS industry-level production account for the US: integrated sources of growth, intangible capital, and the US recovery

STEVEN ROSENTHAL, MATTHEW RUSSELL,
JON D. SAMUELS, ERICH H. STRASSNER,
AND LISA USHER

11.1 Introduction

There is a long history of innovation within the United States statistical system to measure and provide relevant, accurate, and timely information on the state of the US economy.[1] The fourteenth comprehensive revision of the national income and product accounts (NIPA) described in (McCulla, Holdren, and Smith 2013) details one of the latest innovations: recognizing research and development (R&D) spending as investment spending.[2] This spending has since been incorporated into official measures of US multi-factor productivity (MFP) growth, helping to narrow a long standing gap between new growth theory and empirical measures on the sources of growth.[3] This is just one example of efforts within the statistical system to integrate concepts, methods, and frameworks to provide relevant economic statistics on the US economy.

The purpose of this chapter is to describe the ongoing integration effort within the US statistical system to provide an industry-level production account for the United States and use the account to analyze the sources of economic growth during the ongoing

---

[1] We thank Matt Calby, Thomas F. Howells III, and Amanda Lyndaker of Bureau of Economic Analysis (BEA), and Mark Dumas and Randy Kinoshita of Bureau of Labor Statistics (BLS) for their work on the data. We are grateful to Carol Moylan of BEA and John Ruser of BLS for their support on this project. We also thank seminar participants at the World KLEMS conference, Lucy Eldridge of BLS, and Dale Jorgenson for useful questions and comments. The views expressed in this chapter are solely those of the authors and not necessarily those of the BEA, US Department of Commerce, and the BLS, US Department of Labor.
[2] See BEA website, www.bea.gov.   [3] See BLS MFP website, www.bls.gov/mfp.

US recovery. The production account combines industry-level output and intermediate inputs with information on capital and labor inputs to form an industry-level production account that is consistent with the aggregate gross domestic product (GDP) account published with the January 2014 comprehensive revision of the Industry Economic Accounts.[4] The integrated industry-level production account that we present follows work on an integrated aggregate production account described in Harper, Moulton, Rosenthal, and Wasshausen (2008) and builds off of the prototype industry-level production account described by Fleck, Rosenthal, Russell, Strassner, and Usher (2014). The production account that we produce serves as a contribution to the World KLEMS initiative, a consortium of statisticians and researchers producing country-level industry-level production accounts within the same basic economic and accounting framework.

We construct the industry-level production account within the framework of the input–output (IO) accounts of the United States. The IO accounts underlying the production account, described in detail in Strassner and Wasshausen (2013), include a time series of annual IO accounts that are consistent with the benchmark IO account that is released at approximately five-year intervals. As of the 2013 comprehensive revision of the NIPAs, previous benchmark accounts are revised to reflect the latest definitions of the national accounts, so that the IO accounts, including the benchmark account, are consistent over time and integrated with the national accounts. The IO accounts provide the current dollar measures of output and inputs at the industry level. By construction, these are consistent with the NIPAs.

We form our industry-level production account by decomposing the nominal values into price and quantity components. The most important innovation within this account is that we construct quantity indexes of primary inputs of capital and labor services that are treated symmetrically with intermediate inputs. In particular, significant detail on heterogeneous types of capital and labor are aggregated with weights that reflect the marginal products of the components. This yields estimates of capital and labor that are adjusted for "composition" or "quality." The issue of incorporating capital and labor services

---

[4] This industry-level production account is somewhat broader in scope. It treats government capital symmetrically with private sector capital input. In particular, in addition to the depreciation cost, there is also a rate of return on government capital assets.

into the national accounts is addressed in the *System of National Accounts 2008* (United Nations 2008), which allows for the inclusion of these inputs, but does not require their inclusion. Price and quantity indexes of intermediate inputs are presented in the KLEMS accounts described in Strassner, Medeiros, and Smith (2005).

Ongoing structural change in the US economy due, in part, to globalization, the spread of information and communications technology, and the Great Recession, reinforces the need for an integrated industry-level production account. Economic growth in the US since 1995 has been characterized as containing several unique episodes: the information technology (IT) investment boom between 1995 and 2000, the period of jobless growth over the 2000–2005 period, and the Great Recession and Recovery period that began around 2007 and continues through today.[5] At the same time, ongoing structural trends that pre-date this period have continued and remain a focal point for both economists and policy-makers: increasing globalization of the market-place, the ongoing spread of information and communications technology, and the continued effect of the skills gap on the US labor market.

These broad trends and unique growth episodes are identifiable at the aggregate level, but the macro perspective obscures many of the pertinent details on the sources of growth. Between 2000 and 2005, estimates at the industry level indicate that almost half of this aggregate productivity was due to productivity growth originating in the IT-producing industries. In Jorgenson, Ho, and Samuels (2014), IT-producing industries accounted for a little over 3 percent of nominal aggregate value added but for almost 50 percent of aggregate MFP! The role of IT in growth and productivity continues to garner attention from the research community, including Gordon (2014), Jorgenson *et al.* (2014), Byrne, Oliner, and Sichel (2013), among others.

Furthermore, the impact of the Great Recession was not balanced across industries. For example between 2007 and 2012, real value added declined in construction and non-durable goods manufacturing, but increased substantially in mining industries, professional and business services, and within the Federal government.[6] Data from Jorgenson, Ho, and Samuels (2016) show that the aggregate college skill premium paid to workers was basically unchanged between 2005 and 2010. But at the

---

[5] Jorgenson, Ho, and Samuels 2016.
[6] See www.bea.gov/industry/gdpbyind_data.htm

industry level over that same period, the college wage premium increased significantly in transportation-related industries and decreased substantially in finance-related industries, again emphasizing the importance of industry-level analysis of aggregate trends.[7] Heterogeneity across industries is an important component in the sources of growth of aggregate output and input. The industry-level production account that we present provides an integrated framework for analyzing the sources of growth over time.

In addition to its importance in analyzing growth, the framework can evaluate growth prospects as the economy continues to recover from the recession. For example, Jorgenson *et al.* (2014) argue that it is important to consider industry-specific sources of growth, and shows how to incorporate this feature into aggregate projections of labor productivity and growth in GDP.

We use our integrated industry-level production account to analyze the role of the "new" sources of growth in recent US history and how these compare to the sources of growth during the ongoing US recovery. The dataset that we present in this chapter is an update of Fleck *et al.* (2014), which laid the framework for the integrated account that we present in this chapter. The "new" sources of growth include the incorporation of expenditures on research and development (R&D) and on entertainment, artistic and literary originals as capital, which, thus, expands the boundary of US GDP and its related measures. The treatment of R&D includes the estimates of own-account spending on R&D as investment and the R&D produced by industry that is sold to others. Expenditures on entertainment, artistic, and literary originals only includes own-account spending. The updated account includes statistics through the year 2012, allowing for a more-current analysis of trends leading up to and after the period of the Great Recession compared to the previously available data.[8]

To summarize our main empirical results, we find that:

- R&D capital input contributed about 0.09 percentage point to aggregate value added growth between 1998 and 2012, about half as much as software.

---

[7] Jorgenson *et al.* 2014.
[8] Data for this project can be found on the BEA website at www.bea.gov/industry/index.htm#integrated and on the BLS website at www.bls.gov/mfp.

- Including R&D reduces estimated MFP growth from about 0.56% per year to 0.47% per year over the 1998–2012 period.
- The smaller contribution of capital input relative to the pre-crisis period more than accounts for the slower growth during the recovery.

The remainder of the chapter proceeds as follows: Section 11.2 describes the framework and the underlying source data for the industry-level production account. Section 11.3 presents estimates of the industry sources of growth over the 1998–2012 period, and Section 11.4 includes results on the industry sources of aggregate value added and productivity growth. Section 11.5 gives the conclusions and next steps.

11.2 Overview of the framework

The objective of the industry-level production account is to present data that is consistent with the national accounts on outputs produced by industry and inputs used by industry, in current and constant prices. Because an objective of the account is to produce estimates that are consistent with the NIPAs and the GDP by industry accounts, the industry-level production account that we construct maintains the definitional and conceptual framework of the national economic accounts.

The organizing principal for the industry-level production account is the time-series of IO accounts for the United States produced by the BEA, which are fully integrated with the national economic accounts. Strassner and Wasshausen (2014) describe in detail the most recent comprehensive revision that integrated the benchmark IO account that is produced every five years, with the annual IO accounts and the NIPAs. The 2014 comprehensive revision of the *Industry Economic Accounts* marked the completion of BEA's effort to fully integrate these sets of accounts. As a result of this most recent revision, future benchmark IO accounts will be revised according to the schedule of BEA's annual revisions to the NIPAs. Thus, allowing for full consistency among the NIPAs, the IO accounts, and GDP by industry accounts over time.

This integration effort was coupled with significant conceptual changes to the accounting framework. In particular, a new category of intangible investment was created – intellectual property products – that is, expenditures on R&D and on entertainment, artistic, and literary originals were added as new intangible capital formation. Software development expenditures were reclassified from the category of private equipment and software investments to the new intellectual property products category. In addition, the scope of capitalized ownership transfer costs of residential fixed investment was expanded to include additional non-financial costs of acquisition and expected disposal to be included with the already-capitalized brokers' commissions. These changes are also covered in detail in Strassner and Wasshausen (2013, 2014), Bureau of Economic Analysis (2013), Kornfeld (2013), and McCulla *et al.* (2013).

The IO accounts contain estimates, in nominal dollars, of outputs produced by industry and inputs used by industry. Consistency between the IO accounts and expenditure-side estimates requires that the sum of value added across industries equals the total purchases of new goods and services by final demanders in each time period. Consistency also ensures that the total domestic supply for the US economy is in balance with its uses by commodity, and that the sum of each industry's value added and intermediate inputs equals its gross output.

Within the production account, the industry-level nominal accounting identity requires that the value of producer output equals the value of spending on all inputs: capital, labor, energy, materials, and purchased services (KLEMS).

The value of self-employed labor is not provided in the IO accounts. To estimate this value, we measure the hours worked for each type of labor input discussed below, and assume that the compensation per hour for each type of worker is equivalent between employees and self-employed. The residual value (output less intermediate inputs less total labor compensation) is defined as the value of capital in the production account.

Defining a production account requires prices and quantities for industry-level outputs and inputs. This is analogous to the price and quantity decomposition within the expenditure-side of the GDP accounts, allowing users to decompose changes in the value of output over time into changes due to prices and changes due to quantities. Our industry-level production account prices for industry outputs and inputs are readily available in BEA's *Industry Economic Accounts*. These accounts, described in detail in Strassner and Wasshausen (2014) contain the prices of industry output and intermediate input that are consistent with BEA's GDP by industry statistics. By construction these are consistent with the US national accounts.[9]

The "integrated" label that we attach to the industry-level production account comes from integrating capital and labor services estimates into the industry accounts. The purpose of this is to decompose nominal dollars spent on capital and labor services into price and quantity terms.

11.2.1 Labor input: price and quantity

The quantity of labor services at the industry level that we employ captures the changing composition of the industry's work force. That is, substitution towards workers with higher productivity manifests an increase in the quantity of labor used by the industry. The basic approach to doing this follows Jorgenson, Ho, and Stiroh (2005), though there are some implementation differences. The basic procedure is to decompose total hours worked by industry into hours worked by a heterogeneous set of workers, and aggregate the hours worked by each group with the price paid to each type of worker.

The measures of total hours worked generally reflect the data and methods underlying the hours used in the BLS industry productivity measures, but have been adjusted where necessary to improve consistency with the BEA Industry Economic Accounts. For most NIPA industries, hours-worked data are based primarily on payroll employment and hours paid data from the BLS Current Employment Statistics (CES) survey. Ratios of hours at work to hours paid, developed from information on employer leave practices in the BLS National Compensation Survey, are used to adjust the CES paid hours (which includes paid holidays, sick leave, and vacation time) to an hours-worked basis. Average weekly hours for production and non-supervisory workers are obtained directly from the CES, while those for non-production and supervisory workers are derived using data from the BLS Current Population Survey (CPS) in conjunction with the CES data. The industry-level employee data are supplemented with data for the self-employed (partners and proprietors) and unpaid family workers from the CPS. Estimates of employment and hours for industries in the farm

---

[9] There are minor differences in aggregating real GDP from the expenditure side and the industry side.

sector are based on data from the US Department of Agriculture. Measures for industries in the non-farm agriculture sector are based primarily on data from the CPS, together with data from the BLS Quarterly Census of Employment and Wages (QCEW). For mining industries, estimates of non-production worker hours are derived from data collected by the Mine Safety and Health Administration. Employment data for the postal service industry are from the CES survey, but estimates of hours for this industry are from the US Postal Service.

Hours for NIPA industries were aggregated from estimates for more detailed industries. Hours for the integrated production account are controlled by aggregate group to NIPA hours worked by full-time and part-time workers by industry to ensure consistency within the national accounts framework.

Labor input is constructed by disaggregating hours worked by industry to a heterogeneous set of workers and aggregating the hours with the price paid to each type. We construct employment, hours worked, and the compensation per hour by industry for 192 unique demographic categories, where workers are divided by gender, class of worker, age (eight categories), and education (six categories). Micro data records from the 2000 census provide the detailed cross-classification in 2000. Estimates for the other years are constructed with the RAS method described in Jorgenson *et al.* (2005). Because the long form of the decennial census has been replaced by the American Community Survey, future work involves evaluating the possibility of using this to refine estimates over this period.

The estimates presented in this chapter modify the accounts published in Fleck *et al.* (2014). Previously, a labor input index was generated using hours measures from BLS and labor matrices of demographic characteristics from the work of Jorgenson, Ho, and Samuels (2011) (JHS). For this update, the complete time series of labor matrices was reestimated to avoid relying on estimates produced outside of the statistical system. Furthermore, the time series was updated to include estimates through 2012. Finally, for the period 1998–2002, our method differs from the JHS approach with respect to converting micro-level Standard Industrial Classification (SIC)-based CPS records to the North American Industry Classification System (NAICS). The approach taken in this chapter uses the CES SIC-to-NAICS employment bridge at the micro-record level. The basic source data is the same: data from the March Supplement of the CPS provides the marginal, while the US Census 2000 1 Percent Public Use Microdata Sample Files provide the 2000 benchmark matrix.

Aggregating worker hours by industry with compensation per hour by industry for each type of worker yields a quantity index of labor input that accounts for compositional changes in the industry's work force over time. The price index for labor input for the industry-level production account is defined by deflating the nominal value of labor by the quantity index of labor input.

11.2.2 Capital input: price and quantity

The fundamental approach to constructing the price and quantity of capital input is analogous to the construction of labor input. We aggregate detailed productive stocks with weights that reflect the marginal product of each asset.

Principal changes in capital input due to the 2013 comprehensive revision of the US NIPAs include the introduction of R&D and entertainment, artistic, and literary originals as fixed investment, the capitalization of ownership transfer costs of residential fixed assets, and revisions to the capital income estimates derived from the Industry Economic Accounts that reflect this new source of capital income.

Capital inputs for the industry-level production account are computed in accordance with a service flow concept for physical capital assets and intellectual property products. Capital inputs for major sectors are determined in three main steps: (1) A very detailed array of capital stocks is developed for various asset types in various industries; (2) asset-type capital stocks are aggregated for each industry to measure capital input for the industry; and (3) industry capital inputs are aggregated to measure sectoral level capital input.

There are ninety asset types for fixed business equipment, structures, inventories, land, and intellectual property products. Data on investment for fixed assets are obtained from BEA. Intellectual property products are composed of three broad classes of assets: software, R&D, and artistic originals. Software is comprised of pre-packaged, custom, and own-account software. R&D is creative work undertaken to increase the stock of knowledge for the purpose of discovering or developing new products or improving existing ones. Artistic originals include theatrical movies, long-lived television programs, books, music, and other forms of entertainment.

The addition of these two new categories of intellectual property products, particularly R&D, is an important feature of this new industry-level dataset. These assets have also been incorporated into the official productivity measures produced by BLS.[10] By treating spending on R&D as an investment that yields a flow of capital services over time, the contribution of intellectual property products to growth and productivity can be analyzed using the same framework as other capital goods in the dataset that we analyze. The incorporation of expenditures on R&D and on entertainment, artistic, and literary originals expands the boundary of US GDP and its related measures. The treatment of R&D includes both the estimates of own-account spending on R&D as investment and the R&D produced by industry that is sold to others. Expenditures on entertainment, artistic, and literary originals only includes own-account spending.

Data on inventories are estimated using BEA and additional information from the Internal Revenue Service (IRS) Corporation Income Returns. Data for land in the farm sector are obtained from the US Department of Agriculture (USDA). Non-farm industry detail for land is based on IRS book value data.

Real stocks are constructed as vintage aggregates of historical investments (in real terms) in accordance with an "efficiency" or service flow concept (as distinct from a price or value concept). The efficiency of each asset is assumed to deteriorate only gradually during the early years of an asset's service life and then more quickly in its later life. These "age/efficiency" schedules are based, to the extent possible, on empirical evidence of capital deterioration.

Current-dollar value added data are used in estimating capital rental prices. The "implicit rental price" of capital is based on the neoclassical principle that inputs should be aggregated using weights that reflect their marginal products. The assumption used to formulate the rental price expression is that the purchase price of a capital asset equals the discounted value of the stream of services (and, hence, implicitly the rents) that the asset will provide. After determining the internal rate of return in each industry, rental prices are computed separately for each type of asset within each industry.

---

[10] See Multifactor Productivity Trends: www.bls.gov/news.release/pdf/prod3.pdf.

Rental prices for R&D assets are treated somewhat differently than other assets. For R&D assets, businesses receive credits for increasing research activities. Unlike all other assets where the effective rate of the investment tax credit is zero, R&D assets do have tax credits factored into the rental price. Given that qualified R&D capital expenses are immediately deductible, the present value of $1 of tax depreciation allowances is given the value of one. Also, given the fact that there is a certain amount of risk to R&D expenditure that is not incurred by other assets, a risk premium of .04 is added to the rates of return of R&D assets.

For the purpose of this industry-level production account, capital measures are conceptually consistent with the total economy production accounts as described in Harper *et al.* (2008).[11] The measures include the government, household, non-profit institutions, and owner-occupied housing capital.

Finally, the nominal value of capital input is decomposed into price and quantity by defining the implicit capital input price as the nominal value of capital services divided by the capital input quantity.

11.2.3 *Integration*

The industry-level production account integrates prices and quantities of capital and labor services into the gross domestic product by industry data. We calculate "integrated MFP" as the ratio of the quantity of output produced by industry to the quantity of input used by industry. To construct total input by industry, we aggregate capital, labor, energy, materials, and purchased services as a Tornqvist aggregate.

The industry-level production account and integrated MFP measures presented here reflect output consistent with GDP for the total economy, but differ in concepts and coverage from the official US MFP measures. Because national accountants and productivity analysts have different objectives, there is an inherent tradeoff between having a set of accounts that add up to the best estimate of GDP and a set of accounts that generates the best productivity measures by industry. GDP statistics that are fully consistent with international guidelines

---

[11] These measures are not consistent with BLS major sector published measures, which exclude government, household, and non-profit institutions, and owner-occupied housing capital.

include measures of economic activities for which there are no market prices. Such activities are excluded from official productivity statistics because output is generally not measured independently from inputs. Furthermore, different concepts of output and aggregation methods are used, and while this integrated account includes an adjustment for labor composition, the official industry MFP estimates does not. It is noteworthy that the official industry multi-factor productivity measures will include labor composition when they are updated to 2013. The appendix to this chapter describes conceptual and empirical differences in deriving MFP growth rates within this integrated production account and the official estimates. For additional details, see "Conceptual and Measurement Challenges" in Fleck *et al.* (2014).

11.3 Sources of industry growth

The fundamental economic entity in our analysis is the industry, and the aggregate economy is divided into sixty-three industries. Each of these industries produces output using primary capital and labor inputs, intermediate input, and the available level of production technology. It is noteworthy that each of these major input groupings at the industry level is, in fact, made up of many heterogeneous inputs, each with its own price and quantity index. For example, under intermediate input, there are all of the commodities that are published in the benchmark IO accounts. Capital input includes estimates for approximately ninety assets within the categories of fixed business equipment, structures, inventories, land, and intellectual property products. Intermediate inputs include items such as energy, materials, and purchased business services. Labor input is cross classified by gender, age, education, and class of worker.[12]

Since productivity is a measure of how efficiently inputs are converted to output, it is important that outputs and inputs are measured in constant units exclusive of inflation, i.e. hours adjusted for labor composition and constant dollar quantity indexes of capital input and intermediates that measure the services provided by that input.

Using the growth accounting framework, industry output growth is expressed as the sum of the share weighted growth rate of industry inputs and the change in MFP. Within this framework, MFP growth

---

[12] Employee, or self-employed.

measures embed underlying changes in the true economic technology, innovation, changes in production management, but also include the effects of inputs that are not properly measured or are unmeasured. For example, prior to the July 2013 comprehensive revision of the NIPAs, spending on R&D did not produce future capital services, so that R&D was missing as a capital input. The set of accounts presented in this chapter includes R&D spending as a capital input.

Table 11.1 presents the comprehensive results from the industry-level production account: industry output growth and the sources of industry output growth for the 1998–2012 period. This table demonstrates the heterogeneity in industry growth and its sources for that period. For example, the support activities for mining industry grew by about 7.2% per year over the period (consistent with the expansion of fracking), due mostly to an expansion of labor input and integrated MFP growth. The data processing, internet publishing, and other information services industry grew by a little over 8% per year as a result of capital investments and purchases of intermediate inputs, consistent with anecdotal evidence of shifts to cloud computing. At the bottom end of the spectrum, the apparel industry shrank by about 10% per year over the period (which is consistent with increased apparel purchases produced abroad), but became slightly more productive in terms of MFP growth. Textile mills had a similar growth experience to apparel. The motor vehicle industry grew by about 0.7% per year over the period, driven mostly by MFP growth, as declines in labor input dampened growth by about 0.4% per year.

Figure 11.1 shows that the contribution of MFP growth to industry output varied considerably by industry. Over the 1998–2012 period, the largest growth in MFP occurred in computer and electronic products, support activities for mining, water transportation, computer systems design and related services, and pipeline transportation. These productivity gains reflect ongoing innovation in information technology, and innovative practices in the mining and transportation industries. In contrast, rental and leasing, management of companies, legal services, and other services, experienced negative productivity growth over the same period. Negative measured MFP growth reflects decreased capability to manage resources, decisions to hoard inputs in uncertain times, but also indicates potential issues in the measurement of outputs and inputs, including but not limited to quality adjustment issues or changes in unmeasured inputs.

Table 11.1 *Sources of industry output growth, 1998–2012*

	Output growth	Capital contribution	Labor contribution	Intermediate contribution	Integrated MFP growth
Farms	0.51	0.18	−0.08	−0.66	1.07
Forestry, fishing, and related activities	−0.20	0.36	0.49	−1.92	0.87
Oil and gas extraction	1.81	−0.16	0.16	0.53	1.28
Mining, except oil and gas	−0.17	0.35	−0.13	−0.68	0.28
Support activities for mining	7.18	0.37	2.34	0.96	3.51
Utilities	−0.36	0.57	−0.09	−1.19	0.35
Construction	−1.44	0.30	−0.11	−0.60	−1.03
Wood products	−2.10	0.00	−0.90	−2.02	0.83
Non-metallic mineral products	−1.94	0.17	−0.51	−1.19	−0.41
Primary metals	0.39	−0.09	−0.58	0.24	0.82
Fabricated metal products	−0.31	0.06	−0.31	−0.07	0.02
Machinery	0.57	0.16	−0.47	0.33	0.56
Computer and electronic products	4.05	0.41	−0.82	−2.01	6.47
Electrical equipment, appliances, and components	−1.83	−0.06	−0.62	−2.05	0.90
Motor vehicles, bodies and trailers, and parts	0.67	0.06	−0.44	0.00	1.06
Other transportation equipment	1.26	0.11	−0.16	0.60	0.72

Furniture and related products	-2.60	0.12	-1.21	-1.44	-0.06
Miscellaneous manufacturing	1.62	0.43	-0.33	0.34	1.19
Food and beverage and tobacco products	0.17	0.16	0.01	-0.07	0.07
Textile mills and textile product mills	-5.25	-0.20	-1.55	-3.70	0.20
Apparel and leather and allied products	-9.99	-0.09	-2.80	-8.10	0.99
Paper products	-1.73	-0.18	-0.60	-0.87	-0.08
Printing and related support activities	-2.49	-0.02	-1.40	-2.58	1.50
Petroleum and coal products	0.77	0.09	-0.02	0.59	0.11
Chemical products	0.45	1.12	-0.15	-0.38	-0.14
Plastics and rubber products	-0.95	0.13	-0.43	-0.76	0.11
Wholesale trade	2.43	0.96	0.13	1.08	0.26
Retail trade	2.10	0.94	0.13	1.17	-0.14
Air transportation	-1.74	0.03	-0.38	-1.18	-0.22
Rail transportation	1.21	0.13	-0.40	1.00	0.48
Water transportation	3.17	-0.21	0.21	0.63	2.54
Truck transportation	0.85	0.36	-0.10	0.30	0.29
Transit and ground passenger transportation	1.15	0.39	0.52	0.57	-0.34
Pipeline transportation	-2.13	1.17	-0.16	-5.46	2.33
Other transportation and support activities	1.67	0.01	0.08	1.25	0.33
Warehousing and storage	6.58	0.49	1.25	3.69	1.15
Publishing industries, except internet (includes software)	1.35	1.28	-0.27	-0.30	0.64

Table 11.1 (*cont.*)

	Output growth	Capital contribution	Labor contribution	Intermediate contribution	Integrated MFP growth
Motion picture and sound recording industries	1.12	1.15	0.22	-1.77	1.51
Broadcasting and telecommunications	4.38	1.69	-0.24	1.64	1.30
Data processing, internet publishing, and other information services	8.36	3.16	-0.48	4.97	0.70
Federal Reserve banks, credit intermediation, and related activities	1.46	1.11	0.34	-0.27	0.29
Securities, commodity contracts, and investments	4.11	0.18	0.45	2.43	1.05
Insurance carriers and related activities	3.40	1.08	0.26	2.08	-0.02
Funds, trusts, and other financial vehicles	2.56	0.96	0.19	1.12	0.29
Real estate	2.52	1.42	0.05	0.60	0.44
Rental and leasing services and lessors of intangible assets	2.06	2.37	-0.10	1.32	-1.54
Legal services	-0.02	1.00	0.30	0.02	-1.35
Computer systems design and related services	4.98	0.23	1.86	0.57	2.32
Miscellaneous professional, scientific, and technical services	2.58	0.76	0.88	1.04	-0.10
Management of companies and enterprises	2.83	1.07	1.11	2.13	-1.47
Administrative and support services	2.23	0.75	0.59	0.21	0.68

Waste management and remediation services	1.47	0.19	0.44	0.41	0.44
Educational services	3.29	0.22	1.74	1.75	-0.43
Ambulatory health care services	3.19	0.22	1.54	1.11	0.32
Hospitals and nursing and residential care	3.02	0.27	1.13	1.85	-0.23
Social assistance	3.52	0.11	1.49	1.99	-0.08
Performing arts, spectator sports, museums, and related activities	2.63	0.14	0.31	1.38	0.80
Amusements, gambling, and recreation industries	2.13	0.69	0.56	1.12	-0.25
Accommodation	0.82	0.95	-0.10	0.11	-0.14
Food services and drinking places	1.73	0.00	0.55	0.88	0.30
Other services, except government	0.00	0.46	0.11	0.78	-1.35
Federal	2.28	0.71	0.01	1.44	0.12
State and local	1.65	0.52	0.62	0.43	0.08

Notes: Average annual percentage growth. A contribution is a share-weighted growth rate. Integrated MFP estimates differ from official estimates produced by the BLS. See: www.bls.gov/mfp for the official estimates.

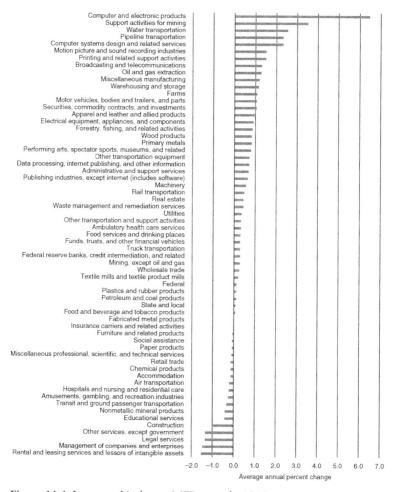

Figure 11.1 Integrated industry MFP growth, 1998–2012

As noted above, the contribution of each broad input (capital, labor, intermediate) incorporates heterogeneous components. For the purpose of exposition, we have divided the measures of capital input into components, specifically, IT capital equipment, software capital, R&D capital, and other capital. Other capital includes about ninety types of other capital equipment and structures, inventories and land. Intermediates include energy, materials, and purchased services. For labor input, we have divided the estimates into those with a college degree and those without. Underlying each of these components of labor is detail on labor input by gender, class, age, and level of educational attainment.

Table 11.2 indicates that the contribution of IT and software capital was spread broadly across industries over the 1998–2012 period, and that R&D capital was important for the growth of a few select industries. IT and software capital played particularly important roles in data processing, broadcasting and telecom, publishing (including software), and management of companies. R&D capital was particularly important for chemical products, computer and electronic products, and miscellaneous manufacturing.

Table 11.3 shows that the declining contribution of non-college workers was spread broadly across industries over the 1998–2012 period. In contrast to the large majority of industries, labor input for non-college workers increased in eighteen of the industries, with sizable gains in support activities for mining and warehousing and storage.

This integrated production account is useful for analyzing the economic changes at the industry level that occurred during the time of the Great Recession and that are taking place during the ongoing recovery. To analyze the ongoing recovery within the 1998–2012 period, we split the sample into three periods: 1998–2007, 2007–2009, and 2009–2012. According to the National Bureau of Economic Research, the official recession began in December 2007, but annual GDP was relatively strong in 2007, so we group 2007 in the pre-recession period. We group 2008 and 2009 as the recessionary period, and 2010–2012 as the recovery period.[13] We also include the 2007–2012 period as a sub-period of comparison.

Figure 11.2 gives the changes to the sources of growth that occurred during the recession period. During the 2007–2009 period, industry output growth fell relative to the earlier period in the large majority of industries, by large percentages. The output of the support activities for mining, wood products, non-metallic mineral, motor vehicles, furniture, and securities industries all fell by about 20 percentage points versus the 1998–2007 period on average. In general, the largest source of the decline was a decrease in intermediate purchases, followed

---

[13] The unemployment rate peaked in October 2009. However, the National Bureau of Economic Research Business Cycle Dating Committee recorded the end of the recession in the United States as June, 2009. See: www.nber.org/cycl es/recessions_faq.html.

Table 11.2 *Sources of capital contribution, 1998–2012*

	Capital contribution	IT capital and software contribution	R&D capital contribution	Artistic originals capital contribution	Other capital contribution
Farms	0.18	0.01	0.00	0.00	0.16
Forestry, fishing, and related activities	0.36	0.00	0.00	0.00	0.36
Oil and gas extraction	−0.16	0.03	0.02	0.00	−0.20
Mining, except oil and gas	0.35	−0.07	0.01	0.00	0.42
Support activities for mining	0.37	0.12	0.03	0.00	0.23
Utilities	0.57	0.10	−0.01	0.00	0.48
Construction	0.30	0.03	0.00	0.00	0.27
Wood products	0.00	0.01	0.02	0.00	−0.04
Non-metallic mineral products	0.17	0.00	0.01	0.00	0.16
Primary metals	−0.09	−0.01	−0.01	0.00	−0.07
Fabricated metal products	0.06	0.03	−0.01	0.00	0.04
Machinery	0.16	0.02	0.10	0.00	0.04
Computer and electronic products	0.41	0.15	0.28	0.00	−0.02

Electrical equipment, appliances, and components	−0.06	0.03	−0.06	0.00	−0.03
Motor vehicles, bodies and trailers, and parts	0.06	0.00	−0.02	0.00	0.07
Other transportation equipment	0.11	0.01	−0.03	0.00	0.14
Furniture and related products	0.12	0.05	0.02	0.00	0.05
Miscellaneous manufacturing	0.43	0.19	0.19	0.00	0.05
Food and beverage and tobacco products	0.16	0.03	0.04	0.00	0.09
Textile mills and textile product mills	−0.20	−0.01	0.00	0.00	−0.19
Apparel and leather and allied products	−0.09	0.00	0.00	0.00	−0.09
Paper products	−0.18	0.00	0.03	0.00	−0.21
Printing and related support activities	−0.02	0.01	0.03	0.00	−0.06
Petroleum and coal products	0.09	0.05	−0.12	0.00	0.17
Chemical products	1.12	0.12	0.94	0.00	0.06
Plastics and rubber products	0.13	0.05	0.03	0.00	0.05

Table 11.2 (*cont.*)

	Capital contribution	IT capital and software contribution	R&D capital contribution	Artistic originals capital contribution	Other capital contribution
Wholesale trade	0.96	0.55	0.00	0.00	0.41
Retail trade	0.94	0.37	0.01	0.00	0.56
Air transportation	0.03	-0.02	0.00	0.00	0.05
Rail transportation	0.13	0.00	0.00	0.00	0.13
Water transportation	-0.21	-0.03	0.00	0.00	-0.17
Truck transportation	0.36	0.16	0.00	0.00	0.20
Transit and ground passenger transportation	0.39	0.02	0.00	0.00	0.38
Pipeline transportation	1.17	0.00	0.00	0.00	1.17
Other transportation and support activities	0.01	0.16	0.00	0.00	-0.15
Warehousing and storage	0.49	0.07	0.00	0.00	0.42
Publishing industries, except internet (includes software)	1.28	1.10	0.06	0.08	0.04
Motion picture and sound recording industries	1.15	0.05	0.02	1.12	-0.04

Broadcasting and telecommunications	1.69	1.45	−0.14	0.31	0.07
Data processing, internet publishing, and other information services	3.16	2.79	0.18	0.00	0.19
Federal Reserve banks, credit intermediation, and related activities	1.11	0.50	0.01	0.00	0.60
Securities, commodity contracts, and investments	0.18	0.16	0.00	0.00	0.02
Insurance carriers and related activities	1.08	1.01	0.01	0.00	0.06
Funds, trusts, and other financial vehicles	0.96	0.06	0.00	0.00	0.91
Real estate	1.42	0.04	0.00	0.00	1.38
Rental and leasing services and lessors of intangible assets	2.37	0.69	0.00	0.00	1.68
Legal services	1.00	0.72	0.00	0.00	0.28
Computer systems design and related services	0.23	0.16	0.04	0.00	0.02

Table 11.2 (*cont.*)

	Capital contribution	IT capital and software contribution	R&D capital contribution	Artistic originals capital contribution	Other capital contribution
Miscellaneous professional, scientific, and technical services	0.76	0.49	0.12	0.00	0.14
Management of companies and enterprises	1.07	1.05	−0.01	0.00	0.03
Administrative and support services	0.75	0.62	0.00	0.00	0.13
Waste management and remediation services	0.19	−0.02	0.00	0.00	0.21
Educational services	0.22	0.10	0.00	0.00	0.12
Ambulatory health care services	0.22	0.19	0.00	0.00	0.04
Hospitals and nursing and residential care	0.27	0.17	0.01	0.00	0.09
Social assistance	0.11	0.03	0.00	0.00	0.07

Performing arts, spectator sports, museums, and related activities	0.14	0.03	0.00	0.01	0.10
Amusements, gambling, and recreation industries	0.69	0.15	0.00	0.00	0.53
Accommodation	0.95	0.07	0.00	0.00	0.88
Food services and drinking places	0.00	0.02	0.00	0.00	-0.01
Other services, except government	0.46	0.31	0.00	0.00	0.15
Federal	0.71	0.25	0.30	0.00	0.16
State and local	0.52	0.09	0.03	0.00	0.40

Notes: Average annual percentage growth. A contribution is a share-weighted growth rate.

Table 11.3 *Sources of labor contribution, 1998–2012*

	Labor contribution	College contribution	Non-college contribution
Farms	–0.08	0.10	–0.18
Forestry, fishing, and related activities	0.49	0.43	0.06
Oil and gas extraction	0.16	0.14	0.02
Mining, except oil and gas	–0.13	0.08	–0.21
Support activities for mining	2.34	1.03	1.30
Utilities	–0.09	0.05	–0.14
Construction	–0.11	0.15	–0.27
Wood products	–0.90	–0.03	–0.87
Non-metallic mineral products	–0.51	0.06	–0.57
Primary metals	–0.58	–0.04	–0.54
Fabricated metal products	–0.31	0.11	–0.43
Machinery	–0.47	0.02	–0.49
Computer and electronic products	–0.82	–0.16	–0.66
Electrical equipment, appliances, and components	–0.62	0.09	–0.71
Motor vehicles, bodies and trailers, and parts	–0.44	–0.07	–0.37
Other transportation equipment	–0.16	0.11	–0.27
Furniture and related products	–1.21	–0.08	–1.13
Miscellaneous manufacturing	–0.33	0.12	–0.45
Food and beverage and tobacco products	0.01	0.03	–0.02
Textile mills and textile product mills	–1.55	–0.32	–1.23
Apparel and leather and allied products	–2.80	–0.76	–2.04
Paper products	–0.60	–0.15	–0.45
Printing and related support activities	–1.40	–0.36	–1.04
Petroleum and coal products	–0.02	0.00	–0.02
Chemical products	–0.15	–0.06	–0.09
Plastics and rubber products	–0.43	–0.05	–0.38
Wholesale trade	0.13	0.23	–0.10
Retail trade	0.13	0.21	–0.09
Air transportation	–0.38	–0.21	–0.16
Rail transportation	–0.40	–0.09	–0.31

Table 11.3 (*cont.*)

	Labor contribution	College contribution	Non-college contribution
Water transportation	0.21	0.06	0.15
Truck transportation	–0.10	–0.02	–0.08
Transit and ground passenger transportation	0.52	0.15	0.37
Pipeline transportation	–0.16	–0.05	–0.11
Other transportation and support activities	0.08	0.02	0.06
Warehousing and storage	1.25	0.21	1.03
Publishing industries, except internet (includes software)	–0.27	0.10	–0.36
Motion picture and sound recording industries	0.22	0.34	–0.12
Broadcasting and telecommunications	–0.24	0.02	–0.26
Data processing, internet publishing, and other information services	–0.48	–0.13	–0.34
Federal Reserve banks, credit intermediation, and related activities	0.34	0.50	–0.16
Securities, commodity contracts, and investments	0.45	0.61	–0.16
Insurance carriers and related activities	0.26	0.36	–0.10
Funds, trusts, and other financial vehicles	0.19	0.24	–0.06
Real estate	0.05	0.06	0.00
Rental and leasing services and lessors of intangible assets	–0.10	0.05	–0.14
Legal services	0.30	0.41	–0.11
Computer systems design and related services	1.86	1.74	0.12
Miscellaneous professional, scientific, and technical services	0.88	0.84	0.04
Management of companies and enterprises	1.11	1.09	0.03
Administrative and support services	0.59	0.50	0.08

Table 11.3 (*cont.*)

	Labor contribution	College contribution	Non-college contribution
Waste management and remediation services	0.44	0.18	0.26
Educational services	1.74	1.51	0.23
Ambulatory health care services	1.54	1.08	0.46
Hospitals and nursing and residential care	1.13	0.81	0.31
Social assistance	1.49	1.11	0.38
Performing arts, spectator sports, museums, and related activities	0.31	0.44	−0.13
Amusements, gambling, and recreation industries	0.56	0.34	0.22
Accommodation	−0.10	0.12	−0.22
Food services and drinking places	0.55	0.24	0.31
Other services, except government	0.11	0.38	−0.26
Federal	0.01	0.09	−0.09
State and local	0.62	0.64	−0.02

Notes: Average annual percentange growth. A contribution is a share-weighted growth rate.

by declines in labor and MFP growth, and lastly declines in the contribution of capital by industry. It is worth noting that these measures of input use during cyclical adjustments do not capture effects such as worker effort, changes in capital utilization, or unmeasured labor effort that average out over the business cycle, but can be important over the course of the business cycle.

Figure 11.3 compares industry output growth and its sources over the 2007–2012 period to the 1998–2007 period. Output growth was slower in all but seven industries, two of which were government sectors. Relative to growth during the 1998–2007 period, the industries with the steepest declines were securities, commodity contracts, and investments, non-metallic mineral products, furniture, construction, and computer and electronic products. The sources of these relative declines was broad based; for each of these sectors all inputs declined relative to the earlier period except labor input in the

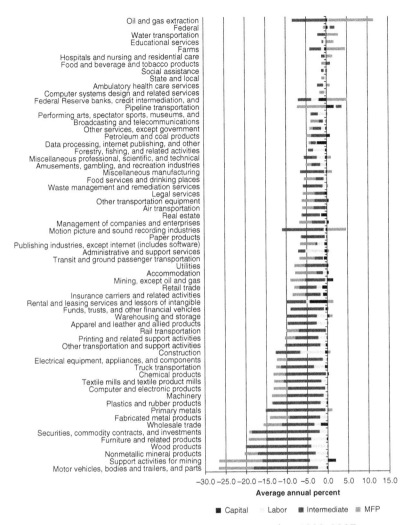

Figure 11.2 Output growth differences, 2007–2009 less 1998–2007

computer and electronic products industry and MFP growth in construction. There are a subset of industries with significant counterbalancing growth of inputs. For example, in motion pictures and sound recording, and rental and leasing, large declines in inputs relative to the 1998–2007 period were counterbalanced by large increases in MFP. In the pipeline transportation industry,

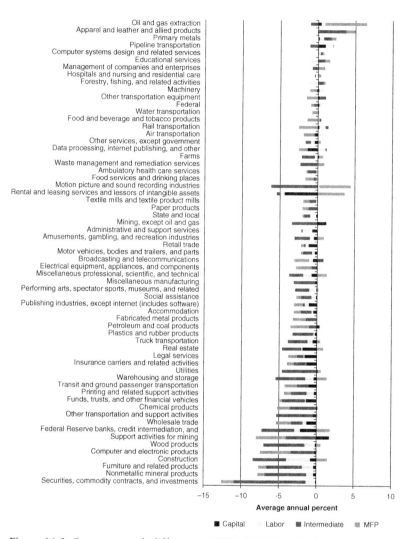

Figure 11.3 Output growth differences, 2007–2012 less 1998–2007

intermediate inputs fell, while the contributions of capital and labor increased. In educational services, declines in labor were offset by increases in intermediate purchases and MFP.

To analyze how the ongoing recovery compares to the pre-crisis expansion, Figure 11.4 compares industry output growth and its sources between 2009 and 2012 with the 1998–2007 period. Of the

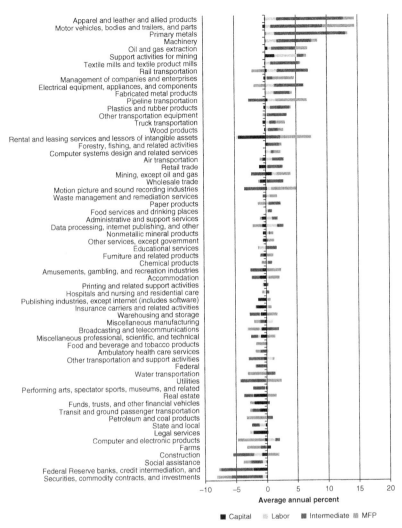

Figure **11.4** Output growth differences, 2009–2012 less 1998–2007

sixty-three industries we analyze, thirty-four industries grew faster during the ongoing recovery period than during the period immediately preceding the crisis, even though aggregate GDP growth was slower during the latter period. The largest relative differences occurred in apparel and leather products, motor vehicles, primary metals, machinery, oil and gas extraction, and support activities for mining. For each of these industries the sources of growth was mostly attributable to labor input, intermediate input, and MFP growth, with contribution of capital not showing much difference compared to the earlier period. The industries with slowest output growth relative to the early period were securities, credit intermediation, social assistance, construction, and farms. This slower growth was due to slower accumulation of inputs and MFP growth in each of these industries, except for relatively higher MFP in construction and a small increase in the contribution of capital in farms. Overall, for the industries that grew faster during the recovery period compared to the 1998–2007 period, the largest source of increased output growth was increased intermediate growth, followed by MFP growth, labor input growth, and then capital input growth, on average. For those industries that declined relative to the 1998–2007 period, the largest source, on average, was the decline in intermediate input, followed by capital input, MFP growth, and labor input. This figure shows that ongoing recovery has not reverted the depth and breadth of the recession.

11.4 Decomposition of aggregate GDP growth

The main empirical contribution of this chapter is to decompose aggregate GDP growth to its sources across industries and factors of production. We do this by means of the direct aggregation of industry approach (Jorgenson, Ho, Samuels, and Stiroh, 2007). With this approach aggregate value added growth is the share weighted growth of industry value added growth. The contribution of primary, or value added, input growth by industry to aggregate value added growth is the Domar-weighted input contribution, and the contribution of industry MFP to aggregate MFP is the Domar-weighted industry MFP growth rate.[14]

Table 11.4 shows that between 1998 and 2012 the majority of aggregate value added growth was due to accumulation of inputs. Of the 2.01% average annual growth in value added, 1.18 percentage points were accounted for by capital (about 60% of growth), 0.36 percentage point by labor (18%), and 0.47 percentage point by MFP

---

[14] Each industry's Domar weight is the ratio of the industry's current-dollar gross output to aggregate current-dollar value added. The industry's contribution to aggregate MFP growth is the industry's MFP growth multiplied by its Domar weight. The contribution of industry intermediate input use drops out in the calculation of aggregate value added and its decomposition.

Table 11.4 *Growth in aggregate value added and the sources of growth*

	Direct aggregation across industries contributions						2009–2012 less 1998–2007
	1998–2012	1998–2007	2007–2012	2007–2009	2009–2012	
Value added	2.01	2.78	0.62	-1.62	2.11	-0.67
Capital input	1.18	1.55	0.52	0.69	0.40	-1.14
IT capital	0.31	0.40	0.14	0.20	0.10	-0.31
R&D capital	0.09	0.09	0.09	0.10	0.08	-0.01
Software capital	0.18	0.23	0.08	0.10	0.06	-0.17
Entertainment originals capital	0.03	0.03	0.02	0.02	0.02	-0.01
Other capital	0.58	0.79	0.19	0.26	0.14	-0.65
Labor input	0.36	0.60	-0.09	-1.31	0.73	0.13
College labor	0.52	0.63	0.34	-0.11	0.63	0.00
Non-college labor	-0.16	-0.02	-0.42	-1.21	0.10	0.12
Integrated MFP	0.47	0.63	0.19	-1.00	0.98	0.35

Notes: Average annual percentages. Aggregate value added growth is the aggregate of share weighed industry value added growth. The contribution of capital, labor, and MFP is the Domar-weighted industry contributions. IT capital is computer, communications and other IT capital. Integrated MFP estimates differ from official estimates produced by the BLS. See www.bls.gov/mfp for the official estimates.

growth (22%). Within capital, about 40% of the capital contribution was due to IT equipment and software (0.48 percentage point), and 0.09 percentage points (about 8%) from R&D capital. The contribution of R&D capital to aggregate value added growth of 0.09 percentage point per year provides a measure of the bias of previously published estimates. If this contribution of capital was excluded, estimated MFP growth would have been higher by about 0.09 percentage point per year; that is, aggregate MFP growth would have been 0.56% per year instead of 0.47% per year. Within labor input, the contribution from workers without a college degree actually fell over the period as a whole.

Table 11.4 demonstrates that the majority of the difference in GDP growth from 2009 to 2012 relative to the 1998–2007 period was due to the difference in the contribution of capital. Comparing the recovery during the 2009–2012 period with the 1998–2007 period, GDP grew slower, by 0.67 percentage point per year. The slower growth was more than accounted for by the smaller contribution of capital input, which contributed 1.14 percentage points less to growth during this period than during the 1998–2007 period. This was split between IT-capital which accounted for 0.31 percentage point, software capital accounted for 0.17 percentage point, and other capital accounted for 0.65 percentage point.

Interestingly, all of the increase of the contribution of labor input during the recovery period was due to the increased contribution of workers without a college degree, reversing the decline in the contribution of non-college workers that took place beginning in the late 1990s.

The direct aggregation across industry approach yields insights into the underlying structural changes that occurred over the 1998–2012 period. Tables 11.5 and 11.6 divide the aggregate value added and productivity growth into contributions from IT-producing industries, industries that use IT relatively intensively, and other industries. Between 1998–2012, IT-producing industries accounted for 3.1% of nominal value added, but 0.31 percentage point of the 2.01 average annual growth, or about 15% of the growth in aggregate valued added. IT-using industries accounted for 0.99 percentage point, or almost 50% of growth, which is slightly larger than its 46.8% share of nominal value added. Non-IT accounted for 0.45 percentage point and government accounted for 0.26 percentage point. Both IT-using (–0.90 percentage point contribution) and non-IT industries (–1.01 percentage points

Table 11.5 *Sector sources of value added growth*

	1998–2012	1998–2007	2007–2012	2007–2009	2009–2012
			Contributions		
Value added	2.01	2.78	0.62	-1.62	2.11
IT-producing industries	0.31	0.37	0.20	0.13	0.24
IT-using industries	0.99	1.42	0.22	-0.90	0.97
Non-IT industries	0.45	0.66	0.05	-1.01	0.76
Government	0.26	0.33	0.15	0.16	0.14
Shares in nominal value added	100.0	100.0	100.0	100.0	100.0
IT-producing industries	3.1	3.1	3.2	3.1	3.2
IT-using industries	46.8	47.2	46.1	46.2	46.1
Non-IT industries	32.6	32.7	32.5	32.4	32.5
Government	17.5	17.1	18.2	18.3	18.1

Notes: Average annual percentages. Aggregate value added growth is the aggregate of share weighed industry value added growth. IT-producing industries are computers and electronic products, data processing, and computer systems design and related services. IT-using industries are those with an IT intensity share above the median share in 2005. Non-IT are the remaining private sector industries. Government includes government enterprise.

Table 11.6 *Sector sources of aggregate integrated MFP growth*

	1998–2012	1998–2007	2007–2012	2007–2009	2009–2012
Integrated MFP growth	0.47	0.63	0.19	-1.00	0.98
IT-producing industries	0.27	0.34	0.14	0.14	0.14
IT-using industries	0.07	0.14	-0.05	-0.53	0.26
Non-IT industries	0.12	0.11	0.13	-0.49	0.53
Government	0.02	0.05	-0.03	-0.13	0.04
Shares in nominal value added	100.0	100.0	100.0	100.0	100.0
IT-producing industries	3.1	3.1	3.2	3.1	3.2
IT-using industries	46.8	47.2	46.1	46.2	46.1
Non-IT industries	32.6	32.7	32.5	32.4	32.5
Government	17.5	17.1	18.2	18.3	18.1

Notes: Average annual percentages. Aggregate value added growth is the aggregate of share weighed industry value added growth. IT-producing industries are computers and electronic products, data processing, and computer systems design and related services. IT-using industries are those with an IT intensity share above the median share in 2005. Non-IT are the remaining private sector industries. Government includes government enterprise. Integrated MFP estimates differ from official estimates produced by the BLS. See www.bls .gov/mfp for the official estimates.

contribution) were hard hit during the recession period of 2007–2009, while IT-producing industries (0.13 percentage point contribution) added to growth. During the recovery period, non-IT industries have contributed a larger share of growth relative to its share during the pre-crisis period, while IT-producing, IT-using, and government all contributed smaller shares of growth.

In terms of aggregate productivity growth in Table 11.6, IT-producing industries accounted for the majority of productivity growth over the 1998–2012 period, when MFP averaged 0.47% per year. The contribution of IT-producing industries to aggregate productivity growth has fallen slightly from 0.34 percentage point per year before the recession to 0.14 percentage point per year during the recession and recovery. Not surprisingly, measured aggregate MFP growth fell significantly during the Great Recession, and recovered during the subsequent period. There does not appear to be a major difference in the decline and recovery between the IT-using and non-IT industries.

Table 11.7 shows that relatively R&D intensive industries made a disproportionate contribution to aggregate MFP growth. Between 1998 and 2012, of the 0.47% per year in aggregate MFP growth, 0.34 percentage point was due to industries that were relatively R&D intensive. Importantly, of this 0.34 percentage point contribution, about 0.27 percentage point was due to productivity growth in the IT-producing industries.[15]

Table 11.8 provides an examination of structural changes at the industry level for twenty-two major industry groups at roughly the two–digit NAICS level of detail, consistent with industry groupings publishing in BEA's Industry Economic Accounts. Finance and insurance accounted for about 42% (0.28 percentage point) of the slower US economic growth during the 2009–2012 period, with capital input accounting for the majority of its slowdown. State and local government accounted for about 29% (0.19 percentage

---

[15] The IT classification is taken from Jorgenson *et al.* (2014). The classification of industries into R&D intensive and non-R&D intensive is based on an R&D intensity index defined as the average share of R&D capital income in capital over the 1998–2012 period. First industries with a share less than 1 percent are allocated to non-R&D. Then industries with shares above the median share of 0.08 are allocated to R&D intensive.

Table 11.7 *Sector sources of aggregate integrated MFP growth*

	1998–2012	1998–2007	2007–2012	2007–2009	2009–2012
Integrated MFP growth	0.47	0.63	0.19	−1.00	0.98
R&D intensive industries	0.35	0.51	0.06	−0.36	0.35
IT-producing industries	0.27	0.34	0.14	0.14	0.14
Other R&D intensive	0.08	0.17	−0.08	−0.50	0.21
Non-R&D intenstive	0.11	0.08	0.15	−0.51	0.59
Government	0.02	0.05	−0.03	−0.13	0.04
Shares in nominal value added	100.0	100.0	100.0	100.0	100.0
R&D intensive industries	16.4	16.6	16.1		16.3
Non-R&D intenstive	66.1	66.3	65.7	100.0	65.6
Government	17.5	17.1	18.2	15.8	18.1

Notes: Average annual percentages. Aggregate value added growth is the aggregate of share weighed industry value added growth. R&D intensive industries are those with an R&D capital income share above the median share, once industries with a share below 1 percent have been dropped. Integrated MFP estimates differ from official estimates produced by the BLS. See: www.bls.gov/mfp for the official estimates.

Table 11.8 Contributions to aggregate value added growth

	1998–2012				1998–2007				2009–2012				2009–2012 less 1998–2007			
	Value added	Capital	Labor	Integrated MFP	Value added	Capital	Labor	Integrated MFP	Value added	Capital	Labor	Integrated MFP	Value added	Capital	Labor	Integrated MFP
Total economy	2.01	1.18	0.36	0.47	2.78	1.55	0.60	0.63	2.11	0.40	0.73	0.98	−0.67	−1.14	0.13	0.35
Agriculture, forestry, fishing, and hunting	0.03	0.00	0.00	0.02	0.03	0.00	0.01	0.02	−0.01	0.02	0.00	−0.03	−0.04	0.01	0.00	−0.05
Mining	0.07	0.00	0.01	0.05	0.02	0.00	0.01	0.01	0.14	0.02	0.04	0.08	0.12	0.02	0.03	0.07
Utilities	0.02	0.02	0.00	0.00	0.01	0.02	0.00	0.00	0.07	0.01	−0.01	0.07	0.06	0.00	0.00	0.07
Construction	−0.07	0.03	0.00	−0.09	0.00	0.05	0.09	−0.14	−0.02	−0.02	−0.02	0.02	−0.02	−0.07	−0.11	0.16
Durable goods	0.25	0.06	−0.05	0.00	0.36	0.06	−0.05	0.09	0.44	0.05	0.01	−0.15	0.08	0.00	0.06	−0.24
Non-durable goods	0.01	0.03	−0.10	0.31	0.09	0.05	−0.11	0.43	−0.09	0.01	0.09	0.35	−0.18	−0.04	0.20	−0.08
Wholesale trade	0.11	0.08	0.01	0.02	0.22	0.12	0.03	0.08	0.13	0.04	0.04	0.05	−0.09	−0.07	0.01	−0.03
Retail trade	0.09	0.09	0.01	−0.01	0.15	0.12	0.02	0.00	0.08	0.02	0.05	0.01	−0.07	−0.10	0.02	0.01
Transportation and warehousing	0.03	0.01	0.00	0.02	0.05	0.02	0.00	0.02	0.09	0.00	0.05	0.05	0.04	−0.02	0.04	0.02
Information	0.21	0.14	−0.02	0.09	0.28	0.17	−0.01	0.12	0.16	0.09	0.00	0.06	−0.12	−0.07	0.01	−0.06
Finance and insurance	0.20	0.12	0.04	0.04	0.31	0.18	0.07	0.05	0.03	−0.02	0.06	−0.01	−0.28	−0.20	−0.02	−0.07
Real estate and rental and leasing	0.30	0.26	0.01	0.04	0.37	0.39	0.02	−0.03	0.28	−0.01	0.00	0.29	−0.10	−0.40	−0.02	0.33
Professional, scientific, and technical services	0.17	0.07	0.09	0.01	0.20	0.10	0.11	−0.01	0.20	0.01	0.10	0.09	0.00	−0.09	−0.01	0.11
Management of companies and enterprises	0.02	0.03	0.03	−0.04	0.01	0.03	0.03	−0.04	0.11	0.02	0.04	0.05	0.11	0.00	0.01	0.09

Table 11.8 (*cont.*)

	1998–2012				1998–2007				2009–2012				2009–2012 less 1998–2007			
	Value added	Capital	Labor	Integrated MFP	Value added	Capital	Labor	Integrated MFP	Value added	Capital	Labor	Integrated MFP	Value added	Capital	Labor	Integrated MFP
Administrative and waste management services	0.08	0.03	0.02	0.03	0.11	0.04	0.04	0.03	0.12	0.01	0.08	0.02	0.01	–0.03	0.04	0.00
Educational services	0.02	0.00	0.03	–0.01	0.02	0.00	0.03	–0.01	0.01	0.00	0.02	–0.01	–0.02	0.00	–0.01	–0.01
Health care and social assistance	0.16	0.02	0.14	0.00	0.17	0.02	0.14	0.00	0.10	0.02	0.15	–0.07	–0.06	0.00	0.01	–0.07
Arts, entertainment, and recreation	0.02	0.01	0.01	0.00	0.02	0.01	0.01	0.00	0.03	0.00	0.01	0.02	0.01	–0.01	0.00	0.02
Accommodation and food services	0.04	0.01	0.02	0.01	0.06	0.01	0.02	0.03	0.09	0.00	0.04	0.05	0.03	–0.01	0.02	0.02
Other services, except government	–0.03	0.02	0.00	–0.05	–0.02	0.02	0.01	–0.06	0.00	0.00	0.01	–0.01	0.02	–0.02	–0.01	0.04
Federal government	0.07	0.06	0.00	0.01	0.06	0.05	–0.01	0.02	0.07	0.06	0.00	0.01	0.01	0.01	0.01	–0.01
State and local government	0.20	0.09	0.10	0.01	0.26	0.10	0.14	0.03	0.07	0.06	–0.02	0.03	–0.19	–0.04	–0.16	0.01

Notes: Average annual percentange growth. A contribution is a share-weighted growth rate. Integrated MFP estimates differ from official estimates produced by the BLS. See: www.bls.gov/mfp for the official estimates.

point) of the slower growth, due mainly to labor input, and non-durable goods manufacturing accounted for about 27% (0.18 percentage point) due to MFP.

In contrast, mining, management of companies, and durable goods manufacturing exhibited stronger growth during the recovery period relative to the pre-crisis period. Mining contributes 0.12 percentage point more to growth during the 2009–2012 period relative to the 1998–2007 period, due mainly to gains in MFP but also from stronger contributions of labor and capital input. Management of companies was also led by stronger relative growth in MFP, while durable goods stronger relative growth was more than accounted for by stronger relative growth in labor input.

The framework and data permits an analysis of the industry sources of the aggregate sources of growth. Figure 11.5 shows the difference in industry contributions to aggregate value added growth during the recovery relative to the 1998–2007 pre-recession period, and extends the more-aggregate analysis from Table 11.8. As noted, aggregate value added growth has been slower during the recovery period compared to the 1998–2007 period, but this is not the case for all industries. For example, motor vehicles, management of companies, machinery, utilities, oil and gas, and computer systems design are all growing more rapidly in the recovery than during the period preceding the recession, as would be expected of most industries during the recovery from a cyclical downturn. Yet all industries are not recovering relative to the 1998–2007 period. State and local governments, computers and electronic products, broadcasting and telecom, and credit intermediation are all growing significantly less rapidly than during the pre-crisis period that we consider.

To understand the sources of slower aggregate value added growth during the recovery period, Figures 11.6–11.8 show the differences in industry contributions to aggregate capital, labor, and MFP between 2009–2012 and 1998–2007. With respect to industry contribution to aggregate capital input, Figure 11.6 indicates that relative to the pre-crisis period, there was a significantly lower contribution of capital input in real estate, credit intermediation, retail trade, rental and leasing, wholesale trade, and construction. Figure 11.7 shows that the small increase in the aggregate contribution of labor input during the 2009–2012 period compared to the 1998–2007 period was spread broadly across a sub-set of industries including computer

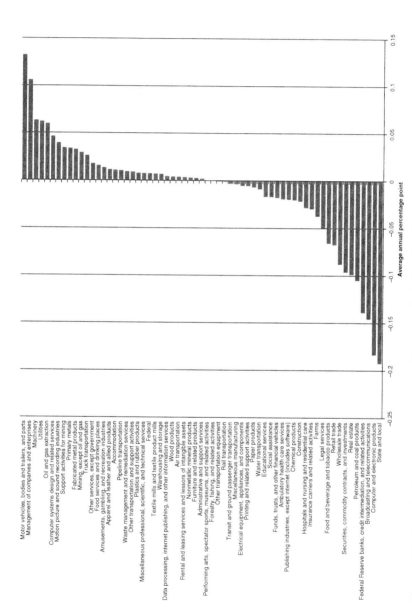

Figure 11.5 Contribution to aggregate value added growth, 2009–2012 less 1998–2007

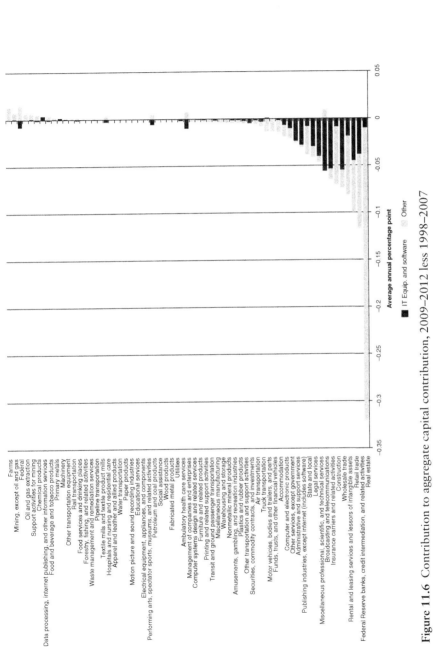

Figure 11.6 Contribution to aggregate capital contribution, 2009–2012 less 1998–2007

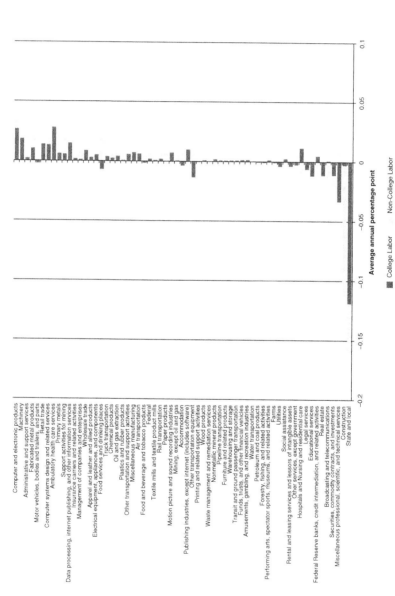

Figure 11.7 Contribution to aggregate labor contribution, 2009–2012 less 1998–2007

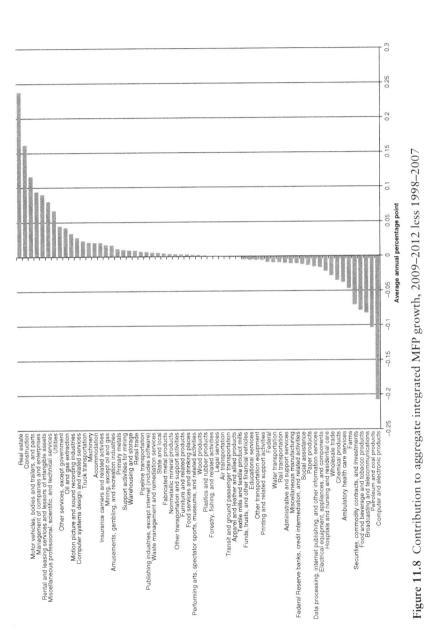

Figure 11.8 Contribution to aggregate integrated MFP growth, 2009–2012 less 1998–2007

and electronic products, machinery, administrative support services, fabricated metal, and motor vehicles. In each of these industries, the contribution of non-college workers outpaced that from the 1998–2007 period.

11.5 Conclusions and next steps

During the ongoing recovery from the financial crisis, US growth continues to be sluggish compared to the period immediately before the crisis. At the aggregate level, our analysis attributes the majority of this sluggishness to a decrease in the contribution of capital services. At the industry level, stronger growth in motor vehicles, management of companies, machinery and utilities is counterbalanced by slower growth in state and local government, computer and electronic products, broadcasting, credit intermediation, and real estate. The large decline in capital services relative to the 1998–2007 period was driven mainly by real estate, credit intermediation, retail trade and wholesale trade.

The purpose of this chapter is to lay the framework for a set of industry-level production accounts that are consistent with aggregate GDP and provide industry detail to analyze the sources of growth. The current update includes an expansion of the scope of the accounts to include investments in R&D and entertainment originals as an investment good. For the period that we consider, R&D capital input accounted for about 0.09 percentage points of aggregate growth, about half as much as software capital. Entertainment originals capital input accounted for about 0.03%. Thus, incorporating R&D lowered MFP growth estimates from about 0.56% per year to about 0.47% per year.

Our analysis is limited by the time series availability of our industry-level production account. Future work includes investigating approaches to extend the industry-level production account backwards in time following Jorgenson *et al.* (2014) and improving estimates of labor composition. In any case, the groundwork for future updates to the industry-level production accounts is now in place, and work is underway to plan for these future updates.

Appendix 11.1 Distinctions between integrated MFP and official US MFP

The industry-level production account presented in this chapter reflects outputs and inputs that are consistent with GDP for the total economy. It is important to draw a distinction between the official MFP measures for the US produced by the BLS, and those from this integrated account. In Section 11.2.3 on integration and covered in detail in the section Conceptual and Measurement Challenges in Fleck *et al.* (2014), the integrated measures of MFP presented in this chapter will differ from the official measures of the BLS.

The US statistical system strives to promote a better understanding of the US economy, however the national economic accounts and the productivity program have unique objectives. The US national economic accounts, produced by BEA, are focused on developing a set of internally consistent macro-economic accounts that are fully integrated, conceptually and statistically, across time and in cross-section. The US productivity statistics, produced by BLS, are focused on producing reliable productivity measures using concepts and methods most appropriate for measuring productivity and to ensure consistency between official measures of labor productivity and MFP. Consequently, there are tradeoffs between having a set of accounts that add up and reconcile to GDP and a set of accounts that generate the best quality productivity statistics by industry. For example, GDP statistics that are fully consistent with international guidelines include measures of economic activity for which there are no market prices. Such activity is excluded from official productivity statistics because output and inputs are not measured independently. In addition, other adjustments are made to outputs and inputs and occasionally alternative source data are used to ensure maximum consistency in calculating official productivity statistics for the US. Another distinction is that the national economic accounts produce measures of value added and gross output, while the official MFP statistics use a concept of sectoral output for major sectors and industries. Furthermore, the use of Tornqvist aggregation differs from the chained fisher index that underlies the official estimate of GDP. As a result, the official US productivity statistics remain separate from the US national economic accounts.

Appendix Table 11.1 documents the empirical differences in the estimates for the 1998–2012 period.

Appendix Table 11.1 *Multi-factor productivity growth: comparison between official measures and integrated production account measures, 1998–2012 (compound annual growth rates)*

NAICS industry code	Sector or industry title	Official	Production accounts	Differences
111, 112	Crop and animal production	1.2	1.1	−0.1
113–115	Forestry, fishing, and related activities	2.0	0.9	−1.1
211	Oil and gas extraction	1.2	1.3	0.1
212	Mining, except oil and gas	−0.7	0.3	1.0
213	Support activities for mining	3.5	3.6	0.1
22	Utilities	0.6	0.4	−0.3
23	Construction	−0.7	−1.0	−0.3
311, 312	Food and beverage and tobacco products	0.5	0.1	−0.4
313, 314	Textile mills and textile product mills	0.7	0.2	−0.5
315, 316	Apparel and leather and applied products	2.2	1.0	−1.2
321	Wood products	1.2	0.8	−0.3
322	Paper products	0.0	−0.1	−0.1
323	Printing and related support activities	1.8	1.5	−0.3
324	Petroleum and coal products	−0.1	0.0	0.2
325	Chemical products	−0.1	−0.1	−0.1
326	Plastics and rubber products	0.4	0.1	−0.3
327	Non-metallic mineral products	−0.4	−0.4	−0.1
331	Primary metals	0.6	0.8	0.2
332	Fabricated metal products	0.3	0.0	−0.3
333	Machinery	0.8	0.6	−0.2
334	Computer and electronic products	7.8	6.7	−1.1

Appendix Table 11.1 (*cont.*)

NAICS industry code	Sector or industry title	Official	Production accounts	Differences
335	Electrical equipment, appliances, and components	1.5	0.9	−0.6
336	Transportation equipment	1.1		
3361–3363	Motor vehicles, bodies and trailers, and parts		1.1	
3364–3366, 3369	Other transportation equipment		0.7	
337	Furniture and related products	0.3	−0.1	−0.4
339	Miscellaneous manufacturing	1.4	1.2	−0.2
42	Wholesale trade	0.8	0.3	−0.5
44,45	Retail trade	0.3	−0.1	−0.4
481	Air transportation	4.4	−0.2	−4.6
482	Rail transportation	0.7	0.5	−0.3
483	Water transportation	2.4	2.6	0.2
484	Truck transportation	0.3	0.3	0.0
485	Transit and ground passenger transportation	−0.2	−0.3	−0.1
486	Pipeline transportation	2.2	2.3	0.1
487, 488, 492	Other transportation and support activities	0.4	0.3	0.0
493	Warehousing and storage	1.1	1.2	0.1
511, 516	Publishing industries	1.0	0.6	−0.4
512	Motion picture and sounds recording industries	2.4	1.5	−0.9
515, 517	Broadcasting and telecommunications	2.4	1.3	−1.1
518, 519	Information and data processing services	−0.6	0.7	1.3
521, 522	Federal Reserve banks, credit intermediation, and related activities	1.1	0.3	−0.8

Appendix Table 11.1 (*cont.*)

NAICS industry code	Sector or industry title	Official	Production accounts	Differences
523	Securities, commodity contracts, and investments	1.4	1.1	−0.3
524	Insurance carriers and related activities	0.7	0.0	−0.7
525	Funds, trusts, and other financial vehicles	0.8	0.3	−0.5
531	Real estate	1.1	0.4	−0.6
532, 533	Rental and leasing services and lessors of intangible assets	−1.4	−1.5	−0.1
5411	Legal services	−0.3	−1.3	−1.0
5415	Computer systems design and related services	2.2	2.3	0.1
5412–5414, 5416–5419	Miscellaneous professional, scientific, and technical services	0.2	−01	−0.3
55	Management of companies and enterprises	−0.8	−1.5	−0.7
561	Administrative and support services	1.1	0.7	−0.5
562	Waste management and remediation services	0.4	0.5	0.0
61	Educational services	0.0	−0.4	−0.4
621	Ambulatory health care services	0.2	0.3	0.1
622, 623	Hospitals and nursing and residential care facilities	0.0	−0.2	−0.2
624	Social assistance	0.7	−0.1	−0.7
711, 712	Performing arts, spectator sports, museums, and related activities	0.3	0.8	0.5
713	Amusements, gambling, and recreation industries	0.0	−0.2	−0.2

Appendix Table 11.1 (*cont.*)

NAICS industry code	Sector or industry title	Official	Production accounts	Differences
721	Accommodation	0.7	−0.1	−0.8
722	Food services and drinking places	0.4	0.3	−0.1
81	Other services, except government	−0.8	−1.3	−0.5

References

Bureau of Economic Analysis. 2013. "Preview of the 2013 Comprehensive Revision of the National Income and Product Accounts: Changes in Definitions and Presentation," *Survey of Current Business*, March.

Byrne, D., S. Oliner, and D. Sichel. 2013. "Is the Information Technology Revolution Over?" *Federal Reserve Board Working Paper*.

Fleck, S., S. Rosenthal, M. Russell, E. Strassner, and L. Usher. 2014. "A Prototype BEA/BLS Industry-level Production Account for the United States." In D. W. Jorgenson, J. S. Landefeld, and P. Schreyer (eds.), *Measuring Economic Sustainability and Progress*. University of Chicago Press, 323–372.

Gordon, R. 2014. "The Demise of US Economic Growth: Restatement, Rebuttal, and Reflections." NBER Working Paper.

Harper, M., B. Moulton, S. Rosenthal, and D. Wasshausen. 2008. *Integrated GDP-Productivity Accounts*.

Jorgenson, D. W., M. S. Ho, and J. Samuels. 2011. "Information Technology and US Productivity Growth: Evidence from a Prototype Industry Production Account," *Journal of Productivity Analysis*, 36(2): 159–175.

2014. "What will Revive U.S. Economic Growth? Lessons from a Prototype Industry-level Production Account for the United States." *Journal of Policy Modeling*. Volume 36, Issue 4, July–August 2014, pages 674–691.

2016. "US Economic Growth – Retrospect and Prospect: Lessons from a Prototype Industry-level Production Account for the US, 1947–2012." In D.W. Jorgensen, K. Fukao, and M.P. Timmer (eds.), *The World Economy: Growth or Stagnation*. Cambridge University Press.

Jorgenson, D. W., M. S. Ho, J. Samuels, and K. Stiroh. 2007. "The Industry Origins of the American Productivity Resurgence," *Economic System Research*, **19**(3): 229–252.

Jorgenson, D. W., M. S. Ho, and K. J. Stiroh. 2005. *Information Technology and the American Growth Resurgence*. Cambridge, MA: MIT Press.

McCulla, S. H., A. E. Holdren, and S. Smith. 2013. "Improved Estimates of the National Income and Product Accounts: Results of the 2013 Comprehensive Revision," *Survey of Current Business*, September.

Strassner, E. H., G. W. Medeiros, and G. M. Smith. 2005. "Annual Industry Accounts: Introducing KLEMS Input Estimates for 1997–2003," *Survey of Current Business*, September, 31–65.

Strassner, E. H. and D. B. Wasshausen. 2013. "Preview of the 2013 Comprehensive Revision of the Industry Economic Accounts," *Survey of Current Business*, June.

   2014. "Industry Economic Accounts: Results of the Comprehensive Revision," *Survey of Current Business*, February.

United Nations. 2008. *System of National Accounts*. Washington, DC: United Nations Statistical Division.

12 Measuring human capital: country experiences and international initiatives

GANG LIU AND BARBARA M. FRAUMENI

12.1 Introduction

Investments in both human and non-human capital are important sources of economic growth. Distinct from other chapters in this volume, the focus of this chapter is on the measurement of human capital.

Within a standard growth accounting framework as frequently employed in this volume, human capital manifests itself, though not explicitly, through the notion of constant quality measures of labor input. It seems plausible to believe that growth accounting can go without caring much about the measurement of human capital because all that is needed is labor services that are generated by human capital.

However, this belief is not true because incorrect measures of human capital are bound to distort the analysis of economic growth. Consider a production possibility frontier that is the foundation of modern growth accounting, the aggregate output consists of both consumption and investment goods.[1] An important component of the latter is provided by the education sector with input by individuals, i.e. investment in human capital.

Once the investment in human capital is inappropriately measured, the estimate of the output of the education sector is biased and the bias generated at the industry level will carry over through aggregation all the way up to the aggregate output for the economy as a whole. In addition, current and future growth is misestimated as the pace of growth depends upon workers' education level. Thus, good measures of human capital are indispensable not only for accounting for the

---

[1] One well-known example of a modern growth accounting framework is that applied in the EU KLEMS project (see O'Mahony and Timmer 2009).

output and productivity of the education sector, but also for better understanding the economic growth more generally.[2]

A number of researchers and organizations have taken steps to produce measures of human capital, relying on various approaches. The diversity of these approaches makes it hard to draw policy implications from comparisons of these measures within and across countries, thus calls for efforts to identify consistent measures that are both theoretically sound and practically feasible.

This chapter makes a review of country experiences and international activities in the field of human capital measurement in terms of the different measuring approaches that have been applied, based on which the two general approaches to measuring human capital, i.e. the indicators-based approach and the monetary approach, are outlined, with pros and cons of each approach being discussed. It also presents and analyzes the growth differences in a production account with and without lifetime income human capital components.

Drawing on the discussion and in observation of the emerging trend from both national studies and international initiatives, a comparison is made of country estimates of human capital up to eighteen countries by three international studies that are carried out based on the most popular approaches.

With the purpose of improving the quality of the existing popular measures of human capital, some of the statistical and methodological challenges are identified and discussed that should be addressed by future researches.

The rest of the chapter is organized as follows. Section 12.2 discusses the concept and definition of human capital, and the subsequent implications for its measurement. Section 12.3 describes country experiences based on national studies employing two most applied monetary approaches. With the United States as an example, this section also shows that the growth pattern differs due to the inclusion of human capital.

In Section 12.4, international initiatives for measuring human capital are reviewed according to the measuring approaches applied. Also in this section, an international comparison is made of country measures

---

[2] Measuring human capital can also serve many other purposes, e.g. to assess the long-term sustainability of a country's development path, and to inform the discussion on "beyond gross domestic product (GDP)" and the quality of life.

of human capital based on different approaches. Main issues and challenges related to the most popular approaches are described in Section 12.5, and Section 12.6 concludes.

12.2 From concept to measurement

The concept of human capital has its roots in the history of economic thought, as reflected in e.g. Petty (1690), Smith (1776), Farr (1853), and Engel (1883), where human beings and their acquired abilities were considered, on a par with traditional assets (e.g. land and fixed capital), as important components of national wealth.

Thanks to the seminal works by Schultz (1961), Becker (1964), and Mincer (1974), the human capital concept regained recognition in 1960s, and since then it has been regularly applied for addressing a variety of issues such as economic growth, education, on-the-job training, migration, and social exclusion.

The extensive applicability of the human capital concept reflects its essentially multi-faceted nature. In recognition of this, the OECD proposed a broad definition of human capital as "the knowledge, skills, competencies and attributes embodied in individuals that facilitate the creation of personal, social and economic well-being" (OECD 2001).

This definition has gradually obtained wide acceptance because it encompasses all the essential constituents that make up human capital, and implies the numerous channels through which human capital is developed, as well as the diverse benefits that human capital delivers. However, it is this all-embracing feature that raises significant challenges for human capital measurement.

In fact, there are so many elements involved in and intertwined with the concept and definition of human capital that getting a full picture of every single element, of the causal links between each type of human capital investment, and the corresponding benefits, and further, of the feedback loop among them, is a daunting task that can not be accomplished in the foreseeable future.[3]

---

[3] For a comprehensive discussion on all the elements pertaining to the concept and definition of human capital, and the complicated relationships among them, please refer to Boarini, *et al.* (2012).

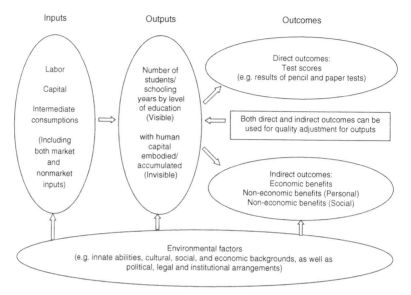

Figure 12.1 Inputs, outputs, and outcomes of education sector

A sensible way is to focus on a narrower range of elements, starting from those aspects characterized as of either lower conceptual challenges or greater data availability. One practically chosen option is to use formal education as the main form of human capital investment; and the economic returns accruing to individuals, as the main benefits due to human capital investment, even if the broader OECD definition is accepted as a useful reference point.[4]

Presently, there exist a number of different ways to measure human capital, even if its definition has been narrowed down to (formal) education only. Figure 12.1 draws a picture about the inputs, outputs, and outcomes of the education sector. When treating the education sector as a production unit, its output should be considered as human capital investment rather than education services as stipulated by the System of National Accounts (SNA).

Although this notion has been widely recognized, to measure the output of the education sector, which is invisible, is never an easy task. Some use the visible indicators, part of them quantitative (e.g. number of students/average schooling years), the others qualitative (e.g. class

---

[4] However, it does not imply that there are no other possible ways to move beyond this option.

size, test scores) as proxies for human capital; these physical measures of human capital can be classified as one category labeled "the indicators-based approach."[5]

Another category to measuring human capital is monetary measures, which can be further divided as the cost-based, the income-based, and the residual approaches. The cost-based approach measures human capital by looking at the stream of past investments undertaken by individuals, households, employers, and governments (e.g. Shultz 1961; Kendrick 1976; Eisner 1985).

This approach relies on information about all the inputs that are incurred when producing human capital. As shown in Figure 12.1, these include market inputs such as monetary outlays as well as non-market inputs such as the imputed value of time devoted to education by students, their parents, and volunteers.

By including non-market inputs, the cost-based approach differs from the way the output of the education sector is currently measured in the SNA, although they are similar. Since many education services are provided by non-market producers (e.g. government), their values are measured by the costs of market inputs following the SNA convention.[6]

The income-based approach measures human capital by looking at the stream of future earnings that human capital investment generates over one's lifetime (e.g. Weisbrod 1961; Graham and Webb 1979; Jorgenson and Fraumeni 1989, 1992a, 1992b). In contrast with the cost-based approach, which focuses on the input side, the income-based approach focuses on the outcomes of human capital investment.[7]

Note that a distinction is deliberately made in Figure 12.1 between outputs and outcomes of the education sector. By using the jargon of national accounting, outputs refer closely to activities or processes that are within the production boundary of the SNA, i.e. the provision of education services here in discussion, while outcomes are further away

---

[5] As qualitative information, class size can be used to explicitly quality-adjust the outputs of the education sector.

[6] The market inputs include teachers' wages and salaries, the consumption of fixed capital, and educational materials, etc.

[7] While the outcomes from human capital investment are of many types (i.e. monetary and non-monetary, private and public), what is measured by the income-based approach is limited to the private monetary benefits that accrue to the person investing in human capital.

from this provision, with indirect outcomes being even further than direct outcomes.

Although the transition from inputs to outputs and further to outcomes are all subject to various environmental factors, it is argued that more and more environmental factors will play a part in the transition from outputs to outcomes. Thus, neither direct nor indirect outcomes are considered to be proper measures of the outputs of the education sector by national accountants.

Consequently, to measure the outputs of the education sector, the current SNA not only excludes many non-market inputs, but also sets the boundary of its measuring scope to the outputs only. However, information about either direct or indirect outcomes, in particular about the contribution of education services to these outcomes, can provide a tool for explicit quality adjustment of the outputs, as indicated by the left-pointing arrow in Figure 12.1.[8]

Another monetary measure is the residual approach that is applied by the World Bank for measuring human capital as the difference between the total wealth and the sum of produced and natural capitals (World Bank, 2006, 2011).[9] A similar approach was also applied by Statistics Norway (Greaker *et al.* 2005) at the country level.

All the approaches as shown in Figure 12.2 have advantages and disadvantages.[10] Depending upon the purpose, different approaches may therefore be used, either individually or jointly. However, given the importance of the SNA in official statistics and for economic analysis, monetary measures, in particular the cost-based and the income-based approaches, are most likely to be used for human capital accounting consistent with the SNA.

---

[8] Therefore, even if within the framework of the current SNA, the results generated from the qualitative indicators (e.g. test scores) as well as from the income-based approach (e.g. earnings differentials) can well be applied for this purpose.

[9] This difference is labeled by the World Bank as "intangible capital residual," of which human capital is found to be the largest component (World Bank 2006, 2011).

[10] The typology as shown in Figure 12.2 is not the only way to classify the various approaches. For instance, a distinction can also be made between parametric and non-parametric approaches to measuring human capital. The former involves econometric techniques (e.g. Kyriacou 1991; Mulligan and Sala-i-Martin 1995; Barro and Lee 2010), while the latter usually does not. More on this is in Section 12.3 and 12.4.

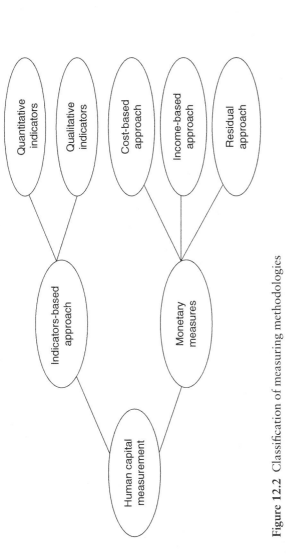

Figure 12.2 Classification of measuring methodologies

12.3 Country experiences

In this section, representative national studies are reviewed of the two monetary measures: the cost-based and the income-based approaches.[11] To demonstrate the importance of human capital for growth accounting, comparison results with US as an example are also presented.

12.3.1 The cost-based approach

The cost-based approach to measuring human capital is similar to the perpetual inventory method (PIM) that is conventionally applied to measuring fixed capital, i.e. the stock of human capital is measured as the accumulated value of all the expenditures occurring to its formation, considered as human capital investment.

This approach is relatively easy to apply, at least when limited to market inputs, because of the ready availability of data on public and private expenditures in formal education. The approach can also be extended to account for expenditures undertaken for on-the-job training.[12]

However, this approach has been criticized on conceptual grounds as the value of human capital should be regarded as determined by demand and supply rather than solely by production costs (Kiker 1966; Le *et al.* 2003). Another problem is that it is hard, if not impossible, to distinguish expenditures between investment and consumption, thus estimates by this approach rely virtually on arbitrarily allocating spending between these two categories in practice.[13]

Challenges are also involved when choosing the price indices used to deflate historical expenditures in order to construct a stock value by PIM. Moreover, the depreciation rate, which matters a great deal when

---

[11] The indicators-based approach and the residual approach will be discussed in Section 12.4 on international initiatives, because the relevant international studies are more representative than national ones. For instance, at the national level, there are just a few countries applying the residual approach (e.g. Norway, the Netherlands).

[12] This point holds only if the skills accumulated through on-the-job training can be separately treated as one specific type of human capital, distinct from that due to formal education.

[13] For instance, during the period of taking education, part of household expenditures is used for paying students' food and clothes, which could serve both consumption and investment purposes.

constructing the stock of human capital by PIM, is usually set arbitrarily as well.

Overall, this approach ignores a fundamental feature of the process of education, i.e. the lengthy gestation period between the current outlays for educational inputs and the emergence of human capital embodied in more competent people (Jorgenson and Fraumeni 1989, 1992a).

The most well-known application of the cost-based approach is provided by Kendrick (1976) for the US. Kendrick's estimates are more inclusive than most other applications, as they include the cost of child rearing, spending on education and other expenditures considered as having educational value. Kendrick also includes the opportunity cost of student time, i.e. earnings forgone when studying. Following the same approach, Eisner (1978, 1985, 1988, 1989) estimated the value of human capital through a number of modifications to the US national income accounts.

Both Eisner and Kendrick included in their estimates of human capital formation the opportunity cost of students' time while in school, as well as the actual costs of education undertaken by both households (e.g. costs for tuition and educational materials) and governments (e.g. costs for salaries and investments of educational institutions). However, unlike Kendrick, Eisner excluded the costs of child-rearing from the investment in human capital.

To resolve the investment-consumption dichotomy, Kendrick included in human capital investments all household expenditures related to child rearing up to the age of 14, as well as half of household expenditures on health and safety, while considering the other half as consumption. Due to a lack of empirical evidences for choosing depreciation rates, Kendrick used a modified double declining-balance method, while Eisner used straight-line depreciation.

The cost-based approach is also applied in Germany (Ewerhart 2001, 2003), the Netherlands (Rooijen-Horsten et al. 2007, 2008), Finland (Kokkinen, 2008, 2010), and Canada (Gu and Wong, 2008).

12.3.2 *The income-based approach*

The income-based approach has been used for measuring human capital at least since the 1960s (e.g. Weisbrod 1961). However, it was the seminal works by Jorgenson and Fraumeni (1989, 1992a, 1992b) that spawned interests in measuring human capital by applying the lifetime income approach (also called the Jorgenson-Fraumeni approach).[14]

The lifetime income approach measures human capital as the present value of the expected future labor incomes that could be generated over the lifetime of the people currently living. By bringing together the influence of a broad range of factors (demography, mortality, education, and labor market aspects), this approach allows comparing the relative importance of these factors and drawing useful policy implications from the estimates.

By focusing on the earning power of each person, this approach values human capital at market prices, under the assumption that market prices are good signals of the value of human capital services that result from the interaction of demand and supply in the labor market.

One clear advantage of this approach is that its extension naturally leads to an accounting system that includes values, volumes, and prices as basic elements, thus opening the way to the construction of a sequence of accounts that are similar to those used for produced capital within the SNA (Fraumeni 2009). This is the main reason that the lifetime income approach is considered as more promising for embracing human capital into the SNA in the future.

However, this approach is not immune from drawbacks. For instance, to calculate expected future earnings, some subjective judgments are necessarily made about the discount rate, real income growth rate, etc. There are also reasons to argue that the labor market does not always function in a perfect way, implying that the wage rate typically used as a proxy for earning power is not always equal to the marginal value of a particular type of human capital.

Moreover, differences in wages may not truly reflect differences in earning power in some cases where trade unions may command a premium wage for their members and where real wages may fall in economic recessions.

Table 12.1 presents a list of national studies that have applied the income-based approach to measuring human capital.[15] As shown in

---

[14] Throughout the chapter, the lifetime income approach and the Jorgenson-Fraumeni approach will be used interchangeably.

[15] The list in Table 12.1 is meant to highlight the broad range of countries (thirteen) for which these estimates exist, rather than being exhaustive of the full range of studies based on this approach.

Table 12.1 *An overview of selected national studies applying the income-based approach*

Examples of national studies	Country	Motivation	Time range	Main data sources	Population covered	Market/non-market activities
Jorgenson and Fraumeni (1989, 1992a, 1992b)	United States	New systems of national accounts, output of education sector	1948–1984, 1947–1987	Rich data based on decades of research	Age 0–75	Both
Ahlroth et al. (1997)	Sweden	Output of education sector	1967, 1973, 1980, 1990	Level of living surveys	Age 0–75	Both
Ervik et al. (2003)	Norway	Output of higher education sector	1995	Register data	Age 20–64	Market only
Wei (2004, 2008)	Australia	Incorporating human capital into the SNA (stock/flow)	1981–2001	Census data	Age 18 (25)–65, labor force/whole population	Market only
Le et al. (2006)	New Zealand	Measuring human capital (stock)	1981–2001	Census data	Age 18–64	Market only

Table 12.1 (*cont.*)

Examples of national studies	Country	Motivation	Time range	Main data sources	Population covered	Market/non-market activities
Gundimeda *et al.* (2006)	India	Accounting for human capital formation	1993–2001	Surveys of employment and unemployment, census of population	Age 15–60	Market only
Gu and Wong (2008)	Canada	Human capital contribution to national wealth account	1970–2007	Census/labor force survey	Age 15–74	Market only
Liu and Greaker (2009)	Norway	Measuring human capital (stock)	2006	Register data	Age 15(16)–67(74), labor force/ whole population	Market only
Christian (2010)	United States	Measuring human capital (stock/ investment)	1994–2006	Rich data	Age 0–80	Both
Coremberg (2010)	Argentina	Measuring human capital (stock)/ output of education sector	1997, 2001, 2004	Household permanent survey	Age 15–65	Market only

Li et al. (2010)	China	Measuring human capital (stock)	1985–2007	Household survey/health and nutrition survey	Urban/rural, age 0–60 (55 for female)	Market only
Jones and Chiripanhura (2010)	United Kingdom	Measuring human capital (stock)	2001–2009	Labor force survey	Age 16–64	Market only
Istat (2013)	Italy	Measuring human capital (stock)	2008	Various surveys	Age 15–64	Both

Table 12.1, data availability varies. For many countries, the data needed is compiled by the researcher, with a number of assumptions made during the data construction process.

In part due to this, and differently from the original studies by Jorgenson and Fraumeni, most of the national studies focused on the working age population (typically based on exogenous age thresholds, e.g. 15 and 64) instead of the whole population and on market activities only.

These limitations reflect a pragmatic way to sidestep a number of conceptual and data issues that arise when applying the full Jorgenson-Fraumeni approach. Incorporating non-market activities into human capital estimates remains controversial and focusing on working age population is also considered more relevant for measuring a country's productive capacity (Wei 2004; Gu and Wong 2008; Greaker and Liu 2008).[16]

Methodological modifications to the original Jorgenson-Fraumeni approach were also made in some national studies. For example, to smooth the business cycle effects that affect the original Jorgenson-Fraumeni approach (which relies exclusively on current cross-sectional information), Wei (2008) applied a cohort-based estimation to simulate future earnings.[17]

Results from national studies suggest that the estimated stock value of human capital is substantially larger than that of conventional produced capital, even when measures of the former are restricted to market activities. In addition, the estimated value of the output of education sector by the income-based approach is also higher than the gross fixed capital formation traditionally measured in the SNA.[18]

---

[16] For example, evaluating non-market activities involves much imputation which should be avoided as much as possible following the tradition of the SNA. Extending the production boundary to incorporate non-market activities (such as cooking, cleaning, and other household unpaid services) will blur the distinction between employment and unemployment, while these terms have been clearly defined, widely accepted, and frequently used for quite a long time.

[17] For more detailed discussions on the technical issues, besides the conceptual, methodological, and data issues, in national studies that applied the lifetime income approach to measuring human capital, see Liu (2012).

[18] As a result, considering educational expenditures as investment rather than consumption would significantly change our understanding of the extent of capital formation in any given year.

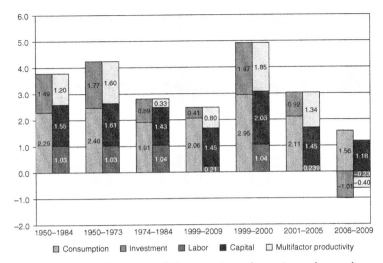

Figure 12.3 Contributions to full gross private domestic product and economic growth without human capital

Measures of human capital by the income-based approach tend also to exceed those by the cost-based approach, a pattern that may reflect that the former approach implicitly attributes the impact of on-the-job training and work experiences to formal education, while the latter effectively ignore the non-market inputs in practice.[19]

The estimated value of human capital by the lifetime income approach are sensitive to the choice of key parameters, i.e. the real annual growth of labor income that is assumed to prevail in the future, and the rate used to discount future earnings. However, the growth of human capital and its distribution across different groups of people are less sensitive.

12.3.3 Production account comparisons for the United States

Including Jorgenson-Fraumeni human capital components in a production account provides a different, and more complete, perspective on economic growth in the US. Figure 12.3 shows production contributions and multi-factor productivity growth, which in a traditional

---

[19] For more discussions on the possible explanations about the large divergence of the human capital estimates between the cost-based and the income-based approaches, Abraham (2010) serves as a good reference.

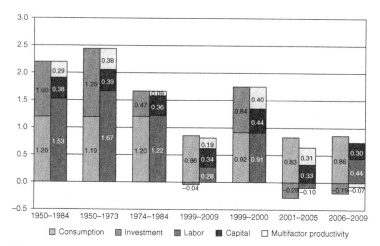

Figure 12.4 Contributions to full gross private domestic product and economic growth with human capital

manner excludes human capital components.[20] Figure 12.4 shows the corresponding results with human capital included.[21]

Although major trends are the same, such as the strong growth in 1950–1973 followed by a slowdown in 1974–1984, the rebound in 1999–2000, and the Great Recession and slow recovery in 2006–2009, the magnitude of the elements are quite different. The maximum rate of growth for the periods shown excluding human capital approaches 5 percent; while that including human capital approaches 2.5 percent, nearly half of the former.

Table 12.2 and 12.3 provide further information on why the two sets of production account estimates differ. Human capital components dominate the inclusive account as the nominal share of human capital accounts are around 75 percent of inclusive output for both output and factor outlay. Human capital quantities (for human investment, non-market consumption, and non-market outlay) grow at a relatively low

[20] Figure 12.3 comes directly from the paper by Fraumeni, Christian, and Samuels (2015). The estimates in Table 12.2 and 12.3 are detailed calculations based upon estimates which underlie the national income and product accounts presented in that paper.

[21] Contributions are calculated as a weighted rate of growth, where the weights are an average of the nominal dollar share in the previous period and this period and the rate of growth is a logarithmic growth rate of the quantities from the previous period to this period.

Table 12.2 *Full gross private domestic product, average nominal shares, and rates of growth, 1949–1984, 1998–2009*

	1949–1984	1949–1973	1973(1974)–1984	1998–2009	1998–2000	2000(2001)–2005	2005(2006)–2009
Human investment							
Average nominal share	0.4183	0.4252	0.4026	0.5481	0.5846	0.5486	0.5201
ROG of constant prices	0.0150	0.0193	0.0056	-0.0022	0.0070	-0.0086	0.0012
ROG of constant prices per capita	0.0019	0.0047	-0.0041	-0.0138	-0.0146	-0.0179	-0.0082
ROG of price index	0.0568	0.0496	0.0725	0.0220	0.0440	0.0078	0.0288
Non-human investment							
Average nominal share	0.0858	0.0848	0.0880	0.0720	0.0704	0.0726	0.0724
ROG of constant prices	0.0431	0.0507	0.0265	0.0107	0.0609	0.0297	-0.0382
ROG of constant prices per capita	0.0300	0.0361	0.0168	-0.0008	0.0393	0.0205	-0.0476
ROG of price index	0.0366	0.0220	0.0682	0.0083	0.0044	0.0103	0.0076
Non-market consumption							
Average nominal share	0.3360	0.3336	0.3414	0.2165	0.1979	0.2185	0.2279

Table 12.2 (*cont.*)

	1949–1984	1949–1973	1973(1974)–1984	1998–2009	1998–2000	2000(2001)–2005	2005(2006)–2009
ROG of constant prices	0.0189	0.0179	0.0210	0.0173	0.0139	0.0159	0.0206
ROG of constant prices per capita	0.0058	0.0033	0.0112	0.0057	-0.0077	0.0067	0.0113
ROG of price index	0.0531	0.0478	0.0646	0.0281	0.0336	0.0286	0.0247
Market consumption							
Average nominal share	0.1599	0.1563	0.1680	0.1634	0.1472	0.1602	0.1796
ROG of constant prices	0.0353	0.0381	0.0292	0.0301	0.0436	0.0306	0.0225
ROG of constant prices per capita	0.0222	0.0235	0.0195	0.0185	0.0220	0.0214	0.0132
ROG of price index	0.0407	0.0260	0.0728	0.0223	0.0088	0.0159	0.0371

Notes: ROG is the abbreviation for rate of growth. Average nominal shares begin in years indicated by a year in parentheses.

Table 12.3 *Full factor outlay, average nominal shares, and rates of growth, 1949–1984, 1998–2009*

	1949–1984	1949–1973	1973(1974)–1984	1998–2009	1998–2000	2000(2001)–2005	2005(2006)–2009
Property outlay							
Average nominal share	0.1029	0.0999	0.1098	0.1006	0.0914	0.0970	0.1119
ROG of constant prices	0.0372	0.0387	0.0339	0.0345	0.0482	0.0351	0.0268
ROG of constant prices per capita	0.0241	0.0241	0.0241	0.0229	0.0266	0.0259	0.0174
ROG of price index	0.0438	0.0287	0.0766	0.0156	-0.0185	0.0215	0.0253
Market labor outlay							
Average nominal share	0.1428	0.1412	0.1463	0.1348	0.1261	0.1359	0.1400
ROG of constant prices	0.0180	0.0177	0.0185	0.0037	0.0180	0.0042	-0.0041
ROG of constant prices per capita	0.0049	0.0031	0.0088	-0.0078	-0.0035	-0.0050	-0.0135
ROG of price index	0.0564	0.0490	0.0724	0.0335	0.0579	0.0314	0.0239

Table 12.3 (*cont.*)

	1949–1984	1949–1973	1973(1974)–1984	1998–2009	1998–2000	2000(2001)–2005	2005(2006)–2009
Non-market labor outlay							
Average nominal share	0.7543	0.7589	0.7440	0.7646	0.7825	0.7671	0.7480
ROG of constant prices	0.0168	0.0187	0.0126	0.0031	0.0087	-0.0019	0.0066
ROG of constant prices per capita	0.0037	0.0040	0.0029	-0.0084	-0.0128	-0.0112	-0.0028
ROG of price index	0.0551	0.0488	0.0689	0.0239	0.0414	0.0136	0.0280

Notes: ROG is the abbreviation for rate of growth. Average nominal shares begin in years indicated by a year in parentheses.

rate and in almost all cases grow at a lower rate than the other quantities (for non-human investment, market consumption, property outlay, and market labor outlay) included both in accounts with and without human capital components.

There are exceptions only in two sub-periods: 1949–1973 and 2005–2009. The quantity of non-market outlay grows at a faster rate than market labor outlay in 1949–1973. Average educational attainment and female labor force participation increased during this early period, with average educational attainment gains slowing around 1980 and female labor force participation gains continuing until about 1990.

The quantity of non-market labor outlay grows at a faster rate than market labor outlay in 2005–2009. With a negative growth rate in market outlay during this Great Recession and slow recovery period, growth in non-market labor outlay for the whole later period, 1998–2009, also exceeds growth in market labor outlay. The positive growth in non-market labor outlay during 2005–2009 is almost all due to growth in the sub-component time in household production and leisure, which occurs because many individuals spent less time in market work.

Multi-factor productivity growth is always lower in the sub-periods shown in Figure 12.4 than those in Figure 12.3 as accounts with human capital components attribute sources of economic growth elsewhere to a greater extent. Given the trends in educational attainment and labor force participation, and the aging of the work force, human capital, which is a major source of growth in the earlier 1949–1984 period, becomes a minor source of growth during the later 1998–2009 period. We conclude that excluding human capital will lead to an over-estimation of economic growth, including multi-factor productivity growth, in the US going beyond the present period.

12.4 International initiatives

In this section, studies focusing on international comparisons of human capital are reviewed of the indicators-based, the income-based, and the residual approaches.

12.4.1 *The indicators-based approach*

This approach has been taken by several international organizations. For instance, the UN publishes a Human Development Index (HDI), which combines measures of average achievements in countries in three basic dimensions of human development, i.e. health, education and knowledge, and standards of living.[22]

The OECD has a long tradition in developing both conceptual and methodological frameworks regarding human capital measurement, reflected by a series of publications (e.g. OECD 1994, 1996, 1998, 2001; Keeley 2007).[23] Using the indicators-based approach, the OECD also collects and disseminates a large range of indicators that are regularly published in *Education at a Glance*.

Recently, two OECD projects attracted increasing attention internationally, i.e. the Programme for International Student Assessment (PISA), which tests 15–16-year-old students for their cognitive skills in terms of reading, mathematics, science, and problem solving; and the Programme for the International Assessment of Adult Competencies (PIAAC), which tests adults for their competencies in terms of literacy, numeracy, and ability to solve problems in technology-rich environments.[24]

Although large-scale international projects such as the PISA and PIAAC can generate important information suitable for policy-taking and decision making, like all surveys, they are subject to limitations (e.g. with respect to sample size, range of variables included, country coverage, etc.).[25]

---

[22] The 2012 Human Development Report includes two measures of education and knowledge, namely school attainment, expressed in terms of the number of years of schooling, and school-life expectancy. More information is available at: http://hdr.undp.org/en.

[23] Other relevant streams of recent OECD on human capital are the "Social Outcomes of Learning project," the OECD Skills Strategy; work on intangible assets undertaken as part of the OECD work on New Sources of Growth; and the OECD Better Life Initiative. For more on these streams of work see the information on the following websites: www.oecd.org/document/9/0,3746,e n_2649_39263294_33706505_1_1_1_1,00.html; www.oecd.org/dataoecd/58/ 28/47769132.pdf; www.oecd.org/dataoecd/60/40/46349020.pdf; www.oecd .org/document/0/0,3746,en_2649_201185_47837376_1_1_1_1,00.html.

[24] For more information on PISA and PIAAC, please visit the following websites: www.pisa.oecd.org/pages/0,2987,en_32252351_32235731_1_1_1_1_1,00 .html; www.oecd.org/document/35/0,3746,en_2649_201185_40277475_ 1_1_1_1,00.html.

[25] More importantly, since these large-scale programs are resource-demanding in terms of both money and time required to implement, administer, process, analyze, and report, they are typically undertaken with low frequency.

Developing internationally comparable indicators has also been pursued by independent researchers. Indicators that are often used as single proxies for human capital include adult literacy rates (e.g. Azariadis and Drazen 1990; Romer 1990), school enrolment ratios (e.g. Mankiw *et al.* 1992; Levine and Renelt 1992), average years of schooling and other measures drawn from the distribution of population across various educational categories (e.g. Benhabib and Spiegel 1994; Islam 1995; Temple 1999; Barro 2001; Krueger and Lindahl 2001).

A well-known example is Barro and Lee (1993, 1996, 2001, 2010, 2013) for developing an international panel dataset on educational attainment, school years, and schooling quality, from 1950 to 2010, for 146 countries by gender and five-year age groupings, based on census and survey information compiled by UNESCO, Eurostat, national statistical agencies, and other sources.

The Barro-Lee dataset is an important resource for researchers attempting to quantify human capital. However, a single physical indicator as a proxy for human capital, though simple, cannot on its own adequately measure the various dimensions of skills and competences (OECD 2001), and sometimes even poorly specifies the relationship between education and human capital (Wößmann 2003; Kokkinen 2010).

Sometimes dashboard type indicators are applied (e.g. *Education at a Glance*; Ederer *et al.*, 2007, 2011). They rely on a number of statistics that, though rich in information, lack a common metric, and as a result cannot be aggregated into an overall measure. This makes them less suitable for comprehensive comparisons of human capital across countries and over time.

Moreover, a set of indicators does not readily allow the comparison of the relative importance of different types of capital, i.e. produced, natural, and human capital (Stroombergen *et al.* 2002), nor is it easily integrated into a consistent accounting framework with which most of national accountants are familiar.[26]

---

[26] This point is also relevant when considering differences between parametric and non-parametric approaches to measuring human capital. Parametric approaches are frequently used in academic research; however, since they rely on econometric techniques, different assumptions and model specifications, even based on the same dataset, will typically lead to different estimates. On the contrary, non-parametric approaches avoid these problems and are more akin to the tools typically used by national statistical offices and other producers of human capital statistics.

12.4.2 *The income-based approach*

To identify the common methodology and data requirements for building human capital accounts for international and inter-temporal comparisons, the OECD project applied a modified Jorgenson-Fraumeni approach and compiled monetary human capital estimates for fifteen OECD and one non-OECD countries, over the years varying from 1997 to 2007 (see Liu 2011).[27]

To reduce estimation difficulties due to data constraints, and to reflect country-specific conditions, the project estimated only market lifetime incomes, and focused on the working age population (between age 15 and 64), based on the categorical data (by five-year or ten-year age groups), rather than data by single year of age.

Results from the project indicate that the estimated human capital is substantially larger than that of conventional produced capital. Ratios of human capital to GDP are in a range from around eight to over ten across countries, in line with those reported in a number of national studies. The distributions of human capital by age, gender, and education reveal a few important conclusions.

While higher educational attainment contributed positively to the change of human capital per capita, this is not always sufficient to offset the negative effect of population ageing; as a result, the volume of human capital per capita appeared to have declined in some countries over the observed period.

In 2012, the UN published its first *Inclusive Wealth Report* (*IWR*), presenting estimates of inclusive wealth (the sum of manufactured, human, and natural capitals) for twenty countries over nineteen years, from 1990 to 2008 (UN-IHDP and UNEP 2012).[28] In this report, human capital is measured by the population's educational attainment and the additional compensation over time of this training.

---

[27] The OECD countries are: Australia (AUS), Canada (CAN), Denmark (DNK), France (FRA), Israel (ISR), Italy (ITA), Korea (KOR), the Netherlands (NLD), New Zealand (NZL), Norway (NOR), Poland (POL), Spain (ESP), the United Kingdom (GBR), and the United States (USA), and the non-OECD country is Romania (ROU); later, estimates for another OECD member country, Japan (JPN), was added to the database (see Liu 2014). For detailed information on the country databases, see www.oecd.org/std/publications documents/workingpapers.

[28] The *Inclusive Wealth Report 2014* covers 140 countries over the period 1990 to 2010 (UNU-IHDP and UNEP 2014).

The methodology applied in the *IWR* is based on Arrow *et al.* (2012), which is also income-based in a broad sense, but is different from the Jorgenson-Fraumeni approach, because the lifetime income as calculated in the *IWR* is at a highly aggregated level, making it hard to analyze the distribution of human capital across different population groups.

More fundamentally, the *IWR* approach does not allow for future education, notably for younger individuals; neither does the approach by the Barro-Lee dataset, because an individual's educational attainment in that dataset is assumed to be unchanged between age 25 and 64. On the contrary, the Jorgenson-Fraumeni approach explicitly allows for future education.

Since further education adds up to the human capital stock already accumulated, the assumption of no further education, made either explicitly or implicitly, may fail to capture the full potential of a country's population, leading to possible bias in policy-making.

12.4.3 *The residual approach*

This approach is internationally represented by the World Bank's well-known work on compiling country comprehensive wealth accounts, which include estimates of human capital, for more than 120 countries over the decade from 1995 to 2005.

As introduced in Section 12.2, the stock of human capital is measured as a residual, i.e. the difference between the total discounted value of each country's future consumption flows (as a proxy for total wealth) and the sum of the tangible components of that wealth, i.e. produced capital and the market component of natural capital (World Bank 2006, 2011; Ruta and Hamilton 2007; Ferreira and Hamilton 2010).

While the residual approach can be applied to a large number of countries based on less-demanding statistical information, it has some limits. First, by taking as its starting point the discounted value of future consumption flows, it obviously ignores the non-market benefits of various capital stocks.

Second, this measure is affected by measurement errors in all the terms entering the accounting identities, resulting in potential biases in the final estimates of human capital. Third, the approach cannot explain what drives the observed change of human capital over time, thus offering less valuable information for policy interventions.

12.4.4 Comparison of country measures

This sub-section presents a comparison of country measures of human capital. The comparison is made for up to eighteen countries, based on four international constructs applying different approaches that have been discussed so far.

As shown in column 2 of Table 12.4, the indicators-based approach is represented by Barro-Lee average educational attainment (in number of years) for individuals in the working age population (aged 15–64), which is drawn from Barro and Lee (2013).

The income-based approach is represented by two variants of Jorgenson-Fraumeni human capital per capita estimates. The first is primarily taken from the OECD project (Liu 2014), with exceptions for China and India. The estimates for China are from Li (2013) and those for India are from Gundimeda *et al.* (2006). The estimates are placed in column 3 of the table.

Note that all the estimates as displayed in column 3 are calculated as the stock of human capital divided by the corresponding working age population. For all the countries listed, except for China and India, the working age population is defined as the sub-population aged 15–64. The ages covered for China are 16 to 54 for females and 16 to 59 for males, while those for India are 15 to 60.

The second variant of Jorgenson-Fraumeni measures is modified human capital per capita estimates, directly drawn from Hamilton and Liu (2014). These per capital measures are calculated based on the whole population in each country, thus allowing for a direct comparison of human capital measures with the World Bank wealth estimates. They are put in column 4 of Table 12.4.

The estimates based on the residual approach are placed in column 5 and are represented by the World Bank intangible capital per capita estimates (World Bank 2011). For the ease of comparison, the corresponding estimates of the World Bank total wealth per capita are presented in column 6 in the same table (World Bank 2011).

As demonstrated in Table 12.4, the Barro-Lee estimates (by the indicators-based approach) are less correlated with other monetary estimates, i.e. the two Jorgenson-Fraumeni human capital per capita estimates (by the income-based approach) and the World Bank intangible capital per capita (by the residual approach). On the contrary, the

Table 12.4 *Country measures and the associated correlations based on different approaches*

Country measures	Indicators-based approach Barro-Lee educational attainment (in number of years) 2005	Income-based approach Jorgenson-Fraumeni human capital per capita (US$ in thousands) 2006	Income-based approach Hamilton-Liu modified Jorgenson-Fraumeni human capital per capita (US $ in thousands) 2005	Residual approach World Bank intangible capital per capita (US$ in thousands) 2005[2]	World Bank total wealth per capita (US$ in thousands) 2005[2]
Australia (AUS)	12.0	457		386	519
Canada (CAN)	12.5	498	350	415	539
China (CHN)	8.1	71		9	19
Denmark (DNK)	10.1	458		591	743
France (FRA)	10.3	459	339	482	586
India (IND)	4.9	94		6	11
Israel (ISR)	11.5	382	197	279	327
Italy (ITA)	10.3	375	269	405	498
Japan (JPN)	12.0	490		399	549
Korea (KOR)	12.3	490	289	190	248
Netherlands (NLD)	11.1	457	333	472	594

Table 12.4 (*cont.*)

| | Indicators-based approach | Income-based approach | | Residual approach | |
	Barro-Lee educational attainment (in number of years) 2005	Jorgenson-Fraumeni human capital per capita (US$ in thousands) 2006	Hamilton-Liu modified Jorgenson-Fraumeni human capital per capita (US $ in thousands) 2005	World Bank intangible capital per capita (US$ in thousands) 2005^2	World Bank total wealth per capita (US$ in thousands) 2005^2
New Zealand (NZL)	12.7	407	305	306	414
Norway (NOR)	12.4	537	503	532	862
Poland (POL)	10.0	223	98	110	136
Romania (ROU)	10.5	126	45	59	81
Spain (ESP)	10.2	456	290	331	408
United Kingdom (GBR)	9.5	558	404	579	663
United States (USA)	13.0	641	410	627	734

Notes: In this column, the figures for Australia and India are for 2001; those for Denmark are for 2002; all figures are in purchasing power parity (PPP, for private consumption) adjusted US$. The figures in these columns are based on the market exchange rates in constant 2005 US$ prices.

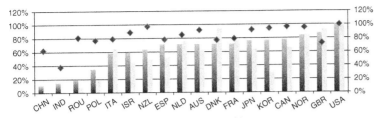

Figure 12.5 Human capital per capita 2006 compared with average education attainment 2005 and World Bank intangible capital per capita 2005

correlations within the three monetary estimates seem to be relatively high.[29]

In Figure 12.5 the estimates for the US are used as a reference point to show the relationship among the three estimates that are of larger country coverage as shown in Table 12.4. The countries in the figure are arranged in ascending order as a percent of the Jorgenson-Fraumeni human capital per capita.

Not surprising, the greatest ranking divergence between the three measures is between the Barro-Lee measures and the other two. Figure 12.5 shows that ranking countries by human capital without being aware of the underlying approaches applied may be misleading.

In addition, policy interventions based solely on educational attainment measures, without further information being taken on the extent to which higher education is significantly rewarded, may also be misleading. For example, such information matters critically for the countries such as Romania (ROU), Poland (POL), and the United Kingdom (GBR).

To sum up, it seems that the income-based, especially the Jorgenson-Fraumeni measures are relatively superior to other measures, because they are capable of capturing the demographic (e.g. age and gender structure of the population), educational (e.g. number of people with different levels of educational attainment, enrolment rates) and labor

---

[29] The sample correlation coefficients between the Barro-Lee estimates (column 2) and the other three are 0.71, 0.40, and 0.52, respectively, while those between the Jorgenson-Fraumeni human capital per capita (column 3) and the others are 0.92 and 0.89, respectively. In addition, the sample correlation coefficient between the last two monetary estimates (one income-based in column 4, and the other in column 5 that is based on the residual approach) is 0.89.

market (e.g. employment probabilities and earnings) factors in a dynamic way, i.e. both at the present and in the future. In contrast, the indicators-based measure (such as Barro-Lee estimates) provides only a snapshot of the present.

12.5 Remaining challenges

Despite that an increasing number of countries have applied, or are planning to apply, the income-based approach to measuring human capital, several issues and challenges remain.

12.5.1 Data issues

The data needed by the income-based approach are currently either not available for some countries or are not in a form suitable for direct use. Based on the OECD experience (Liu 2011), several issues stand out.

First, the quality and sources of earnings data cross-classified by different characteristics of workers vary significantly across countries. Data may refer to different earnings concepts (hourly and weekly earnings in most cases, annual and monthly earnings for some countries) and may include different elements of the remuneration packages of workers.

In some cases, data on earnings refer only to the main job while in other countries they may also cover secondary jobs and other remunerated activities. Finally, earnings data for different countries typically refer to different categories of educational attainment, and may be collected as either point estimates or in the form of earnings brackets.

Second, despite the great progress accomplished in collecting harmonized educational statistics, there remain issues with the quality of data on school enrolment and graduation rates, as definitions and classifications are not always comparable across countries, due for instance to differences in educational systems and in ways of counting students (e.g. students who repeat the year, students who graduate for a second time, etc.).

Third, human capital estimates would ideally require data on survival rates broken down by education.[30] While some national estimates

---

[30] Data on survival rates by age and education is constructed for certain age groups in Barro and Lee (2013).

exist, and they highlight large mortality differentials by socio-economic characteristics, these breakdowns are not available for all countries and they are rarely comparable across countries. Moreover, mortality statistics by educational level are not compiled through common standards across OECD countries, and in several countries they simply do not exist (OECD *et al.*, 2011).

Even more generally, constructing estimates of human capital based on the income-based approach requires that data from a range of sources – e.g. earnings statistics, population census, labor force surveys, mortality records – are integrated and harmonized to meet the requirements of human capital accounting. There are still challenges ahead in this regard.

12.5.2 *Methodological difficulties*

Currently, most human capital estimates rely on the assumption that cross-sectional earnings are good predictors of future cohorts' earnings. However there is ample evidence that cohort effects are typically large.[31] This suggests that it would be appropriate to use longitudinal earnings data that disentangles age and cohort effects, and makes it possible to account for cohort-specific factors.

Likewise, it would be important to separate wage premium due to educational attainment from those due to on-the-job training and other firms' characteristics, as failure to do so may lead to overstate the educational contribution to human capital. With respect to labor market indicators (e.g. employment rates and earnings), it is also important to separate business cycle effects that distort comparisons (e.g. by depressing earnings or employment rates for different categories of workers during a recession).

A further difficulty when applying the lifetime income approach relates to the choice of some of the key parameters required by the method, such as the expected real growth of labor income in the future, the discount rate, and the price deflators used for temporal and country comparisons. While assumptions on these parameters are currently left

---

[31] One implication of the cohort effect is that a person born in the twenty-first century may expect different income flows in the future than a person born in the 1990s.

to the discretion of researchers, their choice would ideally require further theoretical and empirical backup.[32]

Another challenge for developing monetary measures of human capital is represented by the large discrepancies between estimates of human capital by the income-based and the costs-based approaches. These discrepancies should be better understood and reconciled. One way to address this challenge would be to apply the two approaches simultaneously, which would offer an opportunity to identify the main factors accounting for the differences and to reconcile the two methods.

12.6 Concluding remarks

The concept of human capital has many dimensions, implying that its measurement has to be undertaken step by step in practice. Currently, many countries are using the definitions of human capital that focus on the productive capacity of individuals, and restrict the measurement to formal education and the economic returns accruing to individuals, even if the broader OECD definition is accepted as a reference point.

Starting from this narrower focus, human capital measurement initially aimed to develop summary indicators as simple proxies for human capital. While the data requirements are limited, so is the scope of these proxies. In recent years, developing monetary measures of human capital in a systematic way has received increasing interest from independent researchers, national statistical offices, and international organizations.

All the approaches to measuring human capital reviewed in this chapter have strengths and weaknesses. However, the monetary measures generated from the cost-based and income-based approaches should arguably have a core status. Because these measures are more comparable with those for traditional capital covered by the SNA, the construction of the latter is one of the main tasks of national statistical offices.

From country experiences and international initiatives as regards human capital measurement, an international trend is emerging, i.e. the lifetime income approach has been attracting more and more

---

[32] Similar challenges confront the cost-based approach with respect to the choice of depreciation rates and price deflators.

attention. Estimates based on this approach can be used to assess the relative contribution of a range of factors (demographic, education, mortality, and labor market) to the evolution of human capital, facilitating the corresponding policy interventions.

Recent international experiences also suggest the feasibility of producing these types of measures based on the information that is already available within the national and international statistical systems (e.g. Liu 2011). However, the scope for improvements in terms of consistency and comparability of the underlying data remains significant. Therefore, works should be pursued for continuing the compilation and harmonization of the data needed for human capital accounting.

There is also room for improvement on the detailed methodological choices applied by the lifetime income approach for human capital measurement. For instance, to control the cohort and business cycle effects, and to separate wage premiums among different factors, more studies should be carried out, possibly based on new sources of data. Research is also encouraged about how to choose the key parameters required by applying this approach.

To address the divergence between estimates applying the cost-based and the income-based approaches, satellite accounts could be employed for such purpose, as they would allow linking stock and flow measures of human capital in a full-fledged accounting system which is consistent with the rest of the SNA.[33]

Presently, there are more estimates of the stock than of the investment in human capital; studies that directly link the stock and flow in a systematic way are just a few (e.g. Jorgenson and Fraumeni 1989; Wei 2008; Gu and Wong 2010a). To reach an integrated and consistent human capital account, the construction of both stock and flow accounts should also be encouraged.

Up-to-date monetary measures of human capital based on the lifetime income approach have been primarily used for national wealth accounting (e.g. Gu and Wong 2008), for measuring the output of education sector (e.g. Ervik *et al.* 2003), for identifying the driving forces behind the evolution of human capital (e.g. Liu

---

[33] For more details on the rationale and feasibility of developing human capital/ education satellite accounts, please refer to Abraham and Mackie (2005) and Boarini *et al.* (2012).

2011), and for addressing issues related to wellbeing and quality of life (e.g. OECD 2011).

Efforts have been made to use the estimates by the lifetime income approach to quality-adjust the output, so that an output-based estimate of the volume of the education sector can be derived (Gu and Wong 2010b; see also Figure 12.1), making it possible to establish a productivity measure based on independently estimated inputs and outputs (see Schreyer 2010).

Currently, the lifetime income approach has been applied for countries with relatively richer data. However, for the purpose of international comparisons, some kind of streamlined approach should be developed for those countries in which the needed data is not sufficient, or even not available. Despite a few studies in existence (e.g. Fraumeni 2009; Hamilton 2013), more research along this line is very much welcomed.

References

Abraham, K. G. 2010. "Accounting for Investment in Formal Education," *Survey of Current Business*, June: 42–53.

Abraham, K. G., and C. Mackie. 2005. *Beyond the Market: Designing Nonmarket Accounts for the United States*. Washington: The National Academic Press.

Ahlroth, S., A. Björklund, and A. Forslund. 1997. "The Output of the Swedish Education Sector," *Review of Income and Wealth*, 43(1): 89–104.

Arrow, K. J., P. Dasgupta, L. H. Goulder, K. J. Mumford, and K. Oleson. 2012. "Sustainability and the Measurement of Wealth," *Environment and Development Economics*, 17(3).

Azariadis, C. and A. Drazen. 1990. "Threshold Externalities in Economic Development," *Quarterly Journal of Economics*, 105(2): 501–526.

Barro, R. J. 2001. "Human Capital and Growth," *American Economic Review, Papers and Proceedings*, 91(2): 12–17.

Barro, R. J. and J. W. Lee. 1993. "International Comparisons of Educational Attainment," *Journal of Monetary Economics*, 32: 363–394.

1996. "International Measures of Schooling Years and Schooling Quality," *American Economic Review*, 86: 218–23.

2001. "International Data on Educational Attainment: Updates and Implications," *Oxford Economic Papers*, 53(3).

2010. "A New Data Set of Educational Attainment in the World, 1950–2010," *NBER Working Paper Series*, **15902**.

2013. "A New Data Set of Educational Attainment in the World, 1950–2010," *Journal of Development Economics*, **104**: 184–198.

Becker, G. S. 1964. *Human Capital*. New York: Columbia University Press.

Benhabib, J. and M. M. Spiegel. 1994. "The Role of Human Capital in Economic Development: Evidence from Aggregate Cross-Country and Regional US Data," *Journal of Monetary Economics*, **34**(2): 143–173.

Boarini, R., M. Mira d'Ercole, and G. Liu. 2012. "Approaches to Measuring the Stock of Human Capital: A Review of Country Practices," *OECD Statistics Working Papers*, No. 2012/04, OECD Publishing.

Christian, M. S. 2010. "Human Capital Accounting in the United States, 1964–2006," *Survey of Current Business*, June: 31–36.

Coremberg, A. 2010. "The Economic Value of Human Capital and Education in an Unstable Economy: the case of Argentina," Paper Presented at the 31st General Conference of The International Association for Research in Income and Wealth, St. Gallen, Switzerland, August 22–28.

Ederer, P., P. Schuller, and S. Willms. 2007. *Innovation at Work: The European Human Capital Index*, Brussels: The Lisbon Council Policy Brief, Volume **2**, Number 3.

2011. *Human Capital Leading Indicators – How Europe's Regions and Cities Can Drive Growth and Foster Inclusion*. Brussels: The Lisbon Council.

Eisner, R. 1978. "Total Incomes in the United States 1959 and 1969," *Review of Income and Wealth*, **24**(1): 41–70.

1985. "The Total Incomes System of Accounts," *Survey of Current Business*, **65**(1): 2448.

1988. "Extended Accounts for National Income and Product," *Journal of Economic Literature*, **26**(2): 1611–1684.

1989. *The Total Incomes System of Accounts*. University of Chicago Press.

Engel, E. 1883. *Der Werth des Menschen*. Berlin: Verlag von Leonhard Simion.

Ervik, A. O., E. Holmøy, and T. Hægeland. 2003. "A Theory-based Measure of the Output of the Education Sector," *Discussion Paper*, No. **353**, Statistics Norway.

Ewerhart, G. 2001. "Humankapital in Deutschland: Bildungsinvestitionen, Bildungsvermögen und Abschreibungen auf Bildung. Erweiterte Input–Output-Arbeitsmarktanalyse" ("Human Capital Formation in Germany: Investment, Education and Asset Write-downs on Formation. Extended Input–Output Analysis, Labor Market"), *Contributions to the Labour Market and Employment Research*, **247**: 77.

2003. "Ausreichende Bildungsinvestitionen in Deutschland? Bildungsinvestitionen und Bildungsvermögen in Deutschland 1992–1999" ("Sufficient Investment in Education in Germany? Investment in Education and Training Capacity in Germany, 1992–1999"), *Contributions to the Labour Market and Employment Research*, **266**: 65.

Farr, W. 1853. "Equitable Taxation of Property," *Journal of Royal Statistics*, **16**(March): 145.

Ferreira, S. and K. Hamilton. 2010. "Comprehensive Wealth, Intangible Capital, and Development," *Policy Research Working Paper*, **5452**, The World Bank.

Fraumeni, B. M. 2009. "A Measurement Specialist's Perspective on Human Capital," *Presentation at China Centre for Human Capital and Labour Market Research*, Central University of Finance and Economics, Beijing, China, June 11.

Fraumeni, B. M., M. S. Christian, and J. D. Samuels. 2015. "The Accumulation of Human and Nonhuman Capital, Revisited," Paper Presented at the International Association for Research in Income and Wealth Conference "W(h)ither the SNA?" Paris, April 17.

Graham, J. W. and R. H. Webb. 1979. "Stocks and Depreciation of Human Capital: New Evidence from a Present-value Perspective," *Review of Income and Wealth*, **25**(2): 209–224.

Greaker, M. and G. Liu. 2008. "Measuring the Stock of Human Capital for Norway – A Lifetime Labour Income Approach," Paper Presented at the OECD Workshop on "The Measurement of Human Capital," Turin, Italy, November 3–4.

Greaker, M., P. Løkkevik, and M. A. Walle. 2005. "Utviklingen i den norske nasjonalformuen fra 1985 til 2004. Et eksempel på bærekraftig utvikling?" ("Development of the Norwegian National Wealth 1985–2004. An Example of Sustainable Development?"), *Report* 2005/13, Statistics Norway, Oslo.

Gu, W. and A. Wong. 2008. "Human Development and its Contribution to the Wealth Accounts in Canada", Paper Presented at the OECD Workshop on "The Measurement of Human Capital," Turin, Italy, November 3–4.

2010a. "Estimates of Human Capital in Canada: The Lifetime Income Approach," *Economic Analysis Research Paper Series*, No. 062, Statistics Canada.

2010b. "Investment in Human Capital and the Output of the Education Sector in Canada," Draft Working Paper, Statistics Canada.

Gundimeda, H., S. Sanyal, R. Sinha, and P. Sukhdev. 2006. "Estimating the Value of Educational Capital Formation in India," Monograph 5, Green Accounting for Indian States Project (GAISP), TERI Press, New Delhi, India, March.

Hamilton, K. 2013. "Estimating the Value of Human Capital with Limited Data", Unpublished Document, the World Bank.

Hamilton, K. and G. Liu. 2014. "Human Capital, Tangible Wealth, and the Intangible Capital Residual," *Oxford Review of Economic Policy*, 30(1): 70–91.

Islam, N. 1995. "Growth Empirics: A Panel Data Approach," *Quarterly Journal of Economics*, 110(4): 1127–1170.

Istat. 2013. "Il valore dello stock di capitale umano in Italia," Paper Presented at the Conference "*Misurare il capitale umano. Esperienze e prospettive*," Rome, Italy, January 18.

Jones, R. and B. Chiripanhura. 2010. "Measuring the UK's Human Capital Stock," *Economic and Labour Market Review*, UK Office for National Statistics, November, 36–63.

Jorgenson, D. W. and B. M. Fraumeni. 1989. "The Accumulation of Human and Non-human Capital, 1948–1984." In R. E. Lipsey and H. S. Tice (eds.), *The Measurement of Savings, Investment, and Wealth*. University of Chicago Press.

1992a. "The Output of Education Sector." In Z. Griliches (ed.), *Output Measurement in the Service Sectors*. University of Chicago Press.

1992b. "Investment in Education and US Economic Growth," *Scandinavian Journal of Economics*, 94, Supplement: 51–70.

Keeley, B. 2007. *Human Capital: How What you Know Shapes Your Life*. OECD Publishing, Paris.

Kendrick, J. 1976. *The Formation and Stocks of Total Capital*. New York: Columbia University Press.

Kiker, B. F. 1966. "The Historical Roots of the Concept of Human Capital," *Journal of Political Economy*, 74(5): 481–499.

Kokkinen, A. 2008. "Human Capital and Finland's Economic Growth in 1910–2000 – Assessing Human Capital Accumulation by Education inside the National Accounts Framework," Paper Presented at the 30th General Conference of the International Association for Research in Income and Wealth (IARIW), Poster Session I: National Accounts Issues, August 24–30, Portoroz, Slovenia.

2010. "Assessing Human Capital in the National Accounts – Is there a Feedback to Theory?" Paper Presented at the 31st General Conference of the International Association for Research in Income and Wealth (IARIW), Session 8C, August 22–28, St. Gallen, Switzerland.

Krueger, A. B. and M. Lindahl. 2001. "Education for Growth: Why and For Whom?" *Journal of Economic Literature*, 39(4): 1101–1136.

Kyriacou, G. A. 1991. "Level and Growth Effects of Human Capital: A Cross-country Study of the Convergence Hypothesis," *Economic*

Research Reports 19–26, C. V. Starr Centre for Applied Economics, New York University.

Le, T., J. Gibson, and L. Oxley. 2003. "Cost- and Income-based Measures of Human Capital," *Journal of Economic Surveys*, **17**(3): 271–307.

2006. "A Forward-looking Measure of the Stock of Human Capital in New Zealand," *The Manchester School*, **74**(5): 593–609.

Levine, R. E. and D. Renelt. 1992. "A Sensitivity Analysis of Cross-country Growth Regressions," *American Economic Review*, **82**(4): 942–963.

Li, H. 2013. "Human Capital in China," China Center for Human Capital and Labor Market Research, Central University of Finance and Economics, Beijing, China, December.

Li, H., Y. Liang, B. M. Fraumeni, Z. Liu, and X. Wang. 2010. "Human Capital in China," Paper Presented at the 31st General Conference of The International Association for Research in Income and Wealth, St. Gallen, Switzerland, August 22–28.

Liu, G. 2011. "Measuring the Stock of Human Capital for Comparative Analysis: An Application of the Lifetime Income Approach to Selected Countries," *OECD Statistics Working Papers*, No. 2011/06, OECD Publishing.

2012. "The OECD Human Capital Project: A Technical Report," Unpublished Document, OECD Statistics Directorate.

2014. "Measuring the Stock of Human Capital for International and Inter-temporal Comparisons." In D. Jorgenson, S. Landefeld and P. Schreyer (eds.), *Measuring Economic Sustainability and Progress*. National Bureau of Economic Research, University of Chicago Press, 493–544.

Liu, G. and M. Greaker. 2009. "Measuring the Stock of Human Capital for Norway – A Lifetime Labour Income Approach," *Documents*, 2009/12, Statistics Norway.

Mankiw, N. G., D. Romer, and D. N. Weil. 1992. "A Contribution to the Empirics of Growth," *Quarterly Journal of Economics*, **107**(2): 408–437.

Mincer, J. 1974. *Schooling, Experience and Earnings*. New York: Columbia University Press.

Mulligan, C. B. and X. Sala-i-Martin. 1995. "Measuring Aggregate Human Capital," *NBER Working Paper, No. 5016*, Cambridge, MA.

OECD. 1994. *The OECD Jobs Study: Evidence and Explanations*. Paris: OECD Publishing.

1996. *Measuring What People Know – Human Capital Accounting for the Knowledge Economy*. Paris: OECD Publishing.

1998. *Human Capital Investment: An International Comparison*. Paris: OECD Publishing.

2001. *The Well-being of Nations: The Role of Human and Social Capital*. Paris: OECD Publishing.

2011. *How's Life? Measuring Well-being.* Paris: OECD Publishing.

OECD, Eurostat, and WHO. 2011. *A System of Health Accounts 2011.* Paris: OECD Publishing.

O'Mahony, M. and M. P. Timmer. 2009. "Output, Input and Productivity Measures at the Industry Level: the EU KLEMS Database," *Economic Journal*, **119**(538):F374-F403.

Petty, W. 1690. *Political Arithmetic.* Reprinted in C. H. Hull. 1899. *The Economic Writings of Sir William Petty.* Cambridge University Press.

Romer, P. M. 1990. Human Capital and Growth: Theory and Evidence. *Carnegie-Rochester Conference Series on Public Policy*, **32**: 251–286.

Rooijen-Horsten, M. van, D. van den Bergen, and M. Tanriseven. 2007. "Intangible Capital in the Netherlands: A Benchmark," Statistics Netherlands, Voorburg-Heerlen, bpa-no. 2007–20-MNR. See: www.cbs.nl/NR/rdonlyres/DE0167DE-BFB8-4EA1-A55C-FF0A5AFCBA32/0/200801x10pub.pdf.

Rooijen-Horsten, M. van, D. van den Bergen, M. de Haan, A. Klinkers, and M. Tanriseven. 2008. "Intangible Capital in the Netherlands: Measurement and Contribution to Economic Growth," Statistics Netherlands, The Hague-Heerlen, discussion paper no. 08016. See: www.cbs.nl/NR/rdonlyres/7E943807-C553-444D-8690-D21FC35C82D5/0/200816x10pub.pdf.

Ruta, G. and K. Hamilton. 2007. "The Capital Approach to Sustainability." In G. Atkinson *et al.* (eds.), *Handbook of Sustainable Development.* Cheltenham, UK: Edward Elgar Publishing, Inc.

Schreyer, P. 2010. "Towards Measuring the Volume Output of Education and Health Services," *OECD Statistics Directorate Working Paper*, No. 31, OECD, Paris.

Schultz, T. W. 1961. "Investment in Human Capital," *American Economic Review*, **51**(1): 1–17.

Smith, A. 1776. *An Inquiry into the Nature and Causes of the Wealth of Nations*, Book 2. London: W. Strahan and T. Cadell.

Stroombergen, A., D. Rose, and G. Nana. 2002. "Review of the Statistical Measurement of Human Capital," Statistics New Zealand.

Temple, J. 1999. "A Positive Effect of Human Capital on Growth," *Economics Letters*, **65**(1): 131–134.

UN-IHDP and UNEP. 2012. *Inclusive Wealth Report 2012.* Cambridge University Press.

UNU-IHDP and UNEP 2014. *Inclusive Wealth Report 2014, Measuring Progress Toward Sustainability.* Cambridge University Press.

Wei, H. 2004. "Measuring the Stock of Human Capital for Australia," *Working Paper* No. 2004/1, Australian Bureau of Statistics.

2008. "Measuring Human Capital Flows for Australia," *Working Paper* No. 1351.0.55.023, Australian Bureau of Statistics

Weisbrod, B. A. 1961. "The Valuation of Human Capital," *Journal of Political Economy*, **69**(5): 425–436.

World Bank. 2006. *Where is the Wealth of Nations?* Washington, DC: The World Bank.

2011. *The Changing Wealth of Nations: Measuring Sustainable Development in the New Millennium.* Washington, DC: The World Bank.

Wößmann, L. 2003. "Specifying Human Capital," *Journal of Economic Surveys*, **17**(3): 239–270.

13 | A half century of Trans-Pacific competition: price level indices and productivity gaps for Japanese and US industries, 1955–2012

DALE W. JORGENSON, KOJI NOMURA,
AND JON D. SAMUELS

13.1 Introduction

The Trans-Pacific Partnership is a proposed international agreement that would involve Japan, the United States, and ten other countries of the Asia-Pacific region.[1] The agreement would reduce barriers to international trade and investment and increase competition between Japanese and US industries around the Asia-Pacific region. This would provide an opportunity to improve productivity performance and improve standards of living in all the participating countries. In this chapter we analyze the competition between Japanese and US industries that has provided powerful incentives for mutually beneficial international economic co-operation between Japan and the US across the Pacific since Japan regained sovereignty in 1952.[2]

The first objective of this chapter is to present price level indices and productivity gaps between Japan and the US for the period 1955–2012. The price level index is the principal indicator of international competitiveness, often expressed in terms of the over- or undervaluation of currencies, for example, over- or undervaluation of the Japanese yen relative to the US dollar. The productivity gap is an indicator of the relative efficiency with which inputs like capital and labor are transformed into output in the two economies. A key feature of our measures is that they are constructed within the framework of the national

---

[1] For the US perspective, see: https://ustr.gov/tpp.
[2] The views expressed in this chapter are solely those of the authors and not necessarily those of the Research Institute of Economy, Trade and Industry (RIETI), Japan's Ministry of Economy, Trade and Industry (METI), or the US Bureau of Economic Analysis (BEA).

accounts of both countries. We begin with a brief discussion of the two basic concepts, the price level index and the productivity gap.

The price level index is defined as the ratio of the purchasing power parity (PPP) to the market exchange rate. The purchasing power parity represents the price of a commodity in Japan, expressed in yen, relative to the price in the US, expressed in dollars. By comparing this relative price with the market exchange rate of the yen and the dollar, we obtain the price barrier faced by Japanese producers in competing with their American counterparts in international markets.

As a specific illustration, the purchasing power parity of a unit of the gross domestic product (GDP) in Japan and the US in 2005 was 124.9 yen per dollar, while the market exchange rate was 110.2 yen per dollar. The price level index was 1.13, so that the yen was overvalued relative to the dollar by 13%. Firms located in Japan had to overcome a 13% price disadvantage in international markets to compete with US producers. This gives a quantitative measure of the international competitiveness of Japan and the US in 2005.

The first contribution of this chapter is to develop new estimates of price level indices for thirty-six industries in Japan and the US. Our estimates are derived from detailed purchasing power parities for 174 products, constructed within the framework of a bilateral Japan–US input–output table for 2005 by Nomura and Miyagawa (2015). We also develop price level indices for capital stock and capital services for thirty-three types of capital assets, including research and development, land, and inventories. Finally, we develop price level indices for 1,680 categories of labor inputs, cross-classified by gender (2), age (6), education attainment (4), and industry (35) categories. We aggregate the detailed price level indices to construct measures for outputs and for capital (K), labor (L), energy (E), materials (M), and services (S) inputs for the thirty-six industries.

Jorgenson and Nomura (2007) constructed price level indices for forty-two industries for the period 1960–2004. They showed that the price level index for Japan and the US captures a critical turning point in the international competition between the two economies. The Plaza Accord of 1985 was an agreement among the five leading industrialized countries in response to the large US current account deficits in the 1980s. This resulted in depreciation of the US dollar and rapid appreciation of the Japanese yen. The revised estimates in the chapter are broadly consistent with Jorgenson and Nomura (2007). We estimate that the yen was undervalued by 13% relative to the dollar in 1985. The rapid strengthening of the yen reversed this relationship, leading to an overvaluation by 28% in 1990. The revaluation of the yen continued through 1995, leading to an overvaluation of the yen of 75% and a dramatic loss in Japanese international competitiveness.

After 1995 Japanese policy-makers spent more than a decade dealing with the overvaluation of the yen. Domestic deflation and a modest devaluation coincided with a price level index decline of 4.64% annually from 1995 through 2007. A fall in the purchasing power parity of 2.77% per year resulted from modest inflation of 1.92% in the US and deflation in Japan of 0.85%. In addition, the yen–dollar exchange rate fell by 1.87% per year, almost reaching the yen–dollar purchasing power parity in 2007.

The financial and economic crisis that originated in the US in 2007–2009 led to a second sharp revaluation of the yen. Under Chairman Ben Bernanke, the Federal Reserve vastly expanded its balance sheet through quantitative easing but the Bank of Japan under Governor Masaaki Shirakawa failed to react. The yen appreciated to a historic high of 75.5 yen to the dollar in November 2011. Subsequently there was modest depreciation of the yen, but in 2012 the yen was still overvalued by 34%.

The election of Prime Minister Shinzo Abe in December of 2012 coincided with further depreciation of the yen. This accelerated with the adoption of quantitative easing by the Bank of Japan after Governor Haruhiko Kuroda took office in April 2013. By the end of February 2015 the yen–dollar exchange rate had risen to 119.6 yen per dollar, well above our estimate of the purchasing power parity of 107.3 yen per dollar in 2012. We conclude that quantitative easing by the Bank of Japan has restored Japan's international competitiveness relative to the US.

Price level indices between Japan and the US have real counterparts in the productivity gaps between the two countries. We define productivity as output per unit of all inputs. At the economy-wide level total factor productivity (TFP) is defined as the GDP divided by the total of capital and labor inputs. This can be distinguished from labor productivity, the ratio of GDP to labor input, or capital productivity, the ratio GDP to capital input. The productivity gap reflects the difference between the levels of TFP and captures the relative efficiency of production in the two countries.

The second contribution of this chapter is to trace the Japan–US productivity gap to its sources at the industry level. For this purpose we use new industry-level production accounts for Japan and the US that are closely comparable and employ similar national accounting concepts. The US production account was developed by Jorgenson, Ho, and Samuels (Chapter 2, this volume), who have extended the estimates of Jorgenson, Ho, and Stiroh (2005) backward to 1947 and forward to 2012. We extend the Japanese production account presented by Jorgenson and Nomura (2007) backward to 1955 and forward to 2012 with important revisions described below. We derive TFP estimates for each country by aggregating over industries.

The convergence of Japanese economy to US levels of productivity has been analyzed in a number of earlier studies – Jorgenson, Kuroda, and Nishimizu (1987), Jorgenson and Kuroda (1990), van Ark and Pilat (1993), Kuroda and Nomura (1999), Nomura (2004), and Cameron (2005), as well as Jorgenson and Nomura (2007). We define the productivity gap between Japan and the US as the difference between unity and the ratio of levels of total factor productivity in the two countries. For example, in 1955, three years after Japan regained sovereignty at the end of the Allied occupation in 1952, Japan's TFP was 45.4% of the US level, so that the productivity gap between the two economies was 54.6%.

Japanese GDP grew at double-digit rates for a decade and a half, beginning in 1955. This rapid growth is often associated with the "income-doubling" plan of Prime Minister Hayato Ikeda. Ikeda took office in 1960 and immediately announced a plan to double Japanese incomes during the decade 1960–1970. The growth rate of Japanese GDP averaged more than 10% per year from 1955–1970, considerably exceeding the income-doubling rate of 7%. The growth of TFP contributed about 40% of this growth in output, while growth of capital and labor inputs contributed around 60%.

The first oil shock of 1973 slowed Japanese growth considerably, but Japanese GDP doubled more than three times between 1955 and 1991. The growth of TFP accounted for a little under a third of this increase, while growth of capital and labor inputs accounted for slightly more than two-thirds. US economic growth averaged less than half the Japanese growth rate from 1955–1991. Japanese TFP grew at 2.46% per year until 1991, while annual US TFP growth averaged only 0.46%. By 1991 Japanese TFP reached 92.9% of the US level, narrowing the productivity gap from 55% in 1955 to 7% in 1991.

The collapse in Japanese real estate prices that ended the "bubble economy" in 1991 ushered in a period of much slower growth, often called the Lost Decade. The Japanese rate of economic growth plummeted to only 0.70% per year from 1991–2012, less than a tenth of the growth rate from 1955–1991. US economic growth continued at 2.71% during 1991–2012, powered by the information technology investment boom of 1995–2000, when the growth rate rose to 4.40% per year. After 1991 Japanese TFP was almost unchanged, falling at 0.05% per year, while US TFP growth continued at 0.53%. By 2012 the Japan–US productivity gap had widened to 17.3%, the level of the early 1980s.

Hamada and Okada (2009) have employed price level indices to analyze the monetary and international factors behind Japan's Lost Decade. The Lost Decade is discussed in much greater detail by Hamada, Kashyap, and Weinstein (2010), Iwata and ESRI (2011), and Fukao (2013). The Lost Decade of the 1990s in Japan was followed by a brief revival in economic growth. The Great Recession of 2007–2009 in the US was transmitted to Japan by a sharp appreciation of the yen in response to quantitative easing by the Federal Reserve. This led to a downturn in Japan that was more severe than in any of the other major industrialized countries. This provided the setting for a renewed focus on economic growth by the Abe government in 2012.

In summary, this chapter analyzes changes in price competitiveness between Japan and the US and the industry origins of the productivity gap between the two economies over more than five decades beginning in 1955. In Section 13.2 we describe the data sources for comparing outputs, inputs, and productivity at the industry level and constructing price level indices at elementary and industry levels. In Section 13.3 we present the resulting price level indices and productivity gaps. We aggregate these results to obtain indices of output, capital and labor inputs, and total factor productivity for Japan and the US. Section 13.4 concludes the chapter with a discussion of implications for the proposed Trans-Pacific Partnership. We present our methodological framework in the Appendix.

13.2 Data

13.2.1 Industry-level production accounts for Japan and the US

Industry-level production accounts for Japan and the US include industry outputs, factor inputs of capital and labor, and intermediate inputs of energy, materials, and services (KLEMS). We present these data in current and constant prices for the period 1955–2012. Productivity for each industry is defined as the ratio of output to all inputs. Jorgenson, Ho, and Samuels (Chapter 2, this volume) provide details on the data sources and methods of data construction for the US. Adjustments to the US data to ensure consistency between Japan and the US are noted below.

Our industry-level production accounts for Japan take the study by Jorgenson and Nomura (2007) as a point of departure. We have made five major improvements in the data for Japan. The first is greater consistency with the production accounts and commodity flow data from Japan's System of National Accounts (JSNA). These accounts are compiled by the Economic and Social Research Institute (ESRI) of the Cabinet Office. The 2005 benchmark revision of the JSNA was published by ESRI in 2011. We have incorporated commodity flow data from the JSNA.[3]

Second, the estimates of labor services by Jorgenson and Nomura (2007) were based on a limited number of published cross-tabulations, supplemented by sample surveys of educational attainment. Nomura and Shirane (2014) have replaced these sources by custom-made tables with fully cross-classified data for 1980–2010 from the Japanese Census of Population. These tables have been compiled at five-year intervals by the National Statistics Center (NSTAC).[4] Nomura and Shirane (2014) have provided a comprehensive revision of Japanese labor data by industry, with new estimates extended backward to 1955 and forward to 2012.

---

[3] We are indebted to ESRI for the time-series commodity flow data from the JSNA.

[4] The NSTAC is an incorporated administrative agency, created in April 2003 as part of the central statistical organization in Japan. Unpublished tabulations of fully cross-classified data for Japan were made available through full implementation of the Statistics Act implemented in April 2009. See: www.stat.go .jp/english/index/seido/1-1n.htm.

Third, we replace rates of depreciation for produced assets in the JSNA by new estimates developed by Nomura and Suga (2013) for ESRI. They have estimated asset lives and rates of depreciation for a very finely divided classification of assets. This classification distinguishes 369 asset types and uses data on retired assets collected in ESRI's Survey on Capital Expenditures and Disposals in Japan from 2006 to 2012. The survey collected observations on 838,000 asset disposals from business accounts of private corporations. These data were used to estimate asset lifetimes. For about 60,000 observations the assets were sold for continued use and the prices were used to estimate rates of deprecation. Based on this study, many of the depreciation rates that we employ are higher than those used in the JSNA.

Fourth, we have defined the supply and use tables (SUT) at basic prices. Consumption taxes are removed in our compilation of intermediate inputs and factor services. The consumption tax was first introduced in Japan in April 1989. Both deductible and not-deductible consumption taxes are included in indirect taxes in the official benchmark input–output tables and production accounts in the JSNA. By removing these taxes we are able to provide purchasing power parities for Japan–US comparisons that reflect prices received by the producers.

Fifth, we capitalize research and development (R&D) by industry in our time-series SUT and capital services data in order to achieve comparability with the comprehensive revision of the US national accounts published in July 2013. In accord with the *System of National Accounts 2008*, the capitalization of R&D will be included in the benchmark revision of JSNA scheduled for 2016. We developed the R&D investment series covering the period of 1952–2012, based on the Survey of Research and Development by the Statistics Bureau of Japan, and estimated the time-series of capital stock and capital services by industry for 1955–2012.

The public sector is a special challenge in creating a common industry classification. In principle, the public sector under the common classification scheme should include only sectors where market transactions are not available. In practice, to arrive at our common classification, we reclassify a portion of public sector activities to private industries with similar technological characteristics. In particular, we move US government enterprise industries to private sector counterparts. The value for non-market production of capital services by household and government sectors are imputed and are defined as the outputs of government (sector 35) and households (sector 36). We set the productivity gap between Japan and the US equal to zero for the non-market production of capital services by households and the public sector.

The industry-level production accounts for Japan and the US are closely comparable. The required rates of return used in measuring prices and volumes of capital services are determined endogenously to exhaust capital income across all capital assets. The industry-level measures of labor services are adjusted for quality, using similarly detailed cross-classifications of the labor data. For this study we have developed a thirty-six-industry classification that provides greater comparability for the period 1955–2012 than the forty-two-industry classification employed by Jorgenson and Nomura (2007).

13.2.2 PPPs for elementary products

We estimate PPPs for Japan and the US for outputs, factor inputs of capital and labor, and intermediate inputs of energy, materials, and services (KLEMS) for thirty-six industries. Except for labor services, these PPPs are based on price comparisons of 174 elementary products for the benchmark year 2005, where the elementary product refers to the most detailed level at which we have data to define the comparable product. This section describes the concepts and the multitude of data sources used for the elementary price comparisons. Section 13.2.3 describes the industry-level PPPs for output and intermediate inputs. The industry-level PPPs for capital and labor services are presented in Sections 13.2.4 and 13.2.5, respectively.

In this chapter we use a hybrid of the two basic approaches for defining PPPs for elementary products. The first approach uses production-side data for domestically produced products in Japan and the US, the PPPs in producer's prices are ratios of average unit prices, each defined as the monetary value over the physical volume. This approach is especially easy to implement in sectors with outputs defined in homogenous physical units, for example, electricity and mining products. In the second approach PPPs can be estimated from demand-side data by eliminating the wedge between producer's domestic prices and prices of imported products and purchaser's prices of composites of domestic and imported products. The wedges are due to trade and transportation margins and taxes.

The hybrid approach that we use incorporates a new benchmark estimates of PPPs for 174 products from both production-side and demand-side price data for the benchmark year 2005 and is described in detail by Nomura and Miyagawa (2015). We outline the methodology in the appendix to this chapter and discuss the data sources for the PPPs. The elementary level PPPs are based on the 2005 Japan–US input–output table (IOT) published by Ministry of Economy, Trade and Industry (METI) in 2013.

The representation of the trade structure in the 2005 bilateral IOT indicates consistent price differences between the two economies, reflecting differences in freight and insurance rates, duty rates, wholesale and retail trade margins, transportation costs (railway, road, water, air, and others), and import shares of each commodity in Japan and the US. Using demand-side data for purchaser's price PPPs for final demands, we estimate the producer's price PPPs for domestically produced goods.

One of the difficulties in estimating PPPs in producer's prices from demand-side data is to define PPPs for imported goods. These are required to separate PPPs for domestically produced commodities from PPPs for composite products that include imports. Using the Japan–US bilateral IOT, goods purchased in Japan can be separated into domestically produced goods, goods imported from the US, and goods imported from the rest of the world (ROW).

The purchaser's prices in Japan for goods imported from the US can be linked to prices of domestically produced goods in the US. This involves taking account of the wholesale margins and transportation costs in the US, the costs of freight and insurance required for shipment from the US to Japan, the duties levied by Japanese customs, and the margins for wholesale and retail trade and transportation costs in Japan. Similarly, import prices in the US can be linked to domestic output prices in Japan. The prices of imports in Japan and the US from the ROW are not completely observable and we develop a sub-model to determine these prices. The price level indices for domestically produced goods and composite goods are determined simultaneously within the framework of the bilateral Japan–US IOT.

A final challenge to estimation of PPPs from demand-side data is the absence of price comparisons for intermediate products like semiconductors that do not appear in final demands. Although semiconductors play a significant role in productivity comparisons, PPPs are not provided in even the most comprehensive demand-side data, the Eurostat-OECD Purchasing Power Parities. To supply the missing information, METI has carried out a *Survey on Disparities between Domestic and Foreign Prices of Industrial Intermediate Inputs* since 1994. Price differences are defined as purchaser's prices, including the difference in trade margins for intermediate goods. Using these data, the PPPs for domestically produced goods are estimated to be internally consistent based on the accounting identities in the Japan–US IOT.

13.2.3 *PPPs for outputs and intermediate inputs*

We have defined five types of elementary PPPs for each of 174 products: (1) the producer's price PPP for domestically produced goods, excluding net indirect taxes; (2) the producer's price PPP for composite goods sold to households for household final demands; (3) the producer's price PPP for composite goods sold to industry; (4) the purchaser's price PPP for composite goods sold to households; and (5) the purchaser's price PPP for composite goods sold to industry. We use the PPPs for domestically produced goods (1) for outputs, the producer's price PPPs for composite goods sold to industry (3) for intermediate goods, and the purchaser's price PPPs for composite goods sold to industry (5) for investment expenditures.

We aggregate the 174 elementary level PPPs into the thirty-six industry level PPPs for outputs, using the translog price index as of the base year 2005, equation (5) in the Appendix. The weights are the average shares of each industry's output in the two economies from the bilateral Japan–US IOT. We aggregate the elementary product PPPs to industry-PPPs for output in Japan and the US by means of a translog index. The weights are the average shares of product's output in each industry, measured in Supply/Make tables in Japan and the US. Similarly, we aggregate industry-level PPPs for intermediate inputs by means of translog indices from the 174 elementary level PPPs, using the average shares as weights.[5] Given the industry-level PPPs for gross output and intermediate inputs, the industry-level PPPs for value added are measured by a double deflation method. The PPPs

---

[5] In our comparison, all inputs of energy purchased by energy conversion sectors – petroleum refining, electricity, and gas supply – are treated as materials input, not energy inputs.

for non-market production in the government and household sectors set the Japan–US productivity gap equal to zero in these sectors.

13.2.4 PPPs for capital inputs

Our first step in measuring PPPs for capital inputs is to construct a common asset classification for Japan and the US. Our asset classification employs thirty-three assets, including three intellectual property products – R&D, mineral exploration, and software – , inventories, and land. To measure PPPs for the acquisition of each asset, we construct translog indices of the purchaser's price PPPs for the composite goods by asset. These indices are based on our estimates for elementary level PPPs for the 174 products described above. The PPPs for acquisition of inventories are assumed to be the average of PPPs for acquisition of produced goods, except for buildings and construction.

The difference in land prices between Japan and the US has a substantial impact on the PPPs for capital inputs.[6] Compared to the estimates of Jorgenson and Nomura (2007) for the benchmark year of 1990, there has been a drastic change in price level indices for land. The price of land in Japan fell sharply during the real estate price collapse of 1991 that ended the "bubble economy." Our estimate of the average price of land in 2005 is only 56.5% of that in 1990. The US land price increased substantially from the beginning of the 2000s, so that the average price in 2005 is 3.7 times higher than that in 1990. Reflecting these changes in both countries, the price differential for land between Japan and the US has decreased to 1.9 times in our new benchmark estimates for 2005, compared to 11 times in 1990. The price for acquisition of fixed assets, produced assets and land, in Japan is 1.36 times higher than that in the US in 2005 if land is included in capital input, but would be almost identical if land were excluded.

The price of a capital input is the product of the price of acquisition of the corresponding asset and the annualization factor that converts

---

[6] Nomura (2004) showed that Japan's acquisition price of land for commercial and industrial uses was 9.1 times higher than that in the U.S. in 1990. The price for capital acquisition in Japan was 2.9 times higher than that in the U.S. in 1990 if we include land in capital input, but only 24 % higher if land is excluded. Jorgenson and Nomura (2007) ignored the prices of land in measuring the productivity gaps between Japan and the U.S. although land was included in capital inputs in both countries.

the capital stock into a flow of capital services. The final step in measuring PPPs for capital inputs is to determine the relative value of the annualization factors between Japan and the US. A novel feature of our datasets for Japan and the US is that the annualization factors are measured on the basis of comparable formulations of the price of capital input, assuming asset-specific revaluations for all assets and endogenous rates of return for each industry. Tax considerations also provide a key component of the prices of capital inputs.[7]

The annualization factors are described in the appendix and estimated for 105 assets and 47 industries in Japan and 106 assets in 61 industries in the US. The estimates are aggregated into measures for the 33 assets of the Japan–US common asset classification in each industry. In 2005, the aggregate price level index for capital services was 1.14. For comparison purposes, the price level index for capital stock was 1.36 in 2005. The difference between these two price level indexes reflects divergence in measured annualization factors in the two countries, where the primary driver of this divergence is gaps in rates of return to capital across countries.

13.2.5 PPPs for labor input

In defining PPPs for labor inputs, we follow Nomura and Samuels (2003). The elementary level PPPs for labor input as of the base year PPP_{LijT} are measured as average hourly labor compensation in each labor group i in industry j, taking one dollar's worth as the unit at the elementary level. The elementary level PPPs for labor input are aggregated to the industry-level, using the translog index in equation (5) of the Appendix.

For Japanese and US datasets, the labor inputs are cross-classified by gender, age, education, class of worker, and industry. The common labor classification system for Japan and the US enables allows us to compare wages of similar workers. The US dataset has eight age classifications for workers and Japan has eleven. We choose a common classification of six age groups – under 24 years old, 25–34, 35–44, 45–54, 55–64, and over

---

[7] In measuring capital input in Japan, capital consumption allowances, income allowances and reserves, special depreciation, corporate income tax, business income tax, property taxes, acquisition taxes, debt/equity financing, and personal taxes are taken into account. The details are described by Jorgenson, Ho, and Stiroh (2005) for the US and Nomura (2004) for Japan.

65 years of age. As a common education classification, we choose four education categories – less than high school degree, high school degree, some college, and college degree and above.[8]

In both economies workers are classified as employed or self-employed and unpaid family workers. We consider only employed workers when measuring the PPPs for labor input. After cross-classifying the data by all the demographic characteristics, we have 1680 groups in total. The industry-level PPP for labor inputs are calculated as the translog index of the elementary-level PPPs.

13.3 Results

13.3.1 PPPs for output, factor inputs, and intermediate inputs

We now turn to the main results of this chapter. We estimate PPPs for value added at the industry level by a double deflation method. For this purpose, we use industry-level PPPs for gross output, factor inputs of capital and labor, and intermediate inputs of energy, materials, and services for 2005. The PPP GDP is defined as a translog index of the industry-level PPPs for value added, weighted by average industry shares of value added at current prices in the two countries. Similarly, the PPPs for factor inputs and intermediate inputs by industry are defined as translog indexes of PPPs for these inputs at the elementary level, using average industry shares as weights. Taking estimates of the PPPs for 2005 as a benchmark, we derive time-series estimates of the PPPs by extending the benchmark back to 1955 and forward to 2012, using time-series data on prices for outputs and inputs in both countries.

Table 13.1 presents our estimates of PPPs and price level indices (PLIs) for Japan relative to the US. Figure 13.1 represents the long-term trends of PPPs for output and inputs.[9] The yen-dollar exchange rate is

---

[8] In Nomura and Samuels (2003), three education categories for females were used in the common classification of labor input, due to data constraints in Japan. Nomura and Shirane (2014) have estimated wage differentials for the different education categories from the Basic Survey on Wage Structure the late 1950s and the female population shares by education in the Population Censuses.

[9] Our estimates of PPP for GDP are based on outputs, while the Eurostat-OECD PPPs presented in Table 13.1 are based on expenditures. Although the two PPP estimates are nearly identical in 2012, our output-based estimates are higher through the beginning of the 1970s and lower in the 1990s and 2000s.

Table 13.1 *PPPs and price level indices for output and KLEMS*

	1955	1960	1965	1970	1975	1980	1985	1990	1995	2000	2005	2010	2012
PPPs (purchasing power parities)													
Output (GDP)	210.2	215.1	237.0	247.3	279.4	247.3	206.8	185.1	164.3	146.3	124.9	114.0	107.3
Capital	166.6	235.7	217.9	291.2	222.4	227.2	207.9	194.4	145.7	141.9	125.0	112.7	103.2
Labor	60.7	66.2	101.5	123.6	200.2	178.4	153.3	147.7	144.6	114.1	90.4	79.2	75.4
Energy	627.4	625.1	618.9	581.6	600.6	521.3	461.1	308.9	271.9	231.1	169.1	151.3	143.8
Material	270.8	254.3	259.3	255.3	255.8	218.8	193.6	154.3	135.5	128.3	112.3	100.1	93.1
Service	175.2	168.3	197.4	206.4	259.7	246.3	205.6	181.7	163.0	142.5	122.6	108.4	103.3
GDP-expenditure based	–	170.6	204.1	226.0	266.0	245.6	206.9	189.2	174.5	155.0	129.6	111.6	104.6
Exchange rate	360.0	360.0	360.0	360.0	296.8	226.8	238.5	144.8	94.1	107.8	110.2	87.8	79.8
PLIs (price level indices)													
Output (GDP)	0.58	0.60	0.66	0.69	0.94	1.09	0.87	1.28	1.75	1.36	1.13	1.30	1.34
Capital	0.53	0.74	0.68	0.90	0.83	1.09	0.93	1.40	1.59	1.32	1.14	1.29	1.30
Labor	0.17	0.18	0.28	0.34	0.67	0.79	0.64	1.02	1.54	1.06	0.82	0.90	0.95
Energy	1.74	1.74	1.72	1.62	2.02	2.30	1.93	2.13	2.89	2.14	1.53	1.72	1.80
Material	0.75	0.71	0.72	0.71	0.86	0.97	0.81	1.07	1.44	1.19	1.02	1.14	1.17
Service	0.49	0.47	0.55	0.57	0.88	1.09	0.86	1.25	1.73	1.32	1.11	1.24	1.29

Note: The PPP for GDP-output based is defined as a translog index of industry-level PPP for value added, which is calculated by the double deflation method. The Price Level Indices are defined as the ratio of PPP to exchange rate. The PPP and exchange rate are defined by Japanese yen/ US dollar. The PPP for GDP-expenditure based is the estimate by the Eurostat-OECD.

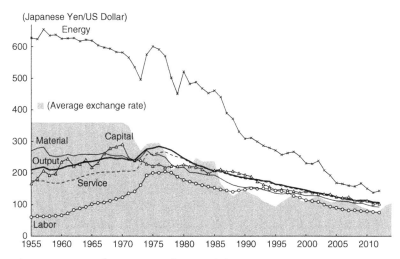

Figure 13.1 PPPs for output and KLEMS during, 1955–2012

represented as a shadow in Figure 13.1. If the PPP is higher than the exchange rate, the Japanese price is higher than the US price. Through the mid-1970s the Japanese price for output (GDP) was lower than the US price. The Japanese prices of inputs of capital, labor, energy, materials, and services (KLEMS), except for energy, were lower than the US prices as well, over this period.

Lower input prices, especially the price of labor input (only 17% of the US level in 1955), provided a source of international competitiveness for Japanese products from the 1950s until the middle of 1970s. During this period the PPP for materials was quite stable and the rise of the PPP for services was nearly proportional to the rise in the PPP for output. The PPPs for capital and labor inputs increased much more rapidly than the PPP for output. With the rise in the price of labor and the yen appreciation in the 1970s, Japan's competitiveness in international markets eroded substantially.

The end of rapid Japanese economic growth in the beginning of the 1970s provided a turning point towards a decrease in the PPP for capital input. After the mid-1970s the PPPs for all inputs began to decrease. Japan's prices of output and all inputs have continued to decline for four decades, relative to prices in the US. For two decades Japan has undergone substantial deflation and the yen has continued to appreciate.

By 1985, the yen was undervalued by 13%, based on our estimate of the PLI for GDP. After the Plaza Accord of 1985, the rapid strengthening of the yen relative to the US dollar in the late 1980s reversed this relationship, leading to an overvaluation of the yen by 28% in 1990. The revaluation of the yen continued through 1995, leading to a huge overvaluation of 75%. At that time the price of labor input was 54% higher in Japan, which posed a formidable barrier to Japanese products in international markets.

Japanese policy-makers required more than a decade to deal with the overvaluation of the yen that followed the Plaza Accord. This was accomplished primarily through domestic deflation, with a modest devaluation of the yen. The PLI for GDP in Japan, relative to the US, declined by 4.64% annually through 2007 from the peak attained in 1995. The decline in the PPP for GDP of 2.77% per year was the result of modest inflation in the US of 1.92% and deflation in Japan of 0.85%. In addition, the yen–dollar exchange rate depreciated by 1.87% per year.

Although the market exchange rate of the yen approached the PPP for GDP in 2007, the yen appreciated sharply in response to quantitative easing by the Federal Reserve that was taken in response to the financial crisis in the US. In November 2011, the market exchange rate reached 75.5 yen per dollar, the highest level since the second world war. By 2012, the PLI for GDP was 34.5% higher in Japan. In response to quantitative easing by the Bank of Japan under Governor Haruhiko Kuroda, the yen sharply declined, reaching 119.6 yen per dollar as of the end of February 2015. This is well below our estimate of the PPP for GDP of 107.3 in 2012 and has restored Japanese international competitiveness.

Figure 13.2 presents PLIs for GDP of 1.13 in 2005 and similar indices for value added in individual industries. Industry-level PLIs for gross output reflect the prices of intermediate inputs as well as value added, so that the PLI for value added is a better measure for evaluating the price competitiveness of individual industries. The second panel of Figure 13.2 gives the contribution of individual industries to the PLI for GDP. For example, Japanese agriculture and electricity and gas sectors, two industries with high PLIs for value added, pushed up the Japanese PLI for GDP by 1.4% and 1.7%, respectively.[10] However the Japanese wholesale and

---

[10] The real estate sector made the greatest contribution to the PLI for GDP. This reflects high prices of buildings and land in Japan and the large share of real estate value added in the GDP.

Figure 13.2 Industry-level PLIs for GDP, 2005

retail industry has the largest contribution to the PLI for GDP. By contrast, Japan's medical care sector in services and motor vehicles and primary metal sectors in manufacturing contributed negatively to the PLI for GDP. All three of these industries are highly competitive with their US counterparts.

13.3.2 Level indices of output, inputs, and productivity

Table 13.2 summarizes the productivity gaps between Japan and the US. This table compares level indices of output, output per capita, input per capita, and TFP between the two countries over the period

Table 13.2 *Volume level indices of output, inputs and productivity*

	1955	1960	1965	1970	1975	1980	1985	1990	1995	2000	2005	2010	2012
Output	0.084	0.125	0.172	0.259	0.302	0.328	0.348	0.381	0.372	0.316	0.289	0.272	0.263
Output per capita	0.155	0.239	0.336	0.508	0.583	0.637	0.684	0.770	0.790	0.703	0.668	0.657	0.646
Input per capita	0.341	0.431	0.563	0.694	0.780	0.789	0.797	0.843	0.886	0.803	0.781	0.788	0.781
Capital input per capita	0.173	0.215	0.334	0.443	0.574	0.607	0.619	0.704	0.794	0.709	0.649	0.638	0.637
Capital stock per capita	0.319	0.380	0.502	0.616	0.727	0.792	0.816	0.853	0.928	0.932	0.919	0.916	0.909
Capital quality	0.541	0.566	0.664	0.719	0.790	0.766	0.758	0.825	0.855	0.761	0.706	0.696	0.701
Labor input per capita	0.606	0.789	0.866	0.988	0.999	0.987	1.002	1.001	0.993	0.919	0.949	0.987	0.970
Hours worked per capita	1.051	1.288	1.308	1.391	1.298	1.225	1.210	1.172	1.150	1.042	1.061	1.097	1.090
Labor quality	0.576	0.612	0.662	0.711	0.770	0.805	0.828	0.854	0.864	0.882	0.895	0.900	0.890
TFP	0.454	0.555	0.597	0.732	0.748	0.808	0.858	0.912	0.892	0.876	0.855	0.833	0.827
Average labor productivity	0.147	0.186	0.257	0.365	0.449	0.520	0.565	0.657	0.686	0.675	0.629	0.599	0.593
Average capital productivity	0.895	1.112	1.008	1.146	1.017	1.051	1.105	1.093	0.995	0.991	1.029	1.030	1.014

Note: All figures present the relative values (Japan/US) in each period.

1955–2012. Differences in output per capita can be decomposed into differences in input per capita and differences in TFP, as defined in equation (11) in the Appendix. For example, Japanese GDP was 26.3% of the US level in 2012. GDP per capita in Japan was 64.6% of the US level, while Japanese input per capita was 78.1% and Japanese TFP was 82.7%.

Differences in input per capita in Table 13.2 result from differences in capital and labor input. In 1955 Japanese labor input per capita was 60.6% of the US level in 1955. The gap of 39.4% was the result of the lower quality of labor in Japan, reaching only 57.6% of the US level. After 1970 the lower quality of Japanese labor was largely offset by longer hours worked per capita, 39.1% longer in 1970. Subsequently, Japan has reduced hours worked per capita and improved labor quality, reducing the gap in labor quality to around 10% in 2010.[11]

Japanese capital input presents a striking contrast to labor input in that the level still remains significantly below the US. In 1955 Japanese capital input per capita was only 17.3% of the US level, but rapidly rising levels of investment in Japan during the period 1955–1973 reduced the gap to 46.3% by 1973. The gap continued to close through 1995, when Japanese capital input per capita reached 79.4% of the US level. The investment slump that followed the collapse of the bubble economy in Japan and the US investment boom of the late 1990s widened the gap to 29.1% in 2000 and 36.3% in 2012. This accounts for most of the remaining gap in input per capita of 21.9% in 2012.

Our estimates of input per capita are revised downward, relative to the study of Jorgenson and Nomura (2007), and the productivity gap has been revised upward. Our new estimate of the Japan–US gap for TFP in 1955 is 54.6%. This gradually declined over the following thirty-six years and reached a low of 7.1% in 1991, as shown in Figure 13.3. Economic growth and its sources for Japan and the

---

[11] By comparison with Jorgenson and Nomura (2007), the PPPs for labor were revised upward, reflecting the shift of the base year from 1990 to 2005 and the revision of Japanese data. Nomura and Shirane (2014) treat full-time, part-time, and temporary employees separately. The PPP for labor was revised upward from 105.0 to 114.1 yen per dollar in 2000. This revision reduced the volume and quality level indices for labor, although the volume level index for hours worked was not affected. The downward revision in the volume of labor increased the level index for TFP.

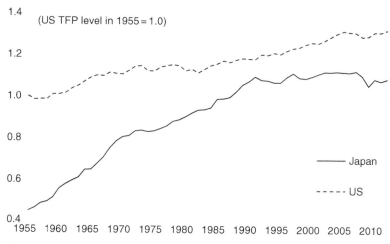

Figure 13.3 Japan–US TFP level indices

US are summarized in Table 13.3. The growth rate of TFP in Japan was 2.46% per year from 1955 to 1991. After 1991 this declined to −0.05%, slightly negative. By comparison the growth rate of TFP in the US was 0.46% per year from 1955–1991 and 0.53% after 1991.

The Japan–US gap in capital input per capita can be decomposed into the gap in capital stock per capita and the gap in capital quality. In equation (9) of the Appendix, capital quality is defined as capital input per unit of capital stock. Relative to the estimates of Jorgenson and Nomura (2007), the PPP for capital input has been revised downward, so that the level index for capita input has been revised upward.[12] Our new estimates include R&D as a capital input, following the recommendations on the treatment of intellectual property products in the *2008 SNA*. In 2005 the R&D stock at current prices accounts for 4.4% of the total capital stock, including land and inventories, in Japan and 3.7% in the US.

We have chosen 2005 as a new benchmark year and this reduces the gap in the average price of land between Japan and the US substantially. The use of benchmark year 2005 also reduces the capital quality level index, reflecting the decrease in the gap in the annualization factors for

---

[12] In 2000 the PPP for capital was revised downward from 157.4 to 141.9 yen per dollar.

Table 13.3 *Growth in aggregate value added and its sources*

	1955–60	1960–65	1965–70	1970–75	1975–80	1980–85	1985–90	1990–95	95–2000	2000–05	2005–10	2010–12	1955–91	91–2012
Japan														
Output	10.45	11.16	11.97	5.82	4.97	4.45	5.33	2.00	1.14	0.96	-0.23	0.34	7.67	0.70
Capital input	3.56	6.46	5.62	4.46	1.97	1.66	2.82	2.00	0.79	0.50	0.43	0.16	3.79	0.73
IT capital	0.09	0.17	0.21	0.23	0.13	0.19	0.37	0.22	0.37	0.46	0.30	0.16	0.20	0.32
(of which quality)	0.00	0.01	0.00	-0.01	0.00	0.01	-0.02	0.00	0.02	0.05	0.02	-0.04	0.00	0.02
Non-IT capital	3.47	6.29	5.41	4.23	1.85	1.48	2.45	1.77	0.42	0.04	0.13	0.00	3.59	0.40
(of which quality)	0.83	1.95	1.21	1.33	0.12	0.32	1.31	0.74	-0.21	-0.21	-0.02	0.13	1.04	-0.02
Labor input	2.68	1.66	2.01	0.67	1.42	1.00	0.86	0.09	-0.17	0.07	-0.06	0.17	1.42	0.02
(of which quality)	0.94	1.02	0.72	1.08	0.78	0.56	0.47	0.36	0.38	0.35	0.33	0.02	0.78	0.33
TFP	4.22	3.03	4.34	0.70	1.58	1.79	1.65	-0.09	0.53	0.39	-0.60	0.00	2.46	-0.05
Agriculture	0.63	-0.10	-0.31	0.03	-0.12	0.09	0.04	-0.07	0.06	-0.07	0.01	0.03	0.03	-0.01
IT-manufacturing	0.08	0.13	0.15	0.15	0.22	0.17	0.28	0.12	0.35	0.29	0.10	-0.03	0.17	0.19
Motor vehicle	0.17	0.11	0.27	0.04	0.24	-0.03	0.07	-0.04	0.00	0.09	-0.05	-0.05	0.12	-0.01
Other manufacturing	1.77	1.86	2.24	0.10	0.73	0.78	0.48	-0.02	0.07	0.00	-0.24	-0.37	1.12	-0.11
Communications	0.15	0.16	0.07	0.07	-0.02	0.05	0.08	0.07	0.10	0.01	0.02	0.07	0.08	0.05
Trade	0.73	1.05	0.88	0.23	0.70	0.02	0.64	0.66	-0.07	0.29	-0.39	0.04	0.62	0.06
Finance and insurance	-0.05	0.29	0.24	0.20	0.23	0.15	0.29	-0.18	0.18	0.10	-0.19	-0.12	0.18	-0.02
Other services	0.73	-0.47	0.81	-0.12	-0.40	0.56	-0.22	-0.63	-0.17	-0.31	0.15	0.44	0.13	-0.20

Table 13.3 (cont.)

	1955–60	1960–65	1965–70	1970–75	1975–80	1980–85	1985–90	1990–95	95–2000	2000–05	2005–10	2010–12	1955–91	91–2012
United States														
Output	2.51	4.78	3.74	2.74	3.31	3.29	3.51	2.47	4.40	2.79	0.96	2.12	3.33	2.71
Capital input	2.00	2.30	2.79	2.10	1.92	1.83	1.98	1.44	2.40	1.78	1.04	0.69	2.11	1.59
IT capital	0.05	0.11	0.16	0.16	0.29	0.42	0.48	0.51	1.02	0.56	0.36	0.21	0.24	0.58
(of which quality)	-0.09	0.14	0.05	0.04	0.09	0.14	0.14	0.16	0.29	0.14	0.07	0.03	0.07	0.15
Non-IT capital	1.95	2.19	2.63	1.94	1.63	1.41	1.50	0.93	1.38	1.22	0.68	0.48	1.87	1.00
(of which quality)	0.59	0.26	0.42	0.51	0.35	0.35	0.53	0.24	0.49	0.53	0.12	-0.02	0.42	0.32
Labor input	0.31	0.92	0.67	0.37	1.38	0.86	1.11	0.65	1.12	0.15	-0.01	1.04	0.76	0.59
(of which quality)	0.28	0.24	0.02	0.20	0.21	0.22	0.13	0.21	0.14	0.20	0.27	0.28	0.19	0.21
TFP	0.20	1.55	0.28	0.27	0.01	0.60	0.41	0.38	0.89	0.86	-0.07	0.39	0.46	0.53
Agriculture	0.12	0.04	0.03	0.02	-0.05	0.24	0.05	-0.01	0.07	0.02	0.00	-0.08	0.06	0.01
IT-manufacturing	-0.03	0.09	0.07	0.14	0.20	0.21	0.20	0.28	0.52	0.19	0.15	0.03	0.13	0.26
Motor vehicle	-0.04	0.12	-0.07	0.01	-0.03	0.05	-0.03	0.05	0.01	0.05	0.01	0.06	0.00	0.03
Other manufacturing	-0.14	0.60	0.15	-0.10	-0.01	0.26	0.16	0.04	0.03	0.14	-0.08	-0.08	0.12	0.02
Communications	0.00	0.05	0.02	0.04	0.14	-0.02	0.04	0.00	-0.02	0.11	0.01	-0.02	0.04	0.03
Trade	0.13	0.23	0.14	0.38	-0.08	0.34	0.15	0.21	0.48	0.21	-0.12	-0.07	0.19	0.16
Finance and insurance	0.00	-0.05	-0.09	-0.06	0.12	-0.17	-0.03	-0.02	0.12	0.08	-0.04	-0.01	-0.04	0.03
Other services	0.16	0.48	0.03	-0.15	-0.27	-0.31	-0.12	-0.17	-0.31	0.05	0.01	0.56	-0.04	-0.02

Note: All figures are average annual growth rates (%). Value added is aggregated from industry GDPs evaluated at basic prices.

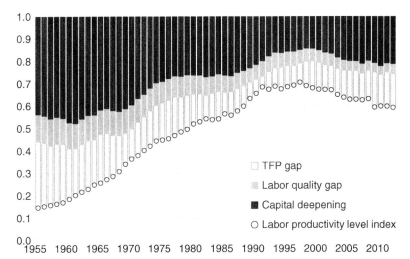

Figure 13.4 Sources of Japan–US gap in labor productivity level index

converting capital stocks to capital inputs. This decrease is due to the fall in Japan's ex-post rate of return. Japanese capital quality, relative to the US, was 54.1% in 1955. This rose to 85.5% by 1995, but declined to 70.1% of the US level in 2012.

Table 13.2 provides volume level indices for labor and capital productivity, defined as output per hour worked and output per unit of capital stock, respectively. Labor productivity in Japan was only 14.7% of the US level in 1955. The labor productivity gap closed rapidly until 1995, when Japanese labor productivity reached almost 70% of the US level. The trends in labor and capital productivity reflect relative factor supplies in the two economies. Japan has had a substantially higher labor/capital ratio than the US throughout the period. This is consistent with the low capital/labor PPPs presented in Table 13.1.

The sources of the Japan–US gap in labor productivity are shown in Figure 13.4. In 1955 lower capital deepening in Japan explained 51.2% of the Japan–US labor productivity gap, while lower Japanese TFP and lower quality of labor input explained 34.6% and 14.2%, respectively. In 2012 lower TFP explains 36.9% of the labor productivity gap, while capital deepening accounts for 52.0%. Figure 13.5 presents the sources of the Japan–US gap in capital productivity. Over the whole observation period, the gap in capital productivity was relatively small, with

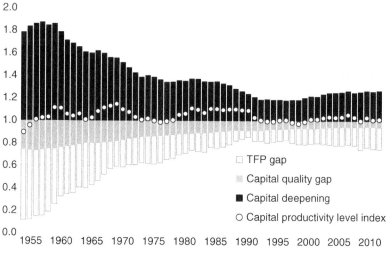

Figure 13.5 Sources of Japan–US gap in capital productivity level index

capital deepening mostly counterbalanced by the gaps in TFP and capital quality.

13.3.3 *Industry origins of Japan–US productivity gap*

Figure 13.6 presents Japan–US gaps in TFP in manufacturing and non-manufacturing sectors for the period 1955–2012. In 1955 both gaps were very large. The TFP gap for manufacturing disappeared by 1980 and the overall TFP gap reflected the lower TFP in non-manufacturing.[13] Japanese manufacturing productivity relative to the US peaked at 103.8 in 1991 and deteriorated afterward, leaving a current gap that is almost negligible. The gap for non-manufacturing also contracted from 1955 to 1991, when the gap reached 8.9%, but expanded until the end of the period in 2012.

Figure 13.7 presents industry-level TFP gap for Japan and the US in 2005 in the first panel and the contributions of each industry to the

---

[13] Cameron (2005) analyzes the convergence of Japan's manufacturing productivity to the US level and estimates the difference in TFP between Japan and the US in 1989 as 91.3. Our estimate is 102.2 in the same year. The main source the difference is that he used the PPP estimates from Jorgenson and Nomura (2007). Our new estimates are considerably revised upward relative to Jorgenson and Nomura (2007).

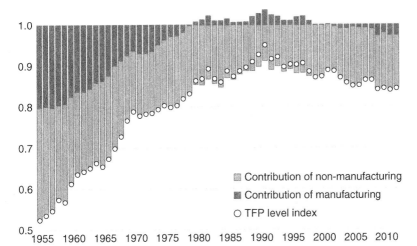

Figure 13.6 TFP gaps in manufacturing and non-manufacturing, 1955–2012

overall TFP gap for the two countries in the second panel. Industries are ordered by their contributions to the TFP gap. The contribution of each industry to the aggregate TFP gap uses Domar weights from equation (13) of the Appendix. Note that TFP gaps for public administration and household sectors are zero by definition, since the outputs of these industries consist entirely of total inputs.

In 2005, Japanese TFP exceeded that in the US for twelve of thirty-six industries included in our study, led by medical care. This industry made a contribution to Japanese TFP, relative to the US, of 4.1 percentage points. This reflects the higher output price of medical care services in the US, as shown in Figure 13.2. Other domestically oriented industries, such as wholesale and retail trade, other services, finance and insurance, construction, electricity and gas, and real estate, have much lower productivity levels than their US counterparts and made negative contributions to the overall TFP gap totaling 16.7 percentage points in 2005.

The agriculture, forestry, and fishery industry has a TFP level that is only a little more than half the level of its US counterpart. Not all of this gap can be traced to differences in the scale of agricultural enterprises or differences in the fertility of land in the two countries. One of the targets for the growth strategy proposed by the Abe Administration is to reform Japanese agricultural cooperatives. These organizations

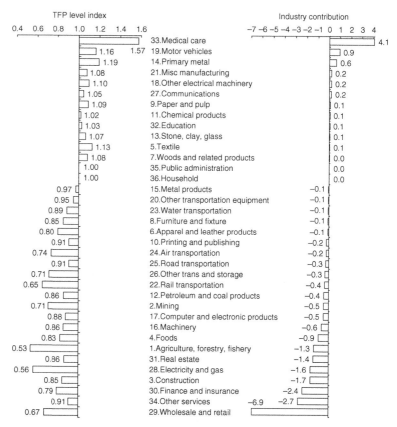

Figure 13.7 Industry origins of TFP gap, 2005

contribute substantially to the higher costs of Japanese agricultural products. In addition, the productivity differences can be traced to the fact that workers over 65 years of age make up 48.6% of the agricultural labor force, compared with 6.1% of the non-agricultural labor force in 2005, based on our labor data.

Manufacturing sectors that produce industrial materials, such as primary metal, paper and pulp, chemical products, stone, clay, and glass, and textiles, have levels of TFP similar to their US counterparts. Since the 1970s, these industries have been concentrating their resources to higher value added products that require more advanced technologies. Motor vehicles and other electrical machinery had higher levels of TFP than their US counterparts in 2005. We conclude that Japan's highly

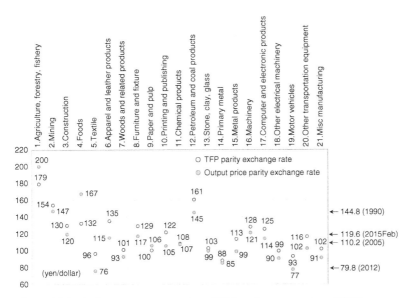

Figure 13.8 Exchange rates to parity of TFP and output prices, 2005

competitive manufacturing industries should be able to find new opportunities in both international and domestic markets under the exchange rate policies of the Bank of Japan. Efforts to improve Japanese productivity should focus on industries in trade and services that are protected from international competition. Agriculture, forestry, and fishery is a special case that will require structural reform, followed by opening to trade.

A depreciation of Japanese yen would enable Japanese producers to decrease the prices of Japan's products in US dollars. However, costs of intermediate inputs may increase directly or indirectly, due to increases in the costs of imports in Japanese yen. Figure 13.8 presents the hypothetical exchange rates required for Japan–US parity in TFP levels and output prices for tradable goods in 2005. The TFP parity exchange rate is measured as the rate that would close the Japan–US TFP gap, considering changes in the prices of output and intermediate inputs by industry.[14]

[14] In this calculation, we use the Japan–US bilateral trade structure described in the 2005 Japan–US IOT and apply the Leontief-type price model to estimate the direct and indirect increases of the intermediate costs by the change in the exchange rate. We assume the Japan–US exchange rate affects all of Japan's imports from the US and the imports from the rest of the world.

Similarly, the output price parity exchange rate is measured as the rate that would equalize prices of gross output.

For example, the TFP advantage of Japan's motor vehicle industry in 2005, 16% in Figure 13.7, would be eliminated at an exchange rate of 93 yen per dollar. The Japanese output price advantage would be eliminated at an exchange rate of 77 yen per dollar. This is almost equal to the exchange rate of 79.8 yen per dollar in 2012, before the change in exchange rate policy by the Bank of Japan. For the primary metal industry the TFP advantage and price competitiveness would disappear at 88 and 85 yen per dollar, respectively. On the other hand, Japan's agriculture, forestry, and fishery and foods industries, which have substantially lower TFP and output price competitiveness, would be equivalent to their US counterparts only at yen to dollar ratios of 200 and 167 yen, respectively.

Figure 13.9 represents long-term trends in TFP levels in Japan and the US for twelve industries that are particularly important in accounting for the productivity differences between the two countries. Productivity levels in each industry are normalized to the US productivity level in 1955. In 1955 the TFP level in Japan's agriculture, forestry, and fishery industry was only slightly below that of the US, but the TFP gap widened dramatically after 1973, reflecting differences in the scale of individual production units, as well as massive public investments in new agricultural technology in the US. Construction showed declining productivity trends in both economies. We find an acceleration of the decline in Japan after the collapse of the "bubble economy" in Japan at the beginning of the 1990s, but productivity growth has recently recovered in both countries.

The US started with an early lead in chemical products but the Japanese industry achieved parity by the end of the 1980s. Relative productivity levels have been very similar over the following two decades with Japan emerging with a slight lead in 2005. Computer and electronic products is the IT-producing sector. The Japanese industry led its US counterpart until the US IT investment boom of the late 1990s. The US rate of productivity growth in US industry accelerated sharply and the US lead in productivity expanded considerably until the deceleration of US productivity growth in the early 2000s.[15] In other

---

[15] The acceleration in US productivity growth in IT production and subsequent deceleration is discussed by Jorgenson, Ho, and Samuels (2015).

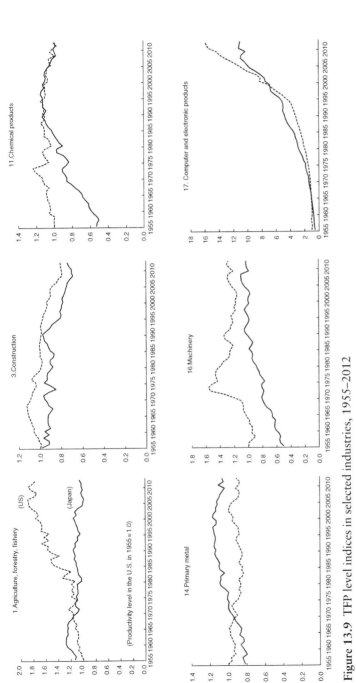

Figure 13.9 TFP level indices in selected industries, 1955–2012

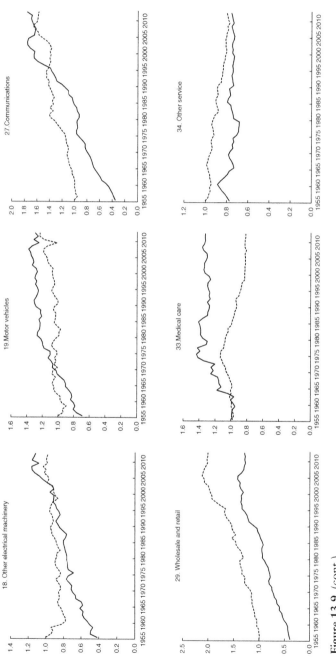

Figure 13.9 (cont.)

electrical machinery the US started with an early lead but the Japanese industry achieved parity in the early 2000s.

The Japanese motor vehicles industry has led its US counterpart since the early 1970s. Although the TFP gap has been fairly constant since the 1980s, the growth of TFP in the US industry has revived dramatically after the financial and economic crisis of 2007–2009. The Japanese communications industry first achieved parity with the US industry in the mid-1990s, but established a sizable lead beginning in the early 2000s, when a policy of competition was implemented in Japan's communications market. This lead disappeared in the late 2000s, due to a decline of TFP in Japan and an improvement in US industry, but the Japanese lead has expanded again in the early 2010s.

Wholesale and retail trade has contributed to the relatively higher TFP in the US since 1955. The TFP gap has widened dramatically since the end of the 1990s, due to a slump in TFP growth in Japan and an acceleration of TFP growth in the US. One possible explanation of the difference in TFP growth could be differences in the effectiveness of using IT between the two countries. In medical care the TFP levels were almost the same between Japan and the US in the 1950s and 1960s. Since the mid-1970s the TFP gap has widened substantially, mainly due to a steady decline in TFP in US industry and a stable TFP level in Japan. A gap of more than 50% has opened up since the end of 1990s. Other services has undergone a steady decline in TFP in both economies, but the US lead is gradually diminishing.

13.4 Conclusions

In this chapter we have analyzed the Trans-Pacific competition between Japan and the US over more than half a century. This has been feasible due to the high quality of economic statistics in both countries, the result of decades of effort by many economic statisticians. Price level indices enable us to summarize international competitiveness of Japanese and US industries at different points of time very succinctly. These indices incorporate purchasing power parities between the two countries as well as the market exchange rate of the Japanese yen versus the US dollar.

Variations in the yen–dollar exchange rate have resulted in substantial fluctuations in international competitiveness between Japan and the US over the period 1955–2012. During the first half of this period, ending with the Plaza Accord of 1985, the yen was undervalued relative to the dollar and many Japanese industries involved in international markets became competitive with their US counterparts. This provided an opportunity for Japan to grow rapidly through mobilization of its high quality labor force, high rates of capital formation, and improvements in productivity.

Although the period of double-digit growth in Japan ended with the first oil shock of 1973, the Japanese economy continued to grow more rapidly than the US until the collapse of the "bubble economy" in Japan in the early 1990s. The overvaluation of the yen relative to the dollar after the Plaza Accord reached a peak in 1995 and led to a drastic decline in the international competitiveness of Japanese industries. This precipitated a decline in Japanese exports and a slowdown in economic growth. The slowdown began as a Lost Decade and has now stretched into more than two decades, marked by a much lower rate of capital formation, much slower growth in labor input, and the disappearance of productivity growth.

Price level indices for Japan and the US have real counterparts in the productivity gaps between the two countries. In 1955, almost immediately after Japan recovered sovereignty in 1952, the productivity gap between Japan and US was more than 50%. This gap closed gradually for more than three decades and Japan nearly achieved parity with the US in 1991. Over the following two decades productivity growth in Japan languished, while US productivity growth slightly accelerated. The Japan–US productivity gap reversed course and has now reached levels that prevailed during the early 1980s.

A major contribution of this chapter is to trace the Japan–US productivity gap to its sources at the level of individual industries. Productivity gaps for Japanese and US manufacturing industries, especially those involved in materials processing rather than assembly, are relatively small. The Japanese motor vehicles industry has had a higher level of productivity than its US counterpart since the 1970s, but the productivity gap has almost closed after the drastic reorganization of US industry in the aftermath of the US financial and economic crisis of 2007–2009.

Two industries stand out as opportunities for improvements in productivity. Medical care in Japan has had a stable level of productivity since the mid-1970s, while the medical care industry in the US has had consistently declining productivity. No doubt substantial improvements are possible in the measurement of outputs in the Japanese and US medical care industries. However, our conclusion about declining US productivity is unlikely to be affected. Resumption in productivity growth in medical care in the US appears to be feasible and would help to relieve much of the budgetary pressure from rapidly growing cost of health care benefits at every level of the US government.

The Japanese agriculture, forestry, and fishery industry has had very little productivity growth since the mid-1970s, while its US counterpart has achieved consistent and relatively high rates of productivity growth. This industry has been targeted by the Abe Administration as a potential opportunity for rapid productivity growth in Japan. This will require major institutional reform, beginning with the Japanese system of agricultural co-operatives. These co-operatives have added enormously to the costs of agricultural production and distribution in Japan and have undermined growth in Japanese standards of living. A reformed agricultural industry could participate in international trade under the Trans-Pacific Partnership agreement now under negotiation between Japan, the US, and ten other countries of the Asia-Pacific region.

The final opportunity for Japan is the six industries that are largely insulated from international competition – real estate, electricity and gas, construction, other services, finance and insurance, and wholesale and retail trade. These industries are largely insulated from domestic competition through government regulation of pricing and entry. The Abe Administration has already directed attention to the electric and gas utilities. Large opportunities remain to improve productivity by removing the barriers to entry in the remaining five industries and eliminating regulations to limit price competition.

We conclude that a half century of Trans-Pacific competition has produced enormous benefits for Japan and the US. However, the two Lost Decades in Japan and the financial and economic crisis that began in the United States in 2007–2009 have created important new opportunities. The successful creation of a Trans-Pacific Partnership through co-operation in international trade and investment will be an important step, creating new benefits to both countries through enhanced competition. This can be combined with the domestic reforms we have outlined, providing a growth strategy for Japan that will end the Lost Decades that began almost a quarter of a century ago.

13.A Appendix

13.A.1 Elementary level price level indices

We begin with definitions of value, price, and volume for output Y and capital (K), labor (L), energy (E), materials (M), and services (S) inputs at the elementary level. The nominal value $V_{\theta ijtc}$ of industry j in country c (Japan and the US) is defined as follows:

$$V_{\theta ijtc} = P_{\theta ijtc} X_{\theta ijtc}, \tag{1}$$

where $P_{\theta ijtc}$ is the constant-quality price index and $X_{\theta ijtc}$ is the volume evaluated in each national currency unit. The suffix i represents a subscript for the elementary components in each category θ (output and KLEMS inputs). For example, the subscript i stands for the elementary level labor input, cross-classified by gender, education, and age. Although the components are different for each θ, we use the same subscript for simplicity.[16] The elementary components i are identical in Japan and the US for our comparisons of the two economies.

For level comparisons we set the unit price $P_{\theta ijTc}$ in the base year T as the unit price in each national currency unit. For example, if the US is the base economy and a "dollar's worth" is the volume unit, the price in the US is one dollar and the price in Japan is the price of the same volume in yen, say, 150 yen. This volume provides the physical unit for each component of i for both economies.

The time series of $P_{\theta ijtc}$ in equation (1) is set to $P_{\theta ijTc}$ in the base year T. We define the purchasing power parity in the base year as the ratio of $P_{\theta ijTc}$ between Japan and the US,

$$PPP_{\theta ijT} = P_{\theta ijTJ}/P_{\theta ijTU}, \tag{2}$$

---

[16] As described in Section 13.2, the number of elementary components defined for Japan and the US is 33 types of assets for capital inputs (K), 1,680 types of labor for labor inputs (L), 173 products for output (Y), and 174 products for intermediate inputs of energy (E), materials (M), and services (S).

as the purchasing power parity (PPP) at the elementary level. The PPP can be interpreted as the relative cost of purchasing a dollar's worth in each economy.

We define the Japan–US price level index (PLI) as the ratio of the PPP to the market exchange rate of the yen to the dollar. In the base year T,

$$PLI_{\theta ijT} = PPP_{\theta ijT}/e_T, \tag{3}$$

where e_T is the exchange rate in year T. If the exchange rate is 100 yen per dollar and the PPP is 150 yen per dollar, the price level index between Japan and the US is 1.5. While the PPP is independent of the exchange rate, the price level index depends on it. In our example, the price in Japan is higher than the price in the US.

The volume measure $X_{\theta ijtc}$ defined as $V_{\theta ijtc}/P_{\theta ijtc}$, provides comparable measures of the quantities purchased in Japan and the US. Thus the Japan–US volume level index (VLI) can be defined as:

$$VLI_{\theta ijt} = X_{\theta ijtJ}/X_{\theta ijtU}. \tag{4}$$

The volume level indices are independent of the exchange rate.

13.A.2 *Industry level aggregation*

To estimate comparable measures between the two economies at the industry level, we define the industry-level PPP in each category θ as of the base year T as a translog index of the elementary-level PPPs:

$$ln\ PPP_{\theta jT} = \Sigma_i w_{\theta ijT}\ ln\ PPP_{\theta ijT}, \tag{5}$$

where the weights $w_{\theta ijT}$ are the two-country average shares of the elementary components in the current value for each category.

We define the value $V_{\theta jtc}$ in industry j as the sum of the values of elementary components in each category and decompose the industry-level price and volume in two ways:

$$V_{\theta jtc} = \Sigma_i P_{\theta ijtc}X_{\theta ijtc} = P_{\theta jtc}X_{\theta jtc} = P^*_{\theta jtc}X^*_{\theta jtc} \tag{6}$$

where $X^*_{\theta jtc}$ is a simple sum of the volumes of elementary components ($\Sigma_i\ X_{\theta ijtc}$) and $X_{\theta jtc}$ is defined as the industry-level translog index of these volumes:

$$\Delta ln\ X_{\theta jtc} = \Sigma_i v_{\theta ijtc}\Delta ln\ X_{\theta ijtc}, \tag{7}$$

where the weights $v_{\theta ijtc}$ are the two-period average shares of the elementary components in the current value in each economy.

The two volume measures as of the base year in Japan are rescaled using the industry-level PPPs in equation (5),

$$X_{\theta jTJ} = X^*_{\theta jTJ} = V_{\theta jTJ}/PPP_{\theta jT,} \tag{8}$$

to be comparable between Japan and the US. The corresponding prices $P_{\theta jtJ}$ and $P^*_{\theta jtJ}$ in equation (6) are defined as the implicit price indices by $V_{\theta jtc}/X_{\theta jtc}$ and $V_{\theta jtc}/X^*_{\theta jtc}$, respectively ($P_{\theta jTJ} = P^*_{\theta jTJ} = PPP_{\theta jT}$ in the base year T).

The translog volume measure $X_{\theta jtc}$ captures the changes in the components with different marginal products in each category. For example, the substitution towards assets with relatively high service prices and high marginal products, for example, information technology equipment, is reflected as the growth of translog volume measure of capital, not in the simple sum volume measure $X^*_{\theta jtc}$. We define the quality indices of the volume and price in each category θ as:

$$Q_{\theta jtc} = X_{\theta jtc}/X^*_{\theta jtc} = P^*_{\theta jtc}/P_{\theta jtc}. \tag{9}$$

The time-series PPPs and PLIs for each category are measured by industry, using the implicit translog price index,

$$PPP_{\theta jt} = P_{\theta jtJ}/P_{\theta jtU} \text{ and } PLI_{\theta jt} = PPP_{\theta jt}/e_t. \tag{10}$$

The two volume level indices and the quality level indices (QLI) are defined as,

$$VLI_{\theta jt} = X_{\theta jtJ}/X_{\theta jtU}, VLI^*_{\theta jt} = X^*_{\theta jtJ}/X^*_{\theta jtU}, \text{ and}$$
$$QLI_{\theta jt} = Q_{\theta jtJ}/Q_{\theta jtU}, \tag{11}$$

where $VLI_{\theta jt} = VLI^*_{\theta jt} QLI_{\theta jt}$.

For example, the volume level index of capital input can be decomposed to the volume level index of capital stock, $VLI^*_{\theta jt}$, and the quality level index of capital, $QLI_{\theta jt}$. The relative measure of values at the US prices between Japan and the US, using the exchange rates, are decomposed to the price level index $PLI_{\theta jt}$, and the volume level index $VLI_{\theta jt}$.

13.A.3 *Productivity level indices*

Under the assumptions of constant returns to scale and competitive markets in both economies, the productivity gap between Japan and the US is defined as a translog index:

$$ln\ TLI_{jt} = \left(ln\ VLI_{Yjt} - \Sigma_\theta w_{\theta jt} ln\ VLI_{\theta jt}\right)$$
$$= \left(\Sigma_\theta w_{\theta jt} ln\ PLI_{\theta jt} - ln\ PLI_{Yjt}\right), \tag{12}$$

where θ includes the intermediate inputs and factor services. The weights $w_{\theta jt}$ are the average, two-country shares of these inputs in the values of output, which are equal to the values of all inputs. The measures of the industry-level productivity gaps from the price and volume data are identical by definition. We define the aggregate TFP gap between Japan and the US as the Domar-weighted average of the industry-level productivity gaps:

$$ln\ TLI_t = \Sigma_j d_{jt} ln\ TLI_{jt}, \tag{13}$$

where d_{jt} weights are the average, two-country shares of the Domar weights.

The Domar weights multiply industry productivity growth by the share of industry value added in GDP and divide by the share of industry value added in industry output. These weights capture the relative importance of the industry in GDP and the relative importance of value added in the industry's output. equation (13) provides the framework for quantifying the industry origins of the productivity gap between Japan and the US.

Finally, the productivity gaps involve prices and quantities of capital inputs. The price of capital input P_{Kijtc} from asset i in industry j in country c is defined as:

$$P_{Kijtc} = \varphi_{ijc} P_{Aijtc}, \tag{14}$$

where P_{Aijtc} represents the unit price for acquisition of a dollar's worth of assets and the coefficient φ_{ijc} is the annualization factor that transforms the acquisition price into the price of capital services. The annualization factors are constant over time periods.

The elementary level PPP for capital input as of the base year T is defined as:

$$PPP_{KijT} = \left(\varphi_{ijJ} / \varphi_{ijU}\right) PPP_{AijT}. \tag{15}$$

The key to measuring the PPP for capital input is the relative value of the annualization factor $\varphi_{ijJ} / \varphi_{ijU}$ and the PPP for the acquisition of assets PPP_{AijT}. The acquisition price is measured as the purchaser's price PPP for composite goods sold to industry, as described in Section 13.2.2. The elementary level PPPs for capital input are aggregated to the industry-level by the translog index in equation (5).

References

Cameron, Gavin. 2005. "The Sun Also Rises: Productivity Convergence between Japan and the USA," *Journal of Economic Growth*, **10**(4): 387–408.

Fukao, Kyoji. 2013. "Explaining Japan's Unproductive Two Decades," *Asian Economic Policy Review*, **8**(2): 192–213.

Hamada, Koichi, Anil K. Kashyap, and David E. Weinstein (eds.) 2010. *Japan's Bubble, Deflation, and Long-term Stagnation*. Cambridge, MA: The MIT Press.

Hamada, Koichi and Yasushi Okada. 2009. "Monetary and International Factors behind Japan's Lost Decade," *Journal of the Japanese and International Economies*, **23**(2): 200–219.

Iwata, Kazumasa and Economic Social Research Institute (ESRI) (eds.) 2011. *The Japanese Economy and Macroeconomic Policies from the Beginnings of the Bubble to the Overcoming of Deflation – What Did We Learn?* Tokyo: Saiki Printing (in Japanese).

Jorgenson, Dale W., Mun S. Ho, and Kevin J. Stiroh. 2005. *Information Technology and the American Growth Resurgence*. Cambridge, MA: The MIT Press.

Jorgenson, Dale W. and Masahiro Kuroda. 1990. "Productivity and International Competitiveness in Japan and the United States, 1960–1985." In C. R. Hulten (eds.), *Productivity Growth in Japan and the United States*. University of Chicago Press, 29–55.

Jorgenson, Dale W., Masahiro Kuroda, and Mieko Nishimizu. 1987. "Japan–US Industry-level Productivity Comparison, 1960–1979," *Journal of the Japanese and International Economies*, **1**, 1–30.

Jorgenson, Dale W. and Koji Nomura. 2007. "The Industry Origins of the Japan–US Productivity Gap," *Economic System Research*, **19**(3): 315–341.

Kuroda, Masahiro and Koji Nomura. 1999. "Productivity Comparison and International Competitiveness," *Journal of Applied Input–Output Analysis*, **5**: 1–37.

Nomura, Koji. 2004. *Measurement of Capital and Productivity in Japan*. Tokyo: Keio University Press (in Japanese).

Nomura, Koji and Kozo Miyagawa. 2015. "*The Japan–US Price Level Index for Industry Outputs*," *RIETI Discussion Paper*, Research Institute for Economy, Trade, and Industry.

Nomura, Koji and Jon D. Samuels. 2003. "Wage Differentials and Structure in Japan and the US, 1960–2000: Purchasing Power Parities for Labor Input," *RCGW Discussion Paper*, No. 28, Research Institute of Capital Formation, Development Bank of Japan.

Nomura, Koji and Hiroshi Shirane. 2014. "Measurement of Quality-adjusted Labor Input in Japan, 1955–2012," *KEO Discussion Paper*, No.133, Keio University, December (in Japanese).

Nomura, Koji and Yutaka Suga. 2013. "Asset Service Lives and Depreciation Rates based on Disposal Data in Japan," *Economic Measurement Group Workshop Asia*, Data Gaps and Economic Measurement Research, University of Tokyo.

van Ark, Bart and Dirk Pilat. 1993. "Productivity Levels in Germany, Japan, and the United States: Differences and Causes," *Brookings Papers on Economic Activity, Microeconomics*, 1–48.

14 | *Searching for convergence and its causes – an industry perspective*

ROBERT INKLAAR

14.1 Introduction

While the recent work of Piketty (2014) and others has drawn great attention to rising inequality of income levels and wealth within many countries, the rapid growth of emerging economies, such as China and India, has led to a decline in global interpersonal income inequality (Milanovic 2013).[1] Even by the exacting standard of Pritchett (1997) – the ratio of gross domestic product (GDP) per capita in the United States relative to the country with the lowest level of GDP per capita – the Great Divergence that had been ongoing since 1870 seems to have ended around the year 2000. This change in the evolution of world income distribution calls for an explanation. One area of the literature has focused on the role of industry productivity in shaping cross-country income differences, the importance of structural change for aggregate outcomes, and identifying drivers of industry productivity growth and whether these have a different impact depending on the level of technological sophistication.[2]

The contribution of this chapter is to provide a more comprehensive analysis of the industry sources of aggregate convergence. The current literature in this area gives a comprehensive coverage of industries, but only for OECD countries. This begs the question whether rich-country results are applicable to emerging economies as well. Alternatively, studies covers a wide range of countries but only for a specific sector

---

[1] The author would like to thank Dale Jorgenson for his helpful comments.
[2] See e.g. Restuccia, Yang, and Zhu (2008), Vollrath (2009), Herrendorf and Valentinyi (2012), Lagakos and Waugh (2013) and Gollin, Lagakos, and Waugh (2014) on industry productivity differences; on structural change, see e.g. Duarte and Restuccia (2010), McMillan and Rodrik (2011) and Herrendorf, Rogerson, and Valentinyi (2014) and on the moderating role of technological sophistication, see the survey of Aghion, Akcigit, and Howitt (2014).

508

of the economy, such as agriculture or manufacturing.[3] This begs the question whether a specific sector truly plays an exceptional role in explaining cross-country differences in economic performance. These shortcomings are remedied in this chapter by covering forty economies at a wide range of development levels and thirty industries making up the entire (market) economy.[4]

In the analysis in this chapter, I will first determine the importance of specific sectors and the role of structural change in accounting for the observed convergence of aggregate productivity. Second, I look at a range of variables that have been suggested to influence productivity growth and (in some cases) to do so differently depending on the industry's distance to the technology frontier. The variables considered are human capital, research and development, (high-tech) imports, foreign direct investment (FDI) and competition.[5] If a particular variable has a larger positive effect on productivity growth in industries that are more distant from the technology frontier, it may help explain convergence.

To estimate relative productivity levels, I estimate prices of industry output and inputs. The data used are comparable to those used in the most recent version of the Penn World Table (see Feenstra, Inklaar and Timmer, 2015), drawing on detailed surveys of final consumption and investment prices and estimates of relative export and import prices by Feenstra and Romalis (2014).[6] Information on the input–output structure and prices of labor and capital are based on the World Input–Output Database (WIOD; Timmer 2012).

---

[3] See e.g. Bernard and Jones (1996), Inklaar and Timmer (2009) and van Biesebroeck (2009) on industry-level convergence across OECD countries. See e.g. Restuccia, Yang and Zhu (2008), Vollrath (2009), and Gollin, Lagakos and Waugh (2014) on the role of agricultural productivity, and see Rodrik (2013) on manufacturing.

[4] Excluded are industries for which the relative output level cannot be determined separately from relative input levels, namely government, health, education, and real estate.

[5] On human capital, see Vandenbussche, Aghion, and Meghir (2006) and Ang, Madsen, and Islam (2011); on research and development, see Griffith, Redding and van Reenen (2004); on imports see Cameron, Proudman, and Redding (2005) and Keller (2004); on FDI, see Alfaro, Chanda, Kalemli-Ozcan, and Sayek (2010), Bloom, Sadun and van Reenen (2012), and Cipollina, Giovannetti, Pietrovito and Pozzolo (2012); and on competition, see Griffith, Harrison, and Simpson (2010).

[6] See e.g. World Bank (2008).

The resulting productivity estimates show that economy-wide productivity levels have moved substantially closer together between 1995
and 2011, helped by rapid productivity growth in countries like China,
India, Russia, and former Communist countries in Central and Eastern
Europe. Of the major sectors of the economy, only productivity levels
in manufacturing have moved substantially closer together while in
agriculture, services, and other goods production the dispersion of
productivity levels has changed only little. Agriculture did contribute
more substantially to aggregate convergence by shrinking in size, with
its average share in value added almost halving over the period and
declining most strongly in countries with low levels of agricultural
productivity. This points to the importance of agriculture's low productivity and high employment share in explaining cross-country
income differences.[7] Overall, structural change has contributed about
one-fifth of total convergence.

To analyze potential drivers of observed industry convergence,
I construct multi-factor productivity growth rates using data from
the Socio-Economic Accounts (SEA) of WIOD. These are KLEMS-
type productivity growth rates, except that the changing composition
of the capital stock is not taken into account. In regression analysis
including a range of productivity-influencing variables, I show that
higher spending on R&D, more imports of high-tech intermediate
inputs, and more inward foreign direct investment (FDI) are associated with faster productivity growth. However, none of these (or
any other) effects vary systematically with proximity to the technological frontier. These results are robust to measurement error in industry productivity levels and robust across major sectors of the
economy. So while we observe that industry productivity is conver-
ging across countries, we do not have a clear understanding why
convergence is taking place and why in some industries and countries
and not in others.

It should be noted that the broad country coverage of the analysis in
this chapter comes at clear cost in terms of measurement quality. First,
the comparison of industry output prices cannot be of as high a quality
as in Jorgenson, Nomura, and Samuels (Chapter 13, this volume), who
rely on more extensive and more price comparisons. More in general,

---

[7] As emphasized in Caselli (2005), Restuccia *et al.* (2008), Herrendorf *et al.* (2014),
Lagakos and Waugh (2013), and Gollin *et al.* (2014).

the data required to compare prices across countries is much less extensive than for comparing prices over time, while at the same time cross-country price differences tend to be much larger. Second, unlike in the standard KLEMS methodology, information about the asset composition of industry capital inputs could not be taken into account. As discussed in OECD (2009), this is a crucial element in measuring productive capital inputs. Taken together, this implies that the resulting estimates of, in particular, comparative productivity levels should be considered as experimental, rather than definitive. The methodological issues mentioned here will be discussed in more detail in the next section. In discussing the results and drawing conclusions, I will argue that the measurement shortcomings likely lead me to overestimate the degree of productivity convergence, while the regression-based analysis is likely to mostly unaffected.

In the remainder of this chapter, I will first lay out the methodology for measuring industry productivity levels and growth, followed by a description of the data and the results from the analysis. Following the results, I discuss where evidence on the sources of industry convergence might be found and some conclusions.

14.2 Methodology

The crucial input for the analysis of convergence is a set of industry productivity level estimates, so this section is mostly devoted to detailing the estimation of industry and aggregate productivity. A more detailed exposition of the underlying production theory is given in Inklaar and Diewert (2015). For comparing industry productivity across countries and time, consider an industry production function with outcomes for country c at time t (omitting industry subscripts for simplicity):

$$Y_{ct} = F(X_{cjt}, A_{ct}),$$ (1)

where industry output Y is produced using inputs $X_j, j \in J$ and productivity level A. The production function is assumed to be identical across countries, but following Caves *et al.* (CCD, 1982a) I assume a translog form to allow for a substantial degree of flexibility. Assuming perfect competition in factor and output markets and constant returns to scale, CCD show that relative productivity across countries can be computed as:

$$\ln(A_{ct}) - \overline{\ln(A)} = \ln(Y_{ct}) - \overline{\ln(Y)} - \frac{1}{2}\sum_{j=1}^{J}(v_{jct} - \overline{v}_j)[\ln(X_{jct}) - \overline{\ln(X_j)}],$$

(2)

where an upper bar indicates the arithmetic mean over the set of countries and years and v_{jct} is the share in total costs of input j in country c at time t. Note that this definition of relative productivity levels is specifically tailored to a multi-country setting where an important aim is that the comparison should be transitive, i.e. $\frac{A_c}{A_k} = \frac{A_c}{A_m}\frac{A_m}{A_k}$ for any set of countries c, m and k. Following CCD, this is achieved by comparing every country to a (hypothetical) average country. Furthermore, to enable a comparison of productivity levels across countries *and* at different points in time, the average of output levels, input levels and cost shares is computed over the countries and year. The approach of comparing a relative output to a relative input level is relevant more generally and is implemented also in Jorgenson *et al.* (Chapter 13, this volume). Their comparison is bilateral, between Japan and the US, which allows them to achieve a level of industry and input detail that cannot be achieved in the forty-country setting of this chapter, but theirs is another example of industry productivity comparisons based on a translog production function. I will discuss the approach to implementing equation (2) – measuring relative industry output and input levels – in some more detail before turning to the data and results.

14.2.1 Industry output

Starting from input–output data (more on which below), we know the value of industry output at national prices but we need relative prices of industry output to compare the quantity of output across countries:

$$\ln(Y_{ct}) - \overline{\ln(Y)} = [\ln(V_{ct}^Y) - \overline{\ln(V^Y)}] - [\ln(P_{ct}^Y) - \overline{\ln(P^Y)}]$$ (3)

Equation (3) expresses the quantity of output in country c (for a given industry at a given point in time) as the ratio of the value of output V_{ct}^Y and the relative price P_{ct}^Y. This relative price is commonly referred to as a purchasing power parity (PPP) and it serves the same purpose as a producer price index for comparing the quantity of output of an industry over time.

Ideally, these PPPs would be based on producer price data, but the lack of dedicated survey data means that alternative approaches have been followed in the literature. When focused only on manufacturing, some have opted to use exchange rates to compare output from different countries, assuming a relative price of one (e.g. Rodrik 2013). An argument in favour of this approach is that many manufactured products are traded and thus more exposed to the pressures of the Law of One Price (LOP). But this argument is not fully convincing given the systematic deviations from LOP even for products that are internationally traded (Feenstra and Romalis 2014; Burstein and Gopinath, 2014) and the very limited trade in some manufactured products, such as ready-mixed concrete (Syverson, 2008).

The main alternative approach, that can also be applied outside manufacturing, is to use relative prices collected as part of the International Comparison Program (ICP). These prices form the basis of the GDP PPPs disseminated by the World Bank (2008, 2014) and are based on prices of consumption and investment goods and services. Relative output prices at the industry level are estimated by selecting and combining the prices of goods that are produced by each, as in Sørensen and Schjerning (2008), van Biesebroeck (2009), and Herrendorf and Valentinyi (2012). Given its broad application, it can be seen as the standard approach, yet it has drawbacks as well. For one, the prices of goods consumed or invested domestically do not take into account the prices of exported products while they are influenced by the prices of imported goods. Furthermore, final consumption and investment prices are not well-suited for comparing prices of industries that produce mostly intermediate inputs.

The most thorough recent approach to resolving these challenges is discussed in Jorgenson *et al.* (Chapter 13, this volume). They compare prices and productivity between Japan and the US and their estimates of relative output prices rely on a variety of sources, including a dedicated survey of intermediate input prices.[8] Most of this information is not available for the broader range of countries covered in this analysis, so I have to rely on ICP prices and relative prices of exports and imports. This still constitutes an improvement over most studies on industry productivity that only use ICP prices, but is some distance removed from the Jorgenson *et al.* (Chapter 13, this volume), "gold

---

[8] See Nomura and Miyagawa (2015) for details.

standard." The possible empirical implications of this will be discussed later.

I take the following approach to estimating industry output prices:[9]

$$
\ln\left(P_{ct}^Y\right) - \overline{\ln\left(P^Y\right)} = \frac{1}{2}\left(r_{ct}^Q + r_{ct}^Z + \bar{r}^Q + \bar{r}^Z\right)\left(\ln\left(P_{ct}^Q\right) - \overline{\ln\left(P^Q\right)}\right)
$$
$$
+ \frac{1}{2}\left(r_{ct}^X + \bar{r}^X\right)\left(\ln\left(P_{ct}^X\right) - \overline{\ln\left(P^X\right)}\right)
$$
$$
- \frac{1}{2}\left(r_{ct}^M + \bar{r}^M\right)\left(\ln\left(P_{ct}^M\right) - \overline{\ln\left(P^M\right)}\right), \tag{4}
$$

where Q refers to goods for domestic final consumption and investment, Z refers to goods for domestic intermediate consumption, X to exports, M to imports, and r^k refers to the share of goods category k in the value of industry output, $r_c^k = V_c^k/V_c^Y$. The r^k's sum to one, satisfying the equality between the value of products supplied – through production or imports – and the value of products used – through (intermediate or final) consumption and investment. Note that only prices for final consumption and investment are available, necessitating the assumption that prices of products for intermediate consumption equal prices for final consumption. Despite this simplifying assumption, equation (4) represents an important step forward by not having to assume that prices of exported and imported products equal the prices of final consumption and investment.

14.2.2 Industry inputs

Gross output of an industry is produced using factor inputs – capital and labor – and intermediate inputs. Following equation (3) for the relative quantity of output, the value of each input is combined with estimates of relative input prices. In the case of domestically produced intermediate inputs, the assumption is made that the relative price of industry output equals the relative price of an intermediate input from that industry; for imported intermediate inputs, actual price data is available. For labor, the available data allow for a distinction between three types of workers, namely high, medium, and low-skilled, each with information on their relative wage. The price of capital input is computed as the relative rental price of capital, P^K:

[9] Except for the output price of agriculture, for which direct output price data is available, see the data section for more details.

$$\ln\left(P_{ct}^K\right) - \overline{\ln\left(P^K\right)} = \left[\frac{r_{ct} + \delta_c - \dot{P}_{ct}^I}{r + \delta - \dot{P}^I}\right]\left[\ln\left(P_{ct}^I\right) - \overline{\ln\left(P^I\right)}\right], \tag{5}$$

where r_{ct} is the required rate of return on capital in country c, δ_c is the average depreciation rate, P_{ct}^I is the price of investment goods and a dot indicates a percentage change from one year to the next. The first term on the right-hand-side of equation (5) is the relative user cost of capital.

Ideally, equation (5) would be applied to individual capital assets and the resulting relative rental prices would be aggregated to an overall capital input PPP using capital compensation shares. This would be the cross-country counterpart of the capital services methodology as outlined in, for example, OECD (2009) and as applied for the Japan–US comparison by Jorgenson *et al.* (Chapter 13, this volume). This is, alas, an area where data limitations lead to a serious methodological shortcoming. While data on capital stocks and compensation by asset and industry is available for a growing number of countries, data availability is still limited and would not allow for a full coverage of countries. The possible implications of this methodological shortcoming will be discussed later. Given the lack of data on the asset composition of industry capital input for all countries, we use country-level average depreciation rates in equation (5).

14.2.3 Aggregation

With measures of relative industry output and relative industry input, industry productivity can be computed based on equation (2), which results in productivity levels on a gross output basis. These industry productivity differences have a magnified impact on the economy-wide productivity since part of the industry's output is used by other industries as intermediate inputs. Formally, Hulten (1978) showed that aggregate productivity (for the economy as a whole or for broad sectors) across N industries can be computed using Domar (1961) weights w:[10]

$$\ln(A_{ct}) - \overline{\ln(A)} = \sum_{i=1}^{N} \frac{1}{2}(w_{ict} + \overline{w}_i)\left(\ln(A_{ic}) - \overline{\ln(A_i)}\right), \tag{6}$$

---

[10] The analysis in Domar (1961) and Hulten (1978) refers to comparisons of productivity over time; equation (7) adapts this to a cross-country setting.

where $w_{ic} = V_{ic}^Y / \sum_i V_{ic}^{VA}$ or the value of gross output in industry i divided by the sum of value added (gross output minus intermediate inputs) across all N industries.

14.2.4 Productivity growth

To measure productivity *growth* based on a translog production function (Diewert 1976; Caves *et al.* 1982b), the change in productivity from $t{-}1$ to t (in a specific industry in country c) is measured as:

$$\ln(A_t) - \ln(A_{t-1}) = (Y_t) - \ln(Y_{t-1})$$
$$-\frac{1}{2}\sum_{j=1}^{J}(v_{jt} - v_{jt-1})[\ln(X_{jt}) - \ln(X_{jt-1})] \qquad (7)$$

This methodology is comparatively straightforward as the required data on changes in volumes of gross output, intermediate inputs, labor of different skill types, and capital are (more) readily available from country national accounts or other sources.

14.3 Data

The approach to estimating industry productivity levels discussed in the previous section requires data on the input–output structure of each country over time and data on relative prices that can be used to infer industry output and input relative prices. For information on country input–output structures, I make use of the World Input-Output Database (WIOD). This is a source of harmonized input–output tables, covering thirty-five industries and forty countries for the period 1995–2011. Together, these countries represent two-thirds of the world population and over 80 percent of world GDP and span much of the development spectrum, from India to the US.

The construction and features of the WIOD are described in detail in Timmer (2012) and the database is also used in Timmer, Los and de Vries (Chapter 15, this volume) to analyze the development of global value chains (GVC) on competitiveness and the labor market. The WIOD is constructed based on national supply and use tables (SUTs), combined with time series data from country national accounts to ensure consistency with trends in industry output and overall economic activity. Importantly for GVC analysis, the SUTs are combined with data on trade in goods and services. This way, it is possible to distinguish the composition of intermediate inputs not only in terms of *what* products are used, but also *where* these products are produced and, in many cases, imported from. For the purposes of this chapter, though, this level of detail is not necessary as only a distinction between domestically produced and imported intermediate inputs (from any country) is needed. Still, the fact that much effort has gone into harmonizing the industrial classifications across countries makes the WIOD ideally suited for this type of cross-country analysis.

However, a crucial difference with, for example, Timmer *et al.* (Chapter 15, this volume) is that the input–output data from WIOD is not sufficient for the analysis in this chapter as these only provide cost shares – the v_{jc} from equation (2) – and nominal output values – V_c^Y from equation (3). We additionally need information on relative prices to allow for comparisons of output and input quantities and thus relative productivity estimates. In part, these are drawn from the Socio-Economic Accounts (SEA) of WIOD. These provide information on the labor compensation and number of hours worked by workers that are high-skilled, medium-skilled and low-skilled (based on their level of education) as well as on capital stocks.[11]

For computing prices of industry output (and hence domestically produced intermediate inputs), relative prices for consumption and investment and relative prices for exports and imports are used (cf. equation (4)). Consumption and investment prices are from the International Comparison Program (ICP), run by the World Bank, and we use the three surveys covering a global sample of countries that were done in the 1995–2011 period, namely for 1996, 2005, and 2011.[12] We use the most detailed publicly available data from each of these years and map consumption and investment categories to industries. Aggregating across expenditure categories is done using the CCD index. ICP prices are based on surveys of purchaser prices rather than producer prices, which means that differences in product taxes and

---

[11] Capital compensation is determined as value added minus labor compensation. Aggregate compensation and employment data from Penn World Table (PWT) is used to extrapolate data from the final year covered in the Socio-Economic Accounts 2009 to 2011 (Timmer *et al.* 2015); note that this extrapolation is only used to update cost shares, not for estimating industry productivity growth.

[12] See World Bank (2008) for the description of the 2005 survey and results and World Bank (2014) for the 2011 results.

distribution margins would lead to a bias in industry output prices. I therefore use tax and margin data from WIOD to adjust the ICP prices.[13] For years not covered by ICP survey data, we use industry deflators to interpolate (for, say, 2007) or extrapolate (e.g. 1995) relative prices, as in Feenstra *et al.* (2015).

For three of the services industries – government, health, and education – the ICP prices do not reflect the prices paid by purchasers of theses services, since public provision or funding makes output prices hard or even impossible to observe. Instead, ICP aims to measure input prices, see Heston (2013). In our framework, this implies equal productivity levels across countries since relative 'output' prices equal relative input prices. These industries are therefore excluded when analyzing productivity differences over time. Similarly, the real estate industry is excluded as (for the most part) its output is the imputed rental cost of owner-occupied housing and the 'private households with employed persons' industry is excluded as its dominant (sometimes only) input is labor (as well as incomplete coverage across countries). The remaining set of thirty industries will be referred to as the market economy.

Relative prices of exports and imports are from Feenstra and Romalis (2014), based on quality-adjusted unit values. Quality differences are inferred using a model of demand and supply of quality as an attribute of a traded good between two countries. Demand for quality is deemed high if observed demand is high but prices are not low; supply of quality is deemed high if supply is high despite high trade costs. We distinguish between prices of imported intermediates and imported final goods using the Broad Economic Classification (BEC) system, aggregating over more detailed products using the CCD index. Final good import prices are used when estimating industry output prices (equation (4)) and intermediates import prices are used when estimating industry intermediate input prices.

In contrast to other industries, there is direct data on producer prices in agriculture, from the Food and Agricultural Organization (FAO). These have been widely used in studying productivity in agriculture, typically based on the relative prices estimated by Rao (1993).[14] For

---

[13] See Inklaar and Timmer (2014) for more details on the mapping procedure and the adjustment for taxes and distribution margins.

[14] Studies using these data are e.g. Caselli (2005), Vollrath (2009), and Restuccia *et al.* (2008).

this analysis, I collected prices and production quantities for crops and livestock directly from FAO and aggregated these to overall agriculture relative output prices for each year using the CCD index.

The relative price of capital – estimated using equation (5) – requires data on investment prices, for which ICP prices can be used directly. The required rate of return is taken as the lending rate, taken from the International Monetary Fund (IMF) *International Financial Statistics*; the depreciation rates are from PWT version 8.0, which provides country-level average depreciation rates in each year; and the investment price change is from WIOD. One drawback is that relative investment prices only cover fixed reproducible assets, so omitting land. This omission can be particularly relevant for agriculture so I also computed relative productivity using the procedure of Vollrath (2009). The results for cross-country differences in agricultural productivity over time are qualitatively similar to those presented below.

14.4 Results

14.4.1 Productivity dispersion

To frame the context of the sectoral analysis, Figure 14.1 presents the trend in market economy productivity dispersion across the set of forty countries covered in the analysis. As discussed above, the market economy refers to the aggregate of all industries except government, health, and education, real estate, and households. Each country's (log) productivity level is multiplied by the share of factor inputs to give greater weight to (e.g.) China and less to (e.g.) Cyprus.[15] The figure shows a substantial and fairly steady decline in the standard deviation, so that in 2011 it is 26 percent lower than it was in 1995.

Aggregate convergence is also found if weighting is omitted (–9%). Furthermore, the 26% decline in Figure 14.1 is both economically substantial and, using the T^3 test of Carree and Klomp (1997), statistically significant at the 10% level. Figure 14.1 also shows that the finding of convergence is a fairly continuous process so the subsequent comparison will be done by comparing the dispersion in 2011 to that in 1995. Aggregate convergence is due in part to rapidly rising productivity levels in China (increasing from 22% to 34% of the US level) and

---

[15] See Inklaar and Diewert (2015) for a more detailed exposition.

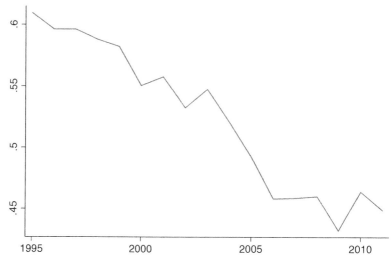

Note: Productivity dispersion is measured as the standard deviation of log productivity levels, weighted using the share of factor inputs. Market economy covers all industries except government, health, education, real estate and households.

Figure 14.1 Market economy productivity dispersion, 1995–2011

India (27% to 38%). However, big increases in relative productivity are also seen in Turkey (35% to 46%) and in Central and Eastern Europe, where big increases can be seen in countries like Estonia (35% to 49%) and Poland (42% to 54%).

To analyze the sectoral pattern of convergence and how these contribute to aggregate convergence, I follow a fairly standard split into major sectors, distinguishing agriculture, manufacturing, market services (transport, distribution, communication, hotels and restaurants, finance, and business services), and other goods (mining, utilities, and construction). Table 14.1 summarises this analysis and shows that productivity convergence is almost entirely driven by convergence in manufacturing, where productivity dispersion fell by 48%. Dispersion in agriculture and other goods was approximately constant, while market services shows an increase in dispersion.

Convergence analyses for OECD countries have typically shown that productivity in services converges more rapidly than manufacturing productivity; this was the main result of Bernard and Jones (1996) and van Biesebroeck (2009) has similar findings. In contrast, the study of

Table 14.1 *Productivity dispersion by main sectors, 1995 and 2011*

	1995	2011	% change	
Market economy	0.610	0.449	−26	*
Agriculture	0.852	0.827	−3	
Manufacturing	1.079	0.565	−48	**
Market services	0.375	0.419	12	
Other goods	0.360	0.342	−5	
Market economy at 1995 structure	0.624	0.492	−21	

Notes: Table reports the standard deviation of log productivity levels, weighted using country shares in the sample population. *(**) indicates that the indicated change is significant at the 10(5) percent level according to the T^3 test of Carree and Klomp (1997).

manufacturing productivity for a much broader set of countries by Rodrik (2013) showed clear evidence of convergence. The results in Table 14.1 suggest that the convergence of productivity in services in OECD countries is specific to that group of countries or to the time period rather than a more general results.[16] The sizeable productivity dispersion in agriculture is consistent with the broader literature (e.g. Caselli 2005) and the relative lack of convergence in this sector shows that this large dispersion is a persistent factor.

The bottom part of the table shows that structural change was an important factor for overall convergence. The line "Market economy at 1995 structure" shows how productivity dispersion would have changed if the value added shares of the thirty industries in the analysis had remained at 1995 levels throughout the period in each country. In this counterfactual case, changes in industry productivity levels would still have led to convergence but much less than actually observed: a reduction in the standard deviation of 21% rather than 26%. Structural change can thus be said to account for about one-fifth of aggregate convergence.

The agricultural sector made a positive contribution to overall convergence as the sector's share of (nominal) market economy value added decreased from an average of 8.5% in 1995 to 4.7% in 2011 and productivity dispersion in the sector is larger than for the market economy as a whole throughout the period. The role of the other

[16] See e.g. Inklaar, Timmer, and van Ark (2008) on diverging productivity growth patterns in market services across Europe and the US after 1995.

sectors is more mixed: there was a clear shift in economic activity away from agriculture and manufacturing (27.8% to 22.9%) and towards market services (50.1% to 57.4%), but the pattern of dispersion in the beginning and end of the period relative to the market economy makes the overall impact of each sector harder to gauge.

At this point, is helpful to step back and consider how the methodological limitations regarding the measurement of industry output prices and capital input prices that were detailed in the previous could affect these results. Regarding the industry output prices, I compared my detailed Japan–US industry output prices for 2005 to those reported in Nomura and Miyagawa (2015, Table 3) and used in Jorgenson *et al.* (Chapter 13, this volume). On an encouraging note, the two sets of industry output prices are positively correlated, but with a correlation of 0.54 there are also notable differences. Some of those differences will cancel out, as there are industries where I find higher relative prices and those where I find lower relative prices than Nomura and Miyagawa (2015). But overall, my estimates seem to overestimate relative industry output pries compared to Nomura and Miyagawa (2015), which would, *ceteris paribus*, lead to lower relative productivity levels in Japan relative to the US in the year 2005. This degree of overestimation of output prices seems to be larger in market services than in manufacturing.

It is harder to draw broader lessons from this comparison for my results regarding productivity convergence. For one, there is no clear pattern or systematic reason for the differences between the two sets of industry output prices, so generalizing the difference for Japan–US in 2005 to other countries and years would not be well-grounded. More generally, for the convergence results to be affected, the degree of overestimation of my estimated industry output prices compared with the "true" industry output prices would have to be (a) larger in manufacturing than in other sectors, (b) larger in lower-income economies, and (c) decrease over time. If all these conditions were met, the productivity dispersion in manufacturing at the start of the period would have been overestimated compared to later years and compared to other sectors, potentially overturning the "faster convergence in manufacturing" result. It is not impossible for these conditions to be met, but there is no evidence pointing in this direction.

It is possible to make a more informed assessment about the potential bias in relative productivity estimates from missing data on the asset composition of industry capital stocks based on economy-wide asset composition. The depreciation rate of structures is low compared to depreciation rates for equipment – around a 2% annual geometric rate for structures, compared to 10–35% depending on the type of equipment. As a result, structures will tend to account for a relatively large share of the value of the capital stock. This is confirmed when looking at economy-wide (weighted) average depreciation rates – as reported in the Penn World Table (Feenstra *et al.* 2015) – of, on average, 4%. Moving from a homogenous capital stock to a (more appropriate) capital services measure will give a lower weight to structures, since the user cost of capital increases with the asset depreciation rate (equation (5)). We also know that relative investment prices of equipment tend to differ less across countries than relative prices of structures (see e.g. Hsieh and Klenow 2007). This is because equipment is largely imported, while investment in structures relies heavily on local (labor) input. As a result of the Balassa-Samuelson effect, the relative price of structures will be lower in lower-income countries. Compared to the capital input prices used in this analysis, lower-income countries would tend to have higher capital services prices and thus higher productivity levels. This would mean that productivity dispersion is overstated in my results, a prediction borne out by the results of Inklaar and Timmer (2009, Table 4). In their sample of mostly high-income countries, productivity dispersion is approximately 15% lower when appropriately accounting for the asset composition of industry capital stocks. As lower-income countries grow richer, this degree of overstatement should decrease. In other words, it seems likely that some of the convergence found in my data is due to mismeasured capital input prices. It is not clear, though, that this problem would be more severe in manufacturing than in other sectors.

14.4.3 *Determinants of productivity growth and convergence*

Though the aggregate productivity convergence is clearly broad-based, Table 14.1 already showed notable differences in the pattern of convergence and divergence of the different sectors. These differences are even larger when analyzing individual industries or countries. In the median industry, productivity dispersion decreased by 21%, similar to the market economy rate but productivity dispersion in the textiles and wearing apparel industry decreased by 58%, while productivity dispersion in air transport increased by 24%. Indeed, six out of thirty industries showed divergence rather than convergence. Also, countries that show larger increases in their aggregate relative productivity levels tend to have more industries with increasing productivity levels, but the correlation is low at 0.09. This raises the question what could be driving these differences.

To answer this question, I use the following general model used broadly in the 'Schumpeterian' growth literature (Aghion *et al.* 2014):

$$\Delta \ln\left(\frac{A_{ict}}{A_{ict-1}}\right) = \beta_1 \ln\left(\frac{A_{ict-1}}{A_{it-1}^F}\right) + \beta_2 X_{ict-1} + \beta_3 X_{ict-1} \times \ln\left(\frac{A_{ict-1}}{A_{it-1}^F}\right)$$

$$+ \eta_{ic} + \eta_t + \varepsilon_{ict} \tag{8}$$

In this equation, productivity growth for industry i in country c - from year $t-1$ to year t (based on equation (7)) is explained using the proximity to the productivity frontier – the productivity level in country c relative to the productivity level of the country with the highest productivity level – (computed based on equation (2)) at $t-1$, explanatory variable X and an interaction between X and the proximity to the productivity frontier. In addition, a full set of country-industry dummies and year dummies is included. We would expect a negative coefficient for $\beta 1$, since a greater proximity to the productivity frontier implies fewer opportunities to achieve productivity growth by imitating frontier technologies.

The main interest is in coefficient $\beta 3$. If this coefficient is significantly different from zero, it implies that variable X has a different effect on productivity growth depending on the proximity to the productivity frontier. So, for example, Griffith *et al.* (2004) find that in countries that are closer to the frontier, research and development (R&D) spending contributes less to productivity growth, indicating that R&D spending helps both innovation (pushing out the frontier) and imitation (catching up to the frontier).

Table 14.2 defines and describes the set of X-variables that are considered in the analysis. The first is the share of hours worked by high-skilled workers, which according the Vandenbussche *et al.* (2006) should contribute positively to productivity growth only in settings of close proximity to the frontier since more high-skilled workers would stimulate the rate of innovation. The second is the share of high-tech imports. As the survey of Keller (2004) discusses, imports of more advanced inputs are an important source of technology transfer, so

Table 14.2 *Potential determinants of productivity growth and determinants*

Variable	Definition	Source
High-skilled	The share of university-educated workers in total hours worked	WIOD, SEA
High-tech M	Industry imports of intermediate inputs of chemicals, machinery, electronics, and transport equipment as a share of industry gross output	WIOD
R&D	Business enterprise research and development expenditure as a share of industry gross output	OECD, Eurostat
FDI	Stock of inward foreign direct investment as a share of gross output	OECD, Eurostat
Lerner	Ratio of price over marginal cost	INDICSER database

Note: WIOD, see www.wiod.org; INDICSER, see www.indicser.com.

these imports would be expected to have a greater impact on productivity growth for industries that are farther from the productivity frontier. Note that "high-tech" uses the OECD definition of high and medium-high technology industries. The third variable is R&D, which according to Griffith *et al.* (2004) would have a greater impact in industries farther from the productivity frontier since R&D helps both innovation and imitation. The fourth variable is FDI, which – again – following Keller (2004) could be a source of foreign technology and thus help growth in industries more distant from the frontier. The final variable is the Lerner index, or price–cost margin, where a higher Lerner index implies less intensive competition. As discussed in Aghion *et al.* (2014), fiercer competition would be particularly beneficial for industries close to the frontier as those industries rely more on innovation for growth and (unless competition turns too cut-throat) competition is beneficial for growth.

Given these predictions, equation (8) can be estimated for each of the variables of interest. As indicated in the equation, the regressions include dummies for each country/industry pair to account for unobserved heterogeneity and year dummies to account for common shocks. In addition, I use two further lags of the explanatory variables (so at $t-2$ and $t-3$) as instruments in a two-step generalized method of moments (GMM) procedure to reduce endogeneity concerns. Though more truly exogenous variables, such as the introduction of the European Single Market Program exploited by Griffith *et al.* (2010), would be preferable, these are typically hard to find. Finally, standard errors are clustered by country-industry pair to allow for correlation of errors within each cross-section.

Table 14.3 shows the results of the analysis. The first row shows industries that are closer to the productivity frontier grow less rapidly, though in the more limited samples for R&D (mostly manufacturing and omitting some emerging economies) and FDI (omitting some emerging economies) these are less significant. In the final column, the coefficient is not significantly different from zero and the sample covers only eight European economies after 2002. Turning to the explanatory variables, the table shows that high-tech imports, R&D, and FDI have a significant positive effect on productivity growth, but the effect does not vary depending on the proximity to the productivity frontier. In fact, none of the interaction coefficients is significantly different from zero, thus failing to contribute to our understanding of why some industries show faster convergence than others.

If the results had shown that a particular variable had a stronger effect on productivity growth for industries farther from the frontier, this would have been clear evidence that this variable enhances the rate of convergence. A more indirect way would be if that variable has a direct effect on productivity growth and takes on higher values in industries farther from the frontier. The high-tech import share is negatively correlated with the proximity to the frontier but at –0.04, the relationship is weak. In contrast, R&D intensity is positively correlated with proximity to the frontier and, at 0.11, this relationship is somewhat stronger. So, if anything, the high-tech import share is a force of convergence, while R&D would lead to divergence. However, it is unclear whether these correlations have systematic drivers or are a coincidence.

To establish the robustness of the results in Table 14.3, I have considered that the industry proximity to the frontier could be measured with error and that, due to the persistence in this variable, this is not adequately addressed by using lagged values of industry proximity. In the first sensitivity analysis, I therefore use two lagged values of the aggregate proximity to the productivity frontier as instruments for industry proximity to the frontier. These are clearly weaker instruments, as indicated by first-stage F-statistics and the pattern of results is the same.

Table 14.3 *Explaining productivity growth and convergence – regression results*

	(1)	(2)	(3)	(4)	(5)
	High-skilled	High-tech M	R&D	FDI	Lerner
Proximity to the frontier	-0.0279***	-0.0334***	-0.0174*	-0.0185*	0.0369
	(0.00765)	(0.00755)	(0.00957)	(0.0108)	(0.0310)
Explanatory variable	-0.00123	0.162***	0.852***	0.00259**	-0.101
	(0.0386)	(0.0582)	(0.329)	(0.00103)	(0.201)
Interaction	-0.0276	0.0663	-0.478	-0.00283	-0.279
	(0.0338)	(0.0430)	(0.395)	(0.00254)	(0.216)
Observations	13435	13435	5676	4398	1955
Overid. restrictions	0.727	0.404	0.129	0.197	0.0482

Notes: Each column represents a separate regression explaining productivity growth using the proximity to the productivity frontier, the explanatory variable that is identified in the column header and an interaction between the proximity to the frontier and the explanatory variable, see also equation (8) for the specification and Table 14.2 for definitions of the explanatory variables. Each regression includes country/industry dummies and year dummies and two lagged values of the independent variables are used as instruments in a two-step GMM procedure. Standard errors, clustered by country/industry pair, are in parentheses. "Overid. Restrictions" gives the p-value of the Hansen J statistic on the overidentifying restrictions of all instruments.

*** p<0.01, ** p<0.05, * p<0.1

In the second sensitivity analysis, I run the regressions for major sectors, i.e. subsets of industries rather than all industries together. Specifically, I run regressions for manufacturing, market services and other goods (including agriculture, as well as mining, utilities and construction). This provides some evidence that the impact of FDI varies with proximity to the frontier, but is unclear why FDI would have a stronger effect on productivity growth when an industry is close to the productivity frontier in manufacturing and other goods production, but a weaker effect in market services.

It is, again, useful to consider how the measurement of relative prices may influence these results. Given the regression context of this analysis, it is helpful to view this as an error-in-variables problem: I measure "true" productivity growth and proximity to the frontier with error. Inklaar *et al.* (2008) consider alternative measures of industry productivity growth and comparative levels, based on EU KLEMS data, and I can compare their measures that do not account for differences and changes in asset composition with those that do. The correlation between these two sets of measures is 0.99 for both productivity growth and comparative levels. Their sample of countries is more limited, covering mostly high-income countries, but there is no obvious reason to suspect that the measurement error from not accounting for asset composition differences and changes would be notably different in a broader sample of countries. In other words, there is little reason to suspect that using the methodologically more appropriate capital services methodology would lead to substantively different regression results.

14.5 Discussion and conclusions

In this chapter, I have analyzed productivity convergence from an industry perspective for an unusually detailed and broad set of countries and industries: forty economies across the development spectrum and thirty industries covering the market economy (i.e. excluding those industries where no sensible productivity measures could be computed). The first aim was to document the sectoral sources of aggregate convergence. Compared with the existing single-sector studies or OECD-sample studies, this analysis offers much more scope for generalizable results.

This analysis showed how only the manufacturing sector contributed to the rapid aggregate convergence. This suggests that some of the evidence showing (faster) convergence in services in OECD countries does not generalize to the current broader set of countries and more recent period. Conversely, the results are more in line with the findings of Rodrik (2013) of (unconditional) convergence of manufacturing productivity.

The second aim of this chapter was to establish why some industries show more rapid convergence than others by testing whether a variety of variables have a greater effect on productivity growth in industries that are more distant from the productivity frontier. While some variables – R&D, FDI, and high-tech imports intensity – were indeed significantly related to productivity growth, others – high-skilled workers and competition – were not. More importantly, none of the variables showed a significantly different effect on productivity growth depending on the proximity to the productivity frontier.

So where to look to better understand productivity convergence? In a volume such as this, a first point for discussion is surely more appropriate data. As I have discussed in some detail, the lack of data on the asset composition of industry capital stocks means that I cannot implement the full KLEMS methodology with a capital services approach. An implication for the convergence analysis of this measurement shortcoming is that I likely overestimate the degree of convergence. Furthermore, the industry output price comparison is based on imperfect source material, which seems to lead to notably difference relative prices than the more extensive price information used by Jorgenson *et al.* (Chapter 13, this volume) for the Japan–US 2005 comparison. This is a source of uncertainty, as the differences for one country pair in one year are hard to generalize. So especially for measuring the degree of productivity convergence, more appropriate data on industry output and capital prices are sorely needed. In the context of the regression results, though, there is likely less impact of the lack of a capital services approach in estimating productivity growth and comparative levels, as data based on EU KLEMS show very high correlations between growth and comparative level measures that do and do not apply the capital services methodology.

There are other concerns about the regressions analysis, though. It could be that the specification chosen here is not appropriate; for instance it could be that learning takes place in proportion to actual trade or investment between specific countries (e.g. Keller, 2004) instead of a common rate of learning from the frontier industry. Beyond that, a first set of alternative candidates are sector- or industry-specific regulations, such as import tariffs and other trade restrictions (e.g. Lileeva and Trefler 2010) or barriers to entry (Nicoletti and Scarpetta 2003). Other candidates are macro variables whose effects differ across industries, such as financial development (Rajan and Zingales 1998), infrastructure (Fernald 1999), or labor market institutions (Bassanini, Nunziata, and Venn 2009). A third possibility would be that a variable considered here has a different effect depending on some other variable that is related to, but not perfectly correlated with (industry) productivity. For example, Alfaro *et al.* (2010) find that FDI has a larger effect on productivity in countries with a greater level of financial development.

All these alternatives are potentially important and may provide further insights into observed convergence patterns. However, existing evidence tends to be limited in terms of countries or industries covered or obtained in empirical frameworks that make it hard to draw firm conclusions on productivity convergence. So given this state of our knowledge, the best we can do is be grateful for any productivity convergence that occurs.

References

Aghion, Philippe, Ufuk Akcigit, and Peter Howitt. 2014. "What do we Learn from Schumpeterian Growth Theory?" In Philippe Aghion and Steven N. Durlauf (eds.), *Handbook of Economic Growth*, vol. **2B**. Amsterdam: Elsevier,515–563.

Alfaro, Laura, Areendam Chanda, Sebnem Kalemli-Ozcan, and Selin Sayek. 2010. "Does Foreign Direct Investment Promote Growth? Exploring the Role of Financial Markets on Linkages," *Journal of Development Economics*, **91**: 242–256.

Ang, James B., Jakob B. Madsen, and Md. Rabiul Islam. 2011. "The Effects of Human Capital Composition on Technological Convergence," *Journal of Macroeconomics*, **33**: 405–476.

Bassanini, Andrea, Luca Nunziata, and Danielle Venn. 2009. "Job Protection Legislation and Productivity Growth in OECD Countries," *Economic Policy*, **24**(58): 349–402.

Bernard, Andrew B. and Charles I. Jones. 1996. "Comparing Apples to Oranges: Productivity Convergence and Measurement across Industries and Countries," *American Economic Review*, **86**(5): 1216–1238.

Bloom, Nicholas, Rafaela Sadun, and John van Reenen. 2012. "Americans do IT better: US Multinationals and the Productivity Miracle," *American Economic Review*, **102**(1): 167–201.

Burstein, Ariel and Gita Gopinath. 2014. "International Prices and Exchange Rates." In Gita Gopinath, Elhanan Helpman, and Kenneth Rogoff (eds.), *Handbook of International Economics, vol. IV*. Amsterdam: Elsevier, 391–451.

Cameron, Gavin, James Proudman, and Stephen Redding. 2005. "Technological Convergence, R&D, Trade and Productivity Growth," *European Economic Review*, **49**: 775–807.

Carree, Martin and Luuk Klomp. 1997. "Testing the Convergence Hypothesis: A Comment," *Review of Economics and Statistics*, **79**: 683–686.

Caselli, Francesco. 2005. "Accounting for Cross-country Income Differences." In Philippe Aghion and Steven N. Durlauf (eds.), *Handbook of Economic Growth*. Amsterdam: North-Holland, 679–741.

Caves, Douglas W., Laurits R. Christensen, and W. Erwin Diewert. 1982a. "Multilateral Comparisons of Output, Input and Productivity using Superlative Index Numbers," *Economic Journal*, **92**: 73–86.

1982b. "The Economic Theory of Index Numbers and the Measurement of Input, Output, and Productivity," *Econometrica*, **50**: 1392–1414.

Cipollina, Maria, Giorgia Giovannetti, Filomena Pietrovito, and Alberto F. Pozzolo. 2012. "FDI and Growth: What Cross-country Industry Data Say," *The World Economy*, **35**(11): 1599–1629.

Diewert, W. Erwin. 1976. "Exact and Superlative Index Numbers," *Journal of Econometrics*, **4**: 114–45.

Domar, Evsey. 1961. "On the Measurement of Technical Change," *Economic Journal*, **71**: 710–729.

Duarte, Margarida and Diego Restuccia. 2010. "The Role of the Structural Transformation in Aggregate Productivity," *Quarterly Journal of Economics*, **125**(1): 129–173.

Feenstra, Robert C., Robert Inklaar, and Marcel P. Timmer. 2015. "The Next Generation of the Penn World Table," *American Economic Review*, **105**(10): 3150–3182.

Feenstra, Robert C. and John Romalis. 2014. "International Prices and Endogenous Quality," *Quarterly Journal of Economics*, **129**(2): 477–527.

Fernald, John G. 1999. "Roads to Prosperity? Assessing the Link between Public Capital and Productivity," *American Economic Review*, **89**(3): 619–638.

Gollin, Douglas, David Lagakos, and Michael E. Waugh. 2014. "The Agricultural Productivity Gap," *Quarterly Journal of Economics*, **129**(2): 939–993.

Griffith, Rachel, Rupert Harrison, and Helen Simpson. 2010. "Product Market Reform and Innovation in the EU," *Scandinavian Journal of Economics*, 112(2): 389–415.

Griffith, Rachel, Stephen Redding, and John van Reenen. 2004. "Mapping the Two Faces of R&D: Productivity Growth in a Panel of OECD Industries," *Review of Economics and Statistics*, 86(4): 883–895.

Herrendorf, Berthold, Richard Rogerson, and Ákos Valentinyi. 2014. "Growth and Structural Transformation." In Philippe Aghion and Steven Durlauf (eds.), *Handbook of Economic Growth*, vol. 2B. Amsterdam: Elsevier, 855–941.

Herrendorf, Berthold and Ákos Valentinyi. 2012. "Which Sectors Make Poor Countries So Unproductive?" *Journal of the European Economic Association*, 10(2): 323–341.

Heston, Alan. 2013. "Government Services: Productivity Adjustments." In World Bank (ed.), *Measuring the Real Size of the World Economy*. Washington, DC: World Bank.

Hsieh, Chang-Tai and Peter J. Klenow. 2007. "Relative Prices and Relative Prosperity," *American Economic Review*, 97(3): 562–585.

Hulten, Charles R. 1978. "Growth Accounting with Intermediate Inputs," *Review of Economic Studies*, 45(3): 511–518.

Inklaar, Robert and W. Erwin Diewert. 2015. "Measuring Industry Productivity and Cross-country Convergence." Presented at the Society for Economic Measurement Annual Conference, Paris, Paper 35, July 23.

Inklaar, Robert and Marcel P. Timmer. 2009. "Productivity Convergence Across Industries and Countries: The Importance of Theory-based Measurement," *Macroeconomic Dynamics*, 13(S2): 218–240.

2014. "The Relative Price of Services," *Review of Income and Wealth*, 60(4): 727–746.

Inklaar, Robert, Marcel P. Timmer, and Bart van Ark. 2008. "Market Services Productivity across Europe and the US," *Economic Policy*, 23(53): 139–194.

Keller, Wolfgang. 2004. "International Technology Diffusion," *Journal of Economic Literature*, XLII: 752–782.

Lagakos, David and Michael E. Waugh. 2013. "Selection, Agriculture, and Cross-country Productivity Differences," *American Economic Review*, 103(2): 948–980.

Lileeva, Alla and Daniel Trefler. 2010. "Improved Access to Foreign Markets Raises Plant-level Productivity ... for Some Plants," *Quarterly Journal of Economics*, 125(3): 1051–1099.

McMillan, Margaret S. and Dani Rodrik. 2011. "Globalization, Structural Change and Productivity Growth," *NBER Working Paper*, no. 17143.

Milanovic, Branko. 2013. "Global Income Inequality in Numbers: in History and Now," *Global Policy*, 4(2): 198–208.

Nicoletti, Giuseppe and Stefano Scarpetta. 2003. "Regulation, Productivity and Growth: OECD Evidence," *Economic Policy*, 18(36): 9–72.

Nomura, Koji and Kozo Miyagawa. 2015. "The Japan–US Price Level Index for Industry Outputs," *RIETI Discussion Paper Series*, 2015-E-059.

OECD. 2009. *Measuring Capital*. Paris: OECD.

Piketty, Thomas. 2014. *Capital in the Twenty-First Century*. Cambridge, MA: Harvard University Press.

Pritchett, Lant. 1997. "Divergence, Big Time," *Journal of Economic Perspectives*, 11(3): 3–17.

Rajan, Raghuram G. and Luigi Zingales. 1998. "Financial Dependence and Growth," *American Economic Review*, 88(3): 559–586.

Rao, D. S. Prasada. 1993. "Intercountry Comparisons of Agricultural Output and Productivity," *FAO Economic and Social Development Paper*, no. 112.

Restuccia, Diego, Dennis Tao Yang, and Xiaodung Zhu. 2008. "Agriculture and Aggregate Productivity: A Quantitative Cross-country Analysis," *Journal of Monetary Economics*, 55: 234–250.

Rodrik, Dani. 2013. "Unconditional Convergence in Manufacturing," *Quarterly Journal of Economics*, 128(1): 165–204.

Sørensen, Anders and Bertel Schjerning. 2008. "Productivity Measurement in Manufacturing and the Expenditure Approach," *Review of International Economics*, 16(2), 327–340.

Syverson, Chad. 2008. "Markets: Ready-mixed Concrete," *Journal of Economic Perspectives*, 22(1): 217–234.

Timmer, Marcel P. (ed.) 2012. "The World Input–Output Database (WIOD): Contents, Sources and Methods," *WIOD Working Paper*, Number 10. See: www.wiod.org/publications/papers/wiod10.pdf.

Timmer, Marcel P., Erik Dietzenbacher, Bart Los, Robert Stehrer, and Gaaitzen J. de Vries. 2015. "An Illustrated User Guide to the World Input–Output Database: the Case of Global Automotive Production," *Review of International Economics*, 23: 575–605.

van Biesebroeck, Johannes. 2009. "Disaggregate Productivity Comparisons: Sectoral Convergence in OECD Countries," *Journal of Productivity Analysis*, 32: 63–79.

Vandenbussche, Jérôme, Philippe Aghion, and Costas Meghir. 2006. "Growth, Distance to Frontier and Composition of Human Capital," *Journal of Economic Growth*, 11(2, June): 97–127.

Vollrath, Dietrich. 2009. "How Important are Dual Economy Effects for Aggregate Productivity?" *Journal of Development Economics*, 88(2): 325–334.

World Bank. 2008. *Global Purchasing Power Parities and Real Expenditures – 2005 International Comparison Program.* Washington, DC: World Bank.

  2014. *Purchasing Power Parities and the Real Size of World Economies. A Comprehensive Report of the 2011 International Comparison Program.* Washington, DC: World Bank.

15 The rise of global manufacturing value chains: a new perspective based on the World Input–Output Database

MARCEL P. TIMMER, BART LOS,
AND GAAITZEN J. DE VRIES

15.1 Introduction

As coordination and transport costs decline, production processes increasingly fragment across borders. This has profound implications for the geographical location of production, the patterns of trade, and the functioning of labor markets (Feenstra 2010). However, national statistical systems were not designed to measure many of the transactions occurring in today's global economy. Houseman and Mandel (2015) provide an overview and identify biases and gaps in national statistics, examine the magnitude of the problems they pose, and propose solutions. As a prominent example, traditional measures of competitiveness such as revealed comparative advantage based on gross export values have lost their meaning. For example, booming exports of electronics suggest that China has rapidly improved in competitiveness since the late 1990s. But recent product case studies suggest that European, Japanese, and US firms still capture major parts of these value chains, as they specialize in high value added activities such as software, design, branding, and system integration. China and other emerging countries are mainly involved in the assembling, testing, and packaging activities, which are poorly compensated. A typical finding is that China keeps less than 4 percent of a product's export value as income for its labor and capital employed in the production process of electronic goods (Ali-Yrkkö *et al.* 2011; Dedrick, Kraemer, and Linden 2010). In today's world countries no longer compete in products. Instead they are specializing in particular activities within a global production network.

The aim of this chapter is to outline a new method and database that have been recently used to analyze the deep changes in international production. It is based on the World Input–Output Database (WIOD) which provides a global input–output table describing flows of goods and services within, as well as across, countries. In addition, it contains data on the factor content of production at the industry level for forty countries. As such the WIOD can be seen as the international equivalent of the national KLEMS databases described elsewhere in this volume. In this chapter we will summarize the main findings of our work analyzing the value that is added in various stages of regionally dispersed production processes.[1] A central concept in this line of work is the income generated in a country by participating in global manufacturing production, abbreviated by the term "GVC income" (for global value chain income). It indicates to what extent a country can compete with other nations in terms of activities related to global manufacturing. These activities take place in manufacturing industries, but also in services industries. We take this concept as a starting point to answer three main questions: how far has international fragmentation progressed? Which countries have increased their competitiveness in global production networks? And is there a change in the factor income distribution within global networks?

The chapter is organized as follows: in Section 15.2 we outline our accounting framework for value added in global value chains. We define a global value chain (GVC) of a final good as the set of all value-adding activities needed in its production. It is identified by the country-industry in which the last stage of production takes place, say the German automobile industry. A GVC includes the value added in this last industry, as well as in all other industries in the same country or abroad where previous stages of production take place. To decompose value added in production, we make use of a standard tool in input–output analysis using Leontief's (1949) demand-driven model in an international setting. New metrics of fragmentation and GVC incomes of countries and production factors are discussed. The empirical analysis is based on the WIOD, which combines national input–output tables, bilateral international trade statistics, and data on production factor requirements. A crucial characteristic of this database is the explicit measurement of national and international

---

[1] In general, research on this topic has been booming since the mid-2000s and we do not aim to provide an overview of all the work. See Amador and Cabral (2014) for an overview and references.

trade in intermediates. In Section 15.3 we discuss the major features of this database.

The remainder of the chapter outlines the main empirical findings, based on an analysis of global production of all manufacturing goods taken together, denoted by the term manufactures.[2] Section 15.4 provides an analysis of the international fragmentation of production and shows how foreign value added in production increases rapidly, in particular outside regional blocs. In Section 15.5 we analyze trends in GVC income shares across regions and major countries in the world. A major shift in production from advanced to emerging regions is established. We also show that only about half of the GVC income originates in the manufacturing sector itself, which indicates the importance of inter-industry linkages in the production of manufacturing goods. In Section 15.6 we focus more in-depth on the role of different factors of production. We show how in advanced countries GVC income generated by capital and high-skilled labor is increasing, while incomes for medium- and low-skilled workers in manufactures production decline. Section 15.7 concludes and argues for the need for a closer integration of national KLEMS-type databases in order to study global production.

15.2 Accounting for value added in global value chains

In this section we outline our new accounting method for value added in global production. It is based on information from world input–output tables to describe the international fragmentation of specific value chains. We decompose the value of a final product into the value added shares generated in all countries that contribute to its value chain. Thus, the measure does not only take into account the value added by the immediate suppliers of intermediates, but also valued added by suppliers further upstream. This can be elucidated by referring to Figure 15.1, which is an extension of a diagram in Hummels *et al.* (2001). It refers to a simplified world economy consisting of three countries and depicts a value chain of a final product for which the last stage of production takes place in country 3. We call this the *country-of-completion*. To produce it, factor inputs are needed in country 3, generating domestic

---

[2] Timmer *et al.* (2015) provides a more detailed analysis of the global automotive industry.

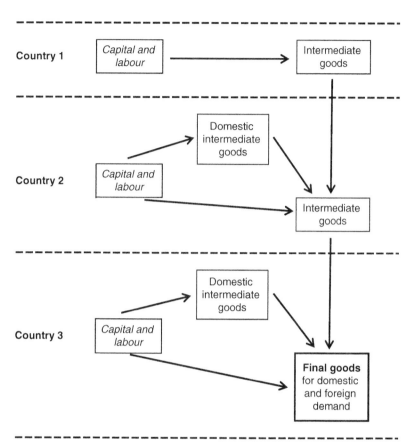

Figure 15.1 Stylized representation of an internationally fragmented value chain

value added. In addition, intermediate inputs are needed, some of which are produced within the country itself and some of which are imported from country 2. To produce these, country 2 in its turn adds value. This is not limited to the industries producing the exported intermediate products (the first-tier suppliers in the production of the final product), but also involves industries in country 2 that act as second-tier suppliers by producing materials and components that are needed for the production by the first-tier exporters. Finally, second-tier suppliers are not only located in country 2, but also in country 1, such that country 1 also adds value. Based on information of the various production linkages in the production of the final product considered, the values added by countries 1, 2, and 3 can be calculated.

More formally stated, we will study value chains of final products that are identified by the last stage of production: a particular industry i located in a specific country j, denoted by (i,j).[3] To produce good (i,j), activities in industries $l = 1, \ldots, L$ in each of the countries $k = 1, \ldots, K$ are needed. To decompose its value, we need to start with finding the levels of gross output associated with the production of (i,j). These can be estimated by applying standard input–output methods to global input–output tables. Global input–output tables contain information on the values of intermediate input flows among all country-industries in the world, as well as on the values of flows from each of these country-industries to final use in each of the countries. These tables also contain information on value added generated in each of the country-industries. Combining information on values of sales and value added per dollar of sales leads to estimates of value added in each of the SN industries as a consequence of final demand for product (i,j). For this we use an equation that has been a standard tool in input–output analysis (see Miller and Blair 2009):

$$\mathbf{g} = \hat{\mathbf{v}}(\mathbf{I} - \mathbf{A})^{-1}(\mathbf{Fe}) \tag{1}$$

In this equation, $\mathbf{g}$ is the vector of value added created in each of the LK country-industries involved in a value chain. The choice for a specific final output matrix $\mathbf{F}$ determines which value chain is considered. Final output is output delivered for household consumption and investment demand.[4] $\mathbf{e}$ is a summation vector. $(\mathbf{I}-\mathbf{A})^{-1}$ is the well-known Leontief inverse, the use of which ensures that value added contributions in all tiers of suppliers are taken into account. $\mathbf{v}$ is a vector with value added over gross output ratios, for each of the country-industries.[5] See Los *et al.* (2015a) for a technical discussion of the derivation of equation (1).

---

[3] Industries producing wholesale and retail services, and transport services industries are not considered as industries-of-completion. Our data is at basic prices and hence the margins generated by these industries in delivery to the final consumer are not taken into account (see Section 15.3).

[4] Note that all final demand for the output of (i,j) is considered, so it includes both domestic and foreign demand. Johnson and Noguera (2012) provide an analysis of value added absorbed by foreign demand, and call this value added exports. See also Los *et al.* (2015b) for an analysis of the importance of foreign demand for Chinese growth.

[5] Matrices are indicated by bold capital symbols and (column) vectors by bold lowercases. Hats denote diagonal matrices with the corresponding vector on the main diagonal.

			Final products of a global value chain, identified by country-industry of completion						Value added
			Country 1		Industry N	...	Country M		Industry N	
			Industry 1	...		...	Industry 1	...		
Value added from country-industries participating in global value chains	Country 1	Industry 1								
		...								
		Industry N								
	...	...								
	Country M	Industry 1								
		...								
		Industry N								
Total final output value										World GDP

Figure 15.2 An accounting framework for global value chains

The main result of this calculation for our purposes is that we are able to decompose the value of a final product into value added contributions in any country in the world. As we are using tables that involve all regions in the world, this decomposition is exhaustive. Denote the final output value of product (i,j) by FINO(i,j) and the value added by industry l in country k in its production by VA$(l,k)(i,j)$. The vector **g** contains the matching VA$(l,k)(i,j)$ levels for each (i,j), such that

$$\text{FINO}(i,j) = \sum_{l,k}\text{VA}(l,k)(i,j) \tag{2}$$

Summed over all countries, the value added contributions to the production of (i,j) are equal to the final output value of (i,j). This accounting scheme is illustrated in Figure 15.2 where global value chains are represented by the columns. There is one column for each final product, characterized by the country-industry-of-completion, with cells showing the origin of the value added. Note that the delivering industries are domestic as well as foreign. The sum across all participating industries in a GVC makes up the gross output value of the final product, given in the bottom row. As all final products are consumed somewhere in the world, final output values will equal global expenditure on the product. Thus the summation of final output across all columns equals world gross domestic product (GDP) which is measured from the expenditure side.

This decomposition framework allows us to define a number of interesting metrics. We define our measure of foreign value added (FVA) as all value added outside the country-of-completion j:

Table 15.1 *Value added shares in final output of automotives from Germany (%)*

Generated in	1995	2008	change
Germany	78.9	66.0	−12.8
Eastern Europe	1.3	4.3	3.0
Other European Union	11.9	14.3	2.4
NAFTA	2.5	3.1	0.6
East Asia	2.1	4.3	2.2
Other	3.3	8.0	4.7
Total	100.0	100.0	

Notes: Decomposition of final output of the transport equipment manufacturing industry in Germany (ISIC rev. 3 industries 34 and 35) based on equation (2). Eastern Europe refers to countries that joined the EU on May 1, 2004 and January 1, 2007. East Asia refers to China, Japan, South Korea, and Taiwan. Numbers may not sum due to rounding.
Source: Authors' calculations based on the World Input–Output Database, November 2013 release.

$$\text{FVA}(i,j) = \sum\nolimits_{k \neq j}\text{VA}(k)(i,j) = \text{FINO}(i,j) - \text{VA}(j)(i,j) \qquad (3)$$

Note that $\text{VA}(j)(i,j)$ is the value added domestically. To measure the importance of foreign value added, we express it as a share of all value added in the production of (i,j):

$$\text{FVAS}(i,j) = \text{FVA}(i,j)/\text{FINO}(i,j) \qquad (4)$$

We will use this share to measure the extent of international fragmentation of value chains in Section 15.4. Subsequently, we decompose $\text{FVAS}(i,j)$ into the value added share of the region to which the country-of-completion belongs, and the remaining value added share that is added outside the region.

As an example, in Table 15.1, we provide the decomposition for the final output of the transport equipment manufacturing industry in Germany, in short "German cars." The table indicates the geographical origin of the final output of German cars in 1995 and in 2008 and reveals striking developments. Between 1995 and 2008, the share of domestic value added decreased rapidly from 79 to 66 percent of the value of a German car. Value added from Eastern Europe increased. This is well documented in case studies: with the new availability of cheap and relatively skilled labor, firms from Germany relocated parts of the production process to Eastern Europe (Marin 2011). But perhaps surprisingly, value added from other countries in Europe increased by nearly the same amount. At the same time, the industry quickly globalized by sourcing more and more from outside Europe. Countries outside Europe actually accounted for more than half of the increase in foreign value added.

A second set of metrics are related to the contribution of countries to global production. It is defined as the income generated in a country by participating in global manufacturing production of a particular set of products, abbreviated by the term "GVC income" (Timmer *et al.* 2013). It answers the question of how much value a country adds to the global production of a particular set of products. Rather than looking at the columns in Figure 15.2, this metric is based on information in the rows. A particular row in Figure 15.2 provides information on the value added from a particular country-industry to all global value chains in the world. Obviously, this includes value added in the production of its own final products, but also value added to production in other GVCs, by means of delivering intermediate inputs. Note that this includes value added delivered directly to the industry-of-completion, but also indirectly through other industries. An element in the final column of Figure 15.2 provides this summation across the row and is equal to the value added in an industry.[6]

In this chapter we focus on the contribution to the global production of final manufacturing goods, denoted by the term "manufactures." Production systems of manufactures are highly prone to international fragmentation, as activities have a high degree of international contestability: they can be undertaken in any country with little variation in quality.[7] GVC income of a country is then defined as the contribution of its industries to the global production manufactures. More formally,

---

[6] Note that VA(l,k) summed across all industries in all countries equals world GDP as measured from the production side. Our accounting framework for GVCs thus obeys an important accounting convention: both the columns and the rows add up to world GDP as global final expenditure must be equal to global value added.

[7] Ideally, one would like to cover value added in all activities that are internationally contestable, and not only those in the production of manufactures. An increasing part of world trade is in services, and only (part of) intermediate services are included in GVCs of manufactures. GVCs of services cannot be analyzed, however, as the level of observation for services in our data is not fine enough to zoom in on those services that are heavily traded, such as for

$$\mathrm{GVC}(k) = \sum_{i \in manu} \sum_{l,j} \mathrm{VA}(l,k)(i,j) \tag{5}$$

The GVC income of country k in global production of manufactures is equal to the sum of value added by all its industries l to the production of all final manufacturing goods i where the last stage of production takes place in any country j in the world. Note that this includes not only activities in the manufacturing sector, but also production activities in all other sectors, such as agriculture, utilities, business services, and so on, that provide inputs in any stage of the production process.[8]

We then define world GVC income as the GVC income summed over all countries. Note that this will be equal to world expenditure on manufacturing goods as we model all regions in the world in our empirical analysis. By definition, any dollar spent on final goods must end up as income for production factors somewhere in the world. The competitiveness of a country in global production of manufactures can then be traced through expressing its GVC income as a share of world GVC income: $\mathrm{GVC(k)} / \sum_{k} \mathrm{GVC(k)}$.

15.3 World input–output database (WIOD)

Central in the WIOD is a time-series of world input–output tables. A world input–output table (WIOT) can be regarded as a set of national input–output tables that are connected with each other by bilateral international trade flows. This is illustrated by the schematic outline for a WIOT involving three countries in Figure 15.3. A WIOT provides a comprehensive summary of all transactions in the global economy

---

example consultancy services. The lowest level of detail in the WIOD is "business services," which for the major part contains activities that are not internationally traded, and hence are much less interesting to analyze from a GVC perspective This is all the more true for other services, such as for example personal or retail services. They require a physical interaction between the buyer and provider of the service and a major part of the value added in these chains is effectively not internationally contestable. More detailed data on trade in and production of services is needed before meaningful GVC analyses of final services can be made.

[8] It is important to note that GVCs of manufactures do not coincide with all activities in the manufacturing sector: some activities in the manufacturing sector are geared toward production of intermediates for final non-manufacturing products and are not part of manufactures GVCs. For example, the production of concrete for the construction industry.

			Use by country-industries						Final use by countries			Total use
			Country 1		...	Country M			Country 1	...	Country M	
			Industry 1	...	Industry N	...	Industry 1	...	Industry N			
Supply from country-industries	Country 1	Industry 1										
		...										
		Industry N										
	...	...										
	Country M	Industry 1										
		...										
		Industry N										
Value added by labour and capital												
Gross output												

Figure 15.3 Schematic outline of a world input–output table (WIOT)

between industries and final users across countries. The columns in the WIOT contain information on production processes. When expressed as ratios to gross output, the cells in a column provide information on the shares of inputs in total costs. Such a vector of cost shares is often referred to as a production technology. Products can be used as intermediates by other industries, or as final products by households and governments (consumption) or firms (stocks and gross fixed capital formation). The distribution of the output of industries over user categories is indicated in the rows of the table. An important accounting identity in the WIOT is that gross output of each industry (given in the last element of each column) is equal to the sum of all uses of the output from that industry (given in the last element of each row).

In addition to a national input–output table, imports are broken down according to the country and industry of origin in a WIOT. This allows one, for example, to trace the country of origin of the chemicals used in the food industry of country A. The combination of national and international flows of products provides a powerful tool for analysis of global production networks as will be shown below. While national tables are routinely produced by national statistical institutes, WIOTs are not, as they require integration of national account statistics across countries. It is this gap that the WIOD project aimed to fill.

The second release of the WIOD in November 2013 provides a time-series of WIOTs from 1995 to 2011. It covers forty countries, including all twenty-seven members of the European Union (as of January 1, 2007) and thirteen other major economies: Australia, Brazil, Canada, China, India, Indonesia, Japan, Mexico, Russia, South Korea, Taiwan, Turkey, and the United States (see Appendix Table 15.1 for a full list). These countries have been chosen by considering both the requirement of data availability of sufficient quality and the desire to cover a major part of the world economy. Together, the countries cover more than 85 percent of world GDP in 2008 (at current exchange rates). In addition, a model for the remaining non-covered part of the world economy is estimated, called the "rest of the world" region. To address several important research questions it is crucial to have a full model of the world economy. The values in WIOTs are expressed in millions of US$ and market exchange rates were used for currency conversion. All transaction values are in basic prices reflecting all costs borne by the producer, which is the appropriate price concept for most applications. International trade flows are accordingly expressed in "free on board" (fob) prices through estimation of international trade and transport margins.

The WIOTs have an industry-by-industry format as many applications require such a square matrix reflecting the economic linkages across industries. They provide details for thirty-five industries mostly at the two-digit ISIC rev. 3 level or groups thereof, covering the overall economy. These include agriculture, mining, construction, utilities, fourteen manufacturing industries, telecom, finance, business services, personal services, eight trade and transport services industries, and three public services industries. This level of detail was dictated by the available data, reflecting the lowest common denominator across countries. The WIOTs are built up from published and publicly available statistics from national statistical institutes around the world, plus various international statistical sources such as OECD and UN National Accounts.

The WIOD has a number of distinguishing characteristics when compared with other data initiatives.[9] First and above all, the WIOTs from the WIOD have been specifically designed to trace developments over time through benchmarking to time-series of output, value added, trade, and consumption from national accounts statistics. Second, WIOD is based on official and publicly available data from statistical institutes to ensure a high level of data quality. In particular, it is constructed within the framework of the international System of National Accounts and obeys its concepts and accounting identities. This obviously restricted the number of countries that could be covered

---

[9] See Tukker and Dietzenbacher (2013) for an overview of existing global input-output databases.

in WIOD as there is a trade-off between quality and coverage. Third, the WIOTs have been constructed on the basis of sets of national supply and use tables (SUTs) that are the core statistical sources from which statistical institutes derive national input–output tables. SUTs provide a more natural starting point for building WIOTs than national input–output tables, which are the basic building blocks in other initiatives. Input–output tables contain less information and are typically derived from SUTs with additional assumptions. Moreover, SUTs can easily be combined with trade statistics that are product-based and employment statistics that are industry-based and allow one to take the multi-product nature of firms into account. Dietzenbacher *et al.* (2013) and Timmer *et al.* (2015) discuss how the WIOD dealt with four major challenges in data construction: harmonization of basic SUTs data; derivation of time-series; disaggregation of imports by country of origin and use category, and global closure.

Fourth, apart from the WIOTs themselves, the WIOD also provides tables with underlying data and statistics that have been used to construct the WIOT. Examples are national and international SUTs, as well as valuation matrices with product-specific trade and transportation margins and net taxes. In addition, the WIOD provides data on the quantity and prices of factors inputs, including data on workers and wages by level of educational attainment and capital inputs. These data are provided in the so-called *Socio-economic accounts* and can be used in conjunction with the WIOTs as similar industry classifications are used. This greatly enhances the scope of analysis, as shown in the next section. Finally, the WIOD is as yet the only database that is publicly available and free at www.wiod.org.

15.4 Increasing international fragmentation of production

Previous studies of globalization tended to claim that international production fragmentation is mainly taking place within regional trade blocs rather than being a truly global phenomenon. This claim is often based on observations of increasingly denser networks of intermediate input flows between countries belonging to the same region (e.g. Baldwin and Lopez-Gonzalez 2013). However, gross trade flows are no longer representative of the value added flows, and the value added content of trade between countries within a region might well be lower than between countries across regions. As shown above, global value chain decompositions provide a particularly useful tool to analyze the geographical distribution of value added in production. In this section we focus on the global production of manufactures and answer the question of whether this process is mainly taking place within a regional bloc (regional fragmentation) or also involves fragmentation outside blocs (global fragmentation).

To analyze the geographical distribution of value added in the production of manufactures we use the decomposition given in equation (1) where F is chosen as one unit of final demand for manufactures coming from a given country-of-completion. For each country-of-completion we indicate the amounts of value added that originates domestically, regionally, and globally. Regional value added is all value that is added outside the country-of-completion, but in the region to which this country-of-completion belongs. Global value added is the value added in all countries outside this region. By definition the domestic, regional, and global value added shares add up to unity as in equation (4). In line with Baldwin and Lopez-Gonzalez (2013), we distinguish three major regional trading blocs: EU, including the twenty-seven member countries of the EU as of 2011; the North-American Free Trade Agreement (NAFTA) countries: Canada, Mexico, and the US; and East Asia, comprising China, Japan, South Korea, and Taiwan. While the latter region does not have an exclusive multi-lateral trade agreement among its members, it is characterized by strong international trade and investment links.

In Table 15.2 we provide decomposition results for 2008, and the change in shares between 1995 and 2008. The results for the twenty-four countries are grouped by trade bloc and sorted within blocs according to final output value. So, for example, the table shows that the final output value of manufactures in Germany in 2008 was US\$950 billion, of which 14 percent was generated within Europe but outside Germany, and 16 percent outside Europe. Since 1995, value added outside Germany has increased by 12 percentage points, of which 8 percentage points outside the EU.

The first major finding is that in all countries, except in Canada, the share of domestic value added has declined between 1995 and 2008, and in some countries even by up to 15 percentage points. Production is indeed fragmenting internationally at a fast pace. Nevertheless, the share of domestic value added is still substantial in 2008. For major countries in Europe, domestic shares are inbetween 65 to 75 percent,

Table 15.2 *Regional value added distribution of final output of manufactures by country-of-completion*

Country of completion	Final output (US$ m) in 2008	Value added shares in 2008			Change in shares (2008 minus 1995)		
		Domestic	Regional	Global	Domestic	Regional	Global
European Union							
Germany	949,854	0.70	0.14	0.16	-0.12	0.04	0.08
Italy	556,645	0.72	0.11	0.16	-0.07	0.00	0.07
France	512,973	0.69	0.15	0.16	-0.09	0.02	0.08
Great Britain	317,244	0.74	0.12	0.14	-0.04	0.00	0.04
Spain	275,311	0.68	0.15	0.17	-0.10	0.02	0.09
Netherlands	160,488	0.54	0.19	0.27	-0.10	-0.01	0.10
Poland	129,775	0.67	0.18	0.15	-0.15	0.06	0.09
Belgium	113,180	0.45	0.34	0.21	-0.10	0.01	0.09
Sweden	100,815	0.60	0.22	0.18	-0.11	0.04	0.07
East Asia							
China	1,655,179	0.79	0.05	0.16	-0.06	-0.01	0.07
Japan	938,876	0.81	0.03	0.16	-0.13	0.02	0.11
South Korea	242,766	0.59	0.12	0.29	-0.15	0.04	0.10

Taiwan	92,895	0.53	0.13	0.34	-0.14	0.02	0.12
NAFTA							
United States	1,961,475	0.80	0.04	0.16	-0.08	0.02	0.06
Mexico	321,788	0.74	0.12	0.14	-0.02	-0.04	0.06
Canada	237,253	0.68	0.15	0.17	0.00	-0.05	0.05
Other							
Brazil	380,110	0.83	0.03	0.14	-0.07	0.01	0.06
Russia	229,801	0.85	0.07	0.09	-0.02	0.00	0.02
Turkey	189,296	0.78	0.09	0.13	-0.07	0.02	0.05

Notes: Domestic, regional, and global value added shares in final output from manufacturing industry in country-of-completion based on equation (2). Regional value added includes value added by countries in the region to which the country-of-completion belongs (EU, NAFTA, or East Asia), but excludes value added in the country-of-completion itself. Global value added is the value added by all countries outside this region. By definition, domestic, regional, and global shares add up to 100 percent. For Brazil the regional value added share refers to the NAFTA countries. For Russia and Turkey the regional value added share refers to countries in the EU.

Source: Authors' calculations based on the WIOD, November 2013 release.

and higher at about 80 percent in the US and Japan. Smaller countries typically have lower domestic shares, which drop to less than 55 percent in the cases of Belgium and the Netherlands. The second finding is that value chains are becoming truly globalized: since 1995 global shares increased much faster than regional shares in all countries as more and more intermediates are sourced from outside the region. Los *et al.* (2015a) provide further evidence that this trend is pervasive across various manufacturing product groups.

15.5 Trends in GVC incomes in global production of manufactures

As shown so far, the value added contribution of countries to domestic production chains is generally declining. This also implies that their contribution to foreign value chains is increasing. To analyze a country's competitiveness one therefore has to measure its contributions to all production chains, domestic and foreign. This was defined in Section 15.2 as a country's "GVC income": the income of all domestic production factors that have been directly and indirectly used in the production of final manufacturing goods, see equation (5). These indirect contributions are explicitly accounted for through the modeling of input–output linkages across sectors. And to calculate this GVC income we choose F in equation (1) as the vector of world-wide consumption of manufactures.

Figure 15.4, Panel A, provides a comparison of the GVC incomes in advanced and emerging regions in the production of final manufacturing goods, based on equation (5). The GVC income share of advanced countries (East Asia plus the US, Canada, Australia, and the EU15) has been declining from almost three-quarters in 1995 to just above half of world GVC income.[10] Emerging regions have rapidly increased their shares, and almost all of this increase was realized after 2003. It should be kept in mind that international competition is not a zero-sum game, and declining shares do not necessarily mean an absolute decline in GVC income in a region. On the contrary, in real terms, world GVC income on

[10] One might hypothesize that shifts in the composition of global manufacturing demand in terms of the type of products being demanded might also be a determinant of the decline of the advanced nations in global manufacturing production. However, the product structure of global demand remained stable over the period 1995 to 2009.

manufactures (deflated by the US Consumer Price Index, or CPI) has increased by about one-third over the period 1995–2008. Panel B shows that the increase in the GVC income in emerging countries has always been higher than in advanced countries, reaching a peak in 2008 at a time when advanced countries' GVC income stalled. The drop in the crisis year of 2009 was large for all countries, but recovery occurred much faster in the emerging economies.

In Figure 15.5 we show the shares of regions in world GVC income in the production of manufactures for the period from 1995 to 2011. The figure plots measures for five groups of countries, namely NAFTA (Canada, Mexico, and the US); the EU, consisting of the twenty-seven EU member states; East Asia, consisting of Japan, South Korea, and Taiwan; China; and Brazil, Russia, India, Indonesia, Australia, and Turkey (BRIIAT). In Table 15.3, additional data for thirty-four major individual economies can be found for 1995, 2002, 2008, and 2011. The table shows that the share of NAFTA countries in world GVC income increased during the information and communications technology (ICT) bubble years, climbing as high as 30 percent, at which point its share was even higher than that of the EU. But it rapidly declined after 2001, reaching a low of 20 percent in 2008. The decline of the advanced nations is particularly due to the demise of East Asia, whose share has been declining rapidly since the mid-1990s. While the shares of South Korea and Taiwan are still increasing, the GVC income share of Japan has been declining rapidly. In contrast, the EU GVC income share has been relatively stable, only slowly declining over the period from 1995 to 2008. France, Italy, and the United Kingdom slowly lost some shares. The German share dropped rapidly in the latter 1990s, but stabilized afterwards. These drops were compensated by increasing shares for other EU countries, in particular the new member states. As is well known, the aftermath of the global financial crisis hit Europe particularly hard, and its share dropped sharply from 32 percent in 2003 to 24 percent in 2011. On the flip side, the share of other regions in the world rapidly increased. China is mainly responsible for the increase of the emerging countries' share, because its share accelerated after its accession to the World Trade Organization (WTO) in 2001. In 2007 it overtook East Asia in terms of share. In 2009, the Chinese GVC income share overtook that of the combined countries of BRIIAT. And in 2011 its share was higher than in the US, making it the number one country in terms of value added in global production of manufactures.

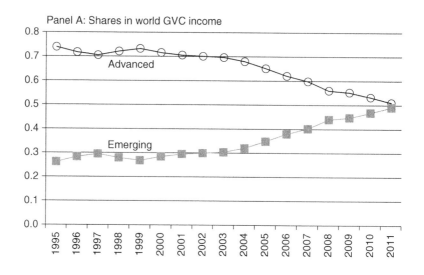

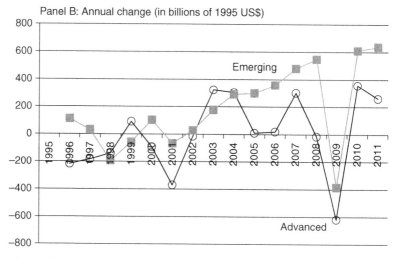

Figure 15.4 GVC incomes in advanced and emerging countries, all manufactures, 1995–2011

One might argue that these shifts in regional GVC income shares are unsurprising, given the faster growth of China and other emerging economies vis-à-vis advanced regions. Higher consumption in the home economy would naturally lead to higher GVC incomes. But this is only true to the extent that demand for manufactures has a strong

Table 15.3 *Country GVC income in production of manufactures (% of world)*

	1995	2002	2008	2011
United States	19.91	23.90	15.81	15.02
Japan	17.52	11.36	7.79	7.59
Rest of the world	11.28	11.39	14.83	15.56
Germany	9.38	7.78	7.64	6.47
France	4.44	4.24	3.79	3.09
Italy	4.39	4.38	4.07	3.15
China	4.21	7.07	12.83	16.73
United Kingdom	3.85	4.18	2.99	2.43
Brazil	2.48	1.63	3.05	3.34
South Korea	2.15	2.08	1.80	2.01
Spain	1.94	1.91	1.97	1.64
Canada	1.88	2.24	2.18	2.40
India	1.72	2.00	2.64	3.20
Mexico	1.50	2.85	2.39	2.17
Netherlands	1.43	1.29	1.37	1.16
Indonesia	1.27	1.07	1.31	1.74
Taiwan	1.26	1.26	0.84	0.83
Russian Federation	1.22	1.26	2.84	2.75
Turkey	1.11	0.90	1.41	1.28
Australia	1.03	1.02	1.29	1.52
Belgium	1.01	0.83	0.80	0.68
Sweden	0.84	0.81	0.81	0.75
Austria	0.76	0.67	0.72	0.60
Denmark	0.55	0.50	0.48	0.37
Poland	0.51	0.61	0.98	0.83
Finland	0.44	0.43	0.42	0.31
Portugal	0.36	0.33	0.31	0.25
Ireland	0.33	0.54	0.47	0.38
Greece	0.31	0.28	0.35	0.25
Czech Republic	0.22	0.32	0.48	0.40
Romania	0.18	0.18	0.37	0.31
Hungary	0.17	0.24	0.31	0.27
Slovenia	0.08	0.09	0.10	0.07
Slovak Republic	0.08	0.10	0.20	0.16

Notes: Contribution of countries to final output of manufactures in any country in the world, based on equation (5). Results for thirty-four most important countries that are covered in the WIOD. Countries ranked on share in 1995.

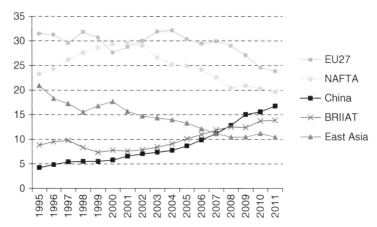

Figure 15.5 Regional shares in world GVC income, all manufactures, 1995–2011 (%)

home production bias – that is, a bias mainly geared towards goods with a high level of domestic value added. Given the high tradability of manufacturing goods, this home bias is not obvious, however. Increased Chinese demand for, say, chemicals or electronic equipment can be as easily served by imports as by Chinese domestic production. And in the latter case, a sizable share could still be captured by advanced countries through the delivery of key intermediate inputs and services. Falling shares in global GVC income for advanced regions in Figure 15.5 indicate that they failed to capture a large part of the value of the increased market for manufacturing goods in emerging economies. At the same time, the domestic value added content of their own production declined. Both trends can be interpreted as a loss of competitiveness.

A number of caveats are in order. Shares in world GVC income are expressed in US dollars using current exchange rates. For income changes over time, we deflate incomes in US dollars to the 1995 US dollar value using the US CPI. Exchange rates have fluctuated over the period considered: the dollar-to-euro rate declined sharply over 1995–2001, followed by a steep rise, which by 2007 had returned it to near its 1995 value.[11] The yen-to-dollar rate fluctuated around

---

[11] The euro was introduced in 2001. For the period before 2001, we refer here to the Deutschmark.

a long-term constant for this period. The yuan-to-US dollar rate was effectively constant over this period, slightly appreciating at the end of the 2000s. The choice of the US dollar as numéraire has no impact on the GVC income measure of a country relative to other countries. For example, calculating GVC income shares of a country in yen or euros would give identical results, but it would affect the absolute levels of GVC incomes and hence comparisons over time within a country.

Second, one has to keep in mind that the location where the value is being added is not necessarily identical to where the generated income will eventually end up. The building of global production chains is not only through arms-length trade in intermediate inputs; it also involves sizable flows of investment, and part of the value added in emerging regions will accrue as income to multi-national firms headquartered in advanced regions through the ownership of capital. What is needed is to analyze capital income on a national rather than a domestic basis as we do in this chapter. Data on foreign ownership is notoriously hard to acquire, not least because of the notional relocation of profits for tax accounting purposes. Hence, further research is needed in this area (Baldwin and Kimura 1998; Lipsey 2010). The decline in East Asian GVC income is likely overestimated, as it is also related to the off-shoring of activities to China, which effectively became the assembly place of East Asia (Fukao *et al.* 2003). Income earned by East Asian capital is allocated to the place of production (in this case China) and not by ownership. This difference is probably larger for East Asian countries than for NAFTA or the EU. The latter regions have larger within-region FDI flows, such that they net out in regional aggregate numbers presented here.

The production of manufacturing goods involves a wide variety of activities, which do not only take place in the manufacturing sector. Using the decomposition technique outlined above, one can trace not only the country but also the sector in which value is added during the production process. Typically, the value that is added by activities in the manufacturing sector itself is around half the basic price value of a good, and it declines over time as services activities are outsourced. In Table 15.4 we provide for each country the share of a sector in the GVC income related to manufactures. This is done for twenty major economies in 1995 and 2008, distinguishing between three broad sectors: (1) natural resources, including the agriculture and mining industries (ISIC Rev. 3 industries A to C); (2) manufacturing, including

Table 15.4 *Sectoral shares in total GVC income, all manufactures (% of total)*

	Natural resources		Manufacturing		Services	
	1995	2011	1995	2011	1995	2011
United States	0.06	0.09	0.56	0.52	0.38	0.39
Japan	0.04	0.03	0.65	0.61	0.31	0.36
Germany	0.03	0.02	0.61	0.56	0.36	0.42
France	0.07	0.04	0.48	0.45	0.46	0.50
United Kingdom	0.07	0.07	0.60	0.49	0.34	0.44
Italy	0.05	0.03	0.57	0.52	0.38	0.44
Spain	0.09	0.05	0.54	0.52	0.37	0.43
Canada	0.12	0.19	0.54	0.44	0.34	0.37
Australia	0.20	0.26	0.42	0.35	0.37	0.39
South Korea	0.10	0.04	0.62	0.68	0.28	0.28
Netherlands	0.11	0.12	0.49	0.43	0.40	0.45
China	0.21	0.17	0.58	0.57	0.22	0.26
Russian Federation	0.20	0.21	0.42	0.39	0.38	0.40
Brazil	0.13	0.17	0.55	0.46	0.32	0.37
India	0.22	0.18	0.42	0.42	0.35	0.40
Mexico	0.21	0.22	0.49	0.49	0.30	0.29
Turkey	0.09	0.13	0.64	0.50	0.27	0.37
Indonesia	0.22	0.30	0.61	0.54	0.18	0.16
Poland	0.15	0.10	0.53	0.49	0.32	0.42

Notes: The numbers represent the share of that sector in total value added for the production of final manufacturing products. "Natural resource" includes the agriculture and mining industries (ISIC Rev. 3 industries A to C), "manufacturing" includes all manufacturing industries (D), and "services" all other industries (E to Q).
Source: Authors' calculations based on WIOD, November 2013 release.

all manufacturing industries (D); and (3) services including all other industries (E to Q). The table shows that the share of value added in the manufacturing sector has declined between 1995 and 2008 in all countries except South Korea. The unweighted average share across all twenty countries declined from 54 percent to 50 percent. This partly reflects a shift away from traditional manufacturing activities, such as those carried out by blue-collar production workers, but also the outsourcing of white-collar activities by manufacturing firms to domestic services firms. Contributions from the natural resources sector are high and have increased over the 1995–2008 period in countries such as

Australia, Canada, Indonesia, Mexico, Russia, and Turkey.[12] This pattern of value added suggests that for resource-abundant countries, activities within manufacturing production networks are reinforcing their comparative advantage. Given its low level of development, services contribute relatively much in India, reflecting its well-developed business services sector, which delivers intermediate services to both domestic and foreign manufacturing firms. In China, the share of natural resources is declining, and activities in the services sector are starting to contribute more, but the level is still well below the contributions of services in Europe and the US. This hints towards a clear pattern of specialization in which advanced countries increasingly focus on non-production activities within manufacturing networks.

15.6 Value added by capital and labor

How much of the GVC income accrues to the various production factors? Our income data on labor and capital allow us to study which production factors have benefited from the changes in the regional distribution of global value added. Increasing trade and integration of world markets have been related to increasing unemployment and stagnating relative wages of low- and medium-skilled workers in developed regions. On the other hand, those factors have offered new opportunities in developing regions for countries to employ their large supply of low-skilled workers. To study these trends, we decomposed value added into capital and three labor types. Labor skill types are classified on the basis of educational attainment levels as defined in the International Standard Classification of Education (ISCED): low-skilled (ISCED categories 1 and 2), medium-skilled (ISCED 3 and 4), and high-skilled (ISCED 5 and 6). Data has been collected for the number of workers involved in production, including employees, self-employed, and family workers. Additional imputations of the labor income of self-employed and family workers were made to adjust for the underestimation of the labor income share in the national accounts statistics, in particular for less advanced nations (Gollin 2002). Capital income is derived as a residual and defined as gross value added minus

---

[12] The share of the natural resource sector in Russia is severely underestimated, since part of the oil and gas production is classified under wholesale services rather than under mining in the Russian national accounts. Adding the wholesale sector would almost double the natural resource share in 2008.

labor income. It represents remuneration for capital in the broadest sense, including physical capital (such as machinery and buildings), land (including mineral resources), intangible capital (such as patents and trademarks), and financial capital.

In Table 15.5 we provide a breakdown of GVC income by labor and capital for major regions. This is a breakdown of the GVC income discussed in the previous section. At the global level, the most important finding is that the share of GVC income that goes to labor is coming down, while the share of capital is increasing. In addition, medium- and low-skilled workers are losing out to high-skilled workers. The income shares for low- and medium-skilled workers dropped by about 4 percentage points over the 1995–2008 period. Income shares for high-skilled workers increased by 1.5 percentage points and for capital more than 6 percentage points. The trends appear to have changed over time. Up to the early 2000s the decline of low-skilled and increase of high-skilled shares dominated. Since then the divergent trends in medium-skilled labor and capital shares dominate, which provides suggestive evidence in favor of the routinization hypothesis. According to the "routinization hypothesis" put forward by Autor *et al.* (2003), information technology capital complements highly educated workers engaged in abstract tasks, substitutes for moderately educated workers performing routine tasks, and has little effect on less-skilled workers performing manual and services tasks. Timmer *et al.* (2014) find similar evidence for a larger set of GVCs and discuss possible reasons. Further econometric analysis is needed to disentangle effects of substitution and possible biases in technical change.

The global trend is reflected within regions. In all regions, the compensation for capital is increasing relative to labor. Particularly in emerging regions, this increase is important and occurs faster than the labor income increase.[13] This might be related to the low wage/rental ratios in these regions that were still characterized by an abundant surplus of low-skilled workers from agricultural and informal urban sectors. In advanced

---

[13] It is important to note that the share captured by capital in emerging markets is known to be overestimated. Our approach is based on domestic production accounting for the location of the production factor and is silent on the ownership, as discussed before. In the case of labor income, this is unproblematic, as for most countries cross-border labor migration is relatively minor. Hence labor income paid out in a particular country mostly benefits the workers of the country in which production takes place.

Table 15.5 *GVC income by production factor and region (shares in world GVC income)*

	Value-added by labor		Value-added by capital		Value-added total	
	1995	2011	1995	2011	1995	2011
EU 27	21.7	19.1	9.8	9.9	31.5	29
US	12.0	8.9	7.9	6.9	19.9	15.8
East Asia	12.9	6.0	8.1	4.5	20.9	10.4
China	2.1	5.1	2.1	7.7	4.2	12.8
BRIIMT	4.1	6.2	5.2	7.5	9.3	13.6
Other	6.3	7.4	7.9	10.9	14.2	18.3
World	59.1	52.6	40.9	47.4	100	100
Advanced	46.6	34	25.7	21.2	72.3	55.2
Emerging	12.5	18.6	15.2	26.1	27.7	44.8

	Value-added by high-skilled		Value-added by medium-skilled		Value-added by low-skilled	
	1995	2011	1995	2011	1995	2011
EU 27	4.9	6.1	10.1	9.0	6.7	4.0
US	4.1	3.9	6.9	4.5	1.0	0.5
East Asia	3.2	2.1	7.1	3.2	2.5	0.6
China	0.1	0.4	0.7	1.8	1.3	2.9
BRIIMT	0.8	1.4	1.7	3.0	1.7	1.7
Other	0.8	1.4	2.2	2.9	3.3	3
World	13.8	15.4	28.7	24.4	16.6	12.8
Advanced	12.3	12.1	24.1	16.7	10.2	5.1
Emerging	1.6	3.2	4.6	7.7	6.4	7.7

Notes: "East Asia" includes Japan, South Korea, and Taiwan. "EU 27" designates the countries that had joined the EU by Januar 1, 2007. "BRIIMT" includes Brazil, Russia, Indonesia, India, Mexico, and Turkey. "Other" is the rest of the world. Skill categories classify workers by their educational attainment levels. World income is equal to world expenditures on manufacturing products at basic prices.
Source: Authors' calculations based on WIOD, November 2013 release.

regions, the increasing importance of capital might be a reflection of the increased investment in so-called intangible assets, which are becoming increasingly important for growth in advanced nations (see Corrado *et al.*, Chapter 9 in this volume).

As expected, GVC income for low-skilled workers has increased strongly in China and in other emerging economies while declining in the advanced regions. In the US and East Asia, the decline was particularly pronounced for medium-skilled workers. Within Europe, medium-skilled workers in Germany lost the biggest share, and in other European countries the income share going to low-skilled workers also declined. Income for high-skilled workers related to global manufacturing went up in most EU countries. This is not simply the result of a strong supply of higher-skilled labor replacing medium-skilled workers but essentially carrying out the same activities. If this were the case, the wages for high-skilled workers should have dropped and the increase in GVC income of high-skilled workers would be limited. However, relative wages for high-skilled workers did not show this pattern (see Timmer *et al.* 2013).

15.7 Concluding remarks

With the availability of new global input–output tables, novel perspectives on trade, growth, and jobs have been developed. In this chapter we introduced the global-value-chain approach which highlights the importance of global production networks and the increasing interrelation of consumption, production, and income across national boundaries through the trade of goods and services. We analyzed the value added of production for a wide set of manufacturing products. This was done through a newly developed accounting method in which we built upon an input–output modeling of the world economy in the tradition of Leontief. The results based on the WIOD show that, first, international fragmentation in the production of manufactures has been ongoing since 1995 as shown by increasing shares of foreign value added in production. In particular, value added from outside the region to which a country belongs has been rising fast. Second, this has been accompanied by a rapid shift towards higher-skilled activities in advanced nations. And third, these activities are increasingly carried out in the services sector and no longer in the manufacturing sector itself. As such, the shift contributes to the so-called job polarization in advanced economies, as the displaced manufacturing workers are likely to be absorbed into personal and distributional services, where low-skilled employment opportunities are still growing (Goos, Manning, and Salomons 2014). Emerging economies are taking up increasing shares in global GVC income, much of which has been driven by rapid growth in China after its accession to the WTO in 2001. We also find increasing intertwining of manufacturing and services activities, which argues against a myopic view of job creation in manufacturing or fears for deindustrialisation. Rather than focusing on the particular sector in which jobs are lost or created, the discussion should be led by a view toward the activities that are carried out in GVCs, irrespective of the sector in which they are ultimately classified. Thinking in terms of sectors is basically a relic of a world where fragmentation of production, both domestically and international, had not progressed far.

Although the model to measure GVC income is relatively straightforward, it is clear that the validity of the findings relies heavily on the quality of the database used. The contributions in Houseman and Mandel (2015) provide a good overview of the various measurement issues that arise, in particular in the context of international trade flows. Possible solutions are discussed as well, indicating future priorities of statistical programs. Alongside new measures of exports and imports there is the ongoing need for high-quality series of national input–output tables, as well as detailed accounts of the labor and capital inputs into production. The KLEMS databases described in this volume provide unique and indispensable information to analyze the impact of trade and technological change on labor markets and more generally welfare. The World KLEMS initiative is therefore highly instrumental in bringing this work forward. We believe that the future development of this type of data should ideally be shouldered by its incorporation in regular statistical programs. Given the international nature of the global input–output tables, this must involve coordination by international agencies. Therefore we welcome the current OECD-WTO initiative in taking this work forward in the international statistical community (OECD and WTO 2013). Together with national KLEMS-type database, the global input–output tables will be an indispensable tool to understand future developments of the global economy.

References

Ali-Yrkkö, J., P. Rouvinen, T. Seppälä and P. Ylä-Anttila. 2011. *Who Captures Value in Global Supply Chains? ETLA Discussion Papers*, No 1240, Helsinki.

Amador, João and Sónia Cabral. 2014. "Global Value Chains: Surveying Drivers and Measures." *Working Paper Series*, 1739, European Central Bank.

Autor, David H., Frank Levy. and Richard J. Murnane. 2003. "The Skill Content of Recent Technological Change: An Empirical Exploration," *The Quarterly Journal of Economics*, **118**(4): 1279–1333.

Baldwin, R. E. and F. Kimura. 1998. "Measuring US International Goods and Services Transactions." In R. E. Baldwin, R. E. Lipsey, and J. D. Richardson (eds.), *Geography and Ownership as Bases for Economic Accounting*. Chicago: NBER, 49–80.

Baldwin, R. E. and J. Lopez Gonzalez. 2013. "Supply-chain Trade: A Portrait of Global Patterns and Several Testable Hypotheses," *NBER Working Paper*, 18957.

Dedrick, J., K. L. Kraemer and G. Linden. 2010. "Who Profits From Innovation in Global Value Chains? A Study of the iPod And Notebook PCs," *Industrial and Corporate Change*, **19**(1): 81–116.

Dietzenbacher, E., B. Los, R. Stehrer, M. Timmer, and G. J. de Vries. 2013. "The Construction of World Input–Output Tables in the WIOD Project," *Economic Systems Research*, **25**(1): 71–98.

Feenstra, R. 2010. *Offshoring in the Global Economy: Microeconomic Structure and Macroeconomic Implications*. Cambridge, MA: MIT Press.

Fukao, Kyoji, Hikari Ishido, and Keiko Ito. 2003. "Vertical Intra-industry Trade and Foreign Direct Investment in East Asia," *Journal of the Japanese and International Economies*, **17**(4): 468–506.

Gollin, D. 2002. "Getting Income Shares Right," *Journal of Political Economy*, **110**(2): 458–474.

Goos, M., A. Manning, and A. Salomons. 2014. "Explaining Job Polarization: Routine-biased Technological Change and Offshoring," *American Economic Review*, **104**(8): 2509–2526.

Houseman, Susan N. and Michael Mandel (eds.) 2015. *Measuring Globalization: Better Trade Statistics for Better Policy*. Kalamazoo, MI: W. E. Upjohn Institute for Employment Research.

Hummels, D., J. Ishii, and K-M. Yi. 2001. "The Nature and Growth of Vertical Specialization in World Trade," *Journal of International Economics*, **54**(1): 75–96.

Johnson, R. C. and G. Noguera. 2012. "Accounting for Intermediates: Production Sharing and Trade in Value Added," *Journal of International Economics*, **86**(2): 224–236.

Leontief, W. 1949. "Structural Matrices of National Economies", *Econometrica*, **17**: 273–282.

Lipsey, R. E. 2010. "Measuring the Location of Production in a World of Intangible Productive Assets, FDI and Intrafirm Trade," *Review of Income and Wealth*, 56(s1): S99–S110.

Los, B., M. P. Timmer, and G. J. de Vries. 2015a. "How Global are Global Value Chains? A New Approach to Measure International Fragmentation," *Journal of Regional Science*, 55: 66–92.

2015b. "How Important are Exports for Job Growth in China? A Demand Side Analysis," *Journal of Comparative Economics*, 43, pp. 19–32.

Marin, D. 2011. "The Opening Up of Eastern Europe at 20: Jobs, Skills, and 'Reverse Maquiladoras'." In M. Jovanovic (ed.), *Handbook of International Economics*, vol. 2. Cheltenham, UK: Edward Elgar.

Miller, R. E. and P. D. Blair. 2009. *Input–Output Analysis: Foundations and Extensions*. Cambridge University Press.

OECD and WTO. 2013. "Trade in Value Added: Concepts, Methodologies and Challenges," Joint OECD-WTO Note. See: www.oecd.org/sti/ind/statisticalqualityoftiva.htm.

Timmer, M. P., E. Dietzenbacher, B. Los, R. Stehrer, and G. J. de Vries. 2015. "An Illustrated User Guide to the World Input–Output Database: The Case of Global Automotive Production," *Review of International Economics*, 23: 575–605.

Timmer, M. P., A. A. Erumban, B. Los, R. Stehrer, and G. J. de Vries. 2014. "Slicing Up Global Value Chains," *Journal of Economic Perspectives*, 28(2): 99–118.

Timmer, M. P., B. Los, R. Stehrer, and G. J. de Vries. 2013. "Fragmentation, Incomes and Jobs. An Analysis of European Competitiveness," *Economic Policy*, 28(76): 613–661.

Tukker, A. and E. Dietzenbacher. 2013. "Global Multiregional Input–Output Frameworks: An Introduction and Outlook," *Economic Systems Research*, 25(1): 1–19.

Index

CPSIA information can be obtained
at www.ICGtesting.com
Printed in the USA
LVOW13s2017170717

541656LV00011B/209/P